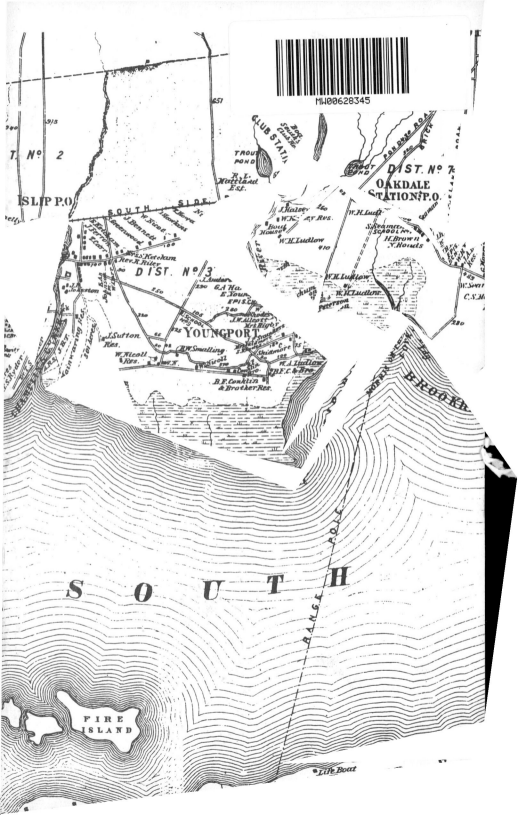

Along the Great South Bay

Along the Great South Bay

From Oakdale to Babylon,
the Story of a Summer Spa,
1840 to 1940

Harry W. Havemeyer

Amereon
House

MATTITUCK, NY

PAGE 1; The Great South Bay off Fire Island from a painting by F. Augustus Silver, 1879. (Courtesy of Coe Kerr Galleries, New York.)

PREVIOUS SPREAD; The Fire Island lighthouse as it appears today. It was built in 1858 to replace the earlier one that had been built in 1826. (Courtesy of the Fire Island Lighthouse Preservation Society.)

The *Olympic Theater* in New York City built c.1840 for which the *Olympic Club,* located in Bay Shore in 1856, was named.

A drawing of *St. Nicholas Church,* Islip, Northamptonshire, England, the parish church of the Nicoll family.

To order, contact
Amereon House,
the publishing division of
Amereon Ltd.
Post Office Box 1200
Mattituck, New York 11952-9500

ISBN 0-8488-1736-2

For my father and mother who
loved Islip and the Great South Bay

PAUMANOK

Sea-beauty! stretch'd and basking!
One side thy inland ocean laving, broad, with copious
    commerce, steamers, sails,
And one the Atlantic's wind caressing, fierce or gentle—
    mighty hulls dark-gliding in the distance.
Isle of sweet brooks of drinking-water—healthy air and soil!
Isle of the salty shore and breeze and brine!

Walt Whitman

TABLE OF CONTENTS

Introduction and Acknowledgements ix
Prologue   Islip, England 1
Chapter I   The Nicoll Family 3
Chapter II   Early Settlers on Long Island 11
Chapter III   The First Summer Residents
               (1840–1860) 23
Chapter IV   August Belmont and the South Side Club
               (1860–1870) 39
Chapter V   William K. Vanderbilt and His Friends
               (1870–1880) 53
Chapter VI   The Gilded Age — The Early Years
               (1880–1890) 91
Chapter VII   The Gilded Age — Its Peak
               (1890–1900) 181
Chapter VIII   The New Century (1900–1914) 265
Chapter IX   The War Years (1914–1919) 305
Chapter X   The Breakup of the Great Estates
               (1920–1929) 345
Chapter XI   Some Endings and a New Beginning
               (1929–1948) 383
Epilogue   The Town of Islip Today 423
Notes   433
Bibliography   447
Index   457

INTRODUCTION AND ACKNOWLEDGEMENTS

The first prominent summer resort in America was established at Saratoga Springs, New York, during the decade of the 1830s. Affluent people from the cities of Boston, New York, and Philadelphia began to go there to enjoy the cooler climate in the summer as well as the mineral springs whose health-giving waters were bottled for consumption. Because of the springs, the resort began to be called a "spa," and the use of the term spread to other resorts that were near the water, even saltwater. Around 1850 horse racing, with both thoroughbred racers and trotters, was established at Saratoga as a sport that entertained, and sometimes made rich, the wagering spectators, to say nothing of the owners. Grand hotels were built with all the comforts expected by their affluent guests. Saratoga Springs was the model for the many summer resorts that would spring up after the Civil War had ended and prosperity returned to the country with the beginning of the Industrial Revolution.

The era from approximately 1870 to 1900 in the United States has been called by historians either the Industrial Revolution, the Age of the Industrial Titans, or the Gilded Age, depending on the point of view of the writer. For the social historian the latter is perhaps the most appropriate name. And for the social historian, the Gilded Age in America rapidly expanded during the 1880s and the 1890s, reaching its apogee at the turn of the century. Although it ended in Europe with the advent of the Great War, it continued in the United States until the start of the Great Depression. The sixty years from 1870 to 1930 are thus generally considered to be the Gilded Age in America.

The economist and historian John Kenneth Galbraith has called the Gilded Age "very specifically a world of competitive ostentation." Louis Auchincloss, the writer and social historian, has labeled those years "the Vanderbilt Era" for the great gusto with which that most prominent family consumed its colossal wealth, acquired and accumulated in rapid fashion and subject to all but nonexistent taxes. When the family founder, Commodore Cornelius Vanderbilt, died in 1877, he left to his son and principal heir an estate of $100 million, a record in America at that time exceeding even that of the hugely wealthy John Jacob Astor. When Vanderbilt's son, William Henry, died in 1885, the value of the estate had risen to $200 million in only eight years. Such an estate in current dollars would be worth in excess of *$20 billion*. The extremes between the rich and the ordinary working men and women were enormous. A chambermaid in Vanderbilt's mansion or a gardener working on the grounds might be paid on average $12 per month, plus room and board if they were fortunate.

William H. Vanderbilt passed on to his son, William K. Vanderbilt, a character in this story, a fortune of about $70 million (the estate of $200 million was not equally divided. Cornelius II and William K., the two elder sons, received far more than their two brothers and four sisters). From 1885 until 1920 when W. K. died, and in spite of a life-style of huge expenditures including those for ten houses, several yachts, racehorses, as well as alimony to his first wife, Alva, and a $25 million wedding gift to his daughter, Consuelo, the Duchess of Marlborough, his estate did not noticeably diminish. He passed on to his two sons most of the $70 million he had inherited, all of which is testimony to the tremendous earning power of his railroad stocks and other investments during the Gilded Age.

In the decade of the 1840s, a few families came from New York to Long Island's South Shore, in the area from Oakdale to Babylon, on the Great South Bay, to build summer houses and to establish an Episcopal church where they could worship in familiar surroundings. This was the beginning of a summer resort, although until after the Civil War it could hardly be called a resort at all, as the residents were so few in number. In the 1850s one club was established and two resort hotels opened, one on Fire Island and the other in East Islip. Nevertheless in hindsight it can be said that the resort along the Great South Bay began during the 1840s and lasted a full hundred years until the advent of World War II.

This is the story of the people who came from New York and from Brooklyn (separate cities then) to spend their summers along a fifteen-mile stretch of waterfront from Oakdale to Babylon, making it a prominent Long Island summer spa.

Some further explanation is necessary. The area from Oakdale to Babylon comprises most, but not all, of the Town of Islip, one of the eight original seventeenth century towns in Suffolk County.* Also in the Town of Islip, to the east of Oakdale, are found the villages of Sayville and Bayport. Babylon, to the west, is today its own town although it once was the southerly part of Huntington town. With the exception of one or two families and one great hotel I have not included Babylon in the narrative. Nor have I included Sayville and Bayport to the east, although many families came there from New York as well, particularly the family of Robert B. Roosevelt (the uncle of President Theodore Roosevelt) to Sayville and the John R. and Walter L. Suydam families to Bayport. Each of these families went back to the early Dutch days in Manhattan prior to 1664. The Sayville and Bayport communities were really separate from the one from Oakdale to Babylon. St. Ann's Episcopal Church in Sayville was their church and they had their own clubs. Only the venerable South Side Sportsmen's Club joined them together in any real way. Consequently I leave Sayville and Bayport to another historian.

---

* The eight original towns of Suffolk County are: Southold, Southampton, East Hampton, Shelter Island, Huntington, Smithtown, Brookhaven, and Islip.

The Town of Islip, which encompasses all of the original patent granted to William Nicoll of the Islip, Northamptonshire, family, has within its boundaries several villages. One village is known as Islip village or Islip hamlet. This creates confusion. When I use the word "Islip" I usually mean the village, unless the words "Town of" are added. Another confusion arises because, although the legal divide between Islip and Bay Shore is Awixa Creek and all the homes on Saxton (later Saxon) Avenue are thus in Islip, many have had Bay Shore mailing addresses for some years. Islip, however, has always had a higher social standing than Bay Shore, almost from the beginning of the age. Contemporary newspapers often labeled residents of Saxton Avenue as from Bay Shore, adding to this confusion. In a third complication, although the village of East Islip lies directly east of Islip, the small hamlet of West Islip is not directly west of Islip, but comes after one has passed through Bay Shore, then Brightwaters, and then West Bay Shore to finally reach West Islip!

In discussing the South Side Sportsmen's Club, that venerable institution founded in 1866 and so important to the early development of the area as a resort, I, like almost all of its former members, have dropped the word "Sportsmen's." It is simply the South Side Club. Also, although the term "estate" was often used to describe the property of the summer residents, it was almost never used by the residents themselves. Their property was their "place" and their house was their "home," never a "mansion."

Primary sources of research for this account have been the two contemporary local weekly newspapers which have been preserved on microfilm and are therefore still available. The first and oldest is the *South Side Signal*, which was published in Babylon beginning in 1869 and lasted until mid 1920. The other is the *Suffolk County News*, published in Sayville from 1884 onward through the end of the period. Without my use of these two papers this book would not have been possible. Bay Shore and Islip also had the *Bay Shore Journal*, the *Islip Herald*, and the *Islip Press* weekly papers, from about 1885 onward. To my knowledge they were not preserved on microfilm, and therefore, whereas certain copies do exist, they are in such a deteriorated state due to the acid used in nineteenth century newsprint that pages cannot be turned without their falling apart, making them useless to the researcher. The *Bay Shore Journal* is available on microfilm from 1931 at the Bay Shore-Brightwaters Library. Microfilms of the *South Side Signal* and the *Suffolk County News* from their beginnings are available at the Brooklyn Historical Society, and I extend my thanks to that institution and in particular to Claire Lamers, Assistant Head Librarian, for all her valuable assistance.

I would also like to recognize the assistance given by that great treasure of Long Island history found in all of the issues of *The Long Island Forum* from its beginning in 1938. Published monthly for many decades, the *Forum*, although not a primary source, was invaluable, and I should like to thank all the authors therein represented, and in particular its former editor — now editor emeritus — Carl A. Starace, for his help and encouragement to me as well as for publishing my article "The Story of Saxton Avenue" in the *Forum*s of Winter and Spring, 1990. While working on that article for the *Forum*, I became convinced that the wider story, "Along the Great South Bay, from Oakdale to Babylon," should be told.

In writing this book I worked in and drew material from the Brooklyn Historical Society (already mentioned), the New York Public Library, the Bay Shore-Brightwaters Public Library, the William K. Vanderbilt Historical Society Library, and the Suffolk County Surrogate's Records office in Riverhead, Long Island. To all of these I am grateful for the help freely given me.

During my research for this book I visited and was informed by gravestones in the following cemeteries:

Babylon Cemetery, Babylon, Long Island
Oakwood Cemetery, Bay Shore, Long Island
Great River Cemetery, Great River, Long Island
Greenwood Cemetery, Brooklyn, New York.

Also I am very grateful for the help of several individuals whose contribution made the story more personal and more accurate. They include the following:

Mariette Russell, great granddaughter of Bradish Johnson Sr.

Hildegarde (Babs) Stevenson Hard and Francis B. Thorne Jr., children of Hildegarde K. Thorne

Charles D. Webster, son-in-law of Harry T. Peters

Ralph D. Howell Jr., grandson of Elmer W. Howell

H. Ward Ackerson, grandson of T. B. Ackerson

Gifford B. Doxsee, great grandson of James Harvey Doxsee

Carl A. Starace

Richard P. Baldwin

the late Lavern Wittlock

Raymond and Judith Spinzia

Preston C. Raynor

Peter and Jane Reilly

Richard A. Milligan, for his photography

Christina Chahal and Loretta Rutigliano for their typing of my manuscript, and

The Old Print Shop, 150 Lexington Avenue, NYC 10016, for photographs of historic prints.

Lastly, I owe special thanks to my editor, Sally Arteseros, my copy editor, Carol Holmes, and to those who read my manuscript, Kate Medina, Carl Starace, Ralph Howell, and Robert MacKay. I appreciate more than I can say their support and encouragement.

Except for the assistance of those people mentioned above, I have done all my own research for this work, which I regard as one of the pleasures and privileges of preparing the text. Any errors or omissions are mine alone.

Harry W. Havemeyer
New York

ALONG THE GREAT SOUTH BAY

Surf Hotel on Fire Island, the first resort hotel on the Great South Bay, was built by David S. S. Sammis in 1856. (Courtesy of Ron Ziel.)

The only known photograph of the first Babylon railroad station, built for the South Side Railroad of Long Island, taken in October, 1878. Babylon was the transfer point on the way to the *Surf Hotel* on Fire Island. (The collection of Ron Ziel.)

Sans Souci, the Johnson family home on the South Country Road west of Bay Shore. (Courtesy of Pictorial Bay Shore)

Bradish Johnson, 1811-1892, first summer resident of the Town of Islip. (Courtesy of Mariette Russell and the Vanderbilt Historical Society Archives.)

Louisa A. Lawrance Johnson, 1819-1870, wife of Bradish Johnson. (Courtesy of Mariette Russell and the Vanderbilt Historical Society Archives.)

Amos Stellenwerf's *Lake House,* East Islip, pictured in 1868 in a Currier & Ives print A Stopping Place on the Road "The Horse Shed drawn by Thomas Worth, Stellenwerf's son-in-law. It opened in the 1850s. (Courtesy of The Old Print Shop.)

La Grange Inn as it appears today. It was founded before the Revolutionary War in West Islip at the corner of Higbie Lane. (Courtesy of Richard A. Milligan.)

A chowder party on the beach on Fire Island in 1873, drawn by Thomas Worth for *Harper's Weekly,* August 23, 1873.

PROLOGUE

ISLIP, ENGLAND

Nestled between the gently rolling hills of Northamptonshire in England lies the small village of Islip. It is one of two villages in England with that name. (The other is in Oxfordshire, ten miles north of the city of Oxford.) Islip, Northamptonshire, is close by the larger village of Thrapston and seven miles east of the town of Kettering. The High Street runs through the middle of the town with its thirty to forty stone houses with mossy tile roofs. One or two small lanes lead off to houses set away from the principal street. The general store, with its red Post Office sign outside, and the local pub, the Rose and Crown, directly across the street are the only public gathering places in immediate view.

Farther along High Street, set back 200 feet from it, is by far the largest and oldest building in the village, the Parish Church of St. Nicholas. It is the dominant landmark of Islip, with a handsome Gothic spire that can be seen from several miles away. The church is surrounded by its ancient grave-yard, in which many ivy covered stones have worn writings, now barely discernible. The building is typical of smaller churches of the Early English Gothic period. The pointed arched windows, the square tower on which the main spire rests with carved mini-spires at its four corners, all have a very graceful effect.

St. Nicholas was completed in 1226, early in the long reign of Henry III and just eleven years after King John was forced to sign the Magna Carta. Its first vicar was known simply as Simon. It has been continuously in use since that time and is today a central part of the life of Islip village.

There is a sense of timelessness about this scene. With only a little imagination one can easily picture Islip as it was in the fifteenth century.

Chapter I

THE NICOLL FAMILY

The mid fifteenth century was a particularly turbulent time in English history. The monarch, Henry VI (1422–1461), was the least competent of all the medieval kings. Meek, pious, physically awkward and mentally unstable, he was totally unfit to steer the ship of state in those troubled times. His reign was marked by the end of the Hundred Years War and the beginning of the War of the Roses. His father, Henry V (1413–1422), had died while his son was still an infant, bequeathing to him the thrones of England and France. It seemed as though a glorious future lay ahead for the child king, but as his reign unfolded it became apparent that its beginning would be the high point of the English conquest of France. In 1429 the tide had turned under the inspired leadership of La Pucelle, the maid, known to history as Jeanne d'Arc, and by 1453 only Calais remained in English hands.

Meanwhile, in England, Henry VI (of the House of Lancaster) had quietly lost his mind, creating a vacuum which culminated in rival quests for power between the Lancasters and the Yorks: the War of the Roses. Although King Henry was weak and at times mad, he had married, by arrangement, the strong-willed French princess Margaret of Anjou, and it was Queen Margaret who in reality carried the royal banner for the Lancasters both during her husband's reign and after his death.

Contesting Henry VI's claim to the throne was Richard, Duke of York. He too was of royal blood and by the law of primogeniture descended directly from Edward III from a son older than Henry's forebear. Sides were taken by all the landed nobles, and civil war was under way.

From 1450 to 1485 the Yorks and the Lancasters battled for the throne of England. In 1461 Henry VI lost his throne to Edward IV (1461–1483), the son of Richard, Duke of York who was killed in 1460. The Yorkshire party was in the ascendancy, but Queen Margaret fought on to restore her husband to his throne. Not until 1471 was Edward IV's reign secure. In May of that year he defeated, in bloody battle, an expedition sent by Margaret from France. Henry VI's only son was killed on that day and the father, the former monarch, was put to death in the Tower of London shortly thereafter.

Edward IV reigned until he died unexpectedly in 1483; to be succeeded by his younger brother, Richard. Richard had seized the twelve-year-old son and heir of Edward IV together with his brother and put them in the Tower of London; they were never seen again. Their uncle declared himself Richard III, king of England. His reign was mercifully short, two years, for in 1485 he died fighting at the Battle of Bosworth and the crown fell to his opponent, the first Tudor king, Henry VII. The War of the Roses was over.

It was during these turbulent years that John Nicoll and his wife, Annys, lived in the small village of Islip (sometimes spelled Islippe) in Northamptonshire. They raised a family of six sons. They were a family of consequence in the country and as such had a coat of arms which was displayed in their parish church. John died in 1467 and was buried in the graveyard of St. Nicholas Church. He was the earliest known ancestor of the family that was to come to the New World some two hundred years later. Little more is known of John Nicoll. Perhaps he was a wool merchant and a member of the market guild of the nearby town. Wool was the lifeblood of English trade in that era and cloth manufactured in English towns, such as Lavenham in neighboring Suffolk, was exported to many cities on the Continent. A merchant's prosperity was recognized by his coat of arms.

John and Annys Nicoll's immediate descendants remained in Islip. There was a son named Henry; a grandson, John; and a great grandson, William; all born in Islip. William, however, moved to the town of Willen in Buckinghamshire for most of his life. For some years the family lived in this part of England. This William had a son named John and a grandson named Matthias; Matthias became a clergyman in the Church of England. He moved his family back to Islip and it was there that his son, Matthias II, was born in about 1621, the seventh generation Nicoll from the original John of Islip.

Matthias Nicoll II grew up in Islip and graduated from Cambridge University. As a son of a priest of the established church he had many educational advantages, and being an ambitious and adventuresome lad he was attracted to the law, becoming a member of the Inner Temple in London. During his formative years, England under Charles I (1625–1649) was for the first time challenging royal authority. The center of that challenge was in Cambridge University and the nearby shires of Lincoln, Norfolk, Suffolk, and Northampton.

After a series of confrontations the king prorogued Parliament in 1629 and ruled for the entire next decade without one. He was kept solvent by resorting to measures considered to be extortionate by the merchants and landed gentry, particularly those from London and the northeast shires. He might have survived, except for the misguided decision to revolutionize the Church of England, an act which alienated a huge majority of the people.

In 1633 Charles I raised William Laud to the see of Canterbury and the new archbishop, together with those he appointed, moved Church doctrine and practice backward to the Roman Catholic practice that Elizabeth I had abandoned fifty years before. Puritan practices were to be abolished and the altar in the churches of the realm was to be moved to the east where it was to be placed on a dais and railed off. (It had usually been placed freestanding in the body of the church.) These acts seemed popish to many and dangerously weakened loyalty to the Crown. The Puritans were incensed.

It was in 1633 that the Great Migration began from the northeast shires of East Anglia to New England in the New World. Most of these people were Puritans who found the "new" religious demands of Archbishop Laud unacceptable. They immigrated to the newly founded Massachusetts Bay

Colony* where they often persecuted each other in the name of Protestant purity. And they immigrated to New Haven, Connecticut, to parts of Long Island, and even to areas of New Netherland, controlled by the more tolerant Dutch.

In the spring of 1635 several ships left England for the New World. The *Elizabeth* and *Ann* sailed for Boston carrying Robert Hawkins, aged twenty-five, and his wife, Mary. They would settle across the river in Charlestown, Massachusetts. In 1636, they were admitted to the First Church, and it was there that their second son, Zachary, was baptized on August 25, 1639.

The ship *Hopewell* left London that same spring of 1635 for Ipswich, Massachusetts. Among its passengers were William Purryer, aged thirty-six, his wife, Alice, and their three children, Mary, seven years old, Sarah, five, and Catherine, one and a half. They had come from the town of Olney in Buckinghamshire. After five years in Ipswich they moved to Southold, Long Island, to be among its first and wealthiest settlers.

The brothers Mapes, John, aged twenty-one, and Thomas, aged six, from Hingham in Norfolk had sailed the previous year (1634) on the ship *Francis* for Salem, Massachusetts. After Thomas had reached manhood he moved to Southold, Long Island, as well, where he and Sarah Purryer were married in 1650. Lastly the Lawrence brothers, John, seventeen years old, and William, twelve, embarked on the ship *Planter* out of London bound for Plymouth, Massachusetts. They had come from an important family of Great St. Albans in Hertfordshire. After ten years or so in Plymouth, they moved to Long Island where they purchased property in the settlement of Flushing, founded by Englishmen under Dutch auspices. A younger brother, Thomas, joined them later and by 1656 was listed among the landowners of Newtown, Long Island, also part of New Netherland. Descendants of each of these earliest immigrant families would play a large role in

---

* Founded in 1630 by Suffolk landowner and lord of the manor, John Winthrop.

the development of the Great South Bay area as a summer colony some two hundred fifty years later.

Tensions in England by 1642 had reached the breaking point. Parliament had been called to sit again in 1640 to finance a war against Scotland. However, it only served as a platform for inflamed passions against the king. Archbishop Laud's changes had convinced many that the system of Church government must be overthrown, the office of bishop abolished and the Prayer Book suppressed. It was too late for compromise, and civil war broke out.

The active military phase of the Civil War did not last for many years. The supporters of the king, the Cavaliers, and those of the Parliament, the Roundheads, clashed in a decisive battle in 1644 at Marston Moor. The forces of Parliament carried the day because of the charge of its well-disciplined cavalry regiment under the leadership of Oliver Cromwell. The most costly battle, in terms of human life, ever to take place on English soil, was over. The forces of Charles I never seriously threatened Parliament's and Cromwell's superiority again. In 1649 the king was beheaded and Cromwell was to rule England as the Lord Protector until his death in 1658.

It is not known on which side of this conflict lay the sympathies of the young lawyer, Matthias Nicoll II. Most landowners, merchants and lawyers alike, sided with Parliament and Cromwell. But the loyalty and support he was to give to Charles I's sons after the Restoration could argue that he was recognized as a Cavalier although perhaps not a prominent one. During the years of the Protectorate he had married Abigail Johns, and they returned to Islip, where their son William Nicoll was born in 1657.

In 1660 the crown of England was restored to Charles II, and a new age of prosperity and overseas settlement began. Early in his reign Charles II had aggravated the worsening relations between England and Holland by granting to his brother James, the Duke of York, the Dutch colony at the mouth of the Hudson River called New Netherland. The grant was accompanied by £4,000 for its conquest. War erupted at sea, and it went badly for the English at first.

James, however, was made head of the Royal Navy and showed himself extraordinarily able at developing English seapower with a large assist from Samuel Pepys at the Admiralty in Whitehall. James also decided to secure possession of his newly granted territory in the New World, and commissioned an expedition to do this in 1664. The Duke of York's patent was "to visit the Colonies and Plantations known as New England," and he chose to head the commission a colonel, Richard Nicoll. Named as secretary to the commission was Matthias Nicoll II.

It was intended before its departure that the commission would remain in the New World to establish England's claim on behalf of the Duke of York. Colonel Richard Nicoll was to become the governor, and Matthias Nicoll II was appointed secretary of the future province of New York. Several of the officers of the commission including Matthias Nicoll were accompanied by their families. Thus it was that Matthias's son, seven-year-old William, first went to the New World. Although he would return to England for education somewhat later, both William and Matthias became permanent residents of New York and never again returned to their family home in Islip, Northamptonshire.

The expedition of only four ships sailed from Portsmouth in May 1664 for Boston, where it got very little help from the colonists there. Upon its arrival in New Amsterdam harbor, the Dutch governor, Peter Stuyvesant, wisely decided to negotiate rather than fight. After receiving promises of free settlement and free trade for the Dutch residents, Stuyvesant surrendered control to Colonel Nicoll of all the Dutch settlements. New Amsterdam was thereafter called New York to honor the royal Duke of York, patron of the expedition. Stuyvesant and the other burghers were allowed to remain, their lives almost entirely unchanged.

Because Colonel Richard Nicoll and Secretary Matthias Nicoll shared the same surname (sometimes spelled Nicolls), some historians have claimed that Matthias was Richard's nephew. Others have maintained that there was no relation between the two. Evidence appears to favor the latter assumption. There is no record of Richard or his immediate ancestors coming from Islip, and more important, he had an entirely different coat of arms from Matthias. However, Nicoll was a common name in England and it is possible that there was some distant relationship. Perhaps Colonel Richard was descended from another son of the first John Nicoll of Islip.

Thus it was that some of the earliest English settlers left the turmoil and religious persecution in the land of their birth to venture across the sea and to establish new communities in a new land. They brought with them strong religious convictions, they were often led by ministers, and they established what have been called Puritan theocracies. Sometimes the lack of tolerance caused groups to break away and establish new settlements. Much of eastern Long Island was first settled by groups from New England searching for their own freedom to worship as they pleased. Matthias Nicoll with his family, coming to New York with the English establishment, not fleeing from it, was to look to parts of Long Island not already settled by earlier colonists. His son, William, was to acquire a large tract of land on the southern part along the Great South Bay, which he would call Islip after the English town of his birth.

Chapter II

EARLY SETTLERS ON LONG ISLAND

Although the God-fearing Puritans from England, 20,000 strong with 65 preachers, all imbued with some form of Calvinism, had come first to settle the Massachusetts towns of Plymouth, Boston, Hingham, Ipswich, Charlestown, and the like in the 1630s, it was not long before many had spread out to more distant parts. In 1636 Cambridge University-educated Roger Williams, having discovered that its religious intolerance was unbearable, left Massachusetts to found Rhode Island. Two years later John Davenport and Theophilus Eaton started the independent town of New Haven in order to protect an even stricter Calvinist-dominated society from the distracting influences they were seeing in Boston. Likewise, the first settlements on eastern Long Island were the result of a divergence from the orthodox Puritanism that Massachusetts had established.

In 1639, the Reverend John Youngs with a small band of followers left Hingham in Norfolk for the New World. They stopped for a time in the town of New Haven, but not finding it much to their liking, moved across Long Island Sound to a neck of land where the local Indians were friendly. They established a permanent settlement there in 1640 and named it for the English port from which they had departed, Southold.* During the next twenty-five years they would maintain a close alliance with New Haven across the sound.

---

*   The English port in Suffolk is spelled Southwold. The "w" was dropped while crossing the Atlantic.

The Southold community led by the Reverend Youngs attracted new settlers in the decade to follow, among whom were the prosperous merchant William Purryer and his family and the young surveyor, Thomas Mapes. To the east was the island that had just been purchased from the Sachem,* Wyandanch, by Lion Gardiner, whose descendants also became property owners along the Great South Bay.

Sharing the claim of being the first English settlement on Long Island in 1640 along with Southold is Southampton. Again, a band of English settlers from Lyon, Massachusetts, led by the Reverend Abraham Pierson and Edward Howell set off for Long Island. They first came ashore, however, too near the usually tolerant Dutch at Cow's Neck (Matinecock) and were promptly put in jail. Only upon promise that they would immediately depart were they released, and they sailed eastward to Long Island's south fork. There they received a friendly reception from the Shinnecock Indians and thus established the settlement of Southampton.

Long Island was settled by the English from east to west and simultaneously by the Dutch from west to east. They met on the western side of what is now called Oyster Bay. The first two English settlements were followed by those at Shelter Island, East Hampton (1648), Oyster Bay (1653), Brookhaven (1655), Smithtown (1665), and finally Islip (1683).

In the spring of 1655 a group of five pioneers from the Boston area came to the north side of Long Island to buy land from the Setalcott Indians. They were joined there by the surveyor, Thomas Mapes. They established a settlement at the head of a bay and named it Ashford. The name was later changed to Cromwell Bay, and then to Setauket. Twenty families from Boston soon followed, one of whom was young Zachary Hawkins, the son of immigrants Robert and Mary Hawkins of Charlestown, Massachusetts. Zachary was to marry and become the progenitor of the large Hawkins family on Long Island. He lived in Setauket until his death in 1698 at age fifty-nine and sired three sons and two daughters.

---

* Native American, meaning 'leader'.

These first settlers were sturdy farmers, deeply imbued with the spirit of liberty and independence. It is likely that the Massachusetts theocracy was too restrictive for their spirit. The common lands were parcelled out to them and the community prospered. As was often the case, worship services were first held in the town hall and then in the newly built meetinghouse. The first minister, the Reverend Nathaniel Brewster (grandson of Elder William Brewster of the *Mayflower*, 1620), having graduated in the first class of Harvard College in 1642, was installed at Setauket in 1665. The first church was not finished until later. Setauket maintained a loose tie with the colony of Connecticut until 1664, when it officially became a part of the Duke of York's grant, New York.

While some English colonists were settling in eastern Long Island, others from Massachusetts were coming to the settlements started by the Dutch in western Long Island, the area they called New Netherland. The Dutch, who had begun their settlement with the purchase of Manhattan Island from the Indians in 1626, looked upon it in the beginning primarily as a trading post. It was not until the 1640s that they began to seriously encourage immigration from Holland, by granting land to those who agreed to stay and raise families. Perhaps because they were always in need of more immigrants, they rarely objected to English settlers, such as John and William Lawrence who arrived from Massachusetts. They were tolerant of all religious groups except the Quakers whom they did persecute.

The five Dutch towns on Long Island grew in the 1640s and 1650s along with New Amsterdam and New Harlem in Manhattan. They were Breukelen, New Utrecht, Flatbush, Bushwick, and Flatlands. Although some English settled there, as well as in Jamaica, Newtown, and Flushing, the Dutch burgher families dominated the political and economic life of New Netherland. Among these burghers were Verveelans, Waldrons, Rikers, Slots, Pieterzens, Demarests (French Huguenot), and Van Cortlandts, descendants of whom have had Great South Bay homes.

Most influential of all was a Dutchman who never came to the New World. Kiliaen Van Rensselaer was a rich and crafty Amsterdam diamond and pearl merchant. A founder (1621) and director of the Dutch West India Company, which controlled the New Netherland settlement, Van Rensselaer saw to it that director generals were appointed that would follow his wishes and agree to his empire building along the Hudson River. From 1630 to his death in 1644 Van Rensselaer's agents purchased from the Indians at nominal prices land along both sides of the river totalling 700,000 acres, what today is all of Albany and Rensselaer counties. This feudal estate was turned over to his sons at his death, some of whom came to America to become patroons, or feudal lords of the manor, over the vast lands. Anna, the widow of Van Rensselaer's grandson, later married William Nicoll, the Islip patentee, uniting these two land-owning families from the Hudson Valley and from Long Island.

The watershed year of 1664 saw New Netherland turned over to English political control, which was hereafter maintained with the exception of the years 1673 and 1674, when the Dutch reinstituted their authority. There was surprisingly little turmoil over this change in authority. Economic life in the new colony of New York was untouched. Although Southold and some of the eastern Long Island towns considered themselves to be part of Connecticut for a time, they soon accepted the reality that Long Island was part of New York under governor Richard Nicoll. In 1665 the Governor promulgated what were called "the Duke's Laws" for the province. These were largely the work of Matthias Nicoll, who with his legal training and as secretary of the province was assigned the task of drafting and disseminating the laws. Patterned after the Yorkshire system of division into two sections called West Riding and East Riding, the laws disappointed many colonists because they did not provide for a General Assembly of the province. Although the local towns could choose their leaders, the provincial leaders were selected by the governor. Matthias Nicoll himself was appointed mayor of New York City in 1671 (then comprising only the lower part of Manhattan Island) by Governor Lovelace. He was followed as mayor by the Dutchman Stephanus Van Cortlandt, showing that English governors were willing to appoint those of Dutch heritage to the office. In 1683 Matthias was appointed a judge of the Supreme Court, capping his service to the Crown in the new province.

As was the custom with the earliest settlers, Matthias Nicoll acquired a large estate on Cow's Neck, Long Island (now known as Manhasset Neck). He and his wife, Abigail, had a large family, including William, who had been born in Islip, England. Legend has it that several of their children were drowned after their boat had capsized off Riker's Island. William, a strong swimmer and perhaps older, was able to reach shore after a struggle in the strong Hell's Gate currents. Matthias died in 1687 at age sixty-five and was buried at his estate in Cow's Neck. No trace of his grave has ever been found. He was the last of his line of the Nicoll family to have lived much of his life in England.

William Nicoll, known as the Islip patentee, was born in 1657, coming to New York, as we have seen, with his father in 1664 when he was seven. In 1677 he returned to England to be educated for the bar and for a time served in the army in Flanders where, it is said, he almost died. After his recovery and return to America, he began a career in law and public service in New York. His name first appears on the public record in 1683 when at age twenty-six he was appointed clerk of Queens County,* a position he held until 1688. He was registrar of the Court of Admiralty in New York as well in that period. He was then attorney general of the province (1687–88), member of the Governor's Council (1691–98), and member of the General Assembly of Suffolk County from 1702 until his death in 1722. He was Speaker of the Assembly for much of that time (1702–18). The province of New York had finally been allowed a general assembly in 1683.

That year, 1683, was significant in William Nicoll's life as well as for the Town of Islip, for at that time he began

---

* Included present day Nassau County as well.

accumulating land from the Secatogue Indians along the Great South Bay. He was granted his first patent by Governor Dongan the following year. Two more patents would follow until his land would exceed 50,000 acres, extending along the bay from Bayport to East Islip. William Nicoll, the first paten-tee, has always been known as the Father of Islip, the last of the eight early English towns on Long Island to be settled.

William and his wife, Anna Van Rensselaer Nicoll, had a large family of ten children. Their son and heir, Benjamin, inherited the Islip Grange, as the patent was called, and was the first supervisor of the town, elected at the first town meeting in 1720. He married Charity Floyd, daughter of Rich-ard Floyd Sr., of Setauket and Margaret Nicoll,* his first cousin, thus uniting two prominent Long Island families. The Nicoll family resided in Islip and retained much of the origi-nal patent until well into the nineteenth century. The last of the line to live in the Islip Grange was William Nicoll (1820–1900), the seventh owner, who left in 1899 and died a year later.

Although William Nicoll was the first and by far the largest of the original patentees of what is today the Town of Islip, there were four others. In chronological order they were: Andrew Gibb, 1692; Thomas and Richard Willets, 1695; Stephanus Van Cortlandt, 1697; and John Moubray, 1708. Andrew Gibb was a lawyer and politician like his friend and associate, William Nicoll. He succeeded Nicoll as clerk of Queens County in 1688 and was elected the first town clerk in the Township of Brookhaven where he resided at the time. He is mentioned as a "marchant" in early records, living in Setauket at first, then in Queens County until about 1690 when it seems he may have lived in Islip for a time. His patent there was for the area of Islip village between the two creeks. Town records mention his son, William, as collector in 1721 and as overseer in 1731. Little more is known about Andrew Gibb. Long Island historian Benjamin F. Thompson called

---

* Their grandson, General William Floyd, signed the Declaration of Independence in 1776.

him "a man of considerable distinction in his day" and added nothing more.

Thomas and Richard Willets, brothers, the third patentees, were grandsons of Richard and Mary Wasburn Willets, who were first settlers of Jericho in Queens County. They had come from Stafford, England, circa 1650, via Huntington, Long Island, where their first son, Thomas, was born. By 1673 they had purchased land in Jericho on which to farm. They were Quakers and as such had to search for areas where persecution could be avoided. The Oyster Bay area lying in between Dutch and English control was reasonably safe, and a number of Quakers settled there. The brothers Thomas and Richard were among nine children of their parents. Their Islip patent was the westernmost of the original five, comprising the area of West Islip today, and had been purchased from the Secatogues in 1692. Their father died in Islip (1714) and their younger brother Amos was born there. The brothers are often mentioned in early town records and their descendants have remained in the area to modern times.

The fourth Islip patentee was the New Amsterdam merchant and politician, Stephanus Van Cortlandt (1643–1700). Son of the wealthy Amsterdam brewer, Olaf Stevens Van Cortlandt, Stephanus was the uncle of William Nicoll's wife as well, and it is likely that it was through Nicoll that the land around "Saghtekoos"* neck became the site of Sagtikos Manor. Stephanus Van Cortlandt, like his younger brother, Jacobus, acquired large tracts of land in and around New York City. The largest part of his estate was a tract extending for ten miles on the east bank of the Hudson River just north of Manhattan Island. His brother acquired what is now called Van Cortlandt Park in the Bronx. Stephanus purchased the 150 acres of Sagtikos Neck just to the east of the Willets grant in 1692 and built the first manor house there that same year. His manor grant (it was known as a minor manor) was received in 1697. The small original Sagtikos Manor house

---

* Indian name for *Sagtikos*; literally meaning 'the snake' or 'the rattlesnake'.

was subsequently enlarged by successive owners and stands today on Montauk Highway between Bay Shore and West Islip. But Sagtikos Manor was not one of Van Cortlandt's principal holdings, and shortly after his death it was sold (1706), partly to Timothy Carll and partly to John Moubray. Stephanus Van Cortlandt was certainly the wealthiest and the most prominent of the five Islip patentees, although his Islip manor was for him small in size and could not compare with that of William Nicoll. Van Cortlandt was primarily associated with New York City. He was mayor of the City in 1677, 1686, and 1687. He was a judge of the admiralty court, an associate justice of the New York Supreme Court, and a commissioner of Customs. He was one of the most prominent citizens of the city, as were many of his relatives and descendants.

The last of the five patentees was the above-mentioned, John Moubray. A Scotsman who immigrated to Southampton, Long Island, by way of New England, he is listed in records for the year 1685 as a teacher and a tailor. He married Elizabeth Anning in Southampton and they had a son, Anning Moubray. Apparently around the year 1694 the Moubray family moved west to the Islip area and began acquiring land from the Secatogue Indians in the present area of Bay Shore. He also acquired land from the heirs of Van Cortlandt so that when he received his patent in 1708 from the governor, Lord Cornbury,* it ran from Orowoc Creek on the east to Appletree Neck on the west (Bay Shore and Brightwaters today).

In 1720 John Moubray was elected one of two assessors of the Town of Islip and in 1721, clerk. His son, Anning, was elected constable in 1725, and descendants were listed in town records for more than two hundred years. John Moubray and his wife built a house on South Country Road** near

---

* Known as the transvestite governor who dressed in women's clothes.

** First laid out in 1732 along the South Shore of Long Island about a mile inland from the bays.

Moubray's Neck (Penataquit Point). He later deeded the neck to his son, Anning. Either with or shortly after the Moubrays came another early settler, Daniel Saxton. Moubray sold to Saxton the land south of South Country Road between Orowoc Creek and Awixa Creek, and it became known as Saxton's Neck. Daniel Saxton thus became the owner of all the land on both sides of the present day Saxton Avenue. Saxton's son, James (Jeans) was elected constable at Islip's first meeting in 1720.

The Town of Islip had been organized, the land had been claimed, but only a few people had chosen to settle in the area. For the next hundred years or so growth would be very slow. In fact, the census of 1810 showed that there were just 885 people in the entire township. Farming and timbering were the major activities. Those who did settle there had to be almost entirely self-sufficient. There were few shops, only one church, and very modest local government. The earliest church established was St. John's in Oakdale, built in 1765 largely at the expense of the Nicoll family. It was a parish of the Church of England, which pledged allegiance to King George III, its head. St. John's was later rebuilt and enlarged but remained the sole church until 1828 when a small Methodist church was built between Bay Shore and Islip on Main Street near Saxton Avenue. It is interesting to note that the minutes of the annual town meetings mention "the Reign of His Majesty King George the Third" until after 1783 when they refer to "the authority of the Good People of the State of New York, and in the eighth year of the American Independence." It would appear that only after the signing of the peace treaty in 1783, did Islip recognize the new American government. This is not so surprising in view of the fact that New York City was the last city to surrender to General Washington and was a Tory stronghold to the end.

There were two inns established in the eighteenth century. They were La Grange Inn in 1739 in West Islip, later renamed La Grange after General Lafayette's home in France, and in 1780 the American House in Babylon (then part of Huntington Township). These fed and housed travellers from

New York and elsewhere. The American House burned down in 1883 but La Grange Inn prospers today at the corner of Higbie Lane, named for its founder Samuel Higbie.

With the advent of the nineteenth century the pace of growth began to quicken but there was still not sufficient economic activity for rapid expansion. Harvesting of the Great South Bay began in earnest by 1815 with the introduction of oysters brought up from Virginia. Another early activity was lumbering. The South Shore with plenty of timber was a good source of wood for an expanding population. There were lumber mills and a paper mill on Orowoc Creek at the South Country Road owned by Ebenezer Hawkins, a descendant of the earliest immigrant family of that name. Salt hay from Captree Island was harvested, boated across the bay, and sold to farmers on the mainland. It was used for bedding cattle, mulching, insulation, and filling cheap mattresses.

As American shipping expanded dramatically after the War of 1812 and after the advent of the steamboat, more and more vessels in the Atlantic trade were grounding on the shoals off Fire Island. The loss of life and cargo forced the federal government to act, and in 1826 the first Fire Island lighthouse was erected to warn ocean vessels of the treacherous currents and shoals.* It was only 74 feet high (less than half the height of the present one) and its lamps, which flashed once every ninety seconds, were fueled by whale oil. Sea captains often complained that they were unable to sight the flashing signal and wrecks continued to occur on the beach. It was apparent that the lighthouse was not high enough, but it was not until the 1850s that anything was done to remedy this tragic situation.

By 1845 Islip's population had reached 2,265. That rural, self-sufficient area along the Great South Bay was poised to enter a new and quite different era, one in which it would

---

* The first lighthouse built in New York State was the Montauk Point lighthouse, commissioned by President George Washington in 1795.

become the host of many people seeking temporary escape from the rapidly expanding cities of New York and Brooklyn. Before that could happen, however, transportation and lodging would be needed. Those came with the development of the railroad and the establishment of the boardinghouses and, particularly, the resort hotel.

First chartered in 1834, the Long Island Railroad started its track in Long Island City across the East River from Manhattan. Its travellers would ferry across the river. Progressing eastward, the track reached Hicksville in 1837, Farmingdale in 1841, and was completed to Greenport in 1844. The first train covered the ninety-five miles to Greenport in July that year. The line roughly bisected Long Island in half from west to east. A separate branch from Brooklyn joined the main track at Jamaica, as it does today. Thus by 1845, the railroad was in reach of the Great South Bay although four to five miles distant at most points, and roads were few and poor. A branch along the South Shore was needed, but would not come for another twenty years.

The coming of the railroad had a dramatic effect on the landscape of Long Island. Many of the trees were cut for railroad ties and sparks from the railroad engines caused forest fires. The use of charcoal for home cooking was also a factor. Amos Stellenwerf, proprietor of East Islip's Lake House, was quoted as saying: "The county used to be famous for its timber [in 1849]. There wasn't a tree to be seen smaller than I am of circumference; and then the trees were gradually burned down. Some say it was from the sparks from the railroad engines, but I think the woods were set fire to by the people who were interested in making charcoal and wanted the charred timber for that purpose. The charcoal business was a great industry here at that time."[1]

The South Shore with its sandy soil took on a barren appearance then and remained that way for many decades. The shipbuilding industry was another huge user of the local wood. It has been estimated that in the years between 1835 and 1885 an average of thirty boats of twenty tons each were built each year on the shores of the Great South Bay.

Along with the railroad and often promoted by it was the seaside resort hotel, an attraction to many city dwellers for an enjoyable and cool summer holiday vacation. The first such resort hotel on Long Island was the Marine Pavilion, built in 1833 on the beach in Far Rockaway. It was a huge success, attracting thousands from New York and Brooklyn. It became the model for the many others to be built throughout the century along or near the Atlantic Ocean and the bays on the South Shore. As the seaside became better known as the place to escape New York's summer heat, it was only natural that New Yorkers and Brooklynites of wealth would build summer homes of their own. So it was that in the 1840s the sons of Captain William M. Johnson, merchant, trader, and planter from New Orleans and New York City, settled in the Town of Islip along the Great South Bay, the first of many to summer there in the decades to follow.

Chapter III
THE FIRST SUMMER RESIDENTS (1840–1860)

Captain William Martin Johnson was born in Connecticut in 1765, the son of Captain Martin Johnson who had emigrated from England to the New England colony as a young man. There he had married Hannah Dean of Stamford. The Johnsons were Loyalists during the Revolution, and they found living in Connecticut increasingly difficult. Near the end of the war they fled to Nova Scotia and were rewarded with the grant of a fine piece of land that swept from Annapolis Bay to the Bay of Fundy. The senior Captain Johnson lived there until his death at age eighty-three.

His son William became a merchant and trader who sailed often to Louisiana to ply his trade once the war was over. With his partner, a Captain Bradish, he acquired a sugar plantation on the Delta and built a home there. Captain Johnson had married Letitia Rice of Digby, Nova Scotia, who had given him two sons. When she died at the age of thirty-seven, he married her sister, Sarah Rice, who was thirty-four at the time. William and Sarah had four children; the eldest born in 1811, was named Bradish, after William's partner in trade. After Captain Johnson's second marriage the wives had difficulty sharing the same plantation house, and after Bradish Johnson's birth, the Johnson family acquired another plantation a few miles to the north. Here the two younger sons John Dean and Edwin Augustus were born.

Captain Johnson had been a great success as a merchant, trader, and sugar plantation owner. He wanted his sons to have the benefits of a good education, which could not be found in the South at that time. Therefore, in 1822 or 1823 he moved his family north to New York City and entered the business of distilling spirits, establishing a distillery on Seventeenth Street between Ninth and Tenth Avenues, way uptown in those days. Believing that New York would one day surpass London in size and prosperity, he invested heavily in real estate in the area of the distillery, bringing him great wealth. It was said that at the time of his death Captain Johnson owned the largest whiskey distillery in America.

Meanwhile, his son Bradish went to Columbia College in New York, from which he was graduated in 1831. Bradish began studying law and was admitted to the bar in New York, but because his father's health had begun to fail at that time, he decided to enter business with him instead. Following the old Captain's death, Bradish continued in the distilling business with a new partner, under the firm name of Johnson and Lazarus. Much later in the 1870s the firm established a sugar refinery during the era of great expansion of that industry in New York and Brooklyn. The refinery, however, only lasted for a decade.

With the death of Captain Johnson, his three sons inherited great wealth and were well known as merchants of New York. The sugar plantation in the Louisiana Delta had been left to Bradish. During the Civil War as the Northern fleet was capturing New Orleans, he freed his slaves and employed them with pay to work the sugar fields. He was among the first to raise the Stars and Stripes in the South. John and Edwin Johnson left the family businesses to pursue lives of sport. It was said of them "they never missed a race on Long Island, and they owned the finest yachts and fastest horses that money could buy."[1]

All three Johnson brothers bought property and built summer residences on the South Shore of Long Island in the 1840s. Bradish, the eldest, had married Louisa Anna Lawrance in 1836 and they were on their way towards raising their large family of eleven children. A home away from New York's summer heat was badly needed. They located on land on the north side of South Country Road between the villages of

Babylon and Bay Shore (it was called Mechanicsville then) and built a home which they named Sans Souci (without a care). Louisa Lawrance Johnson was the third child (out of eleven) of Thomas Lawrance III (1785–1848) and his wife, Margaret Ireland Lawrance (1791–1871), both of whom were descended from Major Thomas Lawrance (1620–1703) who had immigrated to America and settled in Newtown, Long Island, in 1656 (see Chapter I). Sans Souci, a charming Victorian house complete with gables and surrounding front porch, became the family's summer homestead for the remainder of the nineteenth century. Bradish was to die there in 1892 at the grand age of eighty-one years.

The old Captain's younger son, John Dean Johnson (1815–1861), who was born at the family plantation called Woodland in Plaquemine Parish, Louisiana, had married Helen Maria Wederstrandt of that parish. They located on the west side of a lane that ran south from the South Country Road just to the east of Islip village. This became known as Johnson Avenue and later St. Mark's Lane. They built there before St. Mark's Church had been organized. John was a yachtsman. He owned the steam yacht *Bonita*, later chartered as the first ferry from Babylon to the Surf Hotel on Fire Island, and the sloop, *Irene*, built by W. J. Rowland at Port Jefferson.

The youngest son, Edwin A. Johnson, married Ellen Woodruff of St. Louis. He acquired a large amount of land south of South Country Road in the Islip and East Islip areas, much of it from the Nicoll family, the original patentee. He and his wife built a house on the west side of Suffolk Lane in East Islip where they lived from 1846 to 1851. They then built another home farther east near the original Nicoll homestead, which they named Deer Range Farm. Edwin Johnson and later his son, Lee Johnson, who married Fanny Nicoll, were the first developers in the Town of Islip in the sense that they divided their land for sale to others.

The decade of the 1840s saw only a very few other New York families come to summer in Islip Township, and they were related to Bradish and Louisa Johnson, most likely coming to join their kin. Louisa Johnson's father and mother,

Thomas and Margaret Ireland Lawrance, began the very long association of the Lawrance family with the area at that time. Thomas was buried from St. Mark's Church only a year after its founding in 1847. Most of their family of eleven children lived in the area for a time during their lives. Two of their daughters (the second after the death of the first) married William E. Wilmerding, senior partner of the New York auction house of Wilmerding, Priest, and Mount. A younger daughter married Wilmerding's son, George G. The sons, John I. Lawrance, William R. Lawrance (the father of Margaret Knapp), and Francis Cooper Lawrance were all major landowners and all were located near Bradish Johnson between Bay Shore and Babylon on South Country Road. That mile became the first avenue of summer homes by 1850.

All of the earliest summer settlers — the Johnsons, the Lawrances, and the Wilmerdings — were from New York and were Episcopalians. At the time they settled in Bay Shore and Islip, the nearest Episcopal Church was St. John's in Oakdale (see Chapter II) several miles away and too far to reach by horse and carriage. A new church was needed close at hand; a site was donated at the corner of South Country Road and Johnson Avenue to the east of Islip village; and in 1847 St. Mark's Church was organized. The first rector was the Reverend James W. Coe. Among the first churchwardens and vestrymen were John D. and Edwin A. Johnson (1847), William E. Wilmerding (1850), Bradish Johnson (1852), and George G. Wilmerding (1856). Francis C. Lawrance became a vestryman in 1865 and his father-in-law, Thomas Garner Sr., in 1863. Others were year-round residents of Bay Shore and Islip villages. St. Mark's was established before the Methodist,* Presbyterian, or Congregational churches came to the area. This was surely because of the interest and financial support of these early summer families who with many others to follow would be the mainstay of that lovely church well into the twentieth century.

---

* A small Methodist chapel did exist since 1828 (see Chapter II).

The resort hotel was an introduction for many city-dwellers to the seashore summer holiday, and such an introduction often led to residency. Many such hotels came into existence and increased in popularity particularly after the Civil War. The first of these, the Dominy House on Fire Island, started in 1847 in a very modest way.

In 1835 Felix Dominy (1800–1869), a descendant of the early East Hampton family of artisans, and his wife, Phebe, became the second keepers of the original Fire Island lighthouse (see Chapter II). Felix had been a major in the Suffolk County militia. He was also known as a confirmed hunter and fisherman and an excellent host. During the summer of 1836, thirty-eight people from Patchogue had dinner with the Dominys at their adjacent house and stayed the night. A week or so later a Brigadier General Trotter came to shoot ducks and also stayed overnight. Presumably this pattern of informal boarding continued for the remaining years of Dominy's keepership. In 1844 he retired as lighthouse keeper and purchased some land to the east where he built a home on the bay side of Fire Island. The home was said to be built largely from wood salvaged from the many wrecks on Fire Island beach. "There is a record of the barroom being made from a captain's cabin and decorated with salvaged figureheads and nameplates from hapless wrecks."[2] Thus, a small hostelry opened in 1847 for paying guests that featured swimming, fishing, and duck shooting — all conveniently at hand.

The concept of a summer resort with hotels for boarders was not new in the 1840s, although for the Great South Bay area it was still a decade in the future. Resort life in that decade was most popular at Saratoga Springs and by the 1860s it was the most fashionable summer spa in America. "'The fountains of Saratoga,' wrote *Harper's Magazine* in 1876, 'will ever be the resort of wealth, intelligence, and fashion.'"[3] The Grand Hotel there became the model for the many resort hotels that were to spring up in Newport, Rhode Island; Rumson, New Jersey; and around the Great South Bay.

The Dominy House on Fire Island was a very small beginning for resort life for a very few people. In the following decade of the 1850s a much larger hotel was conceived of by a remarkable man from Babylon, David S. S. Sammis. Sammis believed that the attractions of the South Beach for bathing (the Fire Island Beach of today), the Great South Bay for fishing, sailing, and bird shooting, and particularly the cool southwest breezes would draw people by the hundreds from the city during the summer. His Surf Hotel opened for guests in 1856 and was a great success. Located on Fire Island just to the east of the newly built second lighthouse, it was designed at the start to accommodate over a hundred guests who would be brought by ferry from a pier in Babylon. However, for New Yorkers and Brooklynites to get to Babylon was still a great effort, for the South Side Railroad did not come there until 1867. Guests had to be transported by carriage from the main branch of the Long Island Railroad at the Deer Park Station some five miles away. After the South Side Railroad did arrive in Babylon, the Surf Hotel expanded rapidly to become a "grand seashore hotel." "From the three-story main building, covered walks extended to the outlying cottages, giving the hotel the appearance of a modern motel complex. It could accommodate 1,500 guests and was extraordinary for its time in having gas lamps throughout. To facilitate the arrival of his guests, Sammis built a trolley line from the railroad station in Babylon to the dock where his steam yacht, *Bonita* [rented from John D. Johnson of Islip], carried them across to Fire Island."[4] It was a major undertaking to operate such a large establishment far from the source of food and other necessities. Ice for the summer, for example, was shipped by schooner from Maine, packed in the hold in large blocks surrounded by sawdust. The success of the Surf Hotel convinced others that the Great South Bay had great attractions for the holiday-goer.

There followed several less grand summer hotels, some called boardinghouses, on the mainland side of the bay. The Pavilion Hotel and Amos Stellenwerf's Lake House were opened across the South Country Road from each other in East Islip in the mid 1850s near the property of Edwin A. Johnson. Stellenwerf's Lake House was originally an old farmhouse, remodeled to accommodate guests. Some years later Stellenwerf said, "In the old times the fishing was excellent and it was hard work to accommodate the people that came down here. . . . Gold came to Islip in the shape of city boarders. . . . In 1849 you could get good board here for $3.00 a week. When, some years later, I raised it to $2.00 a day there was a terrible outcry, and the people said I would drive the boarders away — but I didn't."[5] Stellenwerf's son-in-law, the artist Thomas Worth, wrote, "Some of the most distinguished people in this country put up at the old-fashioned house with its crooked hall and quaint passages, old fireplaces and Franklyn stoves. Its great attraction was its splendid table, fine old wines and liquors, and its perfect cleanliness. Its proprietor was a man of great intelligence and personal attractiveness. It has also been a great place for shooting and fishing."[6]

The Pavilion Hotel was described in an 1863 advertisement as follows:

The Hotel is fitted up in modern style, lighted with gas, and furnished in a superior manner with every convenience appertaining to a "First-Class Hotel". It is surrounded by handsome grounds, pleasant walks and drives, and has, in connection, a large Garden, Billiard and Bowling Saloons, excellent Stable accommodations, and sailboats, under the charge of experienced boatmen, for fishing — with which the bay abounds in great variety — or sailing parties of pleasure.

It is accessible from New York City by three daily trains of cars each way from James' Slip or 34th Street by the Long Island Railroad stopping at North Islip [the South Shore line was not completed until 1868 to Islip] where stages are in readiness to carry passengers with their baggage to the Hotel. . . . [T]he location is unequaled by any other in the country, while its convenience to New York renders it the most eligible for businessmen desiring to spend much of the day in the City. The house and table will be kept in the best style, and furnished in all respects to accommodate the wishes of every guest, as well as to secure the comforts of a home.

Managed then by New York City hotelier Ira A. Libby and some years later by James Slater, the Pavilion became a great success. It could accommodate up to one hundred guests and had a stable for fifty horses. Many of the New York families who were to build in Islip in the years to follow were first guests at the Pavilion Hotel. Some would spend the entire summer there and the husbands would commute daily to work in the city.

A few years prior to the death of her husband, Felix, Mrs. Phebe Dominy (1807–1891) left Fire Island to open a new Dominy House for guests in the heart of Bay Shore village in 1861. She ran this hotel with great success for many years. More hotels were to follow after the end of the Civil War.

It was mentioned (see Chapter II) that most sea captains found the original Fire Island lighthouse inadequate to prevent disasters, and wrecks along the South Beach continued with alarming frequency. Perhaps the most celebrated wreck of all occurred in July of 1850 and persuaded the U.S. government that a better lighthouse was needed. The bark *Elizabeth* was returning home from Leghorn, Italy, her hold filled with the famous Carrara marble valued at $200,000, a small fortune at that time. The Captain of the *Elizabeth* had died in Italy of smallpox and she was under the command of a totally inexperienced first mate. On board were several notable passengers — the American sculptor Hiram Powers, who had waited three years for a ship to take back to America some of his prize statues (including one of John C. Calhoun), and the American writer Margaret Fuller, travelling with her husband and son. Fuller was closely associated with and much admired by Ralph Waldo Emerson. She was a feminist for her time and very much part of the New England transcendentalists.* The mate in charge of the ship tragically mistook the Fire Island lighthouse for the one on Sandy Hook, New Jersey, turned northward for New York harbor and ran hard aground in the surf off Point O' Woods. As the ship hit bottom, the marble in the hold broke loose and with its great weight remained in the sand. The *Elizabeth* quickly

---

* Her *Woman in the Nineteenth Century* (1845) was the first important American feminist book.

broke up. Margaret Fuller, it is said, never moved from her cabin. Her maid and her son were washed overboard and her husband drowned while trying to save their son. All in her party were lost. A few people from the ship did reach shore by floating on timbers from the broken bark. These survivors were brought to the mainland by the Johnson brothers in their yachts and cared for until they could continue on to New York. The tale is told that the Johnson brothers, upon hearing of the statue of John C. Calhoun lying on the ocean bottom off Point O' Woods, raised it at their own expense and shipped it to its ultimate destination in the South, where it was destroyed in the Civil War some years later.

Although the wreck of the *Elizabeth* and the loss of Margaret Fuller brought agitation for a new and better light-house, Congress was slow to provide the funds. In one thirty month period, November 1854 to June 1857, sixty-four ships were either wrecked or in distress on the beach.[7] Finally, in 1857, $40,000 was appropriated, and construction of a new lighthouse could begin. The new tower was to be 230 feet east of the old one, 167 feet high (the old one was 74 feet high), and the beacon would flash every minute from sunset to sunrise. The color of the tower was a yellowish cream until 1891 when it was changed to the present alternating black and white bands. When it was first lit on November 1, 1858, using whale oil as fuel, it could be seen from twenty miles at sea in clear weather. Over the years the interval of the beacon was shortened to seven seconds. It surely pre-vented many wrecks, but not all, as they continued often in bad weather, until the advent of radio communication could advise ships of their exact location at all times. By the begin-ning of the Civil War the new Fire Island lighthouse and the new Surf Hotel nearby were the main landmarks on the Great South Bay.

Hand in hand with the seaside resort hotel in the 1850s came the sporting club. Whereas the several boardinghouses and hotels were open to all, the sporting club was designed to appeal to those who wished to choose their own friends. The first of these on the Great South Bay was the Olympic

Club. It had been founded in 1841 by several members of a volunteer fire company in New York City who had a great admiration for the Olympic Theatre and for the actress, Mary Taylor, who was performing there that year.* They decided to use the Olympic name for their club. These firemen were also very fond of fish and clams, both catching and eating them. At first they would spend a week or so together in the summer in an outdoor camp set up on the beach on Barren Island** in Sheepshead Bay. The firemen enjoyed the outdoor rustic life away from home and from wives and family. These men were their own cooks, their own hewers of wood, drawers of water, and diggers of clams. They lived on what they caught, clams and fish, and at the end of the time they would pack up their tents and return home. A good supply of clams and fish was essential and it was a shortage of these that caused the firemen to move their campsite. After two or three summers by Sheepshead Bay in Brooklyn, they moved to the Shrewsbury River in New Jersey where for the first time they engaged a cook and consequently had to raise the dues from $1 to $10 a year. Although the clamming was good on the Shrewsbury the fishing was not. Thus, in 1854 a committee was formed to search for a new campsite.

By then the reputation of the Great South Bay for marvelous fishing had spread back to the city and it was thus described in *New York City Illustrated*: "For the glorious

---

* The Olympic Theatre was located on Broadway north of Prince Street in New York City.

** As described in 1930: "Barren Island, directly south of Floyd Bennett Field, is an island in name only — an isolated village in some remote countryside. A cluster of patchwork houses, whose occupants earn a livelihood as housewreckers. To the sound on Dead Horse Inlet, are the ruins of a fertilizer factory where families of Barren Island once found employment.

"The notorious pirate, Gibbs, who met death on the gallows in the early 19 c. was said to have buried a portion of his booty on Barren Island, and legend has it that the treasure is still hidden there."

bluefish, one must go to the Great South Bay, and hire a cat boat; or if you want the finest sport of all, go clear outside to the open ocean. You charter a thirty foot cat boat with one huge sail and with a crew of a man and a boy; the former to manage the boat, the latter to comment sarcastically upon the fish you do not catch. You 'pole' down the creek to the bay through clouds of mosquitos and green-headed flies: then seven miles across the bay and through the inlet to the open sea. . . . Now the gulls are close at hand. Swish! The line is jerked from your nervous fingers and runs out like mad. There's a fish on the line!"[8] It seemed very promising to the committee and they decided to pay a visit. They settled on a low, flat, rather marshy point of land for their campsite that extended into Great South Bay.

It was cool there in the summer with fresh breezes coming off the ocean across the Bay. If they wanted, they could build a dock for small sail boats as well. The mosquitos and flies were a bother, but the strong afternoon breezes drove them inland. This point of land they had found was at the end of Saxton Avenue between Penataquit and Islip villages. It turned out to be the ideal site, and the Olympic Club never moved again, remaining there for sixty years.

An account of that first year is interesting. "A few of us went down on a schooner with the tent and other things belonging to the club and the rest of the boys were to go on the Long Island Railway. The nearest station was four miles away (Central Islip), as the South Side Railway was not yet built, and they had a good walk in the woods, where there were plenty of mosquitos." The schooner was delayed by two days; the men were very angry and hungry; and they almost left. After the schooner did arrive, they unloaded it and went fishing. "We went out into the channel, and in half an hour came back with thirty bluefish, as nice and fat as you would wish to see. . . . We did not hear another word about breaking up the club. It was those bluefish that determined the question for us."

At first the Olympic Club rented the point from a local farmer, probably Captain Hawkins, for five dollars and their patronage in produce. He gradually raised the rent from year to year until the members almost decided to move elsewhere. Some, however, put up money to buy land, seventeen and one half acres, and eventually the club paid them back. With ownership came the move to permanence. Their tent gave way to a small one story house. A second story was added later, a boat was bought and finally a dock was built out into the Bay. The fishing remained excellent. The Olympic Club was the earliest of many sporting clubs that would be important features of the Great South Bay area and influential in developing its prosperity.[9]

Although by the advent of the Civil War quite a number of summer visitors knew of the attractions of the Great South Bay from their stay at boardinghouses and hotels, few had built homes. In the decade of the 1850s however, the Johnsons, Wilmerdings, and Lawrances were joined by Alfred Wagstaff, Benjamin K. True, Robert O. Colt, and Thomas Garner, who also built homes between Babylon and Bay Shore, and by Benjamin Sumner Welles in Islip. A word is in order about each.

Alfred Wagstaff was born in 1804, the son of the eminent New York merchant David Wagstaff who had emigrated from England in 1796. Alfred graduated from Columbia College in 1822, studied medicine and received his degree from Columbia's College of Physicians and Surgeons in 1826. In his early years he practiced medicine in New York City, travelled widely in Europe and tended to the affairs of his wealthy family. He married Sarah Platt DuBois, and together they raised a large family. His eldest son, Alfred, who later became known as Colonel Wagstaff, was born in 1844. In 1859 he purchased a large property on each side of South Country Road to the east of Babylon village in what is now called West Islip. The property extended from the Great South Bay north about four miles to where the railroad would run. Alongside a pond formed by Willets Creek to the north of the road, he built a summer home which he named Tahlulah ('running water'). The Wagstaffs were important to the early development of Babylon and West Islip. The doctor summered at Tahlulah until his death in 1878. His family continued to live there for many years afterwards.

Between the Wagstaffs and the Bradish Johnsons on South Country Road, Robert Oliver Colt also settled at this time. Born in 1812, a veteran of the Mexican War under General Winfield Scott, he was a large stockholder and president of the South Side Railroad Company. He was largely responsible for the building of that railroad, which brought service from the Long Island Railroad in Farmingdale to Babylon village in 1867 and thence eastward along the south shore of Long Island. Later it became a branch of the Long Island Railroad. Colt was a prominent member of the Babylon Presbyterian Church, which he helped build. He was the only pre–Civil War summer settler who was not an Episcopalian. His wife, Adelaide, died in 1865 at the age of thirty. He never remarried but continued to live in his West Islip home and was looked after in his retirement by his daughter, Amy, who had married his neighbor, C. DuBois Wagstaff, a son of Dr. Wagstaff. Robert Colt died in 1885 and was buried beside his wife in the Babylon cemetery.

Thomas Garner Sr. came to summer on South Country Road directly west of Bay Shore village and neighboring to the Francis C. Lawrance land. His property is marked today as Garner Lane, but then it extended from the railroad tracks right down to the bay, a distance of over two miles. After Garner's death in 1867, the property was acquired by Lawrance. Garner, who was born in England, had made a large fortune in cotton milling after his arrival in New York. He and his sons became one of the biggest producers of printed cotton in the world. They were said to have an income of over $2,000,000 a year from their business. Garner married Frances M. Thorn, a descendant of one William Thorne (her branch of the Thorne family had dropped the final e) who was an original patentee of Flushing, Long Island, in 1645. Thomas and Frances Garner had two sons, Thomas Jr. and William Thorn Garner, and four daughters, the eldest of whom, Frances, married neighbor Francis Cooper Lawrance. The Garners, as well as the Lawrances, were avid yachtsmen and did much to bring that sport to the Great South Bay. Garner also became a warden of St. Mark's Church in 1863.

Benjamin K. True, as were most of the early summer residents, was a merchant and a descendant of an early settler in America. His ancestor was Henry True who had emigrated from England in the 1630s to Salem, Massachusetts, and went on to found Salisbury, Massachusetts. Benjamin located on the South Country Road between Wagstaff and Colt.

In Islip, on Johnson Avenue just east of the village and to the south of the home of John Dean Johnson and St. Mark's Church, Benjamin Sumner Welles located in the mid 1850s. Welles had been born in Boston in 1824. He was a grandson of a governor of Massachusetts, Increase Sumner, and descended through his father from Thomas Welles, who came from England to settle in Connecticut in 1636. While in Boston, Benjamin S. Welles had inherited and enhanced a considerable fortune as a dry goods merchant. In 1850 he married Catherine Schermerhorn of New York, who was descended from the Schermerhorns of early Manhattan days (1636) and whose sister, Caroline, was to marry William B. Astor and become *the* Mrs. Astor of the 400 fame.* Welles and his wife moved to New York City soon after their first son, also called Benjamin S., was born and at this time acquired the property

---

* The first Patriarchs of 1872 were twenty-five gentlemen who, in the opinion of Ward McAllister who organized them, "had the right to create and lead society." The list included two Astors, two Livingstons, a Van Rensselaer, a Schermerhorn, a Rutherfurd, Benjamin S. Welles, and, of course, McAllister himself. They vested themselves with the prerogative of saying "whom society shall receive and whom society shall shut out." They sponsored annual subscription balls at Delmonico's to which each Patriarch could invite four ladies and five gentlemen on his individual responsibility. Thus, New York Society was created and controlled. Mr. and Mrs. William B. Astor were naturally first Patriarchs and, with the assistance of McAllister, Mrs. Astor gained dominance over the others until she was recognized by all as the leader of New York Society.

Mrs. Astor also gave an annual ball to which only 400 guests were invited because there was room for no more in her ballroom. McAllister proclaimed in 1892 that in his unquestioned judgment only these 400 ladies and gentlemen constituted "Society." Lloyd Morris, *Incredible New York* (1951) 144.

in Islip where they would summer. Their city home was on West Thirty-ninth Street, a most fashionable area at the time. After the birth of their son they had four daughters. Welles outlived his wife by many years. He was much respected in New York, a patron of the arts, a first Patriach of 1872, and lived to be the oldest member of the Union Club, the most prestigious of New York clubs. He became a vestryman of St. Mark's Church in Islip in 1861 and remained active in the church until his death in 1904 in his eightieth year.

As the decade of the 1850s came to an end and the Civil War was soon to begin, that section of the old South Country Road between Babylon and Bay Shore villages was the preferred spot for summer homes. It was a graceful and elegant road made of hard-packed dirt, of course, but lined with elm and maple trees giving shade in summer to the horse-and-carriages that passed along. Less than a mile from the Great South Bay, the road and the homes along it benefited from the prevailing southwest breezes when the days were very hot. Those who settled here first had bought land running down to the bay, giving them easy access to it, although the marshy border land was a favorite breeding ground for that local pest, the mosquito. It was a quiet, pastoral scene in those days, and people who passed by were attracted.

Second only to this stretch of road was the newly emerging area around St. Mark's Church in Islip. Undoubtedly the location of the church there was important to those who came to build near enough to Islip village to market, but far enough away to feel entirely "in the country." This street, called Johnson Avenue, was to become another major focus of summer homes of the wealthy from New York City. The decades of the 1860s and 1870s, especially after the Civil War had ended, would see many new summer homes, many new hotels, an important new club, and the first farms for the breeding of thoroughbred horses.

Chapter IV

AUGUST BELMONT AND THE SOUTH SIDE CLUB (1860–1870)

As the decade of the 1860s began, no sport was more popular with all classes of people than the sport of kings, horse racing. In New York City's newly opened Central Park there were nearly ten miles of perfect carriage roads and more than five miles of bridle paths. It was fashionable for the affluent to be seen there on horseback or in their carriages. The great "carriage parade" was one of the notable sights of the city, drawing crowds along Fifth Avenue and into the park. Another mania at this time was trotting. The procession of famous trotters bound for exercise along Harlem Lane had drawn the interest and attention of great crowds of spectators. "Men of wealth paid fabulous prices for fast horses. When any exceptional new trotter was to be brought out and shown off, Wall Street became excited. This excitement spread through the city and many bets were made on the newcomer's performance." " 'The opening of Central Park saved horseflesh in New York,' an old jockey asserted, 'and led to the revival of an old sport in circumstances of unprecedented splendor'."[1]

The social leaders of the sport were August Belmont, William R. Travers, and Leonard Jerome. It was Jerome who purchased 230 acres in Westchester County (now part of the Bronx) to lay out an elaborate racetrack with a grandstand seating 8,000 people, and a luxurious clubhouse. A great boulevard to be named Jerome Avenue was built to connect the track with the upper part of New York City. Jerome Park opened in 1866 to the acclaim of thousands, rich and poor. At last, New York had a racetrack close at hand. It was in that year that the American Jockey Club was founded by Belmont, Travers, and Jerome to promote horse racing and trotting and to raise the sport to a high level of elegance and distinction. The leaders of the sport needed to have large stables where their racers were bred, born, and trained under the close supervision of the best trainers that money could buy. Flat land and much space were most desirable, and because of this August Belmont turned to the South Shore of Long Island.

Belmont was the first truly prominent New Yorker to come to the Great South Bay area. Johnson, Wagstaff, Welles, and the others before him were all affluent and most were successful New York merchants. None, however, was a leader of New York Society in the way of August Belmont. By the 1860s he and his wife had been accepted by all but the "Old Guard" families (who never would accept a Jew) as a social arbiter of an extravagant lifestyle financed by merchant banking and epitomized by leadership in the sport of horse racing. It had not always been thus.

Belmont had been born the son of an unsuccessful Jewish merchant named Schonberg, in 1816 in the Rhineland in western Germany near the French border. He was said to have been a wild, unruly, disobedient boy — a cardinal sin in a Jewish household. He left home at the age of thirteen to search for his fortune and was lucky enough to find an apprenticeship in Frankfurt with the House of Rothschild, the leading Jewish banking house in Europe. After only a few years it became evident to the Rothschilds that this rough-spoken, abrupt, often embarrassing boy was a financial genius. At the age of twenty-one he was assigned to Havana, Cuba, to represent the firm in that city. Upon hearing the news of the Great Financial Panic of 1837 in New York he proceeded there immediately and with Rothschild money began to buy distressed stocks at bargain prices. He made a fortune for the firm and for himself in the process. When he appeared in New York that year, his name was not Schonberg any longer but Belmont (both names mean 'Mount Beautiful' in German and in French respectively) and it was no longer evident that his heritage was Jewish. Success followed success in the financial world. The firm of August Belmont & Co. was a lender to other American bankers and even to the U.S. government. Thanks to Rothschild's backing, Belmont became a miniature Federal Reserve system of that day and the profits were enormous. It was not until years later that financial leadership was taken from Belmont by the House of Morgan.

However, financial leadership in New York did not bring social acceptability, and August Belmont very much wanted to be considered a leader of New York Society. He achieved that goal in 1849 with marriage to Caroline Slidell Perry, the daughter of Commodore Matthew Perry who opened Japan to the West with his voyage there, and the niece of Commodore Oliver Hazard Perry, the hero of the War of 1812 and the Battle of Lake Erie. August Belmont and Caroline Perry were married at Grace Episcopal Church, the most fashionable church of that day, in a ceremony attended by most of New York's oldest families including a few Astors. August had been invited a few weeks before to join the Union Club, New York's oldest and most exclusive club. From that day forth no one disputed that the Belmonts were among New York's social leaders, although a very few of the Old Guard abhorred their extravagant lifestyle and would not ignore his blurred-over past. It was their reputation as host and hostess that gave their parties priority over almost anyone's in New York. With a French-trained chef, the Belmonts brought gourmet food to the private home and with dinner parties of up to 200 guests they entertained often. It was said that Belmont spent $20,000 a month on wine alone and had taught society the art of giving a perfect dinner.[2] The Belmonts had three sons, Perry, August Jr., and Oliver. All three would have interesting careers and would become a part of the Long Island story. It was young Perry who led his father to Babylon on the South Shore of Long Island when August was searching for a suitable place to locate stables for breeding his horses.

In August of 1864, Perry had engaged a guide from Babylon, Ras Tucker, to lead him on a bird shooting expedition. They were after quail, partridge, and ducks. The guide took Perry through an area two or three miles north of the village of Babylon where there were several lakes as well as some densely wooded forest. The land was flat and the birds were in abundance. Perry must have impressed his father with his description of that area, because Belmont soon purchased 1,100 acres of property with the intention of establishing a stud and breeding farm for his horses. He called the farm the Nursery. With this huge purchase Belmont became the largest property owner among the "part-time" residents of Babylon and Islip towns. His reputation in New York Society and especially among the horsey set would ensure that Islip would no longer remain an obscure backwater town in the distant countryside. Inevitably now others would follow to take advantage of the South Shore's many assets for sport.

By 1870 Belmont had created a complex to promote his racing interest that was as fine as any in the country at the time. A contemporary observer (1871) described it as follows:

We recently paid a visit to the fine racing stable of August Belmont of Babylon. The farm consists of some eight hundred acres, a good portion of which has been newly cleared and is being rapidly put into a high state of fertility. The agricultural part of the establishment is under the supervision of Alva F. Weld, well-known among us as an experienced farmer. The house, a large two-story villa surmounted with a mansard roof, overlooking the lake and trout preserves, is surrounded by extensive and well-kept grounds that are under the care of John Thompson, who as a landscape gardener, has no equal. The stables are probably the most extensive in the country, owned by a private gentleman. Seventy blooded running horses, among them many imported from England, are here — some very famous in the sporting world. "Kentucky," a famous stallion which Mr. Belmont paid $30,000 for, is sire to a dozen spring colts and a number of yearlings that promise well for the future record of the "Nursery." Jacob Pincus, a gentleman of rare skill in the management and training of horses, has the general supervision over the place as well as care of the horses. The racetrack is said to be the finest in the U.S. The running expenses of the Belmont farm are about $40,000 a year and it is estimated that since the stables were established, the winnings at the races have paid all running expenses.[3]

"The full mile track, not unlike the one at Saratoga [the premier racing spa in America], of dirt and loam with its inside tract of sand, timing stand and cooking sheds is conspicuous, with the numerous paddocks for mares and foals."[4]
The residence [built in 1868] is of the modern villa style, with the attached bowling alley, while immediately in front is Nursery Lake, filled with trout. On the edge of the lake is a plain substantial water tank, high enough to send all over the farm, water which can be drawn from innumerable hydrants.

Nor is the whole estate devoted to horses. The farm is well cultivated, and has its full proportion of cattle, including a fine herd of Alderney cows and plenty of chickens. Hundreds of quail brought from the west last fall, were recently turned out.

With the beginning of the racing season and with the growing popularity of book betting in this country, this stable is of no small interest to the racing public. After an absence of two years, Jacob Pincus again takes charge of the stable. Mr. Pincus has skill, backed by shrewd judgement, and above all, from a phrenological point of view, has secretiveness strongly developed. While in charge of the stable in 1869, 1870, 1871, and 1872, with such horses as: Gleneg and Kingfisher, he kept the "Maroon and Red" at the head of the list of winning stables.[5]

The Belmont racing colors, the maroon and red, or sometimes described as scarlet and maroon, were much in evidence. The coachman's livery consisted of maroon coats, with scarlet piping and silver buttons embossed with the Belmont cross, and black satin knee breeches with silver buckles. All Belmont's carriages were painted maroon with a scarlet stripe on the wheels. Belmont's lifestyle and his image to the public were surely regal.

Belmont was proud of his creation to the north of Babylon and would often show it to visitors. One of those in January 1876 was his patron, the Baron Rothschild of Paris, said to be the richest man in the world. He was apparently very pleased with what he saw and particularly with the trotters, as he purchased a fine pair before his departure for New York. He did not spend the night.

For the Belmonts the Nursery was not a summer residence; that was in Newport. It was, however, a place they often went for long weekends and holidays to oversee their interests, and to retreat from a hectic social life in New York City or in times of sorrow as when their daughter died in 1876. Two of the three sons, Perry and August Jr., were to be especially involved in the area. Perry at age thirty won the first of three consecutive elections as United States Representative to Congress from Babylon. At about that same time, August Jr. with his wife and young son went to live at the Nursery. He went there "to straighten out the place." Apparently it had fallen into decline. "After a year [that was] so dull that even the servants rebelled against staying another winter" he moved back to Hempstead.[6] Decline continued, the stud farm was moved and on November 24, 1890, the senior Belmont died at age seventy-four. His will provided that much of the racing stock and breeding studs at the Nursery be sold, but not the farm itself. Before the year was out many of his famous racers and all his yearlings were sold at auction at the Nursery. Belmont racing interests did not cease, however, as August Jr. had begun a new chapter that would culminate with the creation of the famous Belmont Park track in Hempstead, considered the finest in America when it was built. The Nursery in Babylon remained in family hands well into the twentieth century until it was taken over by the Long Island State Park Commission in 1925 and became Belmont Lake State Park. The "villa" was then torn down but some of the original barns remain today.

In the very early part of the 1860s another prominent New York family came to the Great South Bay area where their descendants would remain for almost a hundred years. Unlike Belmont, they would eventually build summer homes and be very much a part of the Bay Shore, Islip, and East Islip summer community. However, as with Belmont the original attraction to the area was sport, fishing, bird shooting, and trotting. Shepherd Knapp (1790–1875) was a prominent New York banker who for thirty-five years was president of the Mechanics Bank of New York City as well as Chamberlain of the City (treasurer of New York County). His bank, after a succession of many mergers, has become the Chase Manhattan Bank of today. He married Catherine Kumble and from the union four sons were born. Each became in his time an avid sportsman and the family shared the passion of that era for trotting and horse racing. Gideon Lee Knapp (1822–1875), the eldest son, was known as an excellent horseman. Shepherd F. Knapp (1832–1886), the third son, was "a great trotting man," according to his great nephew, "his team of bays 'Charlie Hogan' and 'Sam Hill' being known to all the trotting fraternity."[7] Later he became an organizer and president of the Gentlemen's Driving Association. As youngsters Gideon and Shepherd had become familiar with the Great South Bay. Shepherd was a boyhood friend of George Wilmerding, whose family summered west of Bay Shore. Together they would fish the bays in summer and hunt the birds all the time (there were no restrictions then). Shepherd and his wife located on South Country Road near his friend Wilmerding and directly east of Wagstaff. He would remain in that neighborhood for the rest of his life. The second Knapp son, William K. (1828–1877), with his wife, Maria Meserole Knapp, came to the South Shore as well. They located on Johnson Avenue in Islip across the road from Benjamin S. Welles. W. K. Knapp became a vestryman of St. Mark's Church in 1861.

The 1860s also saw the arrival in East Islip of James Boorman Johnston (whose name is often misspelled "Johnson," causing confusion with the Bradish Johnson family). Boorman Johnston (1823–1887) located between Pavillion Avenue and Champlin's Creek, purchasing land there from Edwin A. Johnson. He built a substantial summer home overlooking the creek, which he retained for twenty years. An active Episcopalian, he soon joined the vestry of St. Mark's, contributing to the upkeep of the church as vestrymen were expected to do. Church records show that he paid to have it painted in 1862, and in 1865 he paid for a new pew. He was also a member of the South Side Sportsmen's Club in the early 1870s.

James Boorman Johnston was the son of the New York merchant John Johnston, who with his partner James Boorman formed the successful importing firm of Boorman, Johnston & Co. shortly after the War of 1812. Of Scots descent and with a sharp trader's eye they captured the market of goods imported from Dundee, Scotland, and later became the exclusive New York agent for importing Swedish iron. The firm was considered among New York's finest mercantile houses and when Boorman retired in 1855 he and his partner, Johnston, had made large fortunes. Sadly, Boorman had no children, but Johnston was able to endow his children handsomely, including James Boorman Johnston, whom he had named after his old partner. Boorman Johnston left East Islip in 1880, selling his home to Charles T. Harbeck. A decade later it was sold again to Bradish Johnson Jr. and was called Woodland after the family's Louisiana sugar plantation. Johnston died in 1887 at his New York residence on West Tenth Street and was buried from the Church of the Ascension.

Islip had already gained a reputation for fishing and hunting. As early as 1820, Eliphalet Snedecor had established a tavern on a site on the Connetquot River* near the South Country Road. Here visitors from New York would come to take a stand on the river and cast for trout or in the fall hunt for deer or fowl. One said, "I, for myself, during residence at Snedecor's, killed five deer in six days hunting, two in one day, and returned to New York, having lived on venison and wild fowl during my four days away and my whole expense did not amount to $10."[8] The famous New York diarist Philip Hone wrote in 1836, "we went on to Snedecor's after dinner, where we found the house so full that, if we had not taken the precaution to write in advance for beds, we might have

---

* The Indian term meaning 'at a tidal river or creek' or 'at the long river.'

lain on the floor."[9] The Connetquot River and the lakes that fed it were an ideal habitat for all kinds of fresh water fish, game, and fowl, a veritable paradise for the field and stream enthusiast.

Eliphalet Snedecor died in 1861 and his son, Obadiah, carried on the tavern for a while. It had become so popular with the sportsmen and space at the inn was so limited that a few of the New York guests felt a change was needed. Among these were Bay Shore and Islip summer residents Bradish Johnson, George G. Wilmerding, and Shepherd F. Knapp. On April 6, 1866, the South Side Sportsmen's Club of Long Island was chartered "for the protection, increase and capture of salmon, trout and game." Its constitution limited the membership to not more than one hundred men of twenty-one years or older. It had an initial capital, raised by subscription, of $50,000. The land on which Snedecor's tavern was located together with the surrounding lakes and fields, almost 900 acres at the start, was donated to the club for one dollar by several of the founders who had purchased it from the Nicoll family a few years before. Improvements began almost immediately. Obadiah Snedecor, who had been paid for his tavern and farm by the club, was persuaded to become the caretaker in charge, host, and manager. Within five years it was described as follows: "Four miles from Islip, a little off the road is the Club House of the celebrated South Side Sportsmen's Club, composed of one hundred wealthy gentlemen. The Club owns 879 acres of valuable land in which are enclosed three preserves, containing ten thousand trout, a spawn tank with over three thousand infant trout, a brook five and one-half miles in length of which only one mile is owned by the Club, an area of ten acres including buildings and plenty of duck, quail, partridge, snipe, deer and all kinds of small game."[10]

The South Side Sportsmen's Club, like the Olympic Club before it (see Chapter III), was to be a club for New York gentlemen. The very first members, in addition to the three mentioned above, were prominent men in New York business and social circles. They included August Belmont,

Charles Louis Tiffany, the founder of the jewelry store of that name, the Lawrances and Wagstaffs, Stephen Whitney (who married Bradish Johnson's daughter), Samuel Milbank, William R. Travers, and many others. Early guests included President U.S. Grant in 1871 and General William Tecumseh Sherman in 1872. By the 1880s the names of Vanderbilt, Lorillard, Cutting, Meeks, Garner, Nicholas, Prince, Robert, Redmond, Hollins, Hollister, Hyde, Livingston, Bourne, Corbin, Peters, and Wood had been added to the membership rolls. It was not a coincidence that all of these were to build summer homes in the Great South Bay area. The sporting attractions of the South Side Club were to introduce to New Yorkers of wealth the South Shore community and make it one of the most fashionable summer resorts on the East Coast by 1890. This was recognized as early as July 1880 when *Harper's New Monthly Magazine* said, "The club life of the South Side is an interesting feature of that region, and has had an important influence in developing its prosperity. Many a man has bought land, and erected a house more or less costly, by reason of having been first attracted to South Bay through club membership, and the money invested in club property is by no means inconsiderable. The principal clubs on or near the bay are the Olympic, the Sportsmen's (South Side Sportsmen's) and the Wa-Wa Yonda."

At the time the gentlemen from New York were creating the South Side Sportsmen's Club, and the South Side Railroad was opened eastward from Babylon, the village of Bay Shore was expanding as well. Directly east of Francis C. Lawrance's property, two roads were opened from Main Street running down to the bay. One, Clinton Avenue, was built by Nathaniel and Hallet Clock of Islip and the second, Ocean Avenue, by Treadwell Smith, a Bay Shore merchant. To encourage more summer visitors it was intended that cottages would be built along them for summer rental. Also at this time a new resort hotel was begun on newly opened Ocean Avenue in Bay Shore and was called the Prospect House. The proprietor, John M. Rogers, had come to Bay Shore from Sag Harbor, Long Island, at the age of forty years. Seeing that insufficient accommodations were available for

Harvesting of salt hay was a major economic activity along the Great South Bay in the 19th century. (Courtesy of Fullerton Collection, the Suffolk County Historical Society.)

The famous trotter *Lady Suffolk,* pictured at the Centerville, L.I., race course in 1849. (Courtesy of The Old Print Shop.)

Shepherd F. Knapp of Bay Shore driving his well-known team of bays, *Charlie Hogan* and *Sam Hill* c.1870s. (Courtesy of We Knapps Thought It Was Nice.)

August Belmont, 1816-1890, prominent New York financier and horse racing figure. (Courtesy of Our Crowd by Stephen Birmingham.)

South Side Sportsmen's Club was founded in 1866 and expanded in the 1890s. The clubhouse as it appears today. (Courtesy of Richard A. Milligan.)

Club House was the private railroad station for the *South Side Sportsmen's Club,* photographed in 1879. (The Collection of Ron Ziel.)

THE YACHT "METEOR" OF NEW YORK.
LEAVING SANDY HOOK AUG 18TH 1869 BOUND TO EUROPE,
TO HER OWNER AND COMMANDER GEORGE L. LORILLARD ESQ MEMBER OF THE N Y YACHT CLUB

The schooner *Meteor*, owned by George L. Lorillard of Great River, was launched in 1869 only to be wrecked off the coast of Africa that same year. (Courtesy of The Old Print Shop.)

The J. Neale Plumb mansion in Great River, remodeled in 1884 to resemble a Chinese pagoda. (Courtesy of the Van Orden family.)

the increasing flow of people, and against the protest of many of his friends, he designed a hotel complex with 200 rooms that could hold 400 guests. It was such a great success that several adjacent guest cottages were added later. All kinds of games, such as tennis, croquet, and bowling, were available, and it was near enough to the bay to be considered a seaside resort. A stage with a team of horses brought guests from the Bay Shore Railroad station to enjoy a few days or weeks of seashore holiday. It attracted many New York and Brooklyn families, one of which was Mr. and Mrs. William M. Parsons and their children. Their son, Schuyler Livingston Parsons, would make Islip his summer home in the 1880s. Together with Dominy House on Main Street, the Prospect House marked the beginning of Bay Shore's reputation as something more than a sleepy village. By 1880 there were twenty-two cottages rented for the summer season, and new-found prosperity had arrived.

Many years later on September 27, 1903, Prospect House burned to the ground and was not rebuilt. Only the cottages were saved. So ended the social rendezvous where many events took place in the summer and on holidays. It had been a meeting place for the elite who often came in evening dress to enjoy the dances, the good food, and conversation.[*]

Meanwhile, in East Islip a new hotel had been opened to join the Lake House and the Pavilion Hotel (see Chapter III). George Westcott had come to the area in the mid 1850s from his native shire of Somerset in England. Seeing the success of the hostelries here, he determined to start another and in about 1860 he opened his Somerset House. It was directly east of Stellenwerf's Lake House. Like its neighbor it was in part a stagecoach stop on the road to the east and in part a local resort hotel. It was used as well by the trotting men of the South Shore who required good food and drink, as well

---

[*] Several guests, who did not like the service at the bar, formed the Growler Club. They decided to christen a new boat built about 1885 and belonging to George Watts, *Growler*. She was often seen on the bay until the 1970s.

as care for their horses. The house itself was a large, low two-story affair set back from the road and facing south to catch the prevailing breeze. The upper floor had bedrooms and the lower floor had the parlor, dining room, and bar-room. The stables were in the back. The horses were well cared for. "These stablemen know what was best to do, and were experts in caring for horses. They had to be; that was their business, and a fat tip often went to the careful groom."[11] The guests often returned. "Thomas Worth, the artist, celebrated for the trotting pictures he 'created' for Currier and Ives, was a constant visitor at the Somerset. He kept a sail-boat in Champions [sic] Creek, just south of the village, and he used to take trips to Fire Island and go blue fishing. After a sail, he would generally spend the night at Somerset House and he gave Westcott some of his original sketches, which used to adorn the walls."[12] Worth married the daughter of Amos Stellenwerf of the neighboring Lake House and lived in Bay Shore for a time.

The Somerset House was the first hostelry in the area to introduce running water for its guests. For the summer season of 1878 George Westcott had built a large water tank on a wooden tower thirty feet above the ground. A small pump kept the tank constantly filled and in a special room beneath the tower guests could take a shower. Each bedroom had running water to a basin from the pressure of the raised tank. In front of the hotel there was a water fountain to display the new attraction to travelers. A contemporary observer noted, "when completed it will be one of the most perfect arrangements for furnishing water that has been introduced on Long Island, and at a reasonable cost."[13]

George Westcott was to join the St. Mark's Vestry in 1876, one of the few local residents so honored. He died suddenly in 1883 and Somerset House went to his sons, John and then Joe, who ran it until 1904 when it went bankrupt and shortly thereafter burned to the ground.

By the start of the new decade in January 1870 a local correspondent noted that "Islip is waking up from its long sleep, and new avenues, new buildings and public improvements are the order of the day. Islip promises to have some of the best roadways on the Island thanks to J.H. Doxsee and the clam shells from his clamming establishment."[14]

The largest commercial enterprise in the Town of Islip was founded by James Harvey Doxsee (1825–1907), whose father came to Islip as a boy and became an extensive landowner in the area. James Harvey conceived of the idea of preserving the great abundance of Great South Bay clams for year-round use by cooking and then canning them. After the Civil War, on the east side of Islip's Orowoc Creek (or Doxsee's Creek as it was then called) he built a canning factory.* Clams brought in by baymen were opened, cooked, and canned to be later shipped to all parts of the United States. In one season in 1874, 17,000 bushels of clams were processed, giving employment to thirty-five hands at the factory. In the off-season, corn, tomatoes and pumpkins were canned there as well. The principal by-product was empty clam shells, which went onto the local roads to make a firm surface. The J. H. Doxsee Co. was to remain in family hands until after World War II.

In spite of the efforts of Doxsee and others to improve the dirt roads, which would get severely rutted in wet weather, there were constant complaints by both travellers and homeowners about the terrible road conditions. Apparently the town did little or nothing and left the matter to groups of individuals and to the early Islip developers.

Although Islip was beginning to awaken, the process was slow. The resort hotels and boardinghouses for rent were popular in the summer and the town was benefiting from this seasonal activity, but very few New York families had built their own homes as yet. The population of the town as shown in the 1870 census had increased only by some 2,300 people in the past twenty-five years, not very much of an awakening. The decade 1870 to 1880 would see many new homes, particularly in the last half and particularly near the village of Islip.

---

* The canning factory operated from 1866 to 1905. Doxsee's deep sea fishing fleet continued to work until after World War II.

Chapter V

WILLIAM K. VANDERBILT AND HIS FRIENDS (1870–1880)

The topography of the South Shore of Long Island around the Great South Bay had much to do with the areas that were eventually chosen for the building of summer homes. Long Island itself is the result of the last glacier, which reached halfway across the island from north to south. When it withdrew, the glacier left a flat, sandy, outwash plain on the south, whereas the north shore was hilly. The Great South Bay is rimmed by a barrier beach known today as Fire Island. This bay, very shallow for the most part and even marshy around its northern perimeter, is a natural haven for wild fowl, saltwater fish, and crustaceans. Several inlets from the Atlantic Ocean keep the saltwater from stagnation and many freshwater streams and rivers feed into the bay from the north. The prevailing summertime breeze is southwest from the ocean, which makes the preferred exposure a south facing one. Recurring coastal storms are a peril to the bay and some protection from them can be sought up the streams or "creeks" as they are called on the South Shore. Although the bay is constantly changing its shape, its essential features are little different today than they were when William Nicoll arrived in the seventeenth century.

As has been seen, the first area chosen for summer homes was between the villages of Babylon and Bay Shore. Here the homes were south facing and the bay could be viewed easily from them. There were few trees then to block the cooling breezes. "The road between Bay Shore and Babylon," wrote the *Signal*, "is one of the finest in the country." "Rich and beautiful country residences of wealthy merchants and businessmen are situated at close distances. Their luxurious homes are surrounded by ornamental lawns and shrubbery, costly hot houses, filled with costly and rare tropical plants and flowers of every hue, while the aid of skilled landscape gardeners has converted everything in nature by the way into artistic and picturesque effects — the whole road in fact being converted into one long beautiful panorama of exceeding loveliness and beauty."[1] Into this panorama in the 1870s two more New York families joined their earlier settling neighbors — those of Richard Arnold and Henry B. Hyde.

The first to come was Arnold, in 1872. He located between Shepherd L. Knapp and Benjamin K. True (see Chapters III and IV). Richard Arnold was the son of the founder of one of the oldest dry goods houses in New York. Born in 1825, he was educated in the city and as a young man joined his father in the business as an apprentice. As the enterprise prospered he was admitted to partnership along with his brother-in-law, James Constable. The firm thereupon was known as Arnold, Constable & Co., which, along with A. T. Stewart & Co., became the two leading department stores of that era in New York. Both stores were located along the famous "Ladies Mile" on Broadway from Eighth Street to Twenty-third Street. Arnold's was a massive white marble building at Eighteenth Street. It was here in the 1870s and 1880s that the daily fashion parade took place, with Broadway filled with carriages and the sidewalks crowded with ladies in their long walking dresses. Shopping had become a favorite pastime for the affluent, and Arnold, Constable was prospering. Arnold built a mansion on Fifth Avenue at Eighty-fourth Street and chose West Islip for his country seat. There he would remain with his family until his sudden death in 1886. He had been twice married and was survived by a son, William, who inherited several million dollars together with the West Islip home. Arnold, like most of his peers, was an Episcopalian, a member of St. Thomas's Church in New York and Christ Church, West Islip. Both he and his son had a great interest in yachting, owning the schooner, *Sachem*. It was this sport that undoubtedly had attracted him to the Great South Bay.

The death of William E. Wilmerding in 1875 caused his property between R. O. Colt and George G. Wilmerding to be put up for sale. The buyer was the founder and head of the Equitable Life Assurance Society of America, Henry Baldwin Hyde (1834–1899). Hyde was descended from an English family who came to New England in the seventeenth century and who followed the Reverend Thomas Hooker to start the Connecticut colony in Hartford. Henry was born in Catskill, New York, the son of Henry Hazen and Lucy Baldwin Hyde. In 1859 he organized the "Equitable" as it became known, and is known today. A mutual insurance company, owned by its policyholders, it became a huge success. Vast sums in premiums were under the control of Hyde and his directors and he became very wealthy in the process. He remained president of the firm until his death in May of 1899. In 1864 he married Anna Finch and they had three children, the last of whom, James Hazen Hyde, was to become a notorious figure in New York after his father's death. Henry B. Hyde became very much a part of New York's merchant establishment. He joined the Union Club, the Union League Club, the Riding and Kennel Clubs, and was a patron of the Metropolitan Museum of Art. In the year of his purchase of the Bay Shore property he became a member of the South Side Sportsmen's Club.

Hyde was to build in Bay Shore what Islip historian George Weeks called "one of the most pretentious country estates on the South Shore of Long Island."[2] Designed by the notable architect, Calvert Vaux, it was called the Oaks. While still under construction in May of 1876 it was described as follows: "Among the many palatial residences one of the prettiest (and must also be the costliest) is the grand residence of H. B. Hyde now in process of completion. Built in a massive and striking style of architecture, reminding one somewhat of an English nobleman's castle, yet amid all its bewildering towers, roofs, etc. its harmony is preserved throughout. Swarms of laborers and mechanics are at work converting order and beauty from neglected natural outlines. When completed this truly grand and noble establishment will be a fit residence for a royal king, or its equally worthy owner."[3]

In addition to the mansion itself, the Oaks included many other buildings in the manner of the great English stately homes. There were stables for nearly a hundred horses kept on the estate and made available for large riding parties and for the famous Tally-Ho coaches of that era. There were cow sheds for the herd of over a hundred cows, a dairy, wagon sheds, a silo, corn cribs, and a windmill. There was a 900 foot long conservatory for roses, carnations, grapes and fruits, palms, orchids, and citrus — the English would have dubbed it the Orangery. There was an entrance lodge, a superintendent's house, a farm office, a gardener's cottage, and two poultry houses. A deer park and two lakes filled with trout completed the estate. It was said that over a hundred people were employed by the Hydes inside the house and on the estate. Lastly, at the north end of the property there was a private railroad siding off the Long Island Railroad tracks where the Hyde private car would be placed for guests to unload. The Oaks was the grandest of the country estates of that decade for only a few years, for soon those of Lorillard and Vanderbilt would rival and even surpass it.

The principal river that feeds into the Great South Bay is called the Connetquot, named for that Indian tribe. Rising from small streams in north shore hills, it meanders southward throughout the forest of oak and pine before widening as it approaches the Great South Bay at what was once called Youngsport and now Great River. The land to the east of the river lies in Oakdale, both towns within the township of Islip. It was along the Connetquot River just north of the country road that the South Side Sportsmen's Club was established (see Chapter IV). South of the country road the river at its wider and deeper part was a natural harbor for yachts, and the surrounding land fronted on water without direct exposure to the occasional bay gales. Three New York families came to this area in the 1870s, George L. Lorillard, J. Neale

Plumb, and William Kissam Vanderbilt. It became the second of the "great estate" sections to be developed.

George L. Lorillard was the last child of Peter and Catherine Griswold Lorillard, a descendant of a French Huguenot family that had fled from France to Holland and thence to Hackensack, New Jersey, to join the Huguenot community there at about the time of the American Revolution. George's grandfather, Peter A. Lorillard, had been a founder (with his brother) of the oldest and most famous tobacco company, Lorillard Company, from which the family fortunes sprung. George's oldest brother was Pierre Lorillard who was the founder of Tuxedo Park, New York (1886), a restricted community for the affluent in the Ramapo Hills. There was also a second brother, Louis.

George had been born in New York City in 1843, had graduated from Yale College in 1862, and had studied medicine for a year at Bellevue Hospital when he decided that being a doctor was not the career he wanted. For a short four years he entered the family tobacco firm with his oldest brother, Pierre, but found that not to his liking either, and in 1868, at the age of twenty-five, he retired from business for good. By then he had discovered the first of the two passions in his life, yacht racing.

George Lorillard had always been good at sports. At Yale his six feet three inch height and 200 pound weight made him a natural for the crew and he was considered a fine oarsman. With the conclusion of the Civil War in 1865, ocean yacht racing became a sport indulged in by the affluent with their great two-masted schooners. For the next seven years Lorillard would own a succession of seven of these huge yachts before retiring from that sport altogether. Two yachts are worth noting. Lorillard's *Vesta* in December of 1866 was one of three schooners to enter the first transatlantic race from Sandy Hook, New Jersey, to Cowes on the Isle of Wight. She was narrowly defeated by James Gordon Bennett Jr.'s yacht *Henrietta*, which crossed the finish line after fourteen days and six hours of sailing to claim the $90,000 prize that had been put up by the members of the New York Yacht

Club, including Bennett and Lorillard, over drinks at the bar earlier that year.*

Transatlantic races, begun in 1866, were repeated in 1867 when *Vesta* returned east to west to New York, and in 1869 when Lorillard, then with the yacht *Meteor*, again raced to Cowes. The schooner *Meteor*, just launched in the spring of 1869, subsequently cruised in the Mediterranean until being wrecked off the coast of Tunis in a storm in December. Commander Lorillard and his party had to pay a $15,000 ransom to be released by the Bey of Tunis. In 1872 Lorillard had tired of yachts and such dangerous exploits. Although his physique was large, he suffered from rheumatism and often had to be assisted by crutches. He decided to give up the sea and devote himself to his second passion, the sport of kings. To do so, he would need some land for a horse farm.

In the 1860s New York tobacco merchant Robert L. Maitland had acquired from the Nicoll family over 600 acres of land north of the country road and directly west of the South Side Sportsmen's Club of which he was an early member. He laid out some trout ponds on his property, which he called Westbrook Farms (the brook feeding the pond being just west of the main Connetquot River). Maitland had scarcely begun to develop the estate when he died suddenly in 1870. Three years later, in June 1873, Maitland's wife and son sold Westbrook Farms to George L. Lorillard for $42,500, a handsome sum at the time.

Suffolk County had achieved a reputation for horse breeding of racers and trotters by then, thanks to August Belmont, and passion for that sport was at its peak. It was Lorillard's intention to turn Westbrook Farms into a breeding and training ground for his stable of fine horses. He began remodeling the dwelling by the road and building the needed barns for the enterprise. It was reported that he "has expended upward of a quarter of a million in acquiring land, erecting residences and out buildings, stables for his long string of

---

* The third yacht was Franklyn and George Osgood's *Fleetwing.*

celebrated horses, racing grounds (including two racing tracks, one a mile and one a half-mile track), drives, shooting grounds and parks."[4]

In 1875 he had built a new stable of unusual dimension. "It is constructed in ten sections forming a circle while covering an acre of ground. The center is left open with a covered track on the outer edge of the opening for exercising the horses in rough weather. Nine sections of stables are to have four stalls in each one, the tenth one being fixed with suitable apartments for the jockey boys. There are 25 horses on the place."[5] When it was completed, Westbrook Farms was as worthy a rival of Belmont's Nursery as their racers and trotters were rivals at Saratoga, Jerome Park, or other top racetracks.

Both Belmont and Lorillard competed in England as well as at home. Lorillard's famous horse, Duke of Magenta, the leading winner at Saratoga in 1877 and 1878, was sent to England for races there. The most famous of all his horses, however, was Islip-trained Iroquois. Sent to England for the June 1881 racing season, this colt won both the Prince of Wales stakes at Ascot and the Derby at Epsom, the first American horse ever to do so. At the conclusion of the 1881 racing season it was reported that Lorillard's stables had won $79,000 in prize money and for three years $366,000, a very successful record by any accounting.

Training horses was not the only activity at Westbrook Farms. Lorillard and his guests would often engage in pigeon shooting matches and usually for stakes. On occasion a shooting match was held with a gun club. Under the rules of the English Gun Club and using double barrel twelve-gauge shotguns, each contestant would try to kill as many birds as possible in an allotted time. In one match the winner killed thirty-three birds out of fifty and collected $5,000 for his team. Lorillard, the host, pocketed $10,000 on another occasion.

Lorillard sold Westbrook Farms in 1884 after only a decade of ownership. He had married late in life but he and his wife, Maria Louise, had no children. His older brother, Pierre, had a horse farm in New Jersey. Perhaps he tired of the sport or of Long Island. Or perhaps he seized upon a good opportunity when it came along, for looking for a great estate was the wealthy New York railroad merchant, W. Bayard Cutting, who purchased Westbrook Farms for his country home. Lorillard's health continued to deteriorate. He would spend the winter at his residence in St. Augustine, Florida, hoping that the mild climate would ease his pain. When not in Florida he traveled to Nice on the Riviera and it was there in the winter of 1886 that George L. Lorillard, age forty-three, died. He was called at that time a patron of all outdoor sports but it was primarily as a yachtsman and turfman that he was remembered and especially as a horse breeder along the Great South Bay.

The land to the south of Lorillard's, fronting along the Great South Bay and on the west side of the Connetquot River, was a densely wooded part of the Nicoll patent. It had been partially cleared by people named Conklin and given the name Deer Range Farm. At the same time that Lorillard bought Westbrook Farm, Deer Range Farm, 690 acres in all, was sold to Sarah Ives Plumb, the wife of J. Neale Plumb, for $42,500 and there began a story that would end in great tragedy many years later.

J. Neale Plumb was a merchant with a reputation for lavish spending and wild speculation. From time to time he was in severe financial straits and once in 1878 was forced to file for personal bankruptcy. At the age of twenty-seven, Plumb won the hand of Sarah Ives of New York, the daughter of a very wealthy merchant. The marriage was opposed by the father and even denounced by a close family friend of the Ives, one Alexander Masterton, a wealthy banker several years older than Plumb. Masterton accused Plumb of being a professional gambler. When Sarah's father died, she was left a trust fund of $800,000 and the named trustee was Masterton. Plumb and his wife lived in great splendor mostly on her money. They built a mansion on Fifth Avenue and Fortieth Street in New York, travelled extensively to Europe, and in 1872 acquired Deer Range Farm (sometimes called Deer

Range Park) for their country estate. They had a son, named J. Ives Plumb, and two daughters.

Deer Range Farm was developed very much in the manner of the estates of the English landed gentry. A contemporary reporter described entry to it as follows: "Perhaps no place here is more talked about than Deer Range Park where the Plumb mansion stands. It is reached by a drive over one of these sylvan roads where Nature comes so close to you that the thickets touch the carriage from either side. An immense field, where a regiment of soldiers could maneuver, without a tree or a stump on it, lies in front of the house and gives the place a cold and lonesome appearance, and this effect is heightened by the house itself."[6] The farm itself consisted of woodlands, meadows, and 260 acres under cultivation for crops of corn, wheat, rye, barley, oats, and fruit trees. A large icehouse, two lodges, piggery, poultry houses, corn crib, barns, carriage house, blacksmith shop, stables, cow barns, a boat house, and a bath house completed the assortment of outbuildings. The thirty-room mansion, formerly built by Edwin A. Johnson, was decorated with a valuable collection of antiquities and works of art collected by the Plumbs during their travel to foreign countries.

Plumb's reputation for eccentricity grew. He imported cattle from Europe. It was reported that he would winter a large part of the menagerie stock of his old friend P. T. Barnum at Deer Range Farm, which would include four elephants. "Look out for rough weather if they stampede some pleasant evening" said our reporter.[7] With their family life under increasing tension as well, the Plumbs left the country for good in 1876 and settled in Paris. Deer Range Farm, however, was not sold. Tragedy struck shortly thereafter with the premature death of Sarah Ives Plumb in the winter of 1877. Her will left her estate including her trust fund and Deer Range Farm in trust for her son, still a minor, and the named trustee was again Alexander Masterton. Her husband was the guardian of their son but had no control over the money or the property — only Masterton held the purse strings.

Meanwhile, Plumb and his three children returned to Deer Range Farm following Sarah's death. Plumb made an attempt at achieving a degree of respectability. He joined the Emmanuel Church in nearby Youngsport (now called Great River). The church had been a chapel of St. Mark's in Islip from 1862. In the spring of 1878 Plumb employed a New York architect to superintend the work of altering the church. "The former entrance on the east end was closed and a memorial window to the late Mrs. Plumb was put in the place where the door had been, and a tower forming a new entrance, with a beautiful spire was built on the south side."[8]

In 1884 Plumb decided to remodel his mansion at Deer Range Park and in so doing expressed his growing eccentricity. One observer commented, "A two-story and mansard roof extension, with double towers, forms the east wing. The west wing is of beautiful design, highly ornamented with fancy architectural designs, and surmounted with a curious single tower of prodigious heights. It somewhat resembles a Chinese pagoda with its carved roofs and fancy cornices. One thing is certain, it makes a very fine appearance and the original house is entirely lost in the new."[9] Another critic said, "It is a peculiar house, and does not at first sight impress the visitor. No one style of architecture is followed, and there is a lack of harmony. The building is pretentious, very much so, but it has more the appearance of a hotel or lunatic asylum than a private residence. It has been in the course of construction for three years. A conspicuous feature about the new house is a tall spire with a clock in it, which can be seen from a distance of ten miles."[10]

As Plumb's children grew to maturity, conflicts with their father grew as well. Plumb opposed the marriage of his son to Anna Burton in 1886. A row followed, and the senior Plumb left Deer Range Farm for good to his son who in reality owned it now outright, having obtained his majority. Plumb's oldest daughter then married an Englishman who Plumb considered "an impecunious fortune hunter" and his younger daughter left him to live with her brother. As family estrangement was now complete, Plumb became more and more neurotic and mentally unstable. All his money had gone and he considered that his life was over.

On May 4, 1899 the *New York Times* reported on page 1; "Alexander Masterton, 72 years old, a wealthy banker was shot and killed yesterday in the Burlington Apartment house at 10 West 30th Street by J. Neale Plumb, a retired merchant, 65 years old of 70 West 38th Street. Plumb admitted the murder was a revenge killing." The article went on to say that Plumb had left a forty-six page statement of his reasons for the killing, which he had prepared well prior to the murder. He blamed Masterton for all the "misfortunes" that befell him, for denouncing him at the time of his marriage, for his son's marriage to a dissolute woman, for his daughter's marriage to an impecunious fortune-hunting Englishman, and for his younger daughter's abandoning him. After the murder he surrendered peacefully to the police and confessed his guilt. He was then taken to the Tombs. Before his trial, at which he was to plead innocent by reason of insanity, he took sick while in the Tombs and was removed to the hospital. Refusing any medical treatment, Plumb died on June 1, 1899, less than a month after the murder.

J. Ives Plumb and his wife had lived at Deer Range Farm after the break-up with his father. In fact, his sister was married there to the Englishman Mr. Ramsey Nares. The Plumbs enjoyed the South Shore life. Eventually they moved closer to Islip village, buying the Meeks property on the west side of Champlin's Pond. They joined St. Mark's Church, but Ives was never asked to join its vestry. The family scandal was, perhaps, too much for the church to overlook.

As the decade of the 1870s progressed, the interest of the affluent in trotting began to wane. Trotting was replaced by the sport of coaching, particularly when the gentleman was the driver. The gentleman driver, properly dressed in bottle green coat with gilt buttons, yellow striped waistcoat, silk topper, and boutonniere, would sit in the driver's seat of the coach, which was pulled by a team of four horses. This was known as four-in-hand driving. In 1874 the Coaching Club of New York was founded by Colonel William Jay, Leonard

Jerome, and DeLancy Kane (an Astor connection) to promote the sport and to maintain its high standards of decorum. To the Coaching Club, form was as important as family. Kane began the practice of driving his coach from the city to the country club for lunch and returning in the afternoon. Occasionally the party would stay overnight at a tavern or better yet as guests in a member's country estate. Kane's four-in-hand coach became known as the Tally-Ho, which promptly became the generic name for all such coaches.

As the summer estates expanded along the Great South Bay in the 1870s so did the number of Tally Ho coaches that were seen on the roads. In 1881 the New York Coaching Club paid a visit to Belmont's Nursery in Babylon. Belmont had driven his own four-in-hand coach years before it became fashionable to do so. The party remained for a weekend of fishing and boating until early on Monday morning the Tally Ho dashed away on the homeward trip. Such an excursion required extensive preparation. The Coaching Club sent grooms out beforehand to check the conditions of the road on the proposed route and often found them bad. They also had to arrange for relays of horses at appropriate points and care for them at local inns such as Somerset House.

Coaching was also used for local travel. A service was begun between the Pavilion Hotel in East Islip and the Babylon Railroad stations in the morning and evening to benefit the commuter to New York. It provided an opportunity for "everyone to enjoy this exhilarating experience."[11]

In May of 1883 the New York Coaching Club planned an outing to the estate in Oakdale of one of their most popular members, who had located there five years before on the east bank of the Connetquot River. He was William Kissam Vanderbilt.

When the old Commodore Cornelius Vanderbilt died in January 1877, he was described in the press as the richest man who had ever died in America up to that time, exceeding even the wealthiest of the deceased Astors. The Commodore left an estate of over $90 million primarily to his eldest son, William Henry Vanderbilt. Upon the latter's death in 1885, a

William K. Vanderbilt, 1849-1920, pictured here in 1899 at the age of 50. (Courtesy of the New York Public Library.)

Alva Smith Vanderbilt, 1853-1933, pictured as dressed for her fancy dress ball on March 26, 1883, at the age of 30. (Courtesy of The New York Historical Society, The Harold Seton Collection.)

Oaks was designed by Calvert Vaux for Hyde. It was later owned by his son, James Hazen Hyde, and then by Louis Bossert of Brooklyn. (Courtesy of John Pullis.)

Henry Baldwin Hyde, 1834-1899,
founder of the Equitable Life
Assurance Society, built the *Oaks*
west of Bay Shore in 1876.
(Courtesy of the New York Public Library.)

The *Prospect House* was built on Ocean Avenue in
Bay Shore in the late 1860s. A large resort hotel,
it attracted hundreds to Bay Shore each summer.
It burned down in 1903. (Courtesy of Historic Bay Shore
by Priscilla Hancock.)

PROSPECT HOUSE.
BAY SHORE, L.I. N.Y.
D. FRANKEL, PROP'R. ALSO CLARENDON HOTEL, BROOKLYN, N.Y.

The above is a reproduction of the flyleaf illustration from
"SOME OF TOWN OF ISLIP'S EARLY HISTORY"
By George Lewis Weeks, Official Historian of the Town of Islip

Idlehour designed by Richard Morris Hunt and built in 1878–79 in Oakdale for W. K. and Alva Vanderbilt. (Courtesy of American Institute of Architects Foundation.)

The Oakdale railroad station was built in 1889 by W.K. Vanderbuilt to replace a wooden one "not in keeping" with *Idlehour* buildings. It is shown here in 1973. (Photo by Ron Ziel.)

substantially larger estate of over $200 million (W. H. Vanderbilt's career as head of the New York Central Railroad had more than doubled the value of the family assets) was left for the most part to his two eldest sons, Cornelius II and William Kissam. The remaining two sons and the four daughters received $10 million each. It has been said that the Vanderbilts, in the grand manner in which they spent money on their personal pleasures, epitomized the age of "the Glitter and the Gold," the title of Consuelo Vanderbilt Balsan's book.[12] This was surely true of William K. Vanderbilt and his wife, Alva Smith Vanderbilt, who were perhaps most famous for the number and the grandeur of their homes. At one time or another in their marriage (married in 1875, they were later divorced and both remarried) they had a dozen homes on two continents, one for each month of the year.

In addition to being the scion of America's largest fortune, Vanderbilt, known as W. K. by his friends, was a very sociable man. "He was tact and kindness personified. Genial, gracious, considerate, and generous to a fault, he was also an amusing raconteur with a huge fund of good stories. Besides native charm he possessed a highly cultivated intelligence. He had been educated in Switzerland, spoke fluent French, and was a connoisseur of European culture, art and manners. He was an intimate of the nobility of the Second Empire of France, very much in demand and a favorite at their luxurious entertainments."[13]

Fortune had yet to give the young Vanderbilts acceptance by New York Society, however. Until 1883 W. K. did not belong to any of New York's prestigious clubs and it was only after the Coaching Club's visit to Idlehour* that he was admitted to the Union, Knickerbocker, Racquet and Tennis, and New York Yacht Clubs. In 1884, the Vanderbilts were at last invited to Mrs. Astor's annual ball. They had "arrived."

---

* The W. K. Vanderbilt country home in Oakdale was often spelled "Idle Hour." However, in her book, *The Glitter and the Gold*, Consuelo Vanderbilt Balsan spelled her girlhood home, "Idlehour." I have chosen to use her spelling.

Alva Smith Vanderbilt was among the most dynamic, iron-willed women of the Gilded Age, a very different personality from her husband. She never took no for an answer and what she wanted, whether acceptance by Society, a mansion to live in, or a titled husband for her daughter, she got. Perhaps her most remarkable achievement was to gain acceptability by New York Society following her divorce (unheard of in that era) from Vanderbilt in 1895 and her marriage to Oliver H. P. Belmont (son of August Belmont Sr.) on January 11, 1896, less than a year later.

W. K. and Alva realized early in their marriage that to become a part of Society in the Gilded Age they must acquire or build a country home, a place where they could establish roots. By 1877, therefore, they had acquired about nine hundred acres of riverfront and bayfront property south of the South Side Sportsmen's Club of which W. K. also became a member that year. The "extensive country villa" as it was locally known, was named Idlehour.[14] The architect most closely associated with Vanderbilt houses, Richard Morris Hunt, was asked to design Idlehour as well. The family liked his work so much that he later built their French Renaissance mansion on Fifth Avenue and Fifty-second Street and their cottage in Newport, called Marble House. He also designed St. Mark's new church building, which Vanderbilt was to donate a year later. Idlehour was ready for occupancy by the fall of 1879, and the Vanderbilts, with their two-year-old daughter, Consuelo, and their year-old son, W. K. Jr., moved into residence.

The estate Idlehour, was planned in the grand manner with some twenty-five outbuildings for every conceivable use, including its own powerhouse, a conservatory, a greenhouse, an enormous coach house designed by Isaac H. Green Jr., an elaborate model farm that provided the estate with livestock and produce, two gatehouses, a caretaker's house, water tower, bowling alley, laundry, an icehouse, and a lovely teahouse overlooking Great South Bay. The property was continuously improved; ornamental canals were dredged from the marshes and scenic drives built throughout. The estate looked out on the quiet Connetquot River, on the other side of which were lovely wooded groves, the southerly part of Westbrook Farms.

The main house that Hunt designed was a dark red Queen Anne style building with an annex known as "the bachelor's quarters," which together contained some sixty rooms. The rambling, picturesque house was a larger clapboarded and shingled version of Hunt's Newport cottages. A local contemporary correspondent described the interior: "The breakfast room is in white and gilt, with a pretty aquarium full of plants nestling around a small fountain. The dining room is oak paneled and hung with life-size portraits of the Vanderbilt family. The main hall is grand and imposing in appearance, lighted by stained glass windows, ornamented with antlered heads of deer and elk, and has a magnificent oak staircase and a huge fireplace, with old fashioned fittings and Yule logs piled within it."[15]

The house stood near a curve in the river, and the river's edge commanded a broad view up and down. The feeling of living at Idlehour is best captured by Consuelo herself who later wrote about her childhood years. "Idlehour, where we spent early summer and autumn months was a rambling frame house close to a river; green lawns swept away to the gardens, stables, woods and farms. Here we crabbed and fished in the river and learned to sail a boat. Good behavior found its reward in the pleasure of cooking our supper in the playhouse. This playhouse was in an old bowling alley. Utterly happy we would cook our meal, wash the dishes, and then stroll home by the river in the cool of the evening."[16]

In the autumn of 1880 Alva Vanderbilt's sister, Mary Virginia Smith, was married at Idlehour to Fernando Yznaga, whose sister had recently married Lord Mandeville. This high society wedding was described by the local reporter and included a description of the estate: "A delightful drive through the woods for a mile or more, past cozy farm houses, brought guests into a broad park of some hundreds of acres lying upon the margin of a broad river curving lazily in and out on its way to the sea. In the midst of these grounds stands a many gabled and gaily painted country house, one of the largest on Long Island. The southern margin of the lawn is defined by a high tower rising out of the thick autumn foliage and by long lines of low green houses and pretty cottages of workmen and other employees. The mansion fronts upon the river, on which lies a small steamer, the *Mosquito*, the only symbol of busy civilization that disturbs the quiet landscape of Idlehour."[17]

Vanderbilt spent over $150,000 to create Idlehour. Although he and his family would only spend a month or two at the most there each year, it was without question the grandest of all the country estates as yet built along the Great South Bay. When the Vanderbilts were in residence festive parties were held for invited house guests, and sporting events such as shooting contests or coaching parties were arranged. It was during this period in the early 1880s that Alva Vanderbilt determined to become the leader of New York Society. Her lavish entertaining, whether in New York, Newport, or at Idlehour, helped her to achieve that goal. The arrival of the Vanderbilts to Long Island's South Shore and the fact that Idlehour would remain in W. K.'s hands until his death in 1920 gave to that area a social prominence that it had not before achieved. There was no question at all after 1880 that to summer near the Great South Bay was to be in a preferred spot for prominent New York families, and many of them would follow.

Although not as large as the Connetquot River, Champlin's Creek, * directly to the west, arises in mid Long Island, flows south to form Champlin's Lake, beside which was Stellenwerf's Lake House (see Chapter III), and finally emerges into the Great South Bay. It was this area that attracted the brothers John D. and Edwin A. Johnson in the 1840s, Benjamin Welles in the 1850s, and William K. Knapp in the 1860s. On the west side of the creek was Johnson Avenue and on the east side Pavilion Avenue (from the Pavilion

---

* Also known by its Indian name, Winganhauppauge Creek, meaning 'brook or spring that burst forth and covered the land.'

Hotel on South Country Road). This would become the third area in which New York families would locate their summer homes. Familiarity with Champlin's Creek locations was undoubtedly a result of the great success of the Pavilion Hotel nearby. In September 1871 a correspondent of the *New York Evening Post* wrote, "The season has been unusually gay. The hotel is crowded with many of the best people of New York and other people who prefer the fine fishing in the Great South Bay and the quiet life to the greater bustle at Saratoga and Long Branch [New Jersey]. The blue fishing is through with in the bay [it was late September] but outside it is as good as ever. Spanish mackerel are plenty and catching them is better sport than blue fishing. Seventy were caught in two hours by the guests of the house. Those who want a good day's sport will find it here. The hotel is situated about half a mile from the bay, two miles east of the Olympic Club, and three miles west of the South Side Club. These clubs are composed exclusively of New York gentlemen."

The Pavilion had its ups and downs. There were several changes in management, and the 1870s saw the addition of several cottages for summer rent besides the main hotel building. These were particularly popular with families who wanted to try out the area. In 1881 the Pavilion "returned to life" again under the new management of James Slater, manager of the Berkeley Hotel on New York's Fifth Avenue. Completely modernized with new plumbing, new wells, and new water treatment, the Pavilion was also advertising that it was on a newly built road that was being maintained by Messrs. Vanderbilt, Lorillard, and Plumb, all of whom were neighbors. In fact, for the summer of 1881, the Hamilton McK. Twomblys (Vanderbilt's sister and brother-in-law), the Bradish Johnson Jrs., and the A. A. Kingslands had taken cottages at the Pavilion. Of course, it still took in transients at the going rate in 1878 of $3 per night and from $10 to $16 per week.

The first two men to build homes for their families in the Champlin's Creek area in the 1870s were Joseph W. Meeks and John D. Prince, both members of the South Side

Sportsmen's Club. Meeks purchased in late 1869 what had been known as Champlin House, located on the west side of Champlin's Pond across from Stellenwerf's Lake House. To transform it into a "proper" country home he constructed a French mansard roof, added a substantial wing, and built several large barns on the property. Meeks had made a fortune in mining and was the owner of the Cottonwood silver mine in Utah. He was an early and active member of the Islip summer colony and remained so until his death in 1878 at age seventy-three in his New York City residence.

John Dyneley Prince, born in Paterson, New Jersey, became a member of the New York Stock Exchange in 1866 and served as a governor from 1871–75. His firm was called Prince and Whiteley. He married Anne Maria Morris of Baltimore and they had two children. In 1874 he bought waterfront property lying between Champlin's Creek and the most southerly end of Johnson Avenue, well south of the W. K. Knapp house. This twelve-acre parcel had been a part of the much larger landholdings of Edwin A. Johnson in the 1840s, which had been sold by his estate to Dr. T. S. Ryder, who in turn sold a lot to Prince. It was extremely desirable land because of bay access through Champlin's Creek and because of the high ground and beautiful beach and oak trees in the area. He paid $5,000 for his twelve acres, an extraordinary sum in 1874. He then built a summer residence on this land and looked forward to many years of enjoyment of his new home.

The Princes were Episcopalians and members of Trinity Parish in New York. John D. had musical interests in particular. In 1875 he was elected to the St. Mark's vestry and in that year he also gave to the parish a cabinet organ and one hundred church hymnals. In 1879 when the new church building was donated by W. K. Vanderbilt, Prince gave the money for the new organ, and at the service of dedication on June 22, 1880, he arranged for the organist and choir of Trinity Church to perform the music. "The music was grand" said the *Signal*, "and was conducted by J. D. Prince and the organist from Trinity Church, New York. The choir was composed of young men from St. Chrysostom's Chapel of Trinity Church of New York."[18] Prince also sponsored and arranged a special concert for choir and organ to benefit the St. Mark's building effort. It was held at the Islip Presbyterian Church to the excellent review of critics. Prince, however, in a letter to the paper said: "An interesting feature of the concert . . . was the large and appreciative audience gathered around the outside of the building, where, as the windows were necessarily open [it was August], the music could be heard almost as well as inside the church, and where the disagreeable formality of paying for a ticket could be comfortably dispensed with. It is somewhat difficult . . . to distinguish between a proceeding of this kind and the actual stealing of a ticket."[19] Perhaps his resentment was heightened by a lack of people inside the church.

By the end of 1881, Prince had tired of his house and decided to build a much grander one, said to cost $50,000, on the same site. The house he had built only six years before was moved across the street and the new work began. During the following spring, while construction was under way, the Prince family traveled to Europe, returning in time to begin a new venture, the sport of yacht racing, and to occupy a new summer home, described as "one of the finest on the south side"[20] and "with every appearance of having been built on a bull market."[21] It was also noted that a telephone line connected the house with that of Captain H. C. Haff in Islip village, one of the earliest telephones in the area.

In June of 1882 John D. Prince purchased one of the most notable sloops of its time, the seven-year-old *Fanny*. She was built in Mystic, Connecticut, 72 feet in length overall with a beam of 24 feet. As was typical of the great centerboard sloops of the 1880s, *Fanny* had a huge single spar, a main boom that extended way beyond her stern, a long bowsprit, the combination of which allowed her to carry a vast amount of sail. A gigantic mainsail, gaff-rigged, a topsail, three jibs for windward sailing, and a huge spinaker for leeward sailing powered the white-hulled *Fanny*. In her seven years as a top competitor in the New York Yacht

Club* races along the east coast (not in the Great South
Bay) *Fanny* had never won a race when Prince bought her.
By the end of the summer of 1882, however, she was the
champion of the NYYC fleet. Owners in that era seldom, if
ever, skippered their yachts. For that purpose sailing mas-
ters were hired with professional crews. Prince, determined
to have a winner, engaged for sailing master the very best,
Islip-born-and-raised Captain Henry C. Haff, known to all as
Hank. Hank Haff, with an experienced local crew of Seth
Wicks, mate, and Warren Clock, James Berry,** and Bert
Haff (A. C. Haff), turned an also-ran into a winner.

The principal test that summer was the New York Yacht
Club cruise and Prince was of course a member. The yacht to
beat was the perennial favorite *Gracie*, owned by Joseph P.
Earle and recently much altered and lengthened to 79 feet.
Also there was the sloop *Vixen* from Bay Shore owned by
Francis C. Lawrance (see Chapter III) and under the command of Captain Samuel Gibson of Bay Shore. The fleet
assembled off Glen Cove, Long Island, for the first day's race,
an eighty-mile run to New London, Connecticut. "With a
score or more of the handsomest and finest yachts in the

---

* The New York Yacht Club was founded on July 30, 1844, on the
deck of the yacht of John C. Stevens who became the first
commodore. Until well after the Civil War it was the only yacht
club in America to sponsor anything but local races. In 1851 it
sent the schooner *America* to England to challenge British yachts
in the race around the Isle of Wight, which race she won deci-
sively. Upon hearing the news of *America*'s victory, Queen
Victoria inquired who finished second. She was told in reply,
"There was no second, madam." In 1868 the club moved its
clubhouse to Stapleton, Staten Island, where the start of the
races could be easily seen. The America's Cup course, the so-
called inner course, ran out the Narrows through the outer bay
to beyond Sandy Hook Light for 20 miles and then returned to
finish off the clubhouse. By the 1880s another course was used
that started off Sandy Hook and went 20 miles out into the
Atlantic Ocean.

** Berry was considered the best light air sailor of his day.

world" said the *Signal*, "there must be many exciting contests in the runs from port to port. The favorites were the schooner *Montauk* and the sloop *Gracie*. The starting gun fired and some twenty-four hours later, after light winds and drifting through typical Long Island Sound August calms, *Fanny* crossed the line first, outsailing the entire fleet. On the second day *Fanny* triumphed again in a race to Saybrook and back, this time defeating *Gracie* by forty minutes. On the third day, a Sunday, the commodore scheduled the leg to Newport, Rhode Island. About 20 yachts started, but Mr. Prince was at church and would not sail. About a dozen boats waited until Monday morning among them, *Gracie*, *Hildegard*, *Vixen* and *Fanny*."[22] *Fanny* won again. The New York Yacht Club cruised on eastward to Marblehead, Massachusetts, sailing under strong winds in Rhode Island Sound. At the conclusion of the regatta *Fanny* was the first boat into port in four runs out of five on the cruise, and won the prize in her class in the three days of races, a record no yacht had made before. The papers concluded: "The regattas this summer have shown three things very plainly — first, that English yachts are no match for ours; second, that 'Fanny' is the fastest sloop afloat if properly handled; third, that Islip can produce the best yachting crew in America."[23] One surely can excuse the local pride. It was a great distinction for such a small village. John D. Prince had suddenly become the owner of the most famous sloop in America, and the call came for a match race, one on one, to be held next season with its great rival, *Gracie*.

Match races were common events at that time and often high stakes were wagered on them. The most prominent of these were the races for the America's Cup sailed in that era in sloops similar to *Gracie* and *Fanny*. In fact, in the competition to defend the Cup just two years before, in 1881, *Gracie* narrowly lost out to the sloop *Mischief*, skippered by Nathaniel Clock of Islip. *Mischief*, nicknamed "the Iron Pot," was the first metal-hulled boat and the first sloop to defend. She defeated the Canadian challenger, *Atalanta*. For the match race between *Gracie* and *Fanny* the date chosen was

October 9, 1883. The course was to be twenty miles to windward and return off Sandy Hook, New Jersey, the America's Cup outer course. *Fanny* was manned by her regular Islip crew under the command of Captain Hank Haff and it was reported in the press that over $75,000 had been wagered on the outcome. The New York Yacht Club, sponsor of the race, had agreed on a $1,000 prize for the victor. On the day of the race, the wind was so light that it was doubtful the yachts could finish within the time limit. However, a large spectator fleet had assembled to watch the contest. They included *Mischief*, the Cup winner, and J. P. Morgan's steam yacht *Corsair*. *Fanny* had rounded the windward mark first and was ahead when time ran out and no race was declared.

Finally on October 25, on the third attempt, the race was completed. Again the wind was light, but after eight hours over the forty-mile course *Fanny* won the prize on corrected time by seven minutes eighteen seconds. She had a two-minute handicap on account of being the shorter of the two sloops. It was an exciting race. *Fanny* was ahead for much of the course, but as the wind freshened near the end, *Gracie* was catching up when *Fanny* crossed the finish line.

John D. Prince had not been able to watch his great yacht take the prize. He had become ill that October. Although he rallied by the end of the month and went to his home in Islip, he died shortly thereafter at his New York City residence at 27 West Thirty-fourth Street. He was only forty years old and was mourned by his many friends. The famous *Fanny* was laid up at Alonzo Smith's yard on Orowoc Creek that winter to be later sold to William R. Travers of New York, Prince's uncle. It was noted that Captain Haff would be retained as her sailing master. Prince's elegant home on Champlin's Creek was rented for a few summers until in 1888 it was sold to Samuel T. Peters of New York for $50,000. Peters had rented in Babylon for several summers and was eager to be permanently settled.

In the same way that horse racing attracted the attention of New York people to the Great South Bay area so did the sport of yachting. And it also was expensive. "Conspicuous

among all out-of-door sports, as the most expensive, therefore the most exclusive, and yet in point of interest one of the
most popular, is yachting" wrote *Shepp's New York City
Illustrated* in 1894. "There are more than one hundred yacht
clubs in America today, and New York has a far greater
number than any other city. The Seawanhaka, the Larchmont,
and The New York Yacht Club are the most prominent."[24]
Such formal yacht clubs on the Great South Bay, however,
did not appear until the 1890s. Yachting began on the bay
because lumber was plentiful, craftsmen were at hand, and
skilled boat handlers were trained by clamming and fishing
from sailboats. Commerce on the water had preceded sport.
The first sailboats built were catboats, with single mast and
single sail, because they were easy to handle and easy to
clam and fish from. They had stability because of their wide
beam. Later to come was the sloop, a single master, but with
jib added to give both more speed and the ability to sail more
closely into the wind. Both catboats and sloops were raced
on the bay informally at first and later under the auspices of
yacht clubs. The natural protection given the bay by the Fire
Island barrier beach made it a popular sailing area, the only
limit to which was its shallow water (maximum depth 8–10
feet), which kept the largest craft away. In July, 1880, *Harper's
New Monthly Magazine* wrote: "In summer the surface of
Great South Bay is dotted with many dozens of sails. The
boats come from the towns and villages that lie along the
shore and from the few islands in and around the bay that
can boast of inhabitants. Sammis's Hotel and Dominy House
on Fire Island Beach send their quota, and there are delega-
tions of catboats from Havemeyer's [see below], and Jesse
Conklings. Patchogue, Bellport, Sayville, Islip, Bay Shore,
Babylon have each and all their miniature fleets."
    The Great South Bay became famous for the sailing mas-
ters born in the area and trained on that body of water.
Nathaniel Clock and Hank Haff became the most notable by
winning the America's Cup (1881, 1887, and 1895). They were
closely followed by Urias Rhodes and Samuel B. Gibson of
Bay Shore and by Leander A. Jeffrey, James Berry, and Albert

C. Haff (Hank's brother) of Islip. These seven men among them had command of many of the finest and fastest schooners and sloops in the period from 1870 to and after the turn of the century.

The bay also became famous for its boat builders and the notable yachts they built. One of the first of these sloops was built for the Olympic Club (see Chapter III) and named *TB Asten* after Thomas B. Asten, the club's president. *TB Asten* was built in 1867 at the shipyard of Warren C. Brown in Orowoc Creek in Islip. Under the command of the Olympic Club's superintendent at the time, Captain Hank Haff, *TB Asten* was used for the sailing pleasure of the club members. She could make the passage from Fire Island Beach back to the club dock (six miles) in less than an hour in a brisk southwest wind, it was reported, and also won several prizes in club races, beating all her competitors on the bay.

By 1874 Brown's shipyard was taken over by Alonzo E. Smith and the demand for his boats increased as they became better known throughout the sailing world. Islip yachts with Bay Shore and Islip captains were sought after by many members of the famous New York Yacht Club. In May of that year a christening ceremony was held at Smith's boatyard to launch the new centerboard schooner *Comet*, 97 feet overall, built for Major William H. Langley, a member of the New York Yacht Club. It was noted that three hundred people were present including Islip Captains Haff, Ellsworth of *Commodore* (built by Smith), McCannon of *Addie V*, and Havens of *Fanny*. The report concluded: "Mr. Smith has quite a number of vessels nearly completed, and judging from appearances is fast building up a fortune to rival the extended reputation he has already gained as a builder."[25] Business was indeed brisk for Alonzo Smith. A large sloop for Bay Shore's Captain J. Henderson and another for Albany Captain Fred Townsend, 58 feet overall, joined the New York Yacht Club squadron in 1876. "None of the yachts built by Mr. Smith from his own models have proved easy to beat"[26] it was noted.

In yachting circles the year of 1876 saw a great tragedy in a freak accident that took the lives of six people including two members of the Garner family of New York and Bay Shore. William T. Garner was the second son of Thomas Garner Sr. (see Chapter III). After the death of their father, William and his brother had inherited a $10 million fortune made from cotton milling. They each summered on the family estate in Bay Shore and were invited to join the vestry of St. Mark's Church, William as a warden in 1866. William also was a member of the South Side Sportsmen's Club. Yachting, however, was his principal sporting interest, and by 1876 he had reached the pinnacle of that sport with his election as vice commodore of the New York Yacht Club. Garner had owned several large sailing craft including *Vixen*, the sloop which he later sold to his brother-in-law, Francis C. Lawrance, and the schooner *Magic*.* He was an experienced yachtsman as were his sailing masters.

In 1875 Garner had ordered a new yacht, which he named *Mohawk*. Launched from her builder's yard in Williamsburg, Brooklyn, on June 9, she was the largest centerboard schooner ever built at that time, 121 feet in length on the waterline, 30 feet in width. She carried an enormous area of sail. The distance from the top of her topsail sprit to the water was 163 feet and from the end of the main boom to the end of the flying jib boom, 235 feet. She was subject to some criticism at the time as being top heavy but enjoyed a successful racing season that summer. Garner had engaged a Captain Oliver Rowland of Setauket, Long Island, as sailing master because Captain Clock was still in charge of *Magic*.

On July 20, 1876, Vice Commodore Garner and his party had boarded *Mohawk* at anchor off the New York Yacht Club's dock in Stapleton, Staten Island. They were going for a sail down the bay. A shower of rain had driven the ladies below deck when tragedy struck. It was described at the time

---

* *Magic*, with a crew of 25 under the command of Captain Nathaniel Clock of Islip, had defeated her archrival *Comet* in a match race sailed over the NYYC course on October 13, 1874. Garner was said to have won a fortune on the race. She also had won the America's Cup in 1870 under a previous owner.

by another yachting captain, Captain R. F. Coffin, as follows: "The *Mohawk* had all her canvas set and was still at anchor. She had her anchor chain up short and the jibs were being set to loosen the anchor when the squall hit. Being still at anchor she could gain no momentum and just lay over. Her ballast shifted and she went down, filled and sank. Mr. Garner drowned while trying to rescue his wife who was pinned below by shifted ballast."[27] In addition to Garner and his wife, Miss Adele Hunter, Frost Thorn, Gardiner G. Howland, and the cabin boy were lost, trapped below deck by the onrushing water. Captain Rowland and all the crew who were on deck were rescued from the water. A public inquiry followed the tragedy, which cleared Captain Rowland of criminal negligence. He testified that Commodore Garner had assured him that there was no danger even after the squall had struck. It was ruled that the accident was a freak and entirely unpredictable. However, Captain Coffin said, "She [*Mohawk*] was lost through the grossest carelessness and in consequence of the over-confidence felt in her stability by both the Captain and the Owner."[28] The weight of evidence certainly seems to support Captain Coffin's view. The death of Garner and his wife left three young orphan daughters. Their guardian and aunt, Frances Garner Lawrance, took them shortly thereafter to live abroad where each eventually married a titled European gentleman.

Although many of the yachts built by Great South Bay shipyards in the 1870s and 1880s were too large to sail in the bay, there were also many that were designed for just this purpose, and bay racing developed in that period as well. It was noted in 1885 that Alonzo Smith's yard was "the liveliest place in Islip"[29] and had built a new sloop yacht, called *Awixa*, for Commodore T. B. Asten of the Olympic Club. In addition to Alonzo Smith, Gilbert E. Smith of Patchogue was busy designing and building boats at this time. He would become the most famous of all the bay shipwrights. There were match races often held for stakes, such as *Henry Stears* vs. *South Side* (two catboats from Babylon) for a $1,000 purse. More common was fleet racing for prize money for both catboats and sloops. A first prize would be $350 for the race of twenty miles. As more and more interest developed in racing on the bay, the need arose for more organization and with it came the yacht clubs, the first of which were the Bay Shore Yacht Club, founded in 1883, and the Great South Bay Yacht Club founded in 1889.

Contributing to the growing interest in yachting on the Great South Bay in the 1870s was the success of the Olympic Club (see Chapter III). Located at the south end of Saxton Avenue in Bay Shore, the club had changed considerably from its humble beginnings twenty years earlier. The dozen acres of land were now shaded by a grove of oak trees and there were several buildings on the property. It was described in 1869 as "a charming resort for the summer months. The grounds are beautifully laid out and the members are furnished with elegant fishing and sailing yachts and row boats, and enjoy themselves to their hearts content."[30] The Club's charter (1865) had stated that it was to provide "facilities for the social intercourse, physical, moral and intellectual improvement and recreation of its members."[31] There was a main clubhouse "with commodious quarters, comprising parlor, dining rooms, some thirty odd rooms for sleeping purposes" and a well stocked library. A dance floor was added at this time as well. Each member could decorate his room to suit his taste. There was a separate building for servants, an icehouse, and a storeroom for provisions. On the cricket lawn a few yards from the main clubhouse was a tall staff for the club burgee. This staff had been made from the main boom of the bark *Elizabeth*, wrecked off Fire Island in 1850 (see Chapter III). The club now had a permanent dock that projected into the bay at the mouth of Awixa Creek, and the club yachts *T. B. Asten* and *Club* would dock alongside it.

An interesting discovery made the care of the members much easier for the staff. "For years the water for all purposes of the Olympic kitchen was brought from a spring a good half mile away. It was thought useless to dig for water on the club grounds, and the managing committee determined to try the experiment, pronounced it a waste of money. Finally the well was made by dropping an iron pipe to a depth of twenty-five feet . . . and when the pump was started, it brought up the purest and sweetest water that one could wish to drink. The supply is inexhaustible."[32] The quality and supply of fresh water from Long Island's aquifers has always been a great asset to the area and remains so today.

The Olympic Club was open only in the summer months. Only men could be members. Upon occasion women were invited for special functions, but they were never permitted in the so-called dormitories. In the early 1870s there were about seventy members, men from New York and from Brooklyn, who shared an interest in the club's activities, particularly sailing and saltwater fishing, which the South Side Sportsmen's Club could not offer. The club's president in those early years was Thomas B. Asten of New York. He was the president of the city's Board of Taxes and Assessments, a powerful political appointment. He had the reputation of being an excellent tax commissioner. The Astens built a summer cottage of their own on a corner of the Olympic Club's property thus becoming the first New Yorkers to do so on Saxton Avenue. Other members were Alonzo Slote and his brother, Daniel, as well as John R. Platt, all prominent New Yorkers and volunteer firemen. Platt, a one-time president of the Fire Department, had the reputation as "one of the quickest firemen in the City."[33] Another member at that time was Daniel D. Conover, who was to become an active developer in Bay Shore and Islip in the 1880s (see Chapter VI).

The club continued to prosper in the 1880s. A new clubhouse was built at the cost of $20,000 to replace the aging old one. It was described then as "charmingly located. It owns several acres of land sloping down to the water, upon which are five cottages and the club house proper. The cottages are two stories high, with broad piazzas surrounding them and all connected with each other. The dining room and kitchen are in separate buildings." The reporter concludes, "Residents of Bay Shore are much indebted to the Olympic Club for the impulse its members have given to the sale of real estate and improvement of property in the vicinity."[34] Following Asten, James F. Wenman became president. He was said to be the oldest living New York City Volunteer Fireman going back to the club's beginnings in 1841. (Wenman Avenue, off Saxon Avenue, was named after him.)

Those who enjoyed a day's sail on the bay or were out to catch the run of bluefish on the evening flood tide did not always want to return to port at nightfall and there were places on Fire Island for them to have a meal or a bed if so desired. Dominy House and the Surf Hotel (see Chapter III) were still popular hostelries, as was a place on the west side of the Fire Island Inlet known as "Uncle Jesse Conklin's." Uncle Jesse, from the Babylon Conklin family, would advertise his inn as follows: "It has every appliance for entertaining any number of transient guests, with every delicacy in the shape of fish, flesh or fowl, with all the et ceteras of a first class place. Located in the direct route to the fishing ground, the place is remarkably convenient, and few parties go outside [the Inlet] without stopping. Uncle Jesse is always in the best of spirits and his roast clams and chowders are a sure prevention against sea sickness. Stop and See."[35] Many sailors did, and Uncle Jesse's place became famous and drew attention to that site by Fire Island Inlet protected from the Atlantic Ocean but convenient to its access. The channel around that point was known as Whig Inlet.

It was here on Whig Inlet next to Uncle Jesse's that the third club to be started in the Great South Bay area was located. It was named Wa-Wa-Yanda Fishing Club (sometimes spelled Way Wayonda). The origin of the name is a mystery. The early members claimed it was Indian, but it seems more likely that a member thought of it as being "far, far away" from the mainland at Babylon where the ferry would depart. In any event, the club was organized in the spring of 1879 by three New York businessmen, Shepherd F. Knapp (see Chapter IV), Charles Banks, and William C. Connor. Knapp and Banks were South Side Sportsmen's

Club members and excellent bird shots. They wanted a club to pursue fishing and bird shooting as well as sailing, and the location by Whig Inlet was excellent for all three sports. The first year's membership was about sixty. A two-story clubhouse was built, consisting of parlors and bedrooms on the second floor. Meals were taken at Jesse Conklin's, connected to the club by a plank walk over the salt marsh. The club owned two steam yachts to take members back and forth to the trains at Babylon. The club was open only in summer and fall and was a bachelor establishment. It was described at the time (1880) as "young and charming. ... The Wa-Wa-Yandans fish, hunt and sail for amusement and health, and a half-dozen boats belonging to the club are kept pretty busy in the fair days of summer. The members boast of cool breezes when New York is mopping its forehead in agony."[36] Many more New Yorkers were learning of the great advantages to summering near the Great South Bay.

There were, however, a few disadvantages and one of those struck the new Wa-Wa-Yanda Club the year it opened. Violent tropical storms, hurricanes in their most severe form, periodically come up along the East Coast to make landfall on Long Island and cause great destruction. Before the days of weather forecasting these storms struck suddenly, without notice, so that no preparation could be made to minimize the damage. Fire Island usually caught the brunt of these gales. On August 18, 1879, a severe gale hit the Great South Bay during the afternoon and night. The paper said that it was the most severe storm of the past twenty-five years. It was so entirely unexpected that it caught all the boatmen unawares. The Surf Hotel lost a part of its roof and its bulkhead walk was destroyed. The most damage occurred to the boats that were anchored. Twelve boats off the Surf Hotel were driven ashore and some of these were badly damaged. A sloop laying at the hotel dock and filled with supplies was a total loss. It was also reported that "the Wa-Wa-Yanda Club's steamer had her top and smoke stack blown off, and was reported sunk."[37] She was later raised and repaired, ready for the next season.

Severe gales also struck Fire Island in the winter. Although not of a tropical nature, they would cause extremely high tides and devastate the ocean beach. On the night of December 26, 1880, "at Fire Island the sea broke solid across the beach between the Surf Hotel and the lighthouse. At one time the hotel itself was in imminent danger of being washed away. The pavilion at the surf was partly undermined by the sea, and all the bathing houses belonging to the hotel, numbering about 100, were swept away, and the materials of which they were composed strewn along the shore. Among the debris thrown up from the sea was the hull of an old steamer that no one has been able to recognize. A number of telegraph poles, forming the land connection with the Fire Island and Babylon submarine cable was washed out, thus breaking communication [there were no telephones as yet], but no damage was done to the submerged cable. The tides were higher in the bay and along the outer shore than noted before in several years."[38] The Surf Hotel was repaired in time for summer and the Wa-Wa-Yanda Club prospered as well, making extensive additions in 1881 on the east and north sides of the main clubhouse for dining and kitchen. Its membership had increased to ninety.

Near the Wa-Wa-Yanda Club and Uncle Jesse Conklin's place on the east end of Oak Island beach (now called Captree Island Boat Basin) there stood a hotel known in 1877 as the Whig Inlet House, the proprietor of which was a Mr. Stone. The success of the Surf Hotel and Uncle Jesse's place had tempted others to try their luck in this popular area. The owner of a hotel on the mainland, for example, had divided it into two halves and shipped it across the bay on a barge to relocate near the Surf on Fire Island beach. Early in 1879 the Whig Inlet House, or Stone's Hotel as it was also known, was sold to Henry Havemeyer, a New Yorker who had recently chosen West Islip for his summer residence. Havemeyer was reported to have spent $150,000 transforming the hotel into a summertime residence where he entertained lavishly. Separate buildings were erected for use as gymnasium, barn, hennery, and quarters for the dozen servants. Thousands of cartloads of soil were transported across the bay to cover the sandy point. (Henry Havemeyer was described in a local paper as "this prince of fellows.") He called his villa the Armory and the point of beach on which it was located became known as Havemeyer's Point. This elaborate villa did not suit Havemeyer (or perhaps his wife) for long, however, and it was leased for the summer of 1883 to be a seaside adjunct of Babylon's newly built Argyle Hotel complex (see Chapter VI). During that summer President Chester A. Arthur and some members of his cabinet spent several days vacationing in the Armory. The villa struggled along, operated as a public inn by a series of proprietors. In 1885 it was promoted by declaring, "Nature and Henry Havemeyer gave the Point [the Armory] a good send off, and the present management will keep it up to the mark. If you don't believe what we say, go and see for yourself."[39] Finally it was sold by Havemeyer's estate in 1889 to become the Fire Island Country Club around the turn of the century. Today that point of Oak Island Beach is known by old-timers as Havemeyer's Point. It is now without buildings and trees at all, just sand.

Havemeyer, very much an entrepreneur, became interested in Oak Island Beach in 1879 because at that time there was a great surge of large, new resort hotels being promoted by the Long Island Railroad and its new president Austin Corbin (see Chapter VI). Many of these hotels were located along the ocean beach, such as the Manhattan Beach Hotel, the Oriental, and the Rockaway Beach Hotel.

Although Havemeyer used the Armory himself for a summer or two, he likely intended to turn it into a beach resort of an exclusive nature. The Babylon Town Board received two applications to lease about four miles of beach lying west of the Oak Island Club for a period of twenty years for development purposes (August 16, 1879). One application was from Franklin H. Kalbfleisch of Brooklyn and Babylon, and the other was from Havemeyer. Kalbfleisch was awarded the lease, although Havemeyer complained he had been prepared to pay more and wanted a decision by auction.

At the same time there were rumors of the intention to build a new railroad across the Great South Bay from Babylon to Oak Island Beach. "On Oak Island and Jones' Beach it is intended to expend $200,000 in hotels, by next season," said the paper in 1880, "not to count the cost of extending the Montauk Railroad thereto. It is not improbable that a few years will see a railroad running to Fire Island direct by way of Oak Island."[40] There had been reports of "an extremely private meeting of railroad men and capitalists held last week at Delmonico's in Broad Street, New York. The proceedings were uncommonly secret, but it was ascertained that several leading brokers of the Stock Exchange had been asked to meet Mr. William H. Vanderbilt, Erastus Corning, Henry N. Smith, James R. Keene, Russell Sage and Isidore Wormser on important business. The meeting organized by electing Henry Havemeyer Chairman and Charles Banks Secretary. It resolved to build a new railroad, to be known as the New York and Oak Island Railroad, to run from New York along Long Island beach to Fire Island."[41] It was thought that the road would be a new way to develop the beach from Rockaway to Fire Island. Such a railroad was never built. However, in September 1879 the Babylon Board of Supervisors did announce that they had granted to Kalbfleisch and his partners the "privilege" of building the bridge across the bay for the railroad. Although a similar railroad bridge, a trestle on piles, had just been completed across Jamaica Bay to Rockaway Beach, the one to Oak Island was never built either. Thus the beach there never became filled with resort hotels and boardwalks like those at Long Beach, Lido Beach, and the Rockaways.

Meanwhile, Havemeyer, thwarted in his endeavor to develop Oak Island Beach, turned his attention to West Islip. Early in 1880 he purchased the Bergen estate, south of South Country Road, directly east of Colonel Wagstaff's home, for $44,000. This property was to be much more suitable for him and his family as a country residence than the Armory could ever have been. It became one of the several showplaces between Babylon and Bay Shore. He named the estate

Sequatogue after the Indian tribe that had lived in that area when the Willets first came in the seventeenth century (see Chapter II). On 160 acres he established a modern farm. There was the principal residence just off the main road, and to the south of it were stables, cow barns, and a carriage house. An extensive greenhouse, vegetable garden, and fruit orchard provided produce of all kinds for the family. In addition, Havemeyer managed a considerable livestock farm. "The stock of the place embraces the best known breeds of imported Jersey and Alderney cattle, Norwegian and other imported horses, and other blooded stock."[42] He had traveled to Europe in the fall of 1882 to purchase livestock for Sequatogue Farm. The farm did not last very long, however, as troubles were looming ahead for this Havemeyer family.

"Henry Havemeyer," wrote the *Huntington Bulletin* a year after his death, "flitted like a meteor and faded like a falling star. Quixotic in his experiments, he was princely in his indiscriminate gifts, and never said 'no' to anyone demanding aid, whether deserving or otherwise. He lived a brief and busy life [forty-eight years], did no willful wrongs, and leaves no enemy to rejoice because he departed."[43] He was born the fourth son of William F. Havemeyer, three times mayor of New York City, and the grandson of William Havemeyer, who had come from Germany in 1799 to found the sugar refinery in Manhattan that later would bring to the family fame and fortune. Henry's father, the mayor, had earlier been in the sugar business himself, but after he entered the political world, he left his family's interests in the hands of his sons. The mayor also had extensive interests in railroads and was said to be the largest stockholder of the Long Island Railroad at the time of his death in 1874. Henry, being entrepreneurial by nature, left the sugar business in the hands of his younger brother, Hector, and concerned himself with new ventures, some entirely untried, and on some of which he lost a great deal of money. One of the latter was the famous iron pier built out into the ocean at Rockaway Beach as a tourist attraction. It was similar to England's popular Victorian amusement piers such as the famous Old

Chain Pier* at Brighton, which he had made a trip to study. In another venture he attempted to develop a business of gathering iron from the sand on the Long Island beach at Quogue where it was said to be of good quality. Separated from the sand by a magnet, the iron particles were shipped to New York for sale there. Needless to say, this was another failure. He did, however, establish a successful new ferry route from Jersey City to Hunter's Point Avenue with stops at Wall Street and in Brooklyn. Passengers could thus come from New Jersey directly to the Long Island Railroad terminus at Hunter's Point Avenue for transit to the island.

After his father's death Henry Havemeyer was much concerned with his family's interest in the Long Island Railroad, which was in a bad state of disorder at that time (1874). He accepted the presidency in May 1875, stating in an interview that "the railroad and its branches would not be sold; that the present condition of the road is as good as any in the State; that he is determined to maintain it as nearly first-class as possible; that new track will be laid where needed; that extra trains will be put on soon after May 15 for summer travel; that the present passenger rates will be maintained; and that the Company intended to extend a branch from Brentwood to Doxsee's Dock, Islip, the right of way for which had been secured and graded a number of years ago."[44] The branch from Brentwood was never undertaken, and all his statements will seem today to the Long Island commuter like a tired refrain. Apparently improvements did take place in 1875 as promised; freight trains were handled more expeditiously, getting produce to New York markets by 2:30 a.m. for early opening; and a daily express commuter from Hunter's Point Avenue to Greenport and to Sag Harbor was established.

---

* Completed in 1823, it rivalled the Royal Pavilion as the town's chief attraction. With its spectacular towers and supporting chains, souvenir shops, and entertainments — including band performances and firework displays — the Chain Pier attracted thousands of sightseers. It was destroyed in a violent storm in December 1896, but was soon replaced by the Palace Pier that continues today to attract holiday goers.

Ownership of the LIRR was not in strong hands, however, and in spite of Havemeyer's earlier denial, control was transferred to the Poppenhusen family in February 1876.* At that time it was reported: "On the demise of Oliver Charlick, Mr. Henry Havemeyer, son of the late Mayor Havemeyer of New York, was elected President, and together with a reorganized Board of Directors, assumed the management of the Company. Under the new regime, the Long Island Railroad exhibited a degree of prosperity and enterprise hitherto unknown in its history."[45] Following the sale, Havemeyer retired from the presidency.

Henry Havemeyer had married Mary Jennie Moller, the daughter of the sugar refiner William Moller. At an earlier time the two families had been associated together in sugar refining, owning the firm of Havemeyers and Mollers on Van Dam Street in Manhattan. Six children were born from the union. The family enjoyed their life on Sequatogue Farm in West Islip. Their eldest son, William M., exhibited his snow-white Norwegian stallion at the annual Madison Square Garden horse show. They were often seen sailing on the bay in their catboat *South Side*.

By 1884, however, there were signs that all was not well. Havemeyer's failed ventures and expansive life-style (he was known to have been an intemperate drinker) were fast dissipating his resources. Sequatogue Farm was unsuccessfully put up for sale or lease. The livestock herd was sold. He tried to lease the farm for the summer of 1886, but finding no takers decided to reside there himself. He had been in the city for the Decoration Day Parade where he was part of the escort for President Grover Cleveland and had thereafter returned to West Islip. On June 2, three days later, he was seized with several hemorrhages and died.

A funeral was held at his New York City residence led by the Reverend Samuel Moran, the rector of Christ Church,

---

* At the time the LIRR owned 30 locomotives, 60 passenger cars, 350 freight cars, and 15 luggage cars. There were 198 miles of track.

West Islip,* and he was buried in the family plot in Woodlawn Cemetery in the Bronx. Sequatogue Farm, together with his valuable library and art collection, were left to his wife, Mary Jennie, who still had four minor children needing support. The library and art were sold soon thereafter as funds were in short supply. However, Mary Jennie was able to keep the farm and spent the summer of 1889 there. That year in October she died, leaving so little that her children were forced to contest the will of their recently deceased uncle, Hector C. Havemeyer (who had never married), for financial support. The farm in West Islip was finally sold in the 1890s.

As was said in his obituary, Henry Havemeyer did indeed "flit like a meteor and fade like a falling star."[46] Although his time along the Great South Bay was shortened by his early death, he was an important figure, well known and well remembered, and Sequatogue Farm added much luster to that procession of grand estates along the South Country Road. He was also a forerunner of his younger second cousin, Henry Osborne Havemeyer, who was to make a large impact in Islip in the 1890s.

By 1880 the area along the Great South Bay from Babylon in the west to Oakdale in the east, roughly fifteen miles long, had taken on the general character that would remain until World War I. Although there were some commercial activities — Doxsee's clamming and fishing, Hawkins's paper mill at Orowoc Creek, some marine railways and shipbuilders — the economy of the Town of Islip was to a greater degree than ever supported by the summer residents from New York and Brooklyn and by the transient summer guests at the hotels and boardinghouses. The population of the town had grown to 6,500, a 40 percent increase in the past decade. The attractions of the area had been tested, and it had passed the test with flying colors. It could provide what the affluent wanted in a summer resort and it was reasonably close to New York City with good rail service from a recently rejuve-

---

*   Founded in 1869.

nated Long Island Railroad under the guidance of Austin Corbin, who himself built in the area (in Babylon).

At the same time, there was still much bayside and creekside property that could be built on. Indeed, most of the roads that in the years ahead were to run south from the South Country Road to the bay were either not yet opened or if they had been, were very sparsely occupied. Saxton Avenue, Awixa Avenue, Penataquit Avenue in Bay Shore, and Ocean Avenue, Johnson Avenue, and Pavilion Avenue in Islip had very few summer homes in 1880. These roads would look very different by 1890, and in the intervening decade the first promoters and developers began to work. The rush to buy and build on prime waterfront property was under way.

Chapter VI

THE GILDED AGE – THE EARLY YEARS (1880–1890)

The period Mark Twain called the Gilded Age was generally considered to have begun around 1880 and to have lasted until World War I. It was characterized by luxury hitherto unknown in America and was centered to a great degree in New York City. Its leaders were the successful merchants of the city that had built its reputation on commerce and had become by then the largest and most important city in America. Louis Auchincloss, the writer and social historian, said, "The new rich of New York in the 1880s were not an aristocracy, nor did they succeed one. . . . An aristocracy must have its base in the ownership and cultivation of land. The tradesmen and money lenders of cities, no matter how long established and no matter what their personal dignity or moral code, can never be other than a bourgeoisie, which is why it never takes one class of capitalists very long to amalgamate with another."[1]

Although the merchant leaders of New York may not have inherited large land-holdings, they exhibited and often consumed their great wealth in an ostentatious display of houses, horses, and yachts, striving to outdo each other in their luxurious life-styles. The public's fascination with these families and their activities was shown by the close monitoring of them in New York's many daily newspapers of that era, often on the front page. The old families of New York — the Rhinelanders, Livingstons, Schermerhorns, and Astors, among many others — often looked upon this conspicuous new wealth with scorn. They used the term "ultra-fashionable dancing people" when referring to such as the Vanderbilts, because in addition to building grand new homes on New York's Fifth Avenue, the "arrivistes" gave a succession of fancy dress balls held from December to April, usually at Delmonicos, dancing sometimes until three o'clock in the morning with time out only for midnight supper and champagne. William K. and Alva Vanderbilt's costume ball of March 26, 1883, announced to Society that they had "arrived" — they had been called upon by Mrs. Astor.

With the advent of the Gilded Age, as has been seen, William K. Vanderbilt came to Oakdale and built Idlehour. Others were sure to follow and did in increasing numbers throughout the decade. Country homes were built; more cottages were built for summer rental and a great new resort hotel was completed. The economy of the Town of Islip flourished after the depressed years following the Panic of 1873 and the population in the decade of the 1880s almost doubled. (It was the largest percentage increase in the Town of Islip until after World War II.) The word of the day in 1880 was promotion, and no one was more responsible for the boom on Long Island than Austin Corbin.

The Corbin family had settled in New Hampshire many generations before Austin was born in Newport in 1827. After early education in his home state he went to the Harvard Law School from which he graduated at age twenty-two. His interest at first was in banking. In 1851 he went west to Davenport, Iowa, where he founded a bank and remained for fourteen years. Following the end of the Civil War he returned east and settled in New York City. He was then thirty-eight years old. Gifted with organizational and promotional skills, Corbin started his own bank in New York, the Corbin Banking Company, which, like many other banks in that era, was heavily involved with the huge railroad expansion of the 1870s. He and his bank specialized in railroad reorganizations and made large profits in the process. Corbin became a man of great wealth who by 1880 had been accepted into Society with the other "arrivistes." He became a member of the Manhattan, the Seawanhaka-Corinthian Yacht, the

Meadowbrook, and the South Side Sportsmen's clubs. In the mid 1870s Corbin saw the great potential for resorts and seaside holidays in the area along Great South Bay. He acquired a 1,000-acre tract of land in North Babylon to the east of Belmont's Nursery on which he built a gracious country house. He eventually cultivated about a third of this huge parcel. He constructed a twelve-acre trout pond that he stocked from the South Side Sportsmen's Club fish hatchery, as well as a wildlife preserve that was opened weekly to the public. He called his estate Forrest Farm.

During 1880 the Long Island Railroad was experiencing another period of difficulty. Shoddy equipment and unreliable service were causing large losses and finally bankruptcy was declared. Corbin, at the head of a syndicate, negotiated for purchase of the railroad and in December of 1880 ownership was awarded to him by the court-appointed receiver of the property. On January 1, 1881, Corbin was named president. The receiver was influenced by the fact that Corbin was already president of the Bay Ridge and Coney Island Railroad and the Manhattan Beach Co., both in Brooklyn; that he knew Long Island well; that he recognized the necessary connection between a successful railroad and successful resorts on the Island; and that for the first time there was solid financial backing to upgrade the equipment and service on the railroad. The occasion marked the start of a sustained period of expansion and good service.

Corbin said upon taking over the presidency, "I have always believed in Long Island, in its advantages as a place of residence, in its agricultural productiveness, in the attractiveness of its summer resorts and in its value for railroad purposes. All the island needs is development and now that development is going to take place. What the railroad needs is to be managed as a sensible man would manage his own business. The demands of travel must be fully complied with and the trains must run rapidly and on time."[2]

He was as good as his word. By June of that year passenger cars and locomotives had been overhauled, new ties and track had been laid down, and the main depot in Long Island

City was in process of being entirely rebuilt. New directors of the railroad had been added to the board, men of experience in the commercial world of business in that era, one of whom was the young sugar merchant, Henry Osborne Havemeyer, age thirty-three, who would go on to form the Sugar Trust (1887), and would summer in Babylon in the 1880s.

Corbin, in his interview, went on to say, "I propose to make the south side of Long Island the greatest watering place in the world. Its natural beauties and advantages are so great that the improvement of the whole stretch of coast is as certain to come as the world is to stand. I have lived there for eight years and I know whereof I speak when I say that the climate, the scenery, and the natural attractions are unsurpassed in any part of this country or Europe. I have not a particle of doubt that within ten years the south side from Coney Island to Montauk Point will be boarded by a continuous chain of seaside summer resorts."[3] The Long Island Railroad began to reflect Corbin's tremendous enthusiasm by publishing brochures describing the various resorts on the South Shore and how they could be reached easily by rail. Some of these resort hotels were built by Corbin's own Manhattan Beach Co. and Long Island Improvement Co. — such as the Manhattan Beach Hotel in Coney Island.

Still, Corbin was somewhat cautious. "We will not go to Montauk just yet," he said: "We may build a railroad there, but there is no need of any at the present and it wouldn't pay."[4] He did have a scheme in mind that would make it pay. Corbin and George Lorillard (see Chapter V) together met with a representative of a large English shipping firm in late 1881 to discuss the creation of a deep water port for European shipping in Fort Pond Bay, Montauk. Corbin said, "When the new route to Europe is established, and the Railroad done between Fort Pond and Long Island City, the 120 miles will be covered in two hours. Sixty miles an hour on the Long Island Railroad."[5] He loved speed and in fact one day in 1882 did ride non-stop from Babylon to Hunters Point Avenue, a distance of thirty-nine miles, in forty-two minutes to show it could be achieved. The Fort Pond Bay deep-water port never materialized. For once Corbin's enthusiasm was overly ambitious, but the railroad, of course, did get to Montauk which became a seaside resort later. In November 1881, Corbin acquired fifteen acres in Babylon (the Electus B. Litchfield property) on the west side of Blythebourne Lake, between the railroad tracks and South Country Road. The property was only a short walk from the Babylon Railroad station. He intended the site for another huge resort hotel, which his Long Island Improvement Company would build and operate. There were fears at the time that it would detract from business at the Surf Hotel on Fire Island, whose guests had to come by way of Babylon on the railroad and who could easily see the great new resort. The fears would prove unfounded, however. Corbin went ahead and built his new lakeside hotel in Babylon, and it was very different from the Surf Hotel on the ocean beach. To build a hotel of three hundred fifty rooms for seven hundred guests in six months was a massive undertaking. The architects, William Field and Son of New York, designed a Queen Anne–style main building three floors high. It was laid out somewhat in the shape of a Maltese Cross with a 300-foot long frontage and a large wing on either end 155 feet deep. Piazzas, planked in Georgia pine and finished in shellac, were constructed on the sides and at the rear of the first and second floors. On top of the main roof were two ornamental towers with a view of "the vast expanse of sea and shore."[6]

Inside the hotel there was "the grand hall on the lower floor, which is lighted and ventilated by large oval openings through the four floors, properly protected by strong ornamental railings. Facing the main entrance is the grand staircase, finished and railed in solid woods — ash predominating. To the left is the dining hall, which is one of the most prominent features of the house. It is 98 feet long by 47 feet wide, and will seat with four private dining rooms adjoining, 700 persons at once. The interior is gothic in natural woods — lighted by large stained glass windows. The ceiling in the highest part is 55 feet above the floor. Adjoining is the kitchen, a room 40 x 50 feet, fitted with patent ranges, steam tables and every first-class kitchen appliance. The balance of the first floor is devoted to suites, private parlors, and sleeping apartments — there being about 300 of these, all connected with the office by patent electric bells. On the second floor the main parlors are located, the balance being devoted to sleeping accommodations. The third floor is nearly a duplicate of the second floor. In the base are the barber shops, baths, billiard saloons, bar, and wine-rooms. . . . The water service of the house is perfect — the water being pumped to a water tower some distance west of the house. On each floor there are three fire plugs of regulation size, with hoses and pipes attached, ready for instant use."[7] Fire was a tremendous hazard in these wooden structures, which were lighted with gas lamps in the halls and rooms. The final demise of a resort hotel in that era was more often than not its burning to the ground. "All the rooms are large, light, easy of access and well ventilated. The halls are wide and roomy and the whole arrangement is as near perfect as it was possible to make it."[8]

Corbin named his new resort hotel the Argyle, after the Duke of Argyll, whose son, Queen Victoria's son-in-law, Lord Lorne, and some English gentry had made substantial investments in the project. It opened for guests on June 20, 1882. It was to become for Babylon what the Prospect House was for Bay Shore and the Pavilion Hotel was for Islip and East Islip — an introduction for a large number of New Yorkers and Brooklynites to the South Shore and the Great South Bay.

John Lee, of Brooklyn, was the contractor for this work. Using several subcontractors from Brooklyn and New York and a work force of a hundred fifty men, he managed to meet the deadline set by Corbin who had already booked reservations for the summer. As opening day approached the reporter was taken to the top of the 87 foot water tower and commented, "from its highest elevation there is furnished a magnificent view of the adjacent country, the bay, and the ocean. Garden City, with its cathedral, and the church spires of Hempstead, distant about 18 miles are plainly visible, and the lofty hills to the north [Dix Hills] loom up in prominence."[9]

It is interesting to note that the lack of large trees on the South Shore at that time made such an unobstructed view possible. They had been cut for use in shipbuilding, for railroad ties and paper mills, or had burned down in the frequent forest fires of the time, set by the railroad locomotives or on purpose for charcoal production. The water tower was a large structure as well as a high one. It also contained the gas tank, as well as apartments for the staff of the hotel. The laundry, complete with steam for washing and ironing, was nearby.

Many of the resort hotels of the 1880s had followed the example of the Grand Union Hotel at Saratoga, which in 1877 announced that it would accept only Christians as guests. Saratoga was then the queen of American resorts and if its preeminent hotel, then owned by the estate of the late retail merchant Alexander T. Stewart, could restrict its guests, many others would as well. Thus resulted the first publicized case of anti-Semitism in America. A boycott of Stewart's New York store began and had much to do with the store's eventual sale to John Wanamaker. However, in spite of the uproar over this outrageous act of prejudice, hotel after hotel in many of the resorts followed suit. On Long Island, Austin Corbin announced the policy that would be followed by his Manhattan Beach Hotel and by the Argyle: "We do not like Jews as a class. There are some well behaved people among them, but as a rule they make themselves offensive to the kind of people who principally patronize our road [Long Island Railroad] and hotel, and I am satisfied we should be better off without than with their custom."[10] Sadly, this restricted policy was carried on well into the twentieth century by many hotels, especially at exclusive resorts.

The Argyle opened on time, but was not an immediate success. In fact only about one-third of the rooms were ever occupied at any one time. It was, however, a boom for the Babylon economy, and when it closed after its first season on September 1, Corbin had every reason to be pleased. He decided to add fourteen cottages on the property, apart from the main hotel building, which would permit more privacy, but still allow dining in the hotel. These were very much sought after and in the summers of 1885 and 1886 one was rented to Henry O. Havemeyer, his new wife, Louisine, and their infant children. In the summer of 1883 the Argyle rented the Armory on Havemeyer's Point (see Chapter V) as a seaside adjunct for the season. Apparently this was not successful as it was not repeated the following year. Finally, a casino, designed by the prestigious New York firm of McKim, Mead and White, was added in the park south of the hotel. Casinos were a popular addition to the resort hotels of the era. They were covered structures designed for entertainment, dancing, dining, and sometime sport. Boating and fishing in the lake were popular activities as well.

By the mid 1880s Corbin's reputation had grown. The LIRR was operating better than ever before and most of his resort hotels were flourishing as well. Undoubtedly both were benefiting from the prosperity of that time. In a feature article in November 1886, under the headline "Austin Corbin's Career, Wonderful Business Enterprises of the Railway King"; the *New York World* said,

> having already accomplished the full measure of a wondrously successful career, the financial world today finds Austin Corbin cheerfully assuming new cares and responsibilities within the endurance and capacity of only the most extraordinary of men of his time of life. His name is widely known on both sides of the Atlantic, but his face is only familiar to those who have come within the circle of his business and social relations.

> From a condition which made it [LIRR] the laughing stock of railroad men, and a delusion and a snare to the unwary traveller, it has become a thoroughly-equipped and completed system, with numerous branches reaching every part of the Island, and one of the most reliable-paying properties in the State.[11]

Although the LIRR was flourishing, as the decade wore on there was evidence that the era of the huge resort hotel was on the wane. In September 1886, the Argyle closed after only "a fair" season. In September 1890, it closed after the least successful season in its history. In March of 1891 it was bought at auction by a real estate syndicate headed by William Ziegler, of the Royal Baking Powder Co. Ziegler reopened the Argyle for the 1891 season and struggled along until 1897 when he closed the hotel for good and sold the cottages on the grounds. The depression following 1893 was just too much for such a large establishment. It, like its rival, the Surf Hotel on Fire Island, had served its purpose. The Argyle remained boarded up until 1904 when it was razed, its lumber being used to build new houses on the grounds. Argyle Park, as it is known today, had been born.

Meanwhile Corbin was at work on another project, which turned out to be premature. In 1889, he proposed for New York City a system of underground railroads (they were all above ground then, both on the ground and elevated), and engaged an English engineer to draw up comprehensive plans because an underground had been established successfully in London. However, due to a lack of financial backing his plan could not be put into effect. It was, however, that plan that later became the beginnings of the New York City subway system.

Corbin, in his last years, spent more time at his estate in Newport, New Hampshire, his birthplace. It was there on June 4, 1896, that his horses took fright and ran away with his carriage, which overturned. He was thrown against a stone wall, suffered a skull fracture, and died that day, at the age of sixty-nine. In an editorial the following week it was said, "Austin Corbin did not devote his time and talents to the improvement of Long Island from philanthropic motives alone; he made money and because he did, so did many others. Long Island owes much to Austin Corbin and should honor his memory."[12] His North Babylon home, Forrest Farm, was sold in 1902.

Austin Corbin and his Long Island Railroad played a major role in the development of the Great South Bay area in the 1880s. Other entrepreneurs saw the great advantages of this part of Long Island as well and bought land that was strategically located on the bay or on the creeks that flowed into the bay. In the area between Bay Shore and Islip the first of these developers was a New Yorker named Daniel D. Conover.

Conover was born in 1822. In his early life he was identified with New York City politics and was an active and influential member of the Volunteer Fire Department, particularly Amity House No. 38, a company noted for the character and prominence of its members. Through this association he became an early member of the Olympic Club and was most likely introduced to Saxton Avenue in Bay Shore when the club moved there in 1856. He was mentioned as a member in 1869 along with Thomas B. Asten and others who were part of New York's municipal government. In 1857, Conover gained prominence through an appointment as street commissioner by New York State Governor King. He was involved in a clash between the metropolitan police under the control of the governor and the municipal police under Mayor Wood. He had obtained a warrant for the arrest of the mayor on the charge of inciting a riot on June 16, 1857. In attempting to serve the warrant on the mayor at City Hall, a fierce struggle between the rival police forces broke out in which several policemen were severely wounded and the Seventh Regiment had to be called out to restore order. Conover then did serve his writ on the mayor. He was also involved with national politics, being a presidential elector on the Frémont ticket in 1856. (Frémont lost to James Buchanan.)

In addition, Conover was identified with several of New York's street railways. He was a promoter of the Broadway line, the granting of a charter for which caused a contest in the Board of Aldermen. He was involved with the Thirty-fourth Street line; the Fullerton Street, Wall Street and Cortlandt Street Railroad Co.; and the Twenty-eighth and Twenty-ninth Streets Railroad Co. He was president of the Forty-second Street Railroad Co. and vice-president of the Metropolitan Surface Railroad Company. All of these franchises for New York City street railroads or trolleys, which were pulled by horses, had to be approved by the Board of Aldermen, many of whom were friends and fellow members of the Olympic Club. Being the sole means of public transit in the expanding city, the horse railways, as they were called then, were valuable franchises and profitable to the owners. Conover's wealth and influence grew.

In 1880, when Corbin was negotiating his purchase of the LIRR, Daniel D. Conover began acquiring property between Bay Shore and Islip, at first on Saxton Avenue near the Olympic Club. He had sensed that the time was ripe for development and that profits could be made. His method was to start by purchasing the land sites, improving the roads, dredging the creeks, and building cottages for rent. His first acquisition was a site just north of the Olympic Club where he built a house for himself and his family. It was a house typical of the period and it was to be duplicated over and over again on many of the local streets leading to the bay. Three stories high with shingle facing and gables on the top floor, this Victorian style cottage had as its most prominent features the conical turret, the mansard roof, and the screened porch or piazza that surrounded the entire house. It was described as "of attractive design and costly in all its interior decorations and furniture."[13] In addition to the house, Conover built a bathhouse which was not common for that time. It had two floors, on the first of which were "five rooms—two bathrooms, one toilet room, one lounging room, and one shower-bath room with copper floor. These rooms are furnished in princely style. The second floor is finished into one grand room."[14]

Conover continued to acquire land on both sides of Saxton Avenue as it became available to him, and by 1884 it was said that he owned a long frontage on Awixa Creek as well as a large quantity of other land on Saxton's Neck. However, to make this creek frontage suitable to moor boats, improvements were necessary. The water there was shallow and the banks were marshy. The smaller creeks that flowed into the Great South Bay did not carry enough fresh water to keep a channel open at all times, and the rain had a tendency to carry silt from the marshy banks to the bottom of the creek. This prevented all but the very smallest boats from using creeks such as Awixa and Champlin's. However, with the use of a steam dredge, the costly process of deepening and widening the creeks could be undertaken, and the banks could be bulkheaded to permit dockside mooring and prevent erosion.

In the winter of 1884, Conover engaged ten men "to cut off the east bank of Awixa Creek and throw the earth on the shore. He will make the creek navigable for good-sized boats" it was said.[15] The work of deepening Champlin's Creek was also begun then, using Islip shipyard owner Alonzo Smith's new steam digger to make a 90-foot-wide channel. In the next year Conover dredged in Orowoc Creek, filling his land on the east side of Saxton Avenue with the valuable fill which would make it suitable for building sites. He was called at that time "a real estate improvement society all in himself." "He has made more improvements in the Main Street between the Paper Mill Brook [Orowoc Creek] and Awixa Brook than any person in the history of the town." "He is now covering several acres of low, muddy ground adjoining Orowoc Brook with earth. This will cost thousands of dollars, but it will make a beautiful piece of property."[16]

Conover was the first person in the Town of Islip to take the large financial risk of investing in land on which costly improvements must be made before any sales or profits could be realized. As common as it seems today, many were skeptical then that Conover could succeed with this new form of real estate development. The *South Side Signal* in a July 1885 editorial said, "Mr. Conover is talking of a big real estate experiment, which, if successful, will solve a much-talked of problem. It has long been a question whether it will pay to cover the soft meadows bordering on the bay with solid earth, so as to make building sites. A good many wise men have shaken their heads doubtfully when asked if it would pay. There is no doubt that the water fronts would sell at a good price, but the expense of filling up is, of course, very great. Mr. Conover is about to attempt it on a large scale, and, if successful, it will revolutionize the water front business of the South Side. There are at present many miles of soft meadow which, if filled up and made habitable, would bring a good price for building lots for city people."

Conover's plan for Awixa Creek was to dredge from the mouth northward toward the South Country Road, near which he would create a freshwater lake with a dam over which a road would run connecting Saxton Avenue with Awixa Avenue. By 1887 this project was completed except for the road connection, which was never built. Meanwhile, Conover was acquiring land along the creeks as well as to the north of the South Country Road until by the end of the decade he became among the largest property owners in the Town of Islip. Orowoc Pond, north of Main Street, in 1889 the property of Conover, became famous as the site of a fishing expedition. Several of Conover's friends invited former President Grover Cleveland for a day of fly fishing. He and Daniel Lamont came to Islip on Saturday, April 20, 1889, and were seen to thoroughly enjoy themselves. It was observed, however, that "Mr. Cleveland's term of office has not worn away his flesh much, as he now turns the scale at nearly three hundred."[17] Conover was surely a proud host that day. .

In addition to dredging the creeks and buying up the land, the roads needed improvement and cottages had to be built for sale or rent. As has been noted, Conover was famous for his good roads. The South Country Road was, of course, a public highway as were the several roads that ran off it north and south. Because the Town of Islip was so remiss in maintaining the roads there was continuing agitation in the 1880s for improvement. There was fear that poor, dusty roads (they were sprinkled with water to keep down the dust) would keep visitors away and halt the summer boom. The affluent summertime residents would meet together to petition the town to act. In the fall of 1888 they wrote to the highway commissioner of the Town of Islip, "We respectfully draw your attention to the dangerous and disgraceful condition of the highways under your charge and request you to take steps for their thorough repair with the utmost speed that is consistent with a proper performance of the work."[18] It was suggested that taxes should be raised "to make such a road as Mr. Conover builds, of full width, flat surface and composed of clam shells and in equal parts. His roads will stand all seasons — hot, cold, wet or dry."[19] Conover even offered to shell the South Country Road from Orowoc Brook to Islip village at his expense if the Town would properly grade it, but nothing was done to improve this poor condition.

In addition to his own house, Conover built several houses for rent — they were known as cottages then — on Saxton Avenue, Awixa Avenue, and the Main Street itself. They were very popular and were occupied in the summer by New York and Brooklyn families, often year after year, who would rent them from $100 to $1,000 a month. Many who would later build their own country houses first summered in a Conover cottage. It is not possible to say whether Conover was financially successful as a real estate developer. He surely accomplished much for the Town of Islip and because of what he did, the town benefited enormously. He was also a forerunner of several developers who were to follow in the next twenty years such as H. O. Havemeyer, W. H. Moffitt, and T. B. Ackerson.

At the age of sixty-four, Conover was described in the New York Tribune: "Of the men who in recent years have been engaged in surface railroad schemes in this city, D. D. Conover is probably the most striking in appearance. Although he is probably considerably beyond sixty years, his erect carriage, his face as rosy as a boy's, and his complexion as clear, give him a much younger look. His most notable feature, however, is his snow-white hair and full beard and mustache. Mr. Conover has all the dash and vigor of a man of thirty."[20] The following spring he and his wife, Catherine, were hosts at the wedding of their daughter Kate, held at their "handsome mansion" on Saxton Avenue. Guests came from New York in special railroad cars engaged for the occasion to enjoy the festivities on the Conover country estate.

Daniel D. Conover continued his development work in the area, in 1891 laying out the road north of the railroad tracks that was to become Moffitt Boulevard, and in 1894 selling property along Brentwood Road to the Oakwood Driving Park Association for a half-mile horse racing track.

On August 15, 1896, in his seventy-fifth year, Conover died suddenly, at his Bay Shore home. He was survived by his widow, Catherine (nee Whitlock), his daughter and his son, Augustus W. Conover, who lived for a short time in the Saxton Avenue home. Catherine Conover died in February 1900, at the family home in New York City, at the age of seventy-eight. She was buried along with her husband in the family plot in Oakwood Cemetery, Bay Shore, testimony that they must have thought of Bay Shore as their real home.

Although Austin Corbin and Daniel D. Conover were promoters, developers, and residents of the Great South Bay area in the 1880s, they were not what the Gilded Age would consider "of Society." They were successful, had New York City residences, and were summertime owners on the South Shore. They were not, however, from old New York families such as the Johnsons, Lawrances, Knapps, Garners, and others that had settled in the area earlier, nor were they among the arrivistes such as the Belmonts and Vanderbilts whose tremendous wealth and extravagant life-styles overcame the original resistance to including them in New York Society. But because of what Corbin and Conover did, many members of New York Society came to the area in the 1880s. One of those was Edward Spring Knapp, who in the winter of 1880 with his new wife, Margaret Ireland Lawrance Knapp, bought land on the west side of Saxton Avenue to the north of Conover's land. Knapp and his bride were as "old family" in New York as it was possible to be.

Edward Spring Knapp (1852–1895) was the son of Gideon Lee Knapp (see Chapter V) who, with his younger brothers Shepherd and William K. Knapp, had come to the South Shore in the 1860s for its fishing and bird shooting. Gideon's wife, Augusta Murray Spring, was the daughter of the Reverend Gardiner Spring, minister of the Brick Church in New York City from 1810 to 1866, and the granddaughter of Samuel Spring who had fought under Benedict Arnold in the battle for Quebec during the American Revolution.

His wife, Margaret Ireland Lawrance, was the daughter of William R. Lawrance and the granddaughter of Thomas Lawrance III and his wife, Margaret Ireland Lawrance, for whom she was named. Thus, her lineage went back to the Thomas Lawrance who settled in Newtown, Long Island, in 1656 (see Chapter I). Margaret's grandparents, as well as many of her aunts and uncles, were the earliest of the summertime residents of Bay Shore in the 1840s (see Chapter III). Her father, William, and her mother, Mary Helen Crandell, had been married at St. Mark's Church, Islip, in 1849. Edward Knapp and Margaret Lawrance surely knew one another from the earliest ages, summering together amidst large numbers of brothers, sisters, aunts, uncles, and cousins, all located along the South Country Road west of Bay Shore village. Margaret was considered a great beauty as a girl; "the beautiful Miss Lawrance" she was called. When her engagement to Edward S. Knapp was announced, Augusta Spring Knapp wrote,

> A year since I last wrote. It seems incredible that I should have left my book so long. And such an eventful year. Ned [E. S. Knapp], my own dear, loving son, married and gone. I was anxious he should marry and urged him to find a nice girl, but I did not realize I should lose him so completely. But it is better for him, and I am glad though I miss him dreadfully.
>
> He married Miss Maggie Lawrance, a young lady we all knew and I think he has made a wise choice.
>
> They had gone to housekeeping at Bay Shore and are very happy. I should be content.[21]

Edward Knapp and Margaret Lawrance were married in the Church of the Heavenly Rest in New York City on December 10, 1878. They rented a small house west of Bay Shore the following summer while searching for a good site on which to build their own home. When the twelve-acre farm of Selah Abbott on the west side of Saxton Avenue became available in the winter of 1880, they purchased the property and immediately began to build a suitable home for their new family; a son, Edward S. Knapp Jr., had been born by then. John Pullis, "the boss carpenter" from Bay Shore, was engaged to build the house and a barn, and by May ground was broken. Work proceeded quickly and by September the house was nearly complete when a fire, started by spilled turpentine, almost destroyed it. The fire was quickly put out, however, and there was only minor damage. By the fall of 1880, the Knapps moved in. They named their new home Awixa Lawn, fronting as it did on Awixa Creek. The original house they built was later described by their son, Edward, as "tiny with a hall, a sitting room and a dining room on the main floor; above that, a small bedroom, which Katie [nursemaid] and I occupied and, across the hall, a large bedroom for Father and Mother, with servants rooms. The coachman slept in a room in the stable."[22] This "tiny" house was added to in 1886 with a big dining room, a very large butler's pantry, and a large bedroom on the second floor. Again in 1889 a southwest wing* was added to include "a very large living room with a truly enormous fireplace, two beautiful adjoining bedrooms above that, and still two more above that to one of which I moved."[23] Awixa Lawn had become a very grand home indeed.

The Knapps had a vegetable garden and a gardener at Awixa Lawn. Two acres on fine ground along Awixa Creek were carefully tilled and all the vegetables the family used were grown there. An adjacent greenhouse enabled the young plants to get an early start each spring. "The most expensive thing in the garden was a very large asparagus bed . . . I remember Father saying to Mother, 'Maggie, that's the best damn asparagus I ever tasted'."[24] There was also a cow named Beauty and a barn where the hay was kept in the loft.

The Knapps were not entirely self-sufficient for their food. They bought eggs and chickens from Captain Bill Hawkins up at the corner, and tradesmen from Bay Shore and Islip made deliveries each day. Edward Knapp Jr. re-

---

* The addition was designed by the Sayville architect Isaac H. Green Jr.

membered the iceman in his yellow covered wagon, marked "D. S. Hubbard — Ice," as well as Dickerson, the butcher, and the grocer's boy who smoked cigarettes.

Knapp described this as "a carefree, lazy, happy life." He is remembering his boyhood and it is the fond memories that dominate. Behind those there were undoubtedly many trials and much hard work to have created such a summer home as he has described.

Although the Knapps had many friends in both the Bay Shore and Islip areas by 1880, none as yet lived on Saxton Avenue. Edward was a member of the Olympic Club, although his interests were not in sailing or yachting, but rather in horses and in shooting birds. He was a member of the South Side Sportsmen's Club and was considered an excellent shot, "as good as there was."[25] Bird shooting on the bay in the summer and fall (there were no restrictions then, and many birds) was his greatest sporting pleasure. He would shoot all sorts of snipe, plover, and shore birds in the summer season. With his brother, Gideon, he would hunt quail each autumn on farms he had leased at Blue Point, and duck shooting, always a favorite sport on the bay, prompted a story he related to his son. Decoys had been put on the river shore where the ducks liked to feed. "A flock of seven red heads came in to their blind and Father shot — just one barrel — and killed all seven."[26] His description of it was that they came in rather high, and that after he shot, "the sky just seemed to rain ducks."[27] My, how the young lad must have been impressed!

When the Knapps located on Saxton Avenue, it was Edward's intention to live there all year round, commuting to New York daily on the Long Island Railroad. In 1880, there was established a railroad depot called Olympic where the train stopped at Saxton Avenue. This was in addition to the Bay Shore and Islip stops. It was primarily for the convenience of Olympic Club members and in the expectation that more commuters would follow Knapp to Saxton Avenue. "The avenue leading to the Olympic Club will now be rapidly taken up for summer residences. The land slopes on each side of the avenue to navigable creeks, opening into the Bay. The building lots can be so laid out that every man can have his pleasure boat to land directly on his own ground, and the distance to the new depot is so small that many like Mr. Knapp will live in the country the year round, and go to the city every morning."[28]

For a time, Knapp did commute daily to New York all the year round. The Olympic station was soon abandoned for lack of commuters, however, and he went to Bay Shore station, two miles or so away, with a fast horse and carriage. The coachman would take him in the morning and bring him home in the evening. A good horse was a necessity then for daily life, and the Knapps, all being good horsemen, took care to have the best. As time went on and the Knapp family grew with another son, Tom, and a daughter, Margaret, they chose to spend the winters in the city, leaving Awixa Lawn in the late autumn to return in the early spring.

Edward S. Knapp's work was the managing of various enterprises owned by his family. His father, Gideon, in 1853 had purchased a charter to run a ferry to Greenpoint, Long Island, from two New York piers at Tenth Street and at Twenty-third Street. Until 1883 when the Brooklyn Bridge opened, all traffic crossed the East River by ferry and they were profitable enterprises. When Gideon Knapp died, Edward was made manager of the Greenpoint Ferry Co. He later took charge of the Thirty-fourth Street ferry, which connected to Austin Corbin's new Long Island Railroad terminal in Long Island City. He was known as an expert in ferry management.

In 1889, Knapp became president of the Queens County Bank, as the result of acquiring a controlling interest in the bank with the aid of a syndicate headed by the New York broker and East Islip resident, Harry. B. Hollins. The bank was moved to Long Island City from Flushing at about the time the Knapps gained control. He remained president of the bank until his premature death. Although he had many and diverse sporting interests, he conscientiously looked after the family's business interests, unlike many with his background in that era.

Horse racing was a passion and a tradition with the Knapp family. Edward's father and his uncle, Shepherd, were much involved (see Chapter IV). In the following generation, Edward himself, with his younger brother, Gideon, and then after their deaths, the youngest brother, Harry K. Knapp, were closely associated with the sport of kings. Their stable of racehorses, named the Oneck Stables, included the famous horse Sir Walter, a champion during the seasons of 1892–98. The races during those years were held at the Jerome Park track and at the seaside race tracks at Gravesend, Coney Island, and Sheepshead Bay. Edward Knapp, although he was two-thirds owner of the stable, was not publicly identified with it because of his banking and ferryboat interests. His brother, Dr. Gideon Knapp, was known as the owner of Oneck Stables. Sir Walter's winnings were large, and the two Knapp brothers were successful racing owners, but for only three short years.

On March 25, 1895, Edward Spring Knapp died suddenly of a cerebral hemorrhage in New York City. He was only forty-three years old. His brother Gideon died the following year at forty. None of the Knapp men were long-lived, but none died as prematurely as those brothers. Edward's wife, Margaret, was left with three children, ages sixteen, nine, and two, and a large country home on Saxton Avenue. Awixa Lawn was rented to others for the summers following Edward's death. In 1896, Margaret built a new house on her Saxton Avenue property nearer the road and to the south of Awixa Lawn.* Possibly the memories of remaining in the old home were too painful. Her son, Edward, went to school in New York City, but the family continued to summer in Bay Shore. In 1903 Edward married Rosalie E. Moran, a boyhood friend from Islip. In 1915, Margaret Lawrance Knapp sold her homes in Bay Shore and moved away from Long Island for good. She lived on in her long widowhood until the 1930s when she died in her seventies. The year 1915 did not mark

---

*   This house, number 52, stands today on the west side of Saxon Avenue in front of the pump station.

the end for the Knapps on the South Shore, however, for Edward's youngest brother, Harry K. Knapp, had by then established his summer home, Brookwood Hall, in East Islip (see Chapter VIII).

As the Gilded Age began, the families in the Town of Islip with the largest land holdings were those of W. K. Vanderbilt, Francis C. Lawrance, George Lorillard, Alfred Wagstaff, and Henry B. Hyde, all prominent New Yorkers. It was Vanderbilt, the most recent arrival of the five, who would have the most influence on the community in that decade. He had scarcely finished his own home in Oakdale in the summer of 1879 when he proposed to the vestry of St. Mark's Church (he was elected to the vestry in 1879) that his architect, Richard Morris Hunt, design an entirely new church and a new rectory all at his expense. He asked that other members of the parish furnish the rectory and the organ, nothing more. The vestry, of course, accepted this generous offer and by the fall of 1879 construction was under way.

To replace the simple, rectangular, thirty-year-old white frame building, Hunt chose to duplicate a particular Norwegian stave church in Fortun near the Sogne Fjord. It was described at the time as "of timber construction, showing the masonry to represent stone, with shingled sides and steep sloping roofs. It has many points and broken gables, but no lofty spire. The porches are very large. Over the front main porch is carved in wood the lion of St. Mark behind a shield bearing the Latin inscription 'Pax Tibi Marce Evangelista Mens'."[29]

The interior of the new church "is very handsome. The side walls are continued up to the roof with white and Georgia pine, paneled and molded like the sides. The staving and seats are in different colors of ash, heavily cased. A stall, equal to three pews, is reserved and railed in ash, furnished with chairs of the same material for the exclusive use of Mr. Vanderbilt's family. The pulpit and lectern are of walnut with crimson and gold trimmings. The windows are of stained glass and were supplied by L. C. Tiffany [Louis Comfort Tiffany] of New York, who also donated a trefoil window.

The architect, Mr. Hunt, takes great pride in the apse. It is broad, deep and domed and circular in form with three pairs of triplet windows of opalescent glass. In the central window is an exquisite representation of St. Mark and his lion riding in the clouds. The dome is surmounted by the figure of an angel carved in wood, but very much resembling bronze, bearing a scroll on which is the inscription 'Spes In Deo'."[30] "The organ is one of the finest and most powerful instruments on the Island, and is also the donation of a few Christian gentlemen and ladies."[31]

On June 19, 1880, the rector, the Reverend Reuben Riley, moved into his new rectory, which had been comfortably furnished by the ladies: Mmes. John D. Prince, William K. Vanderbilt, Harry B. Hollins, Francis C. Lawrance, Bradish Johnson, and Charles Sackett. On June 22, 1880, St. Mark's Church was consecrated by the bishop of Long Island. The Right Reverend Dr. Littlejohn was assisted in the ceremony by fourteen clergymen. Mr. John D. Prince brought the choir and organist from Trinity Church, New York. "The church was handsomely decorated with choice flowers, the chancel being a complete bank of fragrant exotics and roses. The music was grand."[32] The service, which lasted for over two hours, was followed by a luncheon at the home of Mr. and Mrs. H. Duncan Wood nearby. The day was a splendid occasion for all. William K. Vanderbilt had created a beautiful country church to go along with Idlehour, all within two years after he had chosen that setting for one of his several country homes.

Vanderbilt's influence was felt in Islip in other ways as well. It was due to him that three families settled in Islip and East Islip, two of which would remain for a century or more. Vanderbilt's stockbrokers were Harry B. Hollins and H. Duncan Wood. His close friend was Schuyler Livingston Parsons. Each purchased land for a country home in 1880, and Hollins's and Parsons's descendants remained there until the 1970s and 1990s respectively. A new generation of young families was coming to the South Shore as the 1880s began. Vanderbilt himself was thirty years old, Hollins was twenty-

Parade of the *New York Coaching Club* in 1883, in
the four-in-hand or Tally Ho coaches.
(Courtesy of Harper's Weekly June 2, 1883.)

Austin Corbin, 1827-1896, hotel builder and president
of the Long Island Railroad from 1881.
(Courtesy of Old Oakdale History, vol. I.)

The *Pavilion Hotel* in East Islip in 1881 under the
new management of James Slater.
(Courtesy of Long Island of Today, 1884.)

The sloop *Mischief*, skippered by Captain Nathaniel Clock of Islip, winning the America's Cup in 1881. (Courtesy of The Old Print Shop.)

The New York Yacht Club Regatta off the new clubhouse and grounds, Staten Island, 1869. (Courtesy of The Old Print Shop.)

A Stakes Race for $1,000 a side, *Fanny* (white hull) vs. *Gracie* (black hull), October 9, 1883 (from a painting by Michael Keane).

The yacht *Mohawk* of New York owned by Vice Commodore William T. Garner of Bay Shore. *Mohawk* capsized while at anchor off Staten Island on July 20, 1876. Garner and his wife were drowned. (Courtesy of The Old Print Shop.)

The *Olympic Club* on Saxton Avenue, Bay Shore, sponsored sailing and fishing on the Great South Bay, popular sports of the era. (Courtesy of Pictorial Bay Shore.)

six, Wood and Parsons were twenty-eight. These men, together with E. S. Knapp, twenty-eight, and Bradish Johnson Jr., twenty-seven, became the prominent leaders of Islip's summertime community for the next several decades. Each was descended from a distinguished old New York family, was a member of St. Mark's Church, and of the South Side Sportsmen's Club.

In March of 1877, twenty-three-year-old Harry B. Hollins had married Evelina Meserole Knapp, the daughter of Mr. and Mrs. William K. Knapp of Johnson Avenue, Islip (see Chapter IV). Evelina was thus a first cousin of Edward S. Knapp and Harry K. Knapp. The marriage held in St. Mark's Church (the "old" church) united two families of prominence in New York. Sadly, Evelina's father died later that year at the age of fifty. Hollins had grown up in New York City, attending private schools there. At an early age he went to work on Wall Street, gaining the experience needed to start his own stock-brokerage firm of H. B. Hollins & Co. in 1878. Associated with him was his friend H. Duncan Wood. It was his early friendship with the young W. K. Vanderbilt, scion to that huge family fortune (the old Commodore had died just the year before), that gave Hollins his opportunity. As an energetic and successful banker and broker for W. K. his reputation grew along with his wealth. During his long career Hollins was an organizer of the Knickerbocker Trust Co; a vice president of the Central Railroad and Banking Company of Georgia and of the International Bank of Mexico; and a director of the North American Safe Deposit Company, the Central Union Gas Company, and the Corporation Trust Company.

In 1892 and early 1893, Hollins, along with Jacob H. Schiff of Kuhn, Loeb and Co., worked with J. Pierpont Morgan in the reorganization of the Richmond Terminal rail system. The reorganization, which was completed just before the panic of May 1893, saved the railroad from collapse and the railroad went on to become the central part of today's Southern Railway System. It was a crowning achievement for Harry Hollins to be successfully associated with such powerful figures of that era as Morgan and Schiff, both in their prime. Again in 1905, Hollins was on the opposite side of the table from Morgan while negotiating to sell the Cincinnati, Hamilton and Dayton Railroad and the Pere Marquette Railroad to the Erie Railroad. This deal did not work out well for either man. Hollins was accused on Wall Street of unloading the railroads onto Morgan who had to purchase their stock when the Erie refused to accept it, charging misrepresentation by Hollins. It most likely cost Morgan a great deal of money and his relationship with Hollins suffered badly as a result.

In 1880, Harry B. Hollins purchased a large property in East Islip located south of the South Country Road and running to the bay on the south and to Champlin's Creek on the west. It was known at the time as the Mainwaring Farm and could be reached by Pavilion Avenue. It was several hundred acres in size and would be called Meadowfarm. Not to be outdone by his friend Vanderbilt, Hollins built a large country home in the manner of his contemporaries. Three stories high with shingle roof and wood siding, the house's most distinctive characteristics were the many steep gables and the large brick chimneys that rose up above them. Several large, open porches surrounded the house where the cooling southwest winds off the bay could be enjoyed by the family. Awnings extended out from several windows to reflect away the hot summer sun. It must have been a roomy and comfortable home and was expanded in the following decade to meet the needs of the growing family. Outbuildings included the usual stables and carriage house upon which was a distinctive, handsome clock tower. Harry and Evelina Hollins had four sons, Harry B. Jr., Gerald Vanderbilt, McKim, and John Knapp Hollins, and one daughter, Marion Hollins, who later became the women's national golfing champion.

During the 1880s there was growing concern from Islip's year-round residents and their political spokesmen that because all the bayfront land was being purchased by summer people, there would be no access at all to the bay for swimming or the mooring of boats for the rest. There were no public roads to the bay at that time except Maple Avenue in Bay Shore village. In 1884, the Town of Islip, which had no public access to the bay, surveyed a public highway to run from the Somerset Hotel in East Islip south through Lee Johnson land and then between Hollins and Sutton land to the bay. (Bayview Avenue today.) The three landowners donated the needed land, which was accepted by the town. "It should be opened, by all means," said the newspaper. "Give us free access to the bay all along the Island."[33] Later on, after much agitation, the village of Islip would receive a similar gift of access to the bay.

Harry Hollins's sporting interests included bird shooting — 'gunning' it was then called — and fishing on the bay. He was a founder of the Waverly Gun Club (1890) and, of course, a member of the South Side Club. In New York City he was a member of the Union, Knickerbocker, Metropolitan, and Racquet Clubs, the most prominent in town. In the summer of 1887 along with his friends Schuyler Parsons and Edward Knapp from Islip, Benjamin True from West Islip, and Harry I. Nicholas from Babylon, he founded a new club, known as the Short Beach Club. Its charter stated that it was formed for "lawful sporting, gunning, fishing, sailing and yachting purposes." It was to be located on Sexton Island in the Great South Bay, directly across Whig Inlet Channel from the Way Wayonda Club (see Chapter V). The Way Wayonda Club's membership by then was made up of New York City politicians[34] and therefore was no longer compatible with those who formed the new club which a local paper called "a club of *city gentlemen*."[35] Initially forty-five members joined the Short Beach Club and Hollins became the president. Opening day occurred on August 20, 1887, accompanied by music from the Seventh Regiment Band from New York. A Queen Anne–style clubhouse with the usual wide piazzas on all sides had been built for dining on the first floor and with bedrooms on the second. It was a comfortable, pleasant accommodation and located near Fire Island Inlet so members could enjoy ocean bathing and fishing with a privacy that the nearby Surf Hotel could not provide. By 1895 the

Short Beach Club had modestly expanded its membership. It continued to operate until 1912 when it was closed for good. Hollins's business partner, H. Duncan Wood, purchased land on the west side of Champlin's Lake, north of the South Country Road and north of the late Joseph W. Meeks (whose house was then owned by his son, Edward B. Meeks). It was bought from the Stellenwerf family who still ran the Lake House across the lake. Wood was very near to St. Mark's Church where he took an active role, joining the vestry in 1880 and entertaining the clergy upon the consecration of the new church. He became a churchwarden in 1890, which post he held for the rest of his life. Wood, like Hollins, was a part of New York's elite society, of which his membership in the Union and Metropolitan Clubs gave evidence. He was a Columbia University graduate and president of his class in 1872. He had a successful career as a stockbroker. Following his start with Hollins, Wood founded his own firm that generally prospered with the exception of the year of 1893 when it was reported to have suffered "serious losses"[36] along with many other companies after the panic in May of that year and the following depression.

Duncan Wood and his wife, Ellen, had four children, who were brought up in their Islip home, called Ellenwood. On the night of April 7, 1885, a near-tragedy, which almost ended their lives, demonstrates the constant hazard that fire was to home owners of that era. The local paper reported:

> The house of H. Duncan Wood, Esq., burned to the ground at about two o'clock on Wednesday morning. Mr. Wood was awakened by a choking sensation in his throat, and had barely time to arouse his family and take them out of the house. The children and nurses took refuge at St. Mark's rectory. The house was on fire last week, under the hearth tiles, and was totally extinguished, as it was thought; but possibly it may have been smoldering slowly since that time. There is said to be an insurance in the amount of $20,000 on the house and contents. The fire department was out in force, with the engine truck and hose, but nothing could be done toward saving the property, as the house was a sheet of flame in a few minutes after it was discovered. There was a large amount of personal property destroyed. The money and valuables of the inmates

were in total ruin. There was no time to save anything. It is probable that Mr. Wood will re-build immediately."[37]

Rebuild he did, as well as buying a nearby house to occupy that summer. House fires were occasionally started by arsonists, but more often the cause was an accident. With houses built entirely of wood, heated by open fires, and lit by oil or kerosene lamps, an accident could go quickly out of control. More often than not the house was completely destroyed. Edward S. Knapp almost lost Awixa Lawn in 1890. An oil lamp exploded and only quick action by the maid put the flames out. William Wharton's house was entirely destroyed a few years later, most probably the result of arson.

Voluntary Fire Departments were organized in the 1880s in Bay Shore and Islip and in other Long Island villages. They were manned primarily by year-round residents, although the summer people did take part in purchasing the equipment and often acting as chiefs. Knapp, Parsons, and Hollins were all chiefs of Islip Company No. 1 for a time. Speed, so essential to controlling a fire, was impossible to achieve. Edward Knapp Jr. remembered, "In those days there were no fire hydrants and water had to be pumped from some nearby pond [or creek] and carried in buckets to the fire itself. The pumps were worked by hand and the fire apparatus itself was hand drawn. Everything very crude and not a bit efficient. It took a long time for the firemen to get to a fire, and when they did arrive, there was apt to be no water nearby, to put it out with. Also, the houses were built of wood and burned quickly, and the kerosene that was used in the lamps would ignite and make them even more difficult to extinguish. I do not remember any case except one, where a house was saved from destruction."[38]

By 1895 water lines had been laid and fire hydrants installed, but the water pressure was often too low to be very effective. Several of the summer residents wrote to the Town Board of Islip to complain that "the water furnished by the Great South Bay Water Co. is unfit for general use. It has been clearly demonstrated at the fires of recent date — the

Bound residence, Livingston's barn, Pavilion Hotel and others — that the pressure was totally inadequate to be of any service."[39] Considering the inadequacy of the system and the equipment, it is remarkable that more lives were not lost from the many house and hotel fires.

Duncan Wood lived on with his family in their rebuilt home on Champlin's Lake until his death in 1915. He was buried from his beloved St. Mark's Church where he had remained church warden to the end.

It was only natural that Schuyler Livingston Parsons, W. K. Vanderbilt's best friend, would choose Islip for his country home. His father and mother had been coming to the Prospect House in Bay Shore since he was a young boy, and he knew the area as well as anyone. Growing up in Bay Shore he was friends with the various Lawrances, Garners, and Johnsons, living along South Country Road, and friends in particular with Bradish Johnson's youngest daughter, Helena. It was not surprising to anyone when Schuyler, aged twenty-five, and Helena, twenty-one, announced their engagement. They were married on June 13, 1877, by Dr. Reuben Riley, St. Mark's rector, at the Bradish Johnson home, Sans Souci, where Helena had been born. It was a large and festive affair. Many more guests were invited than the "old" St. Mark's Church could seat. Sans Souci was ideal for the ceremony uniting these two old New York families. The only sad note was the absence of Helena's mother, Louisa Lawrance Johnson, who had died prematurely when Helena was only fourteen. Her father, by then sixty-six years old, gave away his young daughter. The occasion was typical of weddings of the affluent in that era.

A special train on Wednesday conveyed a number of guests to Bay Shore, bidden to the marriage of Miss Helena, youngest daughter of Bradish Johnson, to Schuyler Livingston Parsons. A large number of guests from the surrounding villages were also present. At 10 o'clock the ceremony was performed, under a floral bell, and in a perfect bower of evergreens and flowers, Dr. Riley officiating. A wedding breakfast was served in the English fashion, and the beautiful grounds, flower gardens and conservatories were thrown open to the Company.

About three o'clock the bridal party drove off under a perfect shower of rice and old slippers, and were cheered until out of sight. The groups on the lawn then separated into smaller parties, many extending their walks outside the grounds, while a yachting party went out for a sail in the bay. Others passed the time in dancing, which, as the day was moderately cool, was kept up with spirit until the hour of departure.[40]

Few families could trace their American ancestry back further than Helena and Schuyler Parsons, a distinguishing criterion to be considered by old New York Society in the Gilded Age. As has been seen (Chapter III) Helena, through her mother, descended from Thomas Lawrance who had settled in Newtown, Long Island, in 1656. Through his mother, a Livingston, Schuyler was descended from Robert Livingston, 1654–1728, the canny Scotsman who at the age of twenty settled in Albany (1674), married into the Schuyler and Van Cortlandt families, and built the vast estates in the Hudson Valley, which for centuries were known as the Livingston Manor.* Robert, the first Lord of the Manor, began an American dynasty that has often been called the only real European-style aristocracy in America, based primarily on the ownership of land. Schuyler Parsons was also the grandson of William Burrington Parsons, a young British Naval officer whose ship, H.M.S. *Sylph*, was wrecked off Southampton on the Long Island coast on January 17, 1815. Parsons swam ashore, made his way to New York City, and soon married Ann Barclay, a descendant of Trinity Church's second rector, Dr. Henry Barclay.

Following their marriage, Schuyler and Helena Parsons summered in a small cottage on Bradish Johnson's land while looking for a suitable place of their own. Their first child, named for her mother, Helena Johnson Parsons, was born in 1878. In 1881, Evelyn Knapp Parsons, named for H. B. Hollins's wife, arrived and much later in 1892 their

---

*   In 1686 the Manor amounted to 160,240 acres on the east side of the Hudson River, about forty miles below Albany.

only son, Schuyler Jr., was born. It was in 1881 that they purchased forty acres of land on the east side of St. Mark's Lane in Islip, fronting on Champlin's Creek, as a place to set their roots. They were just south of Mrs. W. K. Knapp and north of John D. Prince. They were also within an easy drive of Harry Hollins and W. K. Vanderbilt and their wives, all great friends.

The house they built there was not unlike those of their friends. It was a wooden shingle-style cottage with the typical gables and surrounding piazzas or porches giving an easy view to the creek. It was small at first, but later enlarged after son Schuyler was born. There were the usual stables and a greenhouse on the property. As was the custom, the house needed a name. Schuyler Parsons Jr. recounted how this occurred. "For weeks the two friends [Schuyler Parsons and W. K. Vanderbilt] wrote down every appealing name and finally eliminated all but two, 'Whileaway' and 'Idlehour'. They tossed for the choice, Mr. Vanderbilt won, chose 'Idlehour', and we got 'Whileaway' . . . our home then was 'Whileaway' at Islip and any house we owned or rented from time to time in New York was only a pied-à-terre for the winter. 'Whileaway' was never closed in the fifty years of our residence there."[41] The Parsons had set their roots firmly in Islip. Whileaway remained in the family after Parsons's death in 1917, going to his daughter, Helena, who by then had married Richard Wharton.

Parsons's and Vanderbilt's friendship has been described as most intimate and life-long. "The bond of friendship between Father and W. K., as Mr. Vanderbilt was called, continued until my father's death. It was one of the closest ties between two men that I have ever seen, and was built not only on familiarity, but on mutual respect."[42] Many of Parsons's sporting interests were shared with Vanderbilt, shooting and fishing at the South Side Club as well as horse racing. Parsons was active in the racing world for much of his life. It was "his chief interest," according to his son. He was vice chairman of the Jockey Club under August Belmont, and later a partner with Harry K. Knapp in "one of the finest stables of thoroughbred horses in the country."[43] Coaching in the 1880s was also a favorite sport of his and his friends.

Parsons, like his friends, was a regular commuter to New York on the Long Island Railroad. He was a partner of the firm of Parsons and Petit, wholesale chemical dealers. He was naturally a member of the Union Club in the city and of the Players and Turf and Field Clubs.

In August 1897, Helena Parsons died at Whileaway after a short but debilitating illness. She was only forty-one years old. Her son, Schuyler Jr., was just five. She was buried from St. Mark's Church. Parsons remained a widower for the rest of his life, leaving the care of his young son primarily to his daughter, Helena.

Vanderbilt and his young friends gave an acceptability to Islip as the decade of the 1880s began that it had not previously had. It became more than just a pleasant place, but rather a summer resort where the very oldest and most socially prominent New York families would go to build their country homes, which they would use not only in summer but often for the greater part of the year. Many of this younger generation would follow as the decade unfolded.

Two other families came to Islip in the early 1880s because W. K. Vanderbilt had built there and liked it. However, unlike the Hollinses and the Parsonses, they did not stay long. W. K.'s younger sister, Florence, had married Hamilton McKown Twombly. Descended from an old New England merchant family, Twombly was to become an astute investor in mining ventures, so successful that he built his wife's $10 million inheritance and his own estate into a fortune that rivaled W. K.'s. Florence was "the plainest, the dourest, the longest-lived [she lived to age 98, dying in 1952], and by far the richest of the four daughters of William H. Vanderbilt."[44] The Twomblys had experimented in Bay Shore in the summer of 1881 by renting the Oaks, Henry B. Hyde's summer mansion there. They must have enjoyed the community because they decided to build a cottage on the property of the Pavilion Hotel in East Islip to be ready for the following summer. Here they would be closer to W. K. and his friends who had come to

Islip. The Twomblys left shortly thereafter for New Jersey and Newport where they built huge mansions (for their time) away from New York City. Auchincloss comments, "Moving from house to house at the same points in each year, with scores of servants and endless luggage, must have been in itself a life's occupation for the Vanderbilt sisters." The same could be said about their brother, William K.

William Collins Whitney (1841–1904), several years older than Vanderbilt, had achieved a remarkable degree of prominence by the time he was forty. Educated at Yale and the Harvard Law School, he became active in Democratic politics in New York City, waging a successful fight against Boss Tweed along with the then Mayor William F. Havemeyer (1874). He was corporation counsel of the city from 1872 to 1882 and a strong supporter of New York State Governor Samuel J. Tilden. Whitney married Flora Payne, the sister of his Yale classmate, Colonel Oliver H. Payne, who later became a Standard Oil trustee. In 1881, the Whitneys, who had a passion for houses (they owned ten at the time of his death) came to Islip to join W. K. Vanderbilt and his circle. They rented the comfortable home of the widowed Mrs. William K. Knapp on St. Mark's Lane that summer and began to acquire land south of her home along Champlin's Creek in order to build their own. One can only conclude that having summered in Islip they found they did not like it, for the land they bought was sold to Clarence Tucker of New York the following year. The Whitneys went to the North Shore of Long Island where they and their sons Harry Payne Whitney and Payne Whitney became prominent in the horse racing and polo playing world of the Meadow Brook Club in Old Westbury. William C. Whitney became secretary of the navy under President Grover Cleveland and made a fortune in insurance, mining, and railroads in that expansionist time. Although his flirtation with Islip was extremely short, he, like Vanderbilt, was a person who was continually covered by the New York press on the front pages. Thus, his coming to Islip added to the prominence of the town as a fashionable summer spa.

As more leading New York families came to Islip to build their country homes along the creeks that emptied into the Great South Bay, it is appropriate to examine the American country home of the 1880s and the life-styles of those who lived in them. Richard Guy Wilson writes,

The American country house as a generic type has always been in evolution, but certain essential features stand out. The first principle as a writer at the turn of the century announced, is that the country house must "possess the country," it should "fit the place where it stands." The country house must have or appear to control acreage and if the land is limited the house must be sheltered from its neighbors. A country house must have a garden of some type, either natural or formal, and it should have outbuildings, or support structures, though they can be limited to a garage, pool house, or garden pavilion. The house should have an ease of communication with the out-of-doors, with porches, verandas, and terraces. A country house is built for show, but also for pleasure, relaxation, and sport, and in addition to the nearby country or hunt club, or polo field, it should have its own sports facilities such as a pool, or tennis courts. The house itself must be large and look substantial and contain a luxury of space especially in public areas such as halls, staircases, or conservatory. Specific room types can vary, but space for a library, and multi-sitting rooms help. Furnishings also can vary but art of some type must be evident. The architectural style of the house is important, but there is no one style. Styles have ranged from English half-timber to the more popular classical derivatives.[45]

All of the New York families who built homes along the Great South Bay since Bradish Johnson in the 1840s were establishing their own particular version of the American country house. They varied greatly in size and style from Vanderbilt's and later F. G. Bourne's huge mansions to the somewhat more modest homes of Knapp, Johnson, Lawrance, and the many others who settled along St. Mark's Lane, Pavilion Avenue, Saxton Avenue, and Ocean Avenue in Islip. Each was, however, a picturesque creation of its owner or his architect.

As the style and size of these homes varied, so did their use. The Vanderbilts used Idlehour primarily in spring and fall months (they spent summers in Newport) although often they would host shooting parties and other festivities over the Christmas holidays. On the other hand the Parsons' Whileaway was always open, although the family did spend the winter months in New York. The Knapps at first used Awixa Lawn all year round but when the children became of school age they returned to New York in the winter. Families took their children out of school often in that era to suit their own convenience. It was not unusual for a child to be in school only from December to March. Private tutoring was used to fill in the gaps of the broken school schedule. Many of these families would travel to Europe for a month or two and while they were away their country homes would be rented to a friend or left empty. Or they would go to Saratoga, Newport, or the Adirondacks for the month of August for a change of scenery.

While they were in residence at their country homes, their lives were much more formal during the Gilded Age and much influenced by the life-style of the English country gentleman and his stately home or manor house. The weekend in the country developed into a rigid routine of activity and dress in the Edwardian age following the role model set by the Prince of Wales, later King Edward VII. Schuyler Parsons Jr. said,

> This was the community into which I was born [1892]. I understand that after the religious aspects of my christening were finished, the countryside turned out for a celebration. So many came that the party had to be held outdoors, but no mere buffet was served — these were the days of twelve-course dinners with five to seven wines! Formality was carried into all aspects of life, and only very intimate friends called each other by their first names. The men, however, were good citizens, serving as volunteer firemen, deputy policemen, members of the School Board and active churchmen. They worked hard at home in spite of the tiring daily commute to New York and back, and yet there were many reports of poker parties into the small hours, and two or three times a week there were formal dinners.

The small tennis club* was the center of our activities, but everyone also had a boat, and of course in those days horses were a necessity. There was splendid fishing and shooting on the bay, and many had places in the middle of the island for quail and pheasant shooting. All in all it was a very pleasant life, patterned on what was thought to be the Country life of England.[46]

Often the most festive times were over the Thanksgiving or Christmas holidays when the families would entertain in their country homes before returning to New York for the winter. On January 7, 1893, it was reported that the Duncan Wood home was "ablaze with light and full of merriment with 40 guests"[47] being feted. This was often the time of year when shooting was at its best, but if the birds were not flying there were always clay pigeon contests to occupy the day.

W. K. Vanderbilt's influence was felt in another way in the Town of Islip early in the Gilded Age. As a result of his wife's and his generosity, the Trinity Church Seaside Home was established along the west side of the Connetquot River in 1882. Eight acres north of Emmanuel Church and running down to the river were turned over by the Vanderbilts to the Trinity Church Association for a summer camp for city children. There was a house on the land which had been used occasionally by Mrs. Vanderbilt's mother. The camp was run by the Sisters of St. Mary (Episcopal nuns) and supervised by a board of managers made up of women summer residents who belonged to St. Mark's Church in Islip. Recruited initially by Mrs. Vanderbilt and headed by Mrs. John D. Prince, these ladies provided for the ragged city children "whole sets of fresh clothing for the summer, sending the old ones to be cleaned and mended. They also sent quantities of vegetables, flowers and playthings."[48] Mrs. Vanderbilt herself sent her yacht twice a week to take the children sailing on the Great South Bay.

---

* Islip Tennis Club, located opposite St. Mark's Church on the north side of Montauk Highway, was founded in 1894.

The Seaside Home officially opened on July 1, 1882. On July 3, twenty-four children arrived by train at the Islip station and were taken by carriage to their summer home by the river. During July and August that year the household consisted of thirty-two children on the average (they came for a two-week stay), two adults, two servants, and the four Sisters in charge. The summer was so successful that improvements were made. Mrs. Prince contributed a dormitory and storage cellar as well as a kitchen and a laundry, thus permitting the former kitchen to be transformed into a chapel. The property was later enlarged to fifteen acres. In 1888 the season was extended from June to October and 326 children and 52 working girls were given holidays there.

The guiding spirit behind the Seaside Home was always Alva Smith Vanderbilt and it is doubtful that without her energy the camp would have survived. She was assisted by Mrs. Richard Irvin Jr. of New York, Mrs. Richard Delafield, and Mrs. W. Bayard Cutting of Great River. It is ironic to note that in 1895 when Mrs. Vanderbilt divorced her husband to marry O. H. P. Belmont the following year, she was asked by Trinity Church to remove her name from association with the Seaside Home. The Home responded by no longer publishing the names of the entire board of managers in their annual report. Alva Vanderbilt Belmont continued to lead the board through 1916 in spite of this rebuff.

The Seaside Home had a long history as a camp on the shore of the Connetquot. Women from St. Marks continued their service on the renamed ladies auxiliary. Mrs. Samuel T. Peters served for forty-six years and Mrs. Buell Hollister for forty-seven years, a truly remarkable record. The summer of 1960 was the final season for the Trinity Seaside Home, seventy-eight years after it had opened. The property by then was considered too valuable for a camp. The explosion of new homes in the Town of Islip following World War II had won the day.

Three new families came to Great River in the mid 1880s following the opening of the Seaside Home there. To the north along the Connetquot River, William Bayard Cutting purchased the George Lorillard estate, Westbrook Farm, in 1884. To the south where the Connetquot empties into the bay, Timber Point Farm was sold by the Nicoll family to William L. Breese in 1883. And west of Nicoll Point a large tract of unimproved land was sold by the Nicoll family to George C. Taylor in 1885. Each of the three new owners was from an old and prominent New York family and it is likely that each came to build his country home there because Vanderbilt had done so and because the location was very near the South Side Sportsmen's Club where each man was an active member and therefore familiar with the area.

William L. Breese, born in 1852, was the son of J. Salisbury Breese and Augusta Eloise Lawrence. His father was descended from Sidney Breese who came from England prior to Revolutionary times, was Master of the Port of New York, and was buried in 1767 in Trinity Churchyard. Sidney's son Samuel was a colonel in the Revolutionary army and later a judge in New Jersey. William L. Breese's mother was a Lawrence who was descended from John Lawrence who came to the Plymouth, Massachusetts, colony in 1635 and thence to Newtown, Long Island. She was also descended from the Bogert family of New Amsterdam in early Dutch times. William Breese's lineage was impeccable and because of it he was a member at New York's best clubs, the Union, the Racquet, the Jockey Club among several others. At an early age he went to Wall Street where as a broker he was successful, joining the firm of Breese and Smith. Like Hollins and Duncan Wood, Breese was one of the Islip crowd that would commute to Wall Street daily in the summer. In that era of huge expansion and speculation that went with it, stockbrokers like Breese could make millions on tips and then lose all in a matter of days. Breese was, of course, friends with Hollins and W. K. Vanderbilt and did business with them as well as sporting activities at Great River and the South Side Club.

It was in the early summer of 1884 that rumors went around the clubhouse of the South Side Club that bad blood had developed between Breese and Hollins. Apparently in the breakfast room one Sunday morning a fracas had broken out between the two men and blows were exchanged. Breese had a fiery temperament and was a strong, powerful athlete. However, all was hushed up and the incident almost forgotten until several years later when the *New York Times* reported on May 26, 1888, "It was a Bloodless Fight — Two Brokers Exchange Blows on a Boat — A Sequel to one of Wall Street's Deals that caused considerable talk in the Street." It happened that Breese and Hollins had only begun their regular summer commute that week and thus had not seen each other for a while. Accompanied by B. K. True from Bay Shore and Duncan Wood from Islip they had boarded the ferry to Wall Street from the LIRR terminal. According to Hollins's partner, Wood, "We were standing on the forward deck of the ferry boat when Mr. Breese walked out of the cabin and came toward Mr. Hollins and from the way he looked I thought he was going to speak to him in a friendly way, but he said, addressing Hollins 'before these men I want to say that you are a _____' using an offensive expression. The men came together at once and a few blows were exchanged. Mr. Hollins' umbrella fell out of his hand. We at once separated the men."[49] Another account of the incident was that a few words passed between Mr. Breese and Mr. Hollins when Mr. Breese called Hollins a liar. Whereupon Hollins's umbrella went thumping down on Breese's head, followed by a right-hander from Breese which knocked Hollins over onto some nearby chairs. More blows followed until the other men on board were able to pull apart the combatants. The incident was over for the moment, but it was the talk of Wall Street all day. It was covered by all the New York daily papers; the *New York Times* concluded its report by saying "the social standing of both men is high." When Hollins was interviewed he demanded that Breese put a written apology in the papers, but nothing came of it at that time. Rumors were afoot, however, that Breese was about to sue both Hollins and W. K. Vanderbilt for damages as a result of the Lake Shore collapse.

A typical Queen Anne style cottage such as those built by Daniel D. Conover in Bay Shore and Islip in the 1880s and 1890s.
(Courtesy of Pictorial Bay Shore.)

The Argyle, a resort hotel in Babylon, was built by Austin Corbin in 1882.
(Courtesy of John Pullis.)

Engine #92 of the Long Island Rail Road is shown here in 1897 at the Patchogue Bicycle Path. (The collection of Ron Ziel.)

The only known photo of the first Bay Shore railroad station, taken in September, 1878. (The collection of Ron Ziel.)

Edward Spring Knapp, 1852-
1895, owner of *Awixa Lawn*,
Saxton Avenue, Bay Shore.
(Courtesy of We Knapps Thought It Was
Nice.)

Margaret Lawrance in 1878 before her marriage to Edward Spring Knapp.
(Courtesy of We Knapps Thought It Was Nice).

The *Futurity Race* at the Sheepshead Bay track, where *Sir Walter*, the Knapps' famous thoroughbred, won in 1893 and 1894. (Courtesy of The Old Print Shop.)

Margaret Lawrance Knapp's house on Saxton Avenue, Bay Shore, built in 1896 after the death of her husband. (Courtesy of Richard A. Milligan.)

What was the Lake Shore affair? In the early 1880s the race to build new railroad routes and to consolidate them into great systems under the control of the railroad barons was at its peak. In the northeastern United States Vanderbilt's New York Central Railroad and Jay Gould's Erie were expanding westward rapidly and competing for new routes. During this era there were no rules governing stock speculation and manipulation. Stock pools were often used to manipulate the price of a stock up or down depending on the desires of the syndicate. It was an era of ruthless, cutthroat competition for profit and no one was more successful than Commodore Vanderbilt and his son, William H. They were masters at the game and they made fortunes.

In 1882 William H. Vanderbilt gained control of the Lake Shore and Michigan Southern Railway Co. for his New York Central System by purchasing a huge block of stock from Jay Gould at a large premium over par. Vanderbilt became president of the Lake Shore railroad and was succeeded by his son William K. in 1883. W. K.'s broker, H. B. Hollins, headed the stock pool that included, in addition to the Vanderbilts, William L. Breese. It was said that Breese had put up a half a million dollars. The stock soared to $115 per share, but as soon as Vanderbilt achieved his control he pulled out of the market and the price collapsed. Apparently Hollins had been warned and got out in time, but Breese had not and suffered a huge loss. He never forgave Hollins and later sued Vanderbilt for $1 million in damages on the ground that both he and Gould had advertised that the stock was worth $120 per share. By late 1884 it sold at $53 per share.

Breese and his wife, the former Mary Parsons from Columbus, Ohio, had built their country home on Timber Point Farm. It overlooked the Great South Bay from the end of Great River Road at a point where the bay widens out to its broadest expanse. He had a special interest in livestock, and Timber Point Farm was noted for its fine herd of Holstein cattle grazing along the seashore. Breese was just thirty years old when he bought Timber Point. He was athletic, enjoyed sports of all kinds and was a popular member of the South Side Club. A son and two daughters were born to the Breeses, the eldest daughter being named Eloise after her grandmother Eloise Lawrence Breese. Tragedy struck this young family in the late fall of 1888. Breese, thirty-six years old, in the vigor of health, contracted pneumonia. Three weeks later he died at Timber Point Farm. The local paper said, "In the death of Mr. Breese, Islip loses one of its wealthiest residents, a man whom all could approach, upright and honest in his dealings with his follow citizens, and benevolent in deeds of charity."[50]

Perhaps to escape the sadness of her husband's premature death Mary Breese took her children for longer and longer visits to England, leaving Timber Point largely unoccupied. In 1894 she married Henry Vincent Higgins, London impresario of the Covent Garden Opera, and moved to England for good. Both her daughters would marry English nobility. Eloise in 1905 married Gilbert Heathcote Drummond Willoughby, the Earl of Ancaster, and Anna in 1907 married Lord Alastair Robert Innes-Ker.

The Timber Point Farm was not sold, however, until 1905 when it was purchased by the New York lawyer Julien T. Davies. William L. Breese's time on the South Shore was brief, only five years at Timber Point, and a few years before that at the South Side Club. He was perhaps best known as the sire of daughters who would marry English lords, one of several South Shore families whose daughters would follow that course.

West of Timber Point Farm in the early 1880s was the Plumb estate with its odd mansion topped with a pagoda-like tower (see Chapter V), and west of that was 800 acres of wooded land fronting on Great South Bay, on which was the site of the first homestead, or grange, of the early eighteenth century (see Chapter II). This had belonged to William Nicoll. The house had gone, but there was a foundation and with it a dispute over whether it really was the original homestead.[51] Early in 1885 the 800 acres were bought by George Campbell Taylor of New York for his country home. Taylor differed from those who were settling in the Islip and Great River area in two ways. He was significantly older (fifty years old) than Vanderbilt and his circle of friends, and, most surprisingly, the reclusive, eccentric Taylor lived with a common law wife! However he was hugely wealthy with a fortune that closely rivaled Vanderbilt's which he had inherited three years earlier at the death of his father (1882). George C. Taylor was the son of Moses Taylor, one of the legendary merchants of New York City in the nineteenth century. The story of Moses Taylor and his eccentric son, George, is among the most intriguing tales of the people who came to the Great South Bay in the Gilded Age.

Moses Taylor was born in New York City in 1806, the son of Jacob B. Taylor, whose occupation was agent or rent collector for John Jacob Astor. As a young boy Moses learned the value of money and how to invest one's earnings from Astor, the man who would become New York's first millionaire. After very little schooling Moses clerked at the mercantile firm of G. G. & S. S. Howland for a time to learn his trade. It was not long before he started on his own, importing sugar from Cuba to sell to the New York refiners, all the time accumulating profit. When he needed financial backing, Mr. Astor was always ready to help. By the age of thirty he had become a rich man. It was the financial panic of 1837, however, that brought him a fortune. As bankers and merchants were failing in that disastrous year, Moses Taylor had the courage to lend them money, charging rates of 2 percent to 3 percent per *month*. Like young August Belmont (see Chapter IV) who was backed by the Rothschilds of Europe, young Moses Taylor, backed by Astor, made an enormous fortune. When favorable economic conditions returned, he owned a huge mercantile business with many ships that traded with Cuba and the Orient, as well as parts of the newly emerging railroads in the East and South. In 1855 he became, in addition, president of the City Bank (the predecessor of today's Citicorp), which position he held for twenty-seven years until his death. Moses Taylor was a confidant of President Lincoln and at his request arranged for $200 million to be loaned to the federal government in 1861 to finance the Civil War. He declined, however, to serve as Lincoln's secretary of the treasury. Helping from New York would prove more valuable for the North.

Moses Taylor married as a young man. He and his wife had three daughters and two sons, George being the second son. His daughter Albertina would marry Percy Rivington Pyne, the son of his trading partner, and they would name one son Moses Taylor Pyne, after his illustrious grandfather. Moses Taylor lived on to 1882. He had become known by then as one of the "Old Merchants" of New York, spoken of in the same company as the first John Jacob Astor, the Lorillard brothers, Stephen Whitney, Robert Lenox, Shepherd Knapp, and Bradish Johnson. He was considered "the boldest, most successful, most sagacious merchant of our country — an old fashioned, upright merchant of the first class."[52] When Moses Taylor died, his wealth was considered to be around $50 million, not that far from Commodore Vanderbilt's $90 million. He was succeeded as head of the City Bank by his son-in-law, Percy R. Pyne (and later by James Stillman), not by either of his two sons. They inherited large sums during Moses's lifetime. George C. Taylor was said to amount to $20 million when his father died, and he was to lead a very different life.

Born in 1835, George spent much of his time in his younger days traveling around the world. Thanks to his father's wealth and personal friendship with President Lincoln, he was appointed by Lincoln as consul to Alexandria in Egypt and later had an appointment in the U.S. Navy. It was on one of his European travels that he met a resident of London, Mrs. Betsy Head. They fell in love, but Mrs. Head was not free to marry. Divorce in the Victorian era was impossible except upon the charge of adultery. In that event it was the reputation of the wife that was ruined even if the husband had committed the offense. Thus, it was rare that a woman would agree to a divorce regardless of the circumstances. It was preferable for her to accept the fact that her husband had a mistress or mistresses and to live apart from him. George C.

Taylor and Mrs. Betsy Head came back to New York together where they lived as husband and wife, but never married. And with them came Mrs. Head's infant daughter, who was called Lena Head.

Taylor began building a proper country home for his odd family in 1885 and when it was completed the following year it was described as "the new and elegant mansion of Mr. George Taylor, son of the late Moses Taylor, the New York millionaire. The land faces the bay with an admirable view from the piazza of the house which Mr. Taylor has built this year at a cost of $100,000. The rooms were all frescoed and are finished with different colored woods and in the most elegant style possible without regard to expense. Large oaken pillars, highly polished, support a central dome which is handsomely lighted with colored glass. There are several large outer buildings on the premises and greenhouses hundreds of feet in length. This is one of the bon ton places in Islip."[53]

In fact, Taylor erected thirty buildings in addition to his home. There were carriage barns, stables, dairy barns, quarters for the staff of employees, a boathouse, an icehouse, and many others, only unusual then in the great number of them. The wooded areas were stocked with deer and game birds. On the lawns peacocks strode about in their magnificent plumage. The porch of the mansion overlooked a broad canal, which Taylor had dredged in 1898, stretching a half mile to the bay. Here he kept his yacht for cruising and fishing. In fact, as his eccentricity grew with his age he commissioned a new type of boat for the Great South Bay in the winter of 1901. It was described as a houseboat, 92 feet in length, with a 32-foot beam and a draught of 2-1/2 feet. "It will be sloop rigged. The cabin will be 60 feet in length, containing 25 staterooms, dining hall, drawing room, smoking room and galley. The interior will be furnished in mahogany and the furnishings will be most elaborate. It will probably cost over $25,000 and will conveniently accommodate 100 people. There will be a permanent awning over the entire length of the cabin."[54] Considering the fact that Taylor was a recluse, a houseboat to handle a hundred people was eccentricity at its best. It did give gainful employment to a dozen Bay Shore shipwrights.

It should not have been too surprising to the East Islip villagers when George Taylor appeared one day in the spring of 1898 riding on his new horseless carriage. The local paper said, "One of the greatest novelties ever seen on a local thoroughfare was noticed on Main Street on Monday evening when George C. Taylor, the Great River millionaire, whirled eastward in his new Columbia electric carriage. The machine, a two-seated, open vehicle, was in charge of a representative of the company. It traveled along at the rate of about 10 miles per hour and attracted no little attention. The carriage will be used by Mr. Taylor in traveling about his grounds at Great River."[55] This may well have been for Islipians their first sighting of a horseless carriage.

On this vast estate Taylor and Mrs. Head increasingly isolated themselves. In 1903 Taylor bought the neighboring Deer Range Farm, 700 acres, from J. Ives Plumb, who finally left his father's pagoda-like house to settle in the Meeks house on Main Street on the west side of Champlin's Pond in Islip. With this purchase Taylor owned 1,500 acres of land, two miles of waterfront on the bay, two mansions (Plumb's and his own), the total of which equalled if it did not exceed W. K. Vanderbilt's Idlehour in size. It was better sited on the bay than Idlehour and carried an assessed value that year of $248,000, second only to Vanderbilt's $303,000 in the whole Islip Township.[56] No one else was even close to that amount.

In this environment Mrs. Head's daughter, Lena, grew up. She was rarely seen off the grounds. Taylor hired special tutors from England for her education and when the bicycle craze came to Long Island he hired an English bicycle instructor who brought with him all the newest models of English bicycles. The only men Lena was allowed to see were the imported Englishmen who worked on the estate. Finally, the inevitable happened when Lena married the foreman, one Frederick William Bodley. The marriage was performed by the justice of the peace on the family estate.

As time went on Taylor's health began to deteriorate and his drinking increased. He had several small strokes, quarreled frequently with Mrs. Head, and had an elevator installed in the mansion. Rumors abounded that both Taylor and Mrs. Head were "under the weather" all the time. Finally, in the summer of 1907, Mrs. Head died. It was said that Taylor never fully realized that she had gone, his mind being all but gone as well. In late September 1907 just a month or so after her death, Taylor died also. The newspaper reported: "Death at 72 years followed a long illness covering years of imbecility and a gradual breaking down of a constitution that excesses had previously impaired. For several years a physician had been in daily attendance and nurses were at his beck and call."[57] Taylor had no legal children. He was survived by an older brother, Henry A. C. Taylor,* and by three sisters and many nephews and nieces. In spite of his many excesses he died a wealthy man. He was buried from his Great River home by the rector of St. Mark's Church. It was said, "Mrs. Bodley [Mrs. Head's daughter] did not attend the funeral. It is believed that while the bulk of the Taylor millions will go to his relatives, his heirs have already entered upon an agreement to give Mrs. Bodley sufficient to keep her from want for the remainder of her life."[58]

After Taylor's death, his property was unoccupied except for caretakers for many years. Plumb's mansion was soon torn down to save on taxes. Taylor's nephew, Moses Taylor Pyne, and his son, Percy R. Pyne II, used the property as a bird and game shooting preserve. It was kept under the control of the Taylor-Pyne family corporation, the Deer Range Corporation, until 1924 when it came to the attention of the new Long Island State Park Commissioner, young Robert Moses, and a whole new chapter began (see Chapter X).

Great River, with its wide stream flowing into the Great South Bay, was a strong attraction for Vanderbilt and then for the fiery Breese and the eccentric Taylor. At that same

---

* Henry A.C. Taylor built a mansion in Newport, R.I., in 1885 which was designed by McKim, Mead and White. He died in 1921.

time it also attracted a family that was very different from Vanderbilt's, Breese's, or Taylor's. Mr. and Mrs. William Bayard Cutting would be best described as from "Old New York," members of the most prestigious clubs in the city, recognized members of Mrs. Astor's 400 families of New York Society, and therefore of the establishment in 1880. With the choice of the Great South Bay first by the W. K. Vanderbilts and then by the Bayard Cuttings for their country estates, there could no longer be any doubt that a new summer spa had been born and that it would be a worthy rival of Saratoga and Newport.

Cutting's first American ancestor was from his mother's family. Mrs. Samuel Bayard of Amsterdam, having been left a widow in her youth, sailed in 1647 with four small children for New Amsterdam to join her brother there, the Governor General, Peter Stuyvesant. She was described as being "of imposing appearance, highly educated, alert in business and imperious in manner."[59] She and her son, Colonel Nicholas Bayard, were independent spirits who fought for the freedom of religious worship for the Quakers, the one group who were persecuted by the Dutch in the New World. It was from the Bayard family that Cutting's wealth primarily came. Nicholas Bayard had established the first sugar refinery in New York in 1730, and his descendants became wealthy merchants in trade with Europe and the West Indies. Cutting's maternal grandparents, Mr. and Mrs. Robert Bayard, although they possessed a fortune, lived simply in Edgewater, New Jersey, across the Hudson River from New York. It was with these Bayards that William Bayard Cutting and his younger brother, Robert Fulton Cutting, were brought up after the death of their mother.

The first Cutting to arrive in America was the young graduate of Eton and Cambridge who came from Norfolk, England, in 1747, paying for his passage by indenturing himself to a Virginia plantation owner for a number of years. Leonard Cutting, a free man, his service over, moved to New York to become a classical tutor at King's College there (now Columbia University). While performing these tasks, he studied religion, then returned to England to be ordained a priest, served as a missionary in New Jersey, and was finally called in 1766 to be the rector of St. George's Church in Hempstead, Long Island. Like many priests of the Church of England, Cutting remained loyal to the king during the Revolution and resigned his rectorship at St. George's. After some time in Maryland and North Carolina he returned to New York City where he died in 1794. Leonard Cutting's son, William, married into the Livingston family of the Hudson Valley, as had the inventor of the steamboat, Robert Fulton, so that William Bayard Cutting, the grandson of William Cutting, was a descendant of the famous Robert Livingston, the first Lord of the Manor. With such ancestors as Stuyvesant, Bayard, Cutting, Pintard, and Livingston, it is not strange that William Bayard Cutting would be always considered from "Old New York."

He was born in New York in 1850, the first son of Fulton Cutting and Elise Justine Bayard. His mother died two years later after his brother, Robert Fulton Cutting, was born. Shortly thereafter their father moved to Paris, leaving the two young infants to be brought up by the Bayard grandparents. They did an exceptionally good job. In an atmosphere of "industrious austerity"[60] the boys were taught that they would have to make their own way in the world. The standards set for them were high; the expectations were great. Bayard went to Columbia College, graduating with the class of 1869 and then on to the Columbia Law School. At his graduation from college he first met fourteen-year-old Olivia Murray, the daughter of Bronson and Ann Eliza Peyton Murray. The Murrays were a Presbyterian family that disapproved in principal of all festivities and "dreaded for their daughters any association with children more wealthy than they."[61] At first Bayard called on Olivia's older sister, but while waiting for her was often entertained by Olivia. Slowly a courtship began which seven years later in 1877 resulted in marriage. After a short stay with the grandparents in Edgewater, Bayard could just afford a small house on East Twenty-fourth Street in Manhattan, where he and Olivia had their first home. When a visitor asked why he had brought his wife to so small a house, he replied, "I cut my coat according to my cloth."[62]

A year later in 1878 grandfather Robert Bayard retired. Bayard Cutting had by then been admitted to the New York bar and had assisted in the reorganization of the St. Louis, Alton and Terre Haute Railroad for his grandfather. He was deemed ready, at age twenty-eight, to take on full responsibility for the Bayard fortune, which at that time was primarily invested in railroads. He was elected president of the Terre Haute Line, a director of the Illinois Central Railroad and somewhat later of the Southern Pacific Railroad. His "cloth" had grown considerably in one short year.

Over the next thirty-four years until his death, Bayard Cutting's business career was diverse. He was involved with the opening of new rail lines in Florida and the Middle West. He was responsible for the development of a large tract of then worthless waterfront in South Brooklyn; for the opening of the Ambrose Channel, which made New York harbor available to deeper draught vessels; for the starting of the American Beet Sugar Co. in the Midwest. He was a director of banks, insurance companies, and vice president of the New York Chamber of Commerce for a time. In all of his business dealings he was careful to keep to the high standards that had been expected of him as a boy. His granddaughter Iris Cutting Origo said of him, "My grandfather was always extremely scrupulous in his business dealings and indignant against the sharp practices of the 'Robber Barons' of his time, who bought out the little land-owner and cheated the small investor — so much so, that his children were never allowed, later on, to accept invitations to their houses."[63] In this matter he was very much the exception among his peers and was recognized as such by a later biographer, R. W. B. Lewis, who described him as "one of the most prodigiously successful of the post-Civil War railroad tycoons, a sworn enemy of the 'robber barons'."[64] He was particularly admired by his friend Edith Wharton, whose contempt for the American business tycoon of the late nineteenth century was well known.

Bayard Cutting was also much involved with works of charity — again somewhat against the grain for many of his peers in the Gilded Age whose large expenditures were usually on their private pleasures. With his brother, Fulton, he purchased a large area of property containing run-down city tenements, which he upgraded to provide model houses with affordable rents. He was able to prove that this could be done without a loss. The Improved Dwellings Association of which he was president from 1879 to 1895 was a model for its time and a forerunner of the Phipps Houses in New York today.* He was also a founder of the New York Botanical Garden, reflecting his great interest in botany, a trustee of the Metropolitan Opera Company and of his alma mater, Columbia University.

Both Bayard and his brother, Fulton Cutting, and their wives were lifelong Episcopalians and active in the affairs of their church. This instilled in them a strong sense of charitable duty — not only in terms of money, but also of time and talent. They had been taught, of course, as were most "Old New Yorkers," the precept taught to Edith Wharton by her mother, "Never talk about money, and think about it as little as possible." But think about it they did, to the great thanks of their many beneficiaries including the Episcopal Church. Bayard served the Church on its Board of Domestic and Foreign Missions, as a trustee of the General Theological Seminary, and as a lay deputy to the General Convention from the Diocese of New York from 1883 to 1912. He was a major benefactor with J. Pierpont Morgan in building the Cathedral of St. John the Divine on Morningside Heights and in the building of the Synod House on the Cathedral Close. In Great River, where he built his country home, he built a

---

* The Improved Dwellings Association was succeeded in 1896 by the City and Suburban Homes Company, organized by a group of philanthropists including the Cuttings. The complex of buildings on the south side of East 79th Street from York Avenue to the F.D.R. Drive was built by Cutting's City and Suburban Homes Company.

rectory (1889) and later a parish house (1903) for little
Emmanuel Church where he and his wife worshipped when
they were in residence and where he was senior warden.
Both brothers were the largest contributors — $1,500 each
— to the new parish house of St. Mark's Church in Islip, built
in 1890, although neither was a member of that parish at the
time. Their gifts to St. Mark's were larger than those of
Vanderbilt who was a vestryman. Bayard also made a modest
gift to a new church built in Bohemia, an area to the north of
South Country Road where there lived many of the families
who worked for Cutting, Vanderbilt, and the other large
landowners. Because many of these people came from
Bohemia in Europe, the community in Long Island was named
after their homeland.

Robert Fulton Cutting was likewise a serious churchman
and benefactor of the Episcopal Church. In New York City he
was a member of St. George's Church on Stuyvesant Square,
a vestryman there for fifty years, and its senior warden from
1913 (succeeding J. Pierpont Morgan) until his death in 1934.
In Sayville, Long Island (just east of Oakdale), he and his
wife, Helen Suydam Cutting, together with her brother, Walter
L. Suydam Sr., donated the funds to build the new St. Ann's
church building in 1887–88 in memory of Helen's family, the
Suydams, an old and distinguished New York and Bayport,
Long Island, family. (Her parents were Charles Suydam and
Ann White Schermerhorn Suydam.)* This lovely church, designed by Sayville architect I. H. Green Jr., was the only stone
house of worship in Suffolk County when it was built. It was
noted in the local newspaper that Robert Fulton Cutting had
addressed the young men of Islip village in church on a
Sunday evening about their responsibilities in life devoting
"himself to the task with unflagging zeal. . . . He is now
Superintendent of the Sunday School and St. George's Church.
This school numbers 1700 pupils, which is considerably more

---

* The sister of Mrs. William B. Astor née Caroline Schermerhorn
and of Mrs. Benjamin S. Welles née Catherine Schermerhorn
(see Chapter III).

than the whole population of Islip village. . . . The example which Mr. Cutting furnishes in his unselfish effort to do good to others might well be followed by some other wealthy men we know of who make Islip their summer home."[65]

William Bayard and Robert Fulton Cutting were very close brothers. They invested in many of the same enterprises, were devout churchmen, went to the same university, and were members of the same clubs. Robert Fulton, the younger, married first, but his wife died following the birth of a son. Seven years later in 1883, he married Helen Suydam and they were to have five children. Both brothers were lovers of sport and had become members of the South Side Sportsmen's Club, Bayard in 1884 and Fulton in 1885. The Great South Bay was, of course, familiar to Helen whose family had located in Bayport earlier. Bayard and Olivia had rented a cottage probably at the Pavilion Hotel in East Islip, for the summers of 1883 and 1884. So it was very natural for the Cutting brothers to look for a country home in that area. Here, however, they took a differing course, for Bayard located permanently, whereas Fulton only rented for several years and finally moved to Tuxedo Park.

By 1884, Bayard and his wife, Olivia, had been married for seven years. Their two older children, William Bayard Jr. and Justine Cutting, had been born (two more children, Bronson and Olivia, would follow later). Affluence had come to the family and it was time to set roots and establish a country home. Westbrook Farm in Great River, Long Island, the home and horse breeding farm of George L. Lorillard, was for sale (see Chapter V) and was purchased in October that year by the Cuttings, 931 acres including the Lorillard house for $125,000. It was not their intention to live in the Lorillard house, which was located to the north of the South Country Road and away from the Connetquot River. They intended to build a new home that would be set back somewhat from the river, but from which there would be a wide, open vista sweeping down to the river at the point where it widened towards the bay. They did not immediately start to build, but chose instead to wait a year while studying the possible sites and consulting with architects. It is likely that the summer of 1885 was spent in the Lorillard house. By early in 1886 the Cuttings had made their decision. To land-scape the grounds of their new home (they never liked or used the word "estate") they chose America's most renowned landscape architect, Frederick Law Olmsted, to design a naturalistic environment. For their new house they did not choose Vanderbilt's favorite, Richard Morris Hunt, but in-stead commissioned a man whom Cutting had come to know from his work at Columbia University, Charles Coolidge Haight.

Haight, although he was a decade older than Cutting, had also studied law at Columbia. After the Civil War he decided to change to architecture and apprenticed at the studio of E. T. Littell, a New York architect. There he came in contact with Henry Hobson Richardson, who was to influence some of Haight's later work. Both Haight and Richardson began their own practices in 1867, and went on to achieve fame. Haight's early work was primarily institutional with several buildings designed for Columbia. He would later achieve renown for his work at the General Theological Seminary, particularly its Chapel of the Good Shepherd, often called the "Jewel of Chelsea Square," and for his design of the H. O. Havemeyer residence on Fifth Avenue and Sixty-sixth Street and the Downtown Association on Pine Street. He also de-signed many country estates.

For Cutting, Haight designed a home that was a mix "of the English Queen Anne and Tudor styles as well as the later American Shingle style. The fireplaces and chimneys were given special attention. Shaped bricks on the chimney stacks accentuated their height and importance in the buildings silhouette. A terra-cotta panel set into a major chimney near the entryway charmingly proclaims: 'William Bayard Cutting - He built me - Ano Dmi 1886'."[66] Granddaughter Iris Cutting Origo lovingly remembers,

> "Although constructed in the period in which the monu-
> mental country houses of their friends were still rising in
> Newport along Ocean Drive, it had the great merit of not
> attempting to be either a French chateau, an Elizabethan

manor house or a Florentine villa; its material was the unpretentious indigenous shingle, and its design that of an English cottage if a somewhat overgrown one. ... Indoors the house certainly had a remarkable degree of Victorian spaciousness and comfort; large rooms cool in summer and glowing with heat in winter, a panelled library filled not only with the well-bound sets of an orthodox gentleman's library, but also with first editions of Stevenson, Conrad, and Oscar Wilde; a dining-room and breakfast room in which the old English silver was as fine as the Canton and Lowestoft china, and upstairs, in the bed-rooms, every device to enhance a guest's comfort that the imagination could conceive. A play room in an annex, joined to the main building by a wide arch, provided a billiard table and a ping pong table, and even in my father's time, a small electric organ, and on the edge of the lawn, a wide piazza — enclosed in a wire netting like a meat-safe against the ferocious Long Island mosquitoes.[67]

Iris Origo's "overgrown English cottage" contained twenty-two fireplaces with mantels bought in England and France; an entrance hall with windows by Louis C. Tiffany, panelling and hand-carved woodwork from a three hundred-year-old English estate, an ornately carved hall table on which lay the family Bible and a Roman sculpture of Silenus, a nature deity of woodlands and fountains, and Chinese vases on the fireplace mantel. The dining room contained a large Chippendale table with fourteen chairs where the family would gather for dinner. The elegant main staircase swept upward to a landing graced by a finial of the Beast Royal together with a portrait of Cutting painted in 1904. The Cuttings had taken an extended trip to Europe in the fall of 1886 where they assembled much of the decorative art that would go into their new home. By the spring of 1887 all was ready for them to move in.

Cutting was very interested in horticulture and took a special interest in the design and planting of trees for Westbrook. Most of the older trees that are in the Arboretum today were planted by Cutting himself in the first few years following his purchase of the property. It was perhaps his most distinctive and lasting memorial. His granddaughter described the scene as in a Constable painting. "It was here out-of-doors, that the real charm of Westbrook began with the tall English oaks beside the house, the shrubs and ferns bordering the mossy paths that led into the woods, and the three ponds edged with tall trees and shrubs which reflected in the autumn the brilliant reds and pinks of swamp maple and dogwood, and in the spring, mossed banks of azaleas and hybrid rhododendrons. Best of all, to my mind, was the shaded, winding path along the river's brink, leading to the stretch of natural unplanted woodland and marsh, where one might see a sudden flight of startled wild fowl and smell the faint acrid odor of rotting leaves and fallen boughs, and watch the still, melancholy, expanse of water turn to copper in the sunset light."[68]

In addition to the main house and the connected annex, which was added a few years later, Cutting built a charming, thatched-roof Westgate House in 1893 to guard the principal driveway entrance. It stands today hidden in the corner of the property.* Its thatched roof made it unique in that area. It was designed by Isaac H. Green Jr. after an English lodge. There was also an Eastgate House, a huge greenhouse, a tennis court, vegetable garden, barns, stables, a boathouse, and a bridge made of locust posts to enable Cutting to directly reach the Southside Club without going onto the public highway. Origo remembered in particular "the stables with the English coachman and innumerable grooms as the other chief feature of the place, to which family and guests (since of course no horse was allowed to work on Sunday) all paid a formal visit on Sunday afternoons. We would find the carriage house decorated, my Aunt Justine told me, with bright colored sands, red, blue, yellow and green and braided straw. It must have taken hours of completely useless work, but it was tradition. There were also a proportionate number of carriages from the humble backboard and buggy to the four-horse brake or coach [the Tally Ho coach] and the two

---

* The corner of River Road and Montauk Highway.

horse victoria and brougham."[69] All of these buildings reflected Cutting's many and varied interests.

His interest in agriculture and scientific farming brought about the creation of a model dairy located to the north of the South Country Road and to the west of where the Lorillard racing stables and horse tracks had been. This Westbrook Farm complex was built over a period of time, the cow barn in 1889 and the brick horse stable in 1892, and was the home of his prize herd of Jersey cows, famous for the richness of their milk. The huge barns were similar in style to those of W. K. Vanderbilt at Idlehour, designed by Richard Morris Hunt. However, it is not known for certain who designed the Cutting Farm buildings. In 1895 a disastrous fire burned many to the ground, but Cutting courageously rebuilt them on an even grander scale. The new barns were designed by Stanford White, by then the most sought-after architect in New York.*

The years from 1887 to 1900 were the happiest that the Cutting family spent at Westbrook. Poor health that later handicapped Bayard and his eldest son, Bayard Jr., had not yet appeared. There were festive parties on weekends when friends from New York were entertained in the formal custom of the time. Cutting was constantly adding a building or a new exotic tree to the place and his young children — four by then — immensely enjoyed playing in the woods, canoeing in the river, or sailing on the bay. Although Cutting commuted to New York by train in the summer to attend to his vast business interests, he was able to find leisure time to pursue and enjoy his many hobbies at Westbrook. The family often traveled abroad as did most of the affluent families of that era. The annual or biannual steamer trip became a part of their lives. The Cuttings would also on occasion leave Westbrook in August to rent a cottage in Newport for the season. This was especially true when Bayard Jr. and Justine were becoming young adults and ready to be introduced into Society.

---

* The dairy farm was operated until after World War II.

His granddaughter remembered Bayard Cutting from her very early years. She was ten years old when he died and had seen him very infrequently, as for many of those years she had lived abroad with her mother and ailing father. "I think he must have been a charming man — wise, humorous, and urbane, with an unusually happy touch with people, a cultivated mind, and a tender heart. But I can only remember a warm voice and a kind smile, a pointed beard which pricked [when she kissed him goodnight] . . . Certainly he had paid, by his hard work and his foresight, for the luxury in which we all lived, and which some of his children, later on, found oppressive, but which I suspect he himself chiefly valued as an adornment and setting for his young wife."[70]

These golden years at Westbrook were made more so by the presence nearby of his brother and sister-in-law. Fulton and Helen Cutting after their marriage rented houses in Islip and East Islip for the summer. After Bayard and Olivia had moved into their new home, Fulton and Helen occupied the old Lorillard house across the road where their young family romped in the fields and the young cousins could all play together. It was a particularly idyllic time for both families.

During these years Bayard Cutting decided to build a golf course on his land, the first to be built in the Great South Bay area.* Golf was then a very new sport in America, having come from Scotland in 1888 with the establishment in Yonkers, New York, of a six-hole course, called St. Andrews, after the famous course in that town in Scotland. In 1891 in Shinnecock Hills, Long Island, a twelve-hole course (it was expanded to eighteen holes in the following year) was built and a proper clubhouse was soon after designed for it by the famous Stanford White. It was to become known as one of the finest and most challenging courses in America, and, now over a hundred years old, it is generally thought of as the

---

* Shortly thereafter Richard Hyde built a nine-hole course south of the South Country Road, west of Bay Shore. It was called the Bay Shore Golf Club. Its clubhouse stands there today, owned by Mrs. Neil Riesing.

cradle of American golf. In 1894 the Amateur Golfing Association of America was organized in Newport, Rhode Island, and Theodore A. Havemeyer (cousin of Henry Havemeyer; see Chapter V) was made its first president. There were only four or five courses at that time. The sport quickly became popular and many golf links were started all over the country in the years thereafter. It became essential for a resort to have one to maintain its status.

The Westbrook Golf Club was organized in 1895 by a group of men led by Cutting and his friend Harry B. Hollins, who became the president. The first members included Hollins, three Cuttings, four Knapps, two Suydams from Bayport, John E. Roosevelt from Sayville (Theodore Roosevelt's cousin), C. Dubois Wagstaff from West Islip, Samuel T. Peters from Islip, Frederick G. Bourne from Oakdale, and, of course, William K. Vanderbilt.* The land that Cutting donated was enough for a nine-hole course. Two holes (number 1 and number 9 hole) and a small clubhouse were set to the south of the railroad tracks while the remaining seven holes were to the north. Steps were provided up and down to the sunken track level for the golfers to cross over. The layout of the course was designed by Willie Dunn Jr., the Scotsman who had designed Shinnecock Hills four years earlier.

The Westbrook Golf Club was an immediate success and many of the summer residents in the area joined. It was a particular advantage for it to be located so near the then famous South Side Sportsmen's Club, which was less than a mile away, as its members and guests could play at Westbrook. Golf became a favored activity at the same time as tennis did in the mid 1890s. Harry B. Hollins decided that a club professional was needed at Westbrook, and while he was golfing at the Royal St. George's course in Sandwich, England, during his trip there in 1897, he was much impressed with an unusually pleasant young man who was assigned to be his caddy. A

---

* From the 1896 yearbook of the club.

few days later, having no golf partner, Hollins was given the same boy as an opponent. He seemed an excellent player with a free, beautiful swing. Hollins was impressed and asked the young lad if he would come to America to be the club professional at Westbrook. Arthur G. Griffiths ("Griff" to his many friends) accepted. His longtime American friend Edward S. Knapp Jr. said many years later, "These were the very early days of golf in this country and it was when golf implements were made by hand. Griff had learned the trade of clubmaker in Hunter's Shop at Sandwich, where the finest class of clubs in the world were made, and he was one of Hunter's best clubmakers, so it was not surprising that, after he had been at Westbrook only a short time, he came to be known as possibly the best golf clubmaker in this country. . . . It wasn't long after Griff came to Westbrook, that he became a much respected member of the community, with a splendid reputation for honesty and fairness. He made golf clubs by hand until machines came along and took the place of the old clubmakers."[71] Griff became justice of the peace in the Town of Islip and was sought after for friendly advice by many during a long life. The Westbrook Golf Club remained popular long after Cutting's death and long after eighteen-hole courses* had been established in the bay area. It finally closed for good in the 1940s. Griff stayed there until his retirement and his family were and are today pillars of the Islip community.

The turn of the century saw the beginning of change for the Cutting family. Fulton left the South Shore in 1898 and the old Lorillard house was offered to the U.S. Army for convalescent soldiers from the Spanish-American War and then was torn down. More important, the shadow of ill health fell upon the family. The most feared disease of the nineteenth and early twentieth century until the discovery of penicillin was undoubtedly tuberculosis. It was thought at the time that to slow up or to cure the disease a patient should live in a dry

---

* Proposals to expand the Westbrook course to 18 holes in the 1920s were never carried out.

climate with lots of sunshine and rest. Damp and humid climates were thought to be particularly harmful, and, if anything, the South Shore of Long Island was damp and humid, particularly in the summer. Three of the Cutting's children (all but Justine) contracted tuberculosis by the time they reached adulthood. Their firstborn, Bayard Jr. was a brilliant son, successful at Groton and Harvard, popular with his peers, the golden boy in his youth, a member of Phi Beta Kappa, and Harvard's famous Porcellian Club. He left Harvard his senior year for an appointment as private secretary to the American ambassador in London where he met and became engaged to his future wife. They were married in the spring of 1901, but by the following spring, Bayard Jr., aged twenty-three, had his first hemorrhage. It was thought he had been working too hard the previous winter. He said to a friend at the time, "It is a mere weakness and no disease and they expect I shall be able to lead a normal life after a month or two."[72] Sadly, he had only eight more years to live and died of tuberculosis in 1910, survived by his wife and eight-year-old daughter, Iris. Both Bronson and Olivia, the younger children, struggled with the disease as well, but were cured. These were shattering blows to Bayard whose own health was weakening in the 1900s. Broken-hearted at the death of his oldest son and attacked by the two prevalent complaints of that age, heart disease and gout, William Bayard Cutting died two years later on March 1, 1912. He was sixty-two years old. He died on the train returning from New Mexico where he had been visiting his son Bronson, who had moved there to cure his tuberculosis.

Cutting's will left almost all of his $11 million estate to his wife, Olivia, who had been the owner of both Westbrook and their New York City house at Madison Avenue and Seventy-second Street.* Special bequests were made to the children and a trust provided for his granddaughter, Iris Cutting, who lived with her mother in the Villa Medici in Florence, Italy.

---

*   The house had been bought in 1897 from Mrs. O. H. P. Belmont, formerly Mrs. W. K. Vanderbilt.

The only charitable bequest was $5,000 to the Emmanuel Church in Great River. His great benefactions to the Episcopal Church in New York had been made during his lifetime.

Olivia Murray Cutting, grief stricken at the loss of her eldest son and her husband in so short a time, was left with the magnificent country house in Great River. Her children at that time had little interest in Westbrook and only her youngest daughter, Olivia James, after an unsuccessful marriage, would return to be with her mother during the thirty-seven years of her widowhood. The first chapter in the Westbrook story was complete and the second belongs in the next century. Suffice it to say that the survival of the place was a tribute to the strong spirit of two indomitable women.

Bayard and Olivia Cutting had come to the South Shore of Long Island at a time when many others were following Vanderbilt's lead. They differed from him and from many of his friends in a subtle way which reflected their background, their upbringing, and most likely their beliefs. It had to do with the manner in which they conducted their lives; with the way they spent their great wealth; and with the responsibility they felt for that wealth. They left a mark on the South Shore that can be seen today, a goodly heritage, and although no Cuttings remain any more, it is perhaps through Westbrook — now called the Bayard Cutting Arboretum — that one can best catch a glimmer of the very best of the Gilded Age along the Great South Bay. As daughter Olivia said, "an oasis of beauty and of quiet for those who delight in outdoor beauty remains."[73]

As the Great River area was filling up with the arrival of Breese, Taylor, and Cutting in the 1880s, so was the land on both sides of Champlin's Creek between East Islip and Islip. Along Pavilion Avenue on the east side of the creek came C. T. Harbeck, Colonel H. R. Duval, Lucius K. Wilmerding, and William F. Wharton. On the west side along Johnson Avenue, or St. Mark's Lane, came Clarence Tucker, Robert C. Livingston, Henry H. Hollister, John C. Tappin, and Samuel T. Peters. To the north of Main Street in the Meeks house was Albert V. De Goicouria. All these families were from New

York City and all of the men were young, active members of the South Side Club. They had all bought or built homes by the time the decade was over. They were mostly brokers, bankers, or merchants in trade who commuted daily to town to work. None had the colossal wealth of Vanderbilt or Taylor, but all were men of property, successful in their own right or inheritors of wealth, such as Livingston, who could easily afford a country home. In most cases they rented in the bay area before they bought or built. They were, by and large, Episcopalians, whose church home was St. Mark's.

At the beginning of the 1880s much of the land south of East Islip village was owned by Lee Johnson, son and heir of Edwin A. Johnson who had settled there in the 1840s (see Chapter III). Lee had married the daughter of William Nicoll of Great River, a direct descendant of the first Islip patentee. Lee had built several summer cottages for rent along Pavilion Avenue, which were located conveniently near the Pavilion Hotel. To the south of these he built a house of his own where he and his wife lived the year round. He suffered from poor health for much of his life, rheumatism and increasing paralysis taking their toll. However, he was thought of by the East Islip community as a kind and generous man. In 1885 he decided to leave East Islip and move to Garden City, Long Island, where he could receive better care for his maladies. [*] He sold his house to Colonel Henry Rieman Duval of New York in December of that year.

Colonel Duval — in the traditional southern manner he was always known as Colonel from his wartime rank in the Confederate Army — was one of the more interesting men to locate along the Great South Bay. He was born in 1843 in Baltimore, descended from a French Huguenot who came to Maryland in 1643 and received a huge land grant in Prince George and Arundel counties from King Charles II. Young Duval attended St. Timothy's Hall Military Academy from which at age eighteen he entered the Confederate Army at

---

[*] Lee Johnson died in Garden City in 1895 at the age of fifty years.

the beginning of the Civil War. He served in the Army of Northern Virginia under Generals Robert E. Lee and Stonewall Jackson, rising to the rank of colonel. In June of 1864 he was taken prisoner by the North and interred at Johnson's Island in New York until the war was over. Returning home to Baltimore he entered the employ of the Baltimore and Ohio Railroad, beginning a long and distinguished career in the great age of railroad expansion. Colonel Duval served with the B & O Railroad and then, moving to New York, with the Erie Railroad. By 1885 his reputation had grown to the point where he was named receiver in bankruptcy of the Florida Railway Navigation Company which he managed for four years. Subsequently it was merged into the Florida Central and Peninsula Railroad and Colonel Duval became its president for ten years. In the meantime he had married Anne Gordon, two young sons had been born, and in his early forties, he was attracted to Long Island's South Shore. Like so many before him, Colonel Duval first joined the South Side Club (1883) and knowing that W. K. Vanderbilt had built his home nearby, decided to do likewise. He may have rented a cottage on Pavilion Avenue before deciding to buy Lee Johnson's home and settle there for good.

By then Colonel Duval had become established in New York City. He had a house at 26 West Twenty-first Street, had been invited to join the Union and Metropolitan Clubs, and shortly would be asked to become a director of three of the country's most prominent companies: the Atcheson, Topeka and Santa Fe Railroad, the Santa Fe Pacific Railroad, and the American Car and Foundry Company. His interest and experience with the western United States was growing and because of it and because of his intimate knowledge of railroads, he was asked by his Islip neighbors, the Cutting brothers, to head up a new venture in the West that the three of them would back with new capital and which would eventually run head-on into the creation of another Islip neighbor, Henry O. Havemeyer.

In 1888 Henry T. Oxnard and his brothers, having sold their Brooklyn sugar refinery to the Sugar Trust the year before, organized a new company to build a sugar beet factory in Grand Island, Nebraska, along the Platte River. It was a courageous venture, as prior to that time sugar beets had not been successfully grown on a commercial basis in the United States. Oxnard had visited Europe where the industry was established and had learned firsthand, by working in the factories there, the techniques that were successful. Substantial capital was needed to build a beet sugar factory and there was no guarantee of success. Oxnard found his backers and future stockholders in New York in the persons of Bayard and Fulton Cutting and Colonel Henry R. Duval. The Grand Island factory was completed in 1890 and two others would follow in the next decade.

The success of the fledgling beet sugar industry in the western United States was assured by the passage in 1890 of the McKinley Tariff, which gave protection to sugar produced in the United States, primarily to cane sugar growers in Louisiana. It had the effect of greatly stimulating the new domestic beet sugar industry as well and many new beet factories were built in the 1890s in California, Utah, Idaho, Colorado, Nebraska, Michigan, and Ohio. The industry, always protected by duty, tariff, or quota, grew into a major industry in the next century.

In 1899 the Oxnard Sugar Company built another huge factory in a town in California, which it named Oxnard, and that year reorganized the four factories into the American Beet Sugar Company, incorporated in New Jersey, capitalized at $20 million, and listed on the New York Stock Exchange. The principal owners were still the Oxnards, the Cuttings, and Colonel Duval, who was named chairman of the board. They were so successful by then and producing so much sugar that an ever increasing amount had to be sold away from the locale of their factories and thus into the Missouri and Mississippi River markets which were normally serviced from New Orleans by the Sugar Trust. The Sugar Trust would not tolerate this loss of their market to the protected beet sugar industry. The "youngster" had to be taught a lesson.

The Sugar Trust had been organized in 1887 and was led by the sugar merchant Henry O. Havemeyer, who at the age of forty had demonstrated his mastery of all commercial aspects of the sugar refining industry. Patterned after the Standard Oil Trust of John D. Rockefeller, the Sugar Trust had as its goals to keep sugar prices as low as was consistent with reasonable profit; to share technical information; to furnish protection against unlawful combinations of labor; and to promote the interests of the parties to the agreement. Various independent sugar companies were "invited" to join into this combination for the purpose of controlling production and regulating prices. It was important that most of the major sugar refiners join in, and by the mid-1890s most of them had done so. The Sugar Trust was by then a monopoly. It controlled production and prices throughout the United States except for the new beet sugar industry. In 1895 the Supreme Court in the famous case *U.S. v. E. C. Knight* declared that sugar refining was in fact manufacturing, not commerce, and therefore could not be regulated by the federal government under the Sherman Anti-Trust Act of 1890. The Sugar Trust was vindicated, and H. O. Havemeyer could turn his attention to the beet sugar industry.

He waited until the late summer of 1901, by which time the American Beet Sugar Company had purchased its sugar beets from the farmers based on the normal price they were expecting to get for sugar sold along the Missouri and Mississippi Rivers, i.e., 4 1/2 cents per pound. Havemeyer then announced that in those markets the Sugar Trust would sell their sugar at 3 1/2 cents per pound, a full cent below normal. This was way below its cost of production and caused substantial losses for the American Sugar Beet Company. "It was a trade war," Henry T. Oxnard later explained, "intended to drive the American Beet Sugar Company from the Missouri River markets, and if it had not been for the affluence of its stockholders [the Cuttings and Duval] the company might well have gone under."[74] Though the company did survive, Bayard Cutting was ready to end the struggle and called on Havemeyer in New York to negotiate an end to the price war.

Havemeyer's terms were that, first, the Sugar Trust would act as selling agent for all of American Beet Sugar's sales, thereby controlling the price and amount sold. For this, the Sugar Trust would get a fee based on the sugar sold; and, second, that the Sugar Trust would purchase 75,000 shares of the American Beet Sugar Company's preferred stock at one-fourth its par value. The negotiations dragged on for a second year, during which the beet sugar company again almost failed. Finally in December 1902 Cutting agreed to the terms. The trade war was over, the Sugar Trust had won and in the bargain had become a large owner in the beet sugar business which it would dominate for another decade. [*]

Although Cutting had agreed to the settlement, Colonel Duval, chairman of the board, was very unhappy with it. He believed it was illegal and said so to his board. "I frequently said to the various directors that I did not approve of that contract, that I thought it was contrary to a rigid consideration of the Sherman antitrust law and that I did not believe the benefit was worth what they were paying for it."[75] Cutting continued to insist on its value to the company. However, finally Colonel Duval convinced the board that the agreement should be abandoned, citing doubtful legality, and on December 18, 1906, the Sugar Trust was so advised. No more payments under the agreement would be made. Havemeyer's reaction was to let the matter drop after telling the American Beet Sugar Board that he found their good faith wanting. By then, he too was worried about adverse litigation. However, the Sugar Trust still owned a major part of Colonel Duval's company. Havemeyer died in 1907 and the Sugar Trust was forced to break up a few years later. [**] Duval stayed on as chairman of the American Beet Sugar Company for the rest of his life. The company was successful and remained inde-

---

[*]   A similar strategy was successfully followed with several other beet sugar companies.

[**]   The Sugar Trust sold its interest in the American Beet Sugar Company in 1912.

pendent, although it lost its position as the largest beet sugar company to the Great Western Sugar Company of Colorado, which was founded later with a large infusion of capital from the Sugar Trust and from H. O. Havemeyer himself.

In the 1890s, Colonel Duval added several acres and made extensive improvements to his house on Pavilion Avenue. He had a great interest in show dogs, building kennels on his place to breed and train the very best to be judged at the Westminster Kennel Club's dog shows in New York.* The Colonel, as he was always known, was an Episcopalian, and soon after his arrival in East Islip he was asked to join the vestry of St. Mark's Church (1899). He became a warden of the Church in 1915, succeeding Duncan Wood who died that year. The Colonel was a much admired member of the summer community. With their southern charm he and his wife were gracious hosts and their home was always festive when they were in residence.

On March 19, 1924, the Colonel died in his home in New York in his eighty-first year. He had outlived his wife by ten years, and his second son, Reiman, who had died in 1912 at twenty-nine years. His oldest son and both daughters-in-law remained in East Islip through the 1920s.

Directly to the north of Colonel Duval on Pavilion Avenue another of the Lee Johnson cottages was rented, to Lucius K. Wilmerding for the summer of 1883. Wilmerding was a keen fisherman and excellent bird shot who had been attracted to the area by the life at the South Side Club where he became a member in 1884. His family had long been prominent in the social life of New York City. The son of Henry Augustus and Harriet Kellogg Wilmerding, Lucius was born in 1848, graduated from Columbia in 1868, and thence began a long career as a dry goods importer and merchant, first with the firm of Wilmerding and Huguet and then with Wilmerding and Bissett. In 1876 he married Caroline Murray of New York, and they had a son Lucius (who later married

---

* The Westminster Kennel Club's dog shows began in 1877 at Madison Square Garden. In 1878, 1,000 dogs were entered in the show.

Robert Fulton Cutting's daughter, Helen) and a daughter (later Mrs. John B. Trevor). Wilmerding was very much a part of the New York establishment, a member of the Metropolitan Club and the St. Nicholas Society, and was for some years president of the prestigious Union Club. Like so many of his peers, he was a lifelong Episcopalian, a member of St. James' Church in New York, and of St. Mark's Church in Islip where he joined the vestry in 1886. The Wilmerdings remained in East Islip for almost forty years, until his death in 1922 at the age of seventy-four.

Pavilion Avenue in the early part of the 1880s was still dominated by the Pavilion Hotel and its group of cottages. Its owner then, James Slater, also proprietor of the Berkeley Hotel on New York's Fifth Avenue, said, "The Islip Pavilion is full or nearly full and all the cottages in the vicinity are rented. There is a demand for more summer cottages."[76] For the summer of 1884, the season for the Pavilion was extended from April 1 until November 1 and a new feature was added. The pleasure boat *Pavilion* had been built the previous winter. The hotel's advertisement proclaimed, "She is owned by the Hotel, and is for the pleasure of its guests, their children and nurses. Under the charge of a competent captain she will make two Excursions each day on the Great South Bay. Conveyances to the Dock will leave the Hotel at 9:30 am and 2:30 pm."[77] The availability of a dock nearby was made possible by the town's extending Pavilion Avenue so that it would reach Champlin's Creek, as well as by the large project of widening and deepening the creek, undertaken by the steam digger of Alonzo Smith and Frank Whitman. Champlin's Creek was thus opened with a ninety-foot-wide cut for the use of the Pavilion Hotel, and also for boats belonging to other property owners on both sides of the creek, improving the value of the property in the process. Every evidence testifies to the property boom continuing throughout the decade.

Two more families completed the arrivals on Pavilion Avenue in the 1880s. Charles T. Harbeck from Brooklyn acquired the property along Champlin's Creek at its upper end, formerly owned by James Boorman Johnston (see Chapter IV) in 1880 and kept it until 1892. During three of those summers, the house was rented to Fulton and Helen Cutting. Lastly, near the end of the decade William Fishbourne Wharton rented a cottage on the east side of the road. Wharton had been born in Philadelphia in 1846, a descendant of the famous Thomas Wharton who had emigrated there in the late seventeenth century, and was the son of George Mifflin Wharton. William was a graduate of the University of Pennsylvania who shortly thereafter moved to New York to begin a long career as a member of the New York Stock Exchange. In September, 1871 he married Frances Fisher of Philadelphia and they had three sons, one of whom, Richard, would later marry Schuyler Parsons's daughter, Helena. Being from such an old, prominent Philadelphia family, W. F. Wharton was quickly accepted by New York Society, joining the Union and Metropolitan Clubs. He was a founder of the Riding Club of New York and kept horses and stables at his East Islip home. His granddaughter, Marion Wharton Hallock, would live in Islip until her death in 1989.

As Pavilion Avenue filled up in the 1880s, so did Johnson Avenue to the west of Champlin's Creek. At the corner of South Country Road was the beautiful St. Mark's Church with the rectory just to its south. The Norwegian stave church was an elegant landmark on a street that hereafter would be called St. Mark's Lane. Farther south were the homes of Mrs. William K. Knapp, Schuyler Livingston Parsons, Clarence Tucker, and John D. Prince on the canal side, and that of Benjamin S. Welles on the west side. In 1886 two more families would join this select group, the Robert Cambridge Livingstons and the Henry Hutchinson Hollisters.

Livingston, a cousin of Parsons, was also a direct descendant of Robert Livingston, the first Lord of the Manor in the Hudson Valley, that canny Scotsman who by 1686 had accumulated a land-holding of some 160,000 acres known thenceforth as Livingston Manor. The Robert Cambridge Livingston who was to settle in Islip was descended through Robert, the third proprietor (1708–1790), and his third son, Robert Cambridge (1742–1794). Because of the prolific use of the name Robert in this huge family and the resultant confusion, this latter Robert adopted the middle name Cambridge after attending the university in England of that name. Unlike many of his cousins, he chose not to settle on the Manor, but instead lived in New York City and engaged in international trade. He became one of New York's most respected and richest citizens. His grandson, named Cambridge Livingston (1811–1879), was a prosperous New York lawyer, vestryman of Trinity Church, and a person who financed the first wireless in the United States after its invention by Samuel F. B. Morse. Cambridge Livingston was a lifetime director of the first Western Union Telegraph Company. He married Maria B. Murray of New York and they named their eldest son, who was born in 1846, Robert Cambridge Livingston. It was this Livingston who in 1886 decided to establish his summer home on St. Mark's Lane in Islip. By then he had married Maria Whitney, granddaughter of the legendary New York merchant Stephen Whitney and descendant of the Suydam family of New York. Robert Cambridge and Maria Whitney Livingston were on the way toward raising a family of seven children.[*]

It seemed natural for them to go where his cousin, Schuyler Parsons, had built Whileaway, on pastoral St. Mark's Lane. Robert had joined the South Side Club the year before and there were quite a few friends among the younger group that had followed Vanderbilt to the South Shore. Besides, there was a very adequate house awaiting their arrival. The property they chose on St. Mark's Lane was sixty-eight acres directly across from the church on the east side of the street. Their neighbors to the south were Mrs. Knapp and then Schuyler Parsons. The property extended across Champlin's Creek to adjoin the Pavilion Hotel land. These sixty-eight acres prior to 1880 had been owned by Parmenus Johnson who had built a house on the south part with an entrance from St. Mark's Lane. The estate was sold in 1880 to E. B. Spaulding of New York who spent that year "transforming the house into a first-class modern country seat. Two or three large extensions are to be finished in very expensive style. The dining

---

[*] Their children were: Robert Cambridge IV, John Griswold, Henry Whitney, Maud Maria, Johnston II, Louis, and Caroline Livingston.

room in the new extension is fitted out with handsome cabinet work of oak and Hungarian ash. The sliding doors are of hard wood three inches thick and laid out in handsome panels. Two tanks holding 600 gallons each are located in the top of the building. One of these has an outside pipe which may be attached to a hose and used upon the lawn, or upon the building in case of fire."[78] Apparently Mr. Spaulding overspent his budget, or suffered other financial reversals, for by the following fall (1881) foreclosure was taking place. Luckily for Livingston no buyer was found at the time, and the house was rented until the spring of 1886 when he acquired the entire sixty-eight acres on both sides of Champlin's Creek. Two years later in 1888 Livingston sold the corner part of his property fronting on South Country Road and St. Mark's Lane to another New York family, John C. Tappin and his wife, where they would build a house of their own.

The Livingstons lived happily on St. Mark's Lane for only nine years. In December 1895, at the age of forty-eight, Robert Cambridge died of kidney disease. He was buried at Trinity Church in New York. Among his pallbearers was his close friend and cousin Schuyler Parsons. Maria Whitney Livingston and her children continued to live on St. Mark's Lane for the rest of her life. Several of the children were confirmed at St. Mark's Church and at least one son was married there. Maria died in 1918 and her property on St. Mark's Lane was taken over by her daughter and son-in-law, Mr. and Mrs. Henry Worthington Bull (Maud Maria Livingston). Her land to the east of Champlin's Creek was sold to Jay Carlisle in 1916.

Across St. Mark's Lane from where the Livingstons would reside had been the home of early Islip resident John D. Johnson (see Chapter III), between Benjamin S. Welles to the south and Dr. Abraham Gardiner Thompson to the north. In the fall of 1886 Henry Hutchinson Hollister of New York purchased the Johnson place and immediately began to remodel and expand the house. By June of 1887 it was ready for summer occupancy. Islip was not new for the Hollister family that summer. In 1880 Henry had joined the South Side Club and for several summers thereafter the family had rented a cottage at the Pavilion Hotel. Like so many others he wanted his own country home where roots could grow.

Henry H. Hollister had been born in Vermont in 1842 and grew up in New England. He was descended from John Hollister who came to Connecticut from England in 1642, and through his mother from Major John H. Buell, who, being an officer on General Washington's staff, was an original member of the prestigious Society of the Cincinnati. Henry moved to New York City to become a successful banker on Wall Street. He became a member of the New York Stock Exchange in 1869 soon after the close of the Civil War. His firm was called Hollister and Babcock. During a long career on the Street he was a director of many railroad and mining enterprises including the Burlington, Cedar Rapids and Northern Railroad and the Mexican Mining and Smelting Company. He also was greatly interested in showing horses, being the treasurer of the National Horse Show Association of America for many years. As one might expect he was a member of the Union, Metropolitan, and New York Riding Clubs in the city.

In 1871 Hollister had married Sarah Louise Howell, and three children were born to them: Louise, Henry H. Jr., and Buell. It was when Buell was four years old that they moved to St. Mark's Lane. There Hollister became a stalwart member of the growing summer community, and being an Episcopalian, joined the St. Mark's vestry in 1888. In 1891, following the premature death of his wife, Sarah Louise, Hollister remarried. The marriage, celebrated at St. Mark's Church, was to Miss Anne Willard Stephenson of Boston who was given away by Hollister's friend and neighbor William F. Wharton. It was commented at the time that "She was a governess at the Hollister home. The marriage therefore was slightly unexpected."[79] In spite of this "irregularity," the couple lived happily together for the rest of Henry's life. To the children Islip became very much of a home, and they all would remain residents for the rest of their lives. Hollister was friendly with some of the most prominent men in the country. In 1904 he hosted Andrew Carnegie at the South Side Club after which they drove together through Islip. It was hoped, said the newspaper, that "he may yet endow a library here. A suitable town hall or hospital, however, would be of more benefit to the community."[80] Hollister died in 1909 at age sixty-eight in his home on St. Mark's Lane where he had gone for the Easter holiday. However, it being well before summer, it was decided that the funeral would be at St. Bartholomew's Church in New York City. He named as his trustees his wife, his son, and his longtime friend and Islip neighbor Samuel T. Peters.

Sam Peters and his wife, Adaline Elder Peters, with their two infant children, had discovered the South Shore in the summer of 1885. They rented a cottage that summer on Fire Island Avenue on the south side of Babylon village. Peters loved to sail and was attracted to the opportunities on Great South Bay. He also loved to ride horseback and the flat South Shore was ideal for that as well. Early that summer he bought the sailing sloop *Patience* which had been designed and built by the bay's most notable builder, Gil Smith of Patchogue.*

The sailing master of *Patience* was Captain Charles Suydam

---

* Gilbert E. Smith was born in 1843 near Shinnecock Bay. He was descended from the Hallock and Terry families that had settled in Southold, Long Island, in 1640. He married at the age of twenty and with his wife had five children. After several years at sea on coastal vessels, he moved with his family to Patchogue, Long Island, where in 1876 he started building boats with a partner, Charlie Saxton. The partnership soon split up and Smith was in business for himself. He was an expert sailor who learned by trial and experience how to improve the design of his boats. His reputation grew and his boats became in great demand. At the peak of his career he would build six or seven boats per year. It has been estimated that over his long life Smith may have built 400 boats. He received his greatest compliment from the famous designer Nat Herreshoff who said to a prospective customer, "If you want a boat for shallow water, as the Great South Bay is, don't come to me; the man you want to get to build her is Gil Smith." Smith suffered a crippling stroke in his 93rd year. His son, Asa Smith, who always worked with him, finished his last boats. Gil Smith died soon thereafter. Source: *Gil Smith, Master Boat Builder* by Paul W. Bigelow - *Long Island Forum* - 1966.

of Babylon. The Peters spent the following two summers in Babylon while looking for a place to settle into permanently. For the summer of 1888 they rented a cottage in Bay Shore where Adaline Peters's brother, George W. Elder, had become a well-known resident. It was during that summer that the Peters purchased their country home. "The handsome residence of the late John D. Prince on Johnson Avenue, Islip — one of the finest places in that section of handsome country seats — has been purchased by Samuel T. Peters. Mr. Peters is reported to have paid $50,000 for the Prince property. We regret that he is not to locate in Babylon," said the Babylon paper.[81] The following spring they added to the property, making it the largest waterfront holding in Islip. *

The Prince home had been the most southerly house on St. Mark's Lane (Johnson Avenue), fronting Champlin's Creek. Barely finished before his premature death in 1883, it had been rented to Lorillard Spencer Jr. for several summers. Directly to the north was the Clarence Tucker place. Tucker had lived there for several summers since purchasing the house from William C. Whitney in 1882. However, Tucker was tiring of Islip and spent the summer of 1889 in Seabright, New Jersey. His place was as elegant and well-maintained as was Prince's, a most desirable find as well. Because the two properties were so closely connected, as soon as Peters acquired his, he knew that he wanted a neighbor who would be congenial and who would keep up the place to his standards. Fortunately his close friend and his wife's brother-in-law, Henry O. Havemeyer, was ready to join him on St. Mark's Lane. Havemeyer, like Peters, had summered in Babylon, first at an Argyle Hotel cottage (1884 and 1885), then renting at Effingham Park (1886 and 1887), and finally at the home of G. W. Thompson (1888), where his daughter Electra was born. He especially enjoyed sailing and the seashore. By 1889, he and his wife, Louisine, had three young children, and they wanted a more permanent home. The

---

* There were two purchases one from T. S. Ryder and the other from A. V. De Goicouria, both of New York, in May 1889.

Tucker place was well suited to his needs. Louisine and her younger sister, Adaline, would be right next to each other and their children would grow up together.

Samuel T. Peters was born in 1854, the son of an English family. He entered the coal business in New York with Richard H. Williams and together the firm of Williams and Peters, merchants and dealers, prospered. Peters became a director of several coal mining companies and of the Hanover Bank. His interests included the collecting of Oriental jades. During his life he gave his collection of four hundred specimen jades to the Metropolitan Museum of Art, of which he was a trustee. He was also a collector of Chinese porcelain which filled his New York home and his country house.

By the end of the 1880s all of the waterfront land on St. Mark's Lane along Champlin's Creek had been built on by summer residents, almost entirely New York City people. Islip, East Islip, Great River, and Oakdale were becoming well known to those who lived beyond their borders and considered themselves part of Society. Islip was particularly well known to those in the sailing community because of the skill and exploits of its most notable sailing master of that era, Captain Henry C. Haff.

In the world of international yacht racing, the 1880s were unusual in that there were four challenges made by Great Britain and Canada to regain the America's Cup, the symbol of racing supremacy. The first challenge of the decade, in 1881, saw the *Atalanta* defeated by the sloop *Mischief*, skippered by the Islip veteran Nathaniel Clock.* Again in 1885 the challenger *Genesta* lost to the defender *Puritan*, and in 1886 the *Galatea* lost to the American yacht *Mayflower*. By then it seemed without doubt that the Americans had both better designers and better skippers. The British, however, were undaunted by this string of defeats and in 1887 resolved to make a new and stronger effort to regain supremacy. It had become a matter of national pride.

---

* Nathaniel Clock died in 1887.

The Royal Clyde Yacht Club then asked the eminent Scottish designer George L. Watson to build a new boat for its challenge, and sent him to America to study all the models of boats that had been winning American races throughout the decade. He was instructed to build the fastest yacht he could without regard to expense. Secrecy thus shrouded the building of *Thistle*. She was covered with a tarpaulin until she was put in the water in New York. In fact, she was wider than any previous challenger and had a longer forward over-hang, allowing for more sail to be carried under the rule that limited the waterline length to 90 feet (the rule was new in 1887). In the early preparatory races in British waters she won eleven out of fifteen, and she came to New York the clear favorite.

To meet this formidable challenge the Americans had only six months. Undeterred, General Charles J. Paine, who had defended in the two previous years, again agreed to build a new boat and called on Boston architect Edward Burgess to design a boat faster than *Puritan* or *Mayflower*, which he had also designed for their successful defenses. Burgess, from a wealthy Boston family, had become famous in a short time and was the most sought-after yacht designer in the 1880s in America. He was only to be eclipsed in the next decade by the greatest of all naval architects, Nathaniel G. Herreshoff. In 1887, Burgess designed a boat 85 feet 10 inches on the waterline, but 106 feet in overall length. She was built of steel, 3 feet wider than *Thistle*, with a centerboard that, when extended, was 21 feet down, 2 feet more than *Thistle*, which was a keel boat. She was to carry 300 square feet more sail than her opponent, and more sail than any previous defender. When Burgess designed his new boat, he had no idea, of course, what the challenger would be like. He only knew she was very much faster than any other British boat. *Volunteer* as she was named, was completed in sixty-six days and ready for trials.

General Paine, her owner, never skippered his yachts, but unlike some other owners always sailed aboard them, sitting in the stern wearing his old straw hat. For the second time he called on Captain Hank Haff to be the sailing master. Haff had sailed the first race in which *Mayflower* had defeated *Galatea* the previous year, but due to illness could not continue in the second. Paine was a stickler for crew discipline and efficient sail trimming. He was confident that in Haff he had the best. To complete the afterguard of *Volunteer* (the four or five men who made all the racing decisions during the race itself, including sail trim, navigation, and tactical ones) Haff chose three veteran captains to assist him: Captain Terry was skipper of *Greyling*; Captain Berry of *Mischief* was considered the best light air helmsman of the time; and finally, Captain Jeffrey of *Mystery*, Haff's cousin from Islip, was in charge of sails and strategy. Edward Burgess, the designer, was also part of the afterguard, as were General Paine and his guests, although their role was in reality that of passengers. Interestingly enough, Bay Shore's famous skipper, Samuel B. Gibson, was hired by *Thistle* to act as local pilot for the first race. Thus three sailing masters on the two boats were from Islip and Bay Shore, as were many of the deckhands on *Volunteer* who had worked with Haff on his other boats.

Hank Haff was born in Islip on September 29, 1837. He was the son of a sea captain, also Henry C. Haff, who in 1844, when young Hank was seven years old, was lost with his schooner off Cape Hatteras, the nineteenth century's graveyard of ships. From then until young Hank was seventeen, he was indentured to local farmers to give some support to his mother in raising the rest of his family. After working for the Long Island Railroad for a few years, he learned to sail on the Great South Bay, and at age twenty-five became the mate on his uncle's schooner, which accompanied Union General Burnside's expedition to the South. "While on this expedition, he was a member of the gallant lifeboat crew that performed a memorable deed of heroism in rescuing the crew of the steamship *New York*, wrecked at Hatteras Inlet. The storm was a terrible one and the members of the rescuing crew seemed to invite almost certain death. They made the trip in safety, however, and received the plaudits of the officers of the fleet, who were anxious to make public recognition of the act, but Captain Henry C. Clock's [Haff's uncle] modesty prevented the plan from being carried out."[82] At age thirty, Hank Haff was appointed superintendent of the Olympic Club. For eight years he carried out this task, as well as sailing and racing the Club's yacht, *T.B. Asten*, giving much enjoyment to the members and all the while gaining valuable experience in the art of the racing skipper. By 1879, Hank Haff was ready to accept his first assignment to be sailing master of a large yacht outside the Great South Bay, being given charge of *Onward*, owned by General Fred Townsend of Albany, New York. From *Onward* he was asked in 1882 to take charge of *Fanny* by John D. Prince of St. Mark's Lane, Islip. Such was his success with *Fanny* in New York Yacht Club races and in the famous match race with *Gracie* that by 1886 Captain Hank Haff had gained the reputation of leading skipper in America and was asked by General Paine to command his boats.

In September of 1887 *Thistle* arrived in New York, and after her unveiling for official measurement, it was found that she was almost two feet longer than she was declared to be by the Royal Clyde Yacht Club. Amidst charges of foul play and the threat of immediate disqualification, the dispute raged on. It was finally resolved by penalizing *Thistle* with a handicap on her elapsed time. The race would go on. As it turned out the first race would be the last one sailed on the New York Yacht Club's inside course, beginning in the Narrows off the Staten Island bluffs at Thompkinsville, running out through the Narrows to Sandy Hook, thence eastward to Sandy Hook lightship and returning to the start, a distance of thirty-nine miles. This course was always crowded with spectator boats, subject to local wind shifts and of great advantage to the defender with local knowledge. An earlier description of the course described the usual scene. "The river was crowded with steam boats, who never seemed tired of streaming around us, with their whistles shrieking by way of salutation — but what concerned us was to know where all these steam boats, some of them huge river boats with 300 people on board, would be when the yachts were under way beating through the Narrows."[83] This report was not exaggerated. In 1886 the British challenger actually collided with a schooner anchored in the Narrows.

On the day of the first race, September 27, 1887, the excitement was intense. The Narrows was filled with spectator boats. Aboard the New York Yacht Club's flagship, *Electra*, was its Commodore Elbridge T. Gerry and his guest, Secretary of the Navy William C. Whitney. A morning fog hung over the Narrows obscuring the Staten Island bluffs and causing the race to be delayed. While waiting, *Thistle* was sailing among the spectator boats showing off her speed for which she was famous in the light breezes. Finally, the fog lifted, the cannon sounded, and the race was under way. *Volunteer* crossed the starting line and headed for the Staten Island bluffs, as did *Thistle*.* When they tacked in the light southerly breeze, they were still even, and although *Thistle* had been thought faster in this light air, *Volunteer* was holding her own. Gradually it became clear that Captain Hank could hold his boat closer to the wind and still keep up her speed. Her greater sail area and the marvelous helmsmanship of her skipper were beginning to tell the tale. The teamwork on *Volunteer* was perfect, and as the wind in the outer bay picked up, she began to pull away, always pointing higher than her rival. By the time she reached the Sandy Hook lightship at the halfway mark, she was twenty-one minutes ahead of *Thistle*. The race was all over. *Thistle* stayed even downwind, but at the finish still lagged by twenty minutes after sailing for over five hours.

Much of the credit went to Captain Hank. A contemporary observer said, "*Volunteer* was splendidly handled all through, especially when the wind was light at the beginning. The crew was so placed for the very best trim for the wind at

---

* The yachts were timed as they crossed the starting line during a two minute handicap period after the starting gun. The winner was the yacht with the least corrected time, after any handicap was applied.

the time, acting as a movable ballast. At the wheel stood trusty Captain Haff (he never left the helm in the five hours of racing) looking as cool and unconcerned as if sailing for the America's Cup was nothing more than going out for a day's blue-fishing off Fire Island. By his side were his three able yachtsmen, Captains Jeffrey, Berry, and Terry. *Volunteer* was sailed to perfection."[84]

The second and final race was a tremendous anticlimax. It was sailed over the outer course, forty miles to windward and return, from the Scotland Lightship eastward to a stake boat off Jones Beach. The wind was somewhat fresher, but no more than moderate. It was hoped by *Thistle*'s skipper that this would help, but it didn't. There were almost no spectators present to watch *Volunteer* win again by twelve minutes. On the evening of September 30, 1887, the New York Yacht Club had again retained the America's Cup and Captain Hank Haff, Islip born and bred, became the leading skipper in the world of yacht racing.

Great Britain would not challenge again for six years. *Thistle* went home after a disappointing lack of form to a new owner and much more success. In 1889 *Thistle* was purchased by Kaiser William II of Imperial Germany, and was re-christened *Meteor*. William, an avid yachtsman and at that time a great Anglophile, regularly competed in the Cowes Race Week off the Isle of Wight. *Meteor*, with an English captain and an all English crew, and with the Kaiser himself aboard, began to win races at Cowes and at other important yachting events with such regularity as to cause great embarrassment to the British and especially to the Kaiser's uncle, the Prince of Wales (later King Edward VII). This caused the Prince to ask G. L. Watson to design a boat faster than *Thistle-Meteor* which he did, naming it *Britannia* in 1892. From then until 1895 *Britannia* always won at Cowes. The Kaiser commissioned Watson to build a *Meteor III*, but she did not win and he personally gave up racing at Cowes, much to the relief of his uncle.

With the victories of *Puritan*, *Mayflower*, and *Volunteer*, pride in the accomplishment of American designers and builders, and the skill of American skippers and seamen grew. The sport of yachting by 1890 became a national symbol of the importance of sea power. The supremacy of Burgess-designed yachts heralded an interest in maritime affairs and eventually the need of an all steel navy.

In the years following his victory with *Volunteer*, Captain Hank Haff had charge of several different yachts, always winning many races for their owners. In 1893 the British challenged for the Cup again, and to defend it, four new American yachts were built. Two syndicates chose a new designer whose record was so outstanding that critics claimed a major breakthrough in yacht design had been achieved. In 1891 the *Gloriana*, designed by Nathaniel G. Herreshoff, had won all her races by large margins, astounding the yachting world. Two years later, after receiving the Cup challenge, William K. Vanderbilt and C. Oliver Iselin each asked Herreshoff to build a yacht for the Cup defense. The Vanderbilt yacht was named *Colonia* and would be sailed by Captain Hank. The Iselin yacht was called *Vigilant* and would be sailed by Herreshoff himself. These yachts were the biggest yet to be built under the rule of 90 feet maximum waterline length. Overall, the yachts were 124 feet in length, constructed of bronze below the waterline and steel above with a hollow bronze centerboard extending down 24 feet below the water. They were able to carry over 11,000 square feet of sail. When heeling over on the windward tack, the extra length overall would give them faster speed. An exhausting contest was held that summer of 1893 to choose the yacht to defend. *Vigilant* was chosen over *Colonia* and the other two boats. Captain Hank lost out narrowly to Herreshoff himself, who went on to defeat the British yacht *Valkyrie II* in the Cup races that fall. Herreshoff, whose boat yard was in Bristol, Rhode Island, had the first of his six incredible America's Cup winners, and was becoming known around the world as "the Wizard of Bristol." Hank Haff, however, had yet to achieve the pinnacle of his career. Following his loss to Herreshoff, he took *Vigilant* to Europe for the 1894 season where he did poorly against *Britannia* and *Meteor* at Cowes. It was in

1895 that Captain Hank would achieve his most notable victory, at the age of fifty-eight, considered old for a sailing master in that era.

Hank Haff was in every way an integral part of Islip and its seagoing tradition. He was a part of a large Islip family. In 1860 he married Adelaide Lake of Islip and the couple had five sons, several of whom sailed with him and made their livelihood on the water. Although Haff was away a great deal as his career dictated, he was considered a good citizen, politically a Republican, and at one time was the highway commissioner for the Town of Islip. For over thirty years he was a Freemason, and was Master of the Lodge five times. It was said of him, "Captain Haff was a good citizen, a fine friend and a kind neighbor. He scorned duplicity and hypocrisy, was quick to denounce wrong and especially quick to espouse a cause that he considered just. He played life's battle straight and no one can say aught to the contrary."[85]

As the choice land along the Connetquot River and Champlin's Creek filled up with the country homes of New York City families in the 1880s, the land on the east side of Doxsee's Creek and on the west side of Awixa Creek had begun to be settled upon by families from Brooklyn who were also looking to escape the summer heat. Brooklyn, of course, was a separate city at that time; not until 1898 did it merge into New York City. In the 1880s the two cities were not only separate entities, but also socially they were miles apart. The old New York families looked down on their Brooklyn neighbors across the East River. With very few exceptions Brooklynites were not welcomed in the Union Club nor were they often members of the magic circle of the 400 families invited to Mrs. Astor's ball each year. However, Brooklyn families of affluence did search for summer homes and many found the South Shore of Long Island along the Great South Bay very desirable. They tended to settle along the avenues where other Brooklyn families were located, and stayed away, by and large, from Great River Road, Pavilion Avenue, and St. Mark's Lane. Thus it was that Ocean Avenue in Islip and Awixa and Penataquit Avenues in Bay

Shore were generally considered "Brooklyn Territory." Saxton Avenue was a mixture of both. This was not an absolute separation by any means, but it was clear enough to be recognized even in 1886. "Doxsee's Lane [now Ocean Avenue, Islip] is known as the Brooklyn section of Islip, and as such it is certainly well represented."[86] There were many more Brooklyn families in Bay Shore than in Islip, East Islip, and Great River all together.

Much of the waterfront land along Doxsee's Lane prior to 1885 was owned by James Harvey Doxsee of Islip, who had the clam factory on Orowoc Creek, which was also known then as Doxsee's Creek (the pond to the north of the creek is still called Doxsee's Pond today). The first to summer along this "favored spot of the region in direct line with the sea breezes"[87] which blow off the bay were four men and their families from Brooklyn: Charles A. Tucker, whose brother Clarence was located on St. Mark's Lane, David D. Valentine, William M. Van Anden, and Alden S. Swan, who was a Brooklyn alderman and trustee of the new Brooklyn Bridge (1883). They were joined shortly by the Leander Waterburys from New York who built a cottage in the winter of 1887.

By the end of 1892 there had been several changes along Ocean Avenue, but the predominance of Brooklyn families still remained. In the winter of 1889 William Dick of Brooklyn purchased the Charles Tucker place as well as the adjoining shipyard of Alonzo Smith, who by then had given up shipbuilding to become the largest dredger in the area. It was commented at the time that Mr. Dick "will have all of the buildings renovated and put in first class order. It looks as if Mr. Dick is to be a valuable addition to our village."[88] William Dick and his family spent the first of many summers on Ocean Avenue in 1889. At the same time that the Dicks arrived, Leander Waterbury died of consumption in his New York home. His brand new house on Ocean Avenue was soon sold to Howard Gibb of Brooklyn, the managing partner of the Brooklyn department store, Frederick Loeser and Company.

In the fall of that same year, Charles A. Schieren, soon to be mayor of Brooklyn, acquired a waterfront property alongside his fellow Brooklynites. Schieren had been born in Neuss, Rhenish Germany, in 1842 and had immigrated to New York with his parents in 1856. There he found employment in a leather factory in the city's famous "Swamp." After the Civil War, he started a leather business of his own with his small savings. The business grew to become nationwide and controlled many tanneries. With success, Schieren moved to Brooklyn where he became a major figure in the commercial and political life of the city. He was an organizer of the Hide and Leather National Bank and a trustee of the Germania Bank of Brooklyn. As a Republican, he was elected mayor of Brooklyn in both 1894 and 1895. In 1865, he married Marie Louise Bramm, with whom he had eight children, only four of whom survived to adulthood. He would remain an Islip summer resident until his death on March 10, 1915. His wife died a day later.

In the spring of 1890, William Dick enlarged his holdings by buying the land, known as the Cedars, to the south of him owned by Alden Swan, thus ending a controversy over land use that was threatening the community. Swan had wanted to create a large sand peninsula there on which to build a clubhouse for the new Great South Bay Yacht Club, of which he was commodore. Most of the neighbors were opposed to this, and by buying the property Dick ensured that it could not happen. Lastly in August of 1892 Dick sold the property to the north of him to John Gibb, Howard Gibb's father, who had rented Conover's house on Saxton Avenue previously. John Gibb built a new house on this site which he named Afterglow for the magnificent sunsets over the western bay which could be viewed by all along Ocean Avenue's waterfront.

By 1892, the families of William Dick, John Gibb, Howard Gibb, Charles Schieren, and Alden Swan, all from Brooklyn, were located along the west side of Ocean Avenue. They were the owners of the waterfront property. Inland somewhat were Van Anden, and renting a Doxsee cottage, Roland Redmond from New York, the president of the South Side Club. The waterfront land there, as it was almost all along the bay, was marshy and mosquito filled. Only by building it up with the sand dredged from the bay could it be made desirable for homes. With proper grading and the addition of topsoil a lawn could be grown down to the waterfront, which was often bulkheaded or from which a dock was built. During much of 1889 Alonzo Smith with his steam dredges was at work on Orowoc Creek. Deepening the channel to five feet for Doxsee's fishing fleet and piling up sand on the waterfront of Dick and Gibb land was the task for two of them. "The money spent by property owners for dredging in this creek alone can not be much, if any, short of $25,000. It seems to be a money-making business and as yet only in its infancy so far as the South Bay is concerned. In ten years the whole shorefront will be improved and used for summer residences instead of retreats for mosquitos and muskrats."[89] Of these first Brooklyn families to settle along Ocean Avenue in Islip prior to 1890 a word more should be said about the Gibb family and the Dick family, as they remained in Islip longer than the others. In fact, descendants of Dick live there today.

The backgrounds and careers of John Gibb and William Dick were similar in many ways. Both men were born in Europe, came to the United States around 1845, were apprenticed to merchants, and after a brief period established their own businesses which became extremely successful. Both married in the New World and raised families which joined them in business. Both settled in Brooklyn where their businesses were located, and both in the latter part of their lives came with their grown children to locate next to each other on Ocean Avenue in Islip. They lived to what in the nineteenth century was considered a very old age, Gibb dying at seventy-six and Dick at eighty-nine. Undoubtedly they had known each other for many years in Brooklyn and were good friends long before moving to Islip. There the similarities end.

John Gibb was born in Forfarshire, Scotland, in 1829. After a short apprenticeship with a dry goods merchant, he moved to London at eighteen and was engaged by the merchant house of J. R. Jaffray & Co. By 1850 he was transferred by Jaffray to its New York house where he became the manager in charge. Fifteen years later, with a partner, Philo S. Mills, Gibb established his own dry goods business of importing laces and linens from London for retail sale in Brooklyn. It was called Mills & Gibb and was a great success, with sales quickly spreading throughout the whole country. In 1887 Gibb and his eldest son, Howard, purchased control of the Brooklyn retail department store, Frederick Loeser & Company, which Howard Gibb subsequently managed and greatly enlarged in 1892.

John Gibb and his wife had a large family — four sons and four daughters. They were members of the Episcopal Church, Holy Trinity in Brooklyn Heights and St. Mark's after they came to Islip. John joined the St. Mark's vestry in 1893. He was also a trustee of the Brooklyn Trust Co. and a member of the prestigious Brooklyn Club and Hamilton Club as well as the Olympic Club in Bay Shore. John came to Islip after his retirement from business and after the death of his first wife and remarriage to his second. He was over sixty years old at the time. He followed his son, Howard, to Ocean Avenue. His other sons, J. Richmond and Lewis Mills Gibb, also located in the Great South Bay area, the latter on Saxton Avenue in Bay Shore. But his sons were not blessed with their father's longevity. Howard died before his father, and Richmond and Lewis died quite soon thereafter. It was left to one son, Walter, to carry on the Loeser store, which he did with the help of his brother's son, Lewis Mills Gibb Jr., who became its president in 1933. John Gibb died in 1905 at his Ocean Avenue home, Afterglow, where he had spent the last dozen summers of his life next to his old friend and neighbor, William Dick.

Dick had been born in 1823 in the old kingdom of Hanover which subsequently became part of the German Empire. He immigrated to New York in 1845 speaking only the German language. To his dying day German was always spoken in his home and he managed English only slowly and haltingly. Locating in Manhattan's Lower East Side amongst the many other German immigrants there, he ran a grocery store over which he and his new wife, Anna, lived. Penniless at the start, William Dick worked long hours and saved his pennies. He progressed from grocery clerk to flour merchant to sugar refiner. His only son, John Henry, was born on the Lower East Side in 1851. Soon afterwards, the Dick family moved to the Williamsburgh* section of Brooklyn, where Germans were beginning to settle in large numbers. It was most congenial for them there. Dick, a Lutheran, became active in the church and established himself as a community leader. In 1861 their second and last child, a daughter Anna, named for her mother, was born.

Dick moved his sugar refinery to Williamsburgh after the end of the Civil War when it had become clear that the mile and a half stretch of waterfront land there was fast becoming the center for sugar refineries in New York harbor. He found a new partner, another German, Cord Meyer, and together they built a new sugar refinery on North Seventh Street. For a time it was the largest in Brooklyn and brought to William Dick great wealth. The Dick and Meyer refinery remained an independent partnership managed by Dick until 1887, when the partners decided to join the Sugar Trust which was being organized that year to manage the production and prices of all the New York refiners due to the surplus capacity in the industry. The Sugar Trust was controlled from the beginning and managed throughout his life by Dick's Islip neighbor, Henry O. Havemeyer. Dick became an original trustee of the Sugar Trust and later a director of its successor, the American Sugar Refining Company. He received a large amount of stock for the Dick and Meyer refinery and its business. However, following 1887 he took a much less active role in sugar and started a new career in banking, again in Williamsburgh. Dick's bank was the Manufacturers National Bank. He was a director of it for almost forty years, a vice president, and finally the president for four years before his retirement. He was one of Williamsburgh's most significant figures during his long life there.

---

* Williamsburgh was the original spelling of the town. The final "h" was dropped later.

St. Mark's Church, Islip, built in 1879-80. It was designed by Richard Morris Hunt to copy a Norwegian stave church and was given to the parish by William K. Vanderbilt. (Courtesy of Richard A. Milligan.)

Trolling for Blue Fish by Currier & Ives, 1866. The Cape Cod catboat was sketched by Thomas Worth. The catboat belonged to Captain Hank Haff of Islip here pictured holding the tiller. (Courtesy of The Old Print Shop.)

Home of George C. Taylor, built in Great River in 1885-86 on his land which is now Heckscher State Park. The house was razed in 1933. (Courtesy of Long Island State Park Commission.)

William Bayard Cutting, 1850-1912, owner of *Westbrook* in Great River. He is pictured here in 1899 at the age of 49. (Courtesy of the New York Public Library.)

The Cuttings' church,
Emmanuel Church on Great
River Road, built in 1862,
steeple and wings added in
1877 and pictured today.
(Courtesy of Richard A. Milligan.)

Westbrook, designed by Charles C. Haight for Mr. and Mrs. W. Bayard Cutting. It was built in 1886. Pictured today in the Bayard Cutting Arboretum. (Courtesy of Richard A. Milligan.)

At dinner in the *Westbrook* dining room on October 1, 1898. Various members of the Cutting family. (Courtesy of *Images and Shadows* by Iris Origo).

When Dick located on Ocean Avenue in Islip in early 1889, he was already sixty-five years old. His son John Henry was thirty-eight and had married young Julia Mollenhauer, age twenty-six, two years before. The younger Dicks had a year-old son and Julia was pregnant again. Three more children would follow. Dick's wife Anna was still living, but at the age of sixty-nine she was becoming increasingly homebound. It was certainly his grandchildren who motivated William Dick to search for a country home. He wanted to enjoy them during what was left of his life. Also, he knew that his wife and he himself would need more care as the years went by. Ocean Avenue in Islip, with its Brooklyn neighbors and the Charles Tucker place for sale, seemed just right. Dick had the resources to develop it, to enlarge the house with the help of architect Isaac H. Green Jr., and to build a model farm across the road in the manner of his many peers. The grandchildren could swim, sail, and ride horseback on the sometimes dusty Ocean Avenue. Dick named his country place Allen Winden Farm.[*] It was the most southerly place on the west side of Ocean Avenue and to its south was the then-marsh called Bayberry Point. To the west was an unbroken view across what was called Doxsee's Cove toward Penataquit Point and the Bay Shore waterfront.

To the west of Awixa Creek lay Penataquit Point, once known as Thurber's Neck, where the first Mowbray[**] family lived in the early 1700s. During the 1880s several New York and Brooklyn families either built or rented cottages there. Waterfront on Awixa Creek on the one side, and on East Creek on the other, gave access to the bay. Three roads ran south off the South Country Road toward the neck of Penataquit Point, providing access to many fine property sites. Before the turn of the decade on Awixa Avenue, Albert Young, William H. Gunther, E. P. Jones, W. Wiswall, Dr. J. V. S. Wooley, and William Wray had settled with their

---

[*] German for 'all winds.'

[**] In later years the spelling was changed from Moubray to Mowbray.

families. Young and Gunther were from New York, the others from Brooklyn. On Penataquit Avenue, Dr. Chauncey E. Low from Brooklyn — a cousin of Dr. Seth Low, mayor of Brooklyn and later New York, and president of Columbia College — had located. Finally on Montgomery Avenue the home of Richard E. Montgomery was built in 1884. Montgomery, a real estate broker and developer, had built the road named for him to develop a large part of the area. He lived there for ten years when the cottage was taken over by Brooklynite Robert A. Pinkerton, son of the founder of the famous detective agency.

Many Brooklynites and New Yorkers were also renting along the three principal avenues from Bay Shore village to the bay, Maple Avenue, Ocean Avenue, and Clinton Avenue. To be near the Prospect House on Ocean Avenue and the brand new Linwood Hotel on Clinton Avenue, which opened in June 1888, was a particularly choice location for the summer. It was on Clinton Avenue in 1890 that Mr. Charles C. Gulden of New York, founder of famous Gulden's Mustard, built his first home in Bay Shore. It was to be "the largest and finest home on the avenue."[90] Some of his descendants live in the area today.

Along that elegant section of the South Country Road from Bay Shore to Babylon many new families arrived to join the old timers who had settled there in the 1840s, 1850s, 1860s, and 1870s. Most of these families — such as the Lawrances, Johnsons, Wilmerdings, Hydes, Colts, Thompsons, B. K. Trues, Arnolds, and Wagstaffs — were still there in 1890. Doctor Wagstaff had died in 1878, but two sons, Colonel Alfred and C. DuBois Wagstaff, and a son-in-law, Phoenix Remsen, all maintained homes on Wagstaff land. Robert O. Colt had died in 1885, and George G. Wilmerding and John I. Lawrance in 1889. Richard Arnold died in 1886, but his son William kept up the house. The dean of all the summer residents was the one who had arrived first. At the grand age of seventy-nine Bradish Johnson was the patriarch of his large family, which he looked upon with pride from Sans Souci, his home on the South Country Road.

Towards Babylon there were other summer families, some that had been there for almost two decades, others more recently arrived. The Minor H. Keith home was occupied in the 1880s by William P. Clyde of New York, whose Clyde Steamboat Company of Wilmington, North Carolina, owned ships that plied the Atlantic trade, filling the company's warehouses with goods and the owner's pockets with profit. Nearby was Benjamin D. Silliman, a New York lawyer, who had the distinction of being Yale College's oldest living graduate, having graduated with the Class of 1824. Farther along the road, George B. Magoun of San Francisco had bought part of the Udall farm in 1880 for his summer residence. On the south side of the road near Babylon village was located the home of John Busteed Ireland, a New York lawyer born in 1863 of a family that descended from the Floyd family of Mastic, Long Island. John B. Ireland married the daughter of Robert Livingston Pell and their seven children (one of whom was Robert Livingston Ireland) thus brought together several of the earliest and most prominent American families.

Across South Country Road from Ireland was a piece of land called Effingham Park, the creation of Effingham B. Sutton, who came to West Islip around 1870. Sutton was born in New York City in 1817, for a time was engaged in importing dry goods, and made a fortune by starting a famous line of clipper ships which sailed around Cape Horn to San Francisco, or went on to China, bringing back valuable cargo with record speed. Sutton built his home in West Islip on the east side of the pond that became known as Effingham Pond. Effingham Park was a private park; in addition to Sutton's residence, it included three cottages which were rented to his friends, two of whom were the brothers George* and William F. Kingsland from New York. Sutton, an Episcopalian, was a vestryman and generous benefactor of Christ Church, West Islip, located just to the east of Effingham Park. He died in 1891, two years after the death of his wife, at the age of seventy-four.

---

* The son-in-law of Benjamin S. Welles of Islip.

Last, to the north of Babylon village on Deer Park Avenue was the home of Harry I. Nicholas of New York. Nicholas, born in 1846 in Virginia, was from an old and distinguished Southern family. His grandfather had been a colonel in a Virginia regiment during the Revolutionary War. Nicholas came north to New York as a young man to achieve success as a banker and broker on Wall Street. He married Alice Hollins, the sister of Harry B. Hollins of East Islip, and settled on Deer Park Avenue during the 1870s. He was a vestryman and benefactor of Christ Church for much of his life, and an active participant in many of the sporting endeavors on the bay, including the South Side Club, the Babylon Yacht Club, and the Great South Bay Yacht Club. Nicholas was a well-known and well-liked member of that younger group of men that followed W. K. Vanderbilt to the Great South Bay. He died in his Babylon home in 1901, survived by his widow Alice, a son Harry I. Jr., several daughters, and a brother, George S. Nicholas, who often rented on the South Shore near Harry. Nicholas, his wife Alice, together with three of their daughters, are buried in the Babylon cemetery just yards away from the site of the Nicholas home.

By the start of the new decade many of the prime sites along the waterfront from Oakdale on the east to Babylon on the west had been purchased and built on by New Yorkers and Brooklynites searching for summertime country homes. The character of that area had been established in the minds of those who had come and those who would follow. The livelihood of the local communities was becoming more than ever dependent on "the summer folk," both the residents and the boarders. Islip village in particular had grown in size during the 1880s to become the largest in the township. Bay Shore, as well, was prospering from increased summer tourist trade, but it was the families who had permanently settled along the Great South Bay and its neighboring waterways that had set the tone.

Chapter VII
THE GILDED AGE — ITS PEAK (1890–1900)

The early years of the 1890s were boom times in America; prosperity was becoming more widespread. As the Industrial Age progressed there was more employment, and also an increase in the immigrant population searching for a better life. There was leisure time for a growing group of the population that had never experienced this luxury before. More were escaping the heat and humidity of New York City in the summer, even if only for one week by the seashore or in the mountains. The *New York Herald* proclaimed in June 1890, "Summer resorts are booming everywhere. Saratoga, Newport, the Adirondacks, Seabright and Asbury Park along the Jersey Shore, and the Great South Bay are among the favorite spas. . . . At Babylon, Bay Shore and Islip, almost every house is occupied and the trusting individual who has waited until now [June 22] to find a cottage will find it a difficult matter to procure what he desires. The South [Short] Beach Club and the excellent management of the Wawayanda House add greatly to the attractions of these last named places."

Not only were summer cottages hard to find that year, but the resort hotels around the Great South Bay were generally thriving as well. In East Islip the Lake House and the Pavilion were full for the summer, as were the Prospect House and the Linwood in Bay Shore. It was even commented that "if we had someone with capital and energy enough to put up a large hotel on the waterfront in Islip, it would be the making of the place. . . . The Prospect House made Bay Shore what it is, or contributed largely to its development."[1] However, in Babylon, the Argyle had suffered the least successful season in its history. This was probably because of poor management, as after it was sold to new ownership in March of 1891, it reopened in June to renewed prosperity. And on Fire Island Sammis's Surf Hotel was continuing to attract guests that would enjoy the ocean surf or the blue fishing. * Like the aging lady she was, the Surf Hotel at thirty-five was not quite sure what would happen to her.

Only with hindsight can it now be said that 1890 was the high water mark for these resort hotels on the Great South Bay. From that year on it was all ebb tide. The Surf Hotel suffered an insurmountable blow in September 1892 when it was purchased by New York State Governor Roswell P. Flower to be a quarantine hostelry for passengers arriving from the Mediterranean, some of whom had cholera. The cholera epidemic failed to spread, but the fear of that disease was such that guests never wanted to go to the Surf again. After several unsuccessful years, it was burned down and the land became the first state park on Long Island, Fire Island State Park.

The Pavilion Hotel met a more precipitous end. In August of 1892 it closed for the season early, "having lost too much money."[2] It did not open in 1893, but a new owner began to paint it in the winter of 1894 in preparation for another season. In the early morning hours of March 22 an alarm was turned in to the East Islip Fire Department that the Pavilion was on fire. Firemen from East Islip, Islip, and Bay Shore all responded to the call, but by the time they arrived the old wooden hotel was "a mass of seething flames." They were only able to save the cottages adjoining the hotel and the neighboring homes, helped by a still night and an earlier rain. They were not helped by finding that the water from the nearby hydrant was insufficient and "was apparently without

---

* One of these guests was Herman Melville, author of *Moby-Dick*, who visited often from 1887–1891 so Mrs. Melville could avoid the hay fever from which she suffered.

the usual force."[3] The hotel burned to the ground in "the most disastrous fire ever known in the history of the town. It was a big blaze in every sense of the word."[4] The hotel and all its contents were a total loss. The cause of the fire was thought to be arson, as the hotel was completely unoccupied that night, and the fire was thought to have begun in several different places at once. Also the wrench to turn on the hydrant was missing from the hose truck. However, no one was found or charged for the offense. Adding to suspicions was the fact that the stables of the Pavilion had been burned down in January in equally mysterious circumstances. The Pavilion was gone forever, but the cottages were used for rental until 1898 when the entire property was sold to neighbors H. B. Hollins, C. T. Harbeck, B. Johnson Jr., and Colonel H. R. Duval who bought it for protection, it being the prime site at the entrance to the road to their homes (now called Suffolk Lane).

Within a year of the Pavilion's destruction another fire completely destroyed the house that had been occupied for five years by William F. Wharton, located a short distance down the same road. Again an empty house in the midst of winter in the middle of a snowstorm was burned to the ground. Again arson was suspected, and this time a charge was made which, upon investigation, could not be proved. The reporter thought it must be the work of someone with an "unsound mind, who has a mania for burning buildings."[5] Again the water pressure was lacking, which prompted a sharp letter from twenty of Islip's leading summer and local residents to the president of the Town Board of Islip complaining that the water furnished by the Great South Bay Water Company was "unfit for general use . . . and as demonstrated at the fires of recent date that the pressure was totally inadequate to be of any service."[6]

The destructiveness of fires and the fear of them in that era can not be overestimated. Not only were house fires a common occurrence, but fires in the villages and forest fires that roared on unchecked caused tremendous destruction. Large parts of Islip village were destroyed by fire in 1900 and again in 1905. In 1893 during a particularly dry summer a forest fire, most likely started by lightning, raged on for several days through the scrub pines and oaks to the north of Islip. The firemen were helpless. There was no water to be had, so that nothing could be done but "let her blaze." As the blaze neared Islip village, the St. Mark's church bell sounded the warning that help was needed to try to protect the homes of neighbors. All the volunteer firemen turned out to East Islip where the threat was the greatest and began to water down homes there. Finally at dusk the northwest wind died down and the prevailing southerly blew in off the bay. The fire was driven back from the village over already-burned land and died out. It was the southerly that saved East Islip from total loss.

The Surf and the Pavilion were not the only two hotels to close in the 1890s. Stellenwerf's Lake House, across from the Pavilion, shut its doors as well. In August of 1894 old Amos Stellenwerf, longtime proprietor of this old-fashioned country inn, died and was buried at St. Mark's Church. The inn had been a particularly personal and homey place, which was remembered by its many guests for the striking pictures hanging on its walls drawn by the artist Thomas Worth, Stellenwerf's son-in-law. With the old man's death his heirs decided to close the establishment for good. The contents were then sold at auction and the 200 acres of property put up for sale. At an auction held in 1897 the most valuable portion of this holding, that to the south of the LIRR tracks, was bid in by Edward B. Meeks, another Stellenwerf son-in-law who owned the house across the pond. He held it until the right buyer was found, Harry K. Knapp, the younger brother of Edward S. Knapp who had lived on Saxton Avenue.

The year 1890 marked another important milestone, for in November, August Belmont, one of the earliest and by far the most prominent early South Shore resident, died. Belmont's Nursery in Babylon had been purchased in 1864. He was seventy-four years old at the time of his death. Only Bradish Johnson was senior to Belmont in age, and only Johnson, Benjamin S. Welles and Mrs. W. K. Knapp on St.

Mark's Lane, and Francis C. Lawrance at Manatuck Farm had arrived at an earlier time.* Thus with the 1890s the older generation of summer residents had passed into history, and the newer generation, which Schuyler Parsons Jr. later called "the young couples who were very close friends of W. K. Vanderbilt," became the leaders of society.

In the winter of 1891 the vestry of St. Mark's Church in Islip announced its intention to build a parish house "which will contain a library, gymnasium, and lecture hall."[7] It had chosen the Sayville architect, Isaac H. Green Jr., to design a building that would be compatible with the Hunt-designed church. Local builder George B. Howell was given the contract estimated to cost $20,000. Subscriptions were asked for from the members of the congregation to raise this sum, and the most generous responses were from the Cutting brothers, W. K. Vanderbilt, Harry B. Hollins, and H. Duncan Wood. Henry B. Hyde, Benjamin S. Welles, and many others added to the fund which included a gift of $500 from the employees of W. K. Vanderbilt, an amount half as large as that given by Vanderbilt himself — quite extraordinary generosity!

In September the church sponsored a festival to raise money for the new parish house. It was a grand, festive occasion held on the grounds of the Meeks estate across the South Country Road from the church. Lasting throughout the afternoon until eleven o'clock at night, it was complete with games for children, booths with goods for sale, and popular music and dancing in the moonlight by the side of Champlin's Pond. It brought together the summer residents and the townsfolk and to some extent bridged the gap between the two groups. "At 11 p.m. the band played 'Home Sweet Home' and so ended the second affair of this kind ever held in East Islip. Why cannot it be repeated each year? Added to the general good time $1200 was raised for the St. Mark's Parish House which is now nearly completed."[8]

---

* B. Johnson Sr. died in 1892; B. S. Welles Sr. and Maria M. Knapp both died in 1904; F. C. Lawrance Sr. died in 1911.

Within a month the parish house was ready for use, and a grand opening celebration was planned for the evening of October 26, to be held in the auditorium of the new building. It was a sellout with over six hundred guests seated and a standing room crowd to hear the speeches and a glee club singing hymns. The rector, the Reverend Henry R. Freeman, made welcoming remarks and then introduced the principal speaker for the occasion, the Honorable Chauncey M. Depew, who had undoubtedly been engaged for the evening by his colleague, William K. Vanderbilt. Depew was known throughout the country by that time as a "world-famous silver-tongued orator and statesman."[9] It would have been impossible to attract such a prominent figure to Islip were it not for Vanderbilt.

Depew (1834–1928) was a Vanderbilt man in every sense of the word. Vanderbilt biographer Louis Auchincloss described him as

attorney for and later president of the New York Central. He worked for the Vanderbilts during most of his long life, having turned down the ministry to Japan at the urgency of the Commodore [Cornelius Vanderbilt], whose lawyer and principal assistant he had then become, working with the old man at his home and in his office every day in the last ten years of his life, the decade in which three-quarters of the great fortune was made [1867–1877]. Half a century later Depew was still on the job, a grand old man with large piercing eyes and an aquiline nose, a tall gleaming bald dome and thin, gravely smiling lips, the high priest of the railroad interests who had even got himself elected to the United States Senate* to further their cause, the ultimate apologist of laissez-faire, the smooth promoter of great ends over small means, the genial idealist at banquets, the sharp realist in the smoke-filled rooms, hailed by all as the greatest after-dinner speaker of his time.[10]

Chauncey Depew spoke for about thirty minutes at the opening celebration, a short talk by the standards of the day. His theme was that the progress in the country was good, that wealth was a blessing if administered well and not

---

* U.S. Senator from New York 1898–1911.

hoarded, and that the church and its new building would bring particular benefit to the young people in the community. In conclusion it was reported that "there was not a person in the whole audience who was not well pleased, glad that he or she had come, and during the evening had been made to feel better and been given higher views of life. Mr. Depew's address was loudly applauded, so much so that it was almost an encore, but the speaker refused to answer the entreaty of the multitude and in his place the glee club sang 'Good Night.'"[11] Thanks to a new parish house for St. Mark's Church and to W. K. Vanderbilt, the Islip, Bay Shore, and Babylon communities had for the first time been addressed in person by a speaker of such prominent acclaim.

In Oakdale, to the east of the land acquired by W. K. Vanderbilt, there was a large tract of mostly marshy ground extending south to the Great South Bay at a point east of the widening Connetquot River's delta. This land was part of the Nicoll patent and was still held in that family until 1880 when 830 acres were sold to a New Yorker with an interesting background and very ambitious plans.

Christopher Rhinelander Robert Jr. was born in 1830. He came from a family whose ancestor, Daniel Robert, had fled from France during the time of the persecution of Huguenots. He was also the grandson of a later Daniel Robert and Mary Tangier Smith, whose family had long been associated with the town of Brookhaven on Long Island, as well as with the establishment of Smithtown. Daniel and Mary's son Christopher was in fact born in Brookhaven. Christopher R. Robert Sr. went on to become a wealthy industrialist who is remembered today as the founder of Robert College* in Istanbul, Turkey (1863), to which he left a part of his estate at his death in 1878.

Christopher Jr., after a brief three year childless marriage ended in divorce in 1875, married the widow of a

---

* Robert College, a private school for Turkish students of special ability, preparatory to university, exists today in Bebek on the shores of the Bosporus just to the north of Istanbul.

wealthy New England shipbuilder, Mrs. Charles Morgan, née Julia Remington, who had needed a country home for her family, and with their vast resources they looked to Oakdale. Christopher, a popular club man of that day, belonged to the Knickerbocker, the Meadowbrook, and of course the South Side Club in Oakdale which he had joined in 1873. He and his wife were on the guest list for Mrs. Astor's 1892 ball. As with so many others, it was the South Side Club that introduced him to Oakdale and the Great South Bay. It was only after his father's death that Christopher began his ambitious plan for a vast country estate.

The Nicoll land that Robert bought presented a large challenge. Low and marshy near the bay, it would have to be drained in order to provide solid ground for a site near enough to the bay for the grand view that he wanted. This was a slow, painstaking, and expensive project. Furthermore, Christopher intended to build a huge castle-like home and to import from France virtually everything that was needed to complete it. It was said that he decided to build the castle to commemorate his feudal ancestors, one of whom he claimed was William the Conqueror. It took Robert almost ten years to reclaim the land, find a Normandy chateau, and import it to Long Island stone by stone. The actual rebuilding of the castle in Oakdale did not begin until 1889 or 1890. In the meantime Robert traveled abroad extensively and when in Oakdale lived in a cottage on his estate. During these ten years he developed a farm on the land. "There is the farmer's dwelling, of solid brick and stone, Queen Anne style. There is a brick cow stable . . . filled with thoroughbred cattle; and there is the horse barn, engine house, piggery, and many other buildings, all built of brick. The piggery is a marvel of size and convenience and the inhabitants thereof innumerable. They run in size of the six hundred pounder to the little grunter you could put in your overcoat pocket."[12] He also engaged a New York architect, H. Edward Ficken, to assist with the design and reassembling of the castle.

After a long wait, work in Oakdale finally got under way. Stone by stone, the castle was put together again. Slowly and painstakingly it began to take shape. "Double walls five feet thick stood on deeply laid brick foundations . . . [Inside] its ballroom, music and art galleries were brought in sections from France, including period panels, gold furniture, tapestries, fireplaces and crystal chandeliers. The rooms on the second floor of the main wing were even more luxurious. From Europe he imported mirrors framed in solid gold, paintings by Old Masters, bronze statues, and fireplaces of ancient design. Mrs. Robert's bathroom was panelled in the manner of Fragonard. Her bed was an exact copy of Marie Antoinette's."[13] Nothing like this had been seen before on the South Shore, even in the Vanderbilt house.

Julia Robert was reported to have hated the castle built for her. By the time it was completed (the conservatory was completed in 1894) their marriage was all but over. "Servants reported on the constant quarrels between Robert and his wife, and on the lack of interest she showed in the place. Fewer and fewer guests would come to their parties."[14] In 1893 the Roberts rented a house in Newport for the season and spent almost no time in Oakdale. The end was soon to come.

One day in November 1896 — the castle had not even been entirely completed and work was still progressing on it — Robert left his castle in a rage, went to New York City and arranged to sell it to W. K. Aston in return for some property Aston owned on Wall Street. The exchange was contingent on the election of William McKinley as president of the United States. Fortunately for Robert, McKinley won and the transaction was completed. Robert never returned to Oakdale. W. K. Aston occupied the Normandy chateau for only a few years. He did give it the name of the lovely nyssa or pepperidge tree which turns a deep red in the autumn, Peperidge Hall.

Robert suffered a tragic death. In the late fall of 1897 he and his wife planned to sail for France and had booked their passage, when suddenly he cancelled the trip. A short time later, on January 2, 1898, Christopher Robert was found dead in his New York City apartment, a revolver lying at his side.

The coroner's verdict was suicide. Julia Robert moved to France where she died some years later.

Peperidge Hall passed through several hands after Aston left. * It was a white elephant requiring care and attention which it did not get. "Decay set in as the masonry cracked, the plaster fell away and the bricks followed. Nature reclaimed the grounds."[15] Not until 1940, fifty years after Robert built the castle he hardly lived in, was Peperidge Hall torn down. By then the land was to have a better use.

The last remaining waterfront land of the Nicoll patent that still was owned by that family was situated between the Robert land on the west and West Sayville on the east. It had a frontage on the Great South Bay of about a mile and a half and on the South Country Road of more than a mile. In 1889 it was owned by William H. Ludlow, a longtime resident of Oakdale and former member of the New York State Assembly from Suffolk County. Ludlow had married Frances Nicoll, from whom, following her death, he had inherited the land. At the age of sixty-eight, with his wife deceased and their three sons moved to the West, Ludlow agreed to sell a large portion of this valuable property. The sale was noted in the *New York Evening Post* under the headline "SALE OF INDIAN LANDS."[16] The new owner would name his mansion Indian Neck Hall. It was also noted that he paid $80,000 for 400 acres. After Ludlow's death in 1890, he would acquire more of the land, finally owning the entire tract south of the South Country Road. The new owner was Frederick Gilbert Bourne of New York. Bourne in 1889 joined his three neighbors, C. R. Robert, W. K. Vanderbilt, and W. B. Cutting, to create the fourth of what were to be the largest estates on the South Shore. Indian Neck Hall when finished in 1900 was the largest mansion on Long Island.

Bourne was a contemporary of W. K. Vanderbilt and had the same friendly, affable nature. He enjoyed the fruits of his labor and like Vanderbilt never hesitated to spend his wealth

---

* In 1907 Aston attempted to subdivide and sell lots at the estate. He was unsuccessful. He died in New York City in 1919.

on his estate as well as his grand passion, yachts. Unlike W. K., however, Bourne earned every penny of his enormous fortune. He was born in 1851, the son of a Boston minister of English origin with extremely modest means. The Reverend George Washington Bourne and Harriet Gilbert Bourne moved to New York when Frederick was very young. He went to a public school in the city but was too poor to attend college. Instead he found a job at the Mercantile Library as a clerk. It also happened that he loved music and sang in the choir of his church on Sundays. Good fortune was to shine on young Frederick. Both at the Mercantile Library and at church he was noticed by Alfred Corning Clark, heir to the founder of the Singer Sewing Machine Company. Clark came to know young Bourne and admired his good sense, his mental alertness, and good nature. He was also impressed with his voice in the choir and the fact that he was a churchgoer. The offer of a job followed and Bourne became a clerk at Singer. He was less than eighteen years old at the time. Bourne became the indispensable assistant to Clark, serving him and his company with great ability and loyalty. He was rewarded with rapid promotion and great wealth. When Clark died in 1882 he named Bourne to be the executor of his estate. In 1885 he was named secretary and then in 1888 president of the Singer Sewing Machine Company. He was only thirty-seven years old at the time. Bourne was credited with spreading the name Singer throughout the world until it became a generic term for a sewing machine.

Frederick Bourne had married Emma Keeler of New York in 1875. They were to have twelve children, five of whom pre-deceased them. With his financial success assured as president of the company and with a young and rapidly growing family, Bourne looked to Oakdale to establish his country home. The property was on the water which he loved, relatively near New York City to which he could commute by train, and near to other important New York figures, particularly Vanderbilt and Cutting. Although Bourne had purchased most of it by 1890, he did not begin building Indian Neck Hall until 1897, living in a large pre-Revolutionary house in West Sayville for almost a decade. One can only speculate that the land, marshy by the bay where he intended to build, needed draining and elevating. Perhaps the depression of 1893–1897 brought about caution on his part.

In 1897 Bourne chose the architect Ernest M. Flagg to design Indian Neck Hall. Flagg, only forty years old at the time, had studied at the Ecole des Beaux-Arts in Paris like so many of his profession in that era. He would become closely associated with Bourne and with Singer. He built for Singer its first office tower in New York at 149 Broadway in 1897–98 and later in 1908 the forty-five-story Singer building. The Scribner building at Fifth Avenue and Forty-eighth Street (still standing) built in 1913, the Corcoran Art Gallery in Washington, D.C., and many buildings on Staten Island, where he was a large property owner, were among his work. It was for Bourne, however, that Flagg first made his reputation and Indian Neck Hall was a masterpiece.

It was described at the time of its completion in the *New York Herald,* September 9, 1900, as "strictly Colonial in architecture, red and white [brick and marble]."[17] Modern architecture critic Steven Bedford said, "Flagg, in designing this vast, red brick and marble mansion . . . reflected prominent architects' commitment to the Colonial Revival in the design of country houses. Its great porticos, one pedimented facing the land, and one curving facing the sea, were certainly reminiscent of those for the White House. In stark contrast Bourne insisted on an undecorated landscape so that the house rose up from the landscape without relief or mediation."[18] Vast it was. Indian Neck Hall covered a space 300 feet long by 125 feet deep, the size of a football field. On its three floors and in its basement there were a hundred rooms. A twenty-seven-acre front lawn ran down to the bay with not a tree on it. The landmark was then and still is visible from miles away by sailors on the Great South Bay. It may well have been Bourne's intention to do without trees, but one must remember that the land had been recently filled and much of the waterfront in 1900 was barren of any foliage.

Henry Hutchinson Hollister lived on Johnson Avenue (later St. Mark's Lane) from 1886 until his death. Pictured here in 1899 at the age of 58. (Courtesy of the New York Public Library.)

Schuyler Livingston Parsons, 1852-1917, married Helena Johnson in 1877. He was W. K. Vanderbilt's close friend. He is pictured here in 1911 at age 59. (Courtesy of *Untold Friendships* by Schuyler L. Parsons, Jr.).

Captain Hank Haff of Islip shown here at the wheel of *Volunteer,* America's Cup defender in 1887 (from a contemporary drawing in The Illustrated London News).

William Dick, 1823-1912, of Williamsburg, Brooklyn, and Ocean Avenue, Islip. Sugar refiner and banker, he first summered along the Great South Bay in 1889.

Volunteer winning the America's Cup against the challenger *Thistle* (far right) of the Royal Clyde Yacht Club in 1887. (Courtesy of The Old Print Shop.)

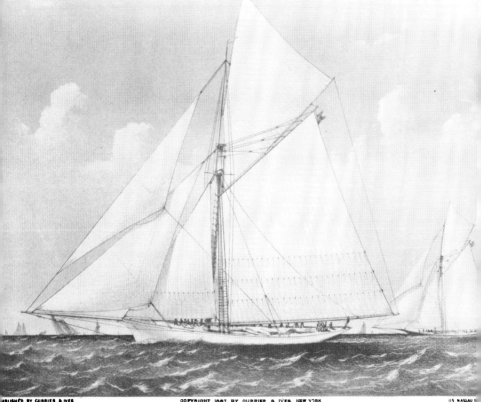

SLOOP YACHT "VOLUNTEER"

Modelled by Edward Burgess of Boston for Genl. C. J. Paine
STEEL HULL BUILT BY PUSEY & JONES, WILMINGTON DEL. SPARS BY GEO. LAWLEY & SON, SOUTH BOSTON.
SAILS BY WILSON & GRIFFIN NEW YORK.

The Scotsman John
Gibb, 1829-1905, built
his home *Afterglow* on
Ocean Avenue in Islip.
He was a dry goods
merchant in Brooklyn.
(Courtesy of the New York
Public Library.)

Charles A. Schieren
lived on Ocean Avenue,
Islip, next to Gibb and
Dick. He was the
mayor of Brooklyn in
1894 and 1895. (Courtesy
of the New York Public
Library.)

The inner court of the French chateau-like home of Mr. and Mrs. Christopher Robert, later called *Peperidge Hall,* in Oakdale. It was built from 1890-94. (Courtesy of Mr. and Mrs. Jack Davies and the W. K. Vanderbilt Historical Society.)

Bradish Johnson, Jr., 1851-1918, lifelong resident of the South Shore and pillar of *St. Mark's Church* in Islip. (Courtesy of Mariette Russell and the W. K. Vanderbilt Historical Society.)

It took three years to complete the mansion and the various improvements on the estate. Some of its special features were three miles of trout-filled canals dug throughout the property, thereby draining the land and providing needed fill. Artificial lakes were created for canoeing, a sport Mrs. Bourne enjoyed. Over 10,000 trees were planted to the north of the house. An entire farm was built to the east of the Hall and Bourne would become known for his champion show horses and his cattle. The entrance drive from the Country Road was a tree-lined straight path which crossed a brick and marble bridge over his canal, said to cost $30,000. In 1912, a clock tower was built to the west of the house from which the chimes rang on the quarter-hour day and night in the tones of Big Ben in London.

The interior of the mansion reflected as much care as the grounds. Unique to the Bournes' home were a skating rink, bowling alley, Turkish bath, and swimming pool, all in the basement with the boilers. The former choirboy had installed in the music room a pipe organ which he found so unsatisfactory that he replaced it in 1908 with a 7,000 pipe organ which its builder, the Aeolian Company, said was "the largest and most complete house organ in the world." It cost Bourne over $100,000 and to achieve the proper acoustics the music room was enlarged to 100 by 40 feet in size.

The housewarming party was held on February 9, 1900, the Bournes' twenty-fifth wedding anniversary. Hundreds of guests were invited, many from New York City on a special train. The current military hero Admiral Dewey, the victor at Manila Bay, came with his wife, as did many of New York Society. The Bournes had not as yet been accepted by Mrs. Astor, but they were taking the traditional path that the Vanderbilts had taken in 1883, entertaining on a huge scale. The *New York Times* commented about the Bourne party, "The entire house was a bower of flowers. The large drawing room was given up to dancing, and the guests were received in the music and morning rooms. The floral decorations were ropes and festoons of laurel and white roses, the latter covered with silver spangles. There was also a profusion of palms, ferns, and banks of lilies and azaleas." It was hard to imagine it was February outside. "Mr. and Mrs. Bourne met their guests in the main hall. Mrs. Bourne was assisted in the receiving by her sister, Mrs. Ballard."[19] The Bournes had a proper country home and a large family. At Indian Neck Hall Bourne could enjoy his family as well as the many avocations that struck his fancy, the principal one of which was yachting.

While Indian Neck Hall was under construction Bourne had a canal from the bay and a boat basin dredged out to accommodate his fleet of boats. A boat house was also built at that time. Later in 1902 he had a special berth dug in the basin to accommodate his 81-foot steam yacht *Artemis*. In 1908 a new and larger boat house was built, which is there today. *Artemis* was one of the largest yachts ever to steam on the bay. Designed to draw only 3 1/2 feet, it just managed to avoid grounding in that shallow body of water. *Artemis* was not, however, Bourne's largest yacht.

In 1902 Bourne was given the signal honor in the yachting world of being elected vice commodore of the most prestigious yacht club in America, the New York Yacht Club, and in 1903 he became its commodore. As such he had to have a flagship that would compare with J. P. Morgan's *Corsair III* (302 feet long) and W. K. Vanderbilt's *Valiant* (331 feet long). It was a matter of status. In England he purchased the steam yacht which he called *Delaware*. She was 350 feet long and had a crew of over a hundred, a truly appropriate flagship for the new commodore. Of course she could not enter the Great South Bay and was usually berthed at the New York Yacht Club dock in Hoboken, New Jersey.* As none of the NYYC races were ever held on the bay, it did not matter at all that *Delaware* was just too large. Bourne had another steam yacht, *Colonia*, 189 feet long, as a back up flagship. When *Delaware* was damaged by fire at the Hoboken dock in 1905, *Colonia* took her place as the flagship.

Bourne was involved with the competition to defend the America's Cup. In 1901 he was a part of the syndicate that

---

* Site of the original NYYC clubhouse, 1846.

built the yacht *Constitution* along with August Belmont II, Colonel Oliver H. Payne, and James Stillman. *Constitution*, however, lost out to *Columbia* in the trials for the right to defend that year. In 1903 he was the New York Yacht Club's commodore when the club chose the giant yacht *Reliance* to defend the Cup. In the era of huge steam yachts and massive sailing boats, *Reliance* was the largest single-masted sailing yacht ever built. Nathaniel Herreshoff again surpassed his previous winners with a 143-foot-long hull with a massive bow and stern overhang of 53 feet to come within the 90-foot waterline rule limit. The mast was 196 feet high, equal in height to a 20-story building. *Reliance* was able to carry 16,000 square feet of sail without capsizing. The mainsail alone weighed one and one half *tons*. Skippered by the veteran Charlie Barr with a crew of sixty-six able-bodied seamen, *Reliance* easily defeated Sir Thomas Lipton's *Shamrock III* from Great Britain in all four races. Bourne was surely pleased.

Bourne was considered one of the most popular commodores the New York Yacht Club ever had. He was a generous man who entertained a great deal and his warm friendly manner drew many to him. He became a great friend of the British tea merchant and perennial Cup challenger Sir Thomas Lipton. Bourne was Lipton's guest aboard his yacht for the naval review off Cowes in honor of the coronation of King Edward VII in 1902. Sir Thomas was often Bourne's guest at Indian Neck Hall and at the New York Yacht Club. Bourne's term as commodore ended in 1905, but he was known by that title for the rest of his life.

At Indian Neck Hall Bourne kept a fleet of many boats smaller than the 81-foot *Artemis*. The 1902 yearbook of the Penataquit Corinthian Yacht Club lists him with *Artemis*, a power launch *Maisie*, the 67-foot steam yacht *Scat*, the sloop *Ginty*, the 48-foot sloop *Reverie*, and the catboat *Meriam*. *Reverie* was designed and built by Gil Smith of Patchogue and was a particularly fast bay racing sloop.

Bourne's tremendous energy and drive brought worldwide success to Singer. It also brought him involvement in

many different sports, including yacht racing, horse showing, and auto racing, and caused him to join many clubs.
Today he would be looked upon as the quintessential club
man. At one time or another, Bourne belonged to fifteen
clubs. There were five yacht clubs, the South Side Sportsmen's
Club, which he joined in 1890, the Westbrook Golf Club, the
Short Beach Club, and the Penataquit Corinthian Yacht Club,
all in the bay area, and several others. In New York City he
was a member of the Metropolitan Club and the Racquet and
Tennis Club, but interestingly, not the Union Club. Perhaps
he still had not quite arrived.

Generosity of spirit would best characterize Frederick
Bourne. He was a contributor to many organizations both in
Oakdale and New York City. He restored the historic St.
John's Church, Oakdale, after he had bought the property on
which it stood from Ludlow's son in 1912. He was a large
benefactor of the Oakdale chapter of the Red Cross during
World War I and gave to various local hospitals. In 1914
Bourne, perhaps remembering his youth as a choirboy in
Trinity Church and later at the Church of the Incarnation,
gave a $500,000 endowment gift to the Cathedral School at
St. John the Divine to support the choir school there. As a
condition of this gift he asked that he be made a member of
the Cathedral choir. He was elected unanimously. Finally
through his will, he remembered many more charities, including Emmanuel Church in Great River and St. Ann's Episcopal Church in Sayville.

On March 9, 1919, Frederick G. Bourne died at Indian
Neck Hall two years after his wife. He was sixty-seven years
old. The bishop of New York, the Right Reverend David
Greer, came to Oakdale to conduct the funeral in his home.
The choir of St. John the Divine, of which he had been a
member, came by train to sing with the organist playing
Bourne's large organ in his music room. Following the service his body was transported by train to Brooklyn where it
was laid to rest in a mausoleum in Greenwood Cemetery that
had been designed for him and his family by his friend,
Ernest Flagg.

At the time of his death, Bourne's fortune was estimated to be worth $48 million. The grand estate in Oakdale, left to members of his family in his will, did not long remain with them. In 1926 most of it was sold to the La Salle Military Academy, including the mansion and much of the grounds, which still owns it today. Only Bourne's son, Arthur, and his daughter, Florence, who had married Anson Wales Hard, stayed on in homes they had built on the vast property. By 1966 they and their heirs had gone as well.

Indian Neck Hall was the last of the vast estates to be developed along the bay. Originally complete in 1900, it was changed and enlarged again in 1907–08 under the direction of Flagg. By the time of Bourne's death only Mrs. William Bayard Cutting at Westbrook remained of the four original great estate builders: Vanderbilt, Cutting, Robert, and Bourne. To those who came in the new century, size of property was not an important factor. Moreover, there was no longer any waterfront land available that measured in the hundreds of acres, as was the case for the original estate builders.

"A GOOD MAN GONE" headlined the local paper on November 12, 1892, when Bradish Johnson died. It was the *Signal*'s way of identifying a milestone in the history of the summer residents who had settled from Oakdale to Babylon along the Great South Bay. The patriarch and first of many residents had died in his home, Sans Souci, west of Bay Shore village. He was eighty-one years old at the time of his death and was survived by a large family of four daughters and three sons. His wife Louisa, three sons, and a daughter had died before him. He had been fortunate in his waning years to have had several of his children near him. His eldest daughter, Lucy Carroll, lived on the South Country Road between Bay Shore and Islip. His sons, Bradish, Henry, and Effingham, lived nearby and his youngest daughter, Helena Parsons, lived on St. Mark's Lane with her husband Schuyler. There were also many grandchildren to lighten his last days. With fifty years along the bay, Bradish Johnson surely deserved the acclaim he received and the title of patriarch. A founder of the South Side Club and one of the first vestrymen of St. Mark's Church, Johnson had seen the area grow from two sleepy villages surrounded by woods and bay to a thriving summer spa where New York's prominent families wanted to come. He himself had had much to do with that transformation and he was justifiably proud. He had lived at Sans Souci as a widower for twenty-two years, but that sadness must have been somewhat alleviated by the devotion of his family.

Following Johnson's death, his children who lived on the South Shore made new plans. His son Henry M. Johnson, who was always called Harry, took over the homestead, Sans Souci, where he lived until his death in 1907. Harry had been born there and died there fifty-two years later. He was survived by his widow and a daughter by his first wife, named Louisa Anna after her grandmother. Louisa had also been born at Sans Souci in 1893.

Bradish Johnson's eldest daughter, Lucy, who had married Dr. Alfred L. Carroll, decided to build a new "cottage" and purchased the land south of the Country Road and directly west of Awixa Pond from Daniel D. Conover. There she built an elegant villa in which she lived until 1907 when it was bought by J. Dunbar Adams of Brooklyn.

Johnson's youngest child, Effingham, took over the cottage that Johnson owned on the Country Road at the corner of Penataquit Avenue in Bay Shore. He and his wife, Amy Scott Johnson, spent most of their time in France, however, where Effingham died in 1897 survived by his widow and one daughter.

It was Bradish Johnson Jr. and his wife, Aimee Gaillard Johnson, whom he had married at St. Mark's Church in 1877, who had the most lasting impact as leader of the summer community. Knowing that his brother Harry would inherit Sans Souci, Bradish Jr. (as was the custom then, he dropped the Jr. from his name following his father's death) had been searching for a home. In December 1892 he was able to buy the house and twenty-six acres of property from C. T. Harbeck on Pavilion Road, south of the hotel and fronting on Champlin's Creek in East Islip. It was the same land that

Harbeck had bought from James Boorman Johnston in 1880. Bradish and Aimee called their house Woodland after his father's sugar plantation in Plaquemine Parish, Louisiana. They happily moved in with their two sons, Bradish G. and Aymar Johnson, ages fifteen and ten, in the summer of 1893. Their third child, a daughter, Marie Gaillard, was not born until 1896. The family would remain on this land for fifty years.

Bradish Johnson Jr. had been born in 1851 in New York City, making him the same age as W. K. Vanderbilt and his circle who came to the South Shore in the 1880s. Johnson, because his mother was a Lawrance, was considered "Old Family" and very much a part of New York social life. He was a Patriarch, a member of the Union and Knickerbocker Clubs and of the St. Nicholas Society. He always maintained a town house in the city. He spent much time managing the family resources, and in so doing became a director of several large corporations including the Equitable Life Assurance Society founded by Bay Shore neighbor Henry B. Hyde. On the South Shore he was a member of the South Side Club and a devoted leader of St. Mark's Church where he served as churchwarden from 1892 until 1915, all following the tradition set by his father.

Bradish and Aimee lived in Woodland in East Islip each summer until October 1905 when a fire completely destroyed their three-story home. Unlike the disastrous nighttime fires at the Pavilion Hotel and the Wharton house a decade earlier, the fire at Woodland began in the daytime under the roof and was thought to have been started by a defective chimney flue. It burned slowly, so slowly that almost all the contents of the house could be removed with the help of firemen and neighbors. "Even the family safe was rolled out."[20] The house could have been saved with minimal damage but for the lack of water. As with the earlier fires, the small hydrant did not produce sufficient water pressure to help at all, and the firemen could only watch the house burn to the ground. Bradish Johnson sent a card of thanks to the newspaper; "I wish to offer most sincere and cordial thanks to the firemen of Islip, East Islip, and Bay Shore, and to the large body of willing citizens, who so promptly on the alarm of fire came to my grounds to render their assistance, and for the good work done by them. Had there been sufficient water their efforts would have brought better results, and my residence now in ashes, would probably have suffered but slight damage. [Signed] Bradish Johnson."[21]

Woodland did indeed rise from its ashes. The Johnsons engaged Isaac H. Green Jr. to design the new home, which was ready by the fall of 1909, and in which they lived for the rest of their lives. Bradish died in 1918 and Aimee in 1929. Their second son, Aymar Johnson, inherited Woodland after his mother's death, and continued to own it until 1942 when he died. His widow then sold it to the Hewlett School of East Islip, a private school that uses it today.

During the first half of the 1890s many New York and Brooklyn families continued to come to the South Shore. It seemed then as though there was no end of those wanting to summer along the Great South Bay. This happened in spite of the financial panic of 1893 that ended the boom years and brought about a four-year depression. Neither the New York Stock Exchange collapse in May, nor the 4,000 bank failures and 14,000 business failures around the country that year, nor the violence, strikes, and Coxey's Army marching on Washington for relief in 1894, slowed the procession of those settling into the area from Oakdale to Babylon. It was reported that stock brokers H. Duncan Wood and Henry H. Hollister were heavy losers in the panic, and it is likely that the other bankers and brokers who commuted to New York with them also suffered losses.

In spite of this, normal life went on along the South Shore; the cottages were all rented for the summer of 1893, and some new arrivals were being reported. H. G. Timmerman of New York, a stockbroker with the firm of Timmerman, Moore and Schley, rented on Maple Avenue, Bay Shore, that summer, as did Juan Manuel Ceballos of New York on Awixa Avenue. It was the first summer for both of these families, who would later buy homes of their own. Timmerman acquired the Howard Gibb house on Ocean Avenue, Islip, in 1898, and Ceballos bought the Mowbray house on the north side of the South Country Road between Saxton Avenue and Brentwood Road in 1895. Part of the house had been occupied by Mowbrays for 175 years. As has been said, from Brooklyn came Robert A. Pinkerton, son of the founder of the Pinkerton Detective Agency, who rented on Ocean Avenue, Bay Shore,* as well as John Mollenhauer, the sugar refiner and his family, who located on the west side of Awixa Avenue in Bay Shore. All four of these families would remain for many years and make their mark on the growing summer community.

The depression of 1893 did not deter another Livingston from building a home on land he had bought overlooking Awixa Creek to the north of Edward S. Knapp on Saxton Avenue. He had previously rented the John I. Lawrance cottage west of Bay Shore and the Conover cottage on Saxton Avenue. Apparently he preferred Saxton Avenue. He was the second prominent New Yorker to settle there after Knapp.

Henry Beekman Livingston was a distant cousin of Robert Cambridge Livingston and Schuyler Livingston Parsons of St. Mark's Lane, Islip. Along with them he was descended from Robert Livingston, the founder, but through the line of Robert R. Livingston, the chancellor,** whose mother was a Beekman. Thus he was descended as well from William Beekman, who came to New Amsterdam with Governor Peter Stuyvesant in 1647, earlier even than the arrival of Robert Livingston.*** Henry was born in 1855 in New York City, the

---

* R. A. Pinkerton purchased the Montgomery house on Montgomery Avenue, Bay Shore, in 1899, after renting it since 1894.

** Robert R. Livingston, the chancellor, gave the oath of office to President-elect George Washington in Federal Hall, New York City, April 30, 1789.

*** William Beekman was born in the Cologne district of North Germany, moved to the Netherlands as a teenager, and came to the New World in 1647. He married Catherine Van Boogh, had five sons and one daughter, and died in 1717. He was the progenitor of the family in America. Beekman Place in Manhattan was named for him.

son of Henry B. Livingston Sr. and Mary Lawrence Livingston. After a short first marriage and the birth of a daughter, Angelica, Henry in 1880 married Frances Redmond who was six years older than he was. Frances was the daughter of William Redmond of New York and the sister of Roland Redmond who was president of the South Side Club and a summer resident in Islip. Henry and Frances Livingston had two daughters, Frances and Lilias. Naturally with their background they were a much entertained young couple and were among those four hundred people invited to Mrs. Astor's ball in 1892.

Henry Livingston was a member of the New York Stock Exchange from 1883 until his retirement. He must have suffered losses in the panic of 1893, but they were probably small. The South Shore provided compatible friends for Livingston and his wife, and most important for his three daughters, who were quickly reaching marriageable age. A typical Victorian shingle-style home with a large porch and many gables was built in the fall of 1893 on Saxton Avenue where this Livingston family would remain for two decades.

Naturally, as the sons and daughters of the first summer families grew up together and saw each other in the summer as well as in the winter in New York City, many marriages between them took place. Most of these weddings were conducted by the rector of St. Mark's Church together with the rector of the bride's New York City church. They were large, festive occasions, usually held at the home of the bride's family, as the many guests from the city and the local area could not possibly fit into St. Mark's Church.* Among the earliest of these were the Hollins-Knapp, Parsons-Johnson, Johnson-Gaillard, and Knapp-Lawrance weddings. In the next generation, many more such marriages would take place. One of these was the union of the Livingston's youngest daughter, Lilias, to Harry B. Hollins Jr., son of the Hollins of Meadowfarm, East Islip. The young couple were married on June 20, 1904, at the Livingston home on Saxton Avenue. It

---

* St. Mark's was enlarged in 1893, doubling the seats.

was the notable event of the social season that year in the Islip community. "The ceremony was witnessed by a very large assemblage of relatives and friends, a special train of three coaches bringing many guests from the city. Rev. Bridges, Rector of St. Mark's P.E. Church, and the Rev. Dr. Huntington of Grace Church* officiated. A wedding breakfast was served immediately after the ceremony by caterers from Delmonico's. . . . Among the many prominent families present were those of H.H. Hollister, W.H. Wharton, H.R. Duval, Harry K. Knapp, Mrs. Edward S. Knapp, Bradish Johnson, Harry M. Johnson, and many others."[22]

As the Livingstons were building on Saxton Avenue in the early 1890s, others were beginning a long association with the area. From New York, Courtlandt D. Moss, a dry goods merchant with Lawrence, Taylor & Company, and his family rented the Meeks house on the west side of Champlin's Pond in 1890 for the decade. They called their home the Ramble. It was here that their daughter Camilla was married on October 16, 1890, to young Charles F. Havemeyer, known by his friends as "Carley." The groom was the eldest son of the sugar refiner Theodore A. Havemeyer.** The wedding was described by the *New York Herald* on October 17, 1890, as "one of the brilliant social events of the year," in every way similar to the Livingston-Hollins union. Guests in attendance included Mr. and Mrs. W. Bayard Cutting of Westbrook, and Mr. and Mrs. R. Fulton Cutting. It was said that Carley's parents were opposed to the marriage. He was only twenty-three at the time and his mother, a devout Roman Catholic, could not have looked favorably upon her son being married in the Episcopal ceremony. The marriage was shaky from the start. Camilla was considered a beauty, "a very handsome girl, and after her marriage one of the leading young matrons

---

* Grace Church on Broadway and Tenth Street was considered the most fashionable New York City church in that era.

** Theodore A. Havemeyer was the older brother of Henry O. Havemeyer of St. Mark's Lane.

in the very fashionable set."[23] A son was born to them in 1892 whom they called Teddy. In 1898 Camilla was pregnant again when Carley was found dead, a pistol at his side. The coroner ruled that the death was accidental, but most accounts said he had committed suicide. Camilla's second child, a son, was named Charles F. Havemeyer after his late father. Camilla's parents died soon thereafter, her mother in 1899 and her father in 1901.* The Ramble was to pass into the hands of Mr. and Mrs. J. Ives Plumb, who finally decided to leave the old mansion on Deer Range Farm and sell it to George C. Taylor.

Also from New York, George H. Macy came to rent a cottage on Penataquit Avenue in Bay Shore for the summer of 1891. Macy was descended from an old Nantucket seafaring family. His sons, T. Ridgeway Macy and W. Kingsland Macy, grew up along the Great South Bay. Kingsland Macy literally married the girl next door, Julia Dick, William Dick's granddaughter, and went on to a long political career in the Republican party in Suffolk County.

From Brooklyn in the mid 1880s came the theatrical producer Richard Hyde (no relation of Henry B. Hyde, owner of the Oaks). Richard Hyde's property was west of the Oaks, between Colt and Turnbull. It went from the bay to north of the LIRR tracks. A keen sailor, Hyde built a 2,000-foot canal north from the bay to a boat basin where his sailboat, *Gaiety*, was moored. The canal was lined up directly with the Fire Island lighthouse, which could be seen flashing at night from the basin. Hyde also built a nine-hole golf course on his land south of South Country Road as Cutting had done at Westbrook. It was called the Bay Shore Golf Club** and used the canal as a water hazard. The clubhouse, designed by Charles Birdsall after a Swiss chalet, was built in 1899. It

---

* Their daughter Natalie married Johnston Livingston, the son of Mrs. Robert C. Livingston of St. Mark's Lane, in May 1901.

** In 1903 the South Shore Field Club succeeded to the Bay Shore Golf Club. Hyde resigned as secretary and treasurer, but continued to own the land which he leased to the club. The new club added tennis courts at this time.

stands today and is owned by Mrs. Neil Riesing. Hyde's daughter, Lillian, became a champion golfer, joining Marion Hollins of East Islip as the area's most accomplished lady golfers. Hyde died in 1912.

Also from Brooklyn came Thomas Adams Jr. to first rent in Bay Shore and then in 1895 to acquire the property of the late Robert O. Colt between Richard Hyde and Henry B. Hyde on South Country Road. Adams was the eldest son of the pioneer chewing gum manufacturer, whose firm Adams & Sons was later merged into the American Chicle Company. As the developer of the Chiclet, the Adams family made a fortune. Thomas Adams Jr., his brother J. Dunbar Adams, and his son-in-law George Ellis, would be longtime residents of Bay Shore.

Lastly, between Richard Hyde and Sagtikos Manor, George R. Turnbull of New York built his house in 1889. Turnbull was a native New Yorker who had fought in the Civil War as a very young man, and later made a successful career in banking. He lived in his Bay Shore home until his death there in 1909.

These were some of the more prominent New York and Brooklyn families who had settled the area from Oakdale to Babylon by 1895.

The year 1895 was to see another challenge for the America's Cup by the same team that had lost two years before, the Earl of Dunraven and the designer George L. Watson. Watson's new boat was named *Valkyrie III*. She was 129 feet in length overall and carried an enormous sail area of over 13,000 square feet, the biggest boat yet to challenge. To meet this formidable British yacht a new American boat had to be built. The cost would be large and the head of the syndicate, C. Oliver Iselin, asked J. Pierpont Morgan and W. K. Vanderbilt to join him, which they willingly did. Again, Nat Herreshoff was entrusted with the job of building a faster boat. The American yacht, *Defender*, had a keel (as opposed to a centerboard) for the first time and was constructed of steel and bronze with aluminum topsides to save weight. To skipper *Defender*, the syndicate turned to the

Islip veteran Captain Hank Haff, who would have the most severe test in his career, as the two boats were remarkably similar and thought to be of equal speed. It would be up to the skipper and crew to make the difference.

As it turned out the contest was filled with controversy. Dunraven accused Haff of cheating by adding ballast in the hold of his boat. Then, because of concern about the large number of spectator craft — it was estimated that fifty thousand people would be in boats watching the contest — Dunraven asked that the races be moved to Marblehead. The race committee refused his request. What he feared would happen came to pass at the start of the second race. "As *Valkyrie* and *Defender* made for the line, a large steamer, the *Yorktown*, blundered across their bows, cutting between them, and when the two contestants came together again they seemed about to collide . . . *Valkyrie* was to weather of *Defender*, and just before they reached the line, the skipper of *Valkyrie*, seeing that he would hit *Defender* if Hank Haff, who had the right of way, held his course, luffed up. As *Valkyrie* turned, the end of her boom raked *Defender*'s deck, and snatching her starboard shrouds from the crosstrees, it snapped the topmast stay with a sound like a pistol shot. *Defender*'s topmast bent like a bow. Haff then spun her head to the wind as Mr. Iselin hoisted the red protest flag."[24]

Captain Hank was able to rig a temporary stay to save his mast. He sailed that race without a jib topsail and with a bent topmast. His skill and seamanship were such that in spite of such an enormous handicap he lost only by 47 seconds. The protest committee later judged that *Valkyrie* had fouled *Defender* and was thus disqualified. In response Lord Dunraven again complained of the interference by spectator craft and was so infuriated that he refused to compete in the third race, dropped his racing flag, and went back to England. Haff had won the America's Cup for the second time.* A later

---

* Only three skippers would surpass that record with three victories apiece: Charles Barr in 1899, 1901, and 1903; Islip-born Harold S. Vanderbilt in 1930, 1935, and 1937; Dennis Connor in 1980, 1987, and 1988.

inquiry about the extra ballast charge found Haff and the crew without blame. His reputation was intact and he returned home in October to the acclaim of one and all. "Islip's brass band and a delegation of citizens met Captain Haff at the depot and escorted him to his home in the lower portion of the village, amid the cheers of the populace. The commander of *Defender* enjoyed the attention hugely, and thanked the citizens most cordially for this demonstration of their regard."[25]

Hank Haff, earlier that summer, had undergone an operation to remove a cancerous growth in his upper jawbone. Part of the bone was removed and the operation considered a success. He soon returned to sailing. His final years, however, were never free of pain. Following his triumph with *Defender*, he remained ashore for two summers, then sailed again until he retired for good in 1903. Cancer finally reoccurred, and after months of suffering Captain Hank died at his Islip home on July 6, 1906, at the age of sixty-eight. His wife had died the year before. He was lain to rest in the Oakwood Cemetery on Brentwood Road. Islip's most famous sailor with his distinctive full white beard was gone. "Captain Haff's career," summed up the paper, "was as remarkable as it was honorable. He possessed a natural gift for the avocation that made him famous in the yachting world and acquired a knowledge that he used at the right time and which gave him a fame that will last as long as there are international yacht races."[26]

Throughout the Gilded Age affluent New Yorkers were accustomed to frequent European travel. A few owned chateaux in France or villas in fashionable resorts elsewhere on the continent. Wives and daughters needed dresses designed by Worth in Paris. Many families went to Italy to refresh their spirits and to acquire works of art. The European trip by luxurious steamer became an annual event in some families and a frequent one in most. One result of this custom was that eligible daughters were introduced to European society and often marriage would follow, sometimes to titled gentlemen. Rarely did sons marry European ladies. When the family did travel abroad, their country home was often rented for the season to friends, who were thus introduced to the area. Several families who ultimately built on the South Shore of Long Island were introduced to it in this way.

The Lawrance family of Manatuck Farm in Bay Shore frequently traveled to Pau, France, located in the foothills of the Pyrennees near the resort of Biarritz. This was a favorite spot for the English and the Germans as well as for the French. It was here that Miss Fanny Lawrance, daughter of Francis Cooper Lawrance and his wife, Frances Garner Lawrance, met George William Henry Vernon, the seventh Baron Vernon of Sudbury Hall in Derbyshire, England. * Within a month Fanny's parents announced the couple's engagement and in July of 1885 they were married in St. George's Church in London surrounded by Dukes, Earls, and Barons. The newspaper noted, "The bridegroom refused any marriage portion (dowry), although Mr. Lawrance is a very wealthy man and would have been very glad to have given a large dowry to his daughter."[27] This was not to be the usual case in the many marriages to follow. Fanny Lawrance, henceforth Lady Vernon, was the first bride from the South Shore to marry into English nobility.

When tragedy struck the Garner family in 1876 (see chapter V) with the drowning of Commodore William T. Garner and his wife, his sister Frances G. Lawrance took the three orphaned daughters to France where they were subsequently brought up. Mrs. Lawrance took a house in Paris and a villa in Pau, and the Garner girls, like their cousin Fanny Lawrance, were introduced to European gentlemen. With the $10 million estate left to them by their father, each was a desirable catch. The eldest, Marcellite, married Henri Charles Joseph le Tonnelie, the Marquis de Breteuil. ** The suave, dashing

---

*   Sudbury Hall is now owned by the National Trust. The seventeenth century house is richly decorated and famous for its wood carvings by Grinling Gibbons.

** Breteuil was a member of the Chamber of Deputies for fifteen years.

French aristocrat was a popular figure in both French and English social circles. As a member of the Marlborough set, the Prince of Wales enjoyed his company. He was an "intimate" friend of Jennie Churchill, who expressed her chagrin when his marriage to Marcellite Garner was announced. "I hope Breteuil's wife will keep sane," she snidely commented. Jennie's husband, Lord Randolph Churchill, was in the latter stages of his fatal illness at the time, and it was thought that Jennie had wanted Breteuil to wait for her. They remained close friends, however, and Breteuil and Marcellite would often entertain Jennie and her son, Winston Churchill, in their Paris home.

Marcellite's sister, Florence Garner, made a tragic marriage to an Englishman twenty-three years older than she was. "She was totally unfitted," said her daughter, "to the milieu in which she lived."[28] Early in 1890, twenty-one-year-old Florence became engaged to Sir William Gordon-Cumming, Baronet, of Gordonstoun* in Scotland where he owned over forty thousand acres of land. Gordon-Cumming was a brilliant soldier and sportsman, but also a high-living club man, once described by *The Sporting Times* as "possibly the handsomest man in London, and certainly the rudest." He was a friend of the Prince of Wales and regular attendee at those weekend house parties that so characterized the Marlborough set. It was at one of these that the trouble began.

During a country house party at Tranby Croft at which the Prince of Wales was present and sitting in on a game of baccarat (the Prince was a devotee of card games, which were a regular part of the weekend activity), Gordon-Cumming was accused by his host of cheating. In order to avert a scandal which would seriously embarrass the Prince, Gordon-Cumming admitted he had cheated and the other guests in return agreed to keep the whole matter quiet. How-

---

* The Gordonstoun estate, near the town of Elgin by the Moray Firth, is the site of the school of that name, founded in 1934 and attended by both Prince Philip, the Duke of Edinburgh, and by Prince Charles, the Prince of Wales.

ever, within days the story was spread all over the newspapers. The outraged Gordon-Cumming, to clear his name, insisted on bringing the matter to court. The Prince of Wales was subpoenaed as a witness, and his reputation plunged to the depths. He was accused by the Church of corrupting the middle classes. Gordon-Cumming lost his case and his reputation as well. He was banished forever from the "Society" that he craved. He tried to release his fiancée from their engagement, but Florence, believing him innocent, refused and the marriage took place quietly on June 10, 1891, at Holy Trinity Church, Sloane Square, in London. They were married by the curate and hurried away. The Prince of Wales in a letter to his son wrote, "Thank God — the Army and Society are now well rid of such a damned blackguard. The crowning point of his infamy is that he, this morning, married an American young lady, Miss Garner (sister to Mme de Breteuil), with money!"[29] Three days later the *Times* said, "Major and Lt. Colonel Sir William Gordon-Cumming, Baronet, is removed from the Army, Her Majesty having no further use for his services."

Their marriage began in gloom and continued in gloom. Florence tried to give parties at their castle in Gordonstoun, but they were failures. When a guest would make a pass at her, she demanded that her husband throw him out. Gordon-Cumming, who had made a career out of making passes at married women, including young Jennie Churchill fifteen years earlier, only replied, "My dear child, don't be so silly. You must learn to take care of yourself."[30] The marriage went from bad to worse. Gordon-Cumming brought a pair of girls to stay at Gordonstoun as his mistresses. Florence in response put on weight and retreated into religious seclusion. She was a victim of a society she could not understand and a way of life to which she could not adjust. She, like many of the American brides of that era, who were attracted by European nobility for their wealth, was not able to accept a standard of morality among the upper classes which was notoriously lax.

The year 1895 was a particularly notable one in American social history because it marked the peak year in international weddings. Nine American brides were married that year to English titled gentlemen. The trend had begun over twenty years earlier when young Jennie Jerome, magnetic daughter of New York merchant, broker, and horse-racing tycoon Leonard Jerome, had married Lord Randolph Churchill, the third son of the seventh Duke of Marlborough.[*] This union was widely publicized at the time on both sides of the ocean, and although it was far from a happy marriage (Churchill had contracted syphilis as a young man and died of the disease in 1895), it was to a great extent a role model for those that followed. Of the nine 1895 weddings, the one that caused the most comment was the marriage of an eighteen-year-old bride with a huge dowry who had grown up in Oakdale, Long Island, Consuelo Vanderbilt.

Consuelo was born in New York City in March 1877, the first child of William K. and Alva Vanderbilt. She was named after her godmother, Alva's childhood friend Consuelo Yznaga (later to become the Duchess of Manchester). The Yznagas were a wealthy Cuban-American family with considerable social standing in New York Society. After the completion of Idlehour in 1879 Consuelo Vanderbilt's family would spend spring, summer, and fall in their new country home. She grew very fond of the place by the Connetquot River and later looked back at her childhood there with happy memories. Life was so free and unstructured, so different from what was to come. It was not until the mid 1880s that her family began to rent a cottage in Newport, Rhode Island, for July and August, using Idlehour only in spring and fall. Since they had been accepted into New York Society by then and W. K. had come into his huge inheritance at the death of his father in 1885, Alva believed her growing daughter should be where the most fashionable people were summering. Mrs. Astor, of course, spent the summer season in Newport.

---

[*] They were wed in Paris on April 15, 1874.

Consuelo was educated entirely at home by governesses and tutors under the direction of her mother. She became a very accomplished young woman. She spoke three languages by the age of eight and conversed at home with her parents in French. Her mother did not spare the rod either. While reciting her lessons to her parents, she was required to wear a metal brace to improve her posture. She wrote, "We suffered a severe and rigorous upbringing. Corporal punishment for minor delinquencies was frequently administered with a riding whip. I have a vivid memory of the last such lashing my legs received as I stood by while my mother wielded her crop. I bore these punishments stoically, but such repressive measures bred inhibitions and even now [1952] I can trace their effects."[31] Consuelo was being molded by her mother for her destiny. Alva was shaping her daughter for the role of wife and mother in that highly structured gilded age, and for her daughter's husband Alva had set her sights very high indeed.

Part of this preparation included confirmation into the Episcopal Church. On May 31, 1893, at the age of sixteen, Consuelo was confirmed by Bishop Littlejohn of Long Island at St. Mark's Church in Islip. She was joined at that service by six other girls and boys, all of whom lived on St. Mark's Lane.* Consuelo remembered the occasion: "The deepest emotion of my young life was born in my confirmation. Bishop Littlejohn, then Bishop of Long Island, was our house guest, and the service took place in the church at Islip which my father helped to build. As I knelt at the altar rails I felt as if I were dedicating my life to God's service, and had anyone suggested my becoming a nun, I might indeed have considered changing the white muslin and veil I was wearing for the more sober garb of the convent. Preparing for this sacrament at a time when the widening rift between my parents was causing me sorrow rendered me particularly susceptible to the emotional appeal of Christianity."[32]

---

* Maud Maria Livingston, Johnston Livingston, George M. Wharton, Richard Wharton, Helena Johnson Parsons, and Lindsley Tappin.

By the time of Consuelo's confirmation the marriage of her parents was in name only. Their personalities were extremely incompatible. W. K. was a man's man, fond of sports and of smoking, drinking, and joking with his friends. As was so often the case in the society of that age, he had liaisons with other women. This double standard was usually tolerated by society provided it was discreetly observed. However it was not acceptable to Alva, and increasingly angry with W. K. she began a liaison of her own with Oliver H. P. Belmont, the third son of August Belmont. The situation between the Vanderbilts was well known to society and to their children as well. As Consuelo was being confirmed at St. Mark's the final blow-up was about to occur. She said, "As I grew older, I was increasingly happy to leave the artificial life of Newport and to return to 'Idlehour' in the autumn. Here when I was 16, a last peaceful interlude awaited me before our departure on a long cruise to India."[33]

On November 23, 1893, W. K. Vanderbilt, accompanied by Alva, Consuelo, and Alva's friend Oliver Belmont, departed on his new 331-foot steam yacht *Valiant* on its maiden voyage. By the end of the cruise in the spring of 1894, Alva had demanded a divorce from her husband, and while visiting the viceroy of India she had learned about his nephew, Charles Spencer-Churchill, the twenty-three-year-old ninth Duke of Marlborough and therefore the master of Blenheim Palace. Consuelo always believed that from that moment her mother was determined that she should become the Duchess. The cruise continued on to England in time for the June season in London where at a ball Consuelo first met her husband-to-be, the Duke, who was always known in his family as "Sunny." She had just turned seventeen. Although Alva was now intent on a divorce from W. K., she was more intent on arranging her daughter's marriage. Within two years she had succeeded in both endeavors.

Early in 1895 Alva obtained her divorce from W. K. She got the right to keep the Vanderbilt name, a large alimony, and Marble House in Newport, the $11 million mansion which W. K. had given to her several years earlier. She also received custody of her three children, removing them from any further contact with their father. W. K. retained the ownership of Idlehour, his official country seat. In spite of the social ostracism brought upon a woman in that era by divorce — in her words "society was by turns stunned, horrified, and then savage" — Alva and Consuelo went to Newport for the summer season of debutante parties. It would have been much worse for them there except for the support they received from none other than Mrs. Astor and her successor-to-be, Mrs. Stuyvesant Fish. When Caroline Astor invited them to her party, it was a sign to others that Alva had not entirely fallen from grace.

At Newport that summer Alva Vanderbilt began her campaign to capture the Duke of Marlborough for her daughter. Although Consuelo considered herself already pledged to New Yorker Winthrop Rutherfurd, her mother, when she learned of this, refused to allow her daughter to see him again. She told her daughter that she "had no right to choose a husband" and must take the man that Alva had chosen, i.e., the Duke. After some early resistance to her mother's iron will and heavy-handed crudeness, Consuelo finally consented. Consent had followed Alva's threat to shoot Rutherfurd and blame her daughter for his murder.

At a ball held at Marble House on August 28, Marlborough proposed and Consuelo accepted the offer to become his Duchess. Her father, who was not present for the party, agreed to his part of the bargain. Consuelo would go to England and Blenheim with a dowry of $100,000 per year for herself and another $100,000 per year for the Duke for the rest of their lives, together with a railroad stock worth $2,500,000 (with which to repair the deteriorating Blenheim Palace). The *New York Times* estimated the dowry to be worth between $15 and $20 million. The Duke and his mother-in-law-to-be had succeeded in their goals. Consuelo was committed to a marriage that would be as much a tragic mismatch as that of her parents.

On November 6, 1895, Fifth Avenue in New York was closed off to traffic from Seventy-second Street to Fifty-third

Street and the sidewalks were packed with spectators. Around St. Thomas's Church at Fifty-third Street the police were having difficulty controlling the crowds that were surging forward to catch a glimpse of the eighteen-year-old girl dressed in a white gown holding a bouquet of flowers. Consuelo had wept profusely for much of the morning. She was escorted to the church by her father. Because of Alva's recent divorce and the ostracism that followed, no other Vanderbilts were present at the church. In fact Alva had returned without a note of thanks all gifts that were sent by W. K.'s family. The Episcopal marriage ceremony was conducted by the bishop of New York, Henry Codman Potter, and it was mercifully short. As they left the church the Duke and Duchess of Marlborough were rushed by carriage to a ferry that took them across the East River to Long Island City where they boarded a special train for the hour journey to Oakdale. Consuelo herself continues the story:

> It was a relief to reach the little station of Oakdale, but there was no carriage awaiting us and we found ourselves surrounded by a large crowd. Rather than remain the objects of their curious scrutiny, we sallied forth on foot, accompanied by members of the press who were overjoyed at the scoop this bit of news would represent in the headlines the next day: 'Duke and Duchess start honeymoon on foot.'

> It was not long before the carriage found us and the gates of "Idlehour" closed behind us. Seeing my old house brought a flood of memories of happy days when my father and my mother had been united and I had my brothers as companions. How different from the present when alone I faced life with a comparative stranger. The house looked cheerful with its blazing fire in the living room hall from which wide steps of polished oak led to the landing above. Here my mother's room had been prepared for me and my room next door for Marlborough. A sudden realization of my complete innocence assailed me, bringing with it fear. Like a deserted child I longed for my family. The problem created by the marriage of two irreconcilable characters is a psychological one which deserves sympathy as well as understanding. In the hidden reaches where memory probes lie sorrows too deep to fathom.

> After a week's seclusion custom had imposed upon reluc-
> tant honeymooners, we returned to New York and spent
> an evening at the fashionable horse show, where our box
> was mobbed by crowds which policemen had to move
> along. It was pleasant to escape from the glare of publicity
> that was focused upon our every act, and I left the city with
> few regrets.[34]

The local papers did indeed take note of the Duke and
Duchess's week-long honeymoon in Oakdale: "The week spent
at 'Idlehour' by the much-talked-of couple was a quiet one for
them, they spending most of the time in driving about the
country and enjoying themselves in a modest quiet way. On
Sunday they attended divine worship at St. Mark's Church,
and heard the gospel expounded by Reverend H. L. Bridges.
Their stay here caused little interest among the more sensible members of the population, and the general impression
seems to have gone forth that the Duke may be 'all kinds of a
good fellow,' but if hung for his good looks or his brilliancy
he would be wronged out of his life."[35] In fact, Sunny was
almost a head shorter than his tall bride and wore the customary moustache of that era. When his wife's beauty was
being praised, he replied, "I don't like tall women."[36] Consuelo
much later remarked, "Of course, I cannot put in a book what
a beast Marlborough was."[37] His inheritance had not been a
good one. His father, the eighth Duke, was widely considered
"one of the most disreputable men ever to have debased the
highest rank in the British peerage."[38]

The week's honeymoon at Idlehour was followed by a
sea voyage back to England with a stop in Paris where
Consuelo could be properly outfitted by Worth for her new
role in life. Now that she was safely married, her mother's
ban on her seeing Vanderbilts was lifted and her father and
many of his family would come to Blenheim to visit her in the
years to follow. Within two months of Consuelo's wedding,
Alva Vanderbilt married Oliver H. P. Belmont in her home on
Seventy-second Street in New York. The mayor performed
the ceremony because no priest could be found who was

willing to do so, as both parties were divorced. Alva Vanderbilt Belmont had finally accomplished both her goals, and most remarkably was still accepted by New York Society.

Consuelo, as the Duchess of Marlborough, was a huge success, although the ten years that she lived with the Duke were filled with much pain and anguish. Immediately upon her arrival at Blenheim, Consuelo was warmly welcomed and henceforth given much moral support by her husband's aunt, Lady Randolph Churchill. Jennie Churchill, by then just widowed, but still the leader of the American women in Great Britain, became a close friend and confidante of the nineteen-year-old Duchess. Jennie was a young forty-one herself, old enough to be a surrogate mother, but young enough to be on the lookout for a new husband. Her guidance of Consuelo undoubtedly helped the new Duchess to learn what was expected of her. Fortunately for Consuelo, Sunny also deeply admired his aunt.

Expectations of Consuelo were many, but by far the most important and most urgent was for her to produce an heir to the Dukedom. The dowager Duchess told her within days of her arrival at Blenheim, "Your first duty is to have a child, and it must be a son, because it would be intolerable to have that little upstart Winston [Churchill] become Duke. Are you in the family way?"[39] Her answer could have been "No, not yet," for the Marlboroughs had to wait until September 18, 1897, for the birth of the heir, christened Albert Edward William John Churchill. (Albert Edward after the Prince of Wales, William after W. K. Vanderbilt, and John after the first Duke of Marlborough.) A second son, named Ivor Spencer-Churchill, arrived a year later.

Many of the American brides were resented by upper class English women. Their feeling was bitter and often expressed: "Why do not American girls marry Americans, and devote their talents and money to their own country?"[40] This was not the case with Consuelo, however, for she became very popular. The Prince of Wales liked her and invited the Marlboroughs to his weekends at Sandringham. Her fel-

low American bride, Mary Leiter Curzon, * knew herself to be
outshone by her compatriot. In May of 1896 they were together for a weekend at Hatfield, the ancestral home of the
then prime minister, Lord Salisbury, along with the Prince
and Princess of Wales, the Landsdownes, and the
Londonderrys. Mary Curzon said, "Everybody raves about
Consuelo, and she is very sweet in her great position, and
shyly takes her rank directly after royalty. She looks very
stately in her marvelous jewels, ** and she looks pretty and
had old lace which makes my mouth water. I never saw
pearls the size of nuts. In a grand party like this George
[Curzon] and I have rather to tag along with the rank and file,
but we are happy and don't mind being small fry."****[41] Nigel
Nicolson commented, "Consuelo never forfeited her essential Americanism." Her rank never went to her head in that
often arrogant and hierarchical society of Edwardian England.

Consuelo returned to America from time to time to connect with her former life. In spite of the harsh treatment she
had received from her mother, she maintained contact with
her and later spoke for the cause to which Alva was devoting

---

* Mary Leiter, daughter of the affluent Chicago retail merchant,
Levi Leiter, married George, Lord Curzon of Kedleston, the heir
of Lord Scarsdale, in St. John's Church, Lafayette Square, Washington, D.C., on April 22, 1895. She was one of the nine American
heiresses to marry English titled gentlemen that year. Mary was
seven years older than Consuelo Vanderbilt.

** As wedding presents her father gave her a diamond tiara; her
husband, a diamond belt to be worn as a stomacher; her mother,
pearl necklaces from the French and Russian royal collections,
which had been worn by both the Empress Eugénie of France
and the Empress Catherine of Russia.

**** Lord George Curzon and his wife, Mary, became the viceroy and
vicereine of India in 1899, and ruled until 1905. Mary fell ill while
in India, returned to England, and died in 1906 at the age of
thirty-six.

her life, women's suffrage. In September 1902 Consuelo, with her youngest brother Harold Vanderbilt, visited the new Idlehour for the first time. Her old home had burned to the ground in 1899. W. K. had commissioned Richard Howland Hunt, son of Richard Morris Hunt who was now deceased, to build the new Idlehour. W. K. wanted a mansion as grand as Frederick G. Bourne's Indian Neck Hall to the east. Idlehour was to be "essentially a luxurious private hotel." [42]

Consuelo and Harold lunched at the South Side Club but apparently did not spend the night. It was commented, "Time had dealt very lightly with her in the last five years and those who saw her said she was but little changed." [43] Five years later she again visited Idlehour, this time with her stepmother, Anne Harriman Sands Rutherfurd Vanderbilt.* She must have found these return visits poignant, filled as they were with happy childhood memories, yet reminding her of her unhappiness since then.

Finally in 1906 Sunny and Consuelo agreed upon a formal separation. She would live in London and have custody of their sons until their majority. Sunny's first cousin, Winston Churchill, wrote a letter to his mother, Jennie: "Sunny has definitely separated from Consuelo, who is in London at Sunderland House. Her father returns to Paris on Monday. I have suggested to her that you would be very willing to go and stay with her for a while, as I can not bear to think of her being all alone during these dark days. If she should send for you, I hope you will put aside other things and go to her. I know how you always are a prop to lean on in hard times." [44] Winston knew that his mother of all people could help this lonely twenty-nine-year-old mother bear her sorrows.

Consuelo was finally free of the man she had agreed to marry ten years earlier, and her life began to improve. She remained close to both her father and her mother. W. K. Vanderbilt and his second wife lived for most of the year at his stud farm in Normandy, where they had remained

---

* W. K. Vanderbilt had married for the second time in 1903.

through the Great War. Only occasionally did they return to New York, and Idlehour remained unused for years at a time. Since the new mansion was built, it had been used less than any mansion in America. Vanderbilt said at the end of his life, "My life was never destined to be quite happy. It was laid out along lines which I could foresee almost from my earliest childhood. It has left me with nothing to hope for, with nothing definite to seek or strive for. Inherited wealth is a real handicap to happiness. It is as certain as death to ambition as cocaine is to morality. If a man makes money, no matter how much, he finds a certain happiness in its possession, for in the desire to increase his business he has a constant use for it. The first satisfaction and the greatest, that of building the foundation of a fortune, is denied him. He must labour, if he does labour, simply to add to an over-sufficiency."[45] With Consuelo and Harold at his bedside in his Normandy chateau, on July 23, 1920, at the age of seventy, William K. Vanderbilt died of heart failure. According to one doctor, he died of a lifetime of heavy smoking. He once averaged a box of cigars a day! Consuelo and Harold took his body home to be laid to rest in the family mausoleum on Staten Island* beside his grandfather, the old Commodore.

In spite of W. K.'s gigantic expenditures of money, his estate after taxes (they were very low in 1920) amounted to $53 million. Because he was officially a resident of Idlehour at the time of his death, Suffolk County collected $2 million, the largest inheritance tax it ever collected up to that time. St. Mark's Church received a $50,000 bequest. Consuelo's sons received a million dollars each and she had been given an outright gift of $15 million just prior to her father's death. His two sons were the remaining beneficiaries, each receiving $21 million. Idlehour, valued at $550,000, went to Harold.

---

* The Vanderbilt Mausoleum was designed by Richard Morris Hunt and is in the Moravian Cemetery in New Dorp, Staten Island.

Consuelo later described her father's death: "I was with him to the end. Whatever his sufferings he made no complaints; not even a gesture of ill-humor troubled the serenity he seemed to emanate. There was a fineness around him that one sensed clearly, and it seemed to me that nothing ignoble would ever touch him. In his business and in his life he lived up to the high standard of integrity he had set himself."[46]

Frank Crowninshield eulogized him as "the greatest supporter of sport, opera, yachting, racing, art, architecture, coaching, and the theater in the American social annals." He surely left his mark wherever he went and very much so along the Great South Bay.

A year after her father's death, Consuelo obtained a divorce from Marlborough, left England, and married a French aviator and financier, Lieutenant Colonel Jacques Balsan. The union was supported by Alva, who then admitted that she had forced her daughter into the tragic first marriage. Jacques and Consuelo lived in France until 1940. They had a home in Paris, built a villa in Eze-sur-Mer on the Riviera, and later bought a chateau in Dreux, fifty miles north of Paris. Despite the divorce from Marlborough, Consuelo was often visited by Winston Churchill who said that she had always been "very nice to me." Her homes were always open to him and his family. Churchill's last visit to Dreux was in August of 1939, only days before Hitler's march on Poland and the Allies' declaration of war.

Marlborough married Gladys Deacon, a Boston heiress and an old friend of Consuelo's in 1921, but that union only lasted until 1931. His abortive political career had fizzled-out much earlier because of his anti-Semitic views. In English Society, he remained unacceptable because of the divorce and remarriage. Neither Kings Edward VII nor George V would receive him in court, and most Duchesses refused to recognize his second wife. The Vanderbilt dowry of 1895 had enabled the Duke to restore Blenheim Palace and its gardens, but during his long forty-two-year Dukedom, the money was all used up. When he died in 1934, he was virtually insolvent. Consuelo had the satisfaction at that time of seeing her son become the tenth Duke of that historic family.

After fleeing from France in the Spring of 1940 upon the Nazi occupation of the country, Consuelo and Jacques lived mostly in New York and Southampton, Long Island, where they had an estate. She regained her U.S. citizenship of which she was very proud and which she had to give up with her marriage to Marlborough. In 1956, she lost both her husband, Jacques, and her second son, Lord Ivor Spencer-Churchill. Finally at the age of eighty-seven, Consuelo Vanderbilt Balsan died on December 6, 1964, at her home in Southampton. Her funeral took place at St. Thomas's Church on Fifth Avenue where sixty-nine years before the young eighteen-year-old bride had marched down the aisle with her father to meet her fate. Many friends and family attended her solemn service. Her eldest son, the tenth Duke of Marlborough, arrived from England with a simple casket to take his mother home to Blenheim, as it had been her wish to be buried in the churchyard at Bladen near her second son and many other Spencer-Churchills. Ironically, before a month had passed, she was joined in the same graveyard by her old friend and Great Britain's most notable figure of the century, Sir Winston Spencer-Churchill.

Consuelo had lived from the Gilded Age to the post-World War II era; from the time of carriages and gaslights to the age of the computer; through two world wars that resulted in the end of the British Empire; and into that period which her first husband's cousin had labeled by saying "an Iron Curtain is falling all over Europe." Only a very few could have experienced the life that she did. It is fair to say, as she said about her father, that Consuelo lived up to the high standard of integrity she had set for herself.

As for Idlehour, Richard Howland Hunt had accomplished his task. No expense had been spared to build a mansion with seventy rooms and over twenty bathrooms. The use of steel beams and twenty-inch thick brick walls permitted a structure that equalled in size some of the stately homes of the English lords. Like the Phoenix, it had arisen from the ashes of its predecessor and was barely finished when W. K. in 1903 enlarged it with the addition of a diagonal wing — called the bachelor annex — and an indoor tennis court. The total expense of building the new Idlehour was estimated to be $3 million.

W. K. had married Anne Rutherfurd soon after the new mansion was finished. As they were both more fond of France than Long Island, the fall weekend parties became less frequent. They did, however, celebrate the opening of the new wing with a house party for fifty people over Thanksgiving in 1903, the new Mrs. Vanderbilt's first as hostess at Idlehour. At the same time in 1905, they entertained thirty-six prominent Society people including financiers J. Pierpont Morgan, John D. Rockefeller Sr., and Schuyler Parsons. It was said "the mansion was never more completely equipped for entertainment than now. All deficiencies discovered by Mr. and Mrs. Vanderbilt in the furnishings and general facilities of the mansion have been overcome and it is said that fully $500,000 has been spent in the adornment of the house and grounds."[47] The house was closed for the rest of the year and by World War I it was not used at all. Vanderbilt had the lawns plowed up and planted with potatoes to support the war effort. After the war all was restored to perfection, waiting for the master who never came. W. K. Jr. had built his own home on the North Shore and Harold much preferred Newport where he could much better engage in the sport for which he became famous, America's Cup yacht racing.[*] By 1930 those races were always held in Rhode Island Sound off Newport.

After W. K.'s death in 1920 Harold sold the country seat he had inherited. It passed through several transformations until becoming Dowling College in 1962. Today, from the outside anyway, it is still possible to imagine the Vanderbilt house party of 1903 in the huge mansion that was so little used.

---

[*]   Harold S. Vanderbilt was a three time victor: 1930 with *Enterprise*, 1935 with *Rainbow*, and 1937 with *Ranger*.

The mid 1890s saw the start of the first planned summer community along the Great South Bay. Although Daniel Conover had been dredging canals, improving roads, and building cottages for the past decade, primarily around Saxton Avenue in Bay Shore, his development did not have a unity of purpose or design that would enable it to be considered a planned community. Furthermore, Conover was willing to rent or to sell his cottages to whoever came along. The most notable planned community for the affluent in the New York area was begun in 1885 when tobacco heir Pierre Lorillard, older brother of George L. Lorillard of Westbrook Farm, purchased 5,000 acres of virgin forest in Tuxedo, New York. There, with the help of architect Bruce Price, Lorillard built thirty miles of roads, a hundred bed clubhouse, and completed several of the forty cottages he intended to build on the site. Tuxedo Park opened in June 1886. It was a huge success, as many of New York's 400 families wanted to have a cottage in this exclusive and restricted colony that had been created in the Ramapo Hills. Pierre Lorillard's name became synonymous with Tuxedo Park. He also became noted in the social annals of that era for his remark, "A man with a $100,000 [income] a year is in the unhappy position where he can see what a good time he could have if he only had the money."

To the south of Islip Village at the end of Ocean Avenue were about a hundred and twenty-five acres of marsh and bog, called wetlands today, fronting on the Great South Bay. The marsh lay between Doxsee's Cove and Champlin's Creek and was called Bayberry Point, for the many bayberry bushes thriving in the damp soil. In 1893 H. O. Havemeyer and his brother-in-law, Samuel T. Peters, purchased this entire parcel of wetland. They were summering next to each other on St. Mark's Lane in Islip and must often have discussed what would become of the marsh to the south of them that was then owned by several local residents. Although Bayberry Point was initially purchased by both brothers-in-law, Peters was the only owner of record — his name was used to disguise the interest of his much more famous relative.

Henry O. Havemeyer by 1893 was well known to the public and the press as the Sugar King. The Sugar Trust, which he had formed in 1887, had become the American Sugar Refining Company in 1891 and Havemeyer was its president. By the end of that decade it would control the price of 90 percent of the refined sugar sold in the United States. It was a complete monopoly, and Havemeyer was watched by the press and investigated by federal and state bodies almost continuously. If he fell ill, the price of the company's shares would fall. He was the subject of cartoons in the papers and by and large received unfavorable press in much the same way that other capitalists did in that age of the moguls. Thus, until he actually owned a property in Islip, he did not want his interest in it disclosed for fear of affecting the price. Both in his purchase of his home on St. Mark's Lane and the land at Bayberry Point, Peters acted for him.

On February 25, 1893, the paper announced the sale of 125 acres of land to S. T. Peters for $45,000 for the purpose of development. It said, "It will be without question a profitable investment and one that will give Mr. Peters an ample return."[48] It was also announced that spring that the Clarence Tucker house north of Peters had been sold to a Mr. R. H. Williams. Williams was Peters's partner in the coal business, and the paper said that the new tenants will probably be "friends of that firm." Thus it was that Havemeyer purchased the home that he had rented in previous summers. He also purchased land for a farm that year to the west of St. Mark's Lane across from his home. Not until the following summer did the reporter say that H. O. Havemeyer was in residence at his home on St. Mark's Lane. Immediately upon his purchase of the Bayberry Point land, Havemeyer applied to the commissioners of the New York State land office for a grant of an additional forty-five acres of land underwater, located to the south and to the west. He acquired this land for $25 per acre. It enabled him to round off and add to the uneven shoreline. By the summer of 1894 he was ready to proceed with his plans for the Bayberry Point community.

Havemeyer wanted to dredge two 100 foot wide canals from the bay north about 2,000 feet. The fill from the canals, consisting of sand for the most part, was to be spread over the marshy land, thereby raising it about 3 feet above water level and providing a firm foundation for building. Fill from the land under the bay was also used to supplement that from the new canals. It was a mammoth undertaking on a scale that had never before been tried on the Great South Bay. Although the contractor was to complete the dredging in a year, in fact it was two and one half years before the property was ready for landscaping. Few of the local dredgers had equipment to handle a project of this scope and only Alonzo Smith bid on the job. Havemeyer, therefore, had to go to Illinois where Charles Vivian had just completed the Chicago Canal. Vivian "employs a rather novel process for dredging which is new in these parts, a rotary pumping machine, with a 24 inch suction and a 20 inch delivery, instead of the ordinary steam dredge. Mr. Vivian's appliance pumps up the material and distributes and grades it at the same time, thereby reducing the labor greatly. The machine will be kept at work for 22 hours out of 24 — a night and day gang being employed."[49]

All did not go smoothly for Vivian. The all-night work bothered the other residents with the continuous noise. John Gibb on Ocean Avenue sued Vivian, claiming that the all-night din over two years had given Mrs. Gibb nervous prostration and that sleep was "absolutely necessary for her recovery." He asked that work be stopped between 10:00 p.m. and 6:00 a.m. He lost his suit, however, and the work went on throughout the night. In the summer of 1896 because of a broken pipe, the dredge filled with water and sank in seventeen feet of water. Much time was lost while the monster dredge was being raised. Finally in the spring of 1897, Vivian had finished his project for Havemeyer and was working for William Dick to the north when the dredge caught on fire and was completely destroyed.* It was said, "The origin

---

* Vivian built a new dredge 70 feet x 42 feet. As a scow it could carry 145 tons of coal.

of the fire is unknown. The machinery had been kept running night and day, including Sundays and must have become over heated."[50] But after two and a half years the land was prepared and building could begin.

To design the houses for the Bayberry Point community, Havemeyer chose a twenty-eight-year-old architect who had been educated at Yale and Columbia, had worked as a draftsman at the offices of McKim, Mead and White, and had then attended the Ecole des Beaux-Arts in Paris. His career was just beginning and it is possible that Bayberry Point was his first commission. It is interesting that Havemeyer did not choose the architect of his New York home, Charles C. Haight, nor the more famous Stanford White, Ernest Flagg, or Richard Howland Hunt, all of whom were at the peak of their careers and designing work for many of Havemeyer's peers. It is likely that he chose young Grosvenor Atterbury (1869–1956) because he wanted to influence him with his own ideas, which would not have been possible with any of the others. Atterbury, at the time of his engagement by Havemeyer, was also working on some shingle-style homes in Southampton and East Hampton, but had yet to establish his reputation. Bayberry Point became one of his most published and widely admired projects. He later went on to great fame as both a house and an institutional architect, with such work as Forest Hills Gardens in Queens,* still considered a landmark American residential and commercial development, the School of Medicine at Yale, and the American Wing at the Metropolitan Museum of Art in New York, which opened in 1924.

Grosvenor Atterbury's plan was ready by the spring of 1897. He had been assisted in his work by the suggestions of Louis Comfort Tiffany, the designer and close friend of the Havemeyers. Tiffany, who had designed the interior of the Havemeyer mansion on Fifth Avenue, undoubtedly discussed Bayberry Point with Havemeyer and Atterbury, and it was probably he who suggested the Moorish style which he greatly admired. On Sunday May 23, 1897, the *New York Times*

---

* Sponsored by the Russell Sage Foundation.

Supplement published an article with illustrations on what it termed "A Modern Venice" on the Great South Bay:

> Bayberry Point is the name of a sandy stretch of beach down on Great South Bay near West Islip, which a year ago was about as barren and uninviting a place as one could find. At high tide a good part of it was submerged, and there was nothing to commend it as a place for human habitation. About that time, however, Henry O. Havemeyer bought the sandy tract, and from the improvements which have already been completed it is evident that the place is destined to become one of the most beautiful and at the same time one of the most novel and picturesque spots anywhere along the coast.
>
> A glance at the accompanying illustration showing the ground plan of the property will give a correct idea of its situation and surroundings. The "point" would more correctly be called a corner, the shore line turning from a westerly course and running almost due north. The illustration shows the extent of the tract and represents about a mile north and south by half that distance east and west.
>
> A "modern Venice" tells in a word what the old Point will become, but not without the expenditure of vast sums of money. One hundred and fifty thousand dollars has already been devoted to the digging of the waterway shown in the center of the illustration, while the other canal at the right will require almost as much more for its completion. The central canal is about 2,000 feet in length, and has a uniform width of 100 feet. The material dredged out has been deposited on the low grounds, so that all parts of the point will be free from danger of encroachment by the sea. The work is being pushed forward rapidly under the supervision of Richard H. Montgomery & Co. of this city, and the season of 1898 will doubtless find the grounds laid out and several villas ready for occupancy.
>
> When the second canal has been completed and the general topography of the place so altered as to conform to the plans, the work of improving the landscape will begin. A broad boulevard will lead down to the grounds from the north. Just at the entrance the road will divide, and, after going to either side a short distance in the arc of a circle, will run straight down to the bay. The semi-circular plot enclosed by the roadways at the head of the canal will be

laid out as a little park and adorned in every way that the landscape architect can devise. Between the roadways and on either side of the canal will be the villas. Twelve of these sites have already been laid out. Each plot contains about one and a half acres, and has a frontage of 200 feet on the canal. The villas will be situated about 150 feet back from the waterway and at a considerable distance from each other, so that the entire place will impress one by its roominess and expanse, and be wholly lacking in everything that might give it a crowded appearance.

In the construction of the villas, this same idea will be carried out. All of them, of course, will be of Venetian design, similar to that shown of Mr. Havemeyer's house, but they will also conform to the general features of the landscape, in that they will be broad and low, not over two stories in height, and wholly without the clusters of pinnacles, turrets, and cupolas which are so often a feature of summer homes by the sea. Broad porticos will replace the conventional veranda or piazza. The villas will be covered with staff, the material used for the World's Fair buildings, with the natural wood of the timbers showing in places. A feature of the structures will be their small cost. Mr. Havemeyer's house will be erected for $11,000, an insignificant sum in view of the amounts frequently expended on such places by wealthy men. In front of each house and extending to the water's edge will be a court, surrounded by a low wall or hedge, and having between the pathways flower beds, fountains, and other adornments.

Mr. Havemeyer has chosen as a site for his house not one of the plots along the waterway, but the extreme southwest corner of the tract overlooking the Great South Bay. It will doubtless be several years before the "modern Venice" will have reached perfection. Lawns and tree-lined boulevards cannot be developed overnight, but with fair time allowance there is every prospect that Bayberry Point will become a Tuxedo of the seaside and a place well worth a visit.

Although the *New York Times* said that twelve sites were laid out, only ten houses would be built, five on each side of the west canal. There were four separate house plans, differing in size and distance from the canal, from which the prospective buyer could choose. The prospectus put out two years later said, "Trees and vegetation are conspicuous by absence. Not only would they detract from the harmony of the design, but more utilitarian purposes are subserved; they draw mosquitos and other pests. It is hoped to keep the Point free from winged insects. Boat houses and pergolas will add to their beauty, as also will bath houses."[51] In addition a foot bridge would be built across the canal to the south of the houses, limiting access to small craft only. Larger sailing and power boats would be moored in the eastern canal. The prospectus went on to say, "The little colony will be an advanced social experiment, on a co-operative plan, entitling each participant to a voice. Membership will be very select, and all elements will be congenial. The grounds will be administered co-operatively." Much was made of the fact that Havemeyer would himself live in one of the houses. This was to be an incentive for others to purchase a home in such an unusual location and so near to their neighbors, a rarity in those days.

Although the general plan was ready by the spring of 1897, it was not until April of 1899 that construction of the houses began. During those two years the eastern canal was completed, Mr. Nathan F. Barrett of New York began the landscaping work, and a scale back from twelve to ten houses was decided upon. The building contract was awarded to Sturges & Hill of New York and it was reported that "a master spike driver is now at work, staving the canals, and a busy time in this section is now anticipated."[52] House building took about eighteen months, and in December of 1900 five carloads of furniture arrived. It was hoped that a furnished house would be more readily saleable. By the spring of 1901 the Bayberry Point community was complete. Havemeyer and his family prepared to move into the southwest house, but as yet, no others had been sold. Would Havemeyer's "modern Venice" on the Great South Bay become Havemeyer's Folly? It was beginning to look that way.

Modern Venice was not the huge success that Tuxedo Park had been. Perhaps the barren landscape or the community living concept kept away those who could afford a summer cottage, or perhaps the affluent wanted for their country residences a year- round home that could be used on weekends as well as in the summer. Bayberry Point would not meet that need. Havemeyer quickly decided to rent the houses, hoping to interest his tenants in buying later on. For the first summer, 1901, George H. Macy rented the northeast cottage and during the summer of 1902 the young Hutton brothers, Edward F. and Franklyn E., each rented a cottage there. The Huttons were to remain in Bay Shore for several summers but not at Bayberry Point. Gradually, however, the Point was catching on, and by 1907 most of the houses were rented by family or friends. Havemeyer was still the sole owner and remained as such until his death.

In both Islip and East Islip there was concern in the villages that the year-round residents would have no public access to the Great South Bay. All the land fronting on the bay had been bought by summer residents by 1893. Pressure was building for the Town of Islip to open a road to the bay for a public beach. They were almost too late. Early in 1906 the Town Board proposed extending Cedar Avenue in Islip to the bay just to the east of Havemeyer's cottages. Naturally, Havemeyer did not take kindly to this proposal and suggested an alternative. South Bay Avenue was laid out on the town map running southward to the bay through property owned by Havemeyer, Peters, and Parsons. At the road's end was land that could be made into a park or public beach without interfering in any way with Bayberry Point. The Islip Town Board authorized $10,000 to buy the needed land. The paper suggested, "It is possible that the owners, realizing the undisputed need of Islip for a park, may donate the land."[53] The town wanted twelve acres and Havemeyer and Peters were only willing to donate one acre. The board resolved on March 16, 1907, to "extend its thanks to Messrs Havemeyer, Peters and Parsons for their generosity in offering without charge one acre of land for a public park . . . this offer is declined with regret in the belief that this acre will be inadequate." Even for the compromise of five acres, Havemeyer demanded full payment. Finally on November 9, 1907,

Havemeyer offered to donate to the Town of Islip 200 feet at the end of South Bay Avenue for bathing purposes and about two acres for bathhouses. "What the Town of Islip wants is a number of shore front parks large enough to be available for future as well as for present day needs," said the reporter, somewhat skeptical of Havemeyer's gift.[54] Within a month Havemeyer had died, but his executors carried out his intentions, and the Islip town public beach became a reality. It was to be the only public beach for Islip villagers. Similarly in East Islip the public beach at the end of Bayview Avenue was given by Harry B. Hollins from his vast estate, Meadowfarm.

Havemeyer enjoyed his new summer home on Bayberry Point although his wife, Louisine, found the constant wind oppressive. He felt close to the water and away from the pressures of business and the press. Their three children, Adaline, Horace, and Electra were seventeen, fifteen, and thirteen in 1901. Horace in particular loved sailing, which was also his father's favorite summertime sport. Havemeyer owned several sailing craft, the largest of which was a huge sloop (for the bay) named *Pleasure*. The *New York Herald* said, "Mr. Henry O. Havemeyer's new Herreshoff sloop yacht has been named the Pleasure and is now ready for delivery [August 1900]. She is 71 feet six inches over all, 16 feet beam and two feet eight inches draft. Captain Suydam and a crew will be sent to Bristol early next week to take possession of the craft for Mr. Havemeyer and sail west with her. The Pleasure will be used on Great South Bay."[55] For competitive racing Havemeyer used his Herreshoff sloop called *Electra*[*] after his daughter. Skippered by Captain Charles L. Suydam of Islip, who divided his time as skipper between Havemeyer and Havemeyer's friend Sam Peters, *Electra* was a regular winner during the summers of 1902 and 1903. Another smaller sloop, called *Adaline* after his older daughter and built by

---

[*]   *Electra* was boat No. 582 of the Herreshoff Manufacturing Co. of Bristol, R.I. Her dimensions were 42 feet 5 inches LOA; 27 feet 6 inches LWL; 12 feet 3 inches beam; 3 feet draught with centerboard raised. She was built in the spring of 1902.

Thomas Muncy in Bay Shore in 1898, was 33 feet long and was used to train his son Horace under the tutelage of Charles Suydam Jr. In 1903 Horace, at the age of seventeen, was given his own boat which he called *Flight*. She was a Herreshoff 30 like *Electra* and under Horace's skillful handling, quickly became known as the boat to beat. Sailboat racing and powerboat yachting were becoming more popular than ever on the bay. There were longer racing sloops and many more races during the summer than had been held in earlier times. This increased interest in the sport of yacht racing brought about the founding of a new yacht club in 1896 called the Penataquit Corinthian Yacht Club of Bay Shore, New York.

The Penataquit Corinthian was not the first of the yacht clubs on the bay. As has been noted, the Bay Shore Yacht Club started in 1883, was abandoned for a time, and restarted in 1890 with a small clubhouse on Main Street. In the spring of 1889 the Great South Bay Yacht Club was organized by a large number of summer residents from Babylon to Sayville. Alden S. Swan was elected commodore and upwards of two hundred members joined. Two regattas for boats of all sizes were scheduled for that summer and were well attended. The main problem was the lack of a clubhouse and mooring on the waterfront. Almost all the available land had been spoken for and Swan's attempt to dredge new land from the bay for the clubhouse had been blocked by nearby residents. The Great South Bay Yacht Club continued to sponsor an annual regatta throughout the 1890s, but without a clubhouse and local mooring, more racing could not be expected. In 1898 it attempted to merge into the Penataquit Corinthian, was rebuffed, and rapidly became a "deceased organization," as almost all its membership had joined the new club.

The Penataquit Corinthian Yacht Club had its beginnings in the winter of 1896. It was the intention of the founders that it be a "real" yacht club with clubhouse, moorings, a paid attendant, and rules that would be patterned after those of the most successful clubs of that era: the New York Yacht Club, the Larchmont Yacht Club, and the Sewanhaka

Corinthian Yacht Club. In April the organizational meeting was held and Harry M. Brewster of Bay Shore was elected the first commodore. It was proposed at that meeting to build a small clubhouse, one story in height, with a broad veranda on the shore front between Ocean Avenue and Maple Avenue in Bay Shore on property owned there by a newly elected governor of the club, J. Adolph Mollenhauer.* Three of the club's founders were from Bay Shore; the other six were summer residents from Brooklyn and New York. The club began slowly in 1896, but by the end of the summer sixteen yachts were reviewed "in the teeth of a howling gale."[56] Although the club had many local residents as members, the vast majority were summertime residents.

At the second annual meeting, held in New York City over dinner in January 1898, Mollenhauer was elected commodore to succeed Brewster. By then there were already ninety members and a fleet of fifty boats, consisting of power yachts, sloops, yawls, and catboats. It was fitting that Mollenhauer had been elected commodore as he was the guiding spirit behind the founding of the club and would remain its leader for its entire life — a relatively short thirteen years.

J. Adolph Mollenhauer was the second son of German immigrant parents, John and Doris Mollenhauer, who had come from Hannover to settle on the Lower East Side in Manhattan in the 1850s. The senior Mollenhauer became a merchant in wines and liquors and then in molasses and syrup, founding the Mollenhauer Molasses Plant in Williamsburgh, Brooklyn, in 1869. The family had moved to Williamsburgh by then to live amongst the growing German community there, and it was there that young Adolph grew up and lived for much of his life. In the 1870s and 1880s John Mollenhauer and William Dick were friendly rivals in business and both became pillars of the German American Williamsburgh community. Their families were neighbors

---

* Mollenhauer sold this property to the Town of Islip in 1903 to be used for the Maple Avenue dock.

and friends and thus it was not entirely unexpected that Dick's son would marry Mollenhauer's daughter, and Mollenhauer's son, Adolph, would marry Dick's daughter, Anna. Nor was it unexpected that soon after William Dick settled on Ocean Avenue in Islip, John Mollenhauer would begin to look for property nearby. In 1893 Mollenhauer, aged sixty-six, bought land on the west side of Awixa Avenue in Bay Shore and built a comfortable Victorian shingle house* where his son Adolph and daughter-in-law Anna joined him for several summers. It was the beginning of a lifelong association for Adolph and Anna Mollenhauer with the Bay Shore community. At the time of his arrival in Bay Shore, Adolph was thirty-six years old, an officer in the Mollenhauer Sugar Refining Co., and a man with a passion for yachts. Although he did not then live on canal-front land, he purchased land on a creek in Bay Shore where he could moor his yachts and it was this parcel that he offered to sell to the new Penataquit Corinthian Yacht Club for their first clubhouse in 1896.

Mollenhauer's passion for yachts almost ended in disaster for him and his wife that first summer of the Penataquit Corinthian's existence. His yacht, *Thelma*, was a 70-foot naphtha powered craft. Popular at that time, naphtha was a forerunner of the gasoline-powered engine of today. It was a very volatile fuel, however, and the risk of fire was greater than in the more traditional steam powered, coal fired yachts. *Thelma*, with the Mollenhauers aboard, was on a trip from Bay Shore via Hell Gate in New York, down Long Island Sound to Newport, Rhode Island. On July 8, the second day out, Anna Mollenhauer spotted flames while sitting on deck. Captain Hendrickson of Bay Shore immediately headed towards a nearby boat which took on the Mollenhauers and all of the crew just as *Thelma* was burning to the waterline. All were saved, but *Thelma* was a total loss. It was commented that she was "the largest naphtha launch afloat. . . . The escape of Mr. and Mrs. Mollenhauer and the crew was mi-

---

* It stands today, at 60 Awixa Avenue.

raculous."[57] This terrifying experience did not discourage Adolph Mollenhauer at all, for he was to go on building and buying new yachts of all sizes for the rest of his life.

Following the burning of *Thelma* in 1896, he acquired in succession the 70-foot steam yacht *Telka*; the *Presto*, which could speed at 30 mph; the 58-foot yacht *Dawn*; and in 1903, the flagship *Corinthia*. *Corinthia* was the grandest of them all. Ninety feet in length overall and 16 feet wide with a draught of 4 feet, she was described by *The Brooklyn Eagle* as follows:

> The keel of the *Corinthia* is of white oak and the craft is planked with yellow pine. The dining saloon is forward in a deck house superbly finished in teak. Aft, below decks, are the owner's living quarters, fitted up in the finest manner possible. The owner's stateroom will be tactfully decorated in white and gold, while those for the use of guests and the saloon are to be furnished in white mahogany.
>
> The sanitary arrangements will be thoroughly up-to-date, providing facilities for hot, cold, fresh and salt baths. Way forward are the quarters for captain Edward Hendrickson of Bay Shore, and a crew of five.
>
> The craft will be propelled by two triple expansion engines driving twin screws. Steam will be generated by a water tube boiler. Steam heat and electric lights will be found throughout. The coal carrying capacity is estimated at 20 tons and a contract speed of 14 knots is required. Two boats will be carried, and the craft will have trisails [for its two masts] to be used in stormy weather.[58]

Corinthia was among the largest, if not the largest, pleasure craft to cruise on the Great South Bay. With a 4-foot draught it was possible for her to navigate throughout much of the bay, but with a very small tolerance in that shallow body of water. Large as she was, *Corinthia* was not in the same class as the great steam yachts that sailed on Long Island Sound and in the Atlantic Ocean. J. P. Morgan's *Corsair III* was 302 feet long and W. K. Vanderbilt's *Valiant* was 331 feet long. The New York Yacht Club listed more than two hundred yachts that were larger than 200 feet in "the golden age of yachting." Commodore Mollenhauer owned *Corinthia* for only two seasons, selling her in the fall of 1904. Apparently she drew too much water for the bay after all and was cumbersome to handle in the narrow creeks. She was replaced by a smaller yacht with shallower draught.

During its first three years the Penataquit Corinthian Yacht Club grew at such a tremendous rate that by 1899 the clubhouse had become inadequate. There was a feeling that the club had to move to a larger site that would allow for a "real" clubhouse which could accommodate overnight guests and where appropriate festivities could be held. Yacht clubs by then in summer resorts had become very formal, almost like resort hotels. An entire section of the by-laws of the Penataquit Corinthian Yacht Club in 1902 was entitled "Yacht Routine." This described in great detail the proper conduct for yachts and yacht club officers. For example, *Section I: Colors, etc., Subsection 1*, Rank said, "In making 'colors,' salutes, etc. the yacht always represents the rank of the owner, whether he is aboard or not." *Subsection 2*: "Yachts in commission should make colors at 8:00 a.m. and haul down at sunset, taking time from the senior officer present." *Subsection 6*: "No guns should be fired for 'colors' except by the yachts giving the time, nor from 'colors' at sunset until 'colors' the next morning, nor on a Sunday." Under *Section II: Officers in Command of Anchorage-duties*, "The Senior Officer present should be in command of the anchorage, should give the time for 'colors,' make and return salutes, visits, etc."[59]

This move to the more formal style of yachting was resisted by some who preferred the simple one-story clubhouse and the informal races to which they had become accustomed. In September 1899, Commodore Mollenhauer purchased from the Mowbrays the whole of Penataquit Point which he considered an ideal location for a new clubhouse for the yacht club. There was more space available in this prominent location for the clubhouse and for many moorings. He offered to sell the end of the point to the yacht club, retaining the rest for his personal use. After much debate and some opposition, the board of governors agreed in October to purchase the end of the point for the club. Funds were found from those members desiring the new three-story club-house with sleeping rooms and restaurant and by the spring of 1900 construction was under way. What emerged was a lovely, shingle-style house with a surrounding veranda on the ground floor and a surrounding balcony or deck on the second floor. A tall flagpole stood in front on which the American flag and the club's red and blue burgee with a single gold star fluttered in the breeze. The Penataquit Corinthian Yacht Club thus became the principal feature on the Bay Shore waterfront as viewed from the bay. A regatta held on the Fourth of July, 1900, marked the opening of the new clubhouse. By then Commodore Mollenhauer had a new boat, the steam yacht *Presto*, and a new home which he appropriately called Homeport.

Adolph and Anna Mollenhauer had wished to have their own home on a canal near his aging parents on Awixa Avenue. So in 1898 they bought land on the east side of that avenue fronting on Awixa Creek. "One of the finest residences now being built in Bay Shore," said the *South Side Signal*, "is that of J. Adolph Mollenhauer on Awixa Avenue. The mansion is after the designs of architect Cornell of New York and was constructed by J.E. Van Orden of Great River." The landscaping for Homeport by N. F. Barrett of New York, the designer for Bayberry Point, was of special note. "The grounds are an innovation in this vicinity and will be a per-fect paradise. A sunken, or depressed Italian garden about five feet below the level of the lawns will adorn the north-easterly portion of the plot. This, with its broad, paved pla-teau, borders of handsome designs, a lily pond also of terracotta and handsome vases with appropriate plants, will add much to the picture. It will be a veritable fairy land when completed. An artificial lake and island, the latter with an elevation of about 20 [5, in fact] feet above the water level, with its paths and natural foliage, will be a very important feature in the work. Access to the island will be had by a very handsome steel and stucco bridge; there will also be a floral garden bordered with boxwood. The designs are very artistic and pretty."[60] Of special interest was the construction of a boat house over the mooring for the Commodore's yacht and a lovely carriage house by the canal to the south of the main house.

In 1913 the Mollenhauers engaged the notable farm architect Alfred Hopkins to design a farm on the west side of Awixa Avenue across from Homeport. There he built a stable, a dairy, silo, greenhouse, and cottage for the farmer, all in white shingle. The Mollenhauer farm buildings became a particularly picturesque part of that quiet street. Homeport was among the most unusual of the South Shore summer homes because of its very Italian feeling and its beautiful farm buildings. Adolph and Anna, who never had children, lived there until their deaths many years later.* Anna left Homeport to her nephew, Adolph Mollenhauer Dick, the grandson of her father, William Dick. Adolph Dick never lived there, however, and in 1936 put the property up for sale.

The Mollenhauers are remembered in Bay Shore today by their gift to the village of the red brick building on the south side of Main Street opposite the Methodist Church. The Soldiers and Sailors Memorial Building was built after World War I to honor those who gave their lives to their country in the Great War.**

The years 1900 to 1907 were the peak years for the Penataquit Corinthian Yacht Club. By 1902 there were 160 members, who owned 25 power or steam yachts, 5 schooners and yawls, 42 sloops, and 15 catboats. The members were largely from New York and Brooklyn with summer homes from Babylon to Bellport on the Great South Bay. The

---

* Adolph Mollenhauer died in 1926, his wife Anna died in 1935. The house at 85 Awixa Avenue and a much reduced garden remain today. The garden and the island, however, have been left to nature's care. The farmer's cottage, 82 Awixa Avenue, is lived in by Mr. and Mrs. George R. Plender Jr.

** J. Adolph Mollenhauer also gave the Bay Shore Fire Department its first piece of motorized equipment in 1914, a Pierce-Arrow limousine whose chassis was used as a horse cart.

largest steam yachts were F. G. Bourne's *Artemis*, 81 feet overall, and Commodore Mollenhauer's *Corinthia*, 90 feet long. The typical racing sloop was the Herreshoff 30, popular at that time, of which there were at least a dozen. The racing season went from the Fourth of July to Labor Day and included day races, weekend races, and an annual cruise down the bay to the east. There was the Lighthouse Cup for the season's champion of the larger sloops (Class "N": 25 to 30 feet waterline length) and several trophies awarded for individual races during the year. In 1903 for the first time on the bay there was a powerboat race over an 8-mile course won by Perry S. Wicks in 1 hour 24 minutes, an average speed of only 5.7 mph.

The Yacht Club became so popular by the end of 1902 that there was demand to increase the facilities for social activity. The governors decided to erect a casino near the clubhouse with a stage suitable for musicals and dramatic productions. A casino in that era did not include gambling in its activities. On the July Fourth weekend in 1903 "the formal opening of the headquarters of the Penataquit Corinthian Yacht Club took place, the occasion being one of the swellest social functions of the summer season here [Bay Shore]. Dancing and feasting marked the course of the evening's festivities, a feature of which was the formal turning over of the new casino to the members by Chairman [William A.] Tucker of the house committee."[61] Other activities sponsored by the club were fireworks over the Fourth of July and an annual water carnival featuring swimming, rowing, and tub races.

The Penataquit Corinthian Yacht Club was the site of an event that had lasting significance for racing on the bay: the organizational meeting of the Great South Bay Yacht Racing Association was held there at the end of September 1906. Organized for the purpose of promoting yacht racing among the clubs on the Great South Bay, its first members that September were the Penataquit Corinthian, Unqua Corinthian, Bellport, and Babylon Yacht Clubs. Others soon joined. Elected president of the Association was Commodore

Frederick G. Bourne, 1851-1919, of New York and Oakdale. He is pictured here in 1899 at the age of 48. Commodore Bourne was the builder of *Indian Neck Hall*. (Courtesy of the New York Public Library.)

Indian Neck Hall was designed by Ernest M. Flagg and built from 1897 to 1900. It was the largest mansion on Long Island when it was completed. A contemporary view of the south side. (Courtesy of Richard A. Milligan.)

John Mollenhauer, sugar refiner
from Williamsburg, Brooklyn,
lived on Awixa Avenue in Bay
Shore from 1895.

The boat house and dock at
Indian Neck Hall built in 1908
to accommodate Bourne's 81 foot
yacht, *Artemis*.
(Courtesy of Richard A. Milligan.)

Robert A. Pinkerton, son of the founder of the Pinkerton Detective Agency, lived in Brooklyn and on Montgomery Avenue in Bay Shore from 1894. (Courtesy of the New York Public Library.)

Woodland, the Bradish Johnson Jr. home on Pavilion Avenue (later Suffolk Lane), East Islip. Designed by Isaac H. Green Jr. in 1906 to replace the home destroyed by fire, it was completed in 1909. It is pictured here as it looks today. (Courtesy of Richard A. Milligan.)

Gilbert E. Smith of Patchogue, born in 1842, was the most notable builder of racing sailboats on the Great South Bay, one of which, *Patience,* was owned by Samuel T. Peters of Islip. He is pictured here c.1895. (Courtesy of Queens Borough Public Library, Long Island Division

The clubhouse of the *South Shore Field Club* was built by Richard Hyde in 1899. It was designed to look like a Swiss chalet and is pictured here as it looks today. (Courtesy of Richard A. Milligan.)

Described by the *New York Times* as "Modern Venice," the ten Moorish houses on Bayberry Point were designed by Grosvenor Atterbury in consultation with Louis Comfort Tiffany and completed in 1901.

Mollenhauer. The GSBYRA continues today to promote racing on the bay most successfully.

The Penataquit Corinthian began to decline in 1907. The great financial panic on Wall Street that October undoubtedly reduced the enthusiasm of many members for expensive yachts and other forms of high living associated with club life. The summer of 1908 was not a good one for the club, and it turned out to be its last. In September of that year the governors discussed a merger with the old Olympic Club on Saxton Avenue, but nothing came of the idea, as their styles of operation were too different. Another proposal then was to build an 80 foot x 130 foot swimming pool filled with saltwater pumped from the bay. "Commodore Mollenhauer who is the father of the project believes that the pool will be a star attraction at the resort next summer."[62] But even Adolph Mollenhauer's enthusiasm could not keep his club alive, although he personally advanced $10,000 for the pool. It was never built. On July 1, 1909, it was announced that the yacht club would not open at all that summer. In the meantime a new yacht club, the Islip Yacht Club with a new, smaller boat, the Islip One-Designs, had come to life in 1909. In the fall of 1910 all hope of re-opening the Penataquit Corinthian had gone. The furniture was sold at auction and the handsome clubhouse was sold to Adolph Mollenhauer who owned the title to the land under mortgage. The era of "grand style" yachting was over on the Great South Bay, never to be revived.

"Grand style" yachting was not the only example of high living at the turn of the century. Whether in sports, in the number of homes, or in the manner of entertaining, the affluent consumed their wealth with passion and exuberance. Elaborate parties or balls, as they were then called, were signs that the host and hostess had achieved acceptability in society. The parties grew more and more expensive and ostentatious, each one topping the last.

The host of one of these was a young man whose father had settled on South Country Road in Bay Shore and built his home, the Oaks, there in 1875. Henry B. Hyde, founder of the

Equitable Life Assurance Society, had amassed a fortune and at his death in 1899, 600,000 individuals held policies in the company said to amount to $1 billion. Hyde had owned 51 percent of the company which was turned over to his twenty-eight-year-old son, James Hazen Hyde, recently graduated from Harvard. Young Hyde became a director of forty-six other corporations as well at that time. This tremendous responsibility should have weighed heavily upon the youth, but as it turned out, his primary interest in life was to enjoy himself. Hyde, who developed a love affair with France and the French, became the epitome of the wealthy playboy.

James Hazen Hyde transformed the Oaks in Bay Shore from a stately country home to a private casino and country club; on his private siding off the Long Island Railroad would come his private car with "actresses" and other friends to his stables where "French costume dramas and other entertainments were performed."[63] Young Hyde bred and raised show horses at the Oaks and to accommodate his yacht in 1901 he built a 60-foot-wide canal from the bay, 2,000 feet north to a basin where she was moored.[*] The Oaks, some four hundred acres with all the various improvements made by Hyde, became the fourth highest assessed property in the Town of Islip in 1903, following those of W. K. Vanderbilt, George C. Taylor, and Frederick G. Bourne.[**] It was commented at the time, "If great wealth in the hands of a few people was an advantage to a township, Islip would certainly be a veritable paradise."[64]

In spite of James Hazen Hyde's reputation for strange goings-on at the Oaks, he was made a vestryman at St. Mark's Church in Islip in 1899 to succeed his father who had served before him. He also gave to the church a Tiffany window in his father's memory.

Hyde's life-style reached a peak in 1905, the last year he was to be in America. He decided to give a ball, and hired

---

[*] Later known as the Landon K. Thorne canal.

[**] J. H. Hyde's assessment was $144,000 in 1903.

"the socialite architect, Whitney Warren, to transform Sherry's ballroom in New York into a garden at Versailles, complete with banks of roses, garlands of orchids, and statuary imported for the evening from France."[65] It was to be a *bal masque* and was to cost Hyde $200,000. The guests were requested to wear court costume, the waiters wore the livery of the French kings, and caviar and terrapin were on the menu together with the most expensive French champagne. The press, who were present, reported on the extravagance, and there was the added suspicion that the party was to be paid for out of the life insurance of the Equitable's policyholders. A major scandal brewed on the horizon.

The financial community rightly suspected that Hyde hadn't the slightest idea how to run an insurance company. At first he sought the help of railroad magnate Edward H. Harriman and his banker, Jacob Schiff of Kuhn, Loeb & Co. Because Harriman and Schiff became involved with Equitable, their great rivals J. Pierpont Morgan and James J. Hill sought to buy out Hyde. The famous battle for control of the Northern Pacific Railroad was repeated with the Equitable. Young Hyde, pressed by both these titans to sell out, finally sold his stock to neither one. Instead, he sold to a lone wolf speculator named Thomas Fortune Ryan, for a startlingly small $2,500,000. Something was obviously fishy and the New York State Legislature appointed a special counsel to investigate. The counsel, Charles Evans Hughes, discovered shady dealings on almost everyone's part. Only Jacob Schiff came out unscathed. Hughes himself made his reputation with this investigation and went on to become governor of New York, a presidential nominee, and finally chief justice of the Supreme Court. When James Hazen Hyde was called to testify before the Hughes committee, he had already left for Paris. He never returned to his country again and died in France many years later.

With Hyde's abrupt departure from the country, the Oaks was quickly put up for sale. Just as quickly, it was purchased by the wealthy Brooklynite, Louis Bossert. Bossert, who was born in Eppingen, Germany, in 1843, had come to Brooklyn with his parents at the age of ten. There, after years of apprenticeship, many of which were frustrating and disappointing, he was able to purchase and develop a lumber business. Determination, vision, and hard work finally brought success and great wealth. The Louis Bossert & Son, Inc. lumber company on Newtown Creek in Brooklyn's Eastern District was widely known for its quality products. Later on he built the Hotel Bossert in Brooklyn Heights, which received special acclaim for its Marine Roof, a nightclub designed like the deck of a ship with glorious panoramic views of New York harbor.

A great devotee of sailing and the sea, Bossert owned many different sailing vessels, the largest of which was *Coronet*, a racing schooner 133 feet long that had many victories to her credit. In addition to his principal residence on elegant Bushwick Avenue, he had a summer house by the sea in Far Rockaway where his growing family could escape the Brooklyn heat and where his boats could be conveniently moored.

After the death of his first wife in 1884, with whom he had three children, he married Philippine Krippendorf and three more children followed. By 1905, Far Rockaway was changing and Bossert wanted a larger house, more outdoor space, and property near, if not on, the water. He had been introduced to Bay Shore by his daughter and son-in-law, Harriet (Hattie) and Max Huber, who had been summering in Brightwaters and then at 48 South Clinton Avenue, Bay Shore, for a few years. The Hyde property was the perfect answer, and it was rumored in the paper that he paid $350,000 for the Oaks. There the family lived in the forty-room mansion for only eight years. In 1913, Louis and Philippine Bossert planned a four-month journey around the world. He was seventy years old by then and wanted to see the many places from which the vessels had come that brought his lumber to Brooklyn. On the last leg of the journey from Hawaii to San Francisco, his appendix ruptured and he died at sea.

Louis Bossert's body was brought to his old home on Bushwick Avenue, then occupied by Hattie and Max Huber and their children, where Pastor J. J. Heischmann of St. Peter's Lutheran Church on Bedford Avenue gave the eulogy at the funeral service. He said, "There was never a finer example of that sterling citizen, the American of German descent, and in all this broad city, there was no happier home life and no more devotion and love than in the family of Louis Bossert."[66] It was this same Pastor Heischmann that had buried Bossert's fellow Brooklyn and Bay Shore neighbor, John Mollenhauer, in 1905 and would bury Mollenhauer's wife, Doris, in 1915. And so the German Lutheran and Brooklyn connection with Great South Bay was repeated with the Bossert and Huber families as it had been with the Dicks and Mollenhauers who had come in an earlier time. The sport of kings, horse racing, and its variations, horse shows and the newer sport of polo, continued to occupy the summer residents from Babylon to Oakdale along the Great South Bay. There had been a race track in Babylon as early as the 1830s, and August Belmont and George Lorillard owned private race courses in the 1860s and 1870s. On Thanksgiving of 1881 the Islip Driving Park opened its doors to trotters and racers.* Among the notable guests that afternoon were W. K. Vanderbilt, Schuyler Parsons, John I. Lawrance, and D. S. S. Sammis. Then in 1894, the same year that the Islip Field Club opened for tennis across from St. Mark's Church, the Oakwood Driving Park purchased land for a half-mile race track from Daniel D. Conover. It was located on Brentwood Road in Bay Shore just to the north of the Oakwood Cemetery. In addition to holding regular trotting and horse races, the Oakwood Driving Park was leased for five years in March 1902 by the recently incorporated (1899) Bay Shore Horse Show Association for its annual shows.** Grandstands, stables, and sheds were erected.

The first of these shows at Oakwood was held on August 7, 8, and 9, 1902, and was described as "the great social event

---

* The Islip Driving Park was located north of the LIRR tracks at a point northwest of Doxsee's Pond.

** Prior to 1902 the show was held on Sagtikos Manor Farm.

of the season on the South Side. Those who had attended the shows at other resorts along the Atlantic coast were unanimous in their verdict that the Bay Shore Show led all the others."[67] Among the winners of blue ribbons were Harry T. Peters, son of Samuel T. Peters, with seven, Jay F. Carlisle with two, and F. G. Bourne with two. The governors of the association, all summer residents, included Samuel T. Peters, J. Adolph Mollenhauer, Edward C. Blum, Simon F. Rothschild, Henry H. Hollister, and Bradish Johnson Jr. For the next year, 1903, they planned thirty-seven classes of horse show events, and the fifty-two boxes in the grandstand were filled with spectators. Bourne won the most blue ribbons that year followed by Harry Peters. By 1904 over thirty summer residents from Babylon to Oakdale had horses competing at the Bay Shore Show.

Interest declined in the following years as the annual event was often marred by rainy weather. After the 1910 show the Bay Shore Horse Show Association went out of existence. It was revived in 1913 under the auspices of the Islip Polo Club in conjunction with a polo match at Oakwood Park, a sport which had come into great popularity by then. Blum, Peters, and Carlisle conducted a neighborhood show for South Shore residents that year.

Polo had been introduced in America by James Gordon Bennett Jr., the publisher of the *New York Herald.* Bennett, who had achieved particular notoriety by sponsoring Henry Morton Stanley's successful expedition to Africa to find Dr. David Livingstone, was especially fond of yachting and for a time was commodore of the New York Yacht Club. While yachting in England one summer he had watched a polo match and was eager to bring that sport back across the ocean. The first match in America was played at Jerome Park in Westchester County in 1876. Five years later the Meadow Brook Club in Old Westbury, Long Island, was founded, and polo was played there in 1884 on a field especially designed and built for the sport. In 1890 the Polo Association was formed to standardize the rules and the equipment and to set ratings for the various players. A ten goal rating was the highest, a one goal rating the lowest. Polo was necessarily a sport for the very affluent, as a stable of specially bred and trained ponies was needed by each player. Eight ponies were required in the match of eight periods or chuckers as they were called. In spite of the large expense, the popularity of the sport grew in the 1890s for players and spectators alike. The Meadow Brook Club became and remained the mecca of American polo until World War II.

Polo came to Bay Shore in the summer of 1903 with the organization of the Bay Shore Polo Association. Matches were played at Oakwood Park by men of the younger generation of summer residents, such as Harry Peters, Arthur Bourne, and Allan Pinkerton. The Peters had their own polo field on St. Mark's Lane where daily practices were held by the Islip team. Polo continued to be played at Oakwood under the auspices of the Islip Polo Club, organized in 1912, which competed with the Smithtown Polo Club and several other Long Island teams. The Islip team in 1913 was made up of Harry Peters, Allan Pinkerton, Horace Havemeyer, and Edward F. Hutton, men in their twenties or early thirties. These were all four or five goal rated players who could play a competent game but were not of international caliber like the nine or ten goalers who played at Meadow Brook such as Devereux Milburn, Watson Webb, Harry Payne Whitney, and young Tommy Hitchcock Jr., considered by many to have been the greatest polo player of all time. Polo was played on the South Shore throughout the 1920s but disappeared with the Depression. The expense of keeping so many thoroughbred ponies was too much of a burden in those difficult times.

Still another member of the prominent Knapp family of New York came to the South Shore in the 1890s to set down roots. During the summer of 1895, the year of his oldest brother Edward Spring Knapp's untimely death, Harry K. Knapp and his wife rented the Wilmerding house west of Bay Shore Village for the summer. Harry was thirty years old at the time. He was the youngest of six children of Gideon Lee and Augusta Spring Knapp, born when his father was forty-three and his mother forty-four. As a youth he was an outstanding student, president of his class at Columbia College and a member of Phi Beta Kappa. He married Caroline Burr and they had two sons, Theodore and Harry K. Jr., and a daughter.

Following the deaths of both of his older brothers, Harry became head of the family, taking on full responsibility for the many Knapp enterprises. He became General Manager of the Union Ferry Co. and a director of the Corn Exchange Bank, the Queens City Bank, and the Kings County Trust Company. He was also a leader in the world of New York Society, a staunch Episcopalian, and for many years president of the Racquet and Tennis Club in New York. He joined the vestry of St. Mark's Church in Islip in 1906, following his brother in that role as well.

It was in the sporting world of horse racing that Harry K. Knapp (his friends called him H. K.) was best known. Harry took over the family's Oneck stables after his brother Edward's death and devoted his effort to making their already good racing record even better. For the next thirty years he pursued the sport with great vigor, often in conjunction with his Islip neighbor Schuyler Parsons. Knapp became a member of the prestigious New York Jockey Club, then a steward of its governing body, then its treasurer, and finally its chairman, the senior position in horse racing in America. He also served as a New York State Racing Commissioner.

Harry and Caroline Knapp rented in Bay Shore and Islip for several summers before finding just the right property on which to build. As has been mentioned, Stellenwerf's Lake House, closed after his death and retained in the Meeks family for several years, was finally sold to Harry Knapp in 1902. By then the Lake House itself had gone, but the property along the east side of Champlin's Pond from the South Country Road north to the Long Island Railroad tracks was wooded with fine trees and would provide an excellent site for a country home overlooking the pond to the southwest. The *South Side Signal* noted on June 28, 1902, "Harry K. Knapp of New York, a well known summer resident of this section, is the purchaser of the Lake House property and will, it is understood, on his return from Europe, erect a handsome colonial villa thereon and occupy the premises as a gentleman's country seat." And on June 27, 1902: "The house is to be located on the wooded section of the property and a driveway 2,200 feet long will lead up to it from the South Country Road." April 18, 1903: "Ground for the handsome new brick colonial villa of Harry K. Knapp was broken this week. The edifice will be 150 feet square, three stories high and will cost about $55,000. The work of laying out the grounds was begun many months ago, and a force of mechanics have just finished building a pretty brick dam. The place, when all is completed, will be one of the grandest on the South Country Road." Knapp would be able to gaze across the pond at his neighbors on the other side, Duncan Wood and J. Ives Plumb. (Plumb had moved to the Meeks house from Deer Range Farm in 1903.) By the summer of 1904 all was ready for the Knapps to move into their new home. They named it Brookwood Hall.

Life for the Knapps at Brookwood Hall during those last years of the Edwardian era was still elegant, even extravagant compared to that of other summer residents on the South Shore where "simplicity" was often bragged about, but not usually adhered to. The Knapps' daughter-in-law* much later recalled that the mansion's kitchen had a staff of three cooks and four dining room attendants. "There were 41 rooms and the place was often filled with family and guests. It was a very glamorous time in life with marvelous food and beautiful furniture. Mrs. Knapp had excellent taste."[68]

Harry and Caroline Knapp summered in Brookwood Hall together until Harry died in January 1926 at the age of sixty-one. A funeral service for him was held at Trinity Church in New York, conducted by the bishop of New York, the Right Reverend William T. Manning, who was assisted by the Reverend William H. Garth, the rector of St. Mark's in Islip. Many

---

* Mrs. Walter R. Herrick, née Elizabeth Mann, was formerly married to Harry K. Knapp Jr.

prominent people from the racing world attended to honor their friend. His wife Caroline died two years later and Brookwood Hall was inherited by their son Theodore, who was not interested in living there. In 1929 it was sold to Francis B. Thorne, the son of Edwin Thorne of Oak Neck Lane in West Islip. Francis, his wife Hildegarde, and their six children lived in Brookwood Hall throughout the 1930s. Harry K. Knapp's other son, Harry Jr., built a new house on Meadowfarm Road in East Islip in 1929. It fronted on Champlin's Creek, was designed by William H. Russell, and was called Creekside. Upon Dr. Alfred Wagstaff's death in 1878 his son, Colonel Alfred, became the head of that family which had settled in West Islip as early as 1859 (see Chapter III). The Doctor's property, which he had called Tahlulah, meaning 'running water,' was among the largest on the South Shore and was assessed by the Town of Islip at the highest value until it was surpassed by that of W. K. Vanderbilt in 1879. It extended several miles to the north of the bay to where Howell's Road is today. Willet's Creek flowed through the land to form a pond on the north side of the South Country Road before flowing on into the bay. The *Brooklyn Eagle* described the property some years later: "The Wagstaff Estate is a broad one, and comprises meadow, upland and forest. The woods are full of quail and other small game, and the several ponds are literally alive with trout. The Colonel enjoys wetting a line during the trouting season, and formerly was a crack shot."[69] It was alongside the pond, which quickly became known as Wagstaff Pond, or sometimes as Lake Tahlulah, that Dr. Wagstaff built his homestead. The residence was distinguished by two classical columns that supported a pediment standing over the front porch and an ornate frieze carved under the eaves which ran around the entire house, giving the square wooden frame building a decidedly classical appearance. On the roof above the second floor stood a small square turret. Tahlulah was not as large as the homes that were to follow, but was sufficiently comfortable for the Doctor and his wife, Sarah, to raise their family. Over the years many festive receptions were held there including the wedding of the Doctor's daughter Mary DuBois Wagstaff to Mr. Henry Gribble of New York, on October 22, 1885.

Colonel Alfred was born on March 2, 1844, in New York City. He was schooled in the city and had entered Columbia College when the Civil War intervened. In 1863 at the age of nineteen, he was commissioned a colonel in the New York State National Guard and assigned to command the Sixteenth Military Regiment that had the difficult assignment of suppressing the Brooklyn draft riots of that year. In 1864 and 1865 he volunteered for service under the Federal flag, rising to lieutenant colonel in that role. From then on throughout his life he was always known as Colonel Wagstaff.

In 1866 the Colonel graduated from Columbia College and in 1868 from the Columbia Law School, ready to begin a legal and political career at the age of twenty-four. Hardly had he started practicing law when he was elected to political office as New York State Assemblyman from Manhattan from 1867–73 and thence as New York State Senator from 1876–78. He became a partner in the law firm of North, Ward and Wagstaff in the city and by the age of thirty-four, when his father died, was recognized as a leading figure of the younger generation in New York legal and political circles. Thereafter, Colonel Wagstaff served many roles. He was president of the New York and Brooklyn Bridge Commission, 1890–91; clerk of the Court of Common Pleas, 1892–95; and after 1896 clerk of the Appellate Division of the New York State Supreme Court. Of all the summer residents from Oakdale to Babylon in the nineteenth century only Colonel Wagstaff and Perry Belmont, son of August Belmont, were to hold political office, and only Belmont represented his summer home district of Babylon.

Colonel Wagstaff was an imposing figure. Six feet six inches tall, very unusual at that time, with a full beard which filled out his slim face, he was noticed wherever he went and was listed among Moses King's *Notable New Yorkers* of 1899. He was a keen sportsman and spent many of his leisure hours alongside Wagstaff Pond or at the South Side Club with rod in hand. In 1880 at the age of thirty-six he married Mary A. Barnard of Poughkeepsie, at the Church of the Transfiguration in New York. They would have four sons and a daughter.

Tahlulah became the country home for many of the Wagstaff family. The Colonel and his wife built their own house to the east of the pond which he called Opekeepsing, meaning safe harbor. His younger brother Cornelius DuBois Wagstaff (1845–1919), who had married his neighbor's daughter, Amy Colt, in 1880 (see Chapter III), located to the west of the original homestead. Lastly the Colonel's older sister, Sarah Louisa, who had married Phoenix Remsen from the old Brooklyn Remsen family in 1870, settled next to the Colonel as well. The widowed Sarah Wagstaff thus had three of her children near her at Tahlulah.

Colonel Wagstaff was a devout and lifelong Episcopalian. In West Islip he was a member of Christ Church where he served as vestryman and senior warden for forty years. The Wagstaff family had been largely responsible for the founding of Christ Church in 1869 as a small mission of St. Mark's Church in Islip. For the Wagstaffs and their neighbors, the five-mile trip to church in Islip on Sundays had become increasingly difficult as the villages in between were rapidly growing. Christ Church was located on the north side of South Country Road just to the west of La Grange Inn and Higbie Lane. It became an active, thriving parish under the rectorship of the Reverend Samuel Moran, attended by most of the summer families from Babylon and West Islip. A rectory was built for the Reverend Moran in 1881 and a new organ was given to the church in 1890 by Harry I. Nicholas of New York and Babylon.

Colonel Wagstaff lived to the age of seventy-seven. On October 2, 1921, he died after a short illness, at his beloved home, Tahlulah, survived by Mary and their five children. He was among the most distinguished men who summered along the Great South Bay and his family was among those which remained there the longest. Today the Wagstaff land is marked by two roads that run south off the Montauk Highway in

West Islip: Wagstaff Lane and Tahlulah Lane. Wagstaff Pond to the north is surrounded by many modern homes. The old mansions have all disappeared. Only the names of the two lanes are a clue to the once grand estate of Tahlulah.

A half mile east of Tahlulah was the Arnold property, inherited by Richard Arnold's son, William, after his father's death in 1886 (see Chapter V). Born in 1863, William Arnold had grown into manhood in West Islip, loved sailing on the bay, and spent most of his time at his home there. In the same year that William was born, Edward M. Cameron was born in New York, the only son of Annanias Cameron. The lives of the Arnold and Cameron families became intertwined in a tragic mix of marriage, death, suicide, and adoption, all in West Islip on the South Country Road.

William Arnold and Edward Cameron were both young men of wealthy families who had become friends while growing up. Both were only sons of parents who also had several daughters. William married Edward's sister, Annie Cameron, and likewise Edward married William's sister. While the Arnolds had no children, the Camerons gave birth to two sons, Edward William Cameron and Alexander Duncan Cameron, and bought a home in West Islip near the Arnold place. All appeared very normal with a future full of hope. It was not to be so.

Three years after Cameron's marriage and the birth of his two sons his wife suddenly died, possibly in childbirth. Cameron soon married again in February 1891 to Annie Carll of Babylon and after a wedding trip to Europe returned to his West Islip home. While they were away the William Arnolds looked after the two baby boys. Suddenly in June of the same year William Arnold died of heart disease at the age of twenty-eight, leaving his wife, Annie, a widow with no children of her own. Meanwhile her brother, Edward Cameron, had become a member of the New York State Stock Exchange, but had lost heavily in the crash of 1893 and the following depression. Most likely despondent from the events that had overcome his life, on August 11, 1895, Cameron shot himself with a pistol through the heart. He was thirty-two years old.

The coroner said only that death had been self inflicted. The family claimed that it was all an accident. The paper said, "Why he should have shot himself, intentionally, if he did so, no one knows. He lost heavily a year or two ago in Wall Street but was still possessed of an ample fortune amounting to a million or more."[70] The incident created a great stir among the West Islip residents. Rumors abounded, but only surmises could be made.

Following this tragedy, the two young Cameron boys without a father or mother, but in the care of their step-mother, were formally adopted by their aunt, Mrs. Annie Cameron Arnold, and took on her married name. They became Edward W. Cameron Arnold and A. Duncan Cameron Arnold. They were both under twelve at the time and were both known as Arnolds for the rest of their lives. Both would be residents of West Islip in adulthood.

Mrs. William (Annie) Arnold in 1906 built a new mansion on the Arnold property to replace the frame house first constructed by her father-in-law in 1873. She called the new home Clovelly, and it stands today in somewhat altered form. Her foster sons owned homes nearby as did her sister. Her son Duncan C. Arnold eloped with youthful Evelyn Hollins Nicholas, daughter of Harry I. Nicholas and his wife, Alice, summer residents of Babylon. This marriage did not last long, but two children were born of it. Duncan Arnold remained "on the bay" for much of his life and was often seen in his later years sailing his Islip One-Designs sloop, *Querida*, in races, sometimes the only boat racing in the "R" Class. His brother, Edward W. C. Arnold, became well known for amassing one of the most complete collections of New York prints and drawings ever assembled. It included the earliest known American historical print of New York, the Burgis view, dated 1716. In 1935 the Arnold collection was loaned indefinitely to the Museum of the City of New York, but in his will Arnold bequeathed the entire 550 works of art to the Metropolitan Museum of Art where the collection resides today.

A half mile east of the Arnold land was the oldest house of all along the South Shore, dating from the original land grant to Stephanus Van Cortlandt in 1692 and his purchase of the land from the Secatogue Indians (see Chapter II). The original manor house, called Sagtikos Manor, was built in the five years following the grant and remained as built until the late eighteenth century when the middle section was added. The final additions were made in 1905. The first house was of simple three story frame and shingle construction with elegant paneling of the doors and dadoes and a graceful stair balustrade inside. The original grant of 1,200 acres ran from the Great South Bay north several miles, the manor house being located on the north side of South Country Road as was the custom with all the first homes along that road from Babylon to Bay Shore.

Van Cortlandt sold Sagtikos (which means 'head of a snake') Manor to Timothy Carll before 1712 and in 1758 it was purchased from the Carll family by Jonathan Thompson of Setauket, Long Island, for £1,200 or £1 per acre. It was to be a wedding gift for Jonathan's son, Isaac Thompson, who in 1772 married Mary Gardiner of East Hampton, a direct descendant of Lion Gardiner. Isaac Thompson was a magistrate for forty years and was well known on Long Island both before and after the Revolution as Judge Thompson. During the period of the Judge's ownership, Sagtikos Manor was occupied for a time during the American Revolution by the British commander Sir Henry Clinton and afterwards by the newly elected president of the United States, George Washington, who during his inspection trip around Long Island spent the night of April 21, 1790, in the manor guest room. The nineteenth and twentieth centuries saw ownership go from Judge Thompson to his son, Jonathan; thence to his son, David; thence to his son, Frederick Diodati (whose mother was a Gardiner); thence to his nephew, David Gardiner; thence to his sister, Sarah Gardiner; thence to her nephew, Robert David Lion Gardiner, who owns it today. The manor has thus remained in the Thompson and Gardiner families for over two hundred thirty years. No other home that stands today from Babylon to Oakdale can make that claim. It has been called "one of the most distinguished historic houses in the United States" by New York State historian, Albert B. Corey.

Although Judge Isaac Thompson was primarily associated with Suffolk County, representing the county in the New York State Assembly as well as serving as a magistrate there, his son Jonathan, the succeeding heir, and Jonathan's son, David, were primarily associated with New York City both in banking and in its political life. Their primary residence was on Lafayette Place where Jonathan died. Sagtikos Manor was used by them as a country homestead. Jonathan's second son, named Abraham Gardiner Thompson after Judge Isaac Thompson's father-in-law, Colonel Abraham Gardiner of East Hampton, had a long and illustrious career on the South Shore.

Born in New York City in 1816, A. G. Thompson graduated from Columbia College at the age of seventeen and four years later from the Columbia College of Physicians and Surgeons. As a young medical resident at Bellevue Hospital he treated a large number of typhus cases during an epidemic that was scourging the city, and as a result he wrote a medical paper that was used by the profession in teaching about the treatment of that disease. Following his residency, Dr. Thompson went to Europe to study medicine for three years, returning to set up a practice of his own in New York in 1840 at age twenty-four.

For ten years, he practiced medicine in the city but also represented his political district in the New York State Assembly in Albany. As the assembly did not meet often and only for very short periods in those years, all assemblymen had other careers. To combine medicine and politics was unusual, but not impossible.

In 1851 Dr. Thompson decided to move his medical practice and took up residence in a house adjoining Sagtikos Manor where he saw his patients. He became recognized as the leading physician in the Babylon-Bay Shore area. Interestingly, he continued his public service, serving as assemblyman from Suffolk County (1857), as examining surgeon for the draft (1862), and as a delegate from Suffolk to the National Democratic Convention which nominated George B. McClellan to oppose President Abraham Lincoln (1864). In 1872 Dr. Thompson, by then age fifty-seven, retired from

The America's Cup winner *Defender* in 1895, on the right, skippered by
Captain Hank Haff of Islip. Note that the topmast is bent like a bow from a
collision with the challenger, *Valkyrie III* (from an oil painting by Tim Thompson).

Consuelo, the Duchess of Marlborough, in her coronation gown in 1902 for the coronation of King Edward VII. (Photograph by Lafayette.)

Charles Spencer-Churchill, known as "Sunny", the ninth Duke of Marlborough was shorter by several inches than his wife. He was known to say that he did not like tall women. (Brown Brothers.)

Consuelo Vanderbilt, only daughter of W. K. and Alva Vanderbilt, at age 16 when she was confirmed at *St. Mark's Church* in Islip. (Courtesy of *The Glitter and the Gold*)

The second *Idlehour* in Oakdale, built from 1899 to 1902 to replace the first which was destroyed by fire. It was designed by Richard Howland Hunt. (Courtesy of W. K. Vanderbilt Historical Society.)

Henry O. Havemeyer, 1847-1907, known in the press as "the Sugar King," was a summer resident of Islip and developed Bayberry Point there in the 1890s.

Havemeyer is pictured crossing the footbridge over the canal, on Bayberry Point c.1903. The Havemeyers' house is in the background.

active medical practice and moved from his Sagtikos house, which his sister took over, to the village of Islip where he settled on land directly south of St. Mark's Church* on Johnson Avenue. In semi-retirement from 1872 to 1887, he continued to be often called upon for consultation.

Abraham Gardiner Thompson died on September 26, 1887, at his Islip home at the age of seventy-one. A funeral was held at the Islip Presbyterian Church, followed by burial at Oakwood Cemetery. His widow and two sons survived him. Dr. Thompson had left his home on the Sagtikos Manor property at the same time that his older brother, David, then lord of the manor, had died (1871) and it was left to his son, Frederick Diodati Thompson. Perhaps uncle and nephew did not get along, it is not known for sure. It is known that Frederick, an inveterate world traveler, had grand designs for the old manor. In the 1890s he bought out his relatives and built the east and west wings in 1905, thereby entirely changing its appearance and creating the much more elaborate country home that is seen today.

Dr. Thompson at the time of his death was recognized as the person who first gave the name of West Islip to the community between Sumpwams Creek, on the east side of Babylon, and Appletree Neck. Of all the long history of the Thompson family in the Town of Islip from Judge Isaac onward, it is perhaps A. G. Thompson who will be remembered by most people as "the good doctor" when there were so few of that profession located there. The local paper described him as follows: "The deceased was a man of much talent and force of character, and was respected by all with whom he came in contact, excepting those unable to appreciate the elements of manhood so prominent in his character. The friends who penetrated beyond the somewhat reserved demeanor which veiled the inner nature of the man found him of generous impulses, cordial and hospitable. He was a firm, unfaltering friend to all whom he once took to his heart, and was a chivalrous, manly opponent of those whose

---

* Dr. Thompson contributed a part of his land to St. Mark's in 1880 for the building of the rectory.

views he differed from or whose methods he antagonized. The various religious bodies of Islip found in him a liberal donator, while to the appeals of the deserving poor he never turned a deaf ear. His death is sincerely mourned by a wide circle of friends, made up of all classes of people resident along the South Side and in New York City."[71]

In West Islip in the 1890s a new road was opened, running south to the bay off the South Country Road opposite the Arnold homestead. It was the only public road to the bay between Babylon and Bay Shore until the Ackerson development began in Brightwaters in 1907. It ran across what was once the old Conklin Farm called Oknock or Okonok toward Conklin's Point which divides Bay Shore from Babylon on the shoreline and was thus named Oak Neck Road.[*] Its opening provided the opportunity for many new summer homes to be built in the same manner as had been done along Saxton Avenue, Ocean Avenue, Awixa Avenue, St. Mark's Lane, and Pavilion Avenue. By the 1890s the South Country Road had twenty-eight homes on the north side and fourteen homes on the south side between Babylon and Bay Shore. It had become "crowded," and it was more desirable to settle off of it on a road to the bay with water access, if possible. Several families located on Oak Neck Road in the 1890s including merchant, author, and longtime trustee of the Metropolitan Museum of Art, William Loring Andrews,[**] William

---

[*] Presently called Oak Neck Lane.

[**] William Loring Andrews, 1837–1920, was born in New York City and was a descendant of William Andrews, who settled in New Haven, Connecticut, in 1638 with John Davenport. Andrews entered the family business, merchandising leather, which he successfully pursued until his retirement in 1878. He was a collector of rare books and prints and was a founder of the Grolier Club in New York. He was a trustee of the Metropolitan Museum of Art from 1878 to 1920 and its honorary librarian. He was a prolific author and a member of the Century Club in New York and the Elizabethan Club of Boston.

McClure, and Edwin Thorne. Thorne and his two sons would remain on the South Shore for many years.

Edwin Thorne (1861–1935) was the eldest son of Samuel Thorne and Phebe Van Schoonhoven. He was descended through his father from William Thorne, who came to Lynn, Massachusetts, in 1638 with the early settlers before moving to Long Island where he became a large landowner in Jamaica. Edwin's father, Samuel, had a successful career in commerce, being president of the Pennsylvania Coal Company. Samuel made his country home in Millbrook, New York, where the Thornes had resided for several generations. Edwin grew up in New York City and Millbrook. He graduated from Yale University and in 1886 married Phebe Ketchum, daughter of Landon Ketchum of Saugatuck, Connecticut. Two sons from their marriage were Landon Ketchum Thorne and Francis B. Thorne. A daughter, Phebe Schoonhoven Thorne, married Harry K. Knapp Jr. of Brookwood Hall in East Islip. A second daughter, Anna Augusta, married Robert Titus.

It was the fishing and bird shooting that attracted Edwin Thorne away from the family homestead in Millbrook in the 1890s. He was an avid fisherman, owning a bay boat named *Gussum* on which he went in search of the blues and the weakfish which were so prevalent then in the bay and in the Fire Island inlet. As a bird shot Edwin was considered the very best of his time, his reputation certainly equaling and perhaps even exceeding that of the brothers Edward and Gideon Knapp (see Chapter VI). The story is told that Edwin Thorne, after a day on the bay one fall, came home with a boat full of 300 ducks, all shot with his one gun. Of course there were no legal limits then and the birds were much more plentiful. He was also famous as a hunter of sharks. He said in 1916: "For the past 15 years I have harpooned sharks in the Great South Bay and during that period there have been seen from my boat probably not less than 2500 between Lindenhurst and Great River on the north side and between Cedar Island and Cherry Grove on the south. The sharks have been taken from June 17 to September 15." Thorne kept careful records of all his forays after sharks. "During the years 1911 to 1916 I went out on 123 occasions. About 1123 sharks were seen, and 146 were taken. Of these only seven were males. Eight females contained young. Young are sometimes born on deck, tail first, after the mother has been caught. ... The greatest number of sharks I have ever taken on any one day was 17 on August 3, 1905. On another occasion I estimated that I sighted 200. They were so thick at times that it would have been impossible to count them with any degree of accuracy."[72] Under these conditions swimming in the bay must have been very restricted then.

Edwin and Phebe Thorne settled on thirteen acres along the east side of Oak Neck Road where they built a large shingle-style summer house that was so typical of that time. It was about halfway down the lane toward the bay and to its east was a small canal where *Gussum* could be moored. They called their home Okonok after the old Conklin farm that had been there. Their children grew up in West Islip along the bay and came to love that area. Landon was to later build his homestead on the south portion of the Henry B. Hyde property west of Bay Shore and Francis would buy Brookwood Hall in East Islip from the Knapp estate, both of them remaining on the South Shore for most of their lives. Edwin Thorne died in 1935 and Okonok on Oak Neck Road was sold at auction in July 1938.

Juan Manuel Ceballos, with his wife and newborn son, rented the Wray Cottage on Awixa Avenue in Bay Shore for their first season along the South Shore, in 1893. They were the fifth family "in sugar" to come to the area. The Havemeyers, the Dicks, the Mollenhauers, and Colonel Duval had preceded them. Juan Ceballos was from a distinguished Spanish family, and with his partner and fellow Spaniard, Manuel Rionda, he had become heavily invested in sugar plantations in Cuba as well as in the shipping, trading, and selling of raw sugar to the importing nations of the world, most importantly the United States. Ceballos and Rionda were partners in the firm of Juan Ceballos & Co. until 1896 when Rionda left to join the English-owned firm of Czarnikow-

MacDougall and Co. (which became Czarnikow-Rionda & Co. in 1909). Both Ceballos and Rionda maintained their headquarters in New York although both travelled often to Cuba where other members of their families lived and managed the sugar estates. Among those estates was Central Rosario, of which both men owned a major part. With the advent of the Spanish-American War in 1898, much damage was done to the canefields at Rosario and the losses were heavy. Ceballos also owned a large share of the Silveira Sugar Company whose sugar mill in Camaguey Province in Cuba was one of the island's largest mills. His partner in this plantation was the firm of D. Stewart & Co. of Glasgow, Scotland.

Because Ceballos had been born in Spain and was heavily involved in Cuban investments, he was appointed by the Spanish government to the commission to negotiate a treaty between Spain and the United States regarding Cuba in March of 1898, following the sinking of the U.S. battleship *Maine* in Havana harbor in February. He proposed that Spain withdraw its troops from Cuba and permit Cuba to form its own government in return for nominal allegiance to the Spanish Crown. However this was not acceptable to the Cubans nor to President McKinley and war soon broke out. Although sugarcane losses were heavy that year, recovery was very rapid and the new independent Cuba continued to be a major supplier to the United States and to world markets. Ceballos and Rionda as well as Henry O. Havemeyer's American Sugar Refining Company made large investments in sugar plantations in Cuba after the end of the war.

Ceballos, however, had a temporary setback in 1908 when his firm had to file for bankruptcy as a result of the disappearance of Manuel Silveira, his partner in the Silveira Sugar Co., with a million dollars of the firm's cash and securities. It was reported that Silveira fled from Havana on a Norwegian cattle steamer which he had chartered and "is now cruising about the ocean with his family."[73] Ceballos reorganized following this loss and the giant sugar mill was henceforth known as Central Stewart after the Scottish partner.

Juan Ceballos had been born in 1859, and he married Lulu Washington. It was with the birth of their son, Juan Jr., in 1893 that they chose to rent for the summer in Bay Shore. In 1894 or 1895 Juan Ceballoses purchased the former Mowbray home, part of which had been occupied by that family for 175 years, since the grant to John Mowbray from the English governor. The house was located on the north side of the South Country Road between Brentwood Road and Saxton Avenue beside Awixa Brook. The Ceballos called their house Brookhurst. It was described at the time as "possessing an originality and quaint, old fashioned appearance which many of the elegant villas on the South road seem to lack. The residence of Mr. Ceballos possesses a far more attractive appearance than if the old house had been torn down and a modern Queen Anne one erected. While lacking nothing in the way of modern improvements, the old style, so suggestive of rest and comfort, has been retained."[74]

The Ceballos family with their son and now their daughter, Lulu (later Mrs. Charles Winter), lived at Brookhurst in the summer for many seasons. The senior Juan died in 1913 at the relatively young age of fifty-four. His widow continued to summer at their Bay Shore house as did the junior Juan who had joined the sugar brokerage firm of his father's old partner, Manuel Rionda, then called Czarnikow-Rionda. Young Juan Ceballos was especially fond of polo and was a part of the group of younger men who formed the Islip Polo Club and played at Oakwood Park prior to World War I. The senior Mrs. Ceballos died at Brookhurst in 1934, more than twenty years after her husband. By then her son had moved away to the North Shore, but her daughter with her family was often with the old lady in the summer. The Ceballoses added an international aspect to the group of summer families which were otherwise predominantly of Anglo-Saxon, New England stock. Juan was an active member of the Olympic Club on Saxton Avenue, a member of the Short Beach Club and the Penataquit Corinthian Yacht Club.

Three more very prominent families came to the Great South Bay in the mid 1890s. Although they rented, not choosing to buy or build, they remained for more than a decade and added to the growing number of distinguished New Yorkers and Brooklynites who by the turn of the century made the area from Oakdale to Babylon one of the most prominent of all the summer spas. It was noted in May of 1896 that the John I. Lawrance home on the south side of South Country Road, west of Bay Shore village, had been rented to Mr. and Mrs. Orme Wilson of New York for the summer. It was also noted that the cottage of Duncan Wood in Islip on Champlin's Pond had been rented to Charles D. Dickey of New York, and that Cord Meyer Jr. and his family were at their seat in Islip.

That the Orme Wilsons rented on the South Shore of Long Island at all is the more remarkable as Mrs. Wilson was the former Caroline Astor, daughter of *the* Mrs. Astor who summered, of course, in Newport, Rhode Island. Perhaps the Wilsons wanted to have a place of their own for at least a part of the summer before going to Newport for the obligatory August season. In any event their presence along the Great South Bay was noted until the advent of World War I.

Charles D. Dickey, his wife, Mary Witherspoon Dickey, their son, Charles D. Dickey Jr., with his wife, Louise L. Whitney Dickey, and their daughter, Mary Dickey, were all summer residents of Islip for a time. The Dickeys, father and son, were both associated with the private banking firm of Brown Brothers at 59 Wall Street and both were among its senior partners for a time. They were widely connected with banking and insurance companies and were members of the most prestigious clubs in New York. They were both also listed among the names of "Notable New Yorkers" by Moses King in 1896. Mr. Dickey, senior, was a "Patriarch" in New York Society. Their participation in the Islip summer community added luster in that era. The senior Mr. Dickey died at his home there in 1897 at the age of seventy-nine.

Finally, Cord Meyer Jr. was the son of a German immigrant who was a contemporary, a friend, and for a long time, a business partner of William Dick. Cord Meyer Sr. had been born in 1823, the same year as Dick was born, in the small town of Rhade, in Hannover. Rhade was only a mile or so from Hanstadt where Anna Vagts, William Dick's wife-to-be, was born in 1819. Surely Cord Meyer and Anna Vagts knew each other from childhood. Dick and Meyer became business partners with the building in 1873 of a new sugar refinery in the Williamsburgh section of Brooklyn. The Dick and Meyer refinery operated until 1889 when it burned to the ground and was not rebuilt because the two partners had sold out to the Sugar Trust two years before.

Cord Meyer Jr., the second son in the family, was born in 1854 in Maspeth, Queens. He matriculated at New York University and joined Dick and Meyer in 1874. His career, first in sugar refining, later developed into the promotion and building of residential real estate property in Queens at Elmhurst and then in Forest Hills. In fact it was Cord Meyer Jr. himself in 1904 who chose the name Forest Hills, which would later become synonymous with the championship tennis played at the club there. Meyer and his wife, Cornelia Covert, with their family of five sons, would depart from the city in the summers of the 1890s for the South Shore of Long Island where they rented a cottage at William Dick's farm on Ocean Avenue in Islip. The Meyer family and the younger Dick family (John Henry and Julia) joined together in sports there as their parents had in business two decades earlier. They were members of the Short Beach Club on Sexton Island where the sea breezes and the saltwater were always cool.

Chapter VIII

THE NEW CENTURY
(1900–1914)

As the new century arrived, Queen Victoria's long reign in England ended, and the new era became that of her son and successor, Edward VII. At the outset of the Edwardian era only very modest changes were observed in the life-styles of the affluent. The great country homes of the landed gentry and the weekend house parties that were so popular in England and America continued in much the same manner as they had before. Prosperity brought on by the fruits of the Industrial Revolution grew in both countries. The advent of the electric light bulb and the automobile made the life of the affluent both easier and at the same time added an element of risk; the early car models often broke down with engine failure or a flat tire.

England was slowly heading toward the end of its century-long domination of the world and the advent of the Great War, which would destroy a whole generation of its manhood, particularly of the upper classes. The United States in 1900 was just beginning to become a nation with world interests. The Spanish-American "short war" was over and Spain had been warned not to return to the Western Hemisphere. In September of 1901 Theodore Roosevelt became president and began an activist era both abroad and at home. The first years of the new century in America were a time of steady economic prosperity except for the financial panic of October 1907, which although severe, was very short lived and successfully managed by two strange bedfellows, President Theodore Roosevelt and the dominant financier of the day, J. Pierpont Morgan, then at the height of his power and influence. By and large America was prosperous from 1897 until the end of 1913.

The life-styles of the affluent in America did not change much in the so-called Edwardian era (1901–10). There were new fortunes made, and the tax on inheritance was so low that old fortunes could be passed along to the younger generation, if they had not been consumed by the older. The population grew, fueled by immigration from Europe to fill jobs created by the Industrial Revolution. In the Town of Islip from 1900 to 1910 the population increased by almost 50 percent, a staggering amount. Most of the country homes that had been built there in the nineteenth century were used by the original settler, or in some cases by the younger generation that stayed on to summer along the bay. There were also several new arrivals. As a summer spa the area from Oakdale to Babylon still maintained much of the luster of earlier times although by 1900 it was beginning to have many more competitors, particularly East Hampton and Southampton on Long Island, Bar Harbor in Maine, and, of course, Newport, which had long since claimed the title of *the* most exclusive summer resort in America.

In Islip village in 1900, according to historian Carl Starace, there were four churches, the finest school building in Suffolk County, the Doxsee canning factory that sent its products all over the world, shipyards, marine railways, and a planing mill. It was the most important business center in the area. There were many shops on each side of Main Street, including the Orowoc Hotel and the offices of the local paper, *The Islip Herald*. This busy complex served not only the local residents but also the growing number of summer residents who employed many of the local people on their "places."

The new decade for Islip village, however, began with a tragedy. On February 28, 1900, fire broke out in the cellar of the Clock and Eastman store. Before it could be contained by the Islip Fire Department, the fire destroyed all of the buildings on the south side of Main Street between Monell and

Union Avenues. It was a very bad blow to the economy of the village and caused much economic hardship. As bad as it was, however, the fire was much less severe than the conflagration that occurred five years later.

In February 1905, in the photo studio of Miss Susie Clark, located in a building on the north side of Main Street, a candle accidentally ignited some lace curtains that decorated the studio. "The little building was gutted and the adjacent Vail block [the block owned by John H. Vail] then went up. This included the Post Office, *The Islip Herald* office and the Town Clerk's office. Then the Lennon block, next to the Vail group, caught fire and was destroyed in spite of efforts by firemen from East Islip and Bay Shore who had arrived to help the local vamps. On the south side of Main Street the Orowoc Hotel and other structures were scorched by the intense heat and many windows were broken, but they were saved. In all 17 business places and five apartments were destroyed."[1] These two terrible fires slowed Islip's growth for several years but did allow the village to rebuild with new structures.

In Bay Shore village in that first decade of the new century the grand resort hotels were reduced in number when one of the earliest of them, John M. Rogers's Prospect House on Ocean Avenue, burned to the ground in 1903 after having been struck by lightning in a violent thunderstorm. There was not sufficient incentive to rebuild it as the era of these large hostelries was on the wane by then. Bay Shore still had the Linwood Hotel on Clinton Avenue and several hotels in the village itself.

The year 1900 also marked the beginning of longtime service to the Great South Bay community by a soon-to-be notable physician. Twenty-two year old George S. King had graduated the year before from the New York Medical School (Flower Hospital), and the lad who had grown up on the Great South Bay at Patchogue established himself as Dr. King in Bay Shore Village on Main Street. For the first few years he practiced at a small hospital in Babylon until in 1915 he started a makeshift twelve-bed hospital as a part of his home on Maple Avenue in Bay Shore. In 1918 he built a new hospital of thirty-five to forty beds adjacent to his home and "Dr. King's Private Hospital" became a permanent fixture in the village. Dr. King himself devoted a lifetime to the care of the people of the South Shore and was the twentieth century successor to Drs. Thompson, Mowbray, and Huntington. Fire Island's first summer community had been at Point O' Woods. Founded in 1894 as a Chautauqua assembly* which proved unsuccessful, it was reorganized in 1898 as a private association in which members could purchase lots on which to build cottages. W. K. Vanderbilt's steel hulled, side wheeler *Connetquot* was purchased in 1895 to ferry passengers from Sayville on the main land to the Point O' Woods dock. The five-mile trip took thirty-seven minutes.

On July 28, 1900, the Point O' Woods Club opened for business to serve the first few summer families. In spite of a slow start, Point O' Woods gained popularity and became solidly established by the end of the century's first decade when the large building that was first called the Inn, and later, the Club,** was built.

Many of the new arrivals from New York and Brooklyn at the dawn of the new century chose to locate in the area between Bay Shore and Islip villages along Saxton, Awixa, and Penataquit Avenues. The land there was not entirely

---

* A Chautauqua assembly was a program of self-improvement, popular in the 1890s. The program was religious in nature, generally Protestant, and was named for the town, Chautauqua, New York, where the Methodist campground was located and where the first assembly was held in 1874. At Point O' Woods the purchase of a share for $10 entitled the buyer to one week's admission to the program. For five shares the owner could obtain a 99-year lease on a lot provided he built a house within three years. The rule for everyone was that no intoxicating drinks could be used at Point O' Woods by anyone at any time. The Chautauquans, as they were known, totally abstained from alcohol.

** It was renamed the Club in 1956.

filled up and the waterfront was close at hand. Two prominent Brooklyn families, both connected with Abraham and
Straus, the dry goods store, or retail department store as it is
called today, came for their first summer to rent in Bay Shore
in 1899. The men were not only business partners but also
close friends. Their wives were sisters, the daughters of
Abraham Abraham, founder of the Brooklyn store. Simon F.
Rothschild and his wife, Lillian, rented the large Thurber
cottage on Penataquit Avenue, and Edward C. Blum and his
wife, Florence, took the neighboring Ryan cottage. After
three summers of renting, both decided that the area was
right for them and that the time had come to own.

Blum asked Islip contractor Benjamin S. Raynor to build
a new home for him farther south on the west side of
Penataquit Avenue across from Mrs. Chauncey Low's house.
Ground was broken in January of 1902 and by July the Blum
family was ready to move in. Their house was a three-story
Victorian shingle-style cottage with a circular turret on the
roof and a covered ground floor veranda so typical of those
built in the 1890s.

Meanwhile, Rothschild had decided to move to Saxton
Avenue. In the fall of 1902 at an auction sale he purchased
land from the Conover estate on the west side directly south
of Mrs. Edward S. Knapp's cottage. (He would expand his
land by the purchase of eight more acres to the south in
1907.) By the fall of 1903 a three-story house of brick and
stucco, called "a villa" in the parlance of that time, was
completed. Of Mediterranean style, it featured a covered
veranda around the ground floor from which were hung
canvas awnings to keep off the hot summer sun. It took
somewhat longer to build than was normal because the local
contractors were extremely busy during the building boom
of 1902 and 1903 in Bay Shore and Islip. "All indicators point
to Bay Shore being hit squarely by a phenomenal building
boom," the paper reported.[2] The new Rothschild place, like
all the others on the west side of Saxton Avenue, fronted on
Awixa Creek with its easy access to the bay. This was important to those who enjoyed boating and the bay life. Both

Blum and Rothschild were among those enthusiasts. Although Blum was not located directly on a creek, a private road gave him access to the small man-made canal that divides off Penataquit Point and feeds into Penataquit Creek. In this small canal the Blums kept their boat.

Edward C. Blum had been born in 1863 in Manhattan, but due to the death of his father a year later, his mother returned to Germany from whence she had come. Edward went to school in Baden until he was twelve, when his mother moved to Paris. He continued his schooling there until 1885 when at age twenty-two he traveled to Brooklyn to look for work. After several years in different jobs, in 1896 he was employed by the firm that would profoundly affect his future.

At the time Edward Blum joined the now prominent Brooklyn department store Abraham and Straus, it had just undergone a major transition. It had been founded in 1865 by Abraham Abraham (1843–1911) on Fulton Street in Brooklyn. Mr. Abraham had been trained in dry goods merchandising as a salesman in a small shop in Newark, New Jersey, where his fellow sales clerks were Benjamin Altman and Lyman G. Bloomingdale. All three men would go on to start successful department stores in their names. Abraham Abraham's business grew so fast that its further expansion required new capital and a new partner, and Nathan Straus joined him in business just before young Edward Blum was hired.

Blum went forward with great success at Abraham and Straus, eventually becoming chairman of the board. He became a cultural leader in Brooklyn as well with a special interest in the Brooklyn Institute of Arts and Sciences of which he became a trustee in 1912 and chairman of the board in 1938. He was also a leader of the Jewish American Community in Brooklyn, president of the Jewish Hospital, and a trustee of the Dime Savings Bank and the Kings County Trust Co.

Edward Blum's career at Abraham and Straus must have been helped by Mr. Abraham's acceptance of him not only as a junior partner but also as a son-in-law. Edward married

Florence Abraham and from this union a son, Robert E. Blum, and a daughter, Alice (later Alice Bigelow Taliaferro), were born.

The Blum's life in Bay Shore in the summer was a busy, active one from the beginning. He soon joined the Penataquit Corinthian Yacht Club, as did his father-in-law, Abraham Abraham. The latter's steam yacht, called *Rose*, was 85 feet long and with a 5-foot draught could not have often been used on the bay. Edward was a governor of the club in 1902 and after its demise in 1909 he became and remained a member of the Bay Shore Yacht Club for the rest of his life. The Blum family was often seen boating on the bay in their black-hulled Matthews cruiser. Edward was also a governor of several Bay Shore horse shows that were held from 1903 to 1906. The recognition of him as a leading citizen along the Great South Bay came as early as 1908 when at the age of forty-five he was appointed one of the first commissioners of the Fire Island State Park Commission by New York State governor Charles Evans Hughes.

In the fall of 1907 about twenty-five Bay Shore and Islip men, including Town Supervisor John H. Vail, ex-mayor of Brooklyn Charles A. Schieren, John C. Doxsee, and J. Ives Plumb, had gathered to share their concern that Fire Island beach might either be closed to the public or developed in a manner detrimental to the public interest. Fears of a new Coney Island or the suggestion "that the state prison now at Sing Sing be moved to this site"[3] were in the air then. All remembered the cholera scare of 1892 when the Surf Hotel had been taken over by the state and was subsequently closed. From that time New York State owned Fire Island from the hotel west to Point Democrat at the inlet.

The meeting in Islip's town hall organized under the name of the Fire Island State Park Association, elected J. H. Vail chairman, and planned to lobby the public in the townships of Islip and Babylon to support the creation of a state park on Fire Island. They gave as reasons: "First, it is needed for a present and future public recreation ground. There should be some place fronting on the Atlantic Ocean where any man, woman, or child could go at will and not be subject to anybody's bounty or caprice; where it would be a matter of right and not of privilege. It would afford a breathing space not only for Suffolk County but for the rapidly increasing population of New York and Brooklyn. The other reason is that the property in its present condition is a constant menace to the welfare of every Long Islander who is either directly or indirectly interested in South Bay industries [oysters and fishing]."[4]

The efforts of this group of citizens brought success to the undertaking, as in 1908 the New York State legislature authorized the creation of Long Island's first state park. The governor named five commissioners: Samuel L. Parrish, Henry W. Sackett, John C. Robbins, John H. Vail, and Edward C. Blum. Since that year many millions of people have enjoyed the magnificent sand beaches and ocean breakers at Fire Island State Park (later named Robert Moses State Park).

Edward and Florence Blum lived in the Victorian house on Penataquit Avenue for the rest of their long lives. Edward died in November 1946, in his apartment in the Hotel Bossert in Brooklyn. He was eighty-three years old. Florence lived on until 1959, when she died at the age of eighty-seven.

Blum's colleague, neighbor, and brother-in-law, Simon F. Rothschild, was a member of "the Brooklyn branch," as he used to say, of the large family of European merchant bankers so dominant in the nineteenth century, whose founder was Mayer Amschel Rothschild of Frankfurt, Germany. Simon was born in 1861 in Alabama, the son of Frank and Amanda Rothschild who had settled there from Baden in Germany. Following the Civil War the family moved to New York and Simon attended City College before going to work for his father's banking firm, F. & A. Rothschild. Simon's younger brother, Louis, was born in New York in 1869. Having received his training in finance, Simon was invited to join his father-in-law's store, Abraham & Straus, where he rose to vice president in 1920, president in 1925, and chairman from 1930 to his death in 1936. Although his early background was different from Edward Blum's, his career in Brooklyn was much the same. He was active in the Federation of Jewish Charities there and was a director of the Brooklyn Academy of Music. He was widely known as a Brooklyn civic leader and philanthropist. He and his wife, Lillian, had a son, Walter N. Rothschild (1892–1960), who would later marry Carola Warburg, granddaughter of the financier Jacob H. Schiff, and have a distinguished career at Abraham and Straus as well.

Simon Rothschild's sporting interest was sailing on the Great South Bay. An early member of the Penataquit Corinthian Yacht Club, he acquired a 37-foot Herreshoff sloop which he named *Lillian* after his wife. He was often seen sailing out of Awixa Creek and competing in the yacht club regattas. He was later a member of the Bay Shore Yacht Club as well. Unlike his friend Blum, Rothschild left Saxton Avenue long before his death, which occurred in 1936. He had lost Lillian in 1927. Their charming "country villa" was sold to others before going on the auction block in 1944. Two other men from Brooklyn had come with their families to summer in the early 1890s, John Gibb to Ocean Avenue, Islip, and Robert Allan Pinkerton to Montgomery Avenue, Bay Shore (see Chapter VII). Their children, seeing each other every summer, would intermarry and establish their own summer homes in the new century.

Robert A. Pinkerton was the second son of Allan Pinkerton, who had made his reputation as a detective by successfully protecting President-elect Abraham Lincoln from assassination during his slow trip from Springfield, Illinois, to his inauguration in Washington, D.C., on March 4, 1861. Robert, from Brooklyn, along with his brother, William, from Chicago, succeeded their father in the management of his company, and they made the Pinkerton National Detective Agency famous throughout the country. When Robert and his wife, Anna, came to Bay Shore, their family consisted of a son, Allan, aged seventeen, and two younger daughters, Anna and Mary. Their Montgomery Avenue home, called Dearwood, which had been bought from R. H. Montgomery himself, must have been a lively and happy summer home filled with the laughter of teenagers.

John Gibb and his wife had an even larger family, nine children, the youngest son of which, Lewis Mills Gibb, was twenty-four when his father built Afterglow on Ocean Avenue in Islip. As the new century began, Lewis Mills Gibb was married to Anna Pinkerton and the couple looked to Saxton Avenue for their own home. At almost the same time Allan Pinkerton, Anna's brother, married Franc Woodworth and they looked to Saxton Avenue as well. In the winter of 1902–03 just as Rothschild was planning his home on the west side of Saxton, the young Gibbs were planning for theirs on the east side of the street. Until that time all of the summer homes on Saxton had been built on the west side and thus were fronting on Awixa Creek. The east side fronting on Doxsee's Creek* had remained vacant and had been owned by the Daniel Conover estate. Two other Brooklynites were also planning homes on the east side of Saxton Avenue then, Julian D. Fairchild, president of the King's County Trust Co., and Robert A. Pierrepont. However Fairchild's was never built and he later chose Awixa Avenue, where in 1904 he purchased the Emil Frank house. Pierrepont did build north of Gibb, but did not remain very long, selling before World War I. Directly south of the land chosen by the young Gibbs, Allan Pinkerton and his wife purchased land for their new home and by September of 1903 it was under way as well. Referring to both Gibb and Pinkerton the local paper said, "The new colonial villas are being erected on the east side of Saxon Avenue adjoining each other and will be similar in design and finish. They will be about 40 x 90 feet with extensions 22 x 45 feet in size and will cost over $20,000 each. Each house will be replete with modern improvements, having four baths, electric bell, etc. The houses will be heated with hot air and will be lighted with gas and electricity. Benjamin S. Raynor is the contractor. The property has water front of nearly 800 feet and is especially desirable."[5] By the summer of 1904 the Gibbs and the Pinkertons were in residence in their new homes. It was reported, "With the new

---

* Doxsee's Creek became known as Orowoc Creek.

villas [Rothschild, Pierrepont, Gibb, and Pinkerton] under-
way, the Saxton Avenue section will doubtless soon become
one of the swellest thoroughfares."[6]

Before the young married Pinkertons had settled on
Saxton Avenue, Allan, called Bud by his friends, was already
an active sailor on the Great South Bay, a member and then a
governor (1902) of the Penataquit Corinthian Yacht Club. He
was only twenty-five when he ordered a new sloop to be built
after the Herreshoff design that was popular at the time. The
41-foot sailing yacht, which he named *Pinkie*, arrived for the
racing season of 1901 and was a fast and competitive boat in
the "N" class of sloops which raced on the bay in that era.
Her principal opponents were H. O. Havemeyer's *Electra*,
S. T. Peters's *Patience*, Horace Havemeyer's *Flight*, T.
Ridgewood Macy's *Arrow*, and John E. Roosevelt's *Wanda*.
In the fall of 1904 *Pinkie* was totally destroyed by fire while
moored at night in the Pinkerton boat basin off Orowoc
Creek. The fire was believed to have been set by an arsonist
although none was ever found. That sad occurrence ended
racing for Allan Pinkerton and he turned his interests to-
wards horses and polo.

The Pinkertons owned sufficient property on the east
side of Saxton Avenue to have a farm, which was located to
the south of the main house. In 1912 they purchased land
from Fairchild to enlarge the farm further. It was primarily a
horse farm where Allan raised and kept his polo ponies. On
the farm a caretaker's house was built which remains today.[*]
At the Bay Shore Horse Show of 1906 Allan Pinkerton's polo
ponies were racing against those of Harry T. Peters and those
of Allan's brother-in-law to be, young Jay F. Carlisle (fiancé
of Mary Pinkerton). Allan also had a hunter in that show.
When the Islip Polo Club was organized in 1912 Allan was a
governor as well as a member of the first team, which played
its home matches at Bay Shore's Oakwood Park, which it
then owned. Other team members were Harry T. Peters,
Horace Havemeyer, and Edward F. Hutton (more of them

---

[*] It is owned by Mr. and Mrs. Charles F. Hayward.

later). Both of Allan's brothers-in-law, Lewis M. Gibb and Jay F. Carlisle, were also governors of the club. Many of the younger generation along the South Shore were taking up the game.* Allan Pinkerton was generally considered the best among them. He joined the Meadow Brook Club in Old Westbury, Long Island, and played there on occasion, but was never ranked with the top goal players of the country. He also was Master of Fox Hunting at Meadow Brook for a time.

Pinkerton and Gibb were interested as well in another sport that was becoming popular in the winter, scootering over the ice on the frozen Great South Bay.** The Islip scooter club sponsored races, and the winters were often cold enough to ensure thick ice. Many of the New York and Brooklyn people who owned homes along the bay would return to them on winter weekends when there was ice on the bay.

Both Pinkerton and Gibb were engaged in the management of their family's business. Allan Pinkerton became president of Pinkerton's National Detective Agency, following his father and his uncle. Lewis Gibb followed his father and older brothers in the importing firm of Mills and Gibb and later joined his older brother, Walter Gibb, in the management of Frederick Loeser & Co. of Brooklyn, the retail department store.

---

* The 1912 governors of the Islip Polo Club were: Horace Havemeyer, Edward C. Blum, Edward F. Hutton, Harry T. Peters, William K. Dick, George A. Ellis Jr., Lewis M. Gibb, August Belmont Jr., Willard F. Thompkins, Juan M. Ceballos, Jay F. Carlisle, William F. S. Hart, Simon Rothschild, Allan Pinkerton.

** The Great South Bay scooter was a duck-shooting boat with a small bowsprit and two metal runners on the bottom, 14 feet in length. There were two sails, a gaff-rigged mainsail and a small jib by which the scooter was steered. The scooter could go over the rough ice of the tidal bay and should there be holes or breaks in the ice, the runners would easily skim over them. If the scooter hit open water, it would not swamp. It could travel at or greater than the speed of the wind, if conditions were perfect, very much in the manner that today's catamaran travels over the water.

On July 5, 1912, Lewis Gibb returned from his office in the store to his home in Bay Shore after a long day at work, but appeared to be in good health. The day before he had refereed a polo match in Bay Shore. During that night he died of a stroke or heart attack. He was only forty-four years old. He was buried from St. Mark's Church in Islip, mourned by his many friends, his widow Anna and their two sons, Lewis M. Jr. and Robert Pinkerton Gibb.

Anna Gibb lived as a widow for thirty years, much of that time with her son Lewis and his family at the home on Saxton Avenue which they called Cedarholme. Lewis Jr. had been born in 1902. After graduating from Harvard he went on to become president of F. Loeser & Co. until 1938 and a director of Pinkerton's National Detective Agency. After the Gibbs' departure, their house on Saxton Avenue has been owned by Judge and Mrs. Charles H. Tenney of New York and Islip and subsequently by several others. Today it stands at the end of Dover Court amidst many modern, smaller houses.

Allan Pinkerton returned from World War I with impaired health, having suffered gas wounds in battle. He died in October 1930 at the age of fifty-four, survived by his widow, Franc, and their son, Robert A. Pinkerton (1904–1967), known as Bobby. With the advent of World War II and Mrs. Pinkerton's death in 1945, their house, unlike the Gibbs', was torn down. Bobby and his wife, Louise, lived in the caretaker's cottage until 1948 when they sold it to Edward J. Martin and moved to Suffolk Lane in East Islip. The Pinkertons, father and son, had lived on Saxton Avenue for forty-four years, a longer span than any family up to that time. In June of 1899 it was duly reported that the Raven cottage on Clinton Avenue, Bay Shore, had been rented to William H. Moffitt of New York. Although Moffitt was a member of the Olympic Club and thus was familiar with the South Shore, this notice was the first indication that he intended to summer in the area with his family on a more permanent basis. Moffitt's business was real estate development, or speculation, as it was then usually called. His W. H. Moffitt Realty Corp. would acquire large amounts of land as an investment, holding the land until the time was right to subdivide and sell the lots or to build houses and sell to the prospective home buyer. He aimed at the mass market and was thus an early forerunner of William J. Levitt, who developed Levittown on Long Island after World War II. As the boom years that followed the depression of the 1890s progressed, Moffitt saw a great opportunity in Bay Shore and Islip to build new housing for those who wanted to escape from the city. He must have presumed that they could find employment locally because the land he purchased was well inland from the Great South Bay and would not have been of interest to the summertime-only resident. His purchase was a huge speculative gamble, which, had it succeeded, would have made Moffitt a fortune and made him as well known as Levitt is today. As it turned out, all that is remembered of Moffitt in Bay Shore and Islip is the name Moffitt Boulevard, which runs from Brentwood Road east to East Islip, north of the railroad tracks.

Moffitt called his first development Bay Shore Manor. It was described as "the greatest real estate speculation Bay Shore has ever experienced."[7] In May 1901, he engaged a surveyor to lay out 648 "villa plots" on 55 acres of land that he had bought between Clinton Avenue on the west and Park Avenue on the east to the north of Bay Shore Boulevard (now called Sunrise Highway). The plots had a 25-foot frontage on new roads that Moffitt built and were 100 feet deep for a total of less than one-tenth of an acre! It is uncertain how many of the side streets were actually built at that time, although some do exist today. It is highly unlikely that many homes were built then. Although Moffitt claimed that he sold most of the lots, he must have realized that his next venture would have to be located nearer the villages of Bay Shore or Islip. People then did not want to be located in the pine barrens along the road to Brentwood.

In the spring of 1906 Moffitt made three separate purchases of land, which he would call Willow Brook Park, Saxon Park, and Olympic Park. Willow Brook Park was situated in Islip north of the railroad tracks up to Islip Boulevard along Athasca Brook. It contained about a hundred sixty acres and included the old Islip Driving Park which Moffitt rejuvenated into a race track to entertain his friends and business associates.* Saxon Park abutted Willow Brook Park on the east and ran to Saxon Avenue. It was purchased from the Estate of Daniel C. Conover, Islip's first developer, for $40,000, "the highest price paid for acreage known in the Town of Islip. It is the intention of the company to parcel it off in lots."[8] Saxon Park continued south of the railroad tracks on the east side of Saxon Avenue to South Country Road. Finally, Olympic Park was located entirely south of South Country Road between Saxon Avenue on the west to Orowoc Creek on the east. It ran south along Saxon for some 1,300 feet and then east to the creek, giving this park water access to the Great South Bay, the only one of the three parks to have this valuable asset. Moffitt paid $65,000 for Olympic Park. By 1910 he had built five new streets off Saxon Avenue running to Orowoc Creek and had constructed five new stucco houses at the corner of three of them.**

In addition to the three parks, Moffitt also purchased for himself, rather than for development, almost all of the land formerly owned by James Harvey Doxsee (who died in 1907), lying north of South Country Road and south of the railroad tracks between Saxon Avenue on the west and Grant Avenue on the east. This included the land on each side of Orowoc Pond and of Athasca (Doxsee's) Pond. It was on this property that he would build his residence. In 1906, Moffitt had acquired over nine hundred acres in Bay Shore and Islip at a huge cost. Together with his other holdings he had added greatly to his inventory of raw land and as yet had sold very little at all.

---

* Islip Driving Park opened in 1881; the new Willow Brook Driving Park opened July 4, 1907.

** The five streets are Kempster, Wenman, Green, Mallar, and Boyd Avenues. The five houses stand at the corners of Saxon Avenue and Kempster, Wenman, and Green Avenues.

Moffitt was enjoying his seeming prosperity. To celebrate the twenty-first birthday of their son, Charles W. Moffitt, he and his wife gave a party at the Olympic Club in September 1907. Occurring only a month before the October financial panic, it could be seen as the last grand extravaganza of that era on the South Shore. The paper said, "the function was the most pretentious ever held within the walls of this famous club."

> The artistic effects produced by the decorators and illuminating artists transformed the clubhouse and grounds into a veritable fairy paradise. From nine o'clock in the evening until nearly three o'clock the dancing and merriment continued unabated, save while the young people were enjoying the tempting viands served by Sherry of New York in his inimitable style. The tables, set about in a large circle, fairly groaned under their wealth of dainty morsels and exquisite decorations, also by Sherry, while the dining room itself resembled a natural arbor, so profuse was the display of greens, palms and flowers. During the courses the Metropolitan Quartette of New York contributed many popular selections. After dinner dancing was resumed in the club pavilion near the water's edge, to the exhilarating music furnished by [an] orchestra of eight pieces (New York). The players were entirely hidden behind rows of palms and potted plants and banks of ferns and cut flowers. The favors were solid silver loving cups bearing the inscription 'C. W. M. 1886-1907'.[9]

In addition to such festivities, the Moffitt family, staunch Roman Catholics, supported the charities of their church. That support included special trips to Fire Island for young children. On an August Saturday in 1908, four hundred children from the Sunday Schools of the Bay Shore and East Islip Catholic Churches (there was no Catholic Church in Islip) were taken to the ocean for a day at the beach. Mrs. Moffitt and her two daughters sponsored and acted as hostesses for the outing. A good time was had by all.

After renting cottages for several summers on Clinton Avenue in Bay Shore, the Moffitts moved to an older residence that stood on the land he had bought around Orowoc Pond. However, as the children grew older, more space was needed, and in the summer of 1910, Moffitt commissioned a new home to be built for his family. It was to be located beside Orowoc Pond. The older Moffitt house and the Hawkins house were removed so that the new home would have an unobstructed view over twenty-five acres of lawn between the two ponds. It took a year to complete the new concrete and steel home that contained twenty-one rooms. It was said to cost Moffitt $100,000, with an additional $30,000 spent on out-buildings and landscaping. By the summer of 1911 the Moffitt family had "one of the most artistic and modern country homes on Long Island,"[10] a suitable residence for a man whose career was such a success.* That summer Moffitt was elected commodore of the Bay Shore Yacht Club as well, and served for three years.

In December of 1910 a news item from the village of Bay Shore said, "W. H. Moffitt, real estate king, county fair promoter, and boomer-in-general of Islip and Bay Shore, it is understood, is to become a newspaper owner. Report says he has planned to purchase the controlling interest on the *Bay Shore Independent*, and that he will continue to publish the same."[11] Boomer of Bay Shore he surely was. A Moffitt Realty Company advertisement showed an aerial view of Bay Shore and Islip with the description, "Nature's Most Beautiful Paradise—Nothing like it anywhere on the American continent—Picturesque Bay Shore and Islip, the most famous yachting and fishing center on the Atlantic Coast." It went on to say: "William H. Moffitt Realty Co. of 192 Broadway, New York City, is the owner and developer of 167 properties in 32 cities and towns suburban to New York" and that "50,000 people have purchased on our easy payment plan."

Moffitt's empire of land-holdings on Long Island, Staten Island, and New Jersey grew larger and larger. By 1914 he was said to have been personally worth over $2 million and to have bought and sold over $20 million worth of real estate over a twenty-year period. The man who had started out as a $3 a week dry goods clerk in Auburn, New York, owned a

---

* Moffitt also had homes on Staten Island and in Connecticut.

mansion in New York City next to the steel magnate Charles Schwab. He was by all appearances a very great success.

In reality, however, during the peak year of 1913 Moffitt had become dangerously overextended, and even before the Great War began in Europe, the real estate bubble in New York burst. The dissolution of his real estate empire began in early 1914. In debt by then and behind on his mortgage payments, Moffitt had to raise cash wherever he could. He sold his four-year-old home on Orowoc Pond to Walter G. Oakman together with most of the property surrounding it.* He sold a factory he owned in Bay Shore as well, but most of his land-holdings had not been developed as yet and were unmarketable. He struggled to survive for three more years, selling what he could to keep the creditors at bay until August of 1917 when he gave up. He said at the time, "I left this city because of the pressure of creditors and the foreclosure of many mortgages and tax liens. More than a year before I had tried to placate this pressure by collecting money from auction sales of property on Long Island. The pressure on me was so strong, however, that I was forced to the wall and some of my friends advised me to go to some other territory and start business anew."[12]

When Moffitt left New York he went to Seattle for six months before settling in San Jose, California. While there, he was indicted by a New York grand jury on the charge of grand larceny resulting from a real estate transaction he was involved in when he lived in New York. He chose to ignore the indictment and became a fugitive from justice, fleeing to London for a time before returning to San Jose where in 1920 he was finally tracked down and arrested. A month later he was returned to New York to face trial and an investigation of his real estate activities, which were said to involve $4 million.

Moffitt's wife, seriously embarrassed by the notoriety, blamed the entire incident, "his terrible mistake" she said, on

---

* Oakman in February 1918 sold the Moffitt house between the ponds to Judge George S. Graham of Philadelphia, who was the senior member of the U.S. House of Representatives.

a Miss Carpen. When Moffitt fled New York, leaving behind his wife and children, he took with him Miss Pearl Carpen, thirty-three years old, from whom he bought his newspapers at a stand in front of his Thirty-fourth Street office. Miss Carpen remained with him during his years as a fugitive, working as his stenographer and known in San Jose as Mrs. Marvin. By then Moffitt was blaming his own family for his troubles, telling the press that they were always too extravagant and that they had had no kind words for him in the past seven years.[13]

In Bay Shore, W. H. Moffitt had been all but forgotten by then. The road that went by his race track, which was soon abandoned for housing, was called Moffitt Boulevard. As the years went by, Willow Brook Park, Saxon and Olympic Parks filled with small houses. Few knew or cared that they had once been the dream of the very enterprising William H. Moffitt. Moffitt slowly recovered from his reverses by developing real estate in California. He returned to Bay Shore briefly in April 1926, having repaid all of his creditors in New York State. The story of Bay Shore's other developer in the first decade of the new century ended differently. His choice of land to develop was far superior, he was careful not to become too over-extended, and when the real estate bubble did burst, he did not evade his responsibilities to his creditors.

In 1907 for a price of "a little under $500,000,"[14] approximately five hundred twenty-five acres of prime property belonging to Charles E. Phelps, located on the bay and extending inland to the railroad tracks between the lands of the Lawrance family and the Johnson family in Bay Shore, was sold to the T. B. Ackerson Construction Company of Brooklyn. Phelps had called his land Brightwaters, and had inherited it from his father, Bethuel Phelps, who had come to Bay Shore in the early 1880s. It contained five small lakes north of the South Country Road which overflowed into a stream leading out into the Great South Bay. It was reported at that time that the Ackerson Company had extensive plans to improve the property and would build at least five hundred houses, macadam roads, and cement sidewalks, spending upwards of $10 million on the development.* One thousand dollars per acre was a very high price to pay for undeveloped land at that time, but the land was far superior, with bay access, to any that Moffitt had bought, and the potential for success was much greater. It was to be the largest bayside development to date, far exceeding H. O. Havemeyer's "Modern Venice" of the 1890s.

The T. B. Ackerson Company of Brooklyn was founded around 1895 by Thomas Benton Ackerson who with his three brothers began to develop real estate with homes, first in the Flatbush section of Brooklyn and then in New Jersey and in suburban Long Island. T. B., as he was usually known, at forty years of age when he began the business, was the leader and the visionary of the brothers. The others were in charge of construction, sales and financing, and special facilities. T. B. was particularly attracted to suburban areas. Much later he expounded his philosophy in a speech before the New York Area real estate board: "There should be none but bright forebodings about Long Island real estate, for, like most well situated home centers, it is on the upward trend and increasing in favor as it becomes better known. . . . The percentage of persons seeking suburban homes is greater now than in the past and rapidly increasing. . . . The ideal suburban community is where there is no suggestion of the city and where bathing, yachting, and good automobiling are easily available. Western Suffolk County and other parts of Long Island have been built up and increasingly occupied by the influx of city residents seeking ideal suburban homes . . . This year and next and so on will witness a real estate movement on Long Island sufficient to satisfy the most enthusiastic optimist and values always respond to demand."[15] Such optimism should be qualified by the fact that he spoke after the ending of the Great War when the world looked "safe for democracy." The spread of suburbia on Long Island was also accelerating after the completion

---

* In 1920 the development cost was estimated to be $3.5 million.

of the railroad tunnels under the East River, allowing the rail commuter direct access to Manhattan and its jobs for the first time.*

The plan for the development of Brightwaters was very ambitious. The centerpiece was to be the widening of the small crooked stream into a 175-foot-wide canal from the bay all the way up to the South Country Road, nearly a mile in length and 10 feet deep. It was the largest dredging job undertaken along the bay to that date and was completed during the year 1909 at a cost of $250,000.[16] It was called the new Venetian Canal and Yacht Harbor and with its completion every home owner in Brightwaters would have a space to moor his boat. It was by far the widest and largest canal built and guaranteed the success of Ackerson's development. At the inland end of the canal two Roman stone pagodas were built on a plaza, while at the bay end on the east pier a two-story bathing pavilion was located so that all residents could swim in seashore waters and enjoy shore dinners in the restaurant there.

In 1910 Ackerson added to Brightwaters in a major way by purchasing 500 more acres of land from his neighbor to the east, Charles L. Lawrance, who had inherited Manatuck Farm from his grandfather, Francis Cooper Lawrance (see Chapter III). This acquisition would almost double the size of the development. Finally he added another 300 acres from the land of Louis Bossert to the west so that by 1912 over 1,300 acres were available for development. The property ran from the east side of Windsor Avenue to the west side of Bay View Avenue and from the Great South Bay to the north of the Long Island Railroad tracks where 400 acres were to be set aside for a group of small farms dedicated to methods of scientific and cooperative farming. North of the South

---

* The Pennsylvania Railroad had bought the Long Island Railroad in 1900. The tunnel under the East River was completed during the summer of 1910, and the first service newly opened from Penn Station directly to Jamaica and points east began on September 8, 1910. The commute to Long Island was thus vastly shortened for everyone.

Country Road the five freshwater lakes were dredged and connected by Venetian concrete bridges. This section was called the Lakes section to contrast with the Bay section to the south and the Pines and Oak sections to the north of the tracks. In 1912 electric lights were available to all and during the following year twenty-five fire hydrants were hooked up to the water supply company. This was crucial as fire was still the principal hazard to homes in that era.

Finally the Brightwaters Casino was built on the corner of the South Country Road and Windsor Avenue and given to the community along with the lakes and Venetian Yacht Harbor. The casino was for the use of members and residents for dining and for parties,* not for gambling as the name would imply today.

The property was divided into lots, usually 100 x 150 feet, much larger than in the Moffitt developments. Ackerson kept to his general plan "not to cut the land into caramel lots and expect to develop them into gingerbread sales. Such a cheap small lot development," he said, referring to Moffitt among others, "is a curse to Long Island, and until this so called 'boom lot' development is wiped out from Long Island, the Island cannot expect to prosper as it should."[17] The prospective plot buyer had options. He could either buy an Ackerson-built house for an average price of $35,000, or, as was more usual, he could build his own using the plans made available by the Ackerson Construction Company, which would also build the house should that be the owner's desire. Ackerson would also provide financing "as far as is consistent with good business practice" and would "lend its advice and assistance to its clients."[18] Ackerson envisaged a year-round community with homeowners commuting daily to Brooklyn and New York on the Long Island Railroad, and to a very large degree those who located in Brightwaters did just that. Their houses were not by and large closed for the winter. By World War I Brightwaters could be called a success. Over three

---

* In September 1914 a large gala was held at the casino to benefit the Southside Hospital of Babylon.

hundred people lived there and in 1916 the community became an incorporated village, no longer a part of Bay Shore. T. B. Ackerson was elected the first mayor.

The T. B. Ackerson Company was not immune to the real estate depression brought on by the war, however. In 1917 and 1918 public auctions were held in an attempt to sell some seven hundred lots, mostly in the north sections of the development. Both were failures, the bidding being disastrously low. Finally in 1920 the company was forced to liquidate in a voluntary bankruptcy action, declaring at the time that it had been doing business "only through the leniency of the creditors, to whom it pays a high tribute."[19] The Brightwaters incorporated village survived the slow war years and went on to expand again in the Roaring Twenties. T. B. Ackerson, who with his family had profited from the creation of Brightwaters, died in 1924, and was succeeded by his son, Henry Ward, who died prematurely two years later. T. B.'s grandson, H. Ward Ackerson, then succeeded to the business and went on to become the dean of real estate on Long Island. He lives today, still active in his nineties, in Brightwaters. It must be rewarding for him to see the village thriving, much as his grandfather conceived of it when Ward was a small boy.

During the first decade of the twentieth century John Dunbar Adams, second son of Thomas Adams (1818–1905), the inventor of Chiclets, decided to permanently settle in the Awixa Creek area of Bay Shore. He and his wife, Susan Burchell Adams, had rented various cottages in Bay Shore since the early 1890s as had his older brother, Thomas Adams Jr. The Adams family would make Bay Shore their summer home for the rest of their lives. Their story is typical of American entrepreneurship in the Gilded Age.

Thomas Adams had been born in New York, and had married Martha Dunbar from which union his two older sons, Thomas Jr. and J. Dunbar, were born in 1846 and 1849 respectively. The senior Adams had been appointed a government photographer in the Civil War. At war's end he and his eldest son began to experiment with a gum substance from the Mexican sapodilla tree that had been given the name of chicle. They believed at first that it could be converted into rubber, but the experiment proved unsuccessful. Their next plan was to manufacture chewing gum using chicle to give the gum its sticky or chewy texture. With a capital of only $35 and some borrowed money they opened a small factory in Jersey City in 1866 only to find that their new product was not being accepted at all. It was sour and had no flavor. To correct this fault they added sugar and a flavoring to the mix, and sales exploded; the Chiclet we know today had been born. In 1869 T. Adams & Sons was organized to manufacture chewing gum on a large scale. The family moved to Brooklyn where a large factory was built in 1888 and the business flourished. It was still very much a family concern at that time.

In 1898 the senior Adams retired as president of the company at the age of eighty and was followed by Thomas Jr. from 1898 to 1922 and thence by J. Dunbar Adams. In 1899 the family firm was the nucleus of the incorporation of the American Chicle Company which expanded its sales throughout the country and then the world by the time of World War I. During that period a larger factory was built in Newark, New Jersey (1903–20), and after World War I still another huge plant was built in Long Island City on the top of which the sign "Chiclets" dominated the skyline.

By the 1890s the Adams brothers had made their fortunes, and in their mid-forties then with wives and children had decided to summer in Bay Shore where several other Brooklyn families had come. Thomas Adams Jr. had married Emma Mills in 1871 and they had three children, Louis R., George J., and Florence Adams who would marry George A. Ellis Jr. of Bay Shore. J. Dunbar Adams and his wife had a son, Dunbar Jr. Thomas Jr. had settled in a permanent home much more quickly than Dunbar. He bought the Robert O. Colt property on South Country Road just west of Henry B. Hyde's Oaks in 1895, but as the house was old and had not been lived in for some years, it needed much rehabilitation. Adams continued to rent on Penataquit Point for several summers.

It was not until the autumn of 1907 that Dunbar Adams decided to purchase a summer home, having rented first on Awixa Avenue for several summers and then for the summers of 1906 and 1907 the house he would eventually buy. The family must have liked it very much, and understandably, as it was located on Awixa Pond surrounded by elegant trees with a driveway off South Country Road but far enough away so there would be no noise. They called their new home Woodlea. Set on about fourteen acres of land, the house had been built in 1895 for Mrs. Lucy A. Carroll, eldest child of the senior Bradish Johnson. Lucy Carroll, a widow when the house was built, had not occupied it in recent years, and when she sold it to Adams, she was over seventy years old. At the time it was reported: "It is one of the show places in this section and Mr. Adams is fortunate in obtaining it."[20] How he obtained title was an interesting tale.

Soon after Lucy Carroll's property had been sold to Adams it was discovered that there was a defect in the title to it. It seemed that in 1832 Messrs Thurber and Clock, who then owned 1,500 acres of land in the Awixa area, including the 14 acres bought by Adams, gave a deed to a Mr. Whelan for the land that required that the owner and any future owners not keep dogs on the premises. This restriction was soon forgotten until the title company brought it to Adams's attention in 1907. Naturally he objected and asked the local court to invalidate the restriction, saying that without clear title he would not buy the property. The restriction covered the lands of many of the neighbors including Adolph Mollenhauer on Awixa Avenue, and Mollenhauer had kennels on his farm. It took almost a year for the court to act. Finally in November of 1908 Justice Jaycox of the State Supreme Court refused to waive the restriction from the deed but said that should the owner violate the restriction and keep a dog, "he would be subject only to an action on the covenant for damages, and such damage could only be nominal."[21] With this assurance Adams proceeded to take title and within a month it was reported that "a large addition 24 x 40 feet in size to include a billiard room on the first floor and sleeping apartments above, is being erected on the front, the cupolas are being removed; five gables erected in their place on the front and tile will take the place of shingles for a roof covering. Two new bathrooms are also being added and the entire exterior and interior of the edifice altered and changed. A water lily garden has been laid out in the rear at a cost of many thousands of dollars. The garden is said to be one of the handsomest on the South Side, in fact there are few equalling it."[22] In the summer of 1909 the Dunbar Adams family moved into Woodlea to remain for the rest of their lives. Mollenhauer and other nearby neighbors continued to keep dogs on their lands, and to the best of anyone's knowledge that odious provision in the original deed was forgotten or never objected to again.

Dunbar Adams and his brother, Thomas, were both active members of the Penataquit Corinthian Yacht Club, although neither owned a sailboat. Dunbar and his wife supported local charities such as the annual fund-raising ball for the Southside Hospital. He succeeded his brother as chairman of the board of the American Chicle Company until failing health forced him to retire. Like his father before him Dunbar Adams lived to a great age for that time. Finally at eighty-five years on November 11, 1934, he died after a long illness at Woodlea in Bay Shore. His wife lived there until her death after which the property was sold in the 1950s to a restaurateur. Woodlea became Mimi's Awixa Pond and after only a few years burned to the ground one night under mysterious circumstances. Today the land is part of the Windemere development.

Thomas Adams Jr., who had bought the Colt house in West Bay Shore and whose son, George Adams, had after his marriage rented in Bay Shore, had a plan to provide a permanent home for his son very nearby. In 1906, the year before the start of the Ackerson development of Brightwaters, Adams purchased a two-acre plot of land from Charles E. Phelps on South Country Road in the area that was soon to become Brightwaters. His plan was to move the Colt house a half mile east to this new location, and after making suitable improvements, give it to George and his family. He would then build a new house for himself and ultimately leave that to his daughter, Florence, and her husband, George A. Ellis Jr., who had been renting in Bay Shore since their marriage. The scheme was not looked upon favorably, although moving houses from one location to another was a common practice then and would be for many years. As it turned out, the plan failed at great cost to Adams, although he was applauded for looking after the public interest.

The paper reported: "Thomas Adams Jr., familiarly known as Tutti Frutti Adams, in consequence of his having made a fortune in a certain brand of chewing gum, has demonstrated that he would rather lose a few thousand dollars than annoy the public or injure his neighbor's property. . . . After getting the [Colt] house cut in two pieces and half of the building started on its journey eastward, he discovered that the progress would be so slow that mid-summer would arrive before the dwelling would again be on its foundation. He also learned that a number of the shade trees in front of the Louis Bossert and Harry M. Johnson [son of Bradish Johnson Sr. who owned Sans Souci] places would have to be more or less mutilated, and he decided to raze the building to the ground. Mr. Adams' loss is between $6,000 and $7,000 as the house was an exceptionally well built one being lined with brick up to the second story."[23]

Although Adams's son George did not get the old Colt house, its demolition allowed the father to build a new home made of stucco on the old site which he called Ardmore and in which he and his wife lived until his death in 1926. In 1919 he had formally transferred Ardmore to his daughter, Florence Adams Ellis. It would remain in the Ellis family for many years and today is owned by the Southward Ho Country Club.

Adams' son-in-law, George A. Ellis Jr., was an active member of the younger generation of summer residents who came of age at the turn of the century. Born in 1875 in Newark, New Jersey, where his father was in the oil business, he received early training in the banking business. In

1904 at the age of twenty-nine he joined with his great friend Edward F. Hutton to co-found the firm E. F. Hutton & Co. George Ellis was called by his contemporary Dr. George S. King "the brain of E.F. Hutton & Co."[24] He ran the firm with the Hutton brothers until his retirement in 1941. Ellis and his wife settled in Bay Shore as early as 1901 and it was very likely that Ellis persuaded Ed Hutton to come as well. Ellis was the principal organizer of the first Bay Shore horse show held at Sagtikos Manor in 1901. He was a member of the Penataquit Corinthian Yacht Club and a part of the younger crowd that played polo with the Islip Polo Club at Oakwood Park. He was president of the club in 1913. Ellis and his wife had two children, a son and a daughter. He died in his Bay Shore home in 1942 at the age of sixty-seven.

The arrival of the Huttons on the South Shore brought a particular mix of glamour and sadness not seen since the days of William K. and Alva Vanderbilt. It was not surprising that the Huttons chose Bay Shore for their summer homes as opposed to the older, more established areas of St. Marks Lane in Islip or Pavilion Avenue in East Islip. By 1900 those roads were looked upon by those living on them as the exclusive homes of the "old" families. The Welles, Hollisters, Livingstons, Knapps, Parsons, Peters, Wilmerdings, Johnsons, Whartons, Hollins, Cuttings, and Vanderbilts had become the aristocrats of Great South Bay and did not welcome newcomers from New York or Brooklyn, especially if they did not have a long lineage of American ancestry and had not been accepted into New York Society. In fact Mrs. Henry O. Havemeyer was teased by her fellow "aristocrats of Islip" when she called upon newcomers Ed and Blanche Hutton who were her neighbors for a summer.[25] According to the protocol of that era it should have been the other way around. Bay Shore was more hospitable, and there was still some good size property available on Saxton and Awixa Avenues.

Edward Francis Hutton had been born in New York City in 1875, the son of James L. Hutton who had come east from his father's Ohio farm to make his fortune. Young Ed attended the New York Latin School, P.S. 69, where he had the good fortune to be noticed by an older man, Bernard Baruch, who was getting rich by buying shares of stock cheaply and selling them dearly, "stock market speculation," it was then called. Ed Hutton learned his trade from the master himself. At the age of seventeen he was a mail boy in the New York office of his uncle, W. E. Hutton, absorbing every aspect of the brokerage business. By the age of twenty, he had become a partner in the firm. By the age of twenty-five, he had made sufficient money to get married, and on October 9, 1900, in St. Thomas's Church on Fifth Avenue he was married to Blanche Horton, daughter of Henry W. Horton. It was not by any means a Society wedding, as the ceremony was performed by the assistant rector. Ed's younger brother, Franklyn, was the best man.

Because the Horton family had a Bay Shore home as did Ed's usher, George Ellis, the young married Huttons for the summer of 1902 rented one of H. O. Havemeyer's homes on Bayberry Point. Ed Hutton loved sailing and became an active member of the Penataquit Corinthian Yacht Club with his new boat *Anita* competing with H. O. Havemeyer's *Electra* and Horace Havemeyer's *Flight*. Ed and Blanche Hutton enjoyed the summer weekends along the Great South Bay. In 1905 they rented one of the Mollenhauer homes on the east side of Awixa Avenue near the South Country Road.

Ed Hutton had decided to start his own securities firm, and E. F. Hutton and Company was organized in 1904 in San Francisco. Ed became the managing partner. He was only twenty-nine years old. His novel idea was to establish a direct wire link from New York City to San Francisco so that customers in California could have an edge in getting news and in executing trades on the New York Exchange. It was a great success. News of the San Francisco earthquake and fire of 1906 reached New York first on the E. F. Hutton wire service. In following years E. F. Hutton offices were opened all over the country. The Hutton name became almost synonymous with stock market tips.

Ed and Blanche Hutton purchased the home they had rented on Awixa Avenue in the mid 1900s and later bought the property up to the corner. Although it was not on a waterway it was of sufficient size to give them privacy. Their neighbor on the east was J. Dunbar Adams and on the south, E. Mildeberger. Ed was a great sportsman. He was a founding member of the Islip Scooter Club and of the Islip Polo Club (1912). He played regularly with Allan Pinkerton, Harry Peters, Horace Havemeyer, and later August Belmont Jr. The Islip team was a formidable competitor for most of the other Long Island teams. In the years between 1912 and 1920 a dozen of the younger generation of summer residents were active "low goal" players (handicap less than seven). Ed and Blanche also always participated in the charity balls for the benefit of the Southside Hospital of Babylon that were held in those years. The Argyle Casino was annually a festive place and Blanche would win awards for the most elegant gown.

This gay, happy, summer life ended abruptly for the Huttons in 1918 when Blanche was stricken and died of the Spanish flu in the epidemic that was sweeping the country that fall. They had been married for eighteen years and had a single child, a son named Halcourt. Ed Hutton was forty-three years old. Two years later, in July 1920, he married the recently divorced daughter and only heir of Charles W. Post, the founder of the hugely successful Postum Cereal Company (later to become the General Foods Corporation). Marjorie Merriweather Post Close and E. F. Hutton would remain married for fifteen years and have one child, a daughter named Nedenia.

Shortly after Ed and Marjorie were married, tragedy struck again. Ed's son Halcourt was eighteen years old at the time and about to enter Yale. An accomplished horseman, he was exercising his horse at his father's estate on Saxton Avenue when the saddle came loose, twisted around the lad's legs, threw him forward and finally upside down. The frightened horse began to gallop, knocking Halcourt's head against the cobblestones in the driveway and fracturing his skull. Doctors were called from New York, and surgery was performed at Doctor King's hospital in Bay Shore, all in vain. Halcourt died two days later on September 26, 1920. This terrible accident ended forever any pleasure Ed Hutton could have received from his Bay Shore home. He and Marjorie soon moved to the North Shore's Gold Coast where in 1921 they built a new seventy-room mansion, called Hillwood, on a 176-acre country estate in Brookville.

If Ed Hutton married an extremely wealthy woman in Marjorie Merriweather Post, as he surely did, his younger brother, Franklyn, did likewise. Franklyn had gone to Yale University after schooling in New York and graduated with the class of 1899. After Ed had started E. F. Hutton & Co., Franklyn had joined him at the new firm where he remained a partner until 1931. He was an attractive, high-spirited young man and certainly a catch for any young woman. On April 24, 1907, at the Church of the Heavenly Rest in New York, at the age of thirty, he wed Edna Woolworth, one of three daughters of F. W. Woolworth, who founded the five and ten cents store in America and amassed a fortune. It was expected that Edna upon the death of her parents would become one of the wealthiest women in the country.

Franklyn and Edna Hutton were a much sought after young couple, entertaining and being entertained in the social whirl that was part of the pre-war era. On November 14, 1912, in New York City, their only child, a daughter whom they named Barbara, was born. With the advent of her birth they decided to purchase a summer home where she could grow up in a suitable environment. They had known Bay Shore well from visits there with Franklyn's brother Ed on Awixa Avenue, and thus in the spring of 1912 they purchased the Daniel Conover house and six acres located directly north of the Olympic Club on Saxton Avenue. The property had access to Awixa Creek and would provide boat moorings for both the Hutton brothers. Five years later they added six more acres to the north side and then adjoined the summer home of Simon Rothschild. Their lavish entertaining continued at their Bay Shore home in the summer.

For five summers young Barbara had a reasonably normal life for a child in that situation, well looked after by nannies, and occasionally seeing her parents in the evenings before supper. She was doted upon by her Woolworth grandparents whom she often visited on the North Shore on their massive estate there. All this "normality" abruptly ended for Barbara on May 2, 1917, when her mother was found dead at her apartment in the Plaza Hotel in New York City. Franklyn had been at their Saxton Avenue home at the time.

The mystery behind Edna Woolworth Hutton's death has never been satisfactorily explained. The *New York Times* said on May 3, 1917, "She had been dead for several hours when she was found. The coroner said an autopsy was not necessary; that she had died of a chronic ear disease which resulted in the hardening of the bones of the ear, causing suffocation." Obviously every effort was being made to protect Barbara from the publicity, and in fact Edna's obituary in the paper did not even mention her daughter. There was apparently no evidence of foul play, however, and death by natural causes became the official verdict. However, in his book *Million Dollar Baby*, Philip Van Rensselaer states that Barbara much later told him that her mother had committed suicide after discovering a letter from her husband to his mistress. The author claims that Barbara found her mother lying dead "on the Turkey-red carpet" in her apartment in the Plaza Hotel "wearing a white lace dress, and the pink enamel and gold parasol she carried was broken in two as if there had been a terrible struggle."[26] Barbara, who was five years old at the time, lived with this memory for her whole life.

With her mother's death, Barbara inherited $18 million, which her father was charged with overseeing while she was a minor. One tragedy was to follow another. When she was seven, her grandfather Woolworth died, to be followed five years later by her grandmother Woolworth. By the time Barbara was twelve years old her fortune had been increased by bequests to $30 million and the press was now constantly referring to her as "the richest child in America." She poignantly described her own childhood, most of which was spent after her mother's death with her Woolworth grandparents and with her aunts' families, the Donohues in Palm Beach and the McCanns on the North Shore of Long Island. "My father was young and very busy. He loved me, of course, but I was only an ordinary, rather stupid little girl and I couldn't be a real companion to a gay, brilliant young man." Of her mother she said, "I hardly remember her at all, but I have missed her all my life." She much later said, "All the unhappiness in my life has been caused by men, including my father."[27] This bitterness towards her father must have resulted from Franklyn's neglect of her and his remarriage in 1926 to Irene Dodds whom Barbara detested and refused to live with. During her early formative years, Barbara's role model was her Aunt Marjorie. "Barbara's aunt, Marjorie Post Hutton, was as beautiful and alluring as the cinema queens. She was a great spender and was attractive to men. Barbara, who was imitative by nature, took on the colors of this vivid woman."[28] Her later life was marred by a series of six unsuccessful marriages and the vast fortune (estimated to be $42 million in 1934 in the midst of the Depression) which caused her nothing but heartache. She had only one child, a son, Lance Reventlow, whom she adored. She lived much of her life in Europe searching for the happiness she never found. Her last years were spent as a partial invalid in Beverly Hills, California, where she died in 1979 at the age of sixty-six. Barbara was buried in the Woolworth mausoleum in the Woodlawn Cemetery in New York. There were only ten people at the burial service to say goodbye. One was her cousin, Nedenia Hutton, by then known as Dina Merrill.

Some time after Edna's death Franklyn Hutton turned the house on Saxton Avenue over to his brother, Ed, and it was there that Halcourt died in the riding accident. Ed had built a new, smaller cottage on the land where his son could come for weekends with his friends and enjoy the riding and the polo. After Halcourt's death, the Huttons sold their property to Philip B. Weld and his wife, Katharine Saltonstall Weld, for $100,000. Land prices had risen considerably by then.

Adding to the glamour on Saxton Avenue in the pre-war decade was another newcomer, whose ancestor had first come to the South Shore in Babylon in the 1860s, August Belmont. Born in New York City in 1882, young August was the grandson and namesake of the famous founder of the family in America. In 1890 when the elder Belmont died, his second son, August, immediately dropped the Jr. from his name and his eight-year-old son became August Jr. It was all in accordance with the usual practice of the time. His mother was Elizabeth Morgan Belmont, daughter of the stockbroker Edward Morgan and granddaughter of Matthew Morgan of the old banking house of that name. As a small child and growing up into manhood, young August had spent a great deal of time at the Nursery in North Babylon, where his father was given the task of "straightening up the place." The family lived there for only one winter but spent many summers there. The stud farm was given up in 1886, but all other aspects of the huge property were run by the family and many happy weekends were spent, fishing, shooting, and working with the livestock there. It was the place where many Bay Shore and Islipians would keep their show horses and later their polo ponies. Young August and his two younger brothers came to know the Great South Bay area from those early years at the farm.

His father and mother decided that their son should go off to St. Mark's School in Massachusetts, and it was while he was there in September of 1898 that his mother died unexpectedly at the age of thirty-six while in Paris on a visit. His father, by then the scion of the banking house of August Belmont & Co., the leading figure in the horse racing world, and founder of the Belmont Park race track on Long Island, was grief stricken. He erected a chapel at the Nursery to commemorate her life and would remain a widower for twelve years before marrying English-born actress Eleanor Robson in 1910 who was twenty-seven years his junior. Young August went on to Harvard from St. Mark's where he was a member of the Hasty Pudding Club and the Porcellian Club, all measures of social success. He graduated in 1904 and went right to work at the family firm, becoming a partner in 1910 at the age of twenty-eight, the same year his father remarried.

Four years earlier, on January 2, 1906, August Belmont Jr. and Alice W. De Goicouria had been wed in New York. Like many other couples in that decade they had come to know each other from summering along the Great South Bay. Alice was the second daughter of Cuban-born Albert V. De Goicouria, one of the most popular members of the South Side Sportsmen's Club and called by his close friends Gerkey. Gerkey was one of the best known all around amateur athletes of his day, a crack bird shot, and avid tennis and golf player. He was a particularly close friend of Edward S. Knapp who often shot with him and likely persuaded him to summer in Islip. Gerkey and his wife first summered along the South Country Road in the mid 1880s, renting at the Pavilion Hotel, the Meeks home, and finally a house next to it on the north side of the road east of the Islip Field Club of which he was an original incorporator. Two daughters were born to the De Goicourias, Rosalie and Alice. By the time Alice and August Belmont Jr. had married, Alice's mother had died at fifty years of age while on holiday with her family at Saratoga Springs "enjoying the gay life at that famous resort."[29] Gerkey, a stockbroker on the New York Stock Exchange, retired the year Alice married. He later remarried and moved to Santa Barbara, California, where he died in 1930 at the age of eighty-one.

August Jr. and Alice Belmont were among the most popular members of the young set in the Great South Bay area in that pre-war decade. Their eldest child, a son named August, was born in 1908 and was followed by two daughters, Bessie Morgan and Alice De Goicouria Belmont. August Jr. was a particularly enthusiastic sportsman with great interest in polo and in yachting. It was not surprising that coming from the family most closely connected with horse racing in America, August Jr. played polo at an early age, and when the Islip Polo Club started in 1912, he was a founder. He was on the team of four in 1914 that was described as "the Islip Freebooters. The men who overthrew the Meadow Brook aggregation constitute the strongest team that the Islip Polo Club has sent on the field in many a day. The Islip players were Allan Pinkerton, Harry T. Peters, Horace Havemeyer, and August Belmont Jr."[30] It should be said that the Meadow Brook team, the Rovers, was not their top team of high goalers (seven to ten rating) but the low goalers (below seven rating). Their top team of that year — Webb, Hitchcock, Stevenson, and Milburn, with a thirty-eight goal rating (out of a possible rating of forty) — was the international champion of the sport. August Jr. was also a member of the Islip Scooter Club and the Short Beach Club. Alice was a prominent and attractive part of the annual Southside Hospital's charity ball. They were leaders in whatever they undertook.

Following the demise of Penataquit Corinthian Yacht Club in 1908, the Bay Shore Yacht Club under the leadership of Commodore J. Adolph Mollenhauer continued to provide occasional races for all classes of boats during the summer. As most of the sailing craft were of different designs, however, competition lagged. There was a need for a one-design class large enough to stimulate competition among the several young men who loved that kind of racing. August Belmont Jr. was one of those enthusiasts.

The Islip Yacht Club was started in the winter of 1909 to promote one-design racing and Belmont was its commodore in its first few years. The men behind the new club were primarily from Bay Shore, Islip, and East Islip, although Sayville was also represented. They were ten in number, all of whom agreed to buy the new boat that had been ordered. They were A. Belmont Jr., H. B. Hollins Jr., Aymar Johnson, Horace Havemeyer, Charles Van Rensselaer, R. C. Watson, William K. Dick, W. R. Simmons, R. B. Potts, and J. O. Law. The group decided to ask the notable yacht designer and naval architect William Gardner to design a racing boat for them which was given the name Islip One-Designs, as it was built solely for the Islip Yacht Club. It was 21 feet long on the waterline with a large overhang giving a 30-foot length over all. It was gaff-rigged in accord with the custom of that day. It was designed with a sleek, streamlined hull making it very fast in the choppy waters of the Great South Bay. All ten boats were identical, thereby providing an equal test for the skipper, his choice of sails, and his sailing ability. One-designs racing was in its infancy then and only in Bellport was there another and different one-design class on the bay.

William Gardner was chosen to design the new boat because his reputation in 1909 was second only to that of the Herreshoff Manufacturing Company whose genius, Nathaniel Herreshoff, had recently died, but whose son, Francis, was carrying on the business. Gardner was a New Yorker who had studied and worked in England at the Royal Naval College in Greenwich and at shipyards in the summer along the Clyde. His reputation, like Herreshoff's, was made designing large sailing yachts in the 1890s and early 1900s. The most famous of these was the three masted, 185-foot schooner *Atlantic* which Gardner designed in 1903 and which in 1905 made yachting history by winning the transatlantic race for the Kaiser's Cup from Sandy Hook, New Jersey, to the Needles off the Isle of Wight in the record time of twelve days and four hours. The record set by *Atlantic* was not surpassed for seventy-five years until 1980! Gardner also designed several America's Cup contenders, notably *Vanitie* in 1914 which was sailed by Captain Hank Haff's son, Harry P. Haff of Islip. The Cup races scheduled for that summer were called off because of the start of the Great War.

Gardner was also interested in designing smaller boats, and in the first decade of the 1900s he designed a one-design class for the Larchmont Yacht Club, called the Larchmont O Class. When the Islip One-Designs were ordered in 1909, one-design racing was fast becoming a sport for everyman and not only for the very affluent. Gardner's greatest and permanent contribution to one-design racing came in 1911 when he created the first Star boat in Port Washington, Long Island. The Star Class became an international one-design success story, but did not come to the Great South Bay until the late 1920s.

During the summer of 1909 there were several races sponsored by the Islip Yacht Club for the one-designs. Belmont was a regular winner of these with his *Goshawk*, as was Havemeyer with his *Electra* and Hollins with his *Nyssa*. Although most of the racing was off Islip, the one-designs did compete in the Great South Bay Yacht Racing Association's regattas and race week held throughout the bay. Although they raced off Sayville and off Bellport, they were primarily an Islip boat, and as so often happened before the advent of the Star Class, with each season the class got smaller, not larger. By 1913 only four or five Islip One-Designs were racing and in 1914 the class did not sail at all. It was reported: "The Islip One-Design Yacht Club which was organized five years ago by well known men of wealth will not be an active body during the coming yachting season. A member of the club claims that the suspension of activities is due simply to a proposed change in the class of boats that will sail under the club burgee of the future. The yachts thus far used have been 30 foot [the One-Designs]."[31] Subsequently, the Islip One-Designs became increasingly scarce on the bay. By the 1930s three or four boats with the new marconi rig raced as a class in bay regattas, but no longer with the burgee of the Islip Yacht Club, which had long ceased to exist. Finally, only Duncan C. Arnold's *Querida* was left to sail with the "R" Class. August Jr. and Alice Belmont did not live at the Nursery in Babylon after their marriage. For several summers they rented cottages in Bay Shore and Islip including Mrs. Edward Knapp's house, Awixa Lawn on Saxton Avenue. Mrs. Knapp had moved to the smaller house she had built on the property after her husband's death. In the spring of 1915 with their three children needing more room and their wanting more permanence to their summer lives, the Belmonts bought Awixa Lawn with its nine acres. They had a spacious summer home at the waterfront at last. The following year Mrs. Knapp sold the house in which she lived and the remaining land to Julius Oppenheimer of Manhattan and left the South Shore.

Margaret Lawrance Knapp had lived on Saxton Avenue for thirty-five years, ever since her marriage. Her three children had been raised in Awixa Lawn and her husband had died while they were living there. She had spent the whole of her life on the South Shore in Bay Shore. If anyone could have been called the doyenne of the South Shore, it was Margaret Lawrance Knapp. Her son Edward described her as "a very regal lady. Her back was very straight and she carried herself beautifully. Within, she was the most full-of-fun person you can imagine, with a twinkle in her eye that denoted a sense of humor and a happy disposition."[32] Edward had married Rosalie Moran, daughter of Amedeé Depau Moran, in 1903, but after some summers spent on Bayberry Point they had left with their children for the North Shore. By 1915 Margaret Knapp's youngest child, Margaret, had reached maturity and left the family home. Thus it was that Mrs. Knapp departed from Saxton Avenue and her girlhood home along the Great South Bay for good. She lived away from Long Island until the 1930s when she died in her late seventies.

The Belmonts made improvements to the old Knapp house, the first one built on Saxton Avenue by a New York family. However their time together there was to be very short. On March 29, 1919, following an operation in a New York City hospital, August Jr. died unexpectedly at the age of thirty-six. His son was ten at the time and his daughters were seven and five. In addition to Alice he was also survived by his father, August Belmont, who would outlive him by five years. In his obituary, as was usual, his clubs were listed to show the scope of his interests and his social standing. He belonged to the Knickerbocker, the New York Athletic, the Downtown Association, the Racquet and Tennis, and the New York Yacht Clubs in New York, and the Meadow Brook Club in Old Westbury, Long Island. His death left a large gap in the firm of August Belmont & Co. and a gap on Saxton Avenue as well.

Alice and the three children continued to live at Awixa Lawn until 1923 when she put the property up for sale. Young

Augie,* as he became known, was fifteen then and off at
boarding school. At the time of the sale the property was
described as follows: "There are nine acres of land, beautifully landscaped, with 600 feet on the Great South Bay [on
Awixa Creek with access to the Great South Bay], boat
houses, stables, and a five car garage. The house has 25
rooms with every improvement. It was offered for $75,000,
and sold to J. Allen Dillon of New York City."[33] In 1924 Alice
De Goicouria Belmont married J. D. Wing. That same year
August Belmont Sr. died at seventy-one years of age. The
Belmont family was gone from the South Shore, having come
in 1864, sixty years and three generations before.

---

* August Belmont IV died in July 1995 at age eighty-six.

Electra, H. O. Havemeyer's Herreshoff 30 sloop, racing off Bayberry Point on the Great South Bay in 1902.

The three-story clubhouse of the *Penataquit Corinthian Yacht Club* was located at the end of Penataquit Point from 1900 to 1909 when the club closed for good. The clubhouse was a landmark from the bay.
(Courtesy of *Pictorial Bay Shore*)

Homeport, the home of
Commodore and Mrs. J. Adolph
Mollenhauer on Awixa Avenue,
Bay Shore, was built in 1899. It
remains standing today on the
west side of Awixa Creek. (Courtesy
of Richard A. Milligan.)

The Islip railroad station is pictured here in 1911. Note the waiting carriage and the unpaved roadway. (The collection of Ron Ziel.)

Brookwood Hall in East Islip was built in 1903-04 for Mr. and Mrs. Harry K. Knapp. They lived there until the late 1920s when the house was acquired by Mr. and Mrs. Francis B. Thorne. It is pictured as it looks today. (Courtesy of Richard A. Milligan.)

Islip village is shown in 1912, seven years after the big fire. Note that Main Street is unpaved. The "Old Town Hall" is in the center of the photo. (Courtesy of the Nassau County Museum, photo by Henry Otto Korten.)

Bird shooting was popular on the Bay in the 1880s and 1890s. Edwin Thorne, an expert shot, was known to have killed as many as 300 birds on a day's outing. (Courtesy of Lightfoot Collection.)

Chapter IX
THE WAR YEARS (1914–1919)

The years of the new century prior to the Great War were years of transition for the area from Oakdale to Babylon. Many of the earliest summer residents who had settled there in the 1870s and 1880s died after the turn of the century. Even more marriages occurred, however, among their sons and daughters, often between childhood acquaintances who had grown up together along the South Shore. These young married couples were deciding to remain in the area they had known as youths. By 1913 there had been a passing of the torch. This was clearly seen at the venerable St. Mark's Church where Benjamin S. Welles Jr. succeeded to his father's vestry seat after the latter's death in 1904, Buell Hollister succeeded to H. H. Hollister's seat in 1915, and Gerald V. Hollins to Harry B. Hollins's seat in 1918. The Bradish Johnsons were on the church vestry for three generations.

Even more striking were the connections between deaths and marriages. During 1904 when seventy-six-year-old Maria M. Knapp died, her grandson, Harry B. Hollins Jr., married Lilias Livingston. They and their children would live in East Islip for many years. Francis Cooper Lawrance Jr. died in 1904 and his father in 1911, while in 1910 his son Charles Lanier Lawrance married Margaret Dix; Charles would live in East Islip for the rest of his life. John Mollenhauer (1905), Henry O. Havemeyer (1907), and William Dick (1912) all died during that time. Only Dick lived long enough to see his granddaughter, Doris Dick, marry Havemeyer's son, Horace, in 1911. They and their offspring would stay in Bay Shore and Islip for most of the century. Robert A. Pinkerton died in 1907 and John Gibb in 1905, only a few years after Lewis M.

Gibb had married Anna Pinkerton and after Allan Pinkerton had married.

The year 1907 saw the death of some other notable figures: the eccentric George C. Taylor and his "wife" from Great River; Bradish Johnson's son, Harry M., of Sans Souci in West Bay Shore; and the dean of the most prominent Islip local family, James Harvey Doxsee. Only a year before, Islip's most notable sailing master, Hank Haff, had passed on to his reward. With the deaths of Haff and Doxsee, Islip village had passed the torch as well. Three more deaths should be recorded: William Bayard Cutting and Richard Hyde in 1912 and Juan M. Ceballos in 1913.

There were many more marriages of summer families between 1900 and 1914. In addition to those noted above, Richard Wharton and Helena Johnson Parsons, Jay F. Carlisle and Mary Pinkerton, Harold H. Weekes and Louisine Peters, August Belmont Jr. and Alice De Goicouria, all married in 1906. Harry T. Peters and Natalie Wells had married the year before. Peter H. B. Frelinghuysen and Adaline Havemeyer would marry in 1907. Toward the end of the period Gerald V. Hollins wed Virginia Kobbe in 1909, Bayard C. Hoppin wed Helen Alexandre in 1910, Harry K. Knapp Jr. wed Phebe Thorne in 1911 and Malcolm McBurney wed Dorothy Moran in 1912. A new generation of summer residents was beginning and many of its members would remain after the war. Although it was not apparent to any of them at the time, the great conflict that lay ahead would alter their lives forever. The end of the Gilded Age or the Edwardian era, as it was often called, was at hand. It was already affecting the resort life along the Great South Bay, forcing the closure of more hotels and two old clubs.

On May 10, 1912, the *Islip Herald* reported: "The Somerset House, one of the oldest remaining road houses on the South Country Road, was sold last week. Included in the sale are the 10 1/2 acres of ground on which the building stands. It has a frontage of 673 feet on Main Street [in East Islip]. It is intended to subdivide the plot into building lots. The hotel will eventually be demolished." Founded by George Westcott in 1860 and later operated by his sons, John and then Joe Westcott, Somerset House had been a popular hostelry, particularly in the days of coaching, but like its neighbor, the Lake House, it suffered badly with the coming of the automobile and for the previous dozen years had struggled along under several different owners.

There were hotels in each of the villages of East Islip, Islip, and Bay Shore then that took care of transient guests, but only the Linwood Hotel on Clinton Avenue, Bay Shore, could properly be called a resort hotel. Its demise would not come until after World War I. In the early morning hours of a Sunday in October 1925, a fire of mysterious origin swept through the empty Linwood Hotel. It had been closed for the winter and was for sale. The big structure which had once held 150 guests was left "a smouldering mass of charred ruins."[1] A high wind and low water pressure prevented the local firemen from doing more than saving the nearby cottages. As was so often the case, the suspected arsonist was never found. Thus ended the last of the great resort hotels in the area from Oakdale to Babylon.

The year 1912 also saw the end of the Short Beach Club on Sexton Island, which had been started with great fanfare in 1887. At the end it had fifty-seven members. The official reason given in the petition to dissolve was "on the ground that conditions have so changed that it is in danger of becoming a losing proposition."[2] The petition went to say that "interest in the club has so greatly fallen off because of changed conditions in the Great South Bay." What the changed conditions were is a matter of speculation. It is likely, however, that the decline of the large sailing yachts on the bay made it increasingly difficult to get from Bay Shore and Islip across the six miles of bay to Sexton Island. The era of the small power craft had not yet arrived, and swimming was much better on Fire Island beach. The concept of club life could not survive if the purpose of coming together had disappeared. This seems to have been the case with the Short Beach Club.

Finally, at the end of the summer season of 1912 the oldest club of all along the Great South Bay closed its doors forever. The venerable Olympic Club had lasted for seventy-one years, for fifty-six of which it had stood at the south end of Saxton Avenue in Bay Shore. Along the way it had its ups and downs. It had undergone a major renovation when women were admitted as guests, with bath houses and cottages having been erected for them. For much of its life it had two hundred or more members mostly from New York and Brooklyn. Although at the end it was not as "exclusive" as were the South Side Club or the Short Beach Club, it did continue to attract the affluent who would board there as well as those who resided in Bay Shore and Islip. Its dues were modest, $100 annually in 1909, but it was always able to avoid losses.

In June 1909, to celebrate its sixty-ninth annual reunion, the club sponsored a special party "on the club's grounds, Saturday afternoon, when about 200 members and invited guests gathered and made merry while partaking of a genuine Rhode Island clambake which was served at 3:30 o'clock. There was nothing missing to make the affair an unqualified success and several hours were consumed in partaking of the appetizing viands. While dinner was in progress, the Islip Yacht Club's one-design class was racing in full view of the dining hall."[3] Although the picturesque setting and the gaiety of the party led the reporter to believe that "the club's future is brighter as each year rolls around,"[4] the end was not far off.

In its last years two figures dominated the Olympic Club. One was its last president, James Kempster, who lived in the house next to the club on Saxton Avenue as his predecessor, Thomas Asten, had done. The other was the club's oldest member, well advanced in his eighties, the retired New York City fireman Captain James F. Wenman. Captain Wenman was one of the charter members of the club and an often seen and popular figure throughout its life. Those who now live on Saxon Avenue (the "t" has been dropped from the Avenue's name today) will recognize the names of Kempster

Avenue and Wenman Avenue in honor of those two men long associated with the Olympic Club.

The club did not open for the 1913 summer season. A foreclosure sale was arranged for August 22 at which "the property including 14 acres [not including Kempster's house which he owned] of excellent upland and six large buildings which constituted the club, besides a good dock, bath houses, bulkheading and in fact all improvements that would be necessary to a first-class club located on the Bay"[5] was sold for $46,000. The buyer was not another club, however. The establishment of a new club on such a large property would have been even more difficult in 1913 than maintaining the failed Olympic Club. The buyers were two neighbors and a friend. To protect their property and to prevent a subdivision of the fourteen acres, Franklyn L. Hutton to the north and Allan Pinkerton to the east with their friend, Edward C. Blum of Penataquit Avenue, acquired the land. "It is possible," said Mr. Hutton, "that the club may be opened in connection with the Islip Polo Club."[6] But that was not to be either. The Polo Club was happy at Oakwood Park.

The syndicate of three began to dispose of the old buildings. The main clubhouse in 1914 was put on a barge and towed across the bay to Ocean Beach on Fire Island where it was used as an annex to the Ocean Beach Hotel. With the start of the war in Europe there was little interest in the land in spite of its marvelous location and the owners continued to hold it until in 1916 it attracted the eye of a man whose young family of three children was getting too big for the cottage on Bayberry Point and who had always wanted to set his roots along the Great South Bay, thirty-year-old Horace Havemeyer. More of that story will come later.

One new family came from New York City to summer on Ocean Avenue in Islip in the first decade of the twentieth century. John B. Stanchfield and his wife, Clara Spaulding, had previously rented in Babylon. For the summer of 1909 they moved to Islip where they engaged Afterglow, the unoccupied home of the late John Gibb. With neighbors John Henry Dick to the south and H. G. Timmerman to the north, they found that Afterglow suited their needs very well, and they purchased the seventeen acres from the Gibb estate by the end of that year.

When the fifty-four-year-old Stanchfield moved to Ocean Avenue he was at the peak of an eminent career in the law. Born in Elmira, New York, and educated at Amherst College and the Harvard Law School, he started practice in Elmira and at the age of twenty-four joined with David B. Hill to form the firm of Hill and Stanchfield. As so often happened then with young lawyers, Stanchfield was attracted to politics, becoming the county district attorney, then mayor of Elmira, then New York State Assemblyman for the district. In 1900 he was nominated to be the Democratic candidate for governor of New York and in 1901 for United States senator. He lost both races against a strong Republican tide running then under the leadership of Theodore Roosevelt.

Following these defeats Stanchfield moved his legal office to New York City, establishing the firm of Stanchfield and Levy on Broadway in lower Manhattan. He represented some very prominent clients and had some notable legal victories. Among these was Harry K. Thaw, the convicted assassin of the famous architect Stanford White, whom he shot on the roof garden of Madison Square Garden for allegedly having an affair with Thaw's wife, the Flora Dora chorus girl Evelyn Nesbit. Stanchfield got Harry K. Thaw acquitted from an asylum after serving nine years of his sentence there on the ground that he was mentally deranged at the time of the shooting. Another Stanchfield victory was the dismissal of the indictment against the famous gambler of that era, Richard Canfield, who ran the most exclusive casino of them all where the affluent would come for entertainment. Canfield's fame was international and his casinos at Saratoga Springs and in Manhattan next to Delmonico's on Forty-fourth Street were the scenes where "Bet-a-Million" Gates and others would sometimes win and often lose huge stakes in a single night. Stanchfield also represented Mrs. James T. Stillman in one of the most notable divorce proceedings of the time.

John and Clara Stanchfield summered at Afterglow for the remaining years of their lives. By the summer of 1920 his health began to fail and in July of 1921 John died at Afterglow. With him at the time of his death were his wife, his son, John Jr., and his daughter, Alice, wife of Dr. Arthur M. Wright of New York. The Wrights inherited the house on Ocean Avenue where they continued to live for many summers and where their son, Stanchfield Wright, named for his grandfather, grew up.

In East Islip, on Pavilion Avenue, soon to be known as Suffolk Lane, several changes were occurring after 1900, and three new families came to set down summer roots there along Champlin's Creek. The old Pavilion Hotel had been destroyed by fire in 1894, and since then the site had been owned by Bradish Johnson Jr. and several neighbors to protect their own residences from unwanted incursion. To the site came Richard T. Dana and his family from New York. The Danas built a new shingle house near the corner of Pavilion Avenue and the South Country Road and would enjoy many years there. Richard was descended from a much earlier Richard Dana who had come from England to Cambridge, Massachusetts, in 1640, as well as from several Richard Danas who made great wealth as merchants in the China trade. He was a cousin of Richard Henry Dana Jr., author of the classic narrative *Two Years Before the Mast* (1840). Dana, a graduate of Yale and a consulting engineer, and his wife, Mary, both had pre-Revolutionary war lineages and were welcome additions to the East Islip summer community. Dana died at his home there in 1928 at the age of fifty-three.

It was not surprising that Percy G. Williams would come to the South Shore to summer. Early in his career he was in business in Brooklyn with Thomas Adams Jr. and was a lifelong friend of Julian D. Fairchild, president of the Kings County Trust Co., both of whom summered in Bay Shore. What was unusual was that a Brooklynite, and one who made his fortune in show business, would choose the enclave in East Islip where he would be surrounded by the Hollins, the

Whartons, the Wilmerdings, and the Bradish Johnsons, all
blue-blood New Yorkers. Williams did not come to East Islip
for sociability, however. He came because he wanted a cool,
comfortable place to retire. He had sold his business and was
looking for a summer house where his invalid wife could be
well cared for even after his death. Their winters were spent
in Palm Beach, Florida.

To the south of Bradish Johnson and fronting on
Champlin's Creek, Charles T. Harbeck had retained about
fifty acres of property at the time he sold his home to Johnson
in 1892. These fifty acres were unimproved land and per-
fectly situated for a house that would face southwest looking
down the creek toward the Great South Bay. In February of
1911 Percy Williams paid $100,000 for Harbeck's land and
proceeded to build his house, which was located directly
across the creek from Schuyler Parsons's Whileaway.
Williams called his home Pineacres, as there were many
large white pine trees on the land.

Williams's career was interesting and altogether different from that of all his Islip and East Islip neighbors. Born in
Baltimore in 1857, he had always had a passion for the
theater, and much of his life was devoted to its promotion.
The son of a respected physician, young Percy was studying
medicine to follow in his father's footsteps when he decided
to try to make a living on the stage.

For five years, first in Baltimore and then in Brooklyn,
he both acted in and managed theater productions, ending
as the leading comedian in a stock company of players known
as the Holliday Street Theater Company. At the age of twenty-
three Williams knew that if he were to follow his passion
and make it a meaningful career, he would have to earn
some money first in a different endeavor, and he turned to
business.

While in Brooklyn Williams had met Thomas Adams Jr.
of chewing gum fame, who was willing to back the young
man in real estate promotion. Adams would remain a financial backer and friend of Williams for the rest of his life.
Several modest successes led to their largest success, the

development of Bergen Beach in Brooklyn. Here was an opportunity for Williams to merge real estate and the theater. "Percy Williams' career as a theatrical magnate had its inception with the organization of summer attractions at Bergen Beach, which followed the extension of the trolley road to the new resort. He managed the erection and conduct of the Casino, which was finished in 1896, and immediately began a successful run of vaudeville."[7] The music hall with its vaudeville acts were the rage in the 1890s, the era of the Flora Dora girls, and Williams was ready to capitalize on that theatrical fashion.

From the casino at Bergen Beach Williams took over the management of the Brooklyn Music Hall in East New York and success quickly followed there as well. He seemed to have the magic touch. At both the casino and the music hall he booked what would become the most famous comedy team of its time, Mr. Gallagher and Mr. Shean. He paid them $150 each per week. By the 1920s they would command $2,500 each for a week's engagement.

Williams next acquired the Novelty Theater in the Williamsburg section of Brooklyn, which then was the center of the prosperous German American community, and in 1900 he built the Orpheum Theater in downtown Brooklyn, one of the finest theaters ever constructed. As his theater empire expanded into Manhattan with the purchase of the Circle Theater and later the Colonial Theater, Williams traveled often to Europe to look for acts that would be attractive in America. He booked many European stars for Brooklyn and New York appearances, and his judgement seemed always to be on the mark.

In 1912 Percy Williams had made his fame and his fortune and was ready to retire. He sold his chain of theaters to the Keith interests for over $5 million. He was fifty-five years old and looked forward to enjoying his retirement with his wife and two sons at his East Islip and Palm Beach homes. The *New York Times* said in summarizing his career, "Percy G. Williams, independent, daring, original, controlling a group of profitable houses in the theatrical center of the country, was a power."[8] Sadly, his retirement was marred by tragedy. His son Victor died in 1913, and shortly thereafter his wife developed mental illness and became incapacitated for the rest of her life.

Williams lived for only eleven summers at Pineacres in East Islip. He died there in July of 1923 "of cirrhosis of the liver complicated by heart disease."[9] He had been ill for much of his last two years. His funeral was conducted by the St. Mark's Church rector Dr. William H. Garth at Pineacres. Williams was honored by the attendance of two hundred members of the Lambs Club, of which he had been treasurer for years, and by many from the Amaranth Society of Brooklyn* where he was twice the president. A prominent member of the Elks Club offered a eulogy.

This honor paid to Williams by his friends in the theatrical community was repaid many times over by his unusual will.** His wife was to be "liberally and luxuriously provided for and for her attendance by nurses, physicians, and other necessary help, as she now is and for a long time has been a helpless invalid, unable to manage her own affairs."[10] Upon her death, his East Islip home was to become an actors' home to be known as the Percy G. Williams Home for the aged, indigent, and infirm members of the drama profession. His will further said, "The residents of the home shall be deemed and referred to as guests. Make their residence home-like and comfortable. Provide in the house a suitable library and diverse means of recreation. Furnish letters, readings, and entertainments to which the guests shall have free access. ... The gardens and grounds are so to be used as to be productive and of profit as well as being maintained for the

---

* One of the few great amateur theatrical organizations, of which Williams was president, stage director, and an actor.

** Williams's lifelong friend Julian D. Fairchild, for thirty-two years president of the Kings County Trust Co. and Bay Shore summer resident, who lived on Awixa Avenue, was named an executor of the will.

health and pleasure of the guests and so far as may be capable, such guests as are not otherwise profitably occupied may be permitted to assist in farming, horticulture, and the cultivation of flowers."[11]

Williams asked that the New York State legislature pass a special act to incorporate a non-profit society known as the Percy Williams Home so that it could receive donations from the public as well as from his estate. This society would be governed by a board of directors of twelve, six chosen by the Lambs and six by the Actors Fund of America. After his wife died, Pineacres became the Percy Williams Home just as he had intended, and with the full cooperation of his one surviving son, Harold. The great debt that Williams felt he owed the acting profession was repaid. For many years until after World War II the actors' retirement home stood on the east bank of Champlin's Creek and hundreds enjoyed the view and the southwest summer breeze that came off the bay. Williams, a Brooklynite and in the theatrical business, had never been entirely accepted by his neighbors on Champlin's Creek, and the Percy Williams Home was always looked upon with some suspicion or largely ignored. But each tolerated the other and separately they enjoyed the South Shore of Long Island.

Joining Richard Dana and Percy Williams in 1916 on the east side of Champlin's Pond came Jay F. Carlisle and his wife, Mary Pinkerton Carlisle. They had both been summer residents along the Great South Bay from a time long before their 1906 marriage. In fact Mary, the youngest of the three Pinkerton children, had grown up in her parents' home on Penataquit Avenue in Bay Shore. It is quite likely that she had known of her husband-to-be as a very young girl, as both families were from Brooklyn and together with the Gibb family and the Dick family were attracted to the South Shore around 1890. Jay Carlisle had been born in 1868 and had graduated from Yale in 1889. He was the same age as Lewis Gibb, his brother-in-law to be, and it is probable that Carlisle was a frequent guest in the John Gibb house, Afterglow, on Ocean Avenue in Islip during the 1890s.

Like so many other summer residents Jay F. Carlisle would make his career as a stockbroker. From 1893 at the age of twenty-five until his death, he was a member of the New York Stock Exchange, and was its governor during the great crash of October 1929. His firm was Carlisle, Mellick & Co. He was well known as a sportsman. The stockbroker's career then had the considerable advantage of providing time for other activities, and Carlisle made full use of that asset. He became a noted horseman and later a dog owner. In fact it was probably the riding, the horse shows, and the polo, in addition to his friendship with Gibb, that kept Jay Carlisle coming back to Islip.

It was reported that he first rented a house of his own in 1902, the Alden Swan house on Ocean Avenue in Islip, only three houses to the north of Afterglow. During that summer and for many afterwards, he was an active participant in the Bay Shore Horse Show, the annual event held at Oakwood Park. Carlisle won ribbons with regularity along with Harry T. Peters, who had similar sporting interests. Both men were proving themselves competent horsemen and both would play polo with the Islip Polo Club after it was organized in 1912.

In the summer of 1906 the engagement of Mary Pinkerton to Jay F. Carlisle was announced by her parents. His friend Lewis M. Gibb had married Mary's older sister, Anna, several years before, and that couple was well settled on Saxton Avenue in Bay Shore. It was noted at the time of Mary's engagement that "the groom is quite a few years his future wife's senior."[12] In fact Jay was thirty-eight at the time and Mary was twenty. They were married before the year was out.

It was not until the spring of 1916 that the Carlisles decided to permanently settle along the Great South Bay. At that time they purchased thirty acres of land together with half of Champlin's Pond that lay south of the South Country Road. Their neighbor to the east was Richard Dana and to the south, Bradish Johnson Jr. The property had been the farm of the Robert Cambridge Livingstons of St. Mark's Lane.

The widowed Maria Whitney Livingston, nearing the end of her life, was happy to sell some of her land to the Carlisles. She retained the rest, which after her death in 1918 went to her daughter, Maud Maria Livingston Bull, who with her husband, Henry W. Bull, would own it for many more years. Maud had grown up in Islip and had been confirmed at St. Mark's at the same time as Consuelo Vanderbilt (1893). Henry Bull, a stockbroker, had a great interest in horse racing and was for many years president of the Turf and Field Club. The Bulls and the Carlisles were the best of friends and shared ownership of Champlin's Pond.

In the fall of 1916 Jay Carlisle engaged the Babylon firm of E. W. Howell and Co. to build a home on his new land. Thirty-year-old Elmer W. Howell had come to Babylon in 1891, and with his father-in-law, George S. Brown, as a partner, began building houses. After ten years Howell bought out his partner. He was on his own and on his way to success. The first large jobs undertaken were the houses for Richard B. Hyde in 1895 and for George Turnbull, both on the South Country Road west of Bay Shore. Later would follow the Ranft house and the W. H. Moffitt house. The Carlisle home, however, was their biggest challenge to date, and with its completion E. W. Howell and Co.'s reputation was made. The firm went on to build some of the largest homes on the North Shore's Gold Coast in the 1920s and many others along the Great South Bay.

Construction of the Carlisle home began in the winter of 1917. It was a huge task. Howell's grandson, Ralph D. Howell Jr., recounts, "The biggest breakthrough in my grandfather's career came when he landed the Carlisle job in East Islip. It was a lump sum job and he made considerable profit which in those days meant capital. No doubt the fact it started in the wintertime and involved pumping (the basement was six feet lower than the lake) scared off the other bidders. In addition, it was really big time compared to the other jobs he had done and gave him the credibility to get a start with the major league players on the north shore. . . . It was of fireproof construction and involved pouring concrete in the winter.

They used coke burning salamanders under the floor arches and after the concrete was poured, they covered the surface with fresh horse manure which gave off its own latent heat. It was a courageous undertaking for a country builder in those days."[13]

The result of all this effort was a magnificent home on the side of the pond which the Carlisles called Rosemary. It became one of the showplaces of the East and was decorated with the very finest antique furnishings in the most tasteful way. Its library was filled with rare first editions. In 1922 it was assessed by the Town of Islip for $125,000, putting it alongside the highly assessed homes of Richard B. Hyde in Bay Shore, S. T. Peters, J. B. Stanchfield, and Horace Havemeyer, all in Islip.* For twenty years Jay and Mary Carlisle summered at Rosemary. Jay established his Wingan kennels there, which, with its green and gold colors, sent a long list of Labrador retrievers to gain blue ribbons at shows in the East. He was president of the Labrador Retriever Club and was noted as one of the foremost breeders and exhibitors in the country.

Jay was also an avid golfer in his day. He played a role in the founding of a new golf club, the Timber Point Club (whose story will be recounted later), and was president of the famous Seminole Golf Club near his winter home in Palm Beach. Mary was particularly active in the new Southside Hospital in Bay Shore. The Carlisles were leaders of the social scene along the South Shore in the 1920s and 1930s until their deaths eight months apart in 1937. Jay was sixty-nine at the time and Mary was only fifty-one.

His funeral was held at Rosemary, and among his twenty-eight honorary pallbearers were his Islip and East Islip neighbors Harry T. Peters, Charles L. Lawrance, Charles H. Theriot, Harry B. Hollins Jr., and William K. Dick. He was a well-liked man of his day.

---

* The highest assessments were still: Vanderbilt's Idlehour; Bourne's Indian Neck Hall; Cutting's Westbrook; and Deer Range Park (formerly George C. Taylor's estate).

The entire contents of Rosemary were sold at auction at Parke-Bernet Galleries in January 1938.* Soon thereafter, the mansion was demolished and the swimming pool filled in. None of their three sons — Jay F. Jr., Allan P., or Lewis G. Carlisle — wished to keep up the mansion. For a time Allan Carlisle lived in another house on Suffolk Lane, but he too soon left the community. For the first time in nearly fifty years there were no Carlisles on the South Shore. The economic cycle had been on the upswing in the country for an unusually long period, about fifteen years, but in 1913 signs of a slowdown were beginning to appear. By the end of that year there was no question that a recession had begun and that it was worldwide in extent in spite of the huge amounts being spent on armaments then by Britain, France, and Germany. The recession would last well into the war years ahead.** The first notice of the recession-to-come in the Islip community was the dramatic failure of the old brokerage house of Harry B. Hollins & Co. on November 13, 1913. With liabilities of over $4 million and very few unpledged assets the stock exchange firm had no course but to declare itself bankrupt. It was noted at the time that no other New York Stock Exchange firm was affected, and that for several years the Hollins firm had only done business outside of the Exchange.

It was perhaps more of a family tragedy than anything else. Harry B. Hollins, aged fifty-nine in 1913, had for thirty-five years been a leading broker on Wall Street. Known widely as the broker for William K. Vanderbilt and a close friend of J. P. Morgan, Hollins was a popular man in the social fraternity of Wall Street during the Gilded Age. The firm's failure was a sign to the South Shore community at

---

* The auction sale was the first for the new partnership of Hiram Parke and Otto Bernet.

** The population of the Town of Islip actually declined by 2,000 from the 1910 census to the 1915 census. It did not surpass the 1910 level until the 1920 census and then by only 2,400.

least that the Gilded Age was indeed over. Hollins was quick to receive the sympathy of his colleagues on the Street as if there had been a death in the family.

The newspapers did not disguise the causes of the failure. "Business with the Hollins firm, in its heyday a very mine of wealth, had steadily declined in late years. It had just evaporated. The closing was the result of causes, coldly summarized in the common expression of Wall Street as 'dry rot.'"[14] Although for a time it was thought that Hollins would have to give up Meadowfarm in East Islip, and on November 21 it was announced that he was moving to a Garden City hotel, he and his family were able to retain that huge estate on Champlin's Creek (see Chapter VI). Indeed his sons Harry Hollins Jr. in 1908 and Gerald V. Hollins had built homes of their own adjacent to and on the property, and Charles L. Lawrance with his wife, Margaret, would soon come from his ancestral home in Bay Shore to join them. During the fateful summer of 1914, life on the Great South Bay appeared to be almost normal. The renting of summer cottages in Bay Shore was only slightly off from the previous year. The Islip Polo Club held its regular matches and even planned a horse show. A normal sailing season was planned by the yacht clubs on the bay. In fact, a major preoccupation of the summer folks appeared to be that perennial foe, the mosquito. A Society for the Extermination of Mosquitoes had been founded and was supported largely by the subscription of the summer families from Oakdale to Babylon. The chairman was J. Ives Plumb and the treasurer, Benjamin S. Welles. The task, begun the previous summer, was to drain the marshes along the bay, the largest of which were on property of the Taylor heirs and of Harry B. Hollins Jr. in East Islip. Following the digging of drainage ditches, oil was spread on the wet land to eradicate the mosquito larvae. The treated area was then set on fire, burning away the dead vegetation. Twenty miles of ditches were dug over many acres of breeding ground. All indications were that the project was effective, as it was expanded in following years to include the marshland west of Bay Shore. The society in its annual report concluded, "it

Colonel Alfred Wagstaff, 1844-1921,
of West Islip, is pictured here in
1899 at the age of 55. He was a
soldier, a lawyer, and a distinguished political figure in New York
State. (Courtesy of the New York Public
Library.)

James Haven Hyde, pictured in
formal dress, entertained lavishly in
New York and at the Oaks in Bay
Shore between 1899 and 1905.
(Courtesy of Brown brothers.)

Simon F. Rothschild, head of Abraham and Straus of Brooklyn, built a home on the west side of Saxton Avenue, Bay Shore, in 1903. (Courtesy of the New York Public Library.)

Vacationers leaving their carriages to catch the ferry to Point O' Woods at the Bay Shore dock in 1908. Note their dress. (Courtesy of the Nassau County Museum, photograph by Henry Otto Korten.)

The Great South Bay scooter,
used by *The Islip Scooter
Club,* is shown here in 1903
off Bellport. Ice boating was
a popular sport on the Bay
prior to World War II. (Courtesy
of Suffolk County Historical Society:
Fullerton Collection.)

Juan Manuel Ceballos was a
Spaniard who came to Bay
Shore in 1893 and located
north of South Country Road
near Saxton Avenue. He was
a sugar merchant with extensive Cuban properties.
(Courtesy of the New York Public
Library.)

Clovelly was the home of Mrs. William (Annie) Arnold in West Islip on the north side of the South Country Road. It was built in 1906 and is pictured today. (Courtesy of Richard A. Milligan.)

Sagtikos Manor, the center part of which was built by Stephanus Van Cortlandt in 1692-97, is the oldest surviving house along the Great South Bay. It has been owned by the Carll, the Thompson, and now the Gardiner family. (Courtesy of Richard A. Milligan.)

is hoped that the society's work will eventually result in the whole matter being taken up by the local health and town boards of Islip. As with the watering and oiling of our roads, which for many years was carried on by private enterprise and subscription, and which is now recognized as a public necessity to stop the dust nuisance, so it will be with the greatest of all nuisances, the mosquito."[15] Not for many years to come would the Town of Islip budget for mosquito control, however, and that pesky insect today often plagues the community in the summer.

Life was so normal on the South Shore on August 14, 1914, that the two principal headlines in the newspaper were, "Yachtsmen Open Cruising Week at Babylon" and "Ladies Planning Hospital Benefit."[16] There was no mention whatsoever that day of the German march into Belgium. And even in December the main notice for Islip read, "The house of Mr. and Mrs. Bradish Johnson here [Woodland on Suffolk Lane] was the mecca of South Shore society last Saturday night on the occasion of the coming out of their daughter, Miss Marie. A special train and many motor cars brought the 400 guests from town and many of the country places were filled with gay weekend parties."[17] During 1914 and for well into 1915 the war in Europe was of little concern to most Americans, who only wanted to stay out of it. Even the often called "rape" of Belgium and the dreadful slaughter on the Western Front did not usually merit coverage in the local papers. In fact the normal summer activities of horse shows, polo matches, hospital fund-raising balls, and sailing regattas would continue in 1915 and in 1916 as well. Even in the summer of 1917, after the United States had declared war on Germany, a horse show was held at Oakwood Park as usual. There was no Great South Bay Regatta that summer, however, and sailboat racing was severely limited until the summer of 1919 after the Armistice had been signed.

The first real evidence of wartime preparation seen on the Great South Bay was the establishment of the Naval Air Station in Bay Shore. Located on about eight acres of property rented from Charles L. Lawrance on the waterfront of his large O-Co-Nee estate, the station began operation in July 1916, with a fifteen-day instruction period for navy pilots of the Naval Militia. It was quite a novelty for the Bay Shore villagers who watched the new pilots being trained in the two seat hydroplanes in flights out over the bay and back, usually only ten minutes in the air at a time. During the summer of 1917 the Air Station was transferred from the Naval Militia to the regular navy. Following the change, over forty-six buildings of a temporary nature were constructed on the property, including hangars, barracks, and even a guard house. By the end of the war the complement amounted to 800 enlisted men and 55 officers. The station was soon closed after the Armistice, however, and disbanded by the navy which turned the property back to Lawrance.

All of this new activity in the air off Bay Shore resulted in a dreadful tragedy to a prominent summer resident in July of 1918. Sixty-one-year-old Gustave Kobbe, veteran music critic for the *New York Herald* and author of many articles on music and grand opera, was the youngest of ten children of Carl Wilhelm Ludwig Augustus Kobbe and his wife, Sarah Lord Sistare Kobbe. The senior Kobbe had emigrated from the German Duchy of Nassau early in the nineteenth century and had married Sarah Sistare of New London, Connecticut, in 1835. Shortly thereafter they moved to New York where all their children were born. In 1882, young Gustave married Carolyn Wheeler and from this union came a son and then four daughters. The children had grown up on the South Shore and three of their daughters, who were considered great beauties, would marry South Shore men. Hildegarde Kobbe married Joseph H. Stevenson and then Francis B. Thorne (son of Edwin Thorne); Virginia Kobbe married Gerald V. Hollins (son of Harry B. Hollins); and Carol Kobbe married Robert W. Morgan (son of Charles Morgan).

While sailing on the bay off Bay Shore on that wartime summer day, Kobbe's boat was struck by a hydroplane which snapped off the mast, striking him on the skull, and killing him instantly. Apparently the aviator had been aware of the accident at the time it occurred. An inquest by the naval authorities followed during which it was said, "The killing of Mr. Kobbe is a happening that those who have had occasion to cross the bay have been expecting, because of the practice of the aviators to see how close they could come to the boats, thus frightening the occupants of the craft and causing children, women and even men to dread what might take place."[18] The navy denied the complaints, saying that such practices were against regulations and that "the accident which recently ended in the death of G. Kobbe was not due to reckless flying. Three machines were maneuvering and were about to go into formation flight. The machine which struck Kobbe endeavored to get out of his way as much as possible without running into the other machines in the formation. This machine was clear of the boat in which Kobbe was [sailing] and had left the water when a gust of wind struck it, throwing it to the left, thereby striking the mast."[19] Finally the navy asked all persons to report any reckless flying whereupon they would take measures to punish the aviators.

At the time he died, Kobbe had almost finished his major opus *The Complete Opera Book*. This important work, a synopsis of and a commentary on over three hundred operas, was published in 1922 and later added to by other distinguished opera critics. It became a memorial of renown to a man who combined a love of music with a love of sailing. Gustave Kobbe was buried at St. Mark's Church in Islip. His death was a wartime tragedy that took place at home, on the Great South Bay.

On Easter morning, April 8, 1917, the country woke up to find itself at war with Germany. President Woodrow Wilson had asked the Congress to declare war in a memorable speech a few days before and it had quickly complied. A Selective Service Law followed in short order and a compulsory draft was under way. Many volunteers enrolled as well and on Long Island, Camp Upton in Yaphank was established as a boot camp for volunteers and draftees alike. By mid August 1917, a second draft quota was announced and Camp Upton began to fill with recruits, including the "Upton Millionaire," Edward W. C. Arnold from West Islip. Arnold, aged thirty, was quoted as saying, "My government needs men and this is the method they have taken to call me to service. I am here and am proud to do my duty, but I wish these boys would let up on the Upton millionaire stuff. They are a fine crowd of men, though. I like every blessed one of them. We are doing our bit."[20] Another recruit at Camp Upton then was moved to write a song, "Oh How I Hate to Get Up in the Morning." His name, of course, was Irving Berlin.

The army established another camp in North Babylon for its aviation service in June of 1918. August Belmont II, then a major in that service, leased 150 acres of his Nursery for one year for one dollar as an aviation training field. The lease did not include Belmont's large home. It did include, however, the one mile race track and nearby land for hangars and for barracks. At first the camp was known as Belmont Field, but later was named Camp Damm after Colonel Henry J. Damm of the aviation service who had been killed in a plane accident the month before. From June through December upwards of twelve hundred men were trained at Camp Damm. With the end of the war the camp was closed. The barracks, mess halls, and other wooden buildings were sold at auction. The steel airplane hangars were dismantled, and the flying field was plowed under. Soon all evidence of its wartime use was gone and Major Belmont had his land back.

The Islip Chapter of the American Red Cross was also doing its bit. It reorganized and greatly expanded its activities, planning a capital campaign to raise funds in response to the president's declaration of Red Cross week on June 18, 1917. Most of the summer resident wives and several of the men, headed by Harry B. Hollins Jr. and Edward C. Blum, were Red Cross Auxiliary members.

Many of the men from Oakdale to Babylon had volunteered for duty and became officers in the American Expeditionary Force in France. One longtime Islip summer resident, Schuyler Parsons Jr., was on active duty with the American Red Cross in France. He wrote home to describe the horror of the warfare during the final German offensive in the spring of 1918: "We saw before us a plain like no man's land with not a structure, and the explosions of the cases of grenades like a barrage. No road led in from our side. We all shouldered stretchers and ran in for half a mile. We dug (literally) out bodies. [Once] I saw only a foot above ground, pulled and when it came out [there was] no head. The sights were too horrible, never have I been so affected. The crowd near was terrific when we returned and pathetic with those who had lost their loved ones. The greatest tragedy I shall ever witness."[21]

Islip and Bay Shore summer residents suffered casualties. Allan Pinkerton, of Saxton Avenue, Bay Shore, had gone to France early in 1917 as a major on the staff of General Pershing's first expeditionary force. He remained with Pershing until the summer of 1918 when a bomb of mustard gas burst at his feet. He was badly burned and inhaled a lot of the deadly fumes, destroying part of his lungs. Crippled for the rest of his life, he had to give up polo, the sport he loved the most. He bought a ranch in Riverside, California, where he could ride leisurely and watch others train the polo ponies. Pinkerton's injury was the cause of his premature death in 1930 at age fifty-four.

The closest that the Great South Bay came to experiencing an enemy attack occurred on July 19, 1918, with the sinking of the navy cruiser USS *San Diego* by a German U-boat just six miles off the Fire Island beaches. German submarines had been actively engaged off the North American coast since the American entry into the war and had sunk merchant shipping, but the destruction of the *San Diego* was the only time in the entire war that a Naval ship had been sunk. Fortunately only six lives were lost. Other ships were in the area to rescue the crew, and two lifeboats rowed the six miles to Point O' Woods to spread the alarm.[22] Air patrols by planes from the Bay Shore station were often made along the beaches to watch for U-boats, but seldom was there a sighting.

During the war years Long Island experienced calamities that were not caused by the Germans, but brought more suffering to those living there than the war did. The month of

January 1918, saw the coldest weather in the forty-year history of weather records on the island. Along the South Shore the temperature dropped to 13 degrees below zero on January 4 and remained well below freezing for the entire month. Such extreme cold caused frozen water pipes and heating systems, forcing schools to close and bringing much hardship to homes. An acute shortage of coal developed, requiring restrictions and the rationing of supplies in Suffolk County. The county administrator for fuel urged the public to burn wood wherever possible and to concentrate public services in churches to save coal which was in short supply throughout the whole state. During the first week in February the mercury dropped to -16 degrees, a new record, and there was great concern that the supply of coal would run out entirely before spring. The Great South Bay was frozen over solid and Fire Island could only be reached by scooter or by the occasional car with chains that traveled over the ice. *The Brooklyn Eagle* reported on the damage on the beach: "The extreme cold weather is proving a severe test for the ocean pier at Lonelyville [a community east of Fair Harbor, started by Dr. George S. King of Bay Shore], which was built a distance of 800 feet into the ocean before it was abandoned. The ice, according to a resident of Fire Island Beach who came across in a scooter a day or two ago, is proving too much for even the big piles and strong braces, and a couple of the sections of the pier have already been carried away."[23] Spring finally arrived, somewhat late, the ice broke up in due course, and the bay returned to normal. It had been a trying winter for those on the South Shore.

As trying as that cold winter was, it paled in comparison to the second and far greater calamity to strike in the early fall of 1918. Just as the Great War appeared to be approaching a possible armistice and peace feelers were being put out by the German government whose generals realized at last that a victory was not possible, in September first evidence began to appear of the pandemic influenza virus that became known as the Spanish flu. Not since the bubonic plague in the fourteenth century was there to be such a dreadful worldwide scourge as the Spanish flu epidemic of 1918–19. In the United States alone 200,000 persons died of it and its complications, usually pneumonia. Millions died throughout the world. Often a person would die within twenty-four hours after being afflicted. In the beginning terror was felt by many communities, and radical measures were taken to isolate the sick and prevent the spread of the disease. It seemed to many who had lost loved ones in the Great War that nature was taking its revenge on mankind.

The pandemic was first noted in local papers in September, 1918. By October 18 the Babylon "village health board, acting under the advice of the village health officer, on Sunday morning placed a general quarantine upon all public assemblages here. They ordered all schools, churches, theaters, dance halls, lodges, and other places of assembly, including the Church Institute, to be closed until further notice."[24] Camp Damm was quarantined for six weeks. For the first time ever there were no church services on Sunday in Babylon. As the small Southside Hospital in Babylon was completely inadequate, most of the sick remained at home. Doctors went to see them when possible or until they became exhausted. Two doctors in Babylon got the flu and a long retired physician tried to help out. There was also a great shortage of nurses. The situation in Babylon seemed to be worse than at points east, as the Town of Islip did not close their schools until the following week when it appeared that the epidemic was spreading from west to east. Most Islip churches began to hold services out of doors except when the weather was particularly bad.

By the end of October there were some signs that the epidemic had peaked on the South Shore. "Never before in the history of Babylon," said the *Signal*, "have so many deaths due to pneumonia been reported within such a short space of time as this week. Most of the cases were preceded by influenza. The epidemic, it is hoped, has reached its height here. All of the doctors are kept busy day and night while the undertakers have had difficulty in obtaining caskets from their supply houses. Throughout the country the epidemic had caused many deaths, but it seems to be now on the decrease [week ending October 25, 1918]."[25] Ironically, on November 11, as the guns became silent on all the battlefields of Europe, thousands were still being stricken by the disease both there and in the United States. One ship returned home that month from France carrying four hundred people with influenza, eighty of whom died en route.

Although the worst of the scourge may have been over by Thanksgiving on the South Shore and the schools and churches were allowed to open by then, the fear persisted throughout the winter of 1918–19, as the flu spread throughout the country. Several of the summer residents who normally would return to New York City for the winter chose to remain in their country homes that winter to avoid the contagion of the crowded city. Particularly those families with young school age children remained in Islip and East Islip where the children were usually tutored at home or went to small private classes of instruction. By the spring of 1919 normalcy began to return to the bay area, the war veterans returned home, and the pandemic was on the wane.

During the war years two New York summer families who had first come to the South Shore in the nineteenth century were planning new ventures which would affect the bay shoreline in the years to come. The first of these was Charles Lanier Lawrance and his development called O-Co-Nee. Lawrance was the grandson of Francis Cooper Lawrance and his wife, Frances Garner Lawrance, whose parents had come to Bay Shore in the 1840s with the very first summer residents. The Lawrance family was one of the earliest to come to America from England (see Chapter I). Charles Lawrance was thus a Garner descendant as well, and through his grandfather's sister was a cousin of the Bradish Johnson family of Bay Shore and of East Islip.* Charles was the son of Francis Cooper Lawrance Jr. and his first wife, Sarah Lanier Lawrance, who was the daughter of Charles Lanier, a suc-

---

* Through the Garner line he was distantly related to Edwin Thorne of West Islip as well.

cessful Wall Street banker. Born in 1882 young Charles lost his mother when he was ten, shortly after the birth of his young sister, Kitty Lanier Lawrance.* His father, a widower for five years, remarried Miss Susan Willing from Philadelphia,** but died of Bright's disease in 1904 at the age of fifty. They had been well known in yachting circles and well liked in New York and Newport society. Young Charles and his baby sister were looked after by the Lanier family in Westchester County until the time came for Charles to attend Groton and then Yale, from which he graduated in 1905. He spent little time in Bay Shore from the time of his mother's death. His Lawrance grandparents, who outlived his parents, spent much of their time at their home in Pau in France, Frances dying there in 1908 and Francis in 1911. Charles, the sole surviving male Lawrance, inherited the family land in Bay Shore at that time.

Although some of the Lawrance land was sold to the Ackerson development of Brightwaters, there remained the family homestead called Manatuck Farm, which was surrounded by land on each side of a stream running into the bay and known locally then as Lawrance Creek. The property Charles inherited ran from the Long Island Railroad south to the bay and in 1912 was one of the largest landholdings left in the area. The house, having hardly been lived in at all for twenty years, was not in good repair. Still it was a substantial inheritance for a young man of twenty-nine. By then Charles had married Margaret Dix (1910), daughter of the Reverend Morgan Dix, longtime rector of Trinity Parish in New York City (1862–1908). Charles had lived in Paris from 1907 to early 1914 studying to be an architect at the Ecole de Beaux Arts where he had obtained a degree just prior to the start of the Great War. Manatuck Farm in Bay Shore was all but ignored.

---

* Kitty Lanier Lawrance later became the first wife of W. Averell Harriman, future governor of New York.

** The sister of Ava Willing, the first wife of Colonel John Jacob Astor IV, who died on the *Titanic* in 1912.

It was while he was studying architecture in Paris that Charles Lawrance discovered his true vocation in life. He had a mind attuned to invention and a passion for speed. Together these led him to the airplane during its earliest days of development, and it was as an airplane engineer that he would make his mark. His first notable invention was the so called Lanier Lawrance wing section, a design which gave more lift to the plane and which was used by both British and German planes in combat in 1914 and 1915. With the advent of hostilities Lawrance and his wife returned to New York. Charles began experimenting with airplane engines on Long Island which was then the center of aviation in America. Mitchell and Roosevelt fields constituted the largest flying center during the war years. He believed that an air-cooled engine could be built that would be lighter and as powerful as the heavier engines then in use. The saving in weight would mean that more fuel could be carried and thus more range would be achieved by the plane.

Charles Lawrance's greatest contribution to aviation, for which he is known today, was the invention and perfection of the Wright Whirlwind air-cooled engine which quickly became known as one of the finest in the world. By 1920 he had constructed two engines, one for the U.S. Army which made 140 horsepower and one for the U.S. Navy which made 200 horsepower (seaplanes required more power for lift off the water). In 1921 both were accepted after a fifty hour running test. Needing more capital to expand further, Lawrance sold his business to the Wright Aeronautical Company with which he worked until 1930. During the Roaring Twenties the engine invented by Lawrance was used by Admiral Richard Byrd on his flights over the North Pole and to Antarctica, by Amelia Earhart, the famous woman aviator, and most notably on the *Spirit of Saint Louis* on May 20, 1927, when young Charles Lindbergh made his solo record-breaking flight to Paris, non-stop over the Atlantic Ocean. By 1928 Lawrance engines made up more than two-thirds of all the airplane engines in use in the country.

After his return from Paris and with the country gradually preparing for war, in January 1916, it was announced that Charles L. Lawrance would develop about a hundred eighty acres of his land south of the South Country Road. It would connect with the Brightwaters development and he would sell it "in large sections under extreme restrictions,"[26] the implication being that Brightwaters was divided into too small parcels. The report went on to say, "For five years up to the commencement of the European War he left the place with its handsome old homestead in charge of a caretaker and made his residence in Paris. The war, however, brought him back to live in America. Nearly every plot sold will be given direct access to the water."[27] Two roads were put in from the South Country Road to the bay on each side of Lawrance Creek and given the names Lawrance Lane (on the west) and Garner Lane (on the east). During that summer and for the duration of the war the Naval Air Station occupied the southerly end of Garner Lane. The dredging and land preparation proceeded slowly, and few new homes were built during the war, but in 1918 a clubhouse was built. The development known today as O-Co-Nee was under way and would become the most attractive and sought after property from Babylon to Oakdale, primarily because Lawrance insisted on plot sizes of four acres or more, the largest in the area. The Charles Lawrance family continued to live at the Manatuck homestead until 1925 when they moved to East Islip to occupy what had been part of the Harry B. Hollins place, Meadowfarm.

If O-Co-Nee was the most attractive residential development to be built in the area, the most striking home to be constructed on the shorefront at almost that same time was the new country home at Olympic Point built for Horace Havemeyer and his family. Named for the Olympic Club that had stood on the site since the 1850s, Havemeyer's new home would become a landmark on the Great South Bay for the next thirty years. It was arguably the most desirable location for a home anywhere along the bay. First of all it was directly on the water, facing to the southwest from where the prevailing, cool, summer breeze came. Only the Bourne home in Oakdale had a similar facing and was sited as close to the bay. All of the other large homes were either on creeks or were much farther away from the bay with more limited views. Secondly, the Havemeyer site had the advantage over the Bourne site of being set back in the Great Cove and thus being protected from the southeast storms by the exposed Bayberry Point and from the commercial harbor of Bay Shore by Penataquit Point to the southwest, the latter being owned at the time of Havemeyer's purchase by his wife's uncle, J. Adolph Mollenhauer. This protection, which the Bourne site did not have, did not impair the broad view of the bay. Lastly, two creeks, Awixa and Orowoc, embraced Olympic Point and provided for the safe mooring of small boats, whereas Bourne had to dredge his own boat harbor. It is a wonder that from the time of the Olympic Club's bankruptcy in September of 1913 until the spring of 1916 when Havemeyer bought the thirty acres that became Olympic Point, no one had bought up the site. The recession, and the fact that the temporary owners, Hutton, Pinkerton, and Blum, were looking for a desirable neighbor, must have been the explanation.

Olympic Point lay at the southerly end of Saxton Avenue, which was named for Daniel Saxton, the first English owner of that neck of land between the two creeks. By 1916, however, the name of the street on the maps and deeds of the area had changed slightly to Saxon's Avenue, and as has been mentioned, it is today called Saxon Avenue. This metamorphosis is hard to explain and one can only speculate that the changes came about by a mapmaker's error or more likely because in common usage each succeeding name is easier to say. Other name changes for roads occurred at about this time as well. In Islip, Johnson Avenue had become St. Mark's Lane. In East Islip, Pavilion Avenue had become Suffolk Street in 1915 and then Suffolk Lane. Finally, although the South Country Road has not entirely disappeared, it is more often known today as the Montauk Highway or the Merrick Road.

Horace Havemeyer, the only son of Henry O. Havemeyer, had spent his summers in Islip from his early childhood, first on Champlin's Creek and then in the family home on Bayberry Point. He had also grown up with horses and shooting on his father's farm in Commack, Long Island, but it was sailing on the Great South Bay that the boy loved the most. He was happiest when summer came and he could sail under the watchful eye of Charles Suydam Jr. Suydam knew the bay as well as anyone, where the fish were and when to look to the northwest for the summer squalls. In search of the bluefish they would sail out of Gilgo Inlet (no longer in existence) and back through Whig Inlet where the tides were strong and the shoals uncertain. Or they would sail over to Carabus Island, owned by Havemeyer Sr. as a duck shooting site, or to nearby Middle Island, owned by Harry B. Hollins. * Young Horace learned about and grew up to love every aspect of the Great South Bay. He would later call it "the most favored spot in the world."

He also learned to race competitively, crewing in his first race at the age of twelve aboard his father's new boat, *Adaline*, built by Thomas Muncy in Bay Shore and skippered by Harry M. Brewster of the Bay Shore sailing Brewsters. When young Horace was seventeen his father gave him a boat of his own which he called *Flight*. It was a Herreshoff 30 similar to his father's *Electra*, and it quickly gained the reputation as the boat to beat at the Penataquit Corinthian Yacht Club races. In July 1903, "in a spirited race, the first of a series sailed during a 'howling sou'wester,' the 'Flight' owned by Horace Havemeyer defeated T. Ridgeway Macy's 'Arrow' by thirty-

---

* Henry O. Havemeyer owned the eastern half of West Island and all of East Island or Carabus Island — both having been purchased from Mrs. Sarah Nicoll. Harry B. Hollins purchased Middle Island from Mrs. Nicoll in 1904. These three islands were part of the so-called Five Islands or Fire Islands, located in the Great South Bay near Fire Island beach between what is today Saltaire and Ocean Beach. They had been in the Nicoll family for over 250 years, having been a part of the original patent granted to William Nicoll.

two seconds [after eight miles]. The gale was the severest known this season, but the race was sailed without an accident occurring. It was a day, however, to test the courage and seamanship of even a professional."[28] Captain Charles Suydam Jr. was usually at the helm of *Flight* that summer, but Horace was a fast learner. At the season's end it was commented that "She [*Flight*] is unquestionably the fastest boat in this end of the bay and so far nothing has been built to beat her."[29] Horace and Suydam sailed *Flight* for five years until the demise of the Penataquit Corinthian club. With the introduction of the Islip One-Design class in 1909, Havemeyer, then twenty-three, was on his own and racing his boat *Electra* in races all over the bay for the five years of the Islip Yacht Club's life. During World War I there was only a temporary hiatus in his yacht racing career. During his sixty years on the bay, he would race in almost every size boat.

Horace lived with his family on Bayberry Point in the early years of the twentieth century in the most southwesterly house of "Modern Venice." In December 1907, his father died suddenly at the Commack farm, and there were thrust upon the twenty-one-year-old son the vast responsibilities that had been carried by the Sugar King both in business and within the family. Horace's only relaxation was in sport, and it was in Islip that he found relief from the tension by playing polo and sailing on the bay. During the summer of 1910 he began to court William Dick's young granddaughter, Doris Dick, who had always summered with her father and mother in the Dick house on Ocean Avenue, Islip, only a few steps away from Bayberry Point. He asked Doris to go sailing with him that summer for the first time. She accepted and remembered years later that she wore a red coat. So embarrassed was he to be seen with a girl wearing a red coat in a sailboat race that he almost asked her to stay home. However they got along well and by the fall became engaged. The wedding took place in New York City at the Church of the Incarnation on February 28, 1911. In the following summers they occupied the Bayberry Point house next to Horace's widowed mother who spent less and less time there, much preferring her Stamford, Connecticut, home. Three children were born to Horace and Doris Havemeyer within the first four years of their marriage, the last of whom, a son named Horace Jr., was born on July 14, 1914, in their Bayberry Point house. By the next summer it was clear that the family was outgrowing this house. Horace knew that he wanted to put down roots permanently on the edge of the bay and to build a proper American country home, and at the end of Saxon Avenue there was the perfect place to do this.

Assembling the thirty acres that were to make up Olympic Point was accomplished speedily in the spring of 1916. Building the house would take much longer. The land was acquired by Havemeyer in three separate transactions, two for the west side of the avenue and one for the east. On the west, the owners of the former Olympic Club property — Hutton, Pinkerton, and Blum — were happy to sell their 13 1/2 acres for $55,000 and to have a friendly new neighbor in their midst. However, James Kempster, former president of the Olympic Club, did not want to move from his house. Since his almost three acres were crucial to the whole parcel, occupying what would become the entrance drive, Havemeyer had no choice but to pay him $25,000 for the small lot and the house, which he promptly had moved away.

On the east side of Saxon Avenue there were fourteen acres lying to the south of Allan Pinkerton's farm that were owned by the Estate of Frank D. Creamer, the Brooklyn sheriff, and Isabella Baird. Creamer, who summered in Bay Shore, and Matthew Baird, a Brooklyn contractor, had bought this land in 1900, hoping to build a large resort hotel and bathing pavilion on the site. At the turn of the century these grand resort hotels were still popular around the bay. In fact another new one was planned that year on West Island by the owner of the Orowoc Hotel in Islip village. Fortunately neither one was ever built. Had they been, they would not have survived for long. By World War I their day was over. Havemeyer paid $52,250 for the Creamer-Baird land where he intended to build his farm.

In summary, he had paid $132,500 for thirty acres — for the best site on the Great South Bay from Oakdale to Babylon. To complete the preparation of the land, he acquired at the same time about one acre of land under water, mostly east of Saxon Avenue, from the State of New York in order to back-fill the entire waterfront which was done while the main house was being built. Finally, two years later he bought several lots in Moffitt's Olympic Park off Saxon Avenue between Green and Mallar Avenues in order to build small houses for employees who would work on Olympic Point.

It is possible that Olympic Point might never have come into existence at that time. In the winter of 1912 it was reported in the *Brooklyn Eagle* that the late Henry O. Havemeyer's 2 1/4 acre island in the Great South Bay, called Cedar or Carabus or sometimes East Island, was to be converted into "a great summer estate." His heirs had applied for a grant of land under water which when filled would create a 3 1/2 acre island. "Plans for its conversion are said to be in process of making by a well known New York architect and will comprise a park with one or more magnificent houses, grounds, wharves, a bathing pavilion and quarters for servants."[30] The article went on to say: "It [Cedar Island] has never been occupied by so much as a shack. It is conspicuous all over the bay by a cluster of large, beautiful red cedars, interwoven with dense masses of poison ivy, the latter offering an effectual barrier to trespassers, without the aid of signs."[31] The other pests found there, the mosquito and the green fly, are not mentioned. But the great summer estate on Cedar Island never came to pass. It was probably a plan or dream that Horace Havemeyer had in order to liquidate an asset held in his father's estate.* As described by the *Eagle*, it was reminiscent of the Armory, Horace's distant cousin Henry Havemeyer's pleasure palace at Havemeyer's Point off Whig Inlet (see Chapter V). It is quite certain that the Horace Havemeyer family would never have lived there.

---

* Carabus or Cedar Island was not sold by the estate of H. O. Havemeyer until 1948, for a total of $1,500.

In much the same way that many had done before him, Havemeyer engaged three prominent architects to design Olympic Point. Harrie T. Lindeberg was chosen to design the main house; Alfred Hopkins was to design the farm; and the famous Boston landscape firm of Olmsted Brothers (son and stepson of Frederick Law Olmsted, America's foremost landscape architect, then deceased) was to prepare a design plan for the residential property west of Saxon Avenue. Of the three, Lindeberg was the youngest (thirty-six years old), and the least notable when he was engaged. Characteristically, Havemeyer, age thirty at the time, picked someone he could work with rather than a more famous name who might be less flexible. That is not to say that Lindeberg was unknown in 1916. In fact he already had several important country homes to his credit.

Harrie T. Lindeberg, 1880–1959, trained for several years with the notable firm of McKim, Mead and White, and in 1906, the year Stanford White was shot, he went into business with a partner under the firm name of Albro and Lindeberg. Around 1914 the partnership broke up and he was on his own. In the beginning Lindeberg specialized in the design of the large country home for the very well to do. Among his first commissions after the partnership had dissolved was a home for the wealthy industrialist Paul Moore, in Convent, New Jersey. It is quite possible that it was the Moore house that influenced Havemeyer's decision to engage Lindeberg. Moore and his wife were close friends of Havemeyer's sister and brother-in-law, the Peter H. B. Frelinghuysens, and it is likely that during a visit Havemeyer and his wife saw the Moore house and were impressed. At almost the same time Havemeyer's house was being built, Lindeberg was also doing homes for Thomas Vietor in Rumson, New Jersey, and Eugene Du Pont in Greenville, Delaware. The similarity of these four houses was striking. Lindeberg went on to do houses for Philip Armour in Lake Forest, Illinois; John Pillsbury in Minneapolis; James Stillman in Pocantico Hills, New York; Michael Van Buren in Newport, Rhode Island, and Nelson Doubleday in Oyster

Bay, New York, all prominent names in American industry of the day.

In April 1924, architectural critic Russell Whitehead said of Lindeberg, "The absence of preconceived ideas on design, this freedom from formula . . . is the keynote of his work. He has invented, or perhaps it would be more accurate to say adapted, more house motives which have become a part of our architectural vocabulary than any other country house architect. What is most evident is the obvious fitness of each house to its site."[32] The house Lindeberg designed for Havemeyer fit that extraordinary site looking out on the Great South Bay to perfection. Whitehead called the house "an extraordinarily interesting, picturesque composition."[33] He also called the entrance facade "superb," continuing to comment, "This house, together with the service group, is of great length, treated very simply and in a single material (or rather combination of materials) along the entire extent, but the expression of the plan is so perfect and the proportion of each of the simple elements so near the ideal both in itself and in its relation to the other elements that one wishes — could wish — no change."[34]

Lindeberg designed a three story house of completely whitewashed brick with a gray slate roof, sharply angled, and with many large, leaded French windows to take maximum advantage of the unique site. As a country house should, it had large rooms and there were a great number of them. The public rooms were spacious and the stairway to the second floor was grand. The master bedroom on the second floor was extremely large with a spectacular view towards the bay. No detail was overlooked to make the house livable and practical as well. Havemeyer, of course, was anxious to move in. However, because the leaded windows had to come from France where the trench war was in stalemate, a long delay occurred, and the house was not completed until the summer of 1919 when the family moved in.[*] The Olympic

---

[*] The builder of the Olympic Point house was Warren Green of New York City.

Point house became a significant landmark from the bay and a comfortable home where three children, and later a fourth, could be raised and from which Havemeyer could enjoy his sailing on the bay.

To design the farm with all the appropriate buildings across Saxon Avenue to the east, Havemeyer chose the most notable farm architect of the day, Alfred Hopkins. Hopkins's barns were classics. At forty-five he had already established his reputation. In the bay area alone he had designed a dairy barn for Frederick G. Bourne at Indian Neck Hall in Oakdale. He designed an entire set of farm buildings for Havemeyer's cousin, Harry T. Peters, on St. Mark's Lane in Islip and for Doris Havemeyer's uncle, J. Adolph Mollenhauer, on Awixa Avenue in Bay Shore. Many more farms for estates, throughout the northeast, were a part of Hopkins work. He was also the author of the definitive book on the planning and design of farms and farm buildings of that era.[*]

For Havemeyer at Olympic Point he designed a complex of shingle barns that were painted white. They consisted of a horse barn at the center with two adjacent wings for stables and for cows and the dairy. A second floor on the horse barn had rooms for the groom. Nearby was the icehouse, various sheds for farm equipment and a four-car garage over which were quarters for the chauffeur. All these barns provided space for the horses, the cows, a bull, and equipment for caring for a vegetable garden, flower garden, and almost twenty acres of mown grass. To the south was an area where the cows and horses could graze.

The landscape designer, Olmsted Brothers, had the advantage of a marvelous feature from which to start their plan. To the west of the main house site stood a row of four 250-year-old English beech trees that must have been planted by Daniel Saxton himself, as the English beech is not indigenous to America. The four trees stood considerably higher than the house was to be and gave the property the appearance of an English park even before any other planting was

---

[*] Alfred Hopkins, *Modern Farm Buildings*, 1913.

done. The Olmsted plan featured two American elms to the south of the house placed inside a yew hedge which surrounded it to the south and west. To the north a gracious circle formed the front entrance driveway, showing off the house to maximum advantage when one entered. To the west was a flower garden surrounded by a beech hedge, a heather garden, and an azalea walk. Trees were located throughout the property to provide open vistas and alleés in the English park manner. Several English oaks were planted by Havemeyer which he had received as a gift from a horticulturalist cousin. On Awixa Creek a boat basin was created to berth the power and sail boats away from the chop of the bay, and a tennis court and nearby playhouse were built in the northwest corner.

By 1919 Havemeyer could claim to have a complete "American Country House" where he could set down his roots and raise his family. For the first year his family spent the winter at Olympic Point. He commuted to the city to his office and the children were tutored in private classes. After that first year, however, winters were spent in New York and the family would be at Olympic Point on weekends only until the summer when school vacation began. During the final year of the Great War a new family came to summer in Islip. This was unusual on two counts. First, during 1917 and 1918 there was little change in residence by anyone, and second, this family did not come from New York or Brooklyn, but from Philadelphia. Furthermore George S. Graham was not a banker, broker, or a man of industry, but a distinguished politician. Born in Philadelphia in 1850, educated at the University of Pennsylvania with both a bachelor of arts and a law degree, Graham was in turn a lawyer, district attorney, judge, and, beginning in 1913, a congressman, all from Philadelphia. When he began to summer in Islip he was a relatively junior Republican member of the House of Representatives, and the shorter congressional sessions then undoubtedly allowed him to spend much time with his family on holiday. He was known as Judge throughout his congressional career. Judge Graham and his family acquired the house in Islip built by

William H. Moffitt north of the South Country Road between the two ponds. Moffitt had sold the house to Walter G. Oakman in 1915 before he disappeared to California. The Oakmans occupied it only for three years. Their son, who had volunteered to serve with the British Expeditionary Force, had been seriously wounded in Flanders in 1916 during the battle of the Somme, and then again in 1917 fighting with the Coldstream Guards at Cambrai. In 1918 the Oakmans decided to sell to Judge Graham, who called his new summer home Lohgrame.

The judge's career was notable for his role as chairman of the House Judiciary Committee during the 1920s when the Republicans controlled the House. Because of his age at that time — he was in his seventies — he was known as the dean of the House of Representatives.

It was in 1930 when he was eighty that Judge Graham as chairman of the committee presided over the hearings to repeal the Volstead Act and prohibition in general, which he had long opposed. He was remembered for his remarks at the hearings: "Let us reason together, not with the fanatic, for he is the foe of religion as well as of religious liberty. Not with him, no, but with broad minded men and women of every faith and belief, and try to relieve our country through reason and by conceiving a new system — one not founded on the bludgeon and a violation of men's conscientious convictions regarding drink. No law can ever be enforced that is destructive of right and individual liberty."[35] Soon after that memorable remark, the long decade of Prohibition was brought to an end.

Judge Graham was a much-respected elder in the Islip summer community of the 1920s. He and his wife were active in the Southside Hospital fund-raising and in the planning for a new golf course in Great River. He died in 1931. "Return to Normalcy," the slogan of the Harding campaign for the presidency in 1920, was very much in evidence around the bay in 1919. Following two wartime summers of almost no racing, the Great South Bay Yacht Racing Association planned to resume at least part of its pre-war schedule. In addition the

Babylon, Bellport, and Bay Shore Yacht Clubs, the latter under the leadership of the venerable Commodore Harry M. Brewster, began to hold two or three races each. Participation was low at first, but gradually it grew until by 1921 normal size fleets were seen on the bay. There was even a revival that year of the Islip One-Design class with five boats from the Bay Shore Yacht Club competing, the best of which was *Yama Yama*, then owned by Roy Brewster. The class continued through the 1920s and into the early 1930s with six to eight boats.

Although returning to normalcy was the desire of almost everyone, they did want to memorialize those among them who had given their lives for their country in the war. However, in Bay Shore there was some disagreement about how best to do so. J. Adolph Mollenhauer of Awixa Avenue chaired a committee to plan a permanent memorial to all who had been in military service. Mollenhauer had purchased a hundred-foot lot on East Main Street opposite the Methodist Church and offered it to the village as a site for the memorial. Some wanted a park, others wanted a playground, and still others a building put on the site. The committee, after much discussion, chose a building and proceeded to raise funds from the community. By November 1920, the money was in hand, including a large additional donation from Mollenhauer himself, and the cornerstone was laid for the Soldiers and Sailors Memorial Building. Constructed of red brick after a design of the architect Charles M. Hart, it is a distinguished building that still graces Bay Shore village. It is also a tribute to the generosity and leadership of Adolph Mollenhauer, who died in 1926 after forty summers spent in Bay Shore.

If the immediate postwar years could be called a return to normalcy, they were also a period of transition for the Town of Islip. The Great South Bay from Oakdale to Babylon as a fashionable summer resort for families from New York Society began a decline then that was never arrested. More people died, or left the area, than arrived, and although the decline was gradual until the Depression, it was noticeable. The completion of other resorts on Long Island, particularly the Gold Coast on the North Shore and Southampton on the East End, was beginning to draw the affluent where they built huge mansions or elaborate summer cottages in the 1920s. One sign of this change occurred in 1919 when for the first time ever, the assessed value for taxation purposes of all real estate in the Town of Islip fell below that of the Town of Southampton. Islip had always had the highest values of all the Suffolk County towns until then. Never again would it be the leader. As the large estates made up by far the greatest part of these values, it was indicative of the decline under way in Islip.

Symbolic as well of the transition were the deaths in 1919 of Frederick G. Bourne and August Belmont Jr. and in 1920 of William K. Vanderbilt. Vanderbilt, Bourne, and Belmont's grandfather (the first August) did more than anyone else to bring the South Shore to the attention of New York Society and make it a fashionable resort. Their deaths and the eventual end of Idlehour and Indian Neck Hall as private residences were signs of decline.

In the world of yachting that had been so much a part of the Gilded Age, a transitional event took place in the summer of 1920. For the last time the America's Cup Challenge races were held off Sandy Hook, New Jersey, and sailed on a course that took them in the Atlantic Ocean off Long Island. The next races in 1930 would be held in Rhode Island Sound off Newport. The British challenge in 1920 was made again by Sir Thomas Lipton with his fourth boat, *Shamrock IV* (he would make five). The defender was *Resolute*, the last winner to be designed by the "Wizard of Bristol", Nathaniel G. Herreshoff. *Resolute* was skippered by Charles Francis Adams of Boston, who became the first amateur to skipper a winner (Captains Haff and Barr had been professionals). *Resolute* and *Shamrock IV* were also the last Cup competitors to be rigged with the traditional gaff rig. In 1930 the boats used the modern marconi rig, so called because the mast resembled a radio transmission tower. The marconi rig was the rig of choice for racing after World War I. The races that summer were among the closest ever. *Shamrock IV* was a very good boat and very well handled. One race was actually a draw, *Resolute* winning on time allowance. By the next challenge these allowances had been abandoned. At the end *Resolute* defeated *Shamrock IV* three races to two and retained the cup. Sir Thomas Lipton was heard to remark, "I canna win," but the indefatigable sailor did come back again in 1930 and lost again against Islip-born skipper Harold S. Vanderbilt, William K.'s second son.

Chapter X

THE BREAKUP OF THE GREAT ESTATES (1920-1929)

Although the Great South Bay as a fashionable resort area had begun a gradual decline, and the largest estates would break up during the decade, the 1920s saw most of the same activities carried on by the summer families. This extravagant and carefree time in American society, when wealth was easy to come by and easier to spend, was best pictured in F. Scott Fitzgerald's novel *The Great Gatsby*, set in another part of Long Island — the North Shore's Gold Coast. To a much lesser extent this life-style could also be found on the South Shore. There were lavish parties in country homes, more polo matches, the building of two new golf clubs, the establishment of a new private hospital, and the creation of two new state parks, in all of which summer families played a major role. Ironically, the Roaring Twenties, as the decade was often known, literally began with the passage of the Volstead Act which provided the machinery for the enforcement of Prohibition. On January 16, 1920, at midnight, the manufacture, sale, or transportation of intoxicating liquors in the United States became illegal. Prohibition, however, created an entirely new activity, albeit an illegal one, on the Great South Bay. Rum-running during the decade would become a large part of the bay scene.

The topography of the South Shore of Long Island with the barrier beach of Fire Island, the inlet from the Atlantic Ocean west of the lighthouse, and the Great South Bay, made it a perfect area in which to bring illicit goods. Unloaded from ships waiting in Rum Row (the name given to the fleet that lay in international waters, three miles offshore [twelve miles after 1924]) onto small, fast rumrunners that would speed through the inlet without lights and across the bay, the cases of alcohol would be off-loaded on the Taylor property or even on Bayberry Point where they were picked up in the night and taken to the market in New York City. Or cases would come ashore at the Fire Island beach on small rafts or in burlap bags floated by a life preserver to be buried in caches hidden among the dunes for later retrieval. Prohibition was so unpopular that it became a game to avoid the law enforcement officials, many of whom looked the other way or accepted bribes. It was generally recognized that the greatest obstacle to effective law enforcement was the corruption of government officials. The rumrunners continued to be seen and heard on the bay until Prohibition was repealed in 1933. Many of them became ferries of people then to the communities on Fire Island.

The post–World War I era brought forth another activity on Long Island from which the South Shore was not immune. More damaging in the long run than the effects of Prohibition was the revival of the Ku Klux Klan. From the earliest time there was prejudice against the black man in Suffolk County, and prior to the Civil War there were a few slaves owned by landholders in the county. The feeling of whites towards blacks ebbed and flowed but was never one of any accommodation. In the 1920s the racist feeling was at a high water mark and the activities of the KKK reflected this feeling not only in the southern United States but also on Long Island.

To celebrate their success in the victory of conservative political candidates in local elections during the fall of 1923, the local Bay Shore Klan organized a huge parade on the following night. The headline in the paper read, "Klan Celebrates with Great Parade." The reporter present went on to say: "The parade, which was a mile long, started at nine o'clock and was led by Major E.D. Smith, the State Kleagle. Major Smith was mounted on a horse and had a staff of fifteen mounted Klansmen, one of whom carried an American flag, and another a 6-foot cross, lighted with red bulbs from a storage battery. About 350 Klan members wore full regalia, excepting masks, and there were about 300 automobiles in the parade."[1] It was estimated that about five thousand people marched in this mile-long parade which went to the local ball field to hear Major Smith's address.

This event was surpassed by the great Klan gathering in April of 1924 in the vicinity of Lake Ronkonkoma, Long Island, when forty acres of field were filled by a crowd to attend a Klan initiation ceremony. From all over Long Island they came in cars to this lonely part of Suffolk County. It was "one of the biggest meetings ever known on Long Island and probably the greatest demonstration of their numbers and power. ... Fiery crosses 12 to 15 feet in height were erected. The crosses of wood were wrapped with excelsior or similar inflammable substances and soaked with oil and gasoline, making a brisk blaze which could be seen for a distance in spite of the fact that the weather was wet."[2] This dramatic scene, so inspirational to those present, was a fearful commentary on the extent to which racism pervaded the area during that decade.

A relatively minor event also held that year was the funeral of a minor Klansman, a watchman on an Islip estate. The service, held at the home of the Klansman, was conducted by the minister of St. Mark's Church in Islip, the Reverend William H. Garth. Mr. Garth must have been very uncomfortable doing his pastoral duty surrounded as he was by "fifty knights of the 3rd degree and thirty women, robed and hooded. At the head of the casket was an electric fiery cross."[3] The Ku Klux Klan very slowly passed into history on Long Island, but the extremely conservative spirit which brought its growth to the area remained among many of the people. Suffolk County has almost always voted with the Republican party, particularly in local elections. The farmers and fishermen in that largely rural area have always maintained their strong and sometimes even fierce independence and their reluctance to accept newcomers to the community.

It was clearly recognized by 1920 that the area from Oakdale to Babylon needed a modern hospital to serve the growing community of the South Shore. The Southside Hospital, which had started in Babylon in 1913, and Dr. King's Hospital on Maple Avenue in Bay Shore were no longer adequate as had been conclusively shown during the Spanish flu epidemic in 1918. Furthermore, there was no other hospital from Amityville to Eastport. Planning for a new fireproof hospital began in the early spring of 1921. It was recognized by all that the wooden building on the corner of George and Cooper Streets in Babylon, which was the old Southside Hospital, would have to be closed. There was a division of opinion, however, as to where to locate the new building. Some preferred Babylon; others wanted to go east to a site in East Islip. It seemed that the East Islip site was carrying the day because it was closer to the middle of the area to be served, when a mass meeting was held at the Babylon town hall to protest the moving of the hospital so far away. As a result of this protest the Board of Managers reconsidered its decision and chose a site on the property of the Mowbray family on the north side of the South Country Road just east of Bay Shore village. It was a compromise solution. Given the distribution of the population along the South Shore in the 1920s Bay Shore was near the mid point. The compromise was equitable and accepted by all but a very few Babylon doctors who did not wish to be associated with the new Southside Hospital of Bay Shore.* The site was purchased in July of 1921. It was 200 feet on the road by 500 feet deep and cost $10,000. A committee consisting of Charles L. Lawrance and William A. Hulse of Bay Shore together with Bayard C. Hoppin of East Islip negotiated the acquisition.

The board of managers of the Southside Hospital in 1921 consisted of residents of the South Shore throughout the

---

* Dr. D. W. Wynkoop from Babylon unsuccessfully opposed a state charter for the hospital in Bay Shore on the ground that four small hospitals should be built instead of one large one. He was subsequently removed from the medical board.

area to be served. The president was Arthur Butler Graham. Several members were summer residents, including Charles L. Lawrance, George A. Ellis Jr., J. Adolph Mollenhauer of Bay Shore; Langdon B. Valentine (husband of Louise Hollister) of Islip; and Jay F. Carlisle, Bayard C. Hoppin of East Islip. Also many more summer families were active in the large fund-raising effort that was about to be launched to raise the $200,000 needed to build the new hospital. The leader in this effort was Mary Pinkerton Carlisle.

The week chosen to focus the fund-raising effort was July 22 to July 29, 1921. Committees had been organized in each village in the area. An evening was set aside for the presentation and the drive was under way. It was commented at that time that it was the women members of the committee, Mrs. Carlisle and Mrs. Gibb (her sister, Anna Pinkerton Gibb) "who aroused genuine enthusiasm by the earnestness of their plea and their own personal willingness to make sacrifice for humanity."[4] Typical of the meetings held that week was the one in Sayville. The chairman paid tribute to the efforts of Mary Carlisle: "If this drive is a success it will be due to her."[5] Mrs. Carlisle was the principal spokesperson at each of the town meetings. Her appeal was personal and moving. She spoke of the defects and overcrowded conditions at the Babylon hospital, which was not fireproof and lacked an elevator. She told of visiting the "new" hospital in Southampton, where the managers pointed out both the mistakes and defects in their building as well as its many advantages. Her talks were a great success and by the end of July the drive was close to completion.

Most of the $200,000 was raised from summer families in the villages of Islip, East Islip, and Bay Shore. Harold S. Vanderbilt gave $10,000 to equip the operating room in memory of his mother, Alva Vanderbilt Belmont. Mrs. Robert Pinkerton gave $5,000 for the babies' ward and an anonymous donor gave $5,000 in memory of an aviator who had trained at the Bay Shore Naval Station. By September the goal had been surpassed; $245,000 had been pledged for the new hospital and the project could proceed.

By then additional land had been acquired, adding depth and more width at the rear to the original plot. A hospital of forty beds with an additional twenty private rooms was designed by the New York architects, York & Sawyer, who were specialists in hospital plans. Construction, however, did not begin until June of 1922 due to the challenge made by the Babylon doctors over the location in Bay Shore. Once that was settled, work proceeded quickly. The board of managers announced that the Southside Hospital would be open to receive patients June 1, 1923; equipment from the Babylon building was moved in late May; and plans were made for the entire South Shore community to celebrate the occasion with a three-day "Dutch Fete" for July 20, 1923. The only public hospital between Mineola and Southampton, a distance of some fifty miles, was then a reality.

The Dutch Fete was held not only to celebrate, but also to raise money for the maintenance fund of the Southside Hospital. It was held on open land across the South Country Road from the hospital, and it had all the makings of a carnival. A huge tent was filled with people watching vaudeville acts, then boxing bouts, and three circus acts. Volunteers dressed in gay Dutch costumes manned the hundred booths selling every conceivable ware. It was estimated that the paid attendance was nine thousand people for each of the three nights, and $30,000 was raised for the hospital. Again much of the planning and organizing for the fete was done by the summer families. Jay and Mary Carlisle, the Langdon Valentines, and the Buell Hollisters all played leadership roles. Most importantly, Anna Pinkerton Gibb was in charge of all publicity for the fete and worked for months ahead of time. Her work was duly recognized. "Mrs. Gibb worked the entire winter and had all the posters, buttons, and advertising well under way at least two months before the Fete. She had a smile for everybody and was never cross no matter what went wrong, and without Mrs. Gibb it can truthfully be said that the Fete never would have been the success it was."[6]

The Southside Hospital had been properly launched and many had reason to be proud of this needed facility. It was not long, however, before there was a severe management crisis. Charles Lawrance and Bayard Hoppin had drafted by-laws and a team of three physicians had drafted medical by-laws. In spite of this effort, tension existed between the board of managers and the medical staff. It all erupted in March 1924, with the resignation of the board president Arthur Butler Graham and nine trustees including Jay Carlisle and Adolph Mollenhauer. Vice President Bayard C. Hoppin remained and became the new president, as did trustees Charles Lawrance, William H. Robbins (a lawyer from Bay Shore), and Langdon Valentine. This split was threatening the existence of the nine-month-old hospital. The eruption was sparked when the medical staff refused to approve the appointment of Dr. George S. King from Bay Shore and several other Long Island doctors to the medical board. When the trustees backed the King appointment, most of the medical staff resigned, but finally were persuaded to withdraw their resignations. Thereupon President Graham and his nine trustees resigned. The hospital issued the following statement: "The Southside Hospital at Bay Shore, Long Island, is reorganizing its methods of internal administration. The former methods of administration were found to be defective, largely because of a lack of definiteness regarding the functions of the medical staff and of the board of managers in their overlapping sphere. The reorganized plans include the election of Bayard C. Hoppin of East Islip, as President of the Board of Managers. Mr. Hoppin is a public spirited citizen who has long taken an active and friendly interest in local civic affairs."[7] After this reorganization there existed a better understanding of the responsibilities of each group.

Bayard Cushing Hoppin, the new board president of the Southside Hospital, was a member of an old New York family descended through his mother from the Beekman clan. Born in 1884 in Oyster Bay, New York, he graduated from Yale in 1907 and went into the stock-brokerage business. In

1910 Hoppin married Helen Alexandré from New York, a marriage which ended in divorce twenty-five years later. He served as a captain in the army in World War I, following which he founded his own brokerage firm of Abbott and Hoppin. Bayard and Helen Hoppin settled on Suffolk Lane in East Islip prior to the start of the war where they summered and were popular members of the younger generation. Bayard was an avid golfer and was a founder of the new golf club at Timber Point, Great River. He was also a clubman who was a member of the prestigious Union and Racquet and Tennis Clubs in New York City. An Episcopalian, he was a member of St. Mark's in Islip and was elected to its vestry in 1923. Much credit should be given to Hoppin for leading the Southside Hospital out of its early period of crisis and into a time of growth during the rest of the decade. During the 1920s many of the largest estates from Oakdale to Babylon began to be split up or used for purposes other than summer residences. As was noted earlier the Lawrance family property, Manatuck Farm, in Bay Shore was slowly changing into the residential development of O-Co-Nee. In Oakdale, Vanderbilt's Idlehour was changing from owner to owner, each in search of a use for that huge estate. It would be years (1962) before the great mansion would finally be used by Adelphi University and then (1968) Dowling College. Most of the land was subdivided into small units.* Next door, Christopher Robert's magnificent chateau, Peperidge Hall, the interior of which came almost entirely from France, stood deserted, as if waiting for another eccentric to claim it for his own. It would wait until 1940 when it was completely leveled. Frederick Bourne's Indian Neck Hall was the subject of a dispute among his seven heirs. For a time it appeared that it would be sold for taxes as three children refused to pay their share. Finally the family was able to agree to sell the Hall and 150 acres of land to

---

* At the first auction sale in June 1925, 114 lots were sold at prices of $100 to $1,000 per lot.

the La Salle Military Academy, a military school for boys.* Two Bourne heirs remained on their portion of the land in homes they had built there. Only the fourth great estate on the Connetquot River, Westbrook, remained mostly unchanged during the 1920s. Mrs. W. Bayard Cutting sold the dairy farm, but she and her daughter, Olivia James, lived in the house until 1949 when the old lady died at ninety-four. Finally in North Babylon the heirs of August Belmont in 1925 had contracted to sell the Nursery with its stables, training track, farm buildings, and fish ponds for a real estate development when the new Long Island State Park Commissioner, Robert Moses, persuaded them to donate it to the state for a park.

In the mid 1920s it was speculated that "within the next few years all of these large estates will be divided into attractive villa sites, where will be located the homes of thousands more from greater New York who are seeking building sites on Long Island."[8] That prediction seemed very likely at the time. Sharply increasing local property taxes, income taxes, and a 1924 immigration law which restricted the procurement of domestic servants, were causing many of the great estates to be given up, often after the death of the original builder-owner. Developers were waiting in the wings, spurred on by improved railroad service and the popularity of the automobile, both of which brought small Long Island villages closer to places of work in the city. Nassau County became America's fastest growing county in the 1920s and Suffolk County was only slightly behind. Suffolk's population increased from 115,000 to 165,000 in the decade, a remarkable 43 percent. In the Town of Islip the population grew from 20,700 to 33,000, a 60 percent jump. The boom times were

---

* The Bourne family sold the Hall and most of the surrounding property in late 1925 to a syndicate headed by Joseph P. Day which had plans to subdivide and develop the land. Day et al sold the mansion and 150 acres to the Clason Point Military Academy in the Bronx in April 1926. By September 1927 the Academy had moved to Oakdale and changed its name to La Salle Military Academy.

creating the psychology that all risks would bring large rewards, that only the fainthearted would lose out. The arrival of the Great Depression, however, and then World War II abruptly ended that thinking. It would be thirty years before growth and development would again come to Long Island. Instead, the large estates were transformed into state parks and private golf courses. Some did remain in single family ownership, and in West Bay Shore a new estate was created. Thus with some imagination at the end of the decade, one could still visualize what had existed at an earlier time.

With the coming of the 1920s the sport of golf was becoming much more popular in America, and on Long Island interest in the game was approaching a mania. Golf courses sprung up everywhere and by the end of the decade there were 108 private and public courses on the Island. When the decade began there were only two courses between Oakdale and Babylon, the Westbrook Golf Club and the South Shore Field Club. Both had been started in the 1890s shortly after golf came to America, and both were nine hole courses. The game had evolved since its beginning to a norm of eighteen holes, but there was insufficient space to expand either Westbrook or South Shore. Only the sale of estates gave to the golfers the opportunity they were waiting for. The first of these came with the death in 1920 of Julien T. Davies, whose place at the mouth of the Connetquot River overlooking the bay in Great River appeared to have the ideal conditions for a seaside golf links, plenty of sand and stiff breezes.

Davies, a prominent New York lawyer and senior partner of the firm of Davies, Auerbach & Cornell, had come to Great River in 1905. At that time he had purchased the house and land of the late William L. Breese, whose widow had married the London impresario Henry V. Higgins (see Chapter VI) and lived in England. Since Breese's death the property had been leased to the South Side Club for gaming and fishing. It was considered a prime site for bird shooting because of its mile and a half of waterfront. The house had fallen into disrepair but that was quickly remedied by Davies who restored it to first class condition.

Davies, aged sixty when he came to South Shore, was a part of the generation of New Yorkers who had arrived in the 1880s and 1890s. He had been born in the city, the son of a judge of the Court of Appeals, and had entered Columbia College where his course of study was interrupted by the Civil War. He fought at Gettysburg as a private in the Twenty-second Regiment of the New York State Militia. After the war he finished at Columbia, joined the law office of Alexander W. Bradford, and was admitted to the New York bar. Davies's law career was notable for his counsel to the builders of the many elevated railways in New York City, helping them establish franchises as well as their liability for property damage. He also was an organizer of the Title Guarantee & Trust Co. in New York, the firm that would guarantee and ensure the title to real estate in the city. In 1869 Davies married Alice Martin, the daughter of an Albany banker. They had several children, the oldest of which, Julien Davies Jr., followed his parents to the South Shore, but located in West Islip where he and his wife lived along the South Country Road with the Arnolds and the Wagstaffs. The son died in 1917 at forty-seven, three years before his father. Julien Davies Sr. and his wife lived happily at their Great River home for fifteen years. They called it Timber Point as had Breese before them. That was the name given the point of land that extended into the bay at the Connetquot River entrance.

Coincidentally with Julien T. Davies's death in May of 1920, a group of Islip and East Islip summer residents of the younger generation began to organize a new golf club. By September the club had a name, the Great River Club, had acquired 150 acres south of the South Country Road adjacent to Cutting's nine-hole Westbrook Golf course, and was preparing to build a second nine holes to use with the older Westbrook course. The Great River Club was led by John B. Stanchfield, George S. Graham, and a much younger Horace Havemeyer. The first directors included twenty-five of the bay area's sportsmen. The new club was to be selective in choosing its members and each had to put up substantial funds to build the new golf course. But construction never began.

It is likely that before commitments were made to begin the nine holes adjacent to Westbrook's nine, the Davies estate began to negotiate to sell Timber Point. It was a far superior site for a classic Scottish seaside links. All that would be required was dredging to turn the marsh into sand and dunes. There was sufficient land for eighteen holes to be laid out from start to finish, and the Breese-Davies mansion could be converted into a clubhouse. Negotiations must have proceeded slowly. Perhaps the buyers were waiting for the estate of Davies to become desperate. In any event, little happened. Davies' daughter and son-in-law, the Archibald Thatchers, spent the summer of 1922 at Timber Point but possibly they did not like it because on July 5, 1923, title to the more than three hundred acres passed to the new club. It was rumored at the time that the selling price was $100,000.

The board of managers of the Great River Club was led at the beginning by W. Kingsland Macy, its first president and for many years to come the leader of the Republican party in Suffolk County. In addition to Macy, Charles and Harry Morgan, Schuyler Parsons Jr., Jay Carlisle, Bayard C. Hoppin, Harry Hollins Jr., Langdon B. Valentine, William K. Dick, and Horace Havemeyer were all governors. It was definitely planned to be the club for the old Islip summer families, and it was their intention at the start to seek a membership of 250 people, each of whom would pay $1,250 to finance the conversion of the Davies house and build the eighteen-hole course.

In the spring of 1925 the club received a new name, the Timber Point Club, to more accurately recognize its location and by which it henceforth was known. The list of charter members was as follows:

CHARTER MEMBERS OF THE TIMBER POINT CLUB
MAY 19, 1925

Jay F. Carlisle	East Islip
William K. Dick	Islip
George A. Ellis	Bay Shore
George S. Graham	Islip
Horace Havemeyer	Islip
William E. Hawkins	Copiague
Harry B. Hollins Jr.	East Islip
Buell Hollister	Islip
Bayard C. Hoppin	East Islip
Aymar Johnson	East Islip
Theodore J. Knapp	East Islip
Charles L. Lawrance	Bay Shore
W. Kingsland Macy	Islip
Charles Morgan	East Islip
Henry Morgan	East Islip
Schuyler L. Parsons Jr.	Islip
Harry T. Peters	Islip
Allan Pinkerton	Islip
Landon K. Thorne	West Islip
Langdon B. Valentine	Islip
Harold H. Weekes	East Islip

To design the golf course the board chose the well-known English architect, C. Hugh Alison. He became very popular in America in the 1920s and had designed the Fresh Meadows course nearby in Great Neck, Long Island. Before the links could be laid out, however, the preparations had to be completed, which consisted of clearing the forest for the front nine and a massive dredging and land building project for the back nine. It was expensive and took two years to finish. Meanwhile the Davies-Breese house was substantially altered by E. W. Howell & Co. of Babylon after a design of New York architects Hart and Shape to create a graceful clubhouse with a colonnaded front porch facing south from which golfers could be seen finishing the last holes. Here, large wedding receptions and other family parties would be held. Davies's fine, electrically operated Aeolian organ was moved to the First Reformed Church of Sayville. Also, during this time a boat basin was dredged in a protected cove of the Connetquot River in which boats could be moored. It was the intention of the governors to have a yacht club combined with a golf club, and to that end a new one-design class of sailboats, to be called a Timber Point class, was purchased by several of the members from a builder in Greenport, Long Island. There would be about twenty of these 23-foot knockabouts racing both at the Timber Point Yacht Club and in the Great South Bay race week regattas beginning in 1926. It was an attempt to again have one-design racing in the manner of the earlier Islip One-Design class of the Islip Yacht Club. Horace Havemeyer, Harry Morgan, and Bayard Hoppin were leaders of the Timber Point Yacht Club. The boats were popular well into the 1930s as residents of Point O' Woods joined with the Islipians in buying them. Gradually, however, they died out on the bay and did not survive World War II, having been supplanted by the increasingly popular Star boat, the most successful one-design class of boat ever built up to that time.

Finally, by 1926 the eighteen-hole golf course at Timber Point was complete and the opening was celebrated by an invitational tournament in June. The members could be proud of the result. In particular, the back nine holes created from the marsh along the bay was as challenging a nine holes in the southwest gales as any nine holes in Scotland. From tee to green over the sand and in the face of the wind, only the very best golfers could make their par. The Timber Point Club was a success, although the membership never reached more than about a hundred. Fewer members had to put up more money, but the club survived until World War II.

While the Davies-Breese estate was being turned into a private golf club, an angry contest was unfolding next door over what should happen to the 1,500 acre estate of the eccentric millionaire George C. Taylor who had died in 1907 (see Chapter VI) almost twenty years before. Taylor had no children of his own. His heirs were the children of his sister and brother-in-law, the Percy R. Pynes, who lived in New York and New Jersey. However, Pyne's son, Moses Taylor Pyne, and grandson, Percy R. Pyne II, used the huge Taylor property as a hunting preserve from 1907 until 1924 when it caught the eye of the new Long Island State Park Commissioner, Robert Moses. Moses wanted the land for a state park and he was opposed by the members of the Timber Point Club who were led by its president, W. Kingsland Macy.

Macy, thirty-five years old at the time, had been born in New York City in 1889. He was the son of George H. Macy who had come to summer along the Great South Bay in the 1890s. Like so many of the early summer families, the Macys were descended from one of New England's first settlers. Thomas Macy had come to Massachusetts in the seventeenth century from England and was one of the purchasers of Nantucket Island in 1659. From this tiny island the family would make its fortune two centuries later. Thomas's descendant Josiah Macy was born on Nantucket Island in 1785. As he grew to manhood the island became the most important center of whaling in America. Whale oil and shipping brought prosperity to many with the foresight and courage to pursue those dangerous paths. Josiah Macy became a merchant captain and later with his son, William Henry Macy, built a shipping empire that brought great wealth to the family. Josiah moved to New York after the Civil War and lived to the great age of eighty-seven. He was one of the remarkable merchants of the nineteenth century.

Josiah's great, great grandson, W. Kingsland Macy, had grown up in Islip from the time he was a small boy. Named for his great aunt's husband, William M. Kingsland, young Macy went to the Groton School, then on to Harvard College, and then joined with his father in the management of the Union Pacific Tea Company. In 1922 he left the family business to join another Islipian, Bayard C. Hoppin, on the New York Stock Exchange in the firm of Abbott, Hoppin, and Co.

In the meantime King Macy, as he was known by his friends, had married William Dick's granddaughter, Julia Dick, and thus became the brother-in-law of Horace Havemeyer, who had married Doris Dick, Julia's older sister. Macy and Havemeyer would be linked together in the contest with Robert Moses.

Ironically it was this battle that thrust King Macy into the political world, where he would spend the remainder of his life. From the age of thirty-five until 1952, when he retired at the age of sixty-three, Macy was the most powerful Republican in Suffolk County, always a Republican county. He held virtually every important political office in the county. He was chairman of the powerful Republican Committee from 1926 to 1951; a congressman from Suffolk County from 1946 to 1952; a delegate to every Republican National Convention from 1928 to 1948 except for 1936; and chairman of the Islip Town Planning Board from 1926 to 1950. Nothing of political significance happened in Suffolk County without the approval of King Macy.

It is strange that such a successful career would begin with a defeat. But from 1924 when Robert Moses was appointed the Long Island State Park Commissioner by Governor Alfred E. Smith, until he retired many years later, Moses almost always had his way in the end. Macy and Moses were less than a year apart in age. Their political careers began in 1924 with the struggle over the disposition of the Taylor estate. Although they fought bitterly to the end over this property, they later became friends and were sometimes close political allies. For more than thirty years they were the most influential men in Suffolk County.

Unlike Macy, Robert Moses (1889–1981) was from a well-to-do German Jewish family, and as a young man he was taught his responsibility to help people. He went to Yale where he was Phi Beta Kappa (1909), then to Oxford, graduating with a First, and then to Columbia for a doctorate in political science. For a time he worked for the administration of New York City Mayor John Purrey Mitchell, but his idealism, optimism, and reforming zeal were too much for

Tammany Hall, so that in 1918 he was without a job. New York State had elected a new governor, Alfred E. Smith, that year and although Smith was taught to be a Tammany man and opposed to civil service reform and all that Moses held important, the two men grew close. Moses held no official post in the Smith administration at that time, but he was the key figure in getting the governor re-elected in 1922. Moses went back to Albany with Al Smith and on April 18, 1924, was rewarded by being appointed president of the Long Island State Park Commission and chairman of the State Council of Parks. He had finally achieved his goal. Over his career Moses served five New York State governors. For him, however, there was only one he called "Governor," Al Smith. The rest he always addressed by their first names.

When Moses became the Long Island State Park Commissioner, there was only one state park on the island. Fire Island State Park (see Chapter VII), without any state funding, was in wretched condition, almost all the buildings having burned in a fire in 1918. As a resident of Babylon by then, Moses, who described himself as a "simple South Shore boy," knew about the conditions at Fire Island and also knew that all the land along the north side of the Great South Bay was privately owned and unavailable for a state park. It appeared that nothing was for sale until the fall of 1924 when the heirs of the Taylor property indicated they would sell the 1,500 acres to the state for $250,000. This was just what Moses was looking for. His idealism and imagination had already envisaged the second state park for Long Island. In fact he called it the Deer Range State Park after the name the Taylor heirs had given their land.

With the prospect of the Taylor land going to the State of New York, Kingsland Macy, Horace Havemeyer, and some other members of the new Timber Point Club put up the $250,000 that the Taylor heirs were asking and bought the property, telling the heirs correctly that the state had no money available to pay for its purchase. Although a state referendum in the fall of 1924 had authorized the purchase, the legislature had not provided any funds. Being under the control of the Republicans, the legislature continued to refuse funding, and it in fact never did provide any. For the state to seize property without compensatory payment was clearly in violation of the New York State Constitution. In spite of having no authority to do so, on December 4, 1924, Robert Moses ordered the Taylor land confiscated in the name of the State of New York and further ordered state troopers to keep out the legal owners Messrs. Macy et al and anyone else without his permission. On December 12, 1924, the *Suffolk County News* headlined the event: "Taylor Estate Now Is A State Park," "Park Commissioner has a squad of state troopers on the fine waterfront property and has plans under way for its development." The article went on: "Bay Shore Attorney William H. Robbins, one of the incorporators of the company [with Macy and Havemeyer] which two weeks ago purchased the 2,000 acres of the George C. Taylor estate, says that he is prepared to fight to the finish the action of the Long Island State Park Commission which on Friday seized the estate for a public park." The battle was joined.

The contest over the rightful ownership of the former Taylor estate, or Moses versus Macy, went on through all the courts of New York State and a petition for certiorari was even made to the United States Supreme Court, which was denied. It took until January of 1929, four years, for the matter to be ultimately decided. Macy won all of the early rounds. Moses had virtually given up when financier August Heckscher, a seventy-six-year-old philanthropist, offered to give the state the $250,000 that the legislature would not provide. The courts held that this was illegal as well, that a private citizen could not give money to pay for compensatory damages. Moses hung on and fought. All the while he was improving the Taylor estate and preparing it for the public park it would become. He used funds out of the small park's department budget for this purpose. Finally Macy and his friends were running out of money. It seemed to some of them senseless to pour good money into legal fees when the park was actually being built. Judge James A. Dunne ruled that although the original confiscation was illegal, the second appropriation with Heckscher's money was legal and thus the state did own the park. Appeals to higher courts failed. Macy et al, having gotten their $250,000 investment back, although not the thousands of dollars in legal fees, surrendered. The Taylor estate became the Heckscher State Park of today, opening with an appropriate ceremony in June of 1929. Governor Al Smith, August Heckscher, and of course Robert Moses were present to welcome over ten thousand guests. The former governor (Smith was out of office by then and had been defeated by Herbert Hoover for president of the United States in 1928) condemned the "wealthy young men who owned the Timber Point Club" for wanting to own the property for $250,000. "I couldn't see that," he declared, while the crowd applauded. Heckscher said, "You owe this park not to me, but to the amazing public spirit of Robert Moses."[9] If he had added tenacity, he would have been exactly right, for Robert Moses fought for what he believed in and would not give up. It was not until the 1960s at the very end of his career that he finally suffered a major defeat over his desire to build a roadway along the length of Fire Island. *

Moses's long career as Long Island State Park Commissioner had begun with particular rapidity and intensity. He had the full support and confidence of Governor Smith and wanted to create parks, parkways, and beaches before a succeeding governor might make it all impossible. From 1924 to 1928 under Al Smith, Moses built fourteen parks, had acquired the right of way for the Southern State Parkway, and had built Jones Beach. Many parcels of land were acquired as gifts without cost to the taxpayer. By the end of 1928 he had only spent $1 million of taxpayers' money. It was from one of those parks, Belmont Lake State Park, acquired from the Belmont family as a gift, that Moses established the

---

* The Taylor mansion was demolished in 1933; the site was marked by a bronze plaque on a stone saying, "Heckscher State Park, a gift from August Heckscher to the people of the State of New York." The other Taylor buildings were used by the park service for various purposes.

headquarters of his Long Island State Park Commission. Inside August Belmont's former home at the Nursery, Robert Moses with his engineers and architects planned their campaigns and ran their department. Moses himself, usually in shirtsleeves, worked in the Belmont dining room. "Belmont had this tremendous dining room, and there was this huge table there, and Moses made it his conference table. The conferences would start at nine o'clock in the morning and sometimes you couldn't leave until after midnight. And you just worked like hell all day long."[10] No doubt old Belmont would have approved. * The Breese-Davies property in Great River was not the only estate that was turned into a golf course in the 1920s, although the Timber Point Club was very much the club of choice of the summer families who lived from Oakdale to Bay Shore. Its bayside setting made it unique among all the courses built near the bay in that decade, as did its combination of golfing and sailing. In the fall of 1921 it was rumored that a group of golfing enthusiasts who lived in the Brightwaters, West Islip, and Babylon areas were eyeing the north part of the Bossert estate as a site for an eighteen hole golf course. Louis Bossert, who had bought the place from James Hazen Hyde, had died. His wife and two sons** were thought to be receptive to selling at least a part of this huge property which carried the fifth highest assessment in the town ($275,000 in 1922). In 1922, an option to acquire 140 acres to build a golf course was given by the Bossert family, but it was not until the spring of 1924 that financing was arranged and the new Southward Ho Land Corporation came into existence. The Bosserts had to take back a mortgage to help the club get started. Located entirely to the north of the South Country Road, it was within a quarter mile of the South Shore Field Club, the golf course south of the road that

---

* The Belmont home was demolished in 1935.

** Louis Bossert's wife was Philippine Bossert; his sons were Charles V. and John Bossert.

had been built by Richard Hyde and was then owned by his son James R. Hyde.* (No relation to James Hazen Hyde mentioned above and in Chapter V.)

To design the Southward Ho golf course the governors turned to the notable American golf architect, A. W. Tillinghast. Tillinghast had created two famous courses, Baltusrol in Springfield, New Jersey, and Winged Foot in Mamaroneck, New York. He was much sought after in that decade. Construction of the new course began in May and took a year to complete. In addition to the golf course, tennis courts, a swimming pool, and a tree-shaded bridle path around the property were planned. The Hyde-Bossert house with its forty rooms was entirely remodeled and redecorated. With its third floor removed altogether, it was transformed into suitable space for a country club with lounges, card rooms, a grill and dining room, a men's locker room, and even squash courts. "An unusual feature of the club are the living quarters both for benedicts ** and bachelors," said the *Babylon Leader* on May 29, 1925.

The first meeting of members of the Southward Ho Country Club was held in September 1924. Henry M. Keith from West Islip was elected president; Wesley M. Oler Jr., secretary (he was also president of the Long Island Golf Association). Among the governors were John Bossert (for the mortgager) and Elmer B. Howell of Babylon (son of Elmer W. Howell). The eighteen-hole golf course was ready for opening day, May 30, 1925, celebrated by a handicap tournament. It was described as "both sporty and picturesque, each hole being individual and distinctive."[11] Shorter than the average eighteen-hole course, it was and is today a challenging

---

* The South Shore Field Club, expanded to 18 holes, continued in existence well into the 1930s. The club office was listed at 33 West 42 St. in New York City. The property was sold to Hans Isbrandtsen for his cattle breeding farm in May 1941.

** A benedict is "a married man; usually, a man newly married, especially one long a bachelor." Webster.

one, with a stream running through to the bay and forming water hazards along the way.

During the Depression, in 1934, the club went bankrupt. It was reorganized that year under a new name, the South Bay Golf Club. The Emigrant Savings Bank of New York owned title to the land but allowed the members to use the facilities for payment of the real estate taxes and $4,000 per year in fees. With the Depression and then World War II there were no buyers for the land. This went on until 1945 when the bank decided to put the property up for sale, it having been appraised on May 1, 1944, for $109,500 by H. Ward Ackerson (grandson of T. B. Ackerson of Brightwaters, see Chapter VIII). Wanting to retain this fine golf course for the community and for his own use (the Timber Point Club had gone bankrupt during the war), Horace Havemeyer bought out the mortgage, took title to the property, and offered the membership ten years to repurchase the property from him at his cost. During those ten years he paid the real estate taxes on the property. In 1954, ten years later, the club exercised its option and again owned its land. Its name was changed back to the Southward Ho Country Club. Thanks to Havemeyer's great generosity, the club had survived when many others failed. The Hyde-Bossert house was remodeled again to suit the modern age. All the upper floors were removed and only the ground floor remains today with its grand entrance hall the sole reminder of the bygone age.

The Southward Ho Country Club took only that portion of the Hyde-Bossert land that lay north of the South Country Road. The portion to the south running to the bay had a different disposition, the makings of another and the last of the great estates to be built from Oakdale to Babylon. As most of the estates were breaking up or were being converted to other uses, Landon K. Thorne of New York and West Islip decided in the mid 1920s to create one for his family.

Landon Ketchum Thorne had been born in 1888 in Saugatuck, Connecticut, the firstborn son of Edwin and Phebe Ketchum Thorne. He was named for his maternal grandfather, Landon Ketchum. As a boy of less than ten Landon would come with his younger brother, Francis, and his two sisters Phebe and Anna to summer in West Islip where the senior Thornes had built their roomy three-story shingle-style home on the east side of Oak Neck Road. Young Landon would go fishing and sharking with his father, and, when he was old enough, duck shooting with him as well. He came to love the Great South Bay with its many sporting opportunities. Landon went away to boarding school at Pomfret, Connecticut, and then on to Yale where he graduated from Sheff in 1910. In September of 1911 the twenty-three-year-old Landon K. Thorne married Julia Atterbury Loomis, daughter of Henry Patterson Loomis, and sister of Alfred A. Loomis who would soon become Thorne's longtime business partner. Landon and Julia Thorne would have two children, sons Landon Jr. and Edwin Thorne.

Thorne started in business after college with the Central Hanover Bank and Trust Co., later joining the investment banking house of Bonbright & Co. He served his country as a captain in the U.S. Army in World War I. Seeing a bright future for the electric utility companies throughout the country, with the assistance of his brother-in-law, Loomis, Thorne acquired control of Bonbright in 1920 just as the Roaring Twenties were beginning. During that decade it was estimated that Bonbright underwrote 15 percent of all electric utility offerings of stocks and bonds in the entire country. Thorne and Loomis made large fortunes. Landon Thorne was asked to join the board of directors of many companies, including utilities, banks, and railroads. Notable among these were the Commonwealth and Southern Corporation, the Public Service Corp. of New Jersey, the Bankers Trust Company, the First National Bank of New York, the Southern Pacific Railroad, and the Federal Insurance Company of New York. By 1933 he was one of the most important industrialists in New York if not in America. When the Glass-Steagall Act of 1933 required the legal separation of commercial and investment banking, Thorne chose to leave Bonbright and devote himself to commercial banks. A wise and prudent investor,

Landon Thorne sold many of his stocks before the crash of October 1929, and thus came through the Depression with his fortune intact. He made a large contribution to the growth of corporate America throughout his entire career. He also had many interests beyond banking. He was a governor of the New York Hospital, a term commissioner of the Long Island State Park Commission (1962), and a trustee of the New York Zoological Society.

Landon was also a sportsman with varied interests, which included golf, sailing, riding, shooting, and especially fishing. While at Yale he rowed on the crew and was a member of the swimming team. Later in 1930 he was a member of the yachting syndicate that built the J boat *Whirlwind*, to defend the America's Cup. *Whirlwind*, a 120-foot-long giant, was defeated in trials by Harold S. Vanderbilt's J boat *Enterprise*, which went on to successfully defend the Cup in the first of many races to be held off Newport, Rhode Island. Vanderbilt would win again in 1934, and in 1937 with his new boat *Ranger*, considered to be the fastest single-masted sailboat ever built.* Thorne also owned Star boats, which he and his two sons sailed in the Great South Bay in the early 1930s. His boat *Mist*, sailed by Ed Fink with Ed Thorne as crew, won the Star Class International Championships on Long Island Sound in 1932, and with Ed Thorne sailing came in second in 1933 off Long Beach, California. Most of all, however, Landon Thorne loved fishing. He spent hours off Montauk Point hunting the swordfish, which could be taken by harpoon while it was basking in the summer sun on the surface of the ocean or by rod and reel which was much more difficult. Fishing was in the Thorne blood and Landon was a true son of his father. He belonged to many clubs in New York City, as would be expected, and to two on Long Island — the South

---

* *Ranger* was 135 feet LOA; beam 21 ft.; draft 15 ft.; sail area 7,546 sq. ft.; mast 165 ft.; designers, W. Starling Burgess and Olin J. Stephens. Of *Ranger*'s thirty-seven races during her first and only season, she was to win all but two. She was broken up for scrap to aid the war effort.

The Islip Polo Club was organized in 1912. Pictured here is a member, Harry T. Peters, practicing at Windholme along Champlin's Creek. (Courtesy of Charles D. Webster.)

Horse shows were held annually at *Oakwood Park* in Bay Shore from 1901 to the end of the 1920s. Shown here is the blue ribbon winner *Steel Trap* in 1919.

Ardmore, built by Thomas Adams, Jr. in 1908, west of the Hyde-Bossert home, was later occupied by his daughter and son-in-law, Florence and George A. Ellis Jr. It is now part of the *Southward Ho Country Club*. (Courtesy of Richard A.Milligan.)

Cedarholme, the home of Lewis Mills Gibb and Anna Pinkerton Gibb on the east side of Saxton Avenue, Bay Shore, which they built in 1903. It was later owned by Judge and Mrs. Charles H. Tenney. (Courtesy of Richard A. Milligan.)

At the head of the Brightwaters
canal stand the two Roman pago-
das built in 1909 by the T. B.
Ackerson Company to decorate
its Brightwaters development
project. They are pictured here
today. (Courtesy of Richard A. Milligan.)

Edward Francis Hutton came to
Bay Shore around 1900 and
remained until 1920. He and his
first wife lived on Awixa and
Saxton Avenues. Their son died as
a result of a riding accident there.
E. F. Hutton is pictured here in
the 1920s. (Courtesy of the Hillwood
Museum.)

The Islip One Design sloop, *Electra,* owned by Horace Havemeyer, racing against *Yama Yama,* owned by Aymar Johnson, off Bellport in 1909 (from *Brooklyn Life* by F. A. Walter)

Rosemary was the home of Jay and Mary Pinkerton Carlisle in East Islip. It was built by E. W. Howell Company of Babylon in 1916-17 on the south side of South Country Road. (Courtesy of E.W. Howell Company, *Noted Long Island Homes.*)

Side Sportsmen's Club and the National Golf Links of America in Southampton. The National, as it was known, had a bayside links course, and a selective membership of prominent men from all over the country. After their marriage Landon and Julia Thorne located in the summer on Oak Neck Road in West Islip across from his parents. They occupied a three-story shingle-style house in an enclave which included the Edward W. C. Arnolds, the Orme Wilsons, the George Wagstaffs, Mrs. Loring Andrews, and Landon's sister, Anna Augusta Thorne. Anna was married in her parents' home on Oak Neck Road to Robert Titus on a lovely Saturday in June 1920, in the most fashionable wedding Oak Neck Road had ever witnessed. The ceremony was performed by the Reverend Henry Sloane Coffin, then pastor of the Madison Avenue Presbyterian Church (later a famous president of Union Theological Seminary of New York). Landon Thorne's other sister, Phebe, the matron of honor, was married to Harry K. Knapp Jr. at the time.

It was during 1925 when Landon, having established his reputation in the investment business, began to plan for a much larger and grander country home. The property he chose, only a mile or so east of Oak Neck Road, was the south part of the Hyde-Bossert estate. To this was added a portion of land from the George G. Wilmerding estate and a strip from the former Bradish Johnson holdings, all south of the South Country Road.* When the acquisitions were completed, Thorne owned 230 acres with a stream running through to the J. H. Hyde-built canal, allowing for the construction of lakes and ponds.

Thorne chose New York architect William F. Dominick to design a comfortable American country home and the Babylon builder E. W. Howell & Co. to construct it. The materials used, red brick with a gray slate roof, gave it a very

_____

* The purchase from the Bossert estate was made on April 1, 1925. The purchases from Julia L. Wilmerding and from the Henry M. Johnson estate were made in January and June 1929, respectively.

similar appearance to Horace Havemeyer's house on Olympic Point built ten years earlier and designed by Harrie T. Lindeberg. Thorne's home, built during 1928, was slightly smaller and not as symmetrical as Havemeyer's. In addition to the main house, Thorne built a "playhouse" consisting of an indoor tennis court, a squash court, and an indoor swimming pool. There were also suitable stables for horses, a five-car garage, a captain's cottage, and a watchman's cottage near the entrance gate. Later in 1941 Thorne built a second home for his son on the property, known as the winter house. To complete this pastoral picture Thorne engaged the leading landscape designer of the time, Umberto Innocenti, to create lakes and ponds and to design an outstanding flower garden. When all was done Landon and Julia Thorne had a lovely, tasteful country home. While not as grand as those built in the nineteenth century, it measured up in every other way. It would be the last to grace the bay area.

In 1958, the Thornes gave the playhouse to St. Peter's Episcopal Church of Bay Shore, which was looking for a new site. A creative transformation changed the tennis court into a church nave and the covered-over swimming pool became a side chapel. Julia Thorne gave more property to the church shortly before her death. On September 13, 1964, Landon K. Thorne died in New York City at the age of seventy-six. Julia lived on until 1973. Except for the gifts to St. Peter's Church and a small parcel that was given to the Bay Shore Yacht Club for a new site, the property had remained intact until the year before Mrs. Thorne's death when about ninety acres of the wetlands near the bay were given to the Nature Conservancy to be kept forever wild. In a final transformation the big house was torn down, and the remaining land was sold to a developer in 1976. He built what is known today as the Admiralty, a clustered condominium community. Much of the feeling of openness with lakes and trees remains. With all of the dispositions of the Thorne land, the community has been thoughtfully served. Penataquit Point in Bay Shore, once the site of the short-lived Penataquit Corinthian Yacht Club, had been owned since the 1890s by J. Adolph

Mollenhauer. From the small canal that cuts through to connect the bay with Bay Shore harbor to the Point's end, Mollenhauer had sold only three parcels prior to his death in 1926.* Two of these on the west side of the point went to Fred Ingraham and to Dr. Charles F. Ash who built houses on them. The third parcel on the east side facing the bay went to the architect Rafael Guastavino (1872–1950) who built a house that is so different in design and construction and is such a prominent landmark on the bay that he deserves further comment.

Rafael Guastavino came to New York from his native Catalonia in Spain with his parents when he was ten years old. His father, also Rafael, was an architect who had become successful as an authority on new methods of construction called "cohesive construction." He was credited as the inventor of the Guastavino arch used in the building of the New York City subway system. The junior Rafael apprenticed with his father's firm and at about the turn of the century gained fame as the inventor of the type of interlocking tile used for elliptical work on the interior of domes. Guastavino tile became even more famous than the Guastavino arch. It was used on many church domes including the 110-foot-span of the dome of the Cathedral of St. John, the Divine, in New York, said to be one of the largest pieces of unsupported dome work in the world. Other church domes using Guastavino tile are St. Bartholomew's, Riverside, and Temple Emanu-El, all in Manhattan. Also notable is the Guastavino tile in the saucer dome of the Gould Library, designed by Stanford White in 1903 at the New York University campus in the Bronx above the Harlem River. With his reputation as an architect in tile secure, Rafael Guastavino sought a summer home for his family — a son and a daughter had been born by then — and settled on the east side of Penataquit Point in Bay Shore. He enjoyed sailing in the bay and owned a Star boat in the late 1920s when that class came to the South Shore. Its name was *Kinkajou*.

---

* The three sales took place between 1910 and 1915.

The Guastavino house, as it is still known by old-timers on the bay, was built just prior to World War I. A Mediterranean style villa, it was faced entirely with tile. A red terracotta roof and sides of glazed red tiles implanted in cement gave it the most distinctive look among Great South Bay homes. A formal grape arbor ran from the house down to the bay. Covered with vine it gave to Guastavino's home a Spanish look which must have reminded him of his native Catalonia. Following Rafael's death in 1950, the house was occupied for a time by his daughter, Louise, and her husband, Frank Gulden Jr. It stands today, one of the very few "old" houses, along with the Bourne-La Salle Military Academy, that can easily be marked by the sailor on the bay from Oakdale to Babylon.

With the death of Adolph Mollenhauer, his Penataquit Point land was put up for auction at a sale held on August 28, 1926.* Prior to that sale Horace Havemeyer had bought the parcel at the point where the clubhouse of the Penataquit Corinthian Yacht Club had stood. He acquired it to protect his own Olympic Point site from an undesirable neighbor. At the auction a hundred lots of varying sizes were offered, ranging from interior ones as small as one-eighth of an acre (there was no minimum-size zoning then) to plots on the water of roughly one half acre. The advertising described the Point as being "bounded on two sides by the beautiful waters of the Great South Bay. Penataquit and Awixa Avenues leading to the property are very beautiful, having many handsome residences of the well-to-do."[12]

Despite the real estate boom of the 1920s, the sale was not a success. The more desirable waterfront lots were the ones sold. On the east side south of Guastavino and facing Olympic Point four lots went to a person who intended to locate a nightclub there. This threat forced Horace Havemeyer to buy the four lots in 1927 at an exorbitant cost to protect his land and his view. A nightclub directly upwind would

---

* Penataquit Gardens, a developer, had bought the land in July 1926 for $125,000 and was the seller at the August auction.

have made Olympic Point a very noisy place indeed. Havemeyer, years later in 1954, would sell the lots to home owners at a loss!

Two more New York families came to Islip in the mid 1920s, Andre De Coppet and his wife, and Kimball Chase Atwood Jr. with his new bride. In May of 1925 De Coppet purchased the property to the north of South Country Road lying between Willowbrook Avenue and Orowoc Lake. The house had been remodeled by William H. Moffitt before he built a second, grander home between the two lakes that later was bought by Judge Graham. The De Coppets called their home the Willows. It was a handsome, stucco house of a style that was popular around 1910. A loggia or porch extended to the east, looking out over Orowoc Lake with several willow trees growing along its banks.

Of Swiss descent, Andre was the son of Edward T. De Coppet who founded the New York brokerage firm of De Coppet & Doremus, notable as a dealer in odd lot securities. [*] Andre was born in 1891, graduated from Princeton University in 1915, and distinguished himself in France in World War I as a lieutenant with the Seventy-seventh Division. General Pershing awarded him the Distinguished Service Cross for "extraordinary heroism in action near Mervel, France, on September 14, 1918. In preparation for an attack by units of his division, he helped establish an observation post. Learning that a wounded officer was in front, he made his way through intense fire from enemy artillery to the wounded officer and assisted in carrying him back to safety."[13] After the war he joined the family firm, of which he became president in 1927. He also owned a sugar plantation in Haiti, which he would visit during the cane harvesting season in the winter. Like so many of his peers, he belonged to the exclusive Union and Racquet and Tennis Clubs in New York.

Andre De Coppet was married three times during the years he summered at the Willows, the last marriage being to Eileen Johnston of the Islip family. Andre and Eileen had two

---

[*] Shares of stock of less than 100 in number.

daughters, Diane and Laura. While vacationing at the family home in Lausanne, Switzerland in 1953, Andre died at sixty-two. Shortly thereafter the Willows on Orowoc Lake was sold for development in the post-war boom.

In 1926, the year after the De Coppets came to Islip, young Kimball Chase Atwood Jr. decided to settle on Ocean Avenue. He had just been married the previous year to Adela Girdner in New York. Atwood was the son of the founder of the Preferred Accident Insurance Company (founded in 1885) and it was there that young Atwood worked, becoming secretary of the company in 1934. The Atwoods were able to purchase the large shingle style house that had been designed by the Sayville architect Isaac H. Green Jr. for Charles A. Schieren, the former mayor of Brooklyn (see Chapter VI). The land was on the west side of Ocean Avenue, south of the small canal that runs from it into Orowoc Creek, and to the north of the H. G. Timmerman property. There was a fine view to the west of the Great South Bay. Although the house was torn down after the Atwoods' death, the land remains in the family. Their son, Frederick L. Atwood, and his wife, Elizabeth, live on the property in a house they built near Ocean Avenue.

The Roaring Twenties was not only the era of the breaking up of great estates on the South Shore; it was also the era of fun and frolicking. In spite of Prohibition, liquor could be easily obtained from bootleggers, and partying was a serious occupation on Long Island. The South Shore had its share of parties, many of which took place along Champlin's Creek in Islip and East Islip. It was there that the social leaders lived and entertained, often turning night into day. As one of them said, "no one gave a thought to a possible end to the times of easy money. I had been speculating wildly on the market, took some profits, and in one day paid cash for my new house and a Rolls-Royce!"[14] Parsons said that the "leaders of the hospitality" were Jay and Mary Carlisle together with Charles and Margaret Lawrance, who by then had moved to East Islip from Bay Shore. He modestly failed to mention himself, but the real leader of partying in Islip and East Islip was in fact Schuyler Livingston Parsons Jr. with his new creation known to all as Pleasure Island.

Parsons, born in 1892, was his parents' youngest child. His mother, Helena Johnson Parsons, died when he was only five. Young Schuyler was then brought up by his older sister, Helena, as his father travelled abroad a great deal and was occupied much of the time with his horse racing interests. Shortly after Helena married Dick Wharton (1906) the senior Parsons turned Whileaway over to them. Young Schuyler looked upon the Whartons as parents and Whileaway as his summer home. He went away to St. Mark's to school and then on to Harvard from which he graduated in three years. From Harvard he went to the Columbia Law School, but hampered by poor eyesight and a strong predilection for debutante parties, he gave up the study of law and at twenty-two years of age became in his words, "a gentleman of leisure." Summers in Europe until the Great War began, weekends in Islip with Helena and Dick, and many parties along the way occupied his time. His poor eyesight kept him from military service in Europe, but he joined the Voluntary Ambulance Service of the American Red Cross and served in France with distinction. In the spring of 1920 Schuyler married, but divorced two years later, and never remarried. Like so many young men after the war, he could not find a meaningful occupation. With plenty of money (his father had died in 1917) he seemed to exist from party to party, drinking too much, and became associated with the theater crowd in New York. He had become a true bon vivant of the Roaring Twenties.

It was in 1924 that Parsons conceived of the idea of building an island in the middle of Champlin's Creek off Whileaway. "I always tried to go to Islip for Sundays, winter and summer, and decided I wanted to build a small house there for my own use. There was a low lying island in the Creek, off the family place, which the town wanted to buy as a dump for the muck from the dredging operations. I had the idea that if I gave them the use of the island, after they had put the muck on top of the fill it would eventually make six or eight feet of rich loam. Experts bore out the theory and it has worked to a remarkable degree. The operation began in the summer of 1923 and by April 1924 'Pleasure Island' was born. Shrubbery came from nearby woods, and birch, cedar, and apple trees were transplanted."[15] Pleasure Island was connected by a bridge to the mainland. A dark green, one-story cottage was built with a living room left unceiled, a great fireplace, and many sofas. "It had three bedrooms (one a servant's room) with two beds in each, and four bunks in the living room disguised as window seats, so that by dividing sexes four ladies could use the bedrooms and four men the living room. Judging from the guest book, it was full every Sunday, winter and summer, til I moved away in 1928. The dock ran out from the front door and there was the fleet, a cabin cruiser, a large and small sea sled, and various small boats."[16] So Schuyler Parsons described what became the focus of party life in Islip from 1924 to 1928. As he aptly put it, "We were really flying high, but money seemed so easy to make that no one cared. Islip was very prosperous at this time, owing to the stock market boom. The commuter train had to have a new private car."[17]

The star boarders at Pleasure Island were the British stage headliners Beatrice Lillie and Gertrude Lawrence, new to New York then, but soon to be the darlings of the Broadway stage. Another notable personality in the summer of 1926 was Rudolph Valentino, the great film idol. Parsons described him as "always quiet at a party, though decidedly decorative. In private life he was a very simple soul, exuding charm. His effect on the public is easy to understand."[18] From time to time the dancer Irene Castle, the songwriters George Gershwin and Rodgers and Hart would be there to add their music to the parties. "They were always generous with songs and skits and getting what is now called 'audience participation.' Sundays we would go by boat to the point of the beach by Fire Island Inlet [Point Democrat], then a stretch of virgin beach. Lunch was a picnic affair, with a great deal of yacht-hopping, as by now every South Shore stockbroker owned a lovely boat. Sunday night would call for another party — at

Islip or in town. We never needed hired musicians or talent, since the guests performed."[19]

Although Pleasure Island may have been the center of all the partying, it did not have a monopoly. The Carlisles' home, Rosemary, was known to be beautiful, gay, and full of warmth and fun. In the early spring of 1927 Charles Lawrance, who was known as the Chief, gave a small party at his home for Colonel Lindbergh, the young aviator who was going to use Lawrance's Whirlwind engine and had come to East Islip to talk to him about it. He had concerns that it might not have enough power to take his plane, the *Spirit of St. Louis*, over three thousand miles of ocean to Paris. The guest of honor was entertained that evening with music played by both George Gershwin and Cole Porter. The following winter Lindbergh, by then the most popular hero in the nation, stayed with the Chief for a week.

Along St. Mark's Lane the younger generation, married before the war, was entering into the fun. Dick and Helena Wharton in Whileaway, Henry and Maud Bull, and Buell and Louise "Tottie" Hollister were a part of this group, as was young William K. Dick and his new wife, Madeleine Force Astor, widowed when Colonel Astor went down with the *Titanic*. They lived on Ocean Avenue. But it was along the former Pavilion Avenue, since called Suffolk Lane, and along its two extensions, Meadow Farm Road and Bay View Avenue in East Islip, that most of those lived who made partying an occupation during that decade. To mention some, there were Harry Jr. and Lilias Hollins; his brother Gerald V. and Virginia Kobbe Hollins; Harry Knapp Jr. and his wife, Elizabeth, who built Creekside in 1929; Aymar Johnson, son of Bradish; Bayard and Helen Hoppin; the three Morgan brothers, Henry (Harry), Charles and Ethel, Robert (Bobby) and Carol Kobbe Morgan (the second Kobbe sister, Hildegarde, had married Francis B. Thorne by then). Lastly on Bay View Avenue lived Malcolm and Dorothy McBurney. Dorothy was the daughter of Amedee Depau Moran and had grown up in Islip since the early 1890s. Many of the men had gone to college together — usually Harvard or Yale — and had been pals for years, either growing up together in Islip or at college.* In fact so many had gone to Harvard that they became known as Islip's Harvard Gang.

The climax to Islip's partying decade and without doubt the grandest party ever held there was the three-day Venetian Fete for the benefit of the Southside Hospital that began on the evening of July 14, 1927. The highlight of the opening night was a fashion pageant entitled "Glorifying the Typical American Girl." It starred Gertrude Lawrence and twelve local debutantes from the Islip summer community including Betsy Duval, Evelina Hollins, Natalie Peters, Carol and Hildegarde Stevenson, Ann Valentine, and Marion Wharton. George Gershwin played several numbers from his new play, *Strike Up the Band*, and Fred and Adele Astaire danced for the audience.** The judges for the beauty contest were Gertrude Lawrence, Jules Glaenzer, Charlie Chaplin, and the impresario for the entire evening was Schuyler Parsons Jr. Who else but Parsons could have brought all that show biz talent to Islip for a benefit? Thirty years later he remembered the occasion in his book *Untold Friendships*:

> That summer [1927] at Islip we made an all-out effort to raise money for the South Side Hospital. Gertie Lawrence, Flo Ziegfeld, Jules Glaenzer and George Gershwin were to judge a Beauty Pageant with an entry from every town in

---

* Bayard C. Hoppin Y '07, Charles L. Lawrance Y '05, Landon K. Thorne Y '10, Stuyvesant Wainwright Y '13, Francis B. Thorne Y '14; W. Kingsland Macy H '11, Harold S. Vanderbilt H '05 ?, Schuyler L. Parsons Jr. H '14, Harry B. Hollins Jr. H '04, August Belmont H '04 and Porcellian Club, Harry Morgan H '05 and Porcellian Club, Charley Morgan H '08 and Porcellian Club, Bobby Morgan H '10 and Porcellian Club, Malcolm McBurney H '05 and Porcellian Club, Aymar Johnson H '05, Anson W. Hard H '08, William H. Russell H '18, George B. Wagstaff H '09, Oliver C. Wagstaff H '07.

** In 1933, Fred Astaire married Phyllis Livingston Potter, niece of Henry W. Bull and Maud Livingston Bull of St. Mark's Lane. Phyllis had grown up with the Bull family in Islip. She died in 1954 of lung cancer at the age of forty-six, greatly mourned by Fred and their two children.

Suffolk County. Charlie Chaplin was in New York and agreed to join the others, and we realized that if we could advertise his presence we could draw a terrific gate, but he was being very temperamental and Jules and I knew he might object to the publicity, so we held our fire until the last moment. Jules, Chaplin and I were to motor down to Islip together on the afternoon of the contest. On the back road, before we came to Babylon, we had placed a series of billboards advertising Gertie, Flo, George, Jules and myself, but with not a word about Chaplin. We had arranged for a scout to follow us from there to Babylon, who, if I raised a handkerchief, was to act. We had three airplanes ready to drop thousands of leaflets telling of Chaplin's presence all over Long Island. Chaplin said nothing at the first sign, but after passing the second he asked, "Why wasn't I given publicity? I'm part of the party, aren't I?" Just what we hoped for. The handkerchief went out, the pamphlets were dropped, and we had a gate we estimated at over twenty thousand people who bought everything we had to sell and at Chaplin's urging poured money into voting for their favorite in the Beauty Pageant. This was no bathing-beauty contest, but on stage set up as a rose garden, the contestants paraded in beautiful Spanish shawls provided by Gertie, who as mistress of ceremonies was herself dressed in a superb white satin Venetian costume with old lace and chinchilla sleeves, a red velvet tricorne and red slippers, and carried a magnificent lace fan. When the judging started, Chaplin was awful. He behaved as if he were judging a horse show. He made the girls show their teeth, felt their feet, and worse, but he gave the crowd their money's worth and they loved him for it. He finally lit on the one girl who we did not consider had won her contest fairly, but there was no arguing with him, so Gertie saved the situation by giving each contestant her shawl and the original first prize to the one who had the most votes. Chaplin spent the night at "Pleasure Island" and the next morning made a clever sketch of himself in the guest book and wrote:

> When pleasure runs high,
> You know you're with Schuy
> And we all know why?
> Cause Schuy's a great guy
> Aloha to you but not goodbye.
> CHARLIE CHAPLIN, July 15, 1927.[20]

A daytime event for the Venetian Fete planned by general chairman Helen Hoppin and Southside trustee Charles L. Lawrance involved the Wright Whirlwind motor then at the height of its fame, having carried Lindbergh across the Atlantic two months earlier. A Fairchild airplane with the Wright motor flew overhead dropping numbered tickets for a lottery to the crowd below. The winner would get a six-cylinder touring car — the grand prize! The Venetian Fete was a tremendous success, thanks to Schuyler Parsons, and the Southside Hospital was much strengthened.

The hospital, again in 1929, raised funds to build a new addition for an X-ray department. This time without Parsons's help, $250,000 was raised. Bayard Hoppin was the leader of this effort and large gifts were received from Mr. and Mrs. Edwin Thorne, Mrs. Bradish Johnson, Mrs. Bayard Cutting, Mr. and Mrs. George A. Ellis, Harry K. Knapp Jr., W. K. and Adolph M. Dick, and many others. The summer community never failed to support its hospital. This drive in the summer of 1929 was to be the last for some years to come. Three months later, after the great crash in October 1929, the world looked very different.

Schuyler Parsons had given up Pleasure Island by the summer of 1928, when he took a house in Newport. Drinking heavily by then, he was searching for new friends and new thrills. As he himself said, "Perhaps my pride brought the fall."[21] In any event he rather dramatically left Islip in August of 1928 on the opening day of the new Islip airport. The airport, located off Islip Avenue to the north of what would become the Sunrise Highway, was sponsored by the Islip Chamber of Commerce and a corporation headed by Charles L. Lawrance, always the promoter of aviation. The twenty-six-acre field had just been cleared of shrub oak and pine when Lawrance and America's most famous female aviatrix, Amelia Earhart, opened it formally with dedication ceremonies on Saturday, August 4, 1928. Shortly thereafter on the first commercial flight from Islip Airport, Schuyler Parsons went to Newport, Rhode Island. His flight took one hour and nine minutes!

In the winter of 1929 Parsons took a calamitous fall down the steps to the cellar of his New York City town house. His skull was fractured and he almost died. His condition was not improved by severe financial losses in the 1929 Crash. His sister and brother-in-law, the Richard Whartons, took over Pleasure Island, while Schuyler divided his time between Newport and Aiken, South Carolina. He became an interior decorator and in 1946 finally joined Alcoholics Anonymous. He died in 1967 at the age of seventy-five. He was certainly one of Islip's more colorful summer residents, providing spirit and gaiety wherever he went. He was also, more than anyone else, Islip's symbol of the Roaring Twenties.

It should be mentioned that of all the notable people who visited Islip in the 1920s, from Parsons's show business friends to Charles Lindbergh, there was one who held a higher ranking on the world's stage. His visit was incognito, however, and thus was never mentioned by the press. In September 1924, during his holiday visit to Long Island where he was the houseguest of Mr. and Mrs. James A. Burden at Syosset (Mrs. Burden was the niece of William K. Vanderbilt), the Prince of Wales paid a visit to the Hollinses at Meadowfarm in East Islip.[22] The thirty-year-old Prince (later King Edward VIII and then the Duke of Windsor) spent most of his American holiday on the North Shore watching the International Polo matches at the Meadow Brook Club and attending a succession of parties in his honor. The grandest of these and arguably the party of the decade was an elaborate dinner dance given by Mr. and Mrs. Clarence H. Mackay (Mrs. Mackay, born Katherine Duer, was a girlhood friend and bridesmaid of Consuelo Vanderbilt) at their 600-acre estate Harbor Hill in Roslyn. The 1,200 guests were entertained by music from bandleader Paul Whiteman as the festivities went on until dawn. The consumption of wine and champagne kept the bootleggers in business for months, but this did not bother anyone, certainly not the Prince of Wales. At these parties he would often "disappear" with his two equerries, not to return to the Burdens until the next day. It was on the eve of one of these disappearances that he came to East Islip. He received such bad press for his behavior on this trip that upon his return home, he was admonished by his father, King George V, and virtually told not to go to America again.

As the decade was ending it seemed to many that there would be no end to the boom. During the summer of 1929 prosperity was still high, built primarily on credit, and it looked as though the stock market would continue to climb upward. Few realized then that the end was so near.

Chapter XI

SOME ENDINGS AND A NEW BEGINNING (1929–1948)

Although the United States economy had begun a modest decline six months earlier, October of 1929 marked the official beginning of the most prolonged and most severe economic depression the industrial world had ever experienced. Its effects were greatest in the United States, Germany, and Great Britain, but its repercussions were felt everywhere. It became known as the Great Depression. By late 1932 or early 1933, the low point in economic activity in the U.S., output was only 54 percent of the 1929 level. Unemployment was at 25–30 percent of the work force. Out of 25,000 banks in the country, 11,000 had failed. On the day following his inauguration, March 6, 1933, President Franklin Delano Roosevelt was forced to proclaim a bank holiday, closing all banks in the country to stop a colossal run on those that were still operating. Only following emergency legislation were sound banks allowed to reopen three days later. The Great Depression would last for more than ten years. As World War II began in Europe in September 1939, the U.S. unemployment rate was still at an unacceptably high 15 percent and did not come down to normal until the attack on Pearl Harbor brought the country to war.

The New York Stock Exchange, the nation's barometer, witnessed stock prices rising through the summer of 1929 to peak at the end of August. Speculation continued to fuel the rise in price as buyers could borrow all the money needed to finance their purchases. There were no margin requirements. In September and early October there was a gradual decline in price levels but few people were concerned. It seemed like only a temporary dip. The first sharp sell-off occurred on October 18, but even then there were buyers to stabilize prices the following day, believing that the sell-off gave them favorable price opportunities. The panic set in on October 24, known ever since as Black Thursday. The wave of selling orders that day found few buyers, and prices plummeted. Again on Monday, October 28, and finally on Black Tuesday, October 29, another huge selling climax occurred, as the market collapsed completely. Historian John Kenneth Galbraith called October 29, "the most devastating day in the history of the New York stock market, and possibly the most devastating day in the history of markets."[1] When November came, some believed the selling was over, only to see three more days of declines that equalled the two "Black" days in October. The stock market bubble clearly had burst, and the Great Depression had begun.

J. P. Morgan was no longer alive to save the banking system as he had in the panic of 1907, and even if he had been alive, any effort would have been futile. John D. Rockefeller Sr. who was still living in 1929 and was by far the richest man in America said to the press, "My son and I are buying common stocks." Even that testimony failed to restore confidence in the stock market. There was a very modest recovery during 1930 after much of the speculation had been wrung out of the market. It was not supported by an increase in economic activity, however, and did not last. By late 1932, stock market prices had dropped to only 20 percent of their pre-crash value.

The losses to investors, brokers, speculators, and their backers in the banking industry were catastrophic. Many were entirely wiped out and declared bankruptcy. Some committed suicide, literally jumping out their office windows. As many of the summer residents on the South Shore were "in the market" in one way or another, the Crash had huge consequences there as well. It was a personal humiliation to have lost everything overnight, as some did. Others tried to keep up appearances in much reduced circumstances,

The *Olympic Point House*, designed by Harrie T. Lindeberg and built from 1917 to 1919, was a landmark from the Great South Bay. The family is playing croquet on the front lawn in 1937.

Horace Havemeyer, 1886-1956, a lifetime summer resident of Bay Shore and Islip, lived with his family on Olympic Point from 1920 to 1956. He is pictured here in 1929 at the age of 43 with a black arm band in mourning for his mother.

The William L. Breese and Julien T. Davies house (above) at Timber Point,
Great River, was converted in 1925 into a clubhouse (below) for the new
Timber Point Club by the E. W. Howell Company. (Courtesy of *Noted Long Island
Homes.*)

An aerial view of Olympic Point taken in September 1938 before the great hurricane. At the top is the home of Mr. and Mrs. H. Cecil Sharp.

The home of Mr. and Mrs. Landon K. Thorne, south of the South Country Road in West Bay Shore, was designed by William F. Dominick and built by the E. W. Howell Company during 1928. (Courtesy of *Noted Long Island Homes*.)

The Southside Hospital was moved from Babylon to Bay Shore and opened there in 1923. To benefit the hospital, a three-day Venetian Fete was held in July 1927. The judges for the beauty contest were Charlie Chaplin, Gertrude Lawrence, and Schuyler L. Parsons, Jr. pictured above. (Courtesy of *Untold Friendships*.)

The home of Rafael Guastavino, the tile architect, was built on Awixa Avenue in Bay Shore in 1910. It is a notable landmark from the Great South Bay. (Courtesy of Richard A. Milligan.)

and still others who were not "in the market" carried on in a life-style largely unchanged. To single out only one man, Jay F. Carlisle from East Islip was a governor of the New York Stock Exchange during the Crash and suffered doubly as a member and as one of its leaders.

The Great Depression hit Suffolk County as hard as it did other parts of the country. The land boom ended and home building slowed to a trickle. Unemployment went way up and labor became much cheaper as those who could find work were willing to do so at very low wages. Public spending projects, such as Robert Moses's parkways and parks and the Town of Islip's new town hall, did provide some work. The summer residents of the South Shore were still able, by and large, to offer jobs both inside and outside the home to local residents. And there were a few new homes built by the summer folk. Times were hard, though, especially for Islip's fishing industry. The market for the product just about dried up. The growth rate in the county was only half as much as it had been in the 1920s. In spite of the depressed conditions, there were some events in the decade that were noteworthy. Horace Havemeyer began his first attempt to sell the property he and his sisters had inherited on Bayberry Point (see Chapter VII).

When H. O. Havemeyer died in 1907, among the many possessions left to his children was "Modern Venice" or Bayberry Point. From then until 1929 the ten Moorish houses were rented with decreasing frequency. After Horace Havemeyer left Bayberry in 1919 for Olympic Point, it was difficult to find renters, although the young Knapps, Edward Jr. and Rosalie, did rent for a few summers. Havemeyer had given a five-acre parcel of land fronting on the bay at the foot of South Bay Avenue to the Town of Islip for a public recreation ground and bathing beach in September 1924. The town, which had been searching for a beach for years, accepted the gift with grateful thanks and immediately voted money to build a bathhouse. It was ready for public use by the summer of 1925. Although the town was very grateful, the gift of land earned Havemeyer the lasting enmity of his cousin Louisine Peters Weekes who had built her home to the north on South Bay Avenue and was bothered by the traffic to the beach, to say nothing of the sight of the pavilion blocking her bay view.

Some time in 1929, as the economy was booming along, Havemeyer organized the Bayberry Point Corporation, transferred the property into it and made plans to further develop and hopefully sell the ten original houses and much of the balance of the land in 117 small lots. To do this, a third canal was dredged to the east of the other two, the surrounding land was raised with fill and leveled, and two new roads were built. The roads were named Elder Road (Elder being his mother's maiden name) and Beech Road. He also extended both East and West Bayberry Roads as the decade progressed.

On March 20, 1930, the *Islip Press* reported as the east canal and the new roads were being built, "Bayberry Point Being Developed," "Scenic Point Promises to be Most Attractive Residential Section of the Island," "Charles O. Doxsee of Islip has the management of the vast improvements and will handle the sales end." The optimism of the promotion was not well timed as the economy had begun to decline. The larger of the ten Moorish houses were priced at $33,000 and the smaller at $15,000. By the end of 1930 only one house had sold. The home of H. O. Havemeyer himself, the most southwesterly of the ten, was sold to Frank Gulden, son of the founder of Gulden's Mustard, Charles Gulden, who had first come to Clinton Avenue in Bay Shore in the 1890s. For the next six years no other house sold. One other was contracted for a sale, which fell through when the buyer could not come up with the payment. Times were indeed hard. Six lots on the east side of East Bayberry Road were sold during these six years, one to Frank Gulden Jr. who built a small stucco home on it; three to Francis B. Thorne who built a boathouse and moored his boat, *Hildegarde*, on the middle canal; and two others to people who never built houses on them. By 1936 it seemed that the development was a complete failure.

In 1937 Havemeyer, in an attempt to revive interest in the project, engaged E. W. Howell & Co. to build three colonial-style houses at the head of the middle canal where there had once been a marine railway. If he could sell those, he reasoned, it would demonstrate to others what a new home on Bayberry Point would be like. Two of the three houses did sell, but not one of the 117 vacant lots was bought by a prospective home owner. Yet, the ten original Moorish houses did begin to sell. Havemeyer's daughter, Adaline, and her husband, Richard S. Perkins, took one in 1936. The William T. Baker and the Schieffelin families from New York took two more. Some year-round Islip residents bought others and one was saved for Havemeyer's son, Horace, and his wife, Rosalind Everdell, whose family had rented on the point earlier in the decade. By 1941 all ten were spoken for. All of the roads on the point were paved and deeded to the Town of Islip by then as well.

Possibly to attract new owners to the many empty lots for sale and also to provide recreation and sport to the community, a new club was formed on April 17, 1937, the Bayberry Beach and Tennis Club. * In the beginning the club leased its land from Havemeyer. It was located at the end of Elder Road, facing the Great South Bay and the new east canal. Two and a half acres provided space for four tennis courts, a small clubhouse, and thirty cabanas on a sand beach running into the bay. In 1940 the lease was converted into a mortgage for $18,750 and the club then owned its own land. The Bayberry Point Corp. which held the mortgage was eventually paid off when a local bank bought it. The Bayberry Beach and Tennis Club was successfully launched. Its members at the start were many who were also members of the Timber Point Club, which by 1937 was nearing its end. They were also principally summer residents of Islip and East Islip, few of whom lived on Bayberry Point. The existence of the club benefited the summer community but did nothing to spur sales on Bayberry Point.

---

* Original incorporators were: Beverley M. Eyre, Ruth A. Horan, Julia D. Macy, Buell Hollister Jr., Carol S. Lovering, Ann Valentine, Mary W. Eyre, and Hildegarde K. Thorne.

With the advent of World War II over a hundred lots remained to be sold. It was only well after the war in 1949 and 1950 that Bayberry Point became a popular place for year-round residents to live. By the time of Horace Havemeyer's death in 1956, all but three of the 117 lots had been sold to homeowners as he had envisaged. Havemeyer's Folly or "Modern Venice" by the bay had finally become, sixty years after its creation, a residential community, albeit a very different one from what H. O. Havemeyer had dreamed of in 1893.

To the north and east of Bayberry Point lay the huge property of the heirs of Samuel T. Peters (see Chapter VI). When Peters died in 1921 Windholme Farm, as it was called, was left to his son, Harry T. Peters, and the portion of land west of South Bay Avenue called Wereholme was left to his daughter, Louisine Peters Weekes (wife of Harold H. Weekes). Windholme Farm consisted of over two hundred fifty acres of upland and marsh fronting on Champlin's Creek and the bay. It was located at the south end of St. Mark's Lane. One might have thought that with Sam Peters's death, the farm would have been broken up like so many estates were in the 1920s. Such was not, however, the case, and the reason lay in the persons of a remarkable man, Harry Twyford Peters, and his mother, Adaline Elder Peters.

Adaline Elder had been born in New York City in 1859, the third daughter of George W. Elder, a grocery merchant, and his wife, Matilda Waldron Elder. Through her father, Adaline was descended from the Riker family that came from Holland to New Amsterdam in the seventeenth century and owned Riker's Island as well as other land. Through her mother Adaline was descended from the Waldron family that also came from Holland to New Amsterdam in the seventeenth century, as well as from the Mapes and the Hawkins families that were among Long Island's first settlers. The Mapeses came to Southold and the Hawkins to Setauket from England in the seventeenth century (see Chapter II).

While growing up in New York, Adaline was particularly close to her next older sister, Louisine Elder, and to Louisine's future husband, Henry O. Havemeyer, who was raised in the Elder home as a teenager. Adaline, Louisine, and Harry Havemeyer would remain close confidants all their lives. In fact it was said later, that when H. O. Havemeyer became known as the Sugar King, his only real confidants were his wife and her sister, Adaline, whose judgement he respected even on business matters. After Adaline had married Samuel T. Peters and Louisine had married H. O. Havemeyer, the two couples remained close. They summered near each other first in Babylon and then on St. Mark's Lane in Islip. Sam and Addie Peters named their two children Harry and Louisine. Harry Peters was born in 1881 and Louisine Peters in 1884.

Samuel and Adaline Peters' property, Windholme Farm, to which they moved in 1889 when Harry T. Peters was an eight-year-old boy, became one of the showplace farms on the South Shore of Long Island. This was so because Sam and Addie, and later Harry, took such a great interest in all aspects of the farm. They always considered it their primary residence, and although they kept an apartment in the city, they were Islipians at heart, in very much the same way as the Johnson and Parsons clans above all loved the South Shore. Windholme Farm demonstrated this affection.

Windholme was a large, elegant Victorian shingle-style house. It was three stories high with surrounding porch or veranda on the first floor, several gables on the third floor, and four massive brick chimneys breaking the skyline. It was sited to face toward Champlin's Creek with a lawn running down to the water and dotted with large elm and copper beech trees. The house had been bought from the John Prince estate and had been enlarged by the Peters family (see Chapter VI). The main house was surrounded by formal gardens and nearby was a large windmill that served to pump fresh water from Long Island's shallow aquifer. The front door entryway was lined with boxwood in the English tradition. Also nearby was an icehouse where ice cut from the ponds in winter was packed in sawdust and stored for year-round use. After his marriage to Natalie Wells in 1905, Harry T. Peters built a house of his own on the property to which he gave the name Nearholme. It was located to the north of Windholme, also facing Champlin's Creek and was a shingle-style house as well, which in most respects resembled the home of his parents.

Perhaps the most remarkable part of Windholme Farm was the farm itself. At about the same time that he designed farms for Havemeyer on Saxon Avenue and for Mollenhauer on Awixa Avenue, Alfred Hopkins also designed one for Sam Peters. It was located to the south of the main house and remains there today in modified form. The central farm buildings included a dairy, horse and cow stables, calf pens, wagon rooms, and an unusual circular bull pen which also served as a dovecote and clock tower. The cow yard in the front square was paved with cobblestones and at its center was the cow trough. Hopkins used the Peters's farm as an example in his book, *Modern Farm Buildings*, concluding, "the buildings depend for their architectural effectiveness entirely on their roof lines and in the simple but effective way in which the structure is spread over the ground."[2] The roof lines referred to were softened by a rounding of the ridges which gave them a thatched-roof appearance. Hopkins also designed a separate three-car garage over which the chauffeur lived that had a machine shop and a space for auto wash within. In addition to these buildings there was a chicken coop, kennels for the hounds, and to the south of them all a piggery, which was designed by Harry Peters himself. It received the unusual compliment of being praised by Hopkins in his book as an "admirable arrangement." Lastly there was a vegetable garden and orchards with a much needed root cellar for over winter storage. Windholme Farm was complete and the Peters family was entirely self-sufficient. *

Somewhat to the southwest of the farm was an old house dating from the early 1880s that had been owned by Dr. T. S. Ryder of New York City when S. T. Peters had bought most

---

* The farm buildings are now on the National Register of Historic Places.

of the land. It had been used as a guest cottage until after World War II, when Harry Peters's daughter, Natalie, and her husband, Charles D. Webster, renovated it, making the house and the surrounding gardens their charming home and private arboretum of almost two hundred fifty species of plants. To the north of the Webster home was the polo field and stables where Harry Peters kept his polo ponies and his fox hunters. On Sunday afternoons the family and friends would gather to watch the informal polo matches or the practices of the Islip team.

Finally, there was the boat dock on Champlin's Creek. Here was berthed the Peters's black-hulled sloop, *Patience*, built in 1882 by Gil Smith, the famous Patchogue boat builder. Sam Peters had bought her in 1885 when he had summered in Babylon and she stayed in the family for three generations, being converted into a powerboat for family outings and for fishing in the later years. In 1941, Harry Peters talked about his life at Windholme Farm: "My mind goes back half a century to my own boyhood in Islip and the boyhood pleasures that were mine as I roamed the fields, went fishing on the bay and did all the other things that are the heritage of an American boy. Incidentally, I still get the same thrill in fishing on the bay from the same boat [*Patience*] my father took me on fifty years ago."[3] Farming, and fishing, and polo were only a part of the life of Harry T. Peters. There was much more.

Harry Peters grew to manhood in New York City and Islip. He graduated from Columbia College in 1903 and immediately entered his father's firm, Williams and Peters, wholesale coal dealers and merchants. He would remain in the coal business throughout his life. He was president of the firm for much of it, and was chairman of the New York State Coal Conservation Committee during World War I. He was also a director of the Peabody Coal Company. He devoted himself to the coal business, but it was far from a full time occupation. As with many of the nineteenth century merchants, there was always time for a diversity of endeavors. When Peters died, the *New York Times* on June 2, 1948, called him "Sportsman" and then "coal merchant, Master of Hounds, and 'pioneer rediscoverer' of Currier & Ives, the printmakers." It was in the latter two roles that he would be most remembered.

Harry Peters had a great love of horses and dogs from his earliest days at Windholme Farm. This love bred knowledge and earned for him the title of "sportsman." The sport was fox hunting and Peters became one of its leaders in America. He hunted on Long Island, in Virginia, and throughout the northeast, and made several trips to England where he hunted with the originators of the sport. A keen student, he became an expert and was so recognized in 1925 by being chosen MFH, Master of Fox Hounds, at the Meadow Brook Hunt, the most prestigious hunt at that time on this side of the Atlantic Ocean. Peters followed two other South Shore men, Harry I. Nicholas, of the Babylon Nicholas family, and Allan 'Bud' Pinkerton of Saxon Avenue, Islip, as MFH at Meadow Brook. When the Meadow Brook Hunt merged with the Smithtown Hunt in 1933, Peters became MFH of both. In 1935 he wrote a book entitled *Just Hunting*, which became a classic in the literature of the fox hunt. He explored the "essential difference between fox hunting in one country [England] and in the other [America], the importance of age and antiquity, the fact that some are born to a thing and others have to acquire it, and above all the fact that climate plays a major part in the sports and pastimes of any people."[4] He concluded that the sport was different in each country and would remain so.

He was also a lifelong member of the Westminster Kennel Club, an exhibitor or judge at their Madison Square Garden shows, and a breeder of hounds at Windholme, where greyhounds, whippets, beagles, dachshunds, and schnauzers were all raised and trained for the hunt or the show. He modestly said in his book, "My one claim to pioneership I regret to state has nothing to do with fox hunting. Harry Nicholas had done all that for Meadow Brook before my time. But in the beagle world I have a claim to distinction. Many years ago three of us decided, urged on by the Bench Show Committee of the Westminster Kennel Club, to attempt to establish something of a definite nature. We showed the first three beagle packs in hunt livery and so started something that is flourishing very well. . . . I still have my costume: green cord breeches, puttees, green melton coat, regulation hunt cap and stock. For the first attempt here it was not so very wide of the mark even though the present livery is a vast improvement."[5]

Harry Peters made a mark as a sportsman, but as a collector of prints he became world renowned and is still remembered today as the first authority on Currier & Ives prints. As a young boy, he began to buy the prints. It was like collecting postage stamps and almost as cheap. Two or three dollars, perhaps ten for a special one, would buy a beautiful print. Small folio prints sold six for a dollar in 1896. The process of lithography had made it possible to pull dozens of prints from the porous stone, all of equally high quality and ready to be hand colored by the artist. Harry would go to the printmaker's shop on Spruce Street in Manhattan and made friends with some of the artists who worked there. Thomas Worth,[*] whose wife came from Islip and who knew the Great

---

[*] Thomas Worth (1834–1917) was born in New York City. At the age of nineteen, he took a sketch he had drawn to the lithographic firm of N. Currier. Mr. Currier was impressed with the young man's talent and paid him $5 for his sketch. Thus began his long career with Currier & Ives. Worth became a principal artist for the firm. He was particularly noted for his "Darktown Comics" as well as for his drawing of trotting horses. Harry T. Peters, who became a close friend of Worth, said that Worth got his inspiration for the well-known print *Trotting Cracks at the Forge* while visiting a blacksmith shop in Bay Shore. His print *A Stopping Place on the Road—the Horse Shed,* very likely pictured the horse barns behind the Lake House in East Islip or the neighboring Somerset House. Worth had married Louise Stellenwerf, daughter of the Lake House proprietor Amos R. Stellenwerf, and at one time in their married lives they lived in Bay Shore. While there, Thomas Worth often sailed a catboat and enjoyed blue fishing. The famous Currier & Ives print (No. 10 of the "Best Fifty" large folio series), *Trolling for Blue Fish,* was the work of two artists: Fanny Palmer who did the ocean and the background, and Thomas Worth who drew the catboat in the foreground. It was said that the catboat's skipper depicted in the print, was Worth's friend, the famous Islip skipper, Captain Hank Haff. Both Thomas Worth and his wife were buried in Oakwood Cemetery in Bay Shore in the Stellenwerf plot.

South Bay, became a particular friend of Harry Peters and gave him some of his original drawings. In fact, Peters attributed his enthusiasm as a collector of Currier & Ives prints to "Uncle Tommy" as he called Worth, whom he first met as a young boy while visiting the Lake House in East Islip which was owned by Stellenwerf, Worth's father-in-law. The walls of the old hotel were then covered with Currier & Ives prints, many drawn by Worth himself. He loved the charm of the lithographs as well as their historical subjects. They became an American history textbook for the young man. They were not appreciated by many others, however, and remained inexpensive for years, primarily a collector's item like matchbooks. This would soon change.

In 1929 Harry Peters completed and published his first volume of the works of the lithographers. It was called *Currier & Ives: Printmakers to the American People*. In 1931 he completed Volume II of the opus. He had looked through more than two thousand prints to select illustrations for the book, and after doing so said, "I have seen the Boston Tea Party and the California Gold Rush; gone down the Mississippi on the old steamboats and penetrated the Rockies; laughed through fifty years of American humor, from Darktown Comics to Barnum's Bearded Lady; traveled in covered wagons and 'lightning express trains'; pondered on the characters, as shown in their faces, of twelve Presidents and their cabinets; felt the chill of isolated farm yards in dead winter; the warmth of 'Home to Thanksgiving'; and gone to practically all the horse races, trotting matches, boat races and prize fights of half a century. To use here the phrase of 'Buffalo Bill,' Currier & Ives have preserved the Romance of America."[6]

When *Currier & Ives: Printmakers to the American People* was complete in 1931, America was in the midst of the Great Depression. The $2 print that Peters had bought in 1895 might have been worth $150, but no more. He then published *America on Stone, the Other Printmakers to the American People*. Interest was growing but the demand was held in check by economic circumstances. In 1932 the New

York print dealer, Harry Shaw Newman, proprietor of the Old Print Shop, together with the art editor of the *New York Sun*, formed a panel of collectors and curators to select the best fifty large folio Currier & Ives lithographs. They were chosen by ten experts at the home of Harry Peters, one of the ten. The interest of the public was greatly stimulated and in the following year, the best fifty small folio prints were designated. Finally in 1942 Harry Peters published *Currier & Ives*. This work contained illustrations of the prints in his own unique collection, was priced at $5, and was recommended by the Book-of-the-Month Club. It sold widely in America. At last Currier & Ives prints had become appreciated and after World War II prices rose dramatically. Today a winter scene in good condition would bring $15,000 for just one print! America had discovered its printmaker and the person principally responsible was Harry T. Peters. As the *New York Times* aptly said, he was the "pioneer rediscoverer" of those marvelous pictures of American life.

In all of his endeavors, whether in the coal business or in sport or in his collecting, Harry Peters was always encouraged and supported by his remarkable mother. Adaline Elder Peters lived on at Windholme near her only son after her husband died in 1921. They were very close. She was a widow for twenty-two years, always retaining her lively and cheerful ways, visited by many nephews and nieces. She was particularly fond of her nephew, Horace Havemeyer, and the affection was reciprocated. During the 1930s she was often seen in Islip village or in her black Model A Ford being driven through the lanes surrounding her home. She was very much the grande dame, along with Olivia Murray Cutting, of the South Shore. On March 11, 1943, Adaline Peters died at her New York City apartment. She was in her eighty-fourth year and had lived along the Great South Bay for sixty summers, most of them on Windholme Farm. She was buried beside her husband in the peaceful cemetery behind the little Emmanuel Church in Great River. Only five years later her son, Harry T. Peters, died and was also buried in Great River by his parents. Harry was sixty-six years old. With their deaths the two great shingle homes, Windholme and Nearholme, were torn down and a new era began at the end of St. Mark's Lane.

Harry Peters had left the farm to his daughter, Natalie Webster, his son having moved to Virginia. Natalie and her husband, Charles D. Webster, took over the management of the property and changed its name to Twyford,* to honor Sam and Harry Peters. They remodeled the cow barn as a small home for Harry's widow, Natalie, who died in 1976. Having lived in the Ryder house since 1945, they knew the land well and loved it. Natalie Webster, like her mother before her, was a president of the Garden Club of America. Her husband, Chuck, as he is known to all, was president of the Horticultural Society of New York for many years. They both had a passion for gardening and for wildlife. Twyford became an arboretum with gardens rivaling the best in England. They determined that their land should remain forever wild and provided that it should be deeded to the U.S. Fish and Wildlife Service of the Department of the Interior as a wildlife refuge; its owner today. Natalie died in 1979 and Chuck lives on at the age of ninety in the old house, a life tenant, gamely enjoying the new research activities that he organized with the establishment of the Seatuck National Wildlife Refuge, the formal name of what was once Windholme Farm over a hundred years ago.

Although the golf clubs that were founded in the 1920s struggled to survive during the Great Depression, sailing activity on the Great South Bay actually increased during the 1930s, largely because of the advent of the Star boat. This popular one-design class finally satisfied those many sailors who were searching for a sailboat that was competitive in testing the skills of the skipper and crew rather than the design of the boat itself. First seen on the bay in 1928 with a fleet of nine boats the class grew quickly and by 1935, twenty-eight Stars competed in the Great South Bay Raceweek Re-

---

* Twyford is the name of the town in England where the Peters's ancestors lived before they moved to America.

gatta. The Star boat did not come to the bay early in its history. It had achieved great popularity elsewhere and by 1928 there were already 555 boats in existence organized into 38 fleets in eight countries. It had already become an International class by then.

Three men stand out above all others in the history of the Star Class, and one of these had Bay Shore and Islip roots. The founder of the class, George A. Corry, known to all as "Pop" Corry, asked the naval architect William Gardner in the fall of 1910 to design a one-design boat that would be similar to but about five feet larger than the "Bug," a Gardner boat that Corry had raced for several years. In Gardner's shop with his draftsman, Francis Sweisguth, the new design took form for a hard chine boat 22 feet 8 inches in length, rigged with a gaff rig. Twenty-two Stars were built in Port Washington, Long Island, that winter and on May 30, 1911, the first race was held on Western Long Island Sound. It was won by Pop Corry. The name Star was given to the boat shortly thereafter by Stuyvesant Wainwright of the American Yacht Club in Rye, New York, although he never owned a Star boat.

William Gardner, who two years before had designed the Islip One-Design for the Islip Yacht Club, and George A. Corry, founder and commodore of the Star Class until his death in 1944, were two of the giants. The third was George Waldron Elder, whose father, G. W. Elder, and whose aunts, Louisine W. Havemeyer and Adaline Elder Peters, were all longtime Bay Shore and Islip summer residents. George had spent his boyhood in Bay Shore. A yacht broker by profession, he became secretary of the class and then president for over forty years. It was he who was primarily responsible for promoting and developing the class into an international organization. It became an Olympic Class in 1932 and remains one today. The Star Class became the greatest success story in international one-design racing thanks to George Elder.

Although the Star boat was developed in 1911 and raced primarily in Western Long Island Sound, it was the years after World War I, from 1922 on, that saw its period of great growth. And it was not until 1930 when the class adopted the tall marconi rig that the modern day boat was born. * With the new rig the Star became a better boat, could point closer to the wind, and in light airs was faster than boats ten feet longer. Other developments, such as the flexible mast, came in 1937, making the boat faster in a heavy wind.

When Star boats came to the Great South Bay in 1928 several of the boats came from as far away as the Westhampton Yacht Club on Moriches Bay to compete. It was not until later that Moriches Bay had its own fleet. The first Star from the Great South Bay to compete in the Internationals held off Newport Harbor, California, that year was *Minx*, owned by W. & J. Atwater. It placed in the middle of the standings, a good performance by the new fleet. In 1929, it placed fifth at New Orleans, an even better result. On the Great South Bay that year a cup was awarded for the first time to the winner of the five race series in the Star Class held during race week; it was called the Corry Cup in honor of Pop Corry and became a prize sought after by many sailors from all over the Eastern United States. At one time over forty Star boats competed for the Corry Cup, which made the start of the race a particularly exciting affair! In 1930 some of the Star racers were the two Atwaters, Harold Halstead from Westhampton, young Ed Ketcham Jr. from Babylon with his number 44 boat *Draco*, who would be heard from often in the future; also the Libaires from Sayville, Rafael Guastavino from Bay Shore, and Charles Lawrance from East Islip. In 1931 they were joined by young Horace Havemeyer Jr. in *Okla II* and by the young brothers Landon and Edwin Thorne in *Mist*. By 1932 the 23 Stars were the largest class of the 103 boats that sailed in race week. Many of the Islip and East Islip summer families stayed with the popular Timber Point class

---

* The original gaff rig had a mast of 18 feet 5 inches. In 1921 the short marconi rig was adopted with a 27 foot mast. In 1930 the mast height was extended to 31 feet 9 inches. With the tall marconi rig the boom was shortened almost 4 feet to 14 feet 7 inches.

well into the 1930s. This one-design class failed to attract any who were not members of the Timber Point Club, however, and thus it began a gradual decline as the decade progressed. The Star boat had clearly won the day on the bay.

During the 1930s and 1940s as the Star Class grew in size and popularity, five sailors dominated the list of victors on the South Shore waters and usually represented the bay fleet at International and Atlantic Coast events. They were the Thorne brothers early in the period; Harold Halstead from Westhampton and latter Bellport; Ed Ketcham Jr. from Babylon; Bill Picken from Bay Shore; and Horace Havemeyer from Olympic Point in Islip. Of the five only the Thornes and Havemeyer were summer families. And of the five only the Thornes, Harold Halstead, and Horace Havemeyer did well in events held away from the familiar bay waters. When the breeze was fresh from the southwest and whitecaps showed on the bay, Picken and Ketcham were unstoppable. No one could get to the weather mark faster than they. In 1947 off Bellport, Ed Ketcham and his regular crew, Bill Hayward, achieved an unheard-of five straight firsts to win the Atlantic Coast Championship.* In that competitive class, with eighteen other fleet champions racing, it was rarer than pitching a no-hitter in the World Series. The Thornes with *Mist* did well in the Internationals of 1932 and 1933, and Halstead with many different boats, all named *Chuckle*, was a fearsome competitor throughout his whole life, competing well into his sixties when he was half blind and had to rely on his crew for more help than ever. Although never winning the Internationals, he won every other event throughout a long career.

Horace Havemeyer did not start sailing Star boats on the bay on a full-time basis until 1936, much later than the others, but he stayed with Stars until health and age prevented him from getting into the cockpit. In total he and his two sons owned thirteen Star boats from 1931 until his death in 1956.

---

* Ketcham and Hayward were then sailing number 1944, *Draco II*.

Always a sharp competitor and having raced since he was a twelve-year-old in 1898, Havemeyer was always searching for the best in one-design racing. The early bay racing in the Herreshoff 30 and then the Islip One-Design was followed by a Shore Bird, named *Doris*, in 1924 and 1925 and then a Timber Point named *Skitty* in 1926 to 1930. From the summer of 1930 through that of 1935 he owned and raced on Long Island Sound three much larger one-design boats — the Ten Meter *Dragon* in 1930 and 1931; the Twelve Meter *Mouette* in 1932, 1933, and 1935; and the Six Meter *Meteor* in 1934. However, it was a long trip from Islip to Glen Cove on the North Shore where the boats were kept and the breezes on the sound in July and August were famous for arriving either in the late afternoon or not at all. Havemeyer learned to sail well in light air and had an outstanding record on *Mouette* in 1932 in particular when he won twenty-one of thirty-two races held for the Twelves that summer. Meanwhile his son, Horace Jr., both crewed for his father on the sound and sailed a Star boat on the Bay, first *Okla II* (1931) and then *Vim* (1934).

In 1936 Havemeyer returned to racing a Star boat on the bay and bought *Whistler* which did not turn out well. In 1937 he bought the first of many boats he named *Gull* number 940. It was an excellent boat, as good as Horace Jr.'s *Vim* number 1019 in which the twenty-two-year-old won one race at the Internationals off Rochester, New York, in 1936 and finished a credible ninth overall. Number 940 had finished eighth in that series, which was perhaps why it caught Havemeyer's eye. Harold Halstead was in his usual third place that year as well. In 1937 Havemeyer and his son sailed *Gull* in the Internationals on Long Island Sound. They did well until the last race when they fouled and had to withdraw. Halstead was third again but the series is noted in Star Class history for four straight wins (after a first race breakdown) for the German boat *Pimm* sailed by Walter Von Hutschler. It had a new wooden mast that would bend in heavy winds — the so-called flexible spar. From then on every other mast was obsolete and by 1938 all competitive Stars had flexible spars.

A modern view of the Moorish house of H. O. Havemeyer on Bayberry Point, Islip built in 1900-01. (Courtesy of Richard A. Milligan.)

Meadowedge was the home of Anson and Florence Bourne Hard, built in 1909 on the vast Bourne property in Oakdale. Today it is the clubhouse of a Suffolk County golf course built there after World War II. (Courtesy of Richard A. Milligan.)

The Islip Town Hall was designed by Adolph M. Dick and built in 1931 at the eastern end of the village. It is pictured here today after the addition of east and west wings. (Courtesy of Richard A. Milligan.)

The Conover barns and windmill
built in the 1880s have been
retained by the several successive
owners of the property. They are
pictured here as they look today.
(Courtesy of Richard A. Milligan.)

By the 1930s and 1940s the Star Class sailboat was the most popular one design class on the bay. Pictured here is Star No. 2010 owned by Horace Havemeyer in the early 1940s. (Courtesy of Morris Rosenfeld.)

Havemeyer sailed *Gull I* throughout the rest of the 1930s. He entered the Atlantic Coast Championship in 1940 with his son Horace but did poorly in the event. In 1941 and 1942 ill health prevented him from racing at all, but as his health recovered very slowly so did his desire to race again. And besides there was his thirteen-year-old son, Harry, then old enough to crew. Havemeyer had regularly taken his son, as a seven-year-old boy, in the Star with him as "ballast." In 1943 Havemeyer purchased boat number 2010 *Rascal*, from Frank E. Campbell of the Western Long Island Sound fleet. She was the fastest (but one) of all the Stars he owned. With Stanley Smith as crew he won the Atlantic Coast Championship on the bay that summer. *Rascal-Gull* was unbeatable off the wind and to windward as well in light air. Only in the strong southwesters could Bill Picken and Ed Ketcham sail faster to windward.

In the summer of 1945, still with *Rascal-Gull*, Havemeyer, then at age fifty-nine, with Harry as crew, reached the pinnacle of his long racing career on the Great South Bay. In the five race series for the Corry Cup against the best of the bay sailors — Halstead, Ketcham, Picken, and Adrian Iselin from the sound, a World Champion sailor of many years experience — Havemeyer took the trophy with two race wins. As he crossed the finish line in the last race amidst the horns from the spectators boats he said to his crew, " Well, Harry, I won the Corry Cup. I never expected it. You did a good job, son." It was high praise, seldom given. The *New York Times* and the *New York Herald Tribune* then reported daily on major sailing events, of which the Corry Cup was one. The *Herald Tribune* said, "Horace Havemeyer's black-hulled Star, Gull, with the veteran himself at the tiller won the Corry Trophy for the Star group. With the exception of yesterday when Eddie Ketcham in Draco II went into a one-point lead over Gull, Havemeyer was a frontrunner the first three days of the regatta, and today the grizzled veteran confirmed his supremacy by leading the fleet of twelve over the finish line."[7] Havemeyer had proven himself that day a worthy successor to the great bay skippers of the past beginning with Captain Hank Haff of Islip.

Late in his sailing career Havemeyer purchased yet another Star boat. Number 2125 called *Shillalah*, built and owned by E. W. "Skip" Etchells of Old Greenwich, Connecticut, was without doubt the most famous Star of the post World War II era. *Shillalah* was built in 1942 in California by Etchells, a naval architect, who had a new idea for the hull design of a Star boat. He was also an excellent skipper. When he moved east with his wife Mary as his crew, Etchells took the East Coast by storm. It was immediately apparent that a breakthrough in design, within the rules which permitted some deviation, had been achieved. It was as dramatic as the new flexible spar of *Pimm* had been in 1937. At the Atlantic Coast Championship off Bellport, Long Island, in 1944, *Shillalah* won all five races by large margins for a clean sweep. Havemeyer wrote in his log, "all other Stars are now obsolete." Etchells set up a boat-building business in Connecticut and within only a few years the Etchells boats became the standard for the class. A competitive skipper had to have one to have any chance for the top placement in a regional series.

Naturally Skip Etchells was reluctant to sell *Shillalah*, even after he had built another boat for himself in which he was racing and winning. But in 1951 Havemeyer was able to buy her with the promise that he would give Etchells first refusal if he ever decided to sell her. Havemeyer himself did not race very often on *Shillalah*. She was sailed by his grandsons, particularly his grandson Danny Catlin. During the last years of his life he took a great interest in coaching them from his power boat, *Sea Gull*. His last summer on the bay was 1956. He died in October of that year. It had been fifty-eight years since the twelve-year-old boy had crewed on *Adaline* for Harry M. Brewster in a sailboat race. He had called the Great South Bay "the most favored spot in the world." His life was a testament to that belief.

There were some changes in residence and a few new houses were built by summer residents as the Great Depression approached. Late in 1929 New York stockbroker Francis B. Thorne and his wife, Hildegarde Kobbe Thorne, both around forty years old at the time with a family of six children (she had two daughters from a previous marriage to Joseph H. Stevenson) and needing more space, decided to purchase Brookwood Hall from Theodore J. Knapp. Brookwood Hall with its fifty acres of beautifully landscaped lawns, gardens, and trees along Champlin's Lake was the creation of Harry K. Knapp Sr. and had passed on to his son, Theodore, after his wife's death. It would be a happy place for the Thorne children to grow to maturity.

Both Francis and Hildegarde had summered along the bay as children. For Francis in particular that body of water always had a special place, a magical quality. Francis, like his older brother, Landon, had gone to the Pomfret School and then on to Yale, graduating with the class of 1914. After a course at Annapolis he was commissioned in the navy and served aboard the destroyer *Wainwright*, during World War I. Following the war and for the rest of his life he worked as a broker on the New York Stock Exchange. In 1933 he founded his own firm. As for so many other brokers the Depression years were difficult years for Francis, but he was able to keep Brookwood Hall until World War II.

In 1920 Francis married Hildegarde Kobbe, the second daughter of Gustave Kobbe, who had been killed in the accident off Bay Shore in 1918. Both Francis and Hildegarde had had short previous marriages. During the 1920s they lived all year round in a house on North Awixa Avenue in Bay Shore with Hildegarde's widowed mother and eventually, six children. In 1925 or 1926 Francis had built the classic bay powerboat, which he named *Hildegarde* and which he berthed in the middle canal at Bayberry Point alongside the land and boathouse he owned there. *Hildegarde* was modeled after *Gussum*, Francis's father's bay boat, with a wide beam and shallow draught. She was the setting for fun and gaiety which would serve to brighten the generally gloomy 1930s. Having sufficient beam to hold a piano in the cabin, *Hildegarde* was the beginning of the musical career of the Thornes' talented son, Francis Jr., who was often at the keyboard in those years, playing the popular tunes of the day. Francis Sr. was a founding member of the Timber Point Club, a member of the South Side Club and in New York City, the Racquet and Tennis Club. Francis Thorne Jr. remembers with great affection growing up in Brookwood Hall during the decade of the 1930s. The charm of the house, the parties, especially the coming out party of his sister, all speak to the graceful elegance of that era.

The Thornes left Brookwood Hall in 1941. Wartime shortages of labor and fuel, together with increased taxes, convinced them like so many others, that Brookwood must be sold. In 1942 the Orphan Asylum Society of the City of Brooklyn bought the property as a refuge for orphan children from the city. The library of the great house was turned into a study hall and sixty children, who attended public school in East Islip, had a new home.

Francis and Hildegarde Thorne moved to Millbrook, New York, where earlier Thornes had lived. Francis, however, missed the bay and after several years they returned to Islip, taking a much smaller house on Maple Avenue across from the Harry T. Peters property. It was there beside the bay he loved that Francis died in December 1950, at the age of fifty-eight. Hildegarde, who was three years older, died in June 1959, at the age of seventy. They were buried together in the little cemetery behind Emmanuel Church in Great River. The South Shore had always been their home.

Two new houses were built along Ocean Avenue in Islip in the late 1920s, both with grand southwesterly views of the Great South Bay. William Hamilton Russell and Marie Johnson Russell had chosen the twelve acres of land lying between Maple Avenue on the north, Orowoc Creek on the west, and the small canal that fed into Orowoc on the south. Their southerly neighbor was K. C. Atwood who had come to Islip in that decade. Both the Atwood and Russell lands had formerly been owned by Brooklyn mayor Charles A. Schieren. The Russells, however, were not newcomers to Islip when they built their new home.

Born in 1896 in New York City, Marie Johnson was the grandaughter of Bradish Johnson Sr., owner of Sans Souci in Bay Shore and the first summer resident along that part of the Great South Bay. Marie was the last child and only daughter of Bradish Johnson Jr. and his wife, Aimee Gaillard. Marie was born after her parents, with her two older brothers Bradish G. and Aymar Johnson, had moved into Woodland on Pavilion Avenue in East Islip. She was a nine-year-old when the old house burned in 1905 and was subsequently rebuilt by her father, and a charming eighteen-year-old when her parents introduced her into society in December 1914 at a fashionable party held at Woodland. Thus Marie's roots were as deeply set in Islip as was possible for a member of a New York family to be.

Her husband-to-be, William Hamilton Russell, was also born in 1896, the son of the notable architect of the same name. Russell senior (1854–1907), also a native of New York, had graduated from Columbia College before starting his career in the office of his great uncle, the famous Gothic Revival architect James Renwick, in 1878.* Later he joined with Charles Clinton to start the firm of Russell and Clinton, which achieved acclaim by designing some important buildings in Manhattan around the turn of the century.** The younger Russell headed toward an architectural career in his father's footsteps. He entered Harvard with the class of 1918, but by January of 1918 with the country at war, Russell like so many other young men left college to serve his country. And like so many other young men at that time he chose to get married. On March 6, 1918, at beautifully decorated St. Bartholomew's Church on Park Avenue in New York, William Hamilton Russell and Marie Johnson became hus-

---

* James Renwick designed Grace Church on Broadway in New York, a masterpiece of the Gothic Revival movement.

** The richly gilded and heavily ornate ballroom of the Hotel Astor in New York was designed by Russell and Clinton c. 1910.

band and wife. They were married by both St. Bart's rector and Mr. Garth, the longtime rector of St. Mark's Church in Islip, Marie's family church in the country. The wedding was distinctive in that the groom and every usher were dressed in military uniforms. Second Lieutenant Russell was attended by Ensign Aymar Johnson, Marie's brother, by Captain Hawkins and by two other lieutenants, all in khaki, a sign of those times. Marie was attended by two Johnson cousins, by Caroline H. Knapp of Brookwood Hall in East Islip and by three other friends.

After the war the Russells lived in Cambridge, Massachusetts, while William studied at the Harvard School of Architecture. This was followed by a time in Paris where he attended the famous Beaux Arts School before coming home to join the firm of Russell and Clinton in New York. Three daughters were born to William and Marie during this period, and following the return from France, summers were often spent on the South Shore with Marie's widowed mother at Woodland (her father had died in 1918, the summer after her wedding) or at her brother's house, Enfin, on St. Mark's Lane.* During one summer month they rented the home of Mrs. August Belmont overlooking Belmont Lake before it was taken over by the Long Island State Park Commission for its headquarters. With the girls growing up and with the hope of a son to come, the Russell family looked for land of its own. William Russell was anxious to design a home for his own family. In 1927 they purchased the land off Maple Avenue in Islip and by the winter of 1927–28 building was under way.

Russell had designed a house that could best be described as an adaptation of the Mediterranean style. It was built of hollow tile with an outside facing of softly tinted pink stucco. The roof was of red slate and the entrance driveway was covered with red slag to match the color of the roof, all of which created a distinctly tropical feeling that was un-

---

* Enfin was later sold to Joseph and Carol Stevenson Lovering.

usual on the South Shore. Only the Guastavino tile house across the cove on Penataquit Point was comparable. The Russell house was much larger, however, and considerably more graceful. The entrance hall was floored with mellow-toned Belgian tiles, the library was paneled in pine, and the living room was sunken with a fireplace at each end. The dining room opened onto a sun porch. The living room, library, and sun porch all faced southwest to take maximum advantage of the view of the Great South Bay. Upstairs, the master bedroom, sleeping porch, and sitting room also faced southwest as did the other bedrooms and a second enclosed sleeping porch. The pantry, kitchen, and six servant's rooms were in the wing of the house which extended to the north.

In addition to the main house the twelve acres contained a spacious guest cottage with nine rooms and three baths, a gardener's house, a four-car garage as well as dog kennels, a stable for horses, and a small cow barn. A formal flower garden with a long vista ending in a bird tower, and many large trees and shrubs completed the landscaping of this lovely Islip home. It was one of the mini jewels along the bay, not as large as some, but in better taste than many.

In 1928 the Russell family moved into its new home in time for the birth of the last child, a son, William Hamilton Russell Jr. Prospects were at their brightest then. Architects were in demand and Russell designed a new house for Harry K. Knapp Jr. (1929), which he called Creekside, on the east side of Champlin's Creek. A decade later it was sold to William H. Gregory Jr. who occupied it in the 1940s, 1950s, and 1960s. Russell was also to design a grand house on Saxon Avenue for Marie's cousin, Ruth Draper Sharp (1932), which will be mentioned later.

The depression of the 1930s put many out of work. With the almost total halt in the building of private homes, architects had to subsist, if they could, on the few public commissions that were financed by the government through the WPA or at the state or local level. The Russell family spent more time in Europe in the 1930s where it was cheaper to live although they did return to Islip in the summers. Their marriage dissolved before World War II and each remarried. Marie Johnson Russell married Gordon Crothers in 1941. To save her beautiful Islip house and to manage it without the staff that once was required, she "remodeled" it by removing the entire eastern part of the house. With the help of her neighbor and architect friend, Adolph M. Dick, she created a livable summer house for herself, her son, and her new husband. Her daughters by then were on their own and could use the guest cottage during visits in the summer. She rented out the gardener's cottage and substantially reduced the upkeep of the grounds.

William H. Russell with his new wife had moved to the North Shore of Long Island. In 1952 he was elected president of the Municipal Art Society of New York City, a recognition of the contribution he and his father had made to the city. In 1958 at the age of sixty-two he died of a heart attack in Glen Cove, Long Island. Marie Johnson Crothers left Islip in 1958 after sixty years and moved to the Boston area. She died in 1977 at the age of eighty-one. Only her son, William H. Russell Jr., remained along the Great South Bay. Ordained an Episcopal priest, Bill served at St. Mark's Church in Islip where his great grandfather, Bradish Johnson Sr., had once been the senior warden, and today he is the rector of St. Paul's Episcopal Church in Patchogue, Long Island.

The second new house to be built along Ocean Avenue in Islip near the start of the Depression was designed by the architect Adolph M. Dick, for himself and his widowed mother, Julia T. Dick, during her few remaining years. She died in the house in the summer of 1931 following a fall which fractured her hip. Adolph Dick and his older brother, William K. Dick, were the grandsons of William Dick and the heirs to Allen Winden, the large property along Ocean Avenue purchased by their grandfather in 1889. From childhood the Dick brothers, with their two sisters, Doris and Julia, had spent summers at Allen Winden. When grandfather Dick died in 1912, his son, John Henry Dick, and daughter-in-law, Julia Mollenhauer Dick, inherited the place. By then the original Victorian frame house, first built by Charles A. Tucker in the

1880s, had been added to several times, and with its great front porch and several Victorian turrets seemed larger than in fact it was. Allen Winden also included a stable and garage of Alfred Hopkins's design built prior to World War I; a playhouse with a squash court, pool room, and bowling alley (the latter was popular in private homes in that era) given to the four Dick children by their uncle and aunt, Adolph and Anna Mollenhauer; and on the east side of Ocean Avenue, a working farm very much like that of the Peters family on St. Mark's Lane. All told the property of the Dick family was almost as large as the Peters's land and Allen Winden was, along with Nearholme and Windholme, the showplace homestead of Islip hamlet prior to the Great War.

Because his father, John Henry Dick, suffered badly from asthma and was in declining health for much of his later years, William K. Dick, as the oldest son, took the leading role in the family's business affairs and in the management of Allen Winden as well. Outgoing and affable by nature he quickly became a part of New York's social scene, joining the many clubs that signified to others that he was accepted as a "club man" of that day. From the time he was a young lad living in Williamsburg, Brooklyn, Will Dick had fallen in love with a Brooklyn friend of his sister, Madeleine Force. He went away to boarding school to Pomfret, Connecticut, and then into the family's banking business in Brooklyn. Meanwhile at the very young age of eighteen, Madeleine surprisingly married the most prominent bachelor in New York Society, the recently divorced forty-seven-year-old Colonel John Jacob Astor IV. Colonel Astor, as he was always known, was the father of Vincent Astor (by his first wife). As was customary then, the Colonel and Madeleine went to Europe on their wedding trip. After an extended stay, they planned to return to New York in April 1912, and chose to travel on the newest, fastest ship on her maiden voyage, the White Star Line's flagship *Titanic*. The rest is history. Madeleine was pregnant at the time and got into a lifeboat as she was instructed to on that terrible night as the ship was sinking. The Colonel, knowing there was not enough room for all, refused to go with his young wife, said goodbye, and with hundreds of others went to his icy grave. Legend has it that after the ship had struck the iceberg and its doom became certain, the Colonel and his valet changed into full evening dress so that they might die as gentlemen.[8] Several months later young John Jacob Astor V was born, and four years later, on June 22, 1916, William K. Dick, then twenty-eight years old, married his childhood sweetheart, Madeleine Force Astor. Two sons were born of this union. Will and Madeleine Dick with their family of three boys rented the Schieren house on Ocean Avenue in the summer, only steps away from Allen Winden. For them to reside at Allen Winden would have been too much of a strain for Will's elderly parents.

In September 1925, John Henry Dick died in the homestead. It soon became obvious that Allen Winden needed another renovation and that the spacious house should be taken over by the Will Dick family. Adolph Dick had not married and was expected by the family to care for his aging mother who adored him. Her two daughters, Doris Havemeyer and Julia Macy, were nearby on Saxon and Ocean Avenues. Thus Adolph Dick designed both a new home, located to the south of the old home, as well as a major renovation and new addition to Allen Winden. As the Depression was beginning both jobs were performed by E. W. Howell Co. of Babylon. A new era for Allen Winden had begun.

During the 1930s Will Dick and Adolph Dick lived next to one another on the west side of Ocean Avenue. Adolph Dick's new house, neo-Georgian in style, added greatly to the beauty of the street. The playhouse was often used by Will Dick for parties. He was an active participant in Islip life, a member of the South Side Club, a vestryman at St. Mark's Church, and a trustee of the Southside Hospital. His marriage, however, had broken up by then and he and Madeleine were divorced in 1933. He married Virginia Connor in 1941.

Adolph Dick, six years younger than his brother, had graduated from Yale in 1917, served as an ensign in the U.S. Navy in World War I, and had graduated from the Columbia

School of Architecture. He worked with the firm of Fuller and Dick. In the Islip area he designed the lovely, Georgian brick town hall, built in 1931 at the eastern entrance to the village.* Adolph's great passion, however, was yachting, and in that regard he took after his uncle and namesake, Adolph Mollenhauer. In the 1930s he owned a large two-masted schooner, *Vega*, in which he cruised throughout the East Coast and Caribbean waters. In 1932 after his mother's death he chartered another two-masted schooner, *Cressida*, for a four-month cruise to Tahiti and back through the Panama Canal. *Cressida* was 145 feet long with a crew of twenty-one. On board as his guests for the long voyage were several friends including Polly Campbell, who would become his wife in 1935. They divorced in 1937 and there were no children.

After World War II Will and Virginia Dick continued to live in Allen Winden. Two children, Direxa and Will, were born and grew up there in the summer. Much of the farm had been given up during the war and the signs were evident that the end of the great place would soon be at hand. William K. Dick died in 1953 at the age of sixty-five. His brother, Adolph, died in 1956 at sixty-two, having spent his last years at his home in Miami Beach. William Dick's widow, Virginia, moved into the Adolph Dick house with her children and razed the original homestead in 1954. It was much too large for her small family. Finally she too moved away, the house was demolished, and the property put up for sale. Only the play-house and garage remain today. For over seventy years the Dick family had lived on Ocean Avenue in Islip, one of the longest of all the summertime residencies.

The last great house to be built in the area from Oakdale to Babylon for a summer resident was completed in 1933 when the Great Depression was at its nadir. It was built on the twelve acres of land on the west side of Saxon Avenue fronting on Awixa Creek land that had been owned first by

---

* Two wings were added later.

Daniel Conover in the 1880s, by the Hutton brothers, Franklyn and Edward F., in the 1912–21 period, and by Philip B. Weld and his wife, Katharine Saltonstall Weld, from 1921 to 1929. The land was directly to the north of the Havemeyers' Olympic Point. When the Welds bought the property from E. F. Hutton in August of 1921, they paid the large price at that time of $100,000 for it. In spite of the fact that they had a large family of six children they were satisfied to live in the Victorian house near the street that had been built by Conover and that had been lived in by the Franklyn Huttons and their daughter, Barbara.

Philip Weld had been born in 1887, of the notable Massachusetts Weld family. He went to Harvard where he graduated in 1908, making him a contemporary of his Saxon Avenue neighbor, Horace Havemeyer. Weld married another Boston Brahmin, Katharine Saltonstall. The Welds then moved to New York where Philip made his career as a cotton broker. He was a member of the New York Cotton Exchange for over twenty years and was its president for several of them. Commuting by train to Bay Shore was easy then, and he and his family enjoyed the cool breezes and sailing on the bay. Philip became a notable yachtsman. However as their six children grew, the old house became too small and in 1929 they decided to move away and put the property on the market.

The same year that the Welds left the South Shore, a thirty-five-year-old ex-marine from Charleston, South Carolina, H. Cecil Sharp, was married to Mrs. Ruth Carroll Draper. Ruth Carroll was the grandaughter of Lucy Carroll and the great grandaughter of Bradish Johnson Sr. Her marriage to Draper ended in divorce. Ruth had thus known of the bay area and had several cousins living in Bay Shore and Islip at the time of her marriage to Cecil Sharp. He became a member of the Timber Point Club in Great River that year.

In July of 1930 the Sharps acquired the Weld property for their summer home. With the Depression deepening in 1932 and labor plentiful and cheap, they asked Bill Russell, the husband of Ruth Sharp's cousin, Marie Johnson Russell, to design a new house for them on the property. They obviously admired Olympic Point to the south because Russell designed a somewhat smaller twin of Harrie T. Lindeberg's masterpiece on the point. It was of red brick with a gray slate roof and from the outside could almost be mistaken for its older sister. Because the Sharps had a smaller family, of two daughters, the rooms tended to be very large in size and fewer in number than in the Havemeyer house. While construction was under way, they rented a cottage in "Modern Venice" on Bayberry Point. The new house was completed in 1933 and the Conover home was removed from the property. The new home was situated closer to Awixa Creek where the view of the canal and of the bay to the south over the Havemeyer tennis court was much more favorable. The Conover barns and windmill were retained, providing an interesting contrast of the old and the new.

The Sharps lived in their new home on Saxon Avenue in the summers until the year 1944, only eleven years. In January of that year Cecil Sharp, then a major in the marine corps, died suddenly of a heart attack in the Norfolk, Virginia, naval hospital. He was only forty-nine years old. Ruth Sharp immediately put the house on the market and it was sold on June 30, 1944, to Frank V. Riggio. Ruth and her two daughters left the South Shore for Connecticut and a new life.

Frank Riggio was the son of Vincent Riggio, a president of the American Tobacco Company. Frank, his wife Margaret, their son and two daughters, occupied the Sharp house all year round until first Frank and then Margaret died in the 1980s. It became known as the Riggio House and stands today with a new owner. Because of the Depression, followed by the Second World War, there were no other grand summer houses built in the area. The few houses that were constructed after the war were of a much smaller scale and indistinguishable from the many other residences dotting the landscape in the 1950s and 1960s.

On September 18, 1938, storm clouds had gathered northeast of Puerto Rico. They were tracked to 200 miles east of Florida, heading north, and were termed by the weather bureau in Jacksonville "a hurricane." No further warnings were beamed to Long Island or Connecticut, although in reality the storm was headed directly there. There was no evacuation of the Fire Island beaches. Speeding ahead, the storm took only ten hours to cover the distance from Cape Hatteras to Long Island, and almost unheralded, it struck on the afternoon of September 21. The equinoctial tides were already high and on that fateful afternoon were rising rapidly. Nature was about to deliver to the South Shore a massive blow, and the area was completely unprepared.

It was not, of course, the first hurricane to strike the Great South Bay. Statistics show that there has been a severe storm every ten years on average and a hurricane every thirty years. As no one lived permanently on Fire Island prior to 1900 (there was only the Surf Hotel and one or two boarding-houses or clubs until then), little is known of the earlier storms. There is evidence, however, of some early violent storms. Long Island historian Benjamin F. Thompson told of a particularly bad storm in the winter of 1690–91. It was also reported that around 1764 a storm caused an inlet to be formed between the Fire Island and Gilgo Inlets. It was called the Cedar Island gut but evidently filled in after a few years. The greatest hurricane of the nineteenth century occurred on the equinox between September 21 and 22, 1815 (note the similarity of dates with September 21 and 22, 1938). Historian Osborn Shaw of Bellport called the 1815 storm "the most destructive ever known on Long Island and all along the Atlantic Coast."* Another dreadful one struck in 1821. Since 1900, when homes were first built on Fire Island at Point O' Woods, there had been no violent hurricanes and thus people were entirely unprepared for what would happen on the night of September 21, 1938.

---

* Coincidentally the following summer of 1816 was the "frozen summer" in North America when frost with snow and ice were often experienced from June through September, likely caused by a volcanic eruption which raised dust particles into the stratosphere, partially blocking the rays of the sun.

The earlier storms had, however, changed the topography of the Fire Island coastline, causing inlets to appear and vanish. Often the winter and early spring storms, although not technically hurricanes as they were not circular and not formed from hot water, did the most damage to the ocean beach. The Fire Island Inlet was opened prior to 1670 as it clearly shows on the Robert Ryder map of Long Island of that date. Colonel Nicoll Floyd reported that around 1754 there had been seven inlets east of the Fire Island Inlet. Over the years all of these seven, including the Old Inlet or Smith's Inlet opposite Bellport, closed up as did the Cedar gut and the Gilgo gut west of the Fire Island Inlet. In 1930 there were only the Jones Beach and the Fire Island Inlets from the Rockaways east to Montauk Point, a distance of almost a hundred miles. That changed in March 1931, when a powerful winter northeaster reopened the long-closed Moriches Inlet. Initially the channel was twenty feet deep and four to five hundred feet wide, but it gradually narrowed and became much more shallow over the years. Today it is only navigable by small boats which must sometimes brave the surf. The Shinnecock Inlet to the east, used today by commercial and pleasure fishermen alike, closed around 1880 only to be blown open again in the 1938 hurricane and is now continually dredged by U.S. Army engineers. The Fire Island Inlet, also continually dredged, moves to the west as the sand flows with the set of the surf. Today it is almost six miles to the west of the lighthouse that was built in 1858 on its edge.

On the afternoon of September 21, 1938, most of the summer tourists had left Fire Island. It was estimated that about four hundred people remained, mostly at Ocean Beach, Fair Harbor, and Saltaire, the three largest communities at that time. As the center of the hurricane approached the beach, the storm surge caused the tides to rise precipitously and the northeast wind reached hurricane force of 75 miles per hour. The protective dunes along the beach began to give way and the ocean began to cover the whole width of the island. The last ferry left the Ocean Beach dock headed across the bay for Bay Shore at 3:00 p.m. It never got there.

Its engines were as nothing against the water and wind. The passengers remained on board, safe at least, throughout the entire storm. When it was all over and the tide had receded to below normal, the ferry was high and dry entirely out of water on its side, it had been driven so far up on Fire Island.

The stories are legion and the damage was catastrophic. At Saltaire, worst of all, four persons died, seventy were saved by boats, although the boats never left the dock. The tidal wave there had been estimated at thirty feet high, breaking right through into the Great South Bay. A new inlet opened, but did not survive the storm. Ninety homes were swept away completely. Seventy-five survived but were heavily damaged, most beyond repair. At Kismet, just to the west of Saltaire, twenty-two houses were lost and only one survived. At Fair Harbor to the east, seventy houses were lost and eight survived. Days later, the bay was covered with wooden boards and planks from houses and piers. Ocean Beach and Point O' Woods got off somewhat more easily as the dunes there were higher and the ocean did not get through. The Way Wayonda Club, long in disuse, on Captree Island disappeared from the landscape forever.

As the eye of that great storm passed over Fire Island and the Great South Bay, an eerie calm developed, the winds dropped to almost normal and blue sky appeared above. One was tempted to think it was all over. But peace lasted for only half an hour or so, and for those on the mainland side of the bay, the worst was still to come. As the storm center passed to the northeast to strike into Westhampton with devastating impact, the wind on the bay shifted into the southwest and regained much of its earlier force. The shoreline was very exposed. Tides had risen eight to ten feet above normal levels and torrential rain had soaked and loosened the soil all along the shore. When trees, still full of leaf, were battered by the southwest gales, they overturned, their roots ripped out of the softened ground. The larger the tree, the more apt it was to come down. Boats were driven up the canals. All power was cut off as lines were down everywhere. Basements of houses along the shore filled with wa-

The home of Mr. and Mrs. William H. Russell off Maple Avenue, Islip, was designed by Russell in a Mediterranean style and built in 1927-28. It is pictured here after being remodeled by removing the eastern wing in the 1940s. (Courtesy of Richard A. Milligan.)

Allen Winden was the Dick homestead on Ocean Avenue in Islip. It is pictured here c.1930 after the addition of a wing by E. W. Howell Company. It was torn down in 1954. (Courtesy of *Notable Long Island Homes*.)

Twyford, the home of Mr. and Mrs.
Charles D. Webster on Peters land,
is a house of the 1880s built by Dr.
T. S. Ryder of New York, enlarged
and occupied by the Websters since
1945. Charles (Chuck) Webster lives
there today. (Courtesy of Richard A.
Milligan.)

The home of Mr. and Mrs. H. Cecil Sharp was designed by William H.
Russell and built on the west side of Saxon Avenue, Bay Shore, in 1932-33
on the former Conover and Hutton land.   (Courtesy of Richard A. Milligan.)

Windholme Farm was designed by Alfred Hopkins and included a circular bull pen which later became a dovecote with a clock tower. It is pictured here as it looks today. (Courtesy of Richard A. Milligan.)

Windholme, the Victorian shingle-style home of Mr. and Mrs. Samuel T. Peters on Johnson Avenue (now St. Mark's Lane) in Islip, was built by John D. Prince c.1880 and expanded by the Peters who bought it in 1889. (Courtesy of Charles D. Webster.)

The home of Mr. and Mrs. W. Kingsland Macy on the east side of Ocean Avenue in Islip. It is pictured here today. (Courtesy of Richard A. Milligan.)

The remodeled Hyde-Bossert house is today the clubhouse of the *Southward Ho Country Club*. The club opened on May 30, 1925. (Courtesy of Richard A. Milligan.)

ter, but most houses themselves continued to stand. Finally the wind abated and shifted back to the west and then the northwest. As the following day dawned, clear and bright, the tide had receded. What was left were downed trees, debris everywhere including much from Fire Island, and the stench of decay from leaves felled before their time. It took several days for the ocean surf to abate on Fire Island and one young boy in Islip remembered looking out the third floor window of his home to see the white of the raging surf over the top of the remaining dunes on the beach over six miles away. Months of clean-up began along the Great South Bay. All of the landmark homes on the mainland side of the bay had stood fast, however, and by the beginning of the summer of 1939 normality resumed and summer went on as before with sailing, fishing, clamming, and bird shooting in the fall.

Other hurricanes followed in 1944, several in the 1950s and 1960s, and Hurricane Gloria in 1985. They were all severe, but the weather bureau had greatly improved its warning system and with the advent of the weather satellite, predictions became very accurate. This helped to save lives and lessen damage somewhat. The Fire Island beaches were also severely damaged in the winter storms of 1962 and 1993 when large numbers of houses were lost to the ocean. The statistic of a major storm every ten years appears to be holding true on average. But as the ocean warms with the globe and the water level rises, hurricanes along the Atlantic Coast could easily become more frequent and cause more damage. That remains to be seen. However, few who were then alive will forget September of 1938 when nature dealt its greatest blow to Long Island. It could have been seen as a signal that the era of the Great South Bay as a summer resort was about to end. That was not ended by the hurricane of '38, however, but rather by the man-made holocaust that was about to follow, World War II.

The Great Depression had significantly changed the South Shore, as has been noted. Conceivably the resort could have recovered with a growing economy had it not been for the war. But the war with its deprivations and disruptions ended that era forever. In 1945 and 1946 when life in America began to return to normal, the area from Oakdale to Babylon began to look entirely different, fast becoming an all-year-round suburban, residential community, part of the population explosion that was about to begin in Suffolk County. It could be argued that from 1939 to 1948 not much actually changed along the Great South Bay. From Oakdale in the east, to Babylon in the west, the only significant difference in the shoreline view was the disappearance of Peperidge Hall, razed in 1940. But the view from a boat sailing along those fifteen miles was deceptive and did not reveal what had happened slightly inland from the water.

Between the start of the Great Depression and the summer of 1948 the Westbrook Golf Club, the Timber Point Club, the Islip Tennis Club, and the South Shore Field Club had either disappeared entirely or, in the case of Timber Point, had changed its ownership to the Republican Party of Suffolk County, thanks to W. Kingsland Macy. The venerable South Side Club, with its massive land-holdings, was kept alive and the South Bay Golf Club barely survived, thanks to Horace Havemeyer's generosity. The Bay Shore and Babylon Yacht Clubs continued in existence, although for a time the former was in peril due to changes in Bay Shore harbor that eliminated its site. Thanks to the Landon Thorne family, a new and better site was found.

With regard to private homes, that period saw the demise of Peperidge Hall (1940), mentioned above, the J. Ives Plumb house in Islip, the Jay Carlisle house in East Islip, the Schuyler Parsons home Whileaway on St. Mark's Lane, the Simon Rothschild house on Saxon Avenue, the George Graham house on Main Street west of Islip, and the Alfred Wagstaff and Bradish Johnson homesteads in West Islip and West Bay Shore. The Rothschild house with its twelve acres of canal-front land was sold at a public auction in 1944. It was purchased by a New York City restaurateur for $5,000 in that depressed wartime year, only to be razed in the 1960s to make way for the single family homes on Angela Lane.

Some homes survived, but their use was changed to other purposes. Brookwood Hall became the property of the Orphan Asylum of Brooklyn. Woodland, the Bradish Johnson Jr. home on Suffolk Lane, East Islip, became the Hewlett School in 1941. Aymar Johnson had died in 1942 and his widow rented the property to the school at first and sold it to them in 1946.

All of the owners of the larger places cut back as far as they could during the war years when, with gas rationing in effect and most able-bodied men away, it was almost impossible to continue the old life-style. Victory gardens, filled with beans and tomatoes, replaced flower gardens on many of the estates. After the war it was apparent that the large houses could no longer be maintained. Staff was not available and the war had changed the aspirations of many. Domestic service was not looked upon with favor anymore. The two large Peters homes, Windholme and Nearholme, were razed then, as was the Allan Pinkerton house on Saxon Avenue. Finally at the end of the summer of 1948 Horace and Doris Havemeyer decided to level their home on Olympic Point, one of the great landmark houses on the Great South Bay.

The Havemeyers knew that the size and the cost of maintaining that great house would preclude the possibility of any of their children wanting to live in it after their deaths. Furthermore, Horace, in declining health and in his sixties then, anticipated that he would die long before his wife who had a great life expectancy. In fact she would be a widow for twenty-six years. Horace wanted his wife to have a home she could manage on that unique site and that might easily in time be taken over by their children. He particularly hoped that his youngest, still unmarried son, Harry, aged eighteen, would remain on the bay throughout his adulthood. Thus the difficult decision was taken to raze the big house and to build another, much smaller frame house on the same site.

Havemeyer asked E. W. Howell and Co. and its young architect partner, Ralph D. Howell Jr., to supervise the demolition of the big house, saving the parts that could be reused, and to design and build the new one. Of course, Havemeyer knew just what he wanted, a New England farm-style house with a long wing added by necessity for a pantry, kitchen, and rooms for three maids. Howell was able to reuse some of the foot-wide floor boards in the front hall, some of the yellow pine in the framing, and many of the two-inch thick doors from the old house.

The demolition was a huge undertaking. The bricks were knocked down by ball and chain and bulldozed into the large basement. Only a single curved brick fence remained, which had divided off the servants' wing of the great house. The project of demolition and rebuilding was complete by September of 1949 when the Havemeyers and their son Harry moved in. They had spent the summer of 1949 in a house on the east side of Saxon Avenue, built by Havemeyer on the site of the original four-car garage which he later turned over to his daughter, Adaline, and her family. With the summer of 1950 the Great South Bay had a new, albeit much smaller, landmark house on Olympic Point.

By the end of 1948 there were still a significant, although fast dwindling, number of grandchildren and great grandchildren of the earliest summer residents who continued to live along the bay. Many of those had become year-round residents who did not have city homes any longer. The men would commute to New York City daily, or in some cases they found work on Long Island or did not work at all, scraping by on their inheritance. Descendants of Bradish Johnson, Francis Cooper Lawrance, Schuyler Livingston Parsons, Edwin Thorne, Harry B. Hollins, Robert A. Pinkerton, Charles Gulden, Amedee Depau Moran, Samuel T. Peters, Henry O. Havemeyer, Gustave Kobbe, Henry H. Hollister, George A. Ellis, Frederick G. Bourne, William Dick, and John Mollenhauer were living in the area between Oakdale and Babylon. Nevertheless the tide had turned. Real estate taxes had begun their geometric rise to support the growing public school system in the Town of Islip, making it difficult to own more than a small parcel of land. Real estate development, in suspension since the 1920s, became feverish again after 1950 with the typical house built on a lot of less than one acre. The suburban sprawl had begun in the Town of Islip and in Suffolk County as a whole.

The age of the Great South Bay as a summer spa was over. Still, its attraction for many of these new residents was the same as it had been for those coming to summer along its glimmering waters long ago. Whether fishing for the blues, walking along the Fire Island beaches, sailing into the southwester, shooting ducks from a hidden blind in the fall, or just cruising about, the appeal had not changed. Many more could now enjoy those activities and sometimes now the bay is very crowded in summer on a Sunday afternoon. But most of the time a contemporary observer can still imagine what it was like back in 1890 to that fisherman when the blues struck: "Now the gulls are close at hand and Swish! The line is jerked from your nervous fingers and runs out like mad. There's a fish on the line!"[9]

EPILOGUE
THE TOWN OF ISLIP TODAY

The Town of Islip no longer in any way resembles the few small villages of the 1840s, nor its quaint namesake in Northamptonshire in England. From Oakdale to Babylon one village now merges into the next, creating a waterfront suburbia that extends inland throughout the old pine barrens to Long Island's North Shore. There is scarcely any open land at all, save what has been set aside and protected by the State of New York, by Suffolk County, or by environmental organizations. Bay Shore, once a thriving village, is now plagued with urban decay and is only saved by the existence of a much enlarged Southside Hospital and many nearby medical offices. The focus of consumer shopping is now along a much widened Sunrise Highway while the old South Country Road, now called Main Street or the Montauk Highway, is filled with stoplights. The population of the Town of Islip at the last census was 300,000, more than seven times greater than it was in 1940, and larger than all of Suffolk County in 1950.

How does the landscape look today? From Oakdale on the east to the Connetquot River, Anson and Florence Bourne Hard's home, Meadowedge, built in 1909, and its surrounding land is now a Suffolk County golf course with the house remodeled into a clubhouse and restaurant. Their six-car garage is now the Long Island Maritime Museum. Next door, the huge landmark of the La Salle Military Academy, with its large wing added since the time it was Commodore Bourne's Indian Neck Hall, still is the largest building seen from the bay. Most of its interior is unaltered and in use. From there to the Connetquot are hundreds of small, modern (since the

1920s) houses on small plots of land. Idlehour is now the principal building of Dowling College, again much remodeled from W. K. Vanderbilt's days. The carriage house, the power house, and the indoor tennis court have been transformed for college use. The Vanderbilt teahouse on the bay is now a popular restaurant. Few who dine there know it was a favorite retreat of Consuelo, Duchess of Marlborough, a hundred years ago. North of the South Country Road was the 3,000-acre property of the venerable South Side Sportsmen's Club, founded in 1866 for only one hundred members. It lasted longer than most private clubs — over one hundred years, until 1973 — but was finally taken over by the State of New York to be used as a limited access park preserve for those who wished to fish or to walk in the woods. The Isaac H. Green Jr. clubhouse remains, watched over by a guardian and of course the property, being State-owned, no longer pays taxes to the community. Nevertheless the open land has been preserved, a good resolution in the overcrowded county, and is enjoyed by those who wish to obtain a permit to enter.

From the Connetquot River west to Champlin's Creek — Great River and East Islip — the Lorillard and then the Cutting property Westbrook is now the Bayard Cutting Arboretum, having been deeded to the Long Island State Park Commission by Mrs. Olivia Murray Cutting and her daughter, Mrs. Olivia James, in 1952. The unfurnished house and grounds are open to the public and remain very much as they were in the past except for the farm and the Westbrook Golf course north of the highway which have been commercially occupied for many years. The Cutting Arboretum provides the best look today at what the past was like in the 1890s when the summer spa along the bay was at its height. All the large houses along Great River Road are gone including Trinity Church's Seaside Home for city children. There remain both Emmanuel Church and the little cemetery to the rear where some of the past can be seen on the gravestones of those buried there. At the end of the road is another Suffolk County golf course where the Timber Point Club once was. Sadly, that exceptional seaside links course at Timber Point was changed from eighteen holes to twenty-seven holes on the same amount of land, effectively destroying its character and challenge. The remodeled Breese-Davies-Timber Point clubhouse remains.

To the west Heckscher State Park continues to attract thousands each summer to its several pavilions along the bay. The park has more than justified Robert Moses's expectation of it. The land to the west, once owned by Harry B. Hollins, is now filled with homes, like the Vanderbilt land in Oakdale. Hollins's son, Gerald, did leave some land to the Town of Islip as a nature preserve. The houses along the east side of Champlin's Creek remain today as they were in the earlier time. On Suffolk Lane only the Bradish Johnson Jr. house, Woodland, now the Hewlett School, survives. To the north of Main Street the Harry K. Knapp-Francis B. Thorne estate Brookwood Hall is today owned by the Town of Islip and used as an annex to the Town Hall — a museum and arts complex. From the outside the Georgian house and grounds have not changed at all.

From Champlin's Creek to Orowoc Creek — the hamlet of Islip — St. Mark's Church, now almost 150 years old, survived a disastrous fire in 1989 and was painstakingly restored, Tiffany windows and all, to its former condition. It is in fact today closer to the original 1880 building than it had been before the fire. Across from the church, the Islip Tennis Club has been replaced by modern homes and none of the old homes exist on St. Mark's Lane. The names of Tappin, Livingston, Knapp, Parsons, Hollister, and Welles are gone and forgotten except that side streets have the name of two of them. At the end of the lane, Twyford, with a sliding gate at the entrance, marks the large property of the Department of the Interior's Fish and Wildlife Service where in former days the Peterses and then the Websters resided. Across South Bay Avenue the National Audubon Society owns the balance of the Peterses' great estate. Those lands will remain open and untouched into the future. At the southern end of the hamlet lies Bayberry Point, with its ten Moorish houses, some of which are now substantially remodeled, still recognizable to a visitor from 1900. Many post-war homes and the Bayberry Beach and Tennis Club, all amongst substantial trees now, complete the scene. The most striking difference today at Bayberry Point, and indeed throughout the whole bay area, from a hundred years ago is the growth of trees and shrubs. It no longer has that barren look of a landscape where most of the trees had been felled for shipbuilding, railroad ties, and charcoal. Along Ocean Avenue in Islip only the Doxsee house on Raymond Avenue, the W. Kingsland Macy house, now owned by the Daughters of Wisdom, and one-half of the Russell house on Maple Avenue, survive. The homes of the Dicks, Gibb-Stanchfield-Wrights, Timmerman-Tobeys, and Schieren-Atwoods are gone, replaced by many more modern ones, including an attractive cluster housing development known as the Club on the former property of W. K. and A. M. Dick. In Islip village the Georgian town hall, with its wings added later, marks the easterly entrance to many small shops along Main Street.

From Orowoc Creek west to Awixa Creek, north of the Main Street, the new Islip High School occupies the Moffitt-Graham-Vatable land. Southward along Saxon Avenue, the second Knapp house, slowly being restored, the Gibb-Tenney house, and lastly the Sharp-Riggio house, also recently restored by a new owner, remain of the older homes. They are protected by the Monfort Seminary — now used for weekend retreats — which occupies the former lands of Edward S. Knapp and Henry Beekman Livingston. At the end of Saxon Avenue, on the west side Horace and Doris Havemeyer's second house (1949) has been joined by another (1960) lived in by their son Harry and his wife, Eugenie Havemeyer. The old Olympic Point farm with its Hopkins barns razed, has been divided into several new houses.

Awixa Avenue starts with the new condominium development called Windemere, located on what was the property of Edward F. Hutton and J. Dunbar (chewing gum) Adams. Farther south, however, it still is the site of several of the old houses of the 1890s. John Mollenhauer's house and his son and daughter-in-law Adolph and Anna Mollenhauer's home, which they called Homeport, are there today. So is a part of Mollenhauer's farm occupied by George and Greta Plender. There are a few others as well, Dr. Woolley's and Thurber's among them. On Penataquit Point, Rafael Guastavino's all-tile house remains a bay landmark, and on Penataquit Avenue, Mrs. Low's house, Dr. Ash's house, and the Robert Pinkerton house remain as well. All of these houses were more manageable in size and thus were saved from the wrecker's ball.

On Mowbray Avenue stands an old Mowbray house across the road from the now huge, modern Southside Hospital complex. Bay Shore's founder, John Mowbray, would be astonished to see the hospital in the 1990s. To the north of the Montauk Highway on Brentwood Road lies Oakwood Cemetery, opened in 1880 to be the principal Protestant burying ground in the whole area. Here are the graves of most of the older families who were year-round residents of East Islip, Islip, and Bay Shore. There are also graves of summer residents, such as the Macy family, although most of those were buried either in the Great River Cemetery or in family plots in Brooklyn and New York. To the north across modern Sunrise Highway there is a large shopping center, featuring Toys R Us, where polo was once played and horse shows were held at Oakwood Park in the bygone age.

All of the avenues that run from Bay Shore village to the Bay — Shore, Maple, Ocean, and Clinton Avenues — have shingle houses of the 1890s on them. One of these on Clinton Avenue, now an old age home, was the home of Charles Gulden, the mustard king. There are no longer any hotels near the water, but the docks are alive with marinas and Fire Island ferries in the summer. West of Bay Shore village the former Garner and Lawrance lands, now called O-Co-Nee, are the location of the most elegant homes in the area. Built on larger lot sizes, thanks to the requirements of Charles L. Lawrance, the original seller, they are the showplace residences on both sides of O-Co-Nee Creek. North of the Main Road the Lawrance homestead, Manatuck Farm, is nowhere to be found, only shops, a Ford dealership, and multiple small houses.

From Brightwater to Babylon — the Ackerson development of Brightwaters village remains much the same today,
graceful homes along the canal and amongst the lakes north
of the highway. The casino along the bay is gone, however, as
is the inn on Windsor Avenue. To the west the area is now
called West Bay Shore. Sans Souci, Bradish Johnson's summer home, is gone, as are his neighbors George Wilmerding's
and John I. Lawrance's. Those first summer residents are
only remembered here by the naming of the small street that
leads to a cluster of new homes, Bradish Lane. The Southward Ho Country Club has become by far the largest and
most popular club in the entire region with a full membership and a waiting list. After the war the club purchased the
George A. Ellis house next door to add to the older Hyde
house, entirely remodeled to suit a modern country club's
needs. To the south across the highway St. Peter's Church of
Bay Shore and a handsome development known as the Admiralty, remind one that once Landon K. Thorne's estate was on
that land. Moving westward the Richard Hyde, then Hans
Isbrandtsen, land is now a development called Sunscape.
Only the small clubhouse of the South Shore Field Club, built
in the late 1890s, is there to remind a visitor that on the site
there was once a golf course where Hyde's daughter, Lillian,
and her friend, Marion Hollins, competed and became famous national champions of their day. To the west stands the
oldest house of all, Sagtikos Manor (1692), owned today by
Robert David Lion Gardiner. Much of the land has become a
county park, but the historic house remains private and is
open in the summer to the public on a limited basis for
conducted visits.

Ironically, West Bay Shore, moving westward, becomes
West Islip before one gets to Babylon. West Islip, a much
older community, was the site of many of the grandest homes
of the 1880s. Today virtually none remain except for the
second Arnold house built by Mrs. Annie Arnold in the decade of the 1900s on the north side of the Montauk Highway
near the entrance to the Moses Parkway, and two or three
old shingle houses on Oak Neck Road (now called Oak Neck

Lane). One of these was the house of the writer William Loring Andrews. Two buildings now dominate West Islip, the modern Good Samaritan Hospital, and the very old hostelry, La Grange Inn, on the corner of Higbie Lane where George Washington was said to have taken a meal during his visit to Sagtikos Manor. Gone are the various Wagstaff houses, including Tahlulah, the original homestead of the doctor. There is, however, a Wagstaff Lane, a Tahlulah Lane, and a Secatogue Lane, the latter commemorating the Indian tribe of so long ago. The small Episcopal Church, Christ Church, West Islip, is no more, although the building still stands and is now the Holy Family Ukrainian Catholic Church. As West Islip blends into Babylon, the Town of Islip comes to an end and the Town of Babylon, once the south part of the Town of Huntington, begins. The village of Babylon today has a prosperous look and has not been afflicted with the decay that has come to Bay Shore. However, only in the cemetery on Deer Park Avenue, north of the railroad can one find a trace of the summer residents of the nineteenth century. There are the stones of Harry I. Nicholas, his wife, Alice Hollins Nicholas, and three of their daughters, buried across the road from their summer home. On the west side of the village is Argyle Lake and the Argyle Park community of homes, also a reminder of the huge Argyle Hotel that once stood on the edge of the lake, a dream of Austin Corbin's which did not last for more than fifteen years.

Across the Great South Bay on Fire Island, in spite of the several storms the changes have not been that great. On the east, Point O' Woods, the oldest community, today retains its essential exclusive character. The massive, oceanfront building, the Club, built in 1910, finally collapsed into the ocean during a northeast storm in the late fall of 1993. There have been some recent developments including a large marina, called Atlantique, for Town of Islip resident boats only, and a purpose-built community called Dunewood, built by Maurice Barbash in 1958–59. Sunken Forest (to the east of Point O' Woods), a unique nature preserve, was founded by a group of conservationists in the 1950s and now is operated by the

National Park Service. Hundreds come each summer to see the old oaks, cedars, and hollies that have been stunted by the wind yet protected by the dunes. From Point O' Woods west to the Fire Island lighthouse there are thirteen distinct communities of which Ocean Beach is still the largest. The lighthouse stands today more than five miles from the inlet. In between, Robert Moses State Park (once Fire Island State Park, Long Island's first state park) attracts thousands to swim in the Atlantic or lie on the beach each summer. It has become the largest public beach facility along the Great South Bay. Fire Island Inlet itself moves continually westward and is kept open by dredging. Without its infusion of new seawater the bay would become brackish, stagnant, and gradually a large marsh. Captree and Oak Islands have small summer cottages much as they did early in the century. The Oak Beach Inn is on the north side of the inlet. Today the Captree Bridge, built in 1959 across the Great South Bay and across the inlet to the Moses Park, connects with the parkway to Jones Beach. That is as far as Robert Moses got with his dream to build a parkway along the entire length of Fire Island. There is no road today between the lighthouse and Smith's Point at the eastern end of the bay. Fishermen's and hunter's shacks dot Sexton, West, and Middle Islands, the latter once owned by Harry B. Hollins of East Islip as a shooting preserve.

Gone are the Short Beach Club, the Fire Island Country Club, and the Way Wayonda Club of an earlier era.

Finally, the principal landmark on Fire Island is and always has been the lighthouse itself. First born in 1825 and then rebuilt in 1858 it had served as a coastal, navigational beacon, often the first sight of America from ships coming from Europe. With all the array of modern technology, especially satellites, available to ships, it was both unsafe and deemed obsolete in 1974 and its beacon was shut down. For several years it was dark, until a not-for-profit group, the Fire Island Lighthouse Preservation Society, was able to raise the funds to restore it to safe working order. On May 25, 1986, the beacon was relit and began again to flash every 7 1/2 seconds around the bay and out to sea. It was as if an old friend had returned home, hopefully forever. In 1964 Fire Island, from the Robert Moses State Park east to the Smith Point County Park, became a National Seashore. Established communities could remain and develop within set boundaries but undeveloped land must remain that way under the federal law. Sunken Forest was given to the National Seashore by its non-profit owners at that time. This Act of Congress has given Fire Island a measure of protection from human hands. What nature will do to it is left for the future to unfold.

It has been 150 years since the Johnson brothers came from New York City to spend their summers along the Great South Bay in the Town of Islip. Today only three families remain there who are descended from the many who followed the Johnsons to buy and build summer homes where they could escape the heat of the city and enjoy the cooling breezes of the bay. Only two of those three families are summertime residents. By the next generation, will any remain at all? Or will the story of a summer spa along the Great South Bay finally be ended?

NOTES

CHAPTER II Early Settlers on Long Island

[1]*Brooklyn Union*, 29 July 1885.

CHAPTER III The First Summer Residents

[1]Joseph A. Scoville, *The Old Merchants of New York City*, (1872) 1:183.

[2]*Fire Island Light*, Fall 1980, an article by Albert Bliss about the Dominy House.

[3]Frederick Lewis Allen, *The American Procession* (1933) unpaged.

[4]Madeleine C. Johnson, *Fire Island, 1650s – 1980s* (1983) 34.

[5]*Brooklyn Union*, 29 July 1885.

[6]Harry T. Peters, *Currier & Ives Printmakers to the American People* (1929) 1:71.

[7]George L. Weeks Jr., *Some of Town of Islip's Early History* (1955) 83.

[8]James W. Shepp and Daniel B. Shepp, *Shepp's New York City Illustrated* (1894) 362.

[9]Thomas W. Knox, "Summer Clubs on the Great South Bay," *Harper's New Monthly Magazine*, July 1880.

CHAPTER IV August Belmont and the South Side Club

[1]Lloyd Morris, *Incredible New York* (1951) 95, 96.

[2]Stephen Birmingham, *Our Crowd* (1968) 61.

[3]*Old Oakdale History*, 1:13.

[4]*South Side Signal*, 22 July 1871.

[5]*Old Oakdale History*, 1:27.

[6]David Black, *The King of Fifth Avenue: The Fortunes of August Belmont* (1981) 665.

[7]Edward S. Knapp Jr., *We Knapps Thought It Was Nice* (1940) 52.

[8]*Smithtown Star*, September 1828.

[9]Philip Hone, *The Diary of Philip Hone*, part 1 (1828–1851).

[10]*South Side Signal*, 29 July 1871.

[11]Knapp, op. cit. 56.

[12]Knapp, op. cit. 57.

[13]*South Side Signal*, 17 August 1878.

[14]Ibid., 23 August 1873.

CHAPTER V William K. Vanderbilt and His Friends

[1]*South Side Signal*, 20 May 1876.

[2]George L. Weeks Jr., *Isle of Shells* (1965) 212.

[3]*South Side Signal*, 20 May 1876.

[4]Ibid., 11 September 1880.

[5]Ibid., 16 October 1875.

[6]Ibid., 7 August 1886.

[7]Ibid., 15 August 1874.

[8]Ibid., 10 July 1880.

[9]Ibid., 18 April 1885.

[10]Ibid., 7 August 1886.

[11]Ibid., 14 June 1884.

[12]Louis Auchincloss, *The Vanderbilt Era* (1989) 3.

[13]John Foreman and Robbe Stimson, *The Vanderbilts and the Gilded Age* (1991) 27, 28.

[14]*South Side Signal*, 20 July 1878.

[15]*Suffolk County News*, 21 July 1888.

[16]Consuelo Vanderbilt Balsan, *The Glitter and the Gold* (1952) 14.

[17]*South Side Signal*, 23 September 1880.

[18]Ibid., 26 June 1880.

[19]Ibid., 23 August 1879.

[20]Ibid., 7 April 1883.

[21]Ibid., 10 July 1886.

[22]Ibid., 2 September 1882.

[23]Ibid., 2 September 1882.

[24]*Shepp's New York City Illustrated* (1894) 355, 357.

[25]*South Side Signal*, 23 May 1874.

[26]Ibid., 28 June 1879.

[27]Fred S. Cozzens, *Yachts and Yachting* (1887) 79.

[28]Ibid., 79.

[29]*South Side Signal*, 25 April 1885.

[30]Ibid., 11 August 1869.

[31]Thomas W. Knox, "Summer Clubs on the Great South Bay," *Harper's New Monthly Magazine*, July 1880.

[32]Ibid.

[33]Kenneth H. Dunshee, *As You Pass By* (1952) 227.

[34]*South Side Signal*, 21 July 1886, as quoted in *The Brooklyn Eagle*.

[35]*South Side Signal*, 8 August 1874.

[36]*Harper's New Monthly Magazine*, July 1880.

[37]*South Side Signal*, 23 August 1879.

[38]Ibid., 1 January 1881.

[39]Ibid., 6 June 1885.

[40]Ibid., 11 September 1880.

[41]*New York World*, 23 August 1879.

[42]*South Side Signal*, 25 August 1883.

[43]Ibid., 23 July 1887, as quoted in the *Huntington Bulletin*.

[44]Ibid., 8 May and 15 May 1875.

[45]Ibid., 5 February 1876.

[46]Ibid., 23 July 1887, as quoted in the *Huntington Bulletin*.

CHAPTER VI The Gilded Age – The Early Years

[1]Louis Auchincloss, *The Vanderbilt Era* (1989) 3.

[2]*South Side Signal*, 4 December 1880.

[3]Ibid., 4 December 1880.

[4]Ibid., 4 December 1880.

[5]Ibid., 4 February 1882.

[6]Ibid., 6 May 1882.

[7]Ibid., 6 May 1882.

[8]Ibid., 6 May 1882.

[9]Ibid., 10 June 1882.

[10]Stephen Birmingham, *Our Crowd* (1968) 147.

[11]*South Side Signal*, 11 December 1886, as quoted in the *New York World*.

[12]Ibid., 13 June 1896.

[13]Ibid., 21 July 1886.

[14]Ibid., 20 August 1881.

[15]Ibid., 19 January 1884.

[16]Ibid., 13 June 1885.

[17]Ibid., 27 April 1889.

[18]Ibid., 6 October 1888.

[19]Ibid., 6 October 1888.

[20]Ibid., 11 December 1886, as quoted in the *New York Tribune*, December 1886.

[21]Edward S. Knapp Jr., *We Knapps Thought It Was Nice* (1940) 29 – 30.

[22]Ibid., 40.

[23]Ibid., 40.

[24]Ibid., 39.

[25]Ibid., 121.

[26]Ibid., 121.

[27]Ibid., 121.

[28]*South Side Signal*, 7 August 1880.

[29]Ibid., 10 July 1880.

[30]Ibid., 10 July 1880.

[31]Ibid., 26 June 1880.

[32]Ibid., 26 June 1880.

[33]Ibid., 19 April 1884.

[34]*New York Herald*, 8 June 1890.

[35]*South Side Signal*, 2 July 1887.

[36]Ibid., 27 May 1893.

[37]Ibid., 11 April 1885.

[38]Knapp, op. cit. 80.

[39]*South Side Signal*, 15 June 1895.

[40]Ibid., 16 June 1877.

[41]Schuyler L. Parsons Jr., *Untold Friendships* (1955) 8. Excerpts from *Untold Friendships*. Copyright 1955 by Schulyer L. Parsons, Jr., (c) renewed 1983. Reprinted by permission of Houghton Mifflin Company. All rights reserved.

[42]Ibid., 8.

[43]*New York Times*, 5 November 1917.

[44]Auchincloss, op. cit. 67.

[45]Richard Guy Wilson, *Picturesque Ambiguities: The Country House Tradition in America* (1988) 33.

[46]Parsons, op. cit. 9.

[47]*South Side Signal*, 7 January 1893.

[48]C. T. Bridgeman, *History of Trinity Church Association* (1957) 152.

[49]*New York Times*, 26 May 1888.

[50]*South Side Signal*, 15 December 1888.

[51]*Long Island Forum*, 1983 and 1984 issues.

[52]James A. Scoville, *Old Merchants of New York City* (1872), 1:315.

[53]*South Side Signal*, 7 August 1886.

[54]*Sayville News*, February 1901.

[55]*South Side Signal*, 2 April 1898.

[56]Ibid., 3 October 1903.

[57]Ibid., 21 September 1907.

[58]Ibid., 21 September 1907.

[59]Iris Origo, *Images and Shadows* (1970) 15.

[60]Ibid., 21.

[61]Ibid., 21.

[62]Ibid., 22.

[63]Ibid., 23.

[64]R. W. B. Lewis, *Edith Wharton: A Biography* (1975) 55.

[65]*South Side Signal*, 2 November 1889.

[66]Liisa Sclare and Donald Sclare, *Beaux Arts Estates: A Guide to the Architecture of Long Island* (1980) 193.

[67]Origo, op. cit. 18, 19.

[68]Origo, op. cit. 19.

[69]Origo, op. cit. 20.

[70]Origo, op. cit. 26.

[71]Knapp, op. cit. 85, 86.

[72]Origo, op. cit. 77.

[73]Origo, op. cit. 39.

[74]House of Representatives, Hardwick Committee Investigation in 1911 and pre-trial testimony in the case of *United States vs. the American Sugar Refining Company* (1912).

[75]Ibid.

[76]*South Side Signal*, 7 July 1883.

[77]Charles M. Heald, "Long Island of Today," as printed in *The Old Oakdale History*, 1:1884.

[78]*South Side Signal*, 5 June 1880.

[79]Ibid., 11 July 1891.

[80]Ibid., 27 February 1904.

[81]Ibid., 11 August 1888.

[82]Ibid., 7 July 1906.

[83]*Field Magazine*, 1870.

[84]Fred S. Cozzens, ed. *Yachts and Yachting* (1887) 195

[85]*South Side Signal*, 7 July 1906.

[86]Ibid., 7 August 1886.

[87]Ibid., 7 August 1886.

[88]Ibid., 27 April 1889.

[89]Ibid., 7 December 1889.

[90]Ibid., 18 October 1890.

CHAPTER VII The Gilded Age – Its Peak

[1]*South Side Signal*, 11 June 1892.

[2]Ibid., 13 August 1892.

[3]Ibid., 24 March 1894

[4]Ibid., 24 March 1894.

[5]Ibid., 15 February 1895.

[6]Ibid., 15 June 1895.

[7]Ibid., 21 February 1891.

[8]Ibid., 26 September 1891.

[9]Ibid., 31 October 1891.

[10]Louis Auchincloss, *The Vanderbilt Era* (1989) 41.

[11]*South Side Signal*, 31 October 1891.

[12]Ibid., 24 March 1883.

[13]*Long Island Forum*, 1948.

[14]Ibid.

[15]Ibid.

[16]*South Side Signal*, 20 April 1889.

[17]*New York Herald*, 9 September 1900.

[18]Steven Bedford, *The Long Island Country House, 1870–1930* (1988) 67.

[19]*New York Times*, 10 February 1900.

[20]*South Side Signal*, 14 October 1905.

[21]Ibid., 14 October 1905.

[22]Ibid., 25 June 1904.

[23]*New York Times*, 9 August 1899.

[24]Ranulf Rayner, *The Winning Moment* (1986) 52.

[25]*South Side Signal*, 12 October 1895.

[26]Ibid., 7 July 1906.

[27]Ibid., 18 July 1885.

[28]Gail MacColl and Carol Wallace, *To Marry an English Lord* (1989) 243.

[29]Philip Magnus, *King Edward the Seventh: The Most Edwardian of Them All* (1964) 228.

[30]MacColl and Wallace, op. cit. 243.

[31]Consuelo Vanderbilt Balsan, *The Glitter and the Gold* (1952) 8.

[32]Ibid., 23.

[33]Ibid., 28.

[34]Ibid., 58.

[35]*South Side Signal*, 16 November 1895.

[36]Auchincloss, op. cit. 48.

[37]Ibid., op. cit. 105.

[38]David Cannadine, *Aspects of Aristocracy* (1994) 133.

[39]Ralph G. Martin, *Jennie* (1971) 2:95.

[40]Nigel Nicolson, *Mary Curzon* (1977) 83, 89.

[41]Ibid., 97.

[42]John Foreman and Robbe Stimson, *The Vanderbilts and the Gilded Age* (1991) 180.

[43]*South Side Signal*, 20 September 1902.

[44]Randolph Churchill, *Winston S. Churchill* (1969) companion vol. 2, part 1:588, letter dated 13 October 1906.

[45]V. S. Pritchett, *Vanderbilt* (1977) 55.

[46]Balsan, op. cit. 237.

[47]*South Side Signal*, 25 November 1905.

[48]Ibid., 25 February 1893.

[49]Ibid., 24 November 1894.

[50]Ibid., 13 March 1897.

[51]Prospectus: "Moorish Houses at Bayberry Point, *Islip, Long Island, Built for Mr. H. O. Havemeyer.*"

[52]*South Side Signal*, 22 April 1899.

[53]Ibid., 9 February 1907.

[54]Ibid., 9 November 1907.

[55]Ibid., 10 August 1900.

[56]Ibid., 26 September 1896.

[57]Ibid., 11 July 1896.

[58]Ibid., 15 February 1903.

[59]Yearbook of Penataquit Corinthian Yacht Club (1902).

[60]*South Side Signal*, 1 April 1899.

[61]Ibid., 11 July 1903.

[62]Ibid., 26 September 1908.

[63]Stephen Birmingham, *Our Crowd* (1967) 299.

[64]*South Side Signal*, 3 October 1903.

[65]Foreman, op. cit. 27.

[66]Liz Howell, *Continuity* (1993) 249.

442 ■ *Along the Great South Bay*

[67]*South Side Signal*, 16 August 1902.

[68]Carl A. Starace, "Brookwood Hall," undated paper.

[69]*Brooklyn Eagle*, 7 April 1911.

[70]*New York Times*, 13 August 1895.

[71]*South Side Signal*, 1 October 1887.

[72]Ibid., 6 October 1916.

[73]Ibid., 13 October 1906.

[74]Ibid., 21 December 1895.

CHAPTER VIII The New Century

[1]Carl A. Starace, a paper dated 28 September 1988.

[2]*South Side Signal*, 27 December 1902.

[3]Ibid., 26 October 1907.

[4]Ibid., 26 October 1907.

[5]Ibid., 12 September 1903.

[6]Ibid., 25 July 1903.

[7]*Suffolk County News*, 28 June 1901.

[8]*South Side Signal*, 28 April 1906.

[9]Ibid., 14 September 1907.

[10]Ibid., 2 July 1910.

[11]Ibid., 2 December 1910.

[12]*New York Times*, 24 February 1920.

[13]*Suffolk County News*, 27 February 1920.

[14]*South Side Signal*, 1 June 1907.

[15]*New York Times*, 16 March 1919.

[16]*New York Tribune*, 22 May 1910.

[17]*South Side Signal*, 22 June 1912.

[18]T. B. Ackerson Co., "Brightwaters, Long Island" (c. 1910).

[19]*Suffolk County News*, 5 March 1920.

[20]*South Side Signal*, 12 October 1907.

[21]Ibid., 14 November 1908.
[22]Ibid., 19 December 1908.
[23]Ibid., 15 June 1907.
[24]George S. King, M.D., *Doctor on a Bicycle* (1958) 106.
[25]Doris Dick Havemeyer, *Memoirs* (1975).
[26]Philip Van Rensselaer, *Million Dollar Baby* (1979) 25.
[27]Cleveland Amory, *Who Killed Society?* (1960) 171, 173.
[28]Van Rensselaer, op. cit. 31.
[29]*South Side Signal*, 20 August 1904.
[30]Ibid., 10 July 1914.
[31]*Suffolk County News*, 15 May 1914.
[32]Edward S. Knapp Jr., *We Knapps Thought It Was Nice* (1940) 210.
[33]*New York Times*, 14 July 1923.

CHAPTER IX The War Years

[1]*Suffolk County News*, 16 October 1925.
[2]*Islip Herald*, 10 April 1912.
[3]*South Side Signal*, 19 June 1909
[4]Ibid., 19 June 1909.
[5]*Suffolk County News*, 29 August 1913.
[6]Ibid., 29 August 1913.
[7]Ibid., 27 July 1923.
[8]*New York Times*, 22 July 1923
[9]Ibid., 22 July 1923.
[10]*Suffolk County News*, 3 August 1923.
[11]*New York Times*, 22 July 1923.
[12]*South Side Signal*, 4 August 1906.
[13]Ralph D. Howell, Jr., letter to author, c. 1990.
[14]*Suffolk County News*, 14 November 1913.

[15]Ibid., 19 June 1914.

[16]Ibid., 14 August 1914.

[17]Ibid., 4 December 1914.

[18]*South Side Signal*, 2 August 1918.

[19]Ibid., 2 August 1918.

[20]Ibid., 28 September 1917.

[21]Ibid., 3 May 1918.

[22]Ralph Hausrath, "The Sinking of the USS *San Diego*," *Long Island Forum*, 1 May 1990.

[23]*Brooklyn Eagle*, 1 February 1918.

[24]*South Side Signal*, 18 October 1918.

[25]Ibid., 25 October 1918.

[26]*Suffolk County News*, 21 January 1916.

[27]Ibid., 21 January 1916.

[28]*South Side Signal*, 25 July 1903.

[29]Ibid., 15 August 1903.

[30]*Brooklyn Eagle*, 16 February 1912.

[31]Ibid., 16 February 1912.

[32]Russell Whitehead, *Harrie T. Lindeberg's Contribution to American Domestic Architecture* (April 1924) 309–371.

[33]Ibid.

[34]Ibid.

[35]*New York Times*, 4 July 1931.

CHAPTER X The Breakup of the Great Estates

[1]*Suffolk County News*, 9 November 1923.

[2]Ibid., 2 May 1924.

[3]Ibid., 24 November 1924.

[4]Ibid., 15 July 1921.

[5]Ibid., 22 July 1921.

[6]Ibid., 20 July 1923.

[7]Ibid., 23 March 1924.

[8]Ibid., 19 June 1925.

[9]Ibid., 7 June 1929.

[10]Robert A. Caro, *The Power Broker* (1974) 226.

[11]*Babylon Leader*, 29 May 1925.

[12]Notice of public auction, 28 August 1926.

[13]*New York Times*, 13 February 1919.

[14]Schuyler L. Parsons Jr., *Untold Friendships* (1955) 125.

[15]Ibid., 98.

[16]Ibid., 98, 99.

[17]Ibid., 102, 103.

[18]Ibid., 125.

[19]Ibid., 125.

[20]Ibid., 130, 131.

[21]Ibid., 150.

[22]Doris Dick Havemeyer, *Memoirs* (1976).

CHAPTER XI Some Endings and a New Beginning

[1]John Kenneth Galbraith, *The Great Crash, 1929* (1988) 111.

[2]Alfred Hopkins, *Modern Farm Buildings* (1913) 145.

[3]Editorial, *Long Island Forum*, July 1941.

[4]Harry T. Peters, *Just Hunting* (1935) 2.

[5]Ibid., 14, 15.

[6]Roy King and Burke Davis, *The World of Currier & Ives* 18.

[7]*New York Herald Tribune*, 4 August 1945.

[8]Christopher Sykes, *Nancy: The Life of Lady Astor* (1972) 147.

[9]James W. Shepp and Daniel B. Shepp, *Shepp's New York City Illustrated* (1894) 362.

BIBLIOGRAPHY

Allen, Frederick Lewis. *The American Procession*. New York: Harper & Brothers, 1933.

Amory, Cleveland. *The Last Resorts*. New York: Harper & Brothers, 1952.

————. *Who Killed Society?*. New York: Harper & Brothers, 1960.

Auchincloss, Louis. *The Vanderbilt Era*. New York: Charles Scribner's Sons, 1989.

Bailey, Paul. *Long Island: A History of Two Great Counties, Nassau and Suffolk*. Lewis Historical Publ. Co., 1949.

Baldwin, Richard P. *Residents: Town of Islip, 1720–1865*. W. K. Vanderbilt Historical Society, 1989.

Balsan, Consuelo Vanderbilt. *The Glitter and the Gold*. New York: Harper & Brothers, 1952.

Bayles, Richard M. *Historical and Descriptive Sketches of Suffolk County*. Published by author, 1874.

————. *History of Suffolk County*, 1882.

Birmingham, Stephen. *Our Crowd*. New York: Harper & Row, 1967.

Black, David. *The King of Fifth Avenue: The Fortunes of August Belmont*. New York: Dial Press, 1981.

Brandt, Clare. *An American Aristocracy: The Livingstons*. New York: Doubleday & Co., 1986.

Bridgeman, C. T. *History of Trinity Church Association, 1879–1956*. New York: Privately printed, 1957.

448 ■ *Along the Great South Bay*

2222
Byrnes, Horace W., B.D. "Pictorial Bay Shore and Vicinity: A Souvenir." Privately printed, 1902.

Cannadine, David. *Aspects of Aristocracy.* New Haven: Yale University Press, 1994.

Caro, Robert A. *The Power Broker.* New York: Alfred A. Knopf, 1974.

Catlin Jr., Daniel. *Good Work Well Done.* New York: Privately printed, 1988.

Churchill, Randolph S. *Winston S. Churchill.* Companion Vol. 2, Part 1. Boston: Houghton Mifflin Co., 1969.

Cozzens, Fred S., ed. *Yachts and Yachting.* New York: Cassell & Company Ltd., 1887.

Dunshee, Kenneth Holcomb. *As You Pass By.* New York: Hastings House, 1952.

Eaton, James W. *Babylon Reminiscences.* Babylon, N.Y.: Babylon Publishing Co., 1911.

Elder, George W. *Forty Years Among the Stars.* Wisconsin: Schanen & Jacque, 1955.

Foreman, John, and Robbe Stimson. *The Vanderbilts and the Gilded Age.* New York: St. Martin's Press, 1991.

Galbraith, John Kenneth. *The Great Crash, 1929.* Boston: Houghton Mifflin Co., 1988.

Garth, Rev. William H., Rector. "Historical Sketch of St. Mark's Church." Islip, Long Island: Privately printed, 1928.

Gregory, Alexis. *Families of Fortune, Life in the Gilded Age.* New York: Rizzoli International Publications, 1993.

Hamm, Margherita A. *Famous Families of New York.* New York: G.P. Putnam, Sons, 1901.

Havemeyer, Harry W. *Merchants of Williamsburgh.* New York: Privately printed, 1989.

Hazelton, Henry I. *History of Counties of Suffolk and Nassau, the Boroughs of Queens and Brooklyn.* New York: Lewis Historical Publishing Co., 1925.

Heald, Charles M. "Long Island of Today," reprinted in *Old Oakdale History,* 1884.

Holbrook, Stewart H. *The Age of the Moguls.* Garden City, N.Y.: Doubleday & Co., 1953.

Hone, Philip. *The Diary of Philip Hone: Part I, 1828–1851.* New York: Dodd & Mead Co., 1889.

Hopkins, Alfred. *Modern Farm Buildings.* New York: McBride, Nast & Co., 1913.

Howell Company, E. W. "Noted Long Island Homes," Babylon, N.Y., 1933.

Howell, Liz. *Continuity: Biography, 1819–1934.* Sister Bay, Wis.: The Dragonsbreath Press, 1993.

Johnson, Madeleine C. *Fire Island, 1650s–1980s.* New Jersey: Shoreland Press, 1983.

King, George S. *Doctor on a Bicycle.* New York: Rinehart & Co., 1958.

King, Moses. *Notable New Yorkers of 1896–1899.* New York: M. King, 1899.

King, Roy, and Burke Davis. *The World of Currier & Ives.* New York: Bonanza Books, n.d.

Knapp Jr., Edward Spring. *We Knapps Thought It Was Nice.* New York: Privately printed, 1940.

Knox-Johnston, Robin. *History of Yachting.* Oxford: Phaidon Press, 1990.

Kobbe, Gustave. *The Complete Opera Book.* n.p., October 1922.

Lewis, R. W. B. *Edith Wharton: A Biography.* New York: Harper & Row, 1975.

MacColl, Gail, and Carol Wallace. *To Marry an English Lord.* New York: Workman Publishing Co., 1989.

MacKay, Robert B., Geoffrey L. Rossano, and Carol A. Traynor. *Between Ocean and Empire: An Illustrated History of Long Island.* California: Windsor Publications, Inc., 1985.

Magnus, Philip. *King Edward the Seventh: The Most Edwardian of Them All.* London: J. Murray, 1964.

Manley, Seon. *Long Island Discovery.* Garden City, N.Y.: Doubleday & Co., 1966.

Martin, Ralph G. *Jennie.* Vols. 1 & 2, New Jersey: Prentice Hall Inc., 1969, 1971.

Mertz, Clinton E. *Old Bay Shore Lives Again.* Bay Shore, N.Y.: Bay Shore Journal, 1934.

Monner, Frederick M. "A Local History of Brightwaters from Colonial Times to the Present," Oswego, N.Y., n.p., 1964.

Morris, Lloyd. *Incredible New York.* New York: Random House, 1951.

Munsell, W. W., and Co. "History of Suffolk County," New York: n.p., 1882.

Nicoll, Edward H. "The Descendants of John Nicoll of Islip, who died in 1467," England: n.p., 1894.

Nicolson, Nigel. *Mary Curzon.* London: Weidenfeld & Nicolson, 1977.

Noyes, Dorothy McBurney. *The World Is So Full of a Number of Things.* Privately printed, 1953.

Origo, Iris Cutting. *Images and Shadows.* New York: Harcourt Brace Jovanovich, 1970.

Parsons Jr., Schuyler. *Untold Friendships.* Boston: Houghton Mifflin Co., 1955.

Pelletreau, William S. *American Families of Historic Lineage.* New York: National Americana Society, 1973.

Peters, Harry T. *Just Hunting*. New York: Charles Scribner's Sons, 1935.

———. *Currier & Ives: Printmakers to the American People*. 2 vols. Garden City, N.Y.: Doubleday, Doran & Co., 1929.

———. *Currier & Ives*. n.p., 1942.

Pritchett, V.S., from *Great American Families*, "Vanderbilt," New York: W.W. Norton & Co., 1977.

Rayner, Ranulf. *The Winning Moment*. New York: W. W. Norton & Co., 1986.

Riker Jr., James. "Annals of Newtown, Queens," n.p., 1852.

Roosevelt, Robert Barnwell. *Love and Luck: The Story of a Summer's Loitering on the Great South Bay*. New York: Harper & Brothers, 1886.

Ross and Pelletreau [sic], *History of Long Island*. 3 vols. New York: Lewis Publishing Co., 1903.

Schegel, Carl W. *German-American Families in the United States*. New York: The American Historical Society, 1916.

Sclare, Liisa, and Donald Sclare. *Beaux-Arts Estates: A Guide to the Architecture of Long Island*. New York: Viking Press, 1980.

Scoville, Joseph A. *The Old Merchants of New York City*. M. Doolady [1863–1866 and later edition to] 1872.

Shepp, James W., and Daniel B. Shepp. *Shepp's New York City Illustrated*. Chicago: Globe Bible Publishing Co., 1894.

Spinzia, Raymond, Judith Spinzia, and Kathryn Spinzia. *Long Island: A Guide to New York's Suffolk and Nassau Counties*. New York: Hippocrene Books Inc., 1991.

Starace, Carl A., Town Historian. *Book One: Islip Town Records*. Town of Islip, 1982.

Sykes, Christopher. *Nancy: The Life of Lady Astor*. London: Collins, 1972.

T. B. Ackerson Co. "Brightwaters, Long Island," n.p.: c.1910.

Thompson, Benjamin F. *History of Long Island*. 3 vols. n.p.: 1849. 3rd ed. New York: n.p., 1918.

Tuttle, Etta Anderson. "A Brief History of Bay Shore," Privately printed, 1962.

Van Rensselaer, Philip. *Million Dollar Baby*. New York: Putnam, 1979.

Weeks Jr., George L. *Isle of Shells*. Islip, N.Y.: Buys Bros., Inc., 1965.
———. *Some of Town of Islip's Early History*. Bay Shore: Consolidated Press, 1955.

Weeks, Lyman Horace, ed., *Prominent Families of New York*. New York: The Historical Company, 1898.

Whitehead, Russell. *Harrie T. Lindeberg's Contribution to American Domestic Architecture*. New York: The Architectural Record, Doubleday & Co., April 1924.

RECORDS, REGISTERS, AND YEARBOOKS

Suffolk County Surrogate's Records
Long Island Social Register, 1929
Social Register: New York, 1887 republished by the Social Register Association in 1986
South Side Sportsmen's Club, yearbooks 1886 and 1892
Penataquit Corinthian Yacht Club, yearbook 1902
Short Beach Club, yearbook 1895
Great South Bay Yacht Club, programme of entries, July 28, 1894
Timber Point Club, yearbook 1930
Bay Shore Yacht Club, yearbook 1983 on the 100th Anniversary Year
Westbrook Golf Club, yearbook 1896
Southward Ho Country Club, a brief history from the club brochure

REFERENCE WORKS

National Cyclopedia of American Biography
Who Was Who in America

MAGAZINES, PAMPHLETS, AND PAPERS

Harper's New Monthly Magazine
Long Island Forum (founded in 1938 by Paul Bailey)
The Old Oakdale History, privately printed by the William K. Vanderbilt Historical Society of Dowling College, Oakdale, Long Island Volume 1, 1983, Volume 2, 1993
"Picturesque Bay Shore, Babylon and Islip," New York: Mercantile Illustrating Co., 1894
Carl A. Starace, "Brookwood Hall"
Carl A. Starace, a paper read before the Old South Islip Civic Association, Sept. 28, 1988
George L. Weeks Jr., "Sagtikos Manor," a history
George Roussos, "Bayard Cutting Arboretum History"
St. Nicholas Church, Islip, Northamptonshire, England, the Parish Leaflet, April 1988
Judith Spinzia, "A Brief History of St. Mark's Church, Islip"
St. Mark's Church, Vestry minutes
Henry R. Bang, "The Story of the Fire Island Light," 1988
War Records of the Town of Islip, "The Air Station at Bay Shore, 1920"
Prospectus of Homes for sale on Bayberry Point, "Moorish Houses at Bayberry Point, Islip, Long Island, Built for Mr. H. O. Havemeyer," circa 1900
Steven Bedford, "The Long Island Country House, 1870–1930," for the Parrish Art Museum, Southampton, Long Island, 1988
Richard Guy Wilson, "Picturesque Ambiguities: The Country House Tradition in America" for the Parrish Art Museum, 1988
Albert Hanford Sr., "History of the Islips," an unpublished memoir, 1928
Ship building and tonnage on Long Island, 1885

Horace Havemeyer, sailing logs: 1932–1956, unpublished papers
Doris Dick Havemeyer, memoirs of a lifetime, 1890–1976 unpublished papers

NEWSPAPERS

Suffolk County

South Side Signal, Babylon, established in 1869
Bay Shore Journal, Bay Shore, established in 1873–74
Babylon Budget, Babylon, established in 1876 merged into *South Side Signal* in 1889
Suffolk County News, Sayville, established in 1884
Islip Herald, Islip, established in 1900
Islip Press, Islip
Fire Island Light, published by the Fire Island Light Preservation Society

Others

New York Herald
New York Tribune
New York Times
New York World
New York Herald Tribune
Brooklyn Eagle

ATLASES AND MAPS

Map of Northamptonshire, England, by John Speede, 1610
Suffolk County: Map of 1858, 4 sheets
Atlas of Long Island, New York, by Frederick W. Beers & Co., 1873
Atlas of Babylon, Bay Shore, and Islip by Wendelken & Co., 1888
Map of Winganhauppauge Neck, by Eugene R. Smith Co., 1887–88
Map of Long Island, by Hyde & Co., 1896

Atlas of Suffolk County, by E. Belcher Hyde, 1902
Map of Long Island, by Hyde & Co., 1906
Atlas of Suffolk County, by E. Belcher Hyde, 1915
Atlas of Suffolk County, by Dolph & Stewart, 1929
Atlas of Suffolk County, by E. Belcher Hyde, 1931
Atlas of Suffolk County, by Hagstrom, 1941
Atlas of Suffolk County, by Hagstrom, 1944
Maps of Bay Shore and Islip, by Sanborn Map Co., 1886, 1890,
    1897, 1902, 1909

INDEX

A

Abbott, Selah, 106
Abraham, Abraham, 269, 270, 271
Abraham, Florence (Mrs. Edward
  C. Blum), 269, 270-71, 272
Ackerson, Henry Ward (son of
  T.B. Ackerson), 287
Ackerson, H. Ward (grandson of T.
  B. Ackerson), xiv, 287, 366
Ackerson, T. B., 104, 287
  and Brightwaters development,
  258, 283-87, 329, 428
Actors' retirement home,
  established by Williams, 315
Adaline (sloop), 232-33, 333, 402
Adams, Charles Francis, 343
Adams, Dunbar Jr. 288
Adams, Florence (Mrs. George A.
  Ellis Jr.), 288, 291, 380
Adams, George J., 288
Adams, John Dunbar, 198, 205,
  287, 288, 289-90
Adams, Louis R., 288
Adams, Martha Dunbar (Mrs.
  Thomas Adams), 287
Adams, Susan Burchell, 287
Adams, Thomas, 287-88
Adams, Thomas Jr., 205, 287, 288,
  290-91, 311, 312
Addie V (yacht), 76
Adelphi University, 352
Admiralty, the, 428
Afterglow (Gibb house), 173, 175,
  274, 309-10, 315-16
Age of the Industrial Titans, ix
Airplane engines, Lawrance's
  contributions to, 330

Airport, Islip, 380
Alexandré, Helen (Mrs. Bayard C.
  Hoppin), 306, 352, 377, 380
Alison, C. Hugh, 357
Allen Winden Farm (Dick country
  place), 177, 408, 410
Altman, Benjamin, 270
America (schooner), 72n
American House, Babylon, 19-20
America's Cup, 72n, 75, 164-66,
  167-70, 194-95, 205-7, 223, 343-
  44, 368
Andrews, Mrs. Loring, 369
Andrews, William, 258n
Andrews, William Loring, 258,
  258n, 429
Angela Lane, 418
Anita (yacht), 293
Anning, Elizabeth, 18
Anti-Semitism, of resort hotels, 97
Ardmore (Adams home), 291
Argyle Hotel, 84, 95-96, 97-99, 429
Argyle Park, 99
Armory, the (Havemeyer villa), 84
  and Argyle Hotel, 98
  and planned Cedar Island estate,
  336
Arnold, Alexander Duncan
  Cameron, 253, 254, 302
Arnold, Annie Cameron (Mrs.
  William Arnold), 253, 254
Arnold, Edward W. C., 253, 254,
  323, 369
Arnold, Evelyn Hollins Nicholas
  (Mrs. A. Duncan Cameron
  Arnold), 254
Arnold, Richard, 54-55, 178, 253

Arnold, William, 54, 178, 253
Arnold family, 178
Arrow (yacht), 275, 333-34
Artemis (steam yacht), 194, 195, 240
Arteseros, Sally, xiv
Arthur, Chester A., 84
Ash, Charles F., 371
Ashford (settlement), 12
Astaire, Astele, 378
Astaire, Fred, 378, 378n
Astaire, Phyllis Potter, 378n
Asten, Thomas B., 76, 78, 80, 100, 308
Aston, W.K., 189, 190, 190n
Astor, Ava Willing (Mrs. John Jacob Astor IV), 329n
Astor, Caroline (daughter of Mrs. William B. Astor; later Mrs. Orme Wilson), 263
Astor, John Jacob, x, 131, 132
Astor, John Jacob IV, 329n, 409-10
Astor, John Jacob V, 410
Astor, Madeleine Force (Mrs. John Jacob Astor IV: later Mrs. William K. Dick), 377, 409-10
Astor, Vincent, 409
Astors, "the"
William B. Astor, 36, 36n
Mrs. William B. Astor (Caroline Schermerhorn), 36, 36n, 65, 92, 140n, 193, 202, 211, 214, 263
and conspicuous arrivistes, 91-92
and "the 400," 36n, 171, 202
and Newport, 211, 263
Atalanta (yacht), 73, 164
Atlantic (schooner), 301
Atterbury, Grosvenor, 227
Atwater, W. & J., 398
Atwood, Elizabeth, 374
Atwood, Frederick L., 374
Atwood, Kimball Chase Jr., 373, 374, 404
Auchincloss, Louis, x, 91, 122, 186
Audubon Society, 425

Automobile, of Taylor, 134
Awixa (sloop), 78
Awixa Avenue, 90, 171-72, 258, 292, 426
Awixa Creek, xii, 101-2, 103, 269, 274, 332, 340
Awixa Lawn (Knapp house), 107, 109, 110, 117, 124, 302, 303, 303-4

B

Babylon, xi, 429
New York Herald on (1890), 181
Babylon Cemetery, xiii, 180
Babylon Yacht Club, 240, 342, 418
Baird, Isabella, 335
Baird, Matthew, 335
Baker, William T., 387
Baldwin, Richard P., xiv
Ballard, Mrs. (sister of Emma Bourne), 194
Balsan, Consuelo Vanderbilt. *See* Vanderbilt, Consuelo
Balsan, Jacques, 221, 222
Banks, Charles, 81-82, 85
Barbash, Maurice, 429
Barclay, Ann, 119
Barclay, Henry, 119
Bar Harbor, 266
Barnard, Mary A., 252
Barnum, P. T., 61
Barr, Charles, 195, 206n, 343
Barren Island, 32, 32n
Barrett, Nathan F., 230, 238
Baruch, Bernard, 293
Bayard, Elise Justine, 137
Bayard, Nicholas, 136
Bayard, Robert, 136, 138
Bayard, Mrs. Robert, 136
Bayard, Mrs. Samuel, 136
Bayard Cutting Arboretum, 150, 424
Bayberry Beach and Tennis Club, 387, 426
Bayberry Point, 177, 224, 346, 426
Bayberry Point community, 225-31, 334, 385, 386-88, 425-26

Hutton's rent in, 293
Bayport, xi
Bay Shore, 25, 180, 423
  Dominy House (second) in, 30
  expansion of, 48-49
  and Huttons, 292
  vs. Islip hospitality, 292
  Naval Air Station in, 321-22, 325, 331
  New York Herald on (1890), 181
Bay Shore-Brightwaters Public Library, xiii
Bay Shore Golf CLub, 204, 204n
Bay Shore Horse Show, 245-46, 275, 316
Bay Shore Journal, xii-xiii
Bay Shore Manor, 278
Bay Shore Polo Association, 247
Bay Shore Yacht Club, 79, 233, 342, 418
Bayview Avenue, 115
Beach(es) for Town of Islip, 231-32, 385
Beech Road, 386
Beekman, William, 201, 201n
Bellport Yacht Club, 240, 342
Belmont, Alice De Goicouria (Mrs. August Belmont III, later Mrs. J. D. Wing), 299, 300, 302, 303, 304, 306, 406
Belmont, Alva Smith Vanderbilt. *See* Vanderbilt, Alva Smith
Belmont, August, 40-42, 131, 184, 298
  and Coaching Club, 64
  and horse racing, 39, 42-44, 58, 120, 245
  in South Side Sportsmen's Club, 47-48
Belmont, August Jr. or II (son), 41, 44, 195, 298, 303
Belmont, August Jr. or III (grandson), 276n, 294, 298-300, 303, 306, 324
  as college pal, 378n
  death of, 343
  and yachting, 302

Belmont, August IV (great-grandson), 299, 303-304, 304n
Belmont, Bessie Morgan, 299
Belmont, Caroline Perry (Mrs. August Belmont), 41
Belmont, Eleanor Robson (second Mrs. August Belmont Jr.), 298
Belmont, Elizabeth Morgan (Mrs. August Belmont Jr.), 298
Belmont, Oliver H. P., 41, 126, 213, 216-17
Belmont, Perry, 41-42, 44, 251
Belmont Lake State Park, 44, 363
Belmont Park track, 44, 298
Bennett, James Gordon Jr.
  and polo, 246
  and yacht race, 57-58
Bergen estate, 85
Berlin, Irving, 324
Bernet, Otto, 319n
Berry, James (Captain), 72, 75, 166, 169
Birdsall, Charles, 204
Bird shooting
  and Belmont, 42
  and Hollins, 115
  and Knapp, 108
  and winter holidays, 125
Blacks, and Ku Klux Klan, 346-47
Black Thursday, 384
Black Tuesday, 384
Bloomingdale, Lyman G., 270
Blum, Alice, 271
Blum, Edward C., 246, 269-71, 272, 276n
  and horse show association, 246
  Olympic Club land bought by, 309, 332, 335
  and Red Cross, 324
Blum, Florence Abraham, 269, 270-71, 272
Blum, Robert E., 271
Boating. *See* Yachting
Bodley, Frederick William, 134
Bohemia (Long Island commmunity), 140

Bonita (steam yacht), 25, 28
Boorman, James, 46
Bossert, Charles V., 364n
Bossert, Harriet (Hattie), 244
Bossert, John, 364n, 365
Bossert, Louis, 243-45, 285, 291, 364, 369
Bossert, Philippine Krippendorf, 244, 364n
Bourne, Arthur, 197, 247
Bourne, Emma Keeler, 191, 193, 196
Bourne, Florence, 197
Bourne, Frederick Gilbert, 123, 190-91, 195-97
   death of, 343
   descendants of, 420
   Hopkins barn for, 339
   as horse show winner, 246
   and Indian Neck hall, 191-94, 352
   town assessment of, 242, 318n
   in Westbrook Golf Club, 147
   and yachting, 194-95, 240
Bourne, George Washington, 191
Bourne, Harriet Gilbert, 191
Bourne family, 48, 352-53, 353n
Bourne home, 332
Bradford, Alexander W., 355
Bradish, Captain, 23
Bradish Lane, 428
Bramm, Marie Louise, 173
Breese, Anna, 130
Breese, Augusta Eloise Lawrence (Mrs. J. Salisbury Breese), 127, 130
Breese, Eloise, 130
Breese, J. Salisbury, 127
Breese, Mary Parsons (Mrs. William L. Breese), 129-30
Breese, Sidney, 127
Breese, William L., 127-28, 129-30, 354, 355
Breteuil, Marquis de, 208, 208n
Breukelen, 13
Brewster, Harry M., 234, 333, 342, 402

Brewster, Nathaniel, 13
Brewster, Roy, 342
Brewster, William, 13
Bridges, Rev. H. L., 203, 216
Brightwaters (Phelps estate), 258, 283-87, 329, 331, 428
Britannia (yacht), 169, 170
Brookhaven, founding of, 12
Brookhurst (Ceballos house), 262
Brooklyn, 171
   Bergen Beach in, 312-13
   South Shore summer residents from, 171-73, 204-5, 245
Brooklyn Historical Society, xiii
Brookwood Hall (Knapp/Thorne house), 249, 250, 403, 404, 419, 425
Brown, George S., 317
Brown, Warren C., 76
Buell, John H., 161
Bull, Henry Worthington, 160, 317, 377, 378n
Bull, Maud Maria Livingston, 159n, 160, 212n, 317, 377, 378n
Burden, Mr. and Mrs. James A., 381
Burgess, Edward, 165, 166
Burgess, W. Starling, 368n
Burr, Caroline (Mrs. Harry K. Knapp), 248-50, 406
Burton, Anna, 62, 63
Bushwick, 13
Byrd, Richard, and Lawrance engines, 330

C

Calhoun, John C., statue of, 30, 31
Cameron, Alexander Duncan, 253, 254
Cameron, Annie (Mrs. William Arnold), 253, 254
Cameron, Edward M., 253-54
Cameron, Edward William, 253, 254
Campbell, Frank E., 401

Campbell, Polly (Mrs. Adolph
    Dick), 411
Camp Damm, 324, 327
Canfield, Richard, 310
Captree Bridge, 430
Captree Island, 20, 430
Captree Island Boat Basin, 83
Carabus Island, 333, 333n, 336,
    336n
Carlisle, Allan P., 319
Carlisle, Jay F., 306, 315-18
    Bull land sold to, 160
    and Great River (Timber Point)
        Club, 356, 357
    in horse shows, 246, 275
    house of, 418
    as Islip Polo Club governor, 276,
        276n
    and partying, 374
    and Rosemary, 318-19, 377
    and Southside Hospital, 349,
        350, 351
    and Stock Market Crash, 385
Carlisle, Jay F. Jr., 319
Carlisle, Lewis G., 319
Carlisle, Mary Pinkerton (Mrs. Jay
    F. Carlisle), 273, 275, 306, 315,
    316-18, 349, 350, 374
Carll, Annie, 253
Carll, Timothy, 18, 255
Carnegie, Andrew, 161-62
Carpen, Pearl, 283
Carroll, Alfred L., 198
Carroll, Lucy Johnson (Mrs. Alfred
    L. Carroll), 197, 198, 289, 412
Carroll, Ruth (Mrs. H. Cecil
    Sharp), 412-13
Casino(s), 98, 240
    at Bergen Beach, 313
    in Brightwaters, 286, 428
    of Canfield, 310
    near Yacht Club, 240
Castle, Irene, 376
Castle in Oakdale, 188-89
Cathedral of St. John the Divine,
    139, 196, 371

Catlin, Danny, 402
Ceballos, Juan Jr., 262, 276n
Ceballos, Juan Manuel, 200-201,
    260-62, 306
Ceballos, Lulu Washington, 262
Cedarholme, 277
Cedar (Carabus or East) Island,
    333, 333n, 336, 336n
Cedar Island gut, 414, 415
Cemeteries, gravestones as
    information in, xiii
Chahal, Christina, xiv
Chain Pier, Brighton, England, 86-
    87, 87n
Champlin's Creek, 68, 102, 157, 374
Champlin's Pond, 317
Chaplin, Charlie, 378, 379
Charles I (king of England), 5, 7
Charles II (king of England), 7
Charlestown, Massachusetts, 6
Charlick, Oliver, 88
Chautauqua assembly, at Point
    O'Woods, 268, 268n
Cholera epidemic, 182, 271
Christ Church, West Islip, 54, 179,
    180, 252, 429
Chuckle (Star boat), 399
Churches
    Cathedral of St. John the Divine,
        139, 196, 371
    Catholic, 280
    Christ Church in West Islip, 54,
        179, 180, 252, 429
    Church of the Ascension in New
        York City, 46
    Church of the Heavenly Rest in
        New York City, 106
    Church of the Incarnation in
        New York City, 196, 334
    Church of the Transfiguration in
        New York, 252
    Emmanuel in Great River, 62,
        139-40, 150, 196, 424
    Episcopal, x-xi, 151
    First Reformed in Sayville, 358
    and flu epidemic, 327

Grace Episcopal in New York
City, 41, 203n
Holy Family Ukrainian Catholic,
429
Islip Presbyterian, 71
Methodist Church between Bay
Shore and Islip, 19, 26n
St. Ann's in Sayville, xi, 140, 196
St. George's in New York, 140
St. John's in Oakdale, 19, 26, 196
St. Mark's in Islip, 26, 37, 111-12,
113, 151, 158, 425 (*see also* St.
Mark's Church)
St. Nicholas in Islip, England, 1, 4
St. Peter's in Bay Shore, 370, 428
St. Thomas's in New York City,
54, 215, 222, 293
Trinity Parish or Church in New
York City, 70, 196, 249
Churchill, Albert Edward William
John, 217
Churchill, Jennie, 209, 210, 217, 219
Churchill, Lord Randolph, 209,
211, 217
Churchill, Winston, 209, 217, 219,
221, 222
City and Suburban Homes
Company, 139n
Clark, Alfred Corning, 191
Clark, Susie, 267
Clason Point Military Academy, 353n
Cleveland, Grover, 88, 103
Clinton, Charles, 405
Clinton, Sir Henry, 255
Clinton Avenue, 48, 178
Clock (Awixa area landowner), 289
Clock, Hallet, 48
Clock, Henry C., 167
Clock, Nathaniel, 48, 73, 75, 77,
77n, 164, 164n
Clock, Warren, 72
Close, Marjorie Merriweather
Post, 294
Clovelly (Arnold home), 254
Club (yacht), 79
Club, the, 426, 429

Clyde, William P., 179
Coaching, sport of, 63-64, 121
Coaching Club of New York, 63-64,
65
Coe, James W., 26
Coffin, Henry Sloane, 369
Coffin, R. F., 78
Colonia (steam yacht), 194
Colonia (yacht), 170
Colt, Adelaide, 35
Colt, Amy (Mrs. Cornelius DuBois
Wagstaff), 35, 252
Colt, Robert Oliver, 34-35, 178,
205, 288
Colt family, 178
Columbia (yacht), 195
Comet (schooner), 76, 77n
Commodore (yacht), 76
Coney Island, and Fire Island
Beach fears, 271
Conklin (Deer Range Farm
owners), 60
Connetquot (side wheeler), 268
Connetquot River, 46-47, 56
Connor, Dennis, 206n
Connor, Virginia (Mrs. William K.
Dick), 410-11
Connor, William C., 81
Conover, Augustus W., 105
Conover, Catherine Whitlock (Mrs.
Daniel D. Conover), 104, 105
Conover, Daniel D., 80, 99-105, 224
Lucy Carroll cottage purchased
from, 198
house of, 101, 173, 201, 295, 412-13
Moffitt's purchase from estate
of, 279
Oakwood Driving Park land
purchased from, 245
Conover, Kate, 104, 105
Constable, James, 54
Constitution (yacht), 194-95
Corbin, Austin, 84, 90, 92-96, 97-98,
99, 105, 429
Corbin family, 48
Corey, Albert B., 255

Corinthia (yacht), 236-37, 240
Cornbury, Lord, 18
Cornell (architect), 238
Corning, Erastus, 85
Coronet (schooner), 244
Corry, George A. ("Pop"), 397, 398
Corry Cup, 398, 401
Corsair (steam yacht), 74
Corsair III (steam yacht), 194, 236
Country homes, 123-24
  life in, 124-25
Covert, Cornelia, 264
Crandell, Mary Helen, 106
Creamer, Frank D., 335
Creekside, 250, 377, 407
Cressida (schooner), 411
Cromwell, Oliver, 7
Cromwell Bay, 12
Crothers, Gordon, 408
Crothers, Marie Johnson Russell, 408
Currier & Ives, 391-92, 393-95
Curzon, George, 218, 218n
Curzon, Mary Leiter, 218, 218n
Cutting (family), 48, 292
Cutting, Bronson, 141, 149
Cutting, Elise Justine Bayard (Mrs.
  Fulton Cutting), 137
Cutting, Fulton, 137, 158
Cutting, Helen (Mrs. Lucius
  Wilmerding), 156-57
Cutting, Helen Suydam (Mrs.
  Robert Fulton Cutting), 140, 141,
  146, 158, 203
Cutting, Iris, 138, 142-44, 146, 149
Cutting, Justine, 141, 144, 145
Cutting, Leonard, 136-37
Cutting, Olivia (daughter; later
  Mrs. Olivia James), 141, 149,
  150, 353, 424
Cutting, Olivia Murray (Mrs.
  William Bayard Cutting), 137,
  141, 146, 149-50, 197, 203
  and Cutting Arboretum, 424
  and Emmanuel Church, 140
  hospital donation from, 380
  and Adaline Elder Peters, 395

and Seaside Home, 126
and Westbrook, 353
Cutting, Robert Fulton, 136, 137,
  140-41, 146
  at Livingston-Hollins wedding, 203
  and model-house project, 139
  and St. Mark's, 185
  and Sugar Trust, 152, 153
Cutting, William, 137
Cutting, William Bayard, 60, 126-
  27, 136-46, 149, 150, 203
  and Bourne, 191
  death of, 306
  as estate builder, 197
  and golf, 146-48
  large mansion of, 190
  and St. Mark's, 185
  and Sugar Trust, 152, 153, 154-55
  town assessment on property of,
    318n
  and Westbrook Farms, 60, 126-
    27, 141-46, 148, 149, 150, 353
Cutting, William Bayard Jr., 141,
  145, 149
Cutting Arboretum, 150, 424

D

Damm, Henry J., 324
Dana, Mary, 311
Dana, Richard Henry Jr., 311
Dana, Richard T., 311
Daughters of Wisdom, 426
Davenport, John, 11, 258n
Davies, Alice Martin, 355
Davies, Julien T., 130, 354-55
Davies, Julien Jr., 355
Dawn (yacht), 236
Day, Joseph P., 353n
Deacon, Gladys, 221
Dead Horse Inlet, 32n
Dean, Hannah, 23
Dearwood (Pinkerton home), 273
De Coppet, Andre, 373-74
De Coppet, Diane, 373-74
De Coppet, Edward T., 373

De Coppet, Eileen Johnston (Mrs. Andre De Coppet), 373-74
De Coppet, Laura, 373-74
Deer Range Farm (Plumb estate), 25, 60-62, 63, 130, 134, 135, 204
Deer Range Park, 318n
Deer Range State Park, 361
Defender (yacht), 205-7
De Goicouria, Albert V., 150, 163n, 299
De Goicouria, Alice W. (Mrs. August Belmont III), 299, 300, 302, 303, 306, 406
De Goicouria, Rosalie, 299
Delafield, Mrs. Richard, 126
Delaware (steam yacht), 194
Delmonicos, 92, 203
Demarest family, 13
Department of Interior Fish and Wildlife Service, Islip property of, 425
Depew, Chauncey M., 186-87
Depression. See Great Depression
Dewey, George, 193
Dick, Adolph M., 380, 408, 410-11
Dick, Anna Vagts (Mrs. William Dick), 176, 177, 264
Dick, Anna (daughter; later Mrs. J. Adolph Mollenhauer), 176, 235, 238-39, 239n, 409
Dick, Direxa, 411
Dick, Doris (Mrs. Horace Havemeyer), 305, 334, 360, 408, 410, 419
Dick, John Henry, 176, 177, 264, 408, 409, 410
Dick, Julia (Mrs. Kingsland Macy), 204, 360, 387n, 408, 410
Dick, Julia T. Mollenhauer (Mrs. John Henry Dick), 177, 264, 408
Dick, Madeleine Force Astor (Mrs. William K. Dick), 377, 409-10
Dick, Polly Campbell (Mrs. Adolph Dick), 411
Dick, Virginia Connor (second Mrs. William K. Dick), 410-11
Dick, Will (son of William K.), 411

Dick, William, 172, 173, 174, 175-77, 234-35, 408
  death of, 305
  descendants of, 420
  Vivian work for, 226
Dick, William K., 408-10, 411
  as Carlisle pall bearer, 318
  and Great River (Timber Point) Club, 356, 357
  hospital support from, 380
  as Islip Polo Club governor, 276n
  and Islip Yacht Club, 300
  and partying, 377
Dick family, 260
Dickerson (butcher), 108
Dickey, Charles D., 263
Dickey, Charles D. Jr., 263
Dickey, Louise L. Whitney, 263
Dickey, Mary, 263
Dickey, Mary Witherspoon, 263
Dillon, J. Allen, 304
Divorce, 66, 132, 214
Dix, Margaret (Mrs. Charles L. Lawrance), 305, 320, 329, 374
Dix, Morgan, 329
Dodds, Irene, 297
Domestic servants
  immigration law restricts, 353
  World War II effect on, 419
Dominick, William F., 369
Dominy, Felix, 27
Dominy, Phebe, 27, 30
Dominy House, 27, 49
Dominy House (second), 30, 75, 81
Dongan (Governor), 16
Doris (yacht), 400
Dowling College, 223, 352, 424
Doxsee, Charles O., 386
Doxsee, Gifford B., xiv
Doxsee, James Harvey, 51, 172, 279, 306
Doxsee, John C., 271
Doxsee's Creek, 172, 274, 274n. *See also* Orowoc Creek
Doxsee's Lane, 172
Draco (Star boat), 398

Draco II (Star boat), 399n, 401
Dragon (yacht), 400
Draper, Ruth Carroll (later Mrs. H.
 Cecil Sharp), 412-13
DuBois, Sarah Platt (Mrs. Alfred
 Wagstaff the elder), 34, 250, 252
Duchess of Marlborough. *See*
 Vanderbilt, Consuelo
Duer, Katherine (Mrs. Clarence
 Mackay), 381
Duke of Argyll, 96
Duke of Magenta (race horse), 59
"Duke's Laws," 14
Dunbar, Martha, 287
Dunewood community, 429
Dunn, Willie Jr., 147
Dunne, James A., 362-63
Dunraven, Earl of, 205, 206
Dutch Fete, 350
Duval, Ann Gordon, 152, 156
Duval, Betsy, 378
Duval, Henry Rieman, 150, 151-52,
 156, 260
 at Hollis-Livingston wedding, 203
 and Pavilion sale, 183
 and Sugar Trust, 152-56
Duval, Rieman, 156

E

Earhart, Amelia
 at airport dedication, 380
 and Lawrance engines, 330
Earle, Joseph, 72
East Hampton
 as competitor, 266
 founding of, 12
East Island (Carabus or Cedar
 Island), 333, 333n, 336, 336n
East Islip, xii
 resort hotel in, xi, 64 (*see also*
 Pavilion Hotel)
Eaton, Theophilus, 11
Edward IV (King of England), 4
Edward VII (King of England), 195,
 265. *See also* Prince of Wales

Edwardian era, 265, 266, 306
Effingham Park, 179
Effingham Pond, 179
Elder, Adaline (Mrs. Samuel T.
 Peters), 126, 162-63, 164, 388-89,
 395, 397
Elder, George W., 163, 397
Elder, George Waldron (son), 397
Elder, Louisine (Mrs. Henry O.
 Havemeyer), 98, 163-64, 232,
 292, 389, 397
Elder Road, 386
Electra (sloop), 232, 232n, 275,
 293, 302, 333
Elizabeth (bark), 30-31, 79
Ellenwood (Wood home), 116
Ellis, Florence Adams (Mrs.
 George A. Ellis Jr.), 288, 291, 380
Ellis, George A. Jr., 291-92
 and Adams, 205, 288
 as Islip Polo Club governor, 276n
 descendants of, 420
 and Hutton, 293
 and Southside Hospital, 349, 380
 in Timber Point Club, 357
Ellsworth (yacht captain), 76
Emmanuel Church, Great River,
 62, 139-40, 150, 196, 424
Enfin (Johnson/Lovering house),
 406, 406n
English Civil War, 7
Enterprise (yacht), 223n, 368
Episcopal church, x-xi
 and Cutting brothers, 139-41, 150
 Islip residents in, 151
 See also Churches; St. Mark's
 Church
Etchells, E. W. "Skip," 402
Etchells, Mary, 402
European nobility, American
 brides of, 130, 207-11, 217
European travel, 207-8
Everdell, Rosalind, 387
Eyre, Beverley M., 387n
Eyre, Mary W., 387n

F

Fairchild, Julian D., 274, 311, 314n
Fanny (sloop), 71-74, 76, 167
Farmingdale, 21
Far Rockaway, 22
Fashion parade in New York City, 54
Ficken, H. Edward, 188
Field, William, 95
Finch, Anna, 55
Fink, Ed, 368
Fire(s), 117, 183-84
    and fire departments, 117
    forest fires, 184
    hydrants as safeguard against, 286
    Idlehour destroyed by, 219
    Johnson home destroyed by, 199-200
    Linwood Hotel destroyed by, 307
    on Main Street (1900), 266-67
    on Main Street (1905), 267
    at Pavilion Hotel, 182-83
    Pinkerton yacht destroyed by, 275
    Prospect House destroyed by, 267
    in resort hotels, 96
    Vivian's dredge destroyed by, 226-27
    and water supply, 117-18, 182-83, 183, 199
    in Wood home, 116-17
    Woodlea destroyed by, 290
Fire Island, 53, 429
    and gales, 83
    and hurricanes, 82, 414, 415-17
    Moses plan for roadway on, 363, 430
    as National Seashore, 431
    and 1918 winter freezing, 326
    resort hotels on, xi, 81
        Dominy House, 27, 30, 75, 81
        Surf Hotel, 28 (*see also* Surf Hotel)
    and sailing, 75
Fire Island Beach, 28
Fire Island Country Club, 84, 430
Fire Island Inlet, 415, 430

Fire Island lighthouse, first, 20, 27, 30-31
Fire Island lighthouse, second, 28, 31, 430-31
Fire Island Lighthouse Preservation Society, 430
Fire Island State Park, 182, 271-72, 361, 430
First Patriarchs of 1872, 36n
First Reformed Church, Sayville, 358
Fish, Mrs. Stuyvesant, 214
Fisher, Frances, 158
Fishing, 32-33, 69
    and Hollins, 115
    memories of, 421
    and Olympic Club, 32, 33-34
    and Thorne, 368
Fish and Wildlife Service, Islip property of, 425
Fitzgerald, F. Scott, 345
Five Islands (Fire Islands), 333n
Flagg, Ernest M., 192, 196, 227
Flatbush (town), 13
Flatlands (town), 13
Flight (yacht), 233, 275, 293, 333, 334
Flower, Roswell P., 182
Floyd, Charity, 16
Floyd, Nicoll, 415
Floyd, Richard, Sr., 16
Floyd, William, 16n
Flushing, Long Island, 6, 13
Force, Madeleine (Mrs. John Jacob Astor IV; later Mrs. William K. Dick), 377, 409-10
Forest fire, 184
Forest Hills, 264
Forrest Farm (Corbin estate), 93, 99
Fort Pond Bay deep-water port, proposal for, 94-95
"400, the," 36n, 171, 202
Four-in-hand driving, 63-64
Fox hunting, and Peters, 392
Frank, Emil, 274
Freeman, Henry R., 186
Frelinghuysen, Adaline Havemeyer, 232, 306, 337

Frelinghuysen, Peter H. B., 306, 337
"Frozen summer," 414n
Fuller, Margaret, 30-31
Fulton, Robert, 137

G

Gaiety (sailboat), 204
Gaillard, Aimee (Mrs. Bradish
    Johnson Jr.), 198-200, 405
Galatea (yacht), 164, 166
Galbraith, John Kenneth, x, 384
Gardiner, Abraham, 256
Gardiner, David, 255
Gardiner, Lion, 12
Gardiner, Mary (Mrs. Isaac
    Thompson), 255
Gardiner, Robert David Lion, 255, 428
Gardiner, Sarah, 255
Gardner, William, 300-301, 397
Garner, Florence, 209-10
Garner, Frances (Mrs. Francis
    Cooper Lawrance), 35, 78, 112,
    208, 328
Garner, Frances Thorn (Mrs.
    Thomas Garner Sr.), 35
Garner, Marcellite (wife of Henri
    Charles Joseph le Tonnelie,
    Marquis de Breteuil), 208-9
Garner, Thomas Jr., 35
Garner, Thomas Sr., 26, 34, 35, 77
Garner, William Thorn, 35, 77-78, 208
Garner family, 48, 105
Garner Lane, 35, 331
Garth, William H., 249, 314, 347, 406
Genesta (yacht), 164
George V (King of England), 382
Gerry, Elbridge T., 168
Gershwin, George, 376, 377, 378
Gibb, Andrew, 16
Gibb, Anna Pinkerton (Mrs. Lewis
    Mills Gibb), 273, 274, 277, 305-6,
    316, 349, 350
Gibb, Howard, 172, 173, 175, 200
Gibb, John, 173, 174-75, 226, 273,
    274, 305, 309

and Afterglow, 173, 175, 274,
    309, 315
Gibb, J. Richmond, 175
Gibb, Lewis Mills, 175, 274, 276-77,
    305-6, 316
Gibb, Lewis Mills Jr., 175, 277
Gibb, Robert Pinkerton, 277
Gibb, Walter, 175, 276
Gibb, William, 16
Gibbs (pirate), 32n
Gibson, Samuel B., 72, 75, 166
Gilded Age, ix-x, 91
    and Adams family, 287
    American ancestry as criterion
        in, 119
    and arrivistes, 91-92, 105
    and charity, 139
    Edwardian era, 265, 266
    end of, 306
    and life in country homes, 124
    and travel in Europe, 207-8
    and women's role, 212
Gilgo Inlet, 333
Ginty (sloop), 195
Girdner, Adela, 374
Glaenzer, Jules, 378, 379
Gloriana (yacht), 170
Gold Coast on North Shore, 342-
    43, 345
Golf, 146-48, 204-5
    1920s expansion of, 354
    and Southward Ho Club, 364-66
    Timber Point (Great River) Club
        organized, 355-58
Good Samaritan Hospital, 429
Gordon, Anne, 152, 156
Gordon-Cumming, Florence
    Garner, 209-10
Gordon-Cumming, Sir William,
    209-10
Gould, Jay, 129
Grace Episcopal Church, New
    York City, 41, 203n
Gracie (sloop), 72, 73-74, 167
Graham, Arthur Butler, 349, 351

Graham, George S. ("Judge"), 282n, 340-41, 355, 357, 373
  house of, 418
Grant, U.S., 48
Great Depression, 383, 383-84
  boom mentality ended by, 354
  building halted by, 407, 413, 417
  Thorne's surviving of, 367-68
Great Gatsby, The (Fitzgerald), 345 Great River, 135-36
Great River Cemetery, xiii
Great River Club, 355-56
Great South Bay, x-xi, 53
  decline of as summer resort, 342-43
  end of age for, 421
  fishing on, 32-33
  freezing of (1918), 326
  and hurricane(s), 414-17
  landmarks on, 31
  New York Herald on (1890), 181
  oyster harvesting in, 20
  as preferred summer spot, 68
  resort hotels in, 22, 27 (*see also* Resort hotels)
  rum-running on, 345-46
  Sammis on attractions of, 28
  shipbuilding on, 21
  waterfront land on, 53-54, 173-74, 192
Great South Bay area, early immigrants in, 6-7
Great South Bay race week regattas, 358
Great South Bay scooter, 276n
Great South Bay Yacht Club, 79, 173, 233
Great South Bay Yacht Racing Association, 240-41, 302, 341
Great War (World War I)
  America's entry in, 323-24
  and cold 1918 winter, 325-26
  description of battlefield in (Parsons), 324-25
  as end of Gilded Age, 306
  and influenza epidemic, 326-28

life at beginning of, 320-21
  and military uniforms at wedding, 406
  and Naval Air Station, 321-22, 325, 331
  Soldiers and Sailors Memorial Building for veterans of, 239, 342
Green, Isaac H. Jr., 66, 107n, 140, 144, 177, 185, 200, 374, 424
Green, Warren, 338n
Greenport, 21
Greenwood Cemetery, xiii, 196
Greer, David, 196
Gribble, Henry, 251
Gribble, Mary DuBois, 251
Griffiths, Arthur G. ("Griff"), 148
Growler (boat), 49n
Growler Club, 49n
Guastavino, Louise (Mrs. Frank Gulden Jr.), 372
Guastavino, Rafael, 371-72, 398
Gulden, Charles C., 178, 386, 420
Gulden, Frank, 386
Gulden, Frank Jr., 372, 386
Gulden, Louise Guastavino, 372
Gull (yacht), 400
Gull I (yacht), 401
Gunning. *See* Bird shooting
Gunther, William H., 177-78
Gussum (fishing boat), 259, 260, 403

H

Haff, Adelaide Lake (Mrs. Henry C. Haff), 171, 207
Haff, Bert (Albert C.), 72, 75-76
Haff, Harry P., 301
Haff, Henry C. (father), 166
Haff, Henry C. (Hank), 72, 76, 164, 166-67, 170-71, 402
  and America's Cup challenges, 75, 168-69, 170, 206-7
  and Currier & Ives print, 393n
  death of, 306
  and Prince, 72, 74
  as professional, 343
  telephone line to, 71

Haight, Charles Coolidge, 142, 227
Hallock, Marion Wharton, 158
Halstead, Harold, 398, 399, 400, 401
Harbeck, Charles T., 46, 150, 157-
    53, 183, 198, 312
Hard, Anson Wales, 197, 378n
Hard, Florence Bourne, 197
Hard, Hildegarde (Babs)
    Stevenson, xiv
Harriman, Edward H., 243
Harriman, W. Averell, 329n
Hart, Charles M., 342
Hart, Lorenz, 376
Hart, William F. S., 276n
Hart and Shape (architects), 357-58
Harvard Gang of Islip, 377-78
Havemeyer, Adaline (Mrs. Peter H.
    B. Frelinghuysen), 232, 306, 337
Havemeyer, Adaline (Mrs. Richard
    S. Perkins), 387, 420
Havemeyer, Camilla Moss (Mrs.
    Charles F. Havemeyer), 203-4
Havemeyer, Charles F. (Carley), 203-4
Havemeyer, Charles F. (son), 204
Havemeyer, Doris Dick (Mrs.
    Horace Havemeyer), 305, 334,
    360, 408, 410, 419
Havemeyer, Electra (Mrs. J.
    Watson Webb), 163, 232
Havemeyer, Eugenie (Mrs. Harry
    Havemeyer), 426
Havemeyer, Harry W. (son of
    Horace Havemeyer), 401, 419,
    420, 426
Havemeyer, Hector, 86, 89
Havemeyer, Henry, 83-89, 336
Havemeyer, Henry Osborne, 89,
    94, 104, 163, 389
    Argyle cottage rented by, 98
    and Bayberry Point community
    ("Modern Venice"), 224-31,
    293, 385
    Carabus Island owned by, 333,
    333n
    death of, 305
    descendants of, 420

and public beach, 231
residence of, 142
and sugar in Cuba, 261
and Sugar Trust, 94, 152-53, 154-
    55, 156, 176, 225
and yachting, 232-33, 275
Havemeyer, Horace, 232, 305, 309,
    333-35
    and Bayberry Point, 385, 386-88
    and Great River (Timber Point)
    Club, 355, 356, 357, 358
    home of leveled, 419-20
    and Macy, 360
    and Olympic Point, 331-32, 335-40
    and Penataquit Point, 372-73
    and Adaline Elder Peters, 395
    on polo team, 247, 294
    as Polo Club governor, 276n
    and public beach, 385-86
    and South Bay Golf Club, 418
    and Southward Ho Club, 366
    and Taylor property, 361, 362
    town assessment on property of,
    318
    and Weld, 412
    and yachting, 233, 275, 300, 333-34
    Star boat sailing, 399-402
Havemeyer, Horace Jr., 335, 387,
    398, 400, 401
Havemeyer, Louisine Elder (Mrs.
    Henry Osborne Havemeyer), 98,
    163-64, 232, 292, 389, 397
Havemeyer, Mary Jennie Moller
    (Mrs. Henry Havemeyer), 88, 89
Havemeyer, Theodore A., 147, 203,
    203n
Havemeyer, William, 86
Havemeyer, William F., 86, 122
Havemeyer, William M., 88
Havemeyer family, 260
Havemeyer's Point, 84, 336
Havens (yacht captain), 76
Hawkins, Bill, 107
Hawkins, Captain (farmer), 33
Hawkins, Captain (participant in
    Russell weddng), 406

Hawkins, William E., 357
Hawkins, Ebenezer, 20
Hawkins, Mary, 6
Hawkins, Robert, 6
Hawkins, Zachary, 6, 12
Hawkins family, 388
Hayward, Bill, 399
Hayward, Mr. and Mrs. Charles F., 275n
Head, Mrs. Betsy (common law wife of George Taylor), 132, 134, 135, 306
Head, Lena, 133, 134, 135
Heckscher, August, 362-63, 363n
Heckscher State Park, 363, 425
Heischmann, J. J., 245
Henderson, J., 76
Hendrickson, Edward, 236
Henrietta (yacht), 57
Henry V (King of England), 3
Henry VI (King of England), 3, 3-4
Henry VII (King of England), 4
Henry Stears (catboat), 78
Herreshoff, Francis, 301
Herreshoff, Nathaniel G., 162n, 165, 170, 195, 205, 232, 301, 343
Herrick, Elizabeth Mann, 249n
Hewlett School, 200, 419, 425
Hicksville, 21
Higgins, Henry Vincent, 130, 354
Highways (roads), poor condition of, 51, 103-4
Hildegard (yacht), 73
Hildegarde (powerboat), 386, 403
Hill, David B., 310
Hill, James J., 243
Hillwood (Hutton mansion), 295
Hitchcock, Tommy Jr., 247
Hollins, Alice (Mrs. Harry I. Nicholas), 180, 254
gravestone of, 429
Hollins, Evelina (1927 debutante), 378
Hollins, Evelina Meserole Knapp (Mrs. Harry B. Hollins), 112, 113, 114

Hollins, Gerald Vanderbilt, 114, 305, 306, 320, 322, 377, 425
Hollins, Harry B., 112-14, 319-20
and Breese, 127-28
college pals of, 378n
descendants of, 420
Middle Island owned by, 333, 333n, 430
and New York society, 116
and Parsons property, 120
and Pavilion sale, 183
public beach given by, 232
and Queens County Bank, 109
and St. Mark's, 185, 305
sporting interests of, 115
as Vanderbilt broker, 112, 129
as voluntary fire-department chief, 117
Hollins, Harry B. Jr., 114
as Carlisle pall bearer, 318
and Great River/Timber Point Club, 356, 357
home of, 320
and partying, 377
as Red Cross volunteer, 324
and Westbrook Golf Club, 147
and St. Mark's, 305
and yachting, 300
Hollins, John Knapp, 114
Hollins, Lilias Livingston (Mrs. Harry B. Hollins Jr.), 202, 202-3, 305, 377
Hollins, McKim, 114
Hollins, Marion, 114, 205, 428
Hollins, Virginia Kobbe (Mrs. Gerald V. Hollins), 306, 322, 377
Hollins family, 48, 292
Prince of Wales visits, 381
Hollister, Anne Willard Stephenson, 161
Hollister, Buell, 305, 350, 357, 377
Hollister, Buell Jr., 387n
Hollister, Henry Hutchinson, 150, 160-62, 200, 203, 246, 305
descendants of, 420
Hollister, John, 161

Hollister, Louise (Mrs. Langdon B. Valentine), 349, 350
Hollister, Louise "Tottie" (Mrs. Buell Hollister), 126, 377
Hollister, Sarah Louise Howell (Mrs. Henry H. Hollister), 161
Hollister family, 48, 292
Holmes, Carol, xiv
Holy Family Ukrainian Catholic Church, 429
Homeport (Mollenhauer mansion), 238, 426-27
Hone, Philip, 46
Hooker, Thomas, 55
Hopkins, Alfred, 239, 337, 339, 390, 409
Hoppin, Bayard Cushing, 306, 351-52, 359
　college pals of, 378n
　and Great River/Timber Point Club, 356, 357
　and partying, 377
　and Southside Hospital, 348, 349, 380
　and yachting, 358
Hoppin, Helen Alexandré (Mrs. Bayard C. Hoppin), 306, 352, 377, 380
Horan, Ruth A., 387n
Horseless carriage, of Taylor, 134
Horse racing, 39, 245
　and Belmont, 42-44, 58, 120, 245
　and Knapps, 45, 110, 120-21, 248
　and Lorillard, 58-59, 245
　and Parsons, 120-21
Horse shows (Bay Shore Horse Show), 245-46, 275, 316
Horton, Blanche (Mrs. Edward F. Hutton), 293, 294
Horton, Henry W., 293
Hospitals
　Good Samaritan, 429
　of Dr. King, 267-68, 348
　Southside, 294, 348-51, 378, 380, 423
Houseboat, of Taylor, 133-34

House design, by Conover, 101
Houses, country, 123-24
Howell, Buell, 161
Howell, Edward, 12
Howell, Elmer B., 365
Howell, Elmer W. (E.W.), 317, 365, 369, 386-87, 410, 419
Howell, George B., 185
Howell, Henry H. Jr., 161
Howell, Louise, 161
Howell, Ralph D. Jr., xiv, 317, 419
Howell, Sarah Louise (Mrs. Henry H. Hollister), 161
Howland, Gardiner G., 78
Hubbard, D. S., 108
Huber, Harriet (Hattie), 244-45
Huber, Max, 244-45
Hughes, Charles Evans, 243, 271
Hulse, William A., 348
Hundred Years War, 3
Hunt, Richard Howland, 219, 222, 227
Hunt, Richard Morris, 66, 111-12, 142, 219, 220n
Hunter, Adele, 78
Hunting. See Bird shooting
Huntington, Rev. Dr., 203
Huntington Township, 19
Hurricane(s), 82, 413-17
　of 1938, 413-14, 415-17
Hutschler, Walter Von, 400
Hutton, Barbara, 295-97, 412
Hutton, Blanche Horton (Mrs. Edward F. Hutton), 292, 293, 294
Hutton, Edna Woolworth (Mrs. Franklyn E. Hutton), 295-96
Hutton, Edward Francis, 231, 247, 275, 276n, 292-95, 297, 412
Hutton, Franklyn E., 231, 293, 295-96, 309, 332, 335, 412
Hutton, Halcourt, 294-95, 297
Hutton, Irene Dodds (Mrs. Franklyn E. Hutton), 297
Hutton, James L., 292
Hutton, Marjorie Merriweather Post (Mrs. Edward F. Hutton), 294-95, 297

Hutton, Nedenia (Dina Merrill), 297
Hutton, W. E., 293
Hyde, Anna Finch, 55
Hyde, Henry Baldwin, 54, 55-56,
    111, 185, 241-42
Hyde, Henry Hazen, 55
Hyde, James Hazen, 55, 242-43,
    364, 365, 369
Hyde, James R., 365
Hyde, Lillian, 205, 428
Hyde, Lucy Baldwin (Mrs. Henry
    Hazen), 55
Hyde, Richard, 146n, 204, 306, 317,
    318, 365
Hyde family, 48, 178

I

Idlehour (Vanderbilt mansion), 65,
    65n, 66-68, 145, 211, 424
    assessment on, 318n
    in Consuelo's memories, 211,
        213, 215, 219
    end of as private residence, 343
    as rebuilt, 219, 220, 222-23
        changing ownership of, 352
    and Vanderbilt divorce, 214
Improved Dwellings Association
    (New York City), 139, 139n
Income disparities, x
Indian Neck Hall, 190, 191-94, 197,
    219, 318n, 339, 343, 352-53, 353n
Industrial Age, 181
Industrial Revolution, ix, 265, 266
Influenza epidemic (1918), 326-28, 348
    and Blanche Hutton, 294
Ingraham, Fred, 371
Inherited wealth, Vanderbilt on, 220
Innes-Ker, Lord Alastair Robert, 130
Innocenti, Umberto, 370
Ireland, John Busteed, 179
Ireland, Robert Livingston, 179
Irene (sloop), 25
Iroquois (race horse), 59
Irvin, Mrs. Richard Jr., 126
Isbrandtsen, Hans, 365n
Iselin, Adrian, 401

Iselin, C. Oliver, 170, 205, 206
Islip, xi, xii
    bayfront land of, 114-15
    Belmont's effect on, 42
    character of
        in 1880-WWI period, 89-90, 92,
            180
        around 1900, 266
        at present, 423-29
    Conover's developments in, 102-3
    decline of as summer resort, 342-43
    and Doxsee clam industry, 50-51
    earlier years of, 19-21, 51
    earliest summer settlers in, 25-26
    first developers in, 25
    founding of, 9, 12
    gap between summer residents
        and townsfolk in, 185
    largest landholders in, 111
    New York Herald on (1890), 181
    and Nicoll family, 16
    original patentees of, 16-19
    population of
        from 1810 census, 19
        from 1870 census, 51
        1900-1910 increase in, 266
        1910-1915 decline in, 319n
        1920s increase in, 353
        present, 423
    public beach for (1906-1907),
        231-32
    public beach for (1924), 385
    real estate taxes in (post-WWII),
        420
    roads of, 103
    and sailing community, 164
    suburban sprawl in, 421
    Vanderbilt's influence in, 111,
        112, 121, 125, 136
    and Whitney, 122
Islip, England, 1, 4
Islip airport, 380
Islip Driving Park, 245, 279, 279n
Islip Field Club, 245
Islip Herald, xii-xiii
Islip High School, 426

Islip Polo Club, 246, 247, 262, 275-76, 292
  and advent of Great War, 320
  and August Belmont, 299
  governors of (1912), 276n
  and Olympic Club property, 309
Islip Presbyterian Church, 71
Islip Press, xii-xiii
Islip Tennis Club, 125n, 418, 425
Islip Yacht Club, 241, 300, 302, 308
Ives, Sarah, 60

J

Jamaica (Long Island), 13, 21
James (Duke of York), 7-8
James, Olivia Cutting, 141, 149, 150, 353, 424
Jay, William, 63
Jaycox (State Supreme Court Justice), 289
Jeffrey, Leander A. (Captain), 75, 166, 169
Jerome, Jennie (Lady Randolph Churchill), 211
Jerome, Leonard, 39-40, 63-64, 211
Jerome Park, 39-40
Johns, Abigail, 7
Johnson, Aimee Gaillard (Mrs. Bradish Johnson Jr.), 198-200, 405
Johnson, Amy Scott (Mrs. Effingham Johnson), 198
Johnson, Aymar, 199, 200, 300, 357, 377, 378n, 405, 406, 419
Johnson, Bradish, 23, 24, 25, 178, 197-98, 405
  and Belmont, 184
  and Ruth Carroll, 412
  and country homes, 123
  death of, 185n, 197
  descendants of, 420
  estate of, 369
  house of, 418
  as "Old Merchant," 132
  and St. Mark's, 26, 197-98
  and South Side Sportsmen's Club, 47

Johnson, Bradish Jr., 46, 113, 198-200
  as Bay Shore Show Association governor, 246
  and father's death, 197
  at Hollins-Livingston wedding, 203
  and Marie Johnson, 405
  and Pavilion Hotel, 69, 183, 311
  and Woodland, 46, 199, 200, 419
Johnson, Bradish G., 199, 405
Johnson, Edwin Augustus, 23, 24, 25, 28, 31, 68
  and Deer Range Farm mansion, 61
  and Prince property, 70
  and St. Mark's, 26
Johnson, Effingham, 197, 198
Johnson, Ellen Woodruff (Mrs. Edwin A. Johnson), 25
Johnson, Fanny Nicoll (Mrs. Lee Johnson), 25, 151
Johnson, Helena (Mrs. Schuyler Parsons), 118-20, 121, 197, 375
Johnson, Henry M. (Harry), 197, 198, 203, 291, 306
  estate of, 369n
Johnson, John D., 23, 24, 25, 26, 28, 31, 68, 160
Johnson, Lee, 25, 151, 151n, 152
Johnson, Letitia Rice (Mrs. William M. Johnson), 23
Johnson, Louisa Anna Lawrance (Mrs. Bradish Johnson), 24-25, 112, 118, 197, 380
Johnson, Louisa Anna (younger), 198
Johnson, Lucy (Mrs. Alfred L. Carroll), 197, 198, 289, 412
Johnson, Marie Gaillard (Mrs. William Hamilton Russell; later Mrs. Gordon Crothers), 199, 321, 404-8
Johnson, Martin, 23
Johnson, Parmenus, 159
Johnson, Sarah Rice (Mrs. William M. Johnson), 23
Johnson, William Martin, 22, 23-24
Johnson Avenue, 25, 37, 90, 332

Johnson family, 34, 105, 178, 292, 389, 431
Johnston, Eileen (Mrs. Andre De Coppet), 373-74
Johnston, James Boorman, 45-46, 157, 199
Johnston, John, 46
Jones, E. P., 177-78
Jones Beach, 85, 363

K

Kalbfleisch, Franklin H., 84, 85
Kane, DeLancy, 63-64
Keeler, Emma (Mrs. Frederick G. Bourne), 191, 193, 196
Keene, James R., 85
Keith, Henry M., 365
Keith, Minor H., 179
Kempster, James, 308, 309, 335
Ketcham, Ed Jr., 398, 399, 401
Ketchum, Landon, 259, 366-67
Ketchum, Phebe (Mrs. Edwin Thorne), 259, 260, 366, 380
King, George S., 267-68, 326, 348, 351
King, Moses, 251, 263
Kingsland, A. A., family of, 69
Kingsland, George, 179
Kingsland, William F., 179
Kingsland, William M., 359
Kinkajou (Star boat), 371
Knapp, Augusta Murray Spring (Mrs. Gideon Lee Knapp), 105, 106
Knapp, Caroline Burr (Mrs. Harry K. Knapp), 248-50, 406
Knapp, Catherine Kumble (Mrs. Shepherd Knapp), 45
Knapp, Edward Spring, 105-10, 113, 115, 117, 247, 259, 299
Knapp, Edward S. Jr., 107-8, 117, 148, 303, 306, 385
Knapp, Elizabeth (Mrs. Harry K. Knapp Jr.), 377
Knapp, Evelina Meserole (Mrs. Harry B. Hollins), 112, 113, 114
Knapp, Gideon, 110, 259

Knapp, Gideon Lee, 45, 105, 109, 110
Knapp, Harry K., 110, 111, 120-21, 184, 203, 247-50, 403
Knapp, Harry K. Jr., 248, 259, 306, 369, 377, 380, 407
Knapp, Margaret (daughter), 109, 303
Knapp, Margaret Ireland Lawrance (Mrs. Edward Spring Knapp), 26, 105, 106-8, 110, 203, 302-3
house of, 107, 302
Knapp, Maria Meserole (Mrs. William K. Knapp), 45, 120, 122, 158, 184, 185n, 305
Knapp, Phebe Thorne (Mrs. Harry K. Knapp Jr.), 259, 306, 367, 369
Knapp, Rosalie Moran (Mrs. Edward Knapp Jr.), 110, 303, 306, 385
Knapp, Shepherd, 45, 132
Knapp, Shepherd F. (son), 45, 47, 81, 105, 110
Knapp, Theodore, 248, 250, 357, 403
Knapp, Tom, 109
Knapp, William K., 45, 68, 105, 113
Knapp family, 105, 292
and Awixa Lawn, 124 (*see also* Awixa Lawn)
Kobbe, Carol (Mrs. Robert W. Morgan), 322, 377
Kobbe, Carl Wilhelm Ludwig Augustus, 322
Kobbe, Carolyn Wheeler (Mrs. Gustave Kobbe), 322
Kobbe, Gustave, 322, 403, 420
Kobbe, Hildegarde (Mrs. Joseph H. Stevenson, later Mrs. Francis B. Thorne), 250, 322, 377, 387n, 403, 404
Kobbe, Sarah Lord Sistare, 322
Kobbe, Virginia (Mrs. Gerald V. Hollins), 306, 322, 377
Krippendorf, Philippine (Mrs. Louis Bossert), 244, 364n
Ku Klux Klan, 346-47
Kumble, Catherine (Mrs. Shepherd Knapp), 45

L

La Grange Inn, 19-20, 429
Lake, Adelaide (Mrs. Henry C.
   Haff), 171, 207
Lake House, 28-29, 49, 116, 181,
   184, 248, 307
Lake Shore affair, 128-29
Lamers, Claire, xiii
Lamont, Daniel, 103
Landon K. Thorne canal, 242n
Langley, William H., 76
Lanier, Charles, 328-29
Lanier, Sarah (Mrs. Francis C.
   Lawrance Jr.), 328-29
Larchmont O Class of yacht, 301
Larchmont Yacht Club, 75, 233
La Salle Military Academy, 197,
   352-53, 353n, 372, 423
Laud, William (Archbishop of
   Canterbury), 5, 7
Law, J. O., 300
Lawrance, Charles Lanier, 305,
   320, 328-31
   and airport, 380
   as Carlisle pall bearer, 318
   college pals of, 378n
   and Lindbergh, 377
   and Manatuck Farm, 285
   and Naval Air Station site, 321-22
   and O-Co-Nee development,
      321-22, 328, 331, 427
   and partying, 374
   and Southside Hospital, 348,
      349, 351, 380
   as Star boat sailor, 398
   and Timber Point Club, 357
Lawrance, Fanny (Lady Vernon), 208
Lawrance, Frances Garner (Mrs.
   Francis Cooper Lawrance), 35,
   78, 112, 208, 328
Lawrance, Francis Cooper, 26,
   111, 185, 328
   death of, 185n, 305
   descendants of, 420
   and Garner land, 35
   and Manatuck Far, 285

and yachting, 72, 77
Lawrance, Francis Cooper Jr., 305,
   328-29
Lawrance, John I., 26, 178, 201,
   245, 263
Lawrance, Kitty Lanier (Mrs. W.
   Averell Harriman), 329, 329n
Lawrance, Louisa Anna (Mrs.
   Bradish Johnson), 24-25, 112,
   118, 197, 380
Lawrance, Margaret Dix (Mrs.
   Charles L. Lawrance), 305, 320,
   329, 374
Lawrance, Margaret Ireland (Mrs.
   Thomas Lawrance III), 25, 25-26,
   106
Lawrance, Margaret Ireland
   (granddaughter; later Mrs.
   Edward S. Knapp), 26, 105, 106-
   8, 110, 203, 302-3
Lawrance, Mary Helen Crandell
   (Mrs. William R. Lawrance), 106
Lawrance, Sarah Lanier (Mrs. Francis
   Cooper Lawrance Jr.), 328-29
Lawrance, Susan Willing (Mrs.
   Francis Cooper Lawrance Jr.), 329
Lawrance, Thomas, 25, 25-26, 106, 119
Lawrance, Thomas III, 25, 106
Lawrance, William R., 26, 106
Lawrance Creek, 329
Lawrance family, 34, 48, 105, 178,
   208, 328
Lawrance Lane, 331
Lawrence, Augusta Eloise (Mrs. J.
   Salisbury Breese), 127, 130
Lawrence, Gertrude (stage star),
   376, 378, 379
Lawrence, John, 6, 13
Lawrence, Thomas, 6
Lawrence, William, 6, 13
Lee, John, 96
Leiter, Mary, 218, 218n
Lenox, Robert, 132
Levitt, William J., 278
Lewis, R. W. B., 138
Libaires (Star boat sailors), 398

Libby, Ira A., 29
Lighthouses
    Fire Island, 20, 27, 30-31
    Fire Island (second), 28, 31, 430-31
    Montauk Point, 20n
Lillian (sloop), 273
Lillie, Beatrice, 376
Lincoln, Abraham, and Moses
    Taylor, 131-32
Lindbergh, Charles, and Lawrance
    engines, 330, 377, 380
Lindeberg, Harrie T., 337, 370, 413
Linwood Hotel, 178, 181, 267, 307
Lipton, Sir Thomas, 195, 343, 344
Litchfield, Electus B., property of, 95
Littell, E. T., 142
Littlejohn (Right Reverend Dr.),
    112, 212
Livingston, Angelica, 202
Livingston, Cambridge, 159
Livingston, Caroline, 159n
Livingston, Frances Redmond (Mrs.
    Henry Beekman Livingston), 202
Livingston, Frances (daughter), 202
Livingston, Henry Beekman, 201-2
Livingston, Henry B. Sr., 202
Livingston, Henry Whitney, 159n
Livingston, John Griswold, 159n
Livingston, Johnston, 204n, 212n
Livingston, Johnston II, 159n
Livingston, Lilias (Mrs. Harry B.
    Hollins Jr.), 202, 202-3, 305, 377
Livingston, Louis, 159n
Livingston, Maria Murray (Mrs.
    Cambridge Livingston), 159, 160
Livingston, Maria Whitney (Mrs.
    Robert Cambridge Livingston),
    159, 160, 317
Livingston, Mary Lawrence (Mrs.
    Henry B. Livingston Sr.), 202
Livingston, Maud Maria (Mrs.
    Henry W. Bull), 159n, 160, 212n,
    317, 377, 378n
Livingston, Natalie Moss (Mrs.
    Johnston Livingston), 204n

Livingston, Robert ("first Lord of
    the Manor"), 119, 137, 158, 201
Livingston, Robert (third
    proprietor), 158
Livingston, Robert Cambridge
    (1742-1794), 158-59, 316
Livingston, Robert Cambridge,
    150, 158-60, 201
Livingston, Robert Cambridge IV,
    159n
Livingston, Robert R., 201, 201n
Livingston family, 48, 292
    and arrivistes, 91-92
Livingston Manor, 119, 158
Lohgrame (Graham home), 341
Lonelyville, 326
Long Branch, New Jersey, 69
Long Island
    Corbin on, 93, 94
    first settlements on eastern part
        of, 11
Long Island Forum, The, xiii
Long Island Railroad, 21, 35, 87-88,
    89-90, 93
    under Corbin, 84, 93-95, 98
    Olympic station of, 108-9
    Parsons and friends as
        commuters on, 121
    purchase of, 285n
    and resort hotels, 84
    and Surf Hotel, 28
Loomis, Alfred A., 367
Loomis, Henry Patterson, 367
Loomis, Julia Atterbury (Mrs.
    Landon K. Thorne), 367, 369, 370
Lorillard, Catherine Griswold, 57
Lorillard, George L., 56-57, 59-60, 111
    and deep-water port plan, 94
    and horse racing, 58-59, 245
    and Pavilion Hotel, 69
    and Westbrook Farms, 58-60, 141
        (*see also* Westbrook Farms)
    and yachting, 57-58
Lorillard, Maria Louise (Mrs.
    George Lorillard), 59
Lorillard, Peter, 57

Lorillard, Peter A. 57
Lorillard, Pierre, 57, 59, 224
Lorillard Company, 57
Lorillard estate, 56
Lorillard family, 48, 132
Lorne, Lord, 96
Lovelace (Governor), 15
Lovering, Carol Stevenson, 378, 387n, 406n
Lovering, Joseph, 406n
Low, Chauncey E., 178
Low, Seth, 178
Ludlow, Frances Nicoll, 190
Ludlow, William H., 190

M

McAllister, Ward, 36n
McBurney, Dorothy Moran, 306, 377
McBurney, Malcolm, 306, 377, 378n
McCannon (yacht captain), 76
McClure, William, 258-59
Mackay, Clarence H., 381
Mackay, Katherine Duer, 381
MacKay, Robert, xiv
McKinley, William
    and Cuba treaty proposal, 261
    property exchange contingent on election of, 189
Macy, George H., 204, 231, 359
Macy, Josiah, 359
Macy, Julia Dick (Mrs. W. Kingsland Macy), 204, 360, 387n, 408, 410
Macy, Thomas, 359
Macy, T. Ridgeway, 204, 275, 333
Macy, William Henry, 359
Macy, W. Kingsland, 204, 356, 357, 359-60
    college pals of, 378n
    and Taylor property, 361, 362
    and Timber Point Club, 418
Macy family, 427
Magic (yacht), 77, 77n
Magoun, George B., 179
Mainwaring Farm, 114
Maisie (power launch), 195
Maitland, Robert L., 58

Manatuck Farm, 285, 329, 331, 352, 427
Manhattan Beach Hotel, 84, 94, 97
Mann, Elizabeth (Mrs. Walter R. Herrick), 249n
Manning, William T., 249
Mapes, John, 6
Mapes, Thomas, 6, 12
Mapes family, 388
Maple Avenue, 178
Maple Avenue dock, 234n
Marble House, Newport, 66, 213
Marconi rig, 302, 343, 398, 398n
Margaret of Anjou (Queen of England), 3-4
Marina, on Fire Island, 429
Marine Pavilion, 22
Martin, Alice (Mrs. Julien Davies), 355
Martin, Edward J., 277
Massachusetts Bay Colony, 5-6, 11
Masterton, Alexander, 60, 61, 63
Matinecock, 12
Mayflower (yacht), 164, 166
Meadow Brook Club, 246-47, 300, 381
Meadow Brook Hunt, 392
Meadowedge (Florence Bourne Hard home), 423
Meadowfarm (Hollins estate), 114, 232, 320, 331, 381
Mechanicsville (former name of Bay Shore), 25
Medina, Kate, xiv
Meeks, Edward B., 116, 184
Meeks, Joseph W., 69-70, 116
Meeks family, 48
Meeks property or house, 63, 134, 185, 203
Melville, Herman, 182n
Meriam (catboat), 195
Merrick Road, 332
Merrill, Dina, 297
Meteor (schooner), 58, 169, 170
Meteor (yacht), 400
Meyer, Cord, 176, 263-64
Meyer, Cord Jr., 263, 264
Meyer, Cornelia Covert, 264

Middle Island, 333, 333n, 430
Milbank, Samuel, 48
Milburn, Devereux, 247
Milligan, Richard A., xiv
Mills, Emma, 288
Mills, Philo S., 175
Mimi's Awixa Pond, 290
Minx (Star boat), 398
Mischief (sloop), 73, 74, 164
Mist (yacht), 368, 398, 399
Mitchell, John Purrey, 360
Moffitt, Charles W., 280
Moffitt, William H., 104, 277-83, 317, 340-41, 373
Moffitt Boulevard, 278, 283
Mohawk (yacht), 77-78
Mollenhauer, Anna Dick (Mrs. J. Adolph Mollenhauer), 176, 235, 238-39, 239n, 409
Mollenhauer, Doris (Mrs. John Mollenhauer), 234, 245
Mollenhauer, J. Adolph, 234-35, 238-39, 239n
    Allen Winden bowling alley given by, 409
    and Club pool, 241
    and horse show, 246
    fire engine donated by, 239n
    and Hopkins, 339
    and Penataquit Point, 332, 370-71
    and property restriction against dogs, 289
    and Southside Hospital, 349, 351
    on war memorial committee, 342
    as yachtsman, 235-37, 238, 240, 240-41, 300, 411
Mollenhauer, John, 201, 234-35, 245, 305
    descendants of, 420
Mollenhauer, Julia T. (Mrs. John Henry Dick), 177, 264, 408
Mollenhauer family, 260
Moller, Mary Jennie (Mrs. Henry Havemeyer), 88, 89
Monfort Seminary, 426

Montauk, deep-water port proposal for, 94-95
Montauk (schooner), 73
Montauk Highway, 332, 423
Montauk Point lighthouse, 20n
Montauk Railroad, 85
Montgomery, Richard H., 178, 273
Moore, Paul, 337
Moran, Amedeé Depau, 303, 377, 420
Moran, Dorothy (Mrs. Malcolm McBurney), 306
Moran, Rosalie E. (Mrs. Edward S. Knapp Jr.), 110, 303, 306, 385
Moran, Samuel, 88, 252
Morgan, Carol Kobbe (Mrs. Robert W. Morgan), 322, 377
Morgan, Charles, 322, 356, 357, 377, 378n
Morgan, Edward, 298
Morgan, Elizabeth (Mrs. August Belmont II), 298
Morgan, Ethel (Mrs. Charles Morgan), 377
Morgan, Henry (Harry), 356, 357, 358, 377, 378n
Morgan, House of, 41
Morgan, J. Pierpont, 265-66
    and Cathedral of St. John the Divine, 139
    and Hollins, 113-14, 319
    and Hyde, 243
    at Idlehour, 223
    and 1929 crash, 384
    and St. George's Church, 140
    and yachting, 74, 194, 205, 236
Morgan, Julia Remington (later Mrs. Christopher Robert), 187-88, 189-90
Morgan, Matthew, 298
Morgan, Robert W. (Bobby), 322, 377, 378n
Moriches Inlet, 415
Morris, Anne Maria (Mrs. John D. Prince), 70, 112, 125, 126
Moses, Robert, 135, 353, 359, 360-64, 385, 425

Mosquito (Vanderbilt steamer), 68
Mosquitoes
  and Cedar Island, 336
  and marshy land, 37
  Society for the Extermination
    of, 320
Moss, Camilla, 203-4
Moss, Courtlandt D., 203, 204
Moss, Natalie, 204n
Moss, Teddy, 204
Moubray, Anning, 18-19
Moubray, Elizabeth Anning, 18
Moubray (Mowbray), John, 16, 18-
  19, 262, 427
Mouette (yacht), 400
Mowbray family, 177, 201, 237
Mowbray family property, 348
Mowbray home, 262
Muncy, Thomas, 232-33, 333
Murray, Ann Eliza Peyton, 137
Murray, Bronson, 137
Murray, Caroline (Mrs. Lucius K.
  Wilmerding), 156
Murray, Maria B. (Mrs. Cambridge
  Livingston), 159, 160
Murray, Olivia. *See* Cutting, Olivia
  Murray

N

Nantucket Island, and Macy
  family, 359
Nares, Ramsey, 63
Nassau County, population growth
  of, 353
National Audubon Society, 425
National Golf Links of America, 369
Nature Conservancy, 370
Naval Air Station, Bay Shore, 321-
  22, 325, 331
Nearholme, 390, 395-96, 409, 419
Nesbit, Evelyn, 310
New Amsterdam, 8, 13
New Harlem, 13
New Haven, 11
Newman, Harry Shaw, 394-95
New Netherland, 6, 7, 13, 14

Newport, Rhode Island, 136, 266
  America's Cup at, 223, 343
  Astors at, 211, 263
  Belmont residence in, 44
  as booming, 181
  country homes residents to, 124
  resort hotels in, 27
  Vanderbilts at, 211, 223
Newtown, Long Island, 6, 13
New Utrecht, 13
New York (ship), wreck of, 166-67
New York (State)
  beginning of, 8
  under English control, 14
New York City
  Conover in street railways of,
    100-101
  early days of, 14-15
  fashion parade in, 54
  and Gilded Age, 91
  horseback riding in, 39
New York City subway system, 99
  Guastavino arch in, 371
New York and Oak Island Railroad
  (proposed), 85
New York Public Library, xiii
New York Society, 36n
New York Yacht Club, 57-58, 72,
  72n, 75, 167, 233
  and Bourne, 194
Nicholas, Alice Hollins, (Mrs.
  Harry I. Nicholas), 180, 254
  gravestone of, 429
Nicholas, Evelyn Hollins (Mrs.
  Duncan C. Arnold), 254
Nicholas, George S., 180
Nicholas, Harry I., 115, 180, 252,
  254, 392
  gravestone of, 429
Nicholas, Harry I. Jr., 180
Nicholas family, 48
Nicoll, Abigail, 15
Nicoll, Anna Van Rensselaer, 14, 16
  and Van Cortlandt, 17
Nicoll, Annys, 4
Nicoll, Benjamin, 16

Nicoll, Fanny (Mrs. Lee Johnson), 25, 151
Nicoll, Frances (Mrs. William H. Ludlow), 190
Nicoll, Henry, 4
Nicoll, John, 4, 9
Nicoll, John (grandson), 4
Nicoll, John (son of William), 5
Nicoll, Margaret, 16
Nicoll, Matthias, 5
Nicoll, Matthias II, 5, 7, 8-9, 14-15
Nicoll, Richard, 8-9, 14
Nicoll, Mrs. Sarah, 333n
Nicoll, William, xii, 4-5,
Nicoll, William (1820-1900), 16, 151
Nicoll, William (son of Matthias Nicoll II), 7, 8, 9, 14, 15-16, 130, 333n
Nicoll family, 47, 127
Nicolson, Nigel, 218
Nobility, American brides of, 130, 207-11, 217
North Shore Gold Coast, 342-43, 345
Nursery, the (Belmont farm), 42, 44, 184, 298, 302, 324, 353
as Robert Moses headquarters, 364
Nyssa (yacht), 302

O

Oakdale, castle in, 188-89
Oak Island, 430
Oak Island Beach, 84-85
Oakman, Walter G., 282, 282n, 341
Oak Neck Road (now Oak Neck Lane), 258, 428-29
Oaks, the (Hyde mansion), 55-56, 121, 241, 243
town assessment of, 242
Oakwood Cemetery, xiii, 105, 207, 393n, 427
Oakwood Driving Park Association, 105, 245
Ocean Avenue, 48, 90, 123, 171-72, 173, 178, 258
Ocean Beach, 430
Ocean Beach Hotel, 309

O-Co-Nee estate, 321-22, 328, 331, 352, 427
Okla II, 398, 400
Okonok (Thorne home), 260
Old Guard families, and Belmont, 40, 41
Old Print Shop, The, xiv
Oler, Wesley M. Jr., 365
Olmsted, Frederick Law, 142
Olmsted Brothers, 337, 339-40
Olympic Club, 31-34, 47, 76, 79-81, 100, 308-9
Haff as superintendent of, 167
Long Island Railroad station for, 108
in news account, 69
and Penataquit Corinthian, 241
Olympic Park, 278, 279, 283
Olympic Point
Havemeyer home(s) on, 331-32, 335-40, 372, 420, 426
and Sharps, 412-13
Oneck Stables, 110, 248
Onward (yacht), 167
Opekeepsing (Wagstaff house), 252
Oppenheimer, Julius, 302
Oriental hotel, 84
Origo, Iris Cutting, 138, 142-44, 146, 149
Orowoc Creek, 20, 51, 102, 103, 172, 174, 274n, 332
Orowoc Hotel, 267
Orphan Asylum Society of the City of Brooklyn, Brookwood Hall bought by, 404, 419
Osgood, Franklyn, 58n
Osgood, George, 58n
Oxnard, Henry T., 152-53, 154
Oyster Bay
first settlements in, 12
founding of, 12
and Quakers, 17

P

Paine, Charles J., 165-66, 167
Palmer, Fanny, 393n

Panic of 1837, 131
Panic of 1893, 116, 200, 253
Panic of 1907, 241, 265-66, 280, 384
Parke, Hiram, 319n
Parrish, Samuel L., 272
Parsons, Evelyn Knapp, 119
Parsons, Helena Johnson (Mrs.
    Schuyler Parsons), 118-20, 121,
    197, 375
Parsons, Helena Johnson
    (daughter; later Mrs. Richard
    Wharton), 119, 120, 121, 158,
    212n, 306, 375, 377, 381
Parsons, Mary (Mrs. William L.
    Breese), 129-30
Parsons, Schuyler Livingston, 49,
    112-13, 118-22
    descendants of, 420
    home of, 158
    and horse racing, 245, 248
    at Idlehour, 223
    and Livingston, 160, 201
    and public beach, 231
    and Short Beach Club, 115
    as voluntary fire department
        chief, 117
    and Whileaway, 120, 418 (see
        also Whileaway)
Parsons, Schuyler Livingston Jr.,
    119-20, 121, 124-25, 324-25, 380-81
    college pals of, 378n
    and Great River (Timber Point)
        Club, 356, 357
    on newer generation, 185
    and Pleasure Island, 375-77, 380
    and Venetian Fete performance,
        378
Parsons, William Burrington, 119
Parsons, Mr. and Mrs. William M., 49
Parsons family, 292, 389
Parties and partying
    by Belmonts, 41
    by Bournes, 193-94
    as ostentatious display, 241
    during Roaring Twenties, 374-
        79, 381

over Thanksgiving or Christmas,
    125
by Vanderbilts, 68, 92
Patience (sloop), 162, 275, 391
Pavilion (pleasure boat), 157
Pavilion Avenue, 90, 123, 157, 258,
    292, 311, 332
Pavilion Hotel, 28, 29-30, 64, 69,
    118, 157, 181, 182, 311
Payne, Flora, 122
Payne, Oliver H., 122, 195
Pell, Robert Livingston, 179
Penataquit Avenue, 90, 171-72
Penataquit Corinthian Yacht Club,
    233, 235, 237-38, 239-41, 300,
    333, 370
Penataquit Gardens, 372n
Penataquit Point, 177, 332, 370-71,
    372-73, 427
Pennsylvania Railroad, 285n
Peperidge Hall (Robert and Aston
    home), 189, 190, 352, 418
Pepys, Samuel, 8
Percy G. Williams Home, 314-15
Perkins, Adaline Havemeyer, 387, 420
Perkins, Richard S., 387
Perry, Caroline Slidell, 41
Peters, Adaline Elder (Mrs.
    Samuel T. Peters), 126, 162-63,
    164, 388-89, 395, 397
Peters, Harry Twyford, 306, 389,
    391-93
    as Carlisle pall bearer, 318
    and Currier & Ives, 391-92, 393-95
    death of, 395
    and Hopkins, 339
    as horse show winner, 246, 316
    and Nearholme, 390
    and polo, 247, 275, 276n, 294, 300
    and Timber Point Club, 357
    and Windholme Farm, 388, 389-91
Peters, Louisine (Mrs. Harold H.
    Weekes), 306, 385-86, 388, 389
Peters, Natalie (daughter; later
    Mrs. Charles D. Webster), 378,
    391, 396

Peters, Natalie Wells (Mrs. Harry
  T. Peters), 306, 390, 396
Peters, Samuel T., 150, 162-64
  and Bayberry Point, 224, 225
  descendants of, 420
  and Havemeyer, 389
  and horse show, 246
  and Prince home, 74
  property of, 388
  and public beach, 231
  town assessment on home of, 318
  and Westbrook Golf Club, 147
  and yachting, 232, 275
Peters family, 48, 292
Phelps, Bethuel, 283
Phelps, Charles E., 283, 290
Phipps Houses, 139
Picken, Bill, 399, 401
Pierrepont, Robert A., 274
Pierson, Abraham, 12
Pieterzen family, 13
Pimm (yacht), 400, 402
Pincus, Jacob, 42-43
Pineacres, 312, 314-15
Pinkerton, Allan ("Bud"), 273, 275-
  76, 277
  and fox hunting, 392
  house of, 419
  marriage of, 274, 306
  Olympic Club land bought by,
    309, 332, 335
  and polo, 247, 276n, 294, 300
  and Timber Point Club, 357
  wounded in Great War, 277, 325
Pinkerton, Allan (elder), 273
Pinkerton, Anna (Mrs. Robert
  Pinkerton), 273, 349
Pinkerton, Anna (daughter; later
  Mrs. Lewis Mills Gibb), 273, 274,
  277, 305-6, 316, 349, 350
Pinkerton, Franc Woodworth
  (Mrs. Allan Pinkerton), 274, 277
Pinkerton, Mary (Mrs. Jay F.
  Carlisle), 273, 275, 306, 315, 316-
  18, 349, 350, 374

Pinkerton, Robert Allan, 178, 201,
  201n, 273, 277, 305
  descendants of, 420
Pinkerton, William, 273
Pinkie (yacht), 275
Planned communities
  Bayberry Point, 225-31, 293, 334,
    385, 386-88, 425-26
  Tuxedo Park, 224, 230
  See also Real estate development
Platt, John R., 80
Pleasure (sloop), 232
Pleasure Island, 375-77, 380
Plender, George and Greta, 427
Plumb, Anna Burton, 62, 63
Plumb, J. Ives, 61, 63, 134, 204,
  249, 271, 320
  house of, 418
Plumb, J. Neale, 56-57, 60-63
  and Pavilion Hotel, 69
Plumb, Sarah Ives, 60, 61
Point O'Woods, 268, 416, 429
Polo, 246-47, 275-76, 294, 299-300.
  See also Islip Polo Club
Poppenhusen family, 88
Porter, Cole, 377
Post, Charles W., 294
Post, Marjorie Merriweather, 294-
  95, 297
Potter, Henry Codman, 215
Potter, Phyllis Livingston (Mrs.
  Fred Astaire), 378n
Potts, R. B., 300
Powers, Hiram, 30
Presto (steam yacht), 236, 238
Price, Bruce, 224
Prince, Anne Maria Morris (Mrs.
  John D. Prince), 70, 112, 125, 126
Prince, John Dyneley, 69-70
  death of, 74
  estate of, 389
property location of, 120, 158, 163
  and St. Mark's consecration, 112
  and yacht racing, 71-74, 167
Prince family, 48

Prince of Wales (later King Edward VII), 124, 169, 195, 209-10
Prince of Wales (later King Edward VIII), 381-82
Prohibition, 345-46
Prospect House, 48-49, 181-82, 267
Pullis, John, 107
Puritan, 164
Puritanism
  and eastern Long Island settlement, 11
  and opposition to Charles I, 5
Puritan theocracies, 5-6, 9
Purryer, Alice, 6
Purryer, Catherine, 6
Purryer, Mary, 6
Purryer, Sarah, 6
Purryer, William, 6, 12
Pyne, Moses Taylor, 132, 135, 359
Pyne, Percy Rivington, 132, 359
Pyne, Percy R. II, 135, 359

Q

Quail hunting, 108
Quakers, 13, 17, 136
Querida (sloop), 254, 302

R

Racism, and Ku Klux Klan, 346-47
Rainbow (yacht), 223n
Ramble, the (Moss home), 203, 204
Ranft house, 317
Ranger (yacht), 223n, 368, 368n
Rascal (yacht), 401
Raynor, Benjamin S., 269
Raynor, Preston C., xiv
Real estate development
  by Ackerson, 283-87
  and breakup of great estates, 353
  by Conover, 102-3, 104
  by Johnsons, 25
  by Lawrance (O-Co-Nee), 331
  by Moffitt, 277-83
  planned communities

Bayberry Point, 225-31, 293, 334, 385, 386-88, 425-26
Tuxedo Park, 224, 230
post-WWII, 420-21
Recession of 1913, 319
Redmond, Frances, 202
Redmond, Roland, 173, 202
Redmond, William, 202
Redmond family, 48
Reilly, Peter and Jane, xiv
Reliance (yacht), 195
Remington, Julia (Mrs. Charles Morgan; later Mrs. Christopher Robert Jr.), 187-88, 189-90
Remsen, Phoenix, 178, 252
Remsen, Sarah Louisa Wagstaff, 252
Renwick, James, 405, 405n
Resolute (yacht), 343, 344
Reverie (sloop), 195
Resort (summer) hotels, 22, 27, 28, 84, 181
  Argyle Hotel, 84, 95-96, 97-99, 429
  Dominy House, 27, 49
  Dominy House (second), 30, 75, 81
  in 1850s, xi
  1890 as high water mark for, 182
  and end of Gilded Age, 306, 335
  Lake House, 28-29, 49, 116, 181, 184, 248, 307
  Linwood Hotel, 178, 181, 267, 307
  and Long Island Railroad under Corbin, 84, 94
  Manhattan Beach Hotel, 84, 94, 97
  Oriental, 84
  Pavilion Hotel, 28, 29-30, 64, 69, 118, 157, 181, 182, 311
  Prospect House, 48-49, 181-82, 267
  and railroad plans, 85
  Rockaway Beach Hotel, 84
  Somerset House, 49-50, 306-7
  Surf Hotel, 28, 31, 81, 82, 83, 95, 99, 182, 271, 414
  Uncle Jesse Conklin's, 81, 82
  Whig Inlet House (Stone's Hotel), 83-84
Reventlow, Lance, 297

Revolutionary War, 19
Rhinelanders, and arrivistes, 91-92
Rhode Island, 11
Rhodes, Urias, 75
Rice, Letitia, 23
Rice, Sarah, 23
Richard III (King of England), 4
Richardson, Henry Hobson, 142
Riesing, Mrs. Neil, 146n, 205
Riggio, Frank V., 413
Riggio, Vincent, 413
Riggio House, 413
Riker family, 13, 388
Riley, Reuben, 112, 118
Rionda, Manuel, 260-61, 262
Roads, poor condition of, 51, 103-4
Roaring Twenties, 345, 374
    carefree attitude of, 376, 382
    Schuyler Parsons Jr. as symbol
        of, 375, 381
"Robber Barons," 138
Robbins, John C., 272
Robbins, William H., 351, 362
Robert, Christopher Rhinelander
    Jr., 187-90
    as estate builder, 197
    and Peperidge Hall, 189, 190, 352
Robert, Christopher Rhinelander
    Sr., 187, 188
Robert, Daniel, 187
Robert, Julia Remington Morgan
    (Mrs. Christopher Robert Jr.),
    187-88, 189-90
Robert College, 187, 187n
Robert family, 48
Robert Moses State Park, 272, 430
Robson, Eleanor, 298
Rockaway Beach, iron pier at, 86
Rockaway Beach Hotel, 84
Rockefeller, John D. Sr., 223, 384
Rodgers, Richard, 376
Rogers, John M., 48, 267
Roosevelt, Franklin Delano, 383
Roosevelt, John E., 147, 275
Roosevelt, Robert B., xi
Roosevelt, Theodore, 265

Rose (yacht), 271
Rosemary (Carlisle home), 318-19,
    377
Rothschild, Baron, 43-44
Rothschild, Carola Warburg (Mrs.
    Walter N. Rothschild), 273
Rothschild, Lillian Abraham (Mrs.
    Simon F. Rothschild), 269, 273
Rothschild, Louis, 272
Rothschild, Mayer Amschel, 272
Rothschild, Simon F., 246, 269-70,
    272-73, 276n
    house of, 418
Rothschild, Walter N., 273
Rothschild banking family, 131, 272
Rowland, Oliver, 77-78
Rowland, W. J., 25
Rumson, New Jersey, 27
Russell, Bill, 412
Russell, Marie Johnson, 404-8
Russell, Mariette, xiv
Russell, William Hamilton
    (senior), 405
Russell, William Hamilton, 250,
    378n, 404, 405-8
Russell, William Hamilton Jr., 407, 408
Rutherfurd, Anne (Mrs. William K.
    Vanderbilt), 219, 223
Rutherfurd, Winthrop, 214
Rutigliano, Loretta, xiv
Ryan, Thomas Fortune, 243
Ryder, Robert, 415
Ryder, T. S., 70, 163n, 390

S

Sachem (schooner), 54
Sackett, Mrs. Charles, 112
Sackett, Henry W., 272
Sage, Russell, 85
Sagtikos Manor, 17-18, 255, 256, 428
Sagtikos Manor Farm, 245n
Sailing. *See* Yachting
St. Ann's Church, Sayville, xi, 140, 196
St. George's Church, New York
    City, 140

St. John's Church, Oakdale, 19, 26, 196
St. Mark's Church, 26, 37, 113, 151, 158, 425
  Consuelo with Duke at, 216
  and Cuttings, 140
  and Dick, 410
  and Duval, 156
  and Emmanuel Church, 62
  enlargement of, 202n
  and Garners, 35, 77
  Garth as rector of, 406
  and Gibb, 175, 277
  and Hollinses, 185, 305
  and Hollisters, 161, 305
  and Hoppin, 352
  Hunt-designed building of, 66, 111-12
  and Hyde, 242
  and Johnsons, 26, 197-98
  and Johnston, 45-46
  and Knapps, 45, 106, 248
  and Kobbe, 323
  and Lawrance, 26
  and Livingstons, 160
  new parish house of, 185-87
  and Plumb, 63
  and Seaside Home, 125, 126
  and Vanderbilts, 70, 111-12, 185, 186, 212, 220
  weddings in, 202-3
  and Welles, 37, 305
  and Westcott, 50
  and Wilmerding, 157
  and Wood, 116, 118, 156, 185
St. Mark's Lane, 25, 123, 258, 292, 332
St. Nicholas Church, Islip, England, 1, 4
St. Peter's Episcopal Church, Bay Shore, 370, 428
St. Thomas's Church, New York City, 54, 215, 222, 293
Saltonstall, Katharine (Mrs. Philip Weld), 297, 412
Sammis, David S. S., 28, 245

Sammis's Hotel, 75, 182. *See also* Surf Hotel
Sans Souci, 25, 118, 178, 197, 198, 428
Sarataga Springs, New York, ix, 27, 69, 136
  anti-semitic restrictions in, 97
  boom in, 181
  casino at, 310
  country homes residents to, 124
Saxon Park, 278, 279, 283
Saxton, Charlie, 162n
Saxton, Daniel, 19, 332, 339
Saxton, James (Jeans), 19
Saxton (later Saxon) Avenue, xii, 19, 90, 123, 172, 258, 274-75, 292, 332
Saxton's Neck, 19
Sayville, xi
Scat (steam yacht), 195
Schermerhorn, Ann White (Mrs. Charles Suydam), 140
Schermerhorn, Caroline (Mrs. William B. Astor), 36, 36n, 65, 92, 140n, 193, 202, 211, 214, 263
Schermerhorn, Catherine (Mrs. Benjamin S. Welles), 36, 140n
Schermerhorn family, and arrivistes, 91-92
Schieffelin family, 387
Schieren, Charles A., 172-73, 173, 271, 374, 404
Schieren, Marie Louise Bramm, 173
Schiff, Jacob H., 113-14, 243, 273
Scootering over ice, 276, 276n
Sea Gull (power boat), 402
Seaside Home, 125-26, 424
Seaside resort hotel. *See* Resort hotels
Seatuck National Wildlife Refuge, 396
Seawanhaka Yacht Club, 75
Secatogue Indians, 15-16, 17, 18, 255
Sequatogue Farm (Havemeyer estate), 85-86, 88, 89
Servants
  immigration law restricts, 353
  World War II effect on, 419
Setalcott Indians, 12

Setauket, 12-13
Sewanhaka Corinthian Yacht Club, 233-34
Sexton Island, 430
Shamrock III (yacht), 195
Shamrock IV (yacht), 343-44
Shape (architect), 357
Sharks, Thorne as hunter of, 259-60
Sharp, H. Cecil, 412
Sharp, Ruth Carroll Draper, 412-13
Shaw, Osborn, 414
Shelter Island, founding of, 12
Sherman, William Tecumseh, 48
Shillalah (Star boat), 402
Shinnecock Indians, 12
Shinnecock Inlet, 415
Shooting. *See* Bird shooting
Short Beach Club, 115-16, 307, 308, 430
    as exclusive, 308
    New York Herald on (1890), 181
Show business
    at South Shore parties, 376, 377, 378-79
    Williams in, 312, 313-14
Silliman, Benjamin D., 179
Silveira, Manuel, 261
Simmons, W. R., 300
Sing Sing prison, and Fire Island Beach fears, 271
Sir Walter (race horse), 110
Sistare, Sarah, 322
Skitty (yacht), 400
Slater, James, 29, 69, 157
Slote, Alonzo, 80
Slote, Daniel, 80
Slots (family), 13
Smith, Alfred E., 360, 361, 363
Smith, Alonzo E., 74, 76, 78, 102, 157, 172, 174, 226
Smith, Asa, 162n
Smith, E. D., 346-47
Smith, Gilbert E., 78, 162, 162n, 195, 391
Smith, Henry N., 85
Smith, Mary Tangier, 187

Smith, Mary Virginia, 67
Smith, Stanley, 401
Smith, Treadwell, 48
Smithtown, founding of, 12
Smithtown Polo Club, 247
Snedecor, Eliphalet, 46-47
Snedecor, Obadiah, 47
Soldiers and Sailors Memorial Building, 239, 342
Somerset House, 49-50, 306-7
Southampton
    as competitor, 266, 342-43
    founding of, 12
    hospital in, 349
South Bay Golf Club, 366, 418
South Beach, 28
South Country Road, 258, 332
    in present-day Islip, 423
    summer homes on, 26, 37
Southern State Parkway, 363
Southold, Long Island, 6, 11
South Shore Field Club, 146n, 204n, 354, 365n, 418, 428
South Shore of Long Island, x-xi
    Roaring Twenties partying of, 374-79, 381
    rum-running on, 345-46
    topography of, 53
    vanished forests of, 21, 97
    World War II aftermath in, 417-21
South Side (catboat), 78, 88
Southside Hospital, 294, 348, 423
    new facility built for, 348-51
    Venetian Fete for, 378, 380
South Side Railroad, 28, 35, 48
South Side Signal, xii, xiii
South Side Sportsmen's Club (South Side Club), xi, xii, 47-48, 56, 113, 418, 424
    and Breese-Hollins fight, 127-28
    as exclusive, 308
    introductions to South Bay in, 188
    new residents drawn by, 48, 127
    in news account, 69
    and W. K. Vanderbilt, 66

Southward Ho Country Club, 291, 365, 428
Southward Ho Land Corporation, 364
Spa, ix
  South Shore as, xi, 431
Spanish-American War, 265
Spanish flu epidemic, 326-28, 348
  and Blanche Hutton, 294
Spaulding, Clara (Mrs. John B. Stanchfield), 309-11
Spaulding, E. B., 159-60
Spencer, Lorillard Jr., 163
Spencer-Churchill, Charles (Duke of Marlborough), 213, 214-16, 221-22
Spencer-Churchill, Lord Ivor, 217, 222
Spinzia, Raymond and Judith, xiv
Sporting clubs, 31
  Olympic Club, 31-34, 47, 76, 79-81, 100, 308-9 (see also Olympic Club)
  Short Beach Club, 115-16, 181, 307, 308, 430
  South Side Sportsmen's Club (South Side Club), xi, xii, 47-48, 56, 113, 418, 424 (see also South Side Sportsmen's Club)
  Wa-Wa-Yanda Fishing Club, 48, 81-82, 83, 115, 181, 416, 430
Spring, Augusta Murray (Mrs. Gideon Lee Knapp), 105, 106
Spring, Gardiner, 105
Spring, Samuel, 105
Stanchfield, Alice (Mrs. Arthur M. Wright), 311
Stanchfield, Clara Spaulding, 309-11
Stanchfield, John B., 309-11, 318, 355
Stanchfield, John Jr., 311
Starace, Carl A., xiii, xiv, 266
Star boats, 301, 358, 368, 396-402
Stellenwerf, Amos, 21, 28-29, 50, 184
Stellenwerf, Louise, 393n
Stellenwerf family, 116
Stephens, Olin J., 368n
Stephenson, Anne Willard, 161
Stevenson, Carol (Mrs. Joseph Lovering), 378, 387n, 406n

Stevenson, Hildegarde, 378
Stevenson, Hildegarde Kobbe (later Mrs. Francis B. Thorne), 250, 322, 377, 387n, 403, 404
Stevenson, Joseph H., 322, 403
Stewart, Alexander T., 97
Stillman, James, 132, 195
Stillman, Mrs. James T., 310
Stock market crash (1929), 380, 383-84
Stone, Mr. (Whig Inlet House proprietor), 83
Stone's Hotel, 83
Stuyvesant, Peter, 8, 136, 201
Subways in New York. See New York City subway system
Sudbury Hall, 208n
Suffolk County, xi, xin
  Great Depression in, 385
  Macy's political power in, 360
  population growth of, 353
  post-WWII, 418
  suburban sprawl in, 421
Suffolk County News, xii, xiii
Suffolk County Surrogate's Records office, xiii
Suffolk Lane, 183, 311, 332
Suffolk Street, 332
Sugar Trust, 152-56, 176, 225
Summer homes, 37, 53-54
  first avenue of, 26
Summer hotels. See Resort hotels
Summer spa. See Spa
Sumner, Increase, 36
Sunken Forest, 429-30, 431
Sunscape, 428
Surf Hotel, 28, 31, 81, 99, 182, 271
  hurricane rips roof of, 82, 83
  and plan for Argyle Hotel, 95
  and pre-1900 Fire Island, 414
Sutton, Effingham B., 179
Suydam, Ann White Schermerhorn, 140
Suydam, Captain Charles L., 162-63, 232

Suydam, Captain Charles L. Jr., 233, 333, 334
Suydam, Charles, 140
Suydam, Helen (Mrs. Robert Fulton Cutting), 140, 141, 146, 158, 203
Suydam, Walter L., Sr., 140
Suydam family(ies), xi, 140, 159
Swan, Alden S., 172, 173, 233, 316
Sweisguth, Francis, 397

T

Tahlulah (Wagstaff home), 34, 250, 252, 253, 429
Taliaferro, Alice Bigelow, 271
Tally-Ho coach(es), 56, 64, 144
Tappin, John C., 150, 160
Tappin, Lindsley, 212n
Taylor, Albertina, 132
Taylor, George Campbell, 130-31, 132-35, 204, 242, 306, 318n
    estate of, 359, 361-63
Taylor, Henry A. C., 135, 135n
Taylor, Jacob B., 131
Taylor, Mary, 32
Taylor, Moses, 131-32
Taylor property, rum-running on, 346
TB Asten, 76, 79, 167
Telka (steam yacht), 236
Tenney, Charles H., 277
Tennis Club, Islip, 125n, 418, 425
Terry (Captain), 166, 169
Thatcher, Archibald, 356
Thaw, Harry K., 310
Theater. *See* Show business
Thelma (yacht), 235
Theriot, Charles H., 318
Thistle (yacht), 165, 166, 167-69
Thompkins, Willard F., 276n
Thompson, Abraham Gardiner, 256-58
Thompson, Benjamin F., 16-17, 414
Thompson, David, 255, 256, 257
Thompson, Frederick Diodati, 255, 257

Thompson, G. W., 163
Thompson, Isaac, 255-56
Thompson, John, 42
Thompson, Jonathan (elder), 255
Thompson, Jonathan (son of Isaac Thompson), 255, 256
Thompson, Mary Gardiner (Mrs. Isaac Thompson), 255
Thompson family, 178
Thorn, Frances M., 35
Thorn, Frost, 78
Thorne, Anna Augusta (Mrs. Robert Titus), 259, 367, 369
Thorne, Edwin, 250, 259-60, 328n, 366, 380, 398
    descendants of, 420
Thorne, Edwin (son of Landon), 367, 368, 399
Thorne, Francis B., 250, 259, 322, 367, 378n, 386, 403-4
Thorne, Francis B. Jr., xiv, 403-404
Thorne, Hildegarde Kobbe (Mrs. Francis B. Thorne), 250, 322, 377, 387n, 403, 404
Thorne, Julia Atterbury (Mrs. Landon K. Thorne), 367, 369, 370
Thorne, Landon Ketchum, 259, 357, 366-70, 378n, 398, 403
    and Bay Shore Yacht Club, 418
Thorne, Landon Jr., 367, 399
Thorne, Phebe Ketchum (Mrs. Edwin Thorne), 259, 260, 366, 380
Thorne, Phebe Schoonhoven (Mrs. Harry K. Knapp Jr.), 259, 306, 367, 369
Thorne, Phebe Van Schoonhoven (Mrs. Samuel Thorne), 259
Thorne, Samuel, 259
Thorne, William, 35, 259
Thurber (Awixa area landowner), 289
Thurber cottage, 269
Thurber's Neck, 177
Tiffany, Charles Louis, 48
Tiffany, Louis Comfort, 111, 143, 227
Tilden, Samuel J., 122
Tillinghast, A. W., 365

Timber Point class of boat, 398-99
Timber Point Club, 318, 356-58, 359, 363, 364, 366, 387, 399, 404, 418, 424-25
Timber Point Farm, 127, 129, 130, 355, 356
Timmerman, H. G., 200
Titanic, 329n, 409-10
Titus, Anna Augusta Thorne, 259, 367, 369
Titus, Robert, 259, 369
Townsend, Fred, 76, 167
Travel in Europe, 207-8
Travers, William R., 39, 40, 48, 74
Trevor, Mrs. John B., 157
Trinity Church or Parish, New York City, 70, 196, 249
Trinity Church Seaside Home, 125-26, 424
Trotter, General, 27
True, Benjamin K., 34, 35-36, 115, 128, 178
True, Henry, 35-36
Tuberculosis, 148-49
Tucker, Charles A., 172, 177, 408-9
Tucker, Clarence, 122, 150, 158, 163, 172, 225
Tucker, Ras, 42
Tucker, William A., 240
Turnbull, George R., 205, 317
Tuxedo Park, New York, 57, 141, 224, 230
Twombly, Florence Vanderbilt, 69, 121
Twombly, Hamilton McKown, 69, 121-22
Twyford (Webster property), 396, 425

U

"Ultra-fashionable dancing people," 91-92
Uncle Jesse Conklin's, 81, 82
Unqua Corinthian Yacht Club, 240
U.S. v. E. C. Knight, 154

V

Vagts, Anna (Mrs. William Dick), 176, 177, 264
Vail, John H., 267, 271, 272
Valentine, Ann, 378, 387n
Valentine, David D., 172
Valentine, Langdon B., 349, 350, 351, 356, 357
Valentine, Louise Hollister, 349, 350
Valentino, Rudolph, 376
Valiant (steam yacht), 194, 213, 236
Valkyrie II (yacht), 170, 205
Van Anden, William M., 172, 173
Van Boogh, Catherine, 201n
Van Cortlandt, Stephanus, 15-18, 254-55
Van Cortlandt family, 13
Van Cortlandt Park, 17
Van Cortlandt, Jacobus, 17
Vanderbilt, Alva Smith (Mrs. William K. Vanderbilt; later Mrs. O. H. P. Belmont), 65, 66
   alimony to, x
   Consuelo disciplined by, 212
   and Consuelo's marriage, 213, 214-15, 216, 221
   hospital donation in memory of, 349
   marital troubles and divorce of, 66, 126, 213-14
   as party-giver, 68, 92, 193
   and St. Mark's rectory, 112
   and Seaside Home, 125, 126
   second marriage of (Belmont), 66, 126, 149n, 216-17
   and women's suffrage, 218
Vanderbilt, Anne Harriman Sands Rutherfurd (Mrs. William K. Vanderbilt), 219, 223
Vanderbilt, Consuelo (Duchess of Marlborough; later Mrs. Jacques Balsan), 211-19
   and death of father, 220-21
   and Duer, 381
   The Glitter and the Gold by, 65, 65n

and Idlehour, 66, 67, 211, 213, 215, 219, 424
second marriage of, 221, 222
wedding gift to, x
Vanderbilt, Cornelius (Commodore), x, 64, 129, 132, 186
Vanderbilt, Cornelius II, x, 65
Vanderbilt, Florence (Mrs. Hamilton McKown Twombly), 69, 121
Vanderbilt, Harold S., 206n, 218-19, 220, 223, 223n, 344, 349, 368
college pals of, 378n
Vanderbilt, William Henry, x, 64-65, 85, 129
Vanderbilt, William Kissam, x, 57, 64-65, 112-13
and Bourne, 191
and Breese, 127
and Consuelo's wedding, 215
death of, 220, 221, 343
estate of, 220
as estate builder, 197
and Hollins, 319
and horse racing, 245
and Idlehour, 65, 65n, 66-68, 123-24, 145, 214, 219, 223
and Islip, 111, 112, 121, 125, 136
and Lake Shore railroad, 129
and large mansions, 190
lavish entertaining of, 92, 193
marital troubles and divorce of, 66, 213-14
and Parsons property, 120
and Pavilion Hotel, 69
and St. Mark's, 70, 111-12, 185, 186, 212, 220
second wife of, 219-20, 223
town assessment on property of, 242, 250, 318n
in Westbrook Golf Club, 147
and yachting, 170, 194, 205, 236
younger summer residents as friends of, 185
Vanderbilt, W. K. Jr., 66, 223
"Vanderbilt Era," x

Vanderbilt estate, 56
Vanderbilt family, 48, 292
as arrivistes, 92
New York Society's acceptance of, 211
Vanderbilt Mausoleum, 220n
Vanitie (yacht), 301
Van Orden, J. E., 238
Van Rensselaer, Anna (Mrs. William Nicoll), 14, 16, 17
Van Rensselaer, Charles, 300
Van Rensselaer, Kiliaen, 14
Van Rensselaer, Philip, 296
Van Schoonhoven, Phebe, 259
Vaux, Calvert, 55
Vega (schooner), 411
Venetian Canal and Yacht Harbor, 285
Venetian Fete, 378, 380
Verveelan family, 13
Vesta (yacht), 57, 58
Victoria (Queen of England), 72n
Vigilant (yacht), 170
Vim (yacht), 400
Vivian, Charles, 226
Vixen (sloop), 72, 73, 77
Volunteer (yacht), 165, 166, 168-69

W

Wagstaff, Alfred (Doctor), 34, 178, 250
death of, 251
house of, 418
Wagstaff, Alfred (son, "Colonel"), 34, 111, 178, 250, 251-52
Wagstaff, Amy Colt (Mrs. Cornelius DuBois Wagstaff), 35, 252
Wagstaff, Cornelius DuBois, 35, 147, 178, 252
Wagstaff, David, 34
Wagstaff, George B., 369, 378n
Wagstaff, Mary Barnard (Mrs. Alfred Wagstaff younger), 252
Wagstaff, Mary DuBois (Mrs. Henry Gribble), 251
Wagstaff, Oliver C., 378n
Wagstaff, Sarah Louisa (Mrs. Phoenix Remsen), 252

Wagstaff, Sarah Platt (Mrs. Alfred Wagstaff elder), 34, 250, 252
Wagstaff family, 48, 178
Wainwright, Stuyvesant, 378n, 397
Waldron family, 13, 388
Wanda (yacht), 275
Warburg, Carola, 273
Warren, Whitney, 243
War of the Roses, 3-4
Washington, George, 255, 429
Washington, Lulu, 262
Water
    as fire-fighting lack, 117-18, 182-83, 183, 199
    from Long Island aquifers, 80, 389
Waterbury, Leander, 172
Watson, George L., 165, 169, 205
Watson, R. C., 300
Watts, George, 49n
Waverly Gun Club, 115
Wa-Wa-Yanda (Way Wayonda, Way Wayanda) Fishing Club, 48, 81-82, 83, 115, 430
    New York Herald on (1890), 181
        and 1938 hurricane, 416
Wealth
    consumption and exhibition of, 241
    Vanderbilt on inheriting of, 220
Webb, Watson, 247
Webster, Charles D., xiv, 391, 396
Webster, Natalie Peters, 378, 391, 396
Wederstrandt, Helen Maria, 25
Weekes, Harold H., 306, 357, 388
Weekes, Louisine Peters, 306, 385-86, 388
Weeks, George, 55
Weld, Alva F., 42
Weld, Katharine Saltonstall, 297, 412
Weld, Philip B., 297, 412
Welles, Benjamin Sumner, 34, 36-37, 68, 158, 179n, 184, 185, 185n
    death of, 305
Welles, Benjamin S. Jr., 36-37, 305, 320
Welles, Catherine Schermerhorn (Mrs. Benjamin S. Welles), 36-37, 140n

Welles, Thomas, 36
Welles family, 292
Wells, Natalie (Mrs. Harry T. Peters), 306, 390
Wenman, James F., 81, 308-9
Wereholme (Peters property), 388
West Bay Shore, 354
Westbrook Farms (Lorillard estate), 58-60, 67, 424
    Cutting ownership of, 60, 126-27, 141-46, 148, 149, 150, 353
    town assessment on, 318n
Westbrook Golf Club, 147, 148, 148n, 354, 355, 418
Westcott, George, 49, 50, 306-7
Westcott, Joe, 50, 307
Westcott, John, 50, 307
West Island, 333n, 430
West Islip, xii, 17, 34, 257
    Havemeyer estate in, 85-86, 88
Wharton, Edith, 138, 139
Wharton, Frances Fisher, 158
Wharton, George Mifflin, 158, 212n
Wharton, Helena Parsons (Mrs. Richard Wharton), 119, 120, 121, 158, 212n, 306, 375, 377, 381
Wharton, Marion, 378
Wharton, Richard, 120, 158, 212n, 306, 375, 377, 381
Wharton, Thomas, 158
Wharton, William Fishbourne, 117, 150, 158, 161, 183
Wharton, W. H., 203
Wharton family, 292
Wheeler, Carolyn, 322
Whelan (Awixa area landowner), 289
Whig Inlet, 81, 333
Whig Inlet House, 83-84
Whileaway (Parsons house), 120, 124, 159, 375, 418
Whirlwind (yacht), 368
Whirlwind aircraft engines, 330, 377, 380
Whistler (yacht), 400
White, Stanford, 145, 146, 310, 337, 371

Whitehead, Russell, 338
Whiteman, Paul, 381
Whitlock, Catherine (Mrs. Daniel
    D. Conover), 104, 105
Whitman, Frank, 157
Whitney, Harry Payne, 122, 247
Whitney, Maria (Mrs. Robert C.
    Livingston), 159, 160, 317
Whitney, Payne, 122
Whitney, Stephen, 48, 132
Whitney, William Collins, 122, 163,
    168
Wicks, Perry S., 240
Wicks, Seth, 72
Wildlife refuge, Twyford as, 396
Willets, Amos, 17
Willets, Mary Wasburn, 17
Willets, Richard, 16, 17
Willets, Richard (grandfather), 17
Willets, Thomas, 16, 17
William K. Vanderbilt Historical
    Society Library, xiii
Williams, Harold, 315
Williams, Percy G., 311-15
Williams, Richard H., 164, 225
Williams, Roger, 11
Williams, Victor, 314
William II (Kaiser of Germany), 169
Willing, Ava (Mrs. John Jacob
    Astor IV), 329n
Willing, Susan (Mrs. Francis
    Cooper Lawrance Jr.), 329
Willoughby, Gilbert Heathcote
    Drummond, Earl of Ancaster, 130
Willow Brook Driving Park, 278-
    79, 279n, 283
Willows, the (De Coppet home), 373
Wilmerding, Caroline Murray (Mrs.
    Lucius K. Wilmerding), 156
Wilmerding, George, 45
Wilmerding, George G., 26, 47, 178
    estate of, 369
Wilmerding, Harriet Kellogg (Mrs.
    Henry Augustus Wilmerding), 156
Wilmerding, Helen Cutting (Mrs.
    Lucius Wilmerding), 156-57
Wilmerding, Henry Augustus, 156

Wilmerding, Julia L., 369n
Wilmerding, Lucius, 156-57
Wilmerding, Lucius K., 150, 156-57
Wilmerding, William E., 26, 55
Wilmerding family, 34, 178, 292
Wilson, Caroline Astor (Mrs. Orme
    Wilson), 263
Wilson, Orme, 263, 369
Wilson, Richard Guy, 123
Windemere development, 290, 426
Windholme Farm, 388, 389-91, 395-
    96, 409, 419
Wing, Alice De Goicouria Belmont,
    299, 304
Wing, J. D., 304
Winter, Lulu Ceballos (Mrs.
    Charles Winter), 262
Winthrop, John, 6n
Wiswall, W., 177-78
Wittlock, Lavern, xiv
Wood, Ellen, 116
Wood, H. Duncan, 112-13, 118, 156
    as broker, 112, 113, 116, 127
    Dickey rents cottage of, 263
    and 1893 panic, 200
    fire in home of, 116-17
    and Hollins, 113
    as Hollins-Breese witness, 128
    as Knapp neighbor, 249
    and St. Marks, 116, 118, 156, 185
Wood family, 48, 112, 125
Woodland (Johnson home) 46,
    199, 200, 321, 419, 425
Woodlea (Adams home), 289-90
Woodruff, Ellen, 25
Woodworth, Franc (Mrs. Allan
    Pinkerton), 274, 277
Wooley, J. V. S., 177-78
Woolworth, Edna, 295
Woolworth, F. W., 295, 296
World War I. See Great War
World War II
    boom mentality ended by, 354
    South Shore impact of, 417-21
Wormser, Isidore, 85
Worth, Thomas, 29, 50, 184, 393-94
Wray, William, 177-78

Wright, Alice Stanchfield, 311
Wright, Arthur M., 311
Wright Whirlwind engines, 330, 377, 380
Wyandanch (Indian sachem), 12
Wynkoop, D. W., 348n

Y

Yachting, 74-79
America's Cup, 72n, 75, 164-66, 167-70, 194-95, 205-7, 223, 343-44, 368
and Arnolds, 54-55, 254
and Bourne, 194-95
and Adolph Dick, 411
after end of Great War, 341-42
formal style of, 237
and Garners, 35
and Horace Havemeyer, 232-33, 275, 300, 333-34, 399-402
Kaiser's Cup, 301
and Lorillard, 57-58
Marconi rig, 302, 343, 398, 398n
and Mollenhauer, 235-37, 238, 240, 240-41, 300, 411
one-designs racing, 300, 396
Islip One-Designs, 241, 300-301, 302, 308, 334, 342
Larchmont O Class, 301
Star boats, 301, 358, 368, 396-402
Timber Point class, 358, 398-99
and Pinkerton, 275
and Prince, 71-74
and sea power, 170
and Thorne, 368
yacht clubs, 75, 233-34, 237, 239-41
(*see also specific yacht clubs*)
Yama Yama (yacht), 342
Young, Albert, 177-78
Youngs, John, 11-12
Yznaga, Consuelo, 211
Yznaga, Fernando, 67

Z

Ziegfeld, Flo, 378
Ziegler, William, 99